School Subjects and Curriculum Change

Studies in Curriculum History

To My Dad

FREDERICK GOODSON
1903–1983

With Love

School Subjects and Curriculum Change

Studies in Curriculum History

Ivor Goodson

New Revised and Extended Edition

The Falmer Press
(A Member of the Taylor & Francis Group)
London, New York and Philadelphia

UK	The Falmer Press, Falmer House, Barcombe, Lewes, East Sussex, BN8 5DL
USA	The Falmer Press, Taylor & Francis Inc., 242 Cherry Street, Philadelphia, PA 19106-1906

First published in 1983 by Croom Helm Ltd.
This new edition published in 1987

© Copyright 1987 Ivor Goodson

All rights reserved. No part of this publication may be reproduced, stored in a retrieval system, or transmitted in any form or by any means, electronic, mechanical, photocopying, recording or otherwise, without permission in writing from the Publisher.

Library of Congress Cataloging in Publication Data
Goodson, Ivor.
  School subject and curriculum change.
  (Studies in curriculum history; 6)
  Includes bibliographical references and index.
  1. Curriculum planning—Great Britain—Curricula—History. I. Title. II. Series.
  LB1629.5.G7G66 1986 375'.001 86-29360
  ISBN 1-85000-151-0
  ISBN 1-85000-152-9 (pbk.)

Jacket design by Caroline Archer

Typeset in 10/12 Caledonia by
Imago Publishing Ltd, Thame, Oxon

Printed in Great Britain by Taylor & Francis (Printers) Ltd, Basingstoke

Contents

Introduction to New Edition		vi
Part One: Becoming an Academic Subject: Case Studies in the Social History of the School Curriculum		1
1	Introduction	3
2	The Growth of the English Education System: Changing Patterns of Curricula and Examinations	13
3	Academic 'Subjects' and Curriculum Change	24
Part Two: School Subjects: Patterns of Internal Evolution		39
4	Biology: Aspects of Subject History	41
5	Geography: Aspects of Subject History	57
6	Rural Studies: Aspects of Subject History	84
Part Three: Relationships Between Subjects: The Territorial Nature of Subject Conflict		103
7	'Climates of Opinion' with Respect to Education and the Environment, 1960–1975	105
8	Redefining Rural Studies: The Genesis of Environmental Studies	116
9	Construction of an 'A' Level Syllabus	131
10	The Defence of Geography and Biology	145
11	The Negotiation of Environmental Studies	166
Part Four: Conclusions		183
12	Conclusions, Complexities and Conjectures	184
Appendices		199
Index		222

Introduction to New Edition

School Subjects and Curriculum Change developed out of some doctoral research conducted at the University of Sussex in the years 1975–79. But the origins of the work go back to my own cultural and school experiences and to my school teaching days in two comprehensive schools.

The late sixties and early seventies was a fascinating and vivid period to be in school teaching. Both of the brand new comprehensives I taught in were alive with discussion, innovation and contention. Although I had gone to university I had remained very close to my working class home community throughout. My friends, my interests, my values were there. Hence when I arrived to teach in these new schools I was a rather 'odd bird' — part working class student, part teacher (in the latter role I suspect rather 'unsocialised'). In the event this schizophrenia led to some anguished reflections about the nature of schooling.

For here were two schools at the radical edge of the spectrum of comprehensive schooling. Together they combined some almost revolutionary features: no uniforms, no punishments, no sanctions, no compulsion, no team games, no assemblies (even, in one of the schools, no headmaster!). In short, in these schools there were very few of the normal 'oppressions' of schooling which are so often blamed for alienation and hostility. The relationships between the predominantly working class students and the predominantly middle class teachers were at least friendly and at best deeply engaged. The organisational structure of the schools stressed elements of the best of workers' adult education traditions: the students' choice of subject, the students' 'autonomy'.

But from these promising beginnings, from these engaged thresholds the prospects for learning remained deeply problematic. New curriculum areas were pioneered — community studies, urban studies, independent learning in science — but these areas were not judged to be examinable at 'A' level. If Mode 3 'O' levels were negotiated they were most often subsequently closed on grounds of 'cost-efficiency'. So broadly the curriculum for examination courses remained conventional and reminded me greatly of my own experi-

Introduction to New Edition

ences at grammar school. All the curiosity, all the desire to learn, all the promising relationships collided with the intractable form and content of the 'traditional' school subject.

I wrote in a diary at the time (1970) that:

> very possibly a major key to the conundrum of success and failure at school lies in the collision between antecedent curriculum structures and the students' cultural capital — school subjects are most commonly seen as at best beneficial and at worst neutral elements — in fact through their form and content they are deeply active in determining the distribution of life chances.

This was not an original insight at my first school Countesthorpe where a number of staff came to argue that the only way forward was to actually 'reconstruct' the knowledge that was taught. David Hawkins, for instance, argued in *Forum* (Autumn 1975) that:

> as many kinds of subject matter are organized, it is not obvious nor easily possible to transform the teaching of them to a more self-directed and informal style of work in schools. Under these circumstances we are rather likely to fall back into the old polarities. By one party the tradition of the formal course will continue to be seen as for the most part a dreary, ineffective and superficial 'coverage' of subject matter on its way to ossification. By the other party the advocacy of resource-based learning will be seen as a denigration of both rigour and discipline in the mastery of subject matter. What I hope is that this old issue be buried and that we address, instead, the question as to *how* wider ranges of subject matter, of that stuff alluded to in curricula and syllabi, can be revived and reconstituted and extended so as to make it more diversely accessible and appealing to growing minds, more interwoven in the texture of a rich school environment.

If this was a view held by some of us as teachers there is evidence from others about their experience as working class pupils. Albert Hunt blames the 'teachers' assumption that because he is deeply involved with a particular subject that subject must be of value and interest to everybody else'. So a subject is placed at the 'centre of all education' — and a failure to make that subject 'come to life becomes the teachers' failure'. But in Hunt's experience as a pupil it was the 'subject' itself which ensured nothing came to life:

> Virtually nothing in the whole of my formal educational experience had ever connected with me in a way that involved me — me as a person. I had feelings, convictions, commitments to ideas and people. None of these seemed related to my work.... Everything existed for me in fragments.

What Hunt describes is exactly what I had experienced at school myself as a pupil. Now teaching myself I was confronted by waves of kids similar in

School Subjects and Curriculum Change

background to Hunt and myself who quite evidently, and quite justifiably, felt just the same.

Given the centrality of 'subjects' as causes of why so many apparently bright and curious students were turned off school I became progressively fascinated as to where subjects had come from and why they were as they were. Further I was deeply intrigued by the fact that when new subjects were found that apparently motivated large numbers of students (in my experience at both schools environmental studies worked in this way) they were normally judged unacceptable as 'real' or 'examination' subjects.

In the event I had a chance to look for some answers. In 1975 I joined a research project at Sussex concerned to investigate environmental education. This led into the work that is reported herein.

Ivor Goodson
Faculty of Education
University of Western Ontario,
Canada.
November, 1986

Part One
Becoming an Academic Subject: Case Studies in the Social History of the School Curriculum

1 *Introduction*

This book provides a number of historical case studies of school subjects and examines underlying patterns of change and conflict both within and between these subjects. The focus of the case studies is on the 'process of becoming a school subject' and therefore concentrates on the promotion of subjects as they seek establishment in the school curriculum. The concern is not to provide a general explanation of school subjects and curriculum change but rather to raise issues and generate insights about past and current work which does seek to provide such explanatory theories. Central to the book is a belief in a socio-historical approach to curriculum studies.

In particular and in summary the book seeks to present evidence for three hypotheses: firstly, that subjects are not monolithic entities but shifting amalgamations of sub-groups and traditions. These groups within the subject influence and change boundaries and priorities. Secondly, that in the process of establishing a school subject (and associated university discipline) base subject groups tend to move from promoting pedagogic and utilitarian traditions towards the academic tradition. The need for the subject to be viewed as a scholarly discipline will impinge on both the promotional rhetoric and the process of subject definition, most crucially during the passage to subject and discipline establishment. Thirdly, that, in the cases studied, much of the curriculum debate can be interpreted in terms of conflict between subjects over status, resources and territory.

Above all historical case studies of school subjects provide the 'local detail' of curriculum change and conflict. The identification of individuals and sub-groups actively at work within curriculum interest groups allows some examination and assessment of intention and motivation. Thereby sociological theories which attribute power over the curriculum to dominant interest groups can be scrutinised for their empirical potential.[1]

To concentrate attention at the micro level of individual school subject groups is not to deny the crucial importance of macro level economic changes or changes in intellectual ideas, dominant values or educational systems. But it is asserted that such macro level changes may be actively reinterpreted at the micro level. Changes at macro level are viewed as presenting a range of new choices to subject factions, associations and communities. To understand how subjects change over time, as well as histories of intellectual ideas, we need to understand how subject groups take up and promote new ideas and opportunities. It is not contended that subject groups are all-powerful in engineering curriculum change but that their responses are a very important, and as yet somewhat neglected, part of the overall picture.

Besides seeking to examine sociological explanation of the school curriculum the emphasis on the social history of school subjects generates insights and questions of importance for the future of the comprehensive school. The differential status (and available resources) of the various school subjects derive from their origins in the separate educational sectors which preceded comprehensivation. For instance, craft and practical subjects still carry with them the low status which originated through their elementary school background. School subjects, therefore, represent the deep structures of curriculum differentiation at work within contemporary schools. Recent studies of comprehensives have shown how a divisive system arises as these differentiated curricula are allocated to different pupil clienteles. Changing the internal processes of schooling in line with the comprehensive ideal will require detailed understanding of the origins and continuing strengths of the subject-based curriculum. The present pattern of subject definition and syllabus construction, of associated status and resources, ensures that school subjects play their part in preserving entrenched social divisions in the face of organisational change.

Explanations of School Subjects

The juxtaposition of intellectual 'disciplines' and school subjects has for some time been a starting point in the work of certain philosophers of education. Hirst, for instance, talks of school subjects 'which are indisputably logically cohesive disciplines'.[2] But such a philosophical perspective is rooted in particular educational convictions, notably in the assertion that 'no matter what the ability of the child may be, the heart of all his development as a rational being is, I am saying, intellectual'.[3] In accordance with these convictions Hirst (and Peters) argue that 'the central objectives of education are developments of mind'. Such objectives are best pursued by 'the definition of forms of knowledge'[4] (later broadened to include 'fields of knowledge'). These forms and fields of knowledge can provide the 'logically cohesive disciplines' on which school subjects are based.

The philosophy of Hirst and Peters, therefore, provides an explanatory basis for the school curriculum aspiring to promote the intellectual development of its pupils. In this model of school subject definition it is often implied that the intellectual discipline is created by a community of scholars, normally working in a university, and is then 'translated' for use as a school subject. Phenix defines the intellectual discipline base in this way: 'The general test for a discipline is that it should be the characteristic activity of an identifiable organised tradition of men of knowledge, that is of persons who are skilled in certain specified functions that they are able to justify by a set of intelligible standards'.[5]

Once a discipline has established a university base it is persuasively self-fulfilling to argue that here is a field of knowledge from which an 'academic' school subject can receive inputs and general direction. But this version of events simply celebrates a fait accompli in the evolution of a discipline and associated school subject. What is left unexplained are the stages of evolution towards this culminating pattern and the forces which push aspiring 'academic' subjects to follow similar routes. To understand the progression along the route to academic status it is necessary to examine the social histories of school subjects and to analyse the strategies employed in their construction and promotion.

The manner in which philosophical studies offer justification for the academic subject-based curriculum has been noted by sociologists. Thus philosophers such as Hirst present a view of education that Young states: 'appears to be based on an absolutist conception of a set of distinct forms of knowledge which correspond closely to the traditional areas of the academic curriculum and thus justify, rather than examine, what are no more than socio-historical constructs of a particular time'.[6] Whilst accepting Young's critique it is important to note that this book will contend that school subjects represent substantial interest groups. To view subjects as 'no more than socio-historical constructs of a particular time', whilst correct at one level, does severe injustice to all those groups involved in their continuance and promotion over time.

As long ago as 1968 Musgrove made what, at the time, was a fairly original suggestion to sociologists. He recommended that they:

> Examine subjects both within the school and the nation at large as social systems sustained by communication networks, material endowments and ideologies. Within a school and within a wider society subjects as communities of people, competing and collaborating with one another, defining and defending their boundaries, demanding allegiance from their members and conferring a sense of identity upon them ... even innovation which appears to be essentially intellectual in character can usefully be examined as the outcome of social interaction ...

Musgrove remarked that 'studies of subjects in these terms have scarcely begun at least at school level'.[7]

A number of studies have sought to follow Musgrove's exhortation, for instance recent work by Eggleston, but a very influential work in the field of the sociology of knowledge was the collection of papers in 'Knowledge and Control' edited by M.F.D. Young in 1971. The papers reflect Bernstein's contention that 'how a society selects, classifies, distributes, transmits and evaluates the educational knowledge it considers to be public, reflects both the distribution of power and the principles of social control'.[8] Young likewise suggests that 'consideration of the assumptions underlying the selection and organisation of knowledge by those in positions of power may be a fruitful perspective for raising sociological questions about curricula'.[9] The emphasis leads to general statements of the following kind:

> Academic curricula in this country involve assumptions that some kinds and areas of knowledge are much more 'worthwhile' than others: that as soon as possible all knowledge should become specialised and with minimum explicit emphasis on the relations between the subjects specialised in and between specialist teachers involved. It may be useful, therefore, to view curricular changes as involving changing definitions of knowledge along one or more of the dimensions towards a less or more stratified, specialised and open organisation of knowledge. Further, that as we assume some patterns of social relations associated with any curriculum, these changes will be resisted insofar as they are perceived to undermine the values, relative power and privileges of the dominant groups involved.[10]

The process whereby the unspecified 'dominant groups' exercise control over other presumably subordinate groups is not scrutinised, although certain hints are offered. We learn that a school's autonomy in curriculum matters 'is in practice extremely limited by the control of the sixth form (and therefore lower form) curricula by the universities, both through their entrance requirements and their domination of all but one of the school examination boards'. In a footnote Young assures that 'no direct control is implied here, but rather a process by which teachers legitimate their curricula through their shared assumptions about "what we all know the universities want"'.[11] This concentration on the teachers' socialisation as the major agency of control is picked up elsewhere. We learn that:

> The contemporary British educational system is dominated by academic curricula with a rigid stratification of knowledge. It follows that if teachers and children are socialised within an institutionalised structure which legitimates such assumptions, then for teachers high status (and rewards) will be associated with areas of the curriculum that are (1) formally assessed (2) taught to the 'ablest' children (3) taught in homogeneous ability groups of children who show themselves most successful within such curricula.[12]

Young goes on to note that it 'should be fruitful to explore the syllabus construction of knowledge practitioners in terms of their efforts to enhance or maintain their academic legitimacy'.[13]

Two papers by Bourdieu in 'Knowledge and Control' summarise his considerable influence on English sociologists of knowledge.[14] Unlike many of the other contributors to 'Knowledge and Control', Bourdieu has gone on to carry out empirical work to test his theoretical assertions. His recent work, though concentrated at university, not school, level, looks at the theme of reproduction through education and includes an important section on The Examination within the Structure and History of the Educational System.[15] Young also has come to feel the need for historical approaches to test theories of knowledge and control. He wrote recently 'One crucial way of reformulating and transcending the limits within which we work, is to see ... how such limits are not given or fixed, but produced through the conflicting actions and interests of man in history'.[16] Likewise Bernstein has subsequently argued that 'if we are to take shifts in the content of education seriously, then we require histories of these contents, and their relationship to institutions and symbolic arrangements external to the school.'[17]

Towards a Social History of School Subjects

A number of recent studies have employed historical approaches to explore curriculum issues pertinent to the questions addressed in this book. Wilkinson's study of the classical academic curricula of nineteenth-century public schools is of this sort and draws ideas from an earlier study by Weber.[18] Weber investigated Confucian education and identified three crucial elements in the education of Chinese administrators at this time. The main emphasis was on propriety and 'bookishness', with a curriculum largely restricted to the learning and memorising of classical texts. This curriculum comprised a very narrow selection from the available knowledge in a society where mathematicians, astronomers, scientists and geographers were not uncommon. However, all these fields of knowledge were classified by the literati as 'vulgar' or perhaps in more contemporary terms 'non-academic'. The use of examinations, based on this narrow curriculum, for controlling entry into the administrative elite meant that the non-bookish were for the purposes of the Chinese society of the time 'not educated'.[19] Wilkinson draws an analogy between Confucian education and late Victorian public school education in which it is not bookishness but the 'gentleman ideal that maintains the political elite'. The public school curriculum by 'the very criteria themselves, emphasizing classical knowledge and a certain set style, favoured the gentry individual'.[20]

The Wilkinson article appeared in an important collection of papers in 'Sociology, History and Education' edited by P.W. Musgrave. Two other articles rehearse similar arguments to those of Wilkinson. Campbell's study of Latin and the Elite Tradition in Education notes that 'there is a direct relationship between a school's social prestige in the community and the extent to which it is classically based'.[21] Goody and Watts present some general considerations about 'literate culture'. They note that the main characteristics of literate culture are 'an abstraction which disregards an individual's social experience ... and a compartmentalisation of knowledge which restricts the kind of connections which the individual can establish and ratify with the natural and social world'.

Historical studies of the elite education provided in universities have been undertaken, notably by Davie and Rothblatt. Davie's study concerned patterns of curriculum change in the nineteenth-century Scottish universities and pointed to an increasing emphasis on literature rather than oral expression.[23] Rothblatt's study of nineteenth-century Cambridge described the successful strategies which the dons pursued to maintain the dominance of classical studies over the less favoured 'useful knowledge':[24]

> So deeply rooted was the disdain for commerce and industry, for the values which they were supposed to represent, that numerous dons and non-resident M.A.s decided the worth of an academic subject by its usefulness to commerce and industry. In their view no subject which could be turned to the benefit of business deserved university recognition ... whenever it was suspected that the impetus for curricular reform came from commercial or political sources, Cambridge dons arose to denounce the proposed changes as technical, illiberal, utilitarian and soft options.[25]

A number of studies have focused on the traditions within separate subjects and on the pursuit of status and academic acceptability within subjects. Layton's study 'Science for the People' traces a number of traditions in nineteenth-century science which sought to relate science to people's lives. The book generates a number of hypotheses as to why these versions of science were ultimately dominated by a more thoroughly academic version fashioned in laboratories, textbooks and syllabi. The role of subject associations in this pursuit of increased academic status is documented by Hanson with reference to Society of Art Masters. The Society showed great concern for the academic dress and titles which bestowed, or appeared to bestow, high status on other knowledge categories.[27]

Dodd has recently reviewed the history of Design and Technology in the School Curriculum, following earlier work on Design Education by Eggleston.[28] A major theme in the work is the desire among teachers of the subject for higher status:

> Heavy craft activities have been referred to by a number of different titles as their nature and contribution has changed. Concealed in this on-going discussion is the matter of 'status' and 'respectability', and although the most recent change from Handicraft to Design and Technology reflects a change of emphasis, there is something of the former argument. 'Practical' describes quite adequately an essential part of the subject, but it is an 'emotionally charged word'. As the subject has developed there have been efforts made to encourage its acceptability by participation in certain kinds of external examinations (which have not always been the best instruments of assessment), the

Introduction

use of syllabuses (often malformed to make them acceptable by other institutions), and by euphemisms like the 'alternative road', but these have failed to hide the underlying low status which practical subjects have by tradition.[29]

Among more general studies of the history of curriculum, Raymond Williams' brief work, written in 1961, relating educational philosophies to the social groups holding them, is deeply suggestive. He writes: 'an educational curriculum, as we have seen again and again in past periods, expresses a compromise between an inherited selection of interests and the emphasis of new interests. At varying points in history, even this compromise may be long delayed, and it will often be muddled'.[30] This view of the history of curriculum focusing on interest groups has been recently considerably extended by Eggleston who contends that: 'The fundamental conflicts are over the identity and legitimacy of the rival contenders for membership of the groups who define, evaluate and distribute knowledge and the power these confer'.[31]

Bank's study 'Parity and Prestige in English Secondary Education' is a valuable complement to these studies; again the close relationship between curriculum and social class emerges. Williams had noted that the academic curriculum was related to the vocations of the upper and professional classes. The curriculum related to the vocations of the majority was slowly introduced and Banks notes that 'as the proportion of children from artisan and lower middle class homes increased, it was necessary to pay more attention to the vocational needs of the pupils, and even to amend the hitherto academic curriculum to admit subjects of a vocational nature.[32] But the subjects related to majority vocations were persistently viewed as of low status. A TUC pamphlet written in 1937 maintained that school time used for vocational training 'not only gives a bias to study but takes up valuable time and effort better employed in a wider and more useful field. Moreover it stamps at an early and impressionable age, the idea of class and inferior status on the scholar, which it is the aim of a noble education to avoid'.[33] Viewed in this way the notion of vocational training is seen not to refer to the pervasive underlying objective of all education as preparation for vocations but to the low-status concern of preparing the majority for their work. The academic curriculum is, and has historically been, vocational in purpose, but the preparation is for the high-status professions. Indeed Banks' study concludes that 'the persistence of the academic tradition is seen as something more fundamental than the influence, sinister or otherwise, of teachers and administrators. It is the vocational qualification of the academic curriculum which enables it to exert such a pressure on all forms of secondary education'.[34]

The term vocational as applied to the qualification function of the academic curriculum can of course be disputed. The fact that such a curriculum helps people to secure professional jobs, which is an aspect of the selection function of education, does not necessarily imply that it prepares them for the job through the provision of skills relevant to their work. The continuing dominance and high status of academic subjects is undoubtedly grounded in their acceptance as qualifications for desirable jobs. This, however, does not explain why so few new 'academic' subjects are born, nor whether these subjects are 'academic' at 'birth' or only develop a more academic character as they pursue status escalation.

Layton has analysed the evolution of science in England from the nineteenth century and in a brief article has developed a tentative model for the evolution of a school subject in the secondary school curriculum. Layton defined three stages in this evolution. In the first stage:

> the callow intruder stakes a place in the timetable, justifying its presence on grounds such as pertinence and utility. During this stage learners are attracted to the subject because of its bearing on matters of concern to them. The teachers are rarely trained specialists, but bring the missionary enthusiasms of pioneers to their task. The dominant criterion is relevance to the needs and interests of the learners.

In the interim second stage:

> a tradition of scholarly work in the subject is emerging along with a corps of trained specialists from which teachers may be recruited. Students are still attracted to the Study, but as much by its reputation and growing academic status as by its relevance to their own problems and concerns. The internal logic and discipline of the subject is becoming increasingly influential in the selection and organisation of subject matter.

In the final stage:

> the teachers now constitute a professional body with established rules and values. The selection of subject matter is determined in large measure by the judgements and practices of the specialist scholars who lead inquiries in the field. Students are initiated into a tradition, their attitudes approaching passivity and resignation, a prelude to disenchantment.[35]

Layton's model warns against any monolithic explanation of subjects and disciplines. It would seem that, far from being timeless statements of intrinsically worthwhile content, subjects and disciplines are in constant flux. Hence the study of patterns of knowledge in our society should move beyond philosophical or macro-sociological analysis towards a detailed historical investigation of the motives and actions underlying the presentation and promotion of subjects and disciplines.

In this respect the study by Ben-David and Collins provides useful guidelines. They tried to isolate the 'social factors in the origins of a new science'; namely psychology. They postulated firstly that the ideas necessary for the creation of a new discipline are normally available over a prolonged

Introduction

period of time and in several places; secondly that only a few of these potential beginnings lead to further growth, and finally that 'such growth occurs where and when persons become interested in the new idea, not only as intellectual content but also as a means of establishing a new intellectual identity and particularly a new occupational role'.[36]

From a consideration of historical and social factors an alternative set of hypotheses about the way knowledge is organised and promoted begins to emerge. A more traditional explanation is that new knowledge is generated by dispassionate scholarship and taken up according to considerations relating to its intrinsic and pedagogic validity. Sociologists of knowledge counter this with explanations citing the activities of 'dominant interest groups particularly the universities'.

The alternative view would hold that it is really much more complex than that. Subjects and disciplines are made up of teachers and scholars attracted to differing factions and traditions within their subject's concern; and these factions and traditions develop or decline as the subject evolves. By and large, the more 'mature' the subject, the more 'academic' its content and the predispositions of its members. Thus when new intellectual problems or areas arise for solution or enquiry, a differential response would be expected according to the direction and stage of evolution of the various subjects and disciplines involved. New knowledge would be scrutinised for its potential contribution to the furtherance of the subject or the interests of particular factions within the subject. The take-up and promotion of the knowledge could then accord with both the status position of the subject/discipline practitioners involved and their need and perception of its potential in offering new occupational identities.

To pursue this alternative view of school subjects further it is necessary to briefly outline the historical background to curriculum issues, and the main patterns of change in curricula and examinations as the secondary school system has evolved. Describing the changing educational system provides a contextual background for analysing the conflicts over the school curriculum in particular periods of history. The hypotheses that have so far been tentatively formulated can thereby be reformulated in the light of the specific characteristics of the English educational system in the twentieth century.

Notes

1   As in M.F.D. YOUNG (Ed.), *Knowledge and Control*, (London, Collier Macmillan, 1971).
2   P.M. HIRST, 'The logical and psychological aspects of teaching a subject', in R.S. PETERS (Ed.), *The Concept of Education* (London, Routledge and Kegan Paul, 1967), p. 44.
3   Schools Council Working Paper No. 12, *The Educational Implications of Social and Economic Change* (HMSO, 1967).
4   P.M. HIRST and R.S. PETERS, *The Logic of Education* (London, Routledge and Kegan

Paul, 1970), pp. 63–4.
5   P.M. PHENIX, *The Realms of Meaning* (McGraw-Hill, 1964), p. 317.
6   M.F.D. YOUNG, 1971, *op. cit.*, p. 23.
7   F. MUSGROVE, 'The contribution of sociology to the study of curriculum', in J.F. KERR (Ed.), *Changing the Curriculum* (University of London Press, 1968).
8   B. BERNSTEIN, 'On the classification and training of educational knowledge', in M.F.D. YOUNG (Ed.), *op. cit.*, p. 47.
9   M.F.D. YOUNG, 1971, *op. cit.*, p. 31.
10 *Ibid.*, p. 34.
11 *Ibid.*, p. 22.
12 *Ibid.*, p. 36.
13 *Ibid.*, p. 40.
14 P. BOURDIEU, 'Systems of education and systems of thought', *op. cit.* YOUNG (Ed.), 1971.
15 P. BOURDIEU and J.C. PASSERON, *Reproduction in Education, Society and Culture* (London, Sage, 1977).
16 M.F.D. YOUNG, 'Curriculum change: Limits and possibilities', in M. YOUNG and G. WHITTY (Eds.), *Society, State and Schooling* (Falmer Press, 1977), pp. 248–9.
17 B. BERNSTEIN, 'Sociology and the sociology of education', a brief account, in T.J. REX, (Ed.) *Approaches to Sociology* (Routledge and Kegan Paul, 1974), p. 156.
18 R. WILKINSON, *The Prefects* (London, Oxford University Press, 1964).
19 M. WEBER, *Essays in Sociology*, translated and edited by M. CERTZ and C.W. MILLS (London, Routledge and Kegan Paul, 1952).
20 M.F.D. YOUNG, *Knowledge and Control*, p. 30.
21 F. CAMPBELL, 'Latin and the elite tradition in education', in MUSGRAVE, P.W. *Sociology, History and Education* (London, Methuen, 1970), pp. 249–64.
22 J. GOODY and I. WATT, 'Literate culture: Some general conclusions', in MUSGRAVE, *Ibid.*, pp. 75–86.
23 G.E. DAVIE, *The Democratic Intellect* (Edinburgh, Edinburgh University Press, 1961).
24 S. ROTHBLATT, *The Revolution of the Dons* (London, Faber and Faber, 1969).
25 *Ibid.*, pp. 256–7.
26 D. LAYTON, *Science for the People* (London, Allen and Unwin, 1973).
27 D. HANSON, 'The development of a Professional Association of Art Teachers', *Studies in Design Education* 3, 2, 1971.
28 J. EGGLETON, *Developments in Design Education* (London, Open Books, 1971).
29 T. DODD, *Design and Technology in the School Curriculum* (Hodder and Stoughton, London, 1978).
30 R. WILLIAMS, *The Long Revolution* (Harmondsworth, Penguin, 1961), p. 172.
31 J. EGGLESTON, *The Sociology of the School Curriculum* (London, Routledge and Kegan Paul, 1977).
32 O. BANKS, *Parity and Prestige in English Secondary Education* (London, Routledge and Kegan Paul, 1955), p. 5.
33 TUC, *Education and Democracy* (London, TUC 1937).
34 O. BANKS, *op. cit.*, p. 248.
35 D. LAYTON, 'Science as general education', *Trends in Education*, January 1972.
36 T. BEN-DAVID and R. COLLINS, 'Social factors in the origins of a new science: The case of psychology', *American Sociological Review*, August 1966, 31, 4.

2 *The Growth of the English Education System: Changing Patterns of Curricula and Examinations*

The emergence of a national system of education followed in slow and haphazard fashion the rapid series of economic and demographic changes which affected Britain between the mid-eighteenth and mid-nineteenth centuries. In the period from 1751 to 1871 the British population quadrupled. With the development of factories and other urban industry a growing proportion of the population worked in industrial occupations and moved to the rapidly developing industrial towns to be near their work. Williams has contended that at the beginning of the nineteenth century: 'The process of change from a system of social orders based on localities, to a national system of social classes . . . was virtually complete.' The result of this changing pattern he asserted was 'a new kind of class-determined education. Higher education became a virtual monopoly, excluding the new working class, and the idea of universal education, except within the narrow limits of "moral rescue" was widely opposed as a matter of principle'.[1] For the working class the main educational institutions were the Sunday Schools, run by the churches, and the industrial schools set up to provide manual training and instruction, but to classes that often comprised several hundred children. In 1851 the average duration of schooling for working-class children was approximately two years. The Revised Code introduced in 1862, whilst severely limiting the curriculum, attempted to raise and monitor educational standards by introducing payment by results in reading, writing and arithmetic (the three Rs). The limited nature of the educational institutions and experiences available to the working class was acknowledged by the 1870 Education Act which sought to make primary education available for all children. In 1880 attendance was made compulsory up until the age of ten.

For older children education was available in public and grammar schools but, generally speaking, only for the middle and upper classes. The Taunton Commission which reported in 1868 on the state of secondary education defined three grades of education according to the time spent at school: the first grade school continued until 18 or 19 or beyond, the second grade until 16 and the third grade until 14. Taunton asserted:

The difference in the time assigned makes some difference in the very nature of education itself; if a boy cannot remain at school beyond the age of 14 it is useless to begin teaching him such subjects as require a longer time for their proper study; if he can continue till 18 or 19, it may be expedient to postpone some studies that would otherwise be commenced early. Both the substance and the arrangements of the instruction will thus greatly depend on the length of time that can be devoted to it.

In terms of its relationship to the contemporary social structures the convenience of this pattern of curriculum differentiation was duly noted because 'these instructions correspond roughly but by no means exactly, to the gradations of society. Those who can afford to pay more for their children's education will also, as a general rule, continue the education for a longer time.'[2] The curriculum of the public and grammar schools was extremely specialised and, in line with the avowed intention of educating 'Christian gentlemen', stressed classics and religious instruction. The classical educational orientation echoed that in the universities described in Rothblatt's study of nineteenth-century Cambridge.[3] The close connections between secondary and university curricula were far from coincidental for as Williams reminds us: 'By the 1830's, the examination system between these schools [the public and grammar schools] and the universities was firmly established and this, while raising educational standards within the institutions, had the effect of reinforcing the now marked limitation of the universities to entrants from a narrow social class.'[4]

In fact, from this period onwards the curricula of the public schools began, in uneven and idiosyncratic fashion, to broaden. By 1868, when the Public Schools Act was passed, the curriculum covered not only classics but mathematics, one modern language, history, geography, two natural sciences, drawing and music. This broadening curriculum was again partly a reflection of changes in university curricula although some of the changes in the schools in this period did pre-date university developments. Curriculum change was strongly advocated in government circles because of the increasing challenge from countries like Germany and America to Britain's economic and military supremacy. The broadening of the public and grammar school curriculum must not be overstated, however, for inside the new and wider curriculum classical studies for the moment maintained their dominant position. Ryder and Silver noted: 'Science and modern subjects had gained a foothold, but the classical-literary tradition continued to be considered the right kind of cultural and moral contribution to the preparation of an educational and social elite.'[5]

Meanwhile in the elementary school sector, growing rapidly following the 1870 Act, new patterns of curricula began to emerge. The School Boards administering schools that were innovative and responsive to local demands began to provide more vocational curricula covering commercial, technical and scientific subjects. These developments were considered by the 1895 Bryce Commission whose findings helped form the basis of the 1902 Education Act.

One result of the Act was that these schools were removed from the elementary sector and absorbed into the new secondary system defined by Bryce. Vocational and technical curricula were henceforth put on a separate limb in the central schools, which were higher elementary schools for the purposes of administration, and in the junior technical schools: 'Though valuable work was done in both these types of school, and though the junior technical schools came to challenge more orthodox secondary education, the official view was that their status was, and should be, below that of the secondary school.'[6]

The 1902 Act had two main results. Firstly, the 'arenas' in which educational policy were decided were substantially altered and education became the local responsibility of county and borough authorities. Secondly, the secondary sector was to follow the pattern of curriculum then enshrined in the public and grammar schools. The Act ensured that: 'Whatever developments in secondary education might occur, it should be within a single system, in which the dominant values would remain those of the traditional grammar school and its curriculum.'[7]

Other developments, at the national level, confirmed this trend. The Board of Education, formed in 1899, devised a four-year secondary course in 1904. Although this closely echoed public and grammar school curricula the movement within these schools to a broader curriculum was strikingly confirmed. The course covered mathematics, science, English language and literature, geography, history, a language other than English, drawing, manual work, physical training and household crafts for girls. The tendency growing quite markedly in some areas towards the inclusion of technical and commercial curricula in elementary schools was effectively checked. With classical curricula on the other hand the Board's preferences were clear: 'where Latin is not taught the Board will specifically inquire and require satisfaction that the omission of Latin is for the good of the schools'.

The dominant influence of the Board of Education as expressed in the Secondary Regulations was much resented by the local authorities whose own power had been established by the 1902 Act. However, the influence of the Board was not to remain dominant for very long. In 1917 the School Certificate was introduced and from this date onwards the Examination Boards began to exert considerable power in the control of the secondary school curriculum. The examinations were closely tied, as we noted earlier, to the public and grammar schools and by the 1850s 'a system of University Local Examinations, first called "Middle Class Examinations", had enabled endowed and proprietary schools of the first and second grades to aim at some recognised standard of education'.[8]

Control of the curriculum by the University Examination Boards ensured that substantially the same values as those promoted by the Board of Education were enshrined in school curricula. The Joint Matriculation Board, for instance, in 1918 offered the following main subjects for those seeking to pass the Higher Certificate:

Group I: Greek, Latin and Roman History.

Group II: English Literature, French, German, Russian, Spanish, History (either 1(a) or 1(b) and either 2(a) or 2(b)), Latin, Pure Mathematics or Higher Pure Mathematics.

Group II(B): Economics, Geography, History (1 and 2), French, German, Italian, Russian, Spanish.

Group III: Pure Mathematics or Higher Pure Mathematics, Applied Mathematics, Physics, Chemistry, Botany, Zoology.

Candidates had to satisfy the examiners in one of the four groupings (as well as passing one of a broader range of 'subsidiary' subjects).[9] The use of the University Examinations Boards by public and grammar schools facilitated the establishment of viable sixth forms 'able to act as a focal point for . . . academic goals'.[10] These academic goals, linked to specialised course requirements of university departments, developed a common sixth form pattern and 'teacher opinion seemed to accept the value of specialisation. It stimulated interest, maintained high standards of work, kept teachers close to university methods and material and added to their status.'[11]

The linking of the definition of curricula to examination boards controlled by the universities, enabled state education to be established as a 'ladder' leading to professional occupations. Building upon the three-grade classification offered by Taunton, the Bryce Commission had argued for scholarships to offer access for the most talented of all classes to the educational ladder. The ladder to the professions, with the associated curricula thereby implied, affected the social classes differentially. Less than a fifth of the generation of boys born between 1910 and 1929 reached a secondary school; a seventh of these (approximately 3 per cent of the total age group) went on to university. Two-fifths of the middle-class boys and one-tenth of the working-class boys went to secondary school, giving an opportunity ratio of 4:1. For universities the ratio for the same 1910–29 generation of boys was 6:1.[12]

Lacey has traced how the spread of university-controlled school examinations affected the functions of 'Hightown Grammar' school. Up until 1922 the school was: 'used as a jumping-off place, one of higher status than the ordinary or higher elementary school, from which it was possible to obtain the best clerical, commercial, technical and trade apprenticeships in local industry.' The implications for the school curriculum were clear: 'For this purpose a two-year course was often as good as a three-year course. Given the conditions in local industry, academic qualifications were to a large extent ignored in favour of the "secondary school boy" with a good family.'[13] After this date the content and emphasis of the headmaster's reports to the governors underwent a noticeable change and from 1923 onwards there were detailed reports on examinations, school certificates (and later Higher School Certificates) and the number of boys staying on beyond matriculation (at 16 years of age).[14] This has continued to be a major feature of secondary school reporting and associated organisation to this day. Moreover, it is interesting to note that for those boys who stay on beyond compulsory leaving age the same subject-based curriculum has remained almost totally intact for the 60 years following the 1904 Regulations. The major reasons for this stabilised subject-based pattern were the considerable power over the curriculum held by the examination boards and, secondly, the founding and growth of separate subject groups and associations. The combined activities of examination boards and subject groups and associations sustained and developed the secondary school curriculum pattern.

This pattern was critically scrutinised by the Norwood Report of 1943 which argued that throughout Europe, 'the evolution of education' had, 'thrown up certain groups, each of which can and must be treated in a way appropriate to itself.' In England three clear groups could be discerned. Firstly:

> The pupil who is interested in learning for its own sake, who can grasp an argument or follow a piece of connected reasoning, who is interested in causes, whether on the level of human volition or in the material world, who cares to know how things came to be as well as how they are, who is sensitive to language as expression of thought, to a proof as a precise demonstration, to a series of experiments justifying a principle; he is interested in the relatedness of related things, in development, in structure, in a coherent body of knowledge.

These pupils form the continuing clientele of the traditional subject-based curriculum for as Norwood states, 'such pupils, educated by the curriculum commonly associated with the Grammar School, have entered the learned professions or have taken up higher administrative or business posts.'[15] The needs of the intermediate category, 'the pupil whose interests and abilities lie markedly in the field of applied science or applied art,' were to be fulfilled by the technical schools. Finally, Norwood states with a very partial view of educational history, 'There has of late years been recognition, expressed in the framing of curricula and otherwise of still another grouping of occupations.' This third group was to provide the clientele for the new secondary modern schools.

> The pupil in this group deals more easily with concrete things than with ideas. He may have much ability, but it will be in the realm of facts. He is interested in things as they are; he finds little attraction in the past or in the slow disentanglement of causes or movements. His mind must turn its knowledge or its curiosity to immediate test; and his test is essentially practical.[16]

This curriculum, whilst ruling out certain occupational futures, certainly facilitated those destined for manual work. It 'would not be to prepare for a particular job or profession and its treatment would make a direct appeal to interests, which it would awaken by practical touch with affairs'.[17]

The Norwood Report summarises the patterns of curriculum differentiation which had emerged through 'the evolution of education' over the past century or so. The close alliance between patterns of curriculum differentiation and social structure was often conceded (e.g. in the Taunton Report in 1868): different curricula are explicitly linked to different occupational categories. The academic tradition was for the grammar school pupil destined for the learned professions and higher administrative or business posts. The more utilitarian curriculum in the technical schools was for the pupil destined to work in 'applied science or applied art'. Whilst for the future manual worker in the secondary modern the emphasis was on utilitarian and pedagogic curricula; these studies were to 'make a direct appeal to interests which it would awaken by practical touch with affairs'. The close identity between different curriculum traditions, occupational destinations (and social classes) and different educational sectors was confirmed in the 1944 Education Act.

The Tripartite System and the Raising of the School Leaving Age

The 1944 Education Act foreshadowed the tripartite system of grammar, technical and secondary modern schools. The compulsory school leaving age was raised to 15 in 1947. The Act marks the beginning of the modern era of curriculum conflict, not so much because of its details but because from this date onwards curriculum conflict becomes more visible, public and national. Glass has noted that in this respect there was no 'pre-war parallel' for there was now 'a recognition that Secondary education is a proper subject for discussion and study ... in striking contrast to the pre-war position when attempts to investigate access to the various stages of education tended to be looked at by the Government as attacks on the class structure.'[18]

In the emerging secondary modern schools the curriculum was initially free from the consideration of external examinations. This freedom allowed many of the schools to experiment with their curricula and to pursue vocational and child-centred objectives. Social studies and civic courses, for instance, were rapidly established in a number of the schools. Kathleen Gibberd has argued that the secondary modern school as conceived in 1944 was never intended to work to any universal syllabus or external examination: 'It was to be a field for experiment.' She considered that: 'Behind the official words and regulations there was a call to the teacher who believed in education for its own sake and longed for a free hand with children who were not natural learners. Many of those who responded gave an individual character to their schools.'[19] However, the period during which secondary moderns were 'a field for experiment' with vocational, child-centred and integrated curricula was to prove very limited. More parents began to realise that certification led to better jobs, teachers found examinations a useful source of motivation and heads began to use examinations as a means of raising their schools' reputation and status. For some heads support for GCE may have stemmed from an initial rebellious non-acceptance of the whole tripartite philosophy. But soon 'success in this examination started a national avalanche'.[20] By 1961–3, when Partridge studied a secondary modern school, the competitive nature of the 'examination race' was clearly apparent: 'with the public demand for academic attainments, reflecting the fact that education has become the main avenue of social mobility in our society, GCE successes would immeasurably enhance the repute of such a school, and hence the standing and status of the headmaster.'[21] The rapid take-up of the GCE and other examinations in secondary moderns led to an exhaustive inquiry by the Ministry of Education, culminating in the Beloe Report which recommended that secondary modern schools should have their own examinations. In 1965, therefore, the CSE was inaugurated.

The rapidity with which external examinations came to dominate secondary modern school curricula meant that many of the characteristics of grammar school curricula were reproduced. Paradoxically it was the growth of public debate about education which produced this pressure for the convergence of educational patterns whatever sector of the tripartite system was under consideration. But the public debate also identified considerable objections to the whole tripartite philosophy. Evidence accumulated that the 11-plus was often arbitrary and unfair. As a result support grew for a more 'comprehensive system'. The new comprehensive schools, however, also had to justify themselves in terms of examination success. They had to perform as well as the examination-oriented grammar and secondary modern schools; and for many years their examination results were to constitute a major piece of evidence in the 'comprehensive debate'.

The Changeover to a Comprehensive System and the Further Raising of the School Leaving Age

When the Labour Government took office in 1964, an early declaration was made of the intention to end divisions within secondary education along tripartite lines and to move towards a phased introduction of comprehensive schooling. The intention was publicised both in a House of Commons resolution passed in January 1965 and in the two circulars issued by the DES. Circular 10/65, 'The Organisation of Secondary Education', was issued in July 1965 to be followed by Circular 10/66 issued in March 1965 on the subject of 'school building programmes'.

The government's pronouncements met with a patchy response, even though in the year the government took office 71 per cent of all authorities either had established, or intended to establish, some form of comprehensive education.[22] In the years between 1965 and 1970 the number of comprehensive schools grew from 262 to 1,415, a growth in percentage terms from 8.5 to 31 per cent.[23] More important than the actual progress was the fact that more and more local authorities were planning comprehensive schemes: this added a sense of momentum and a growing feeling that all sectors would have to prepare for the inevitable change.

As these figures show, the belief that the Labour Government of the late sixties effected rapid changeover to comprehensives is misleading when examined in detail. The growth of the comprehensive sector in this period took place very largely at the expense of the secondary modern schools. Between 1961 and 1970 the proportion of secondary school pupils attending comprehensive schools increased from 4 per cent to 29 per cent. These pupils came mainly from secondary modern schools whose share of the secondary school population declined by 17 per cent. In comparison the grammar school population declined by only 3 per cent and the proportion of pupils in independent, direct grant and assisted schools by only 2 per cent.[24] For the grammar and independent schools, bastions of traditional academic education in this period, comprehensivisation often remained a threat rather than a reality, albeit a threat often perceived in a highly emotional manner (a common phrase in currency at the time referred to the 'vandals of comprehensivisation'). From 1970, however, comprehensive schooling spread rapidly and in 1979 approximately 80 per cent of secondary school children attended such schools.

Besides the organisational reform considerable curriculum reform was envisaged at this time. A range of influences was at work which partly arose from comprehensiviation and partly from the moves to raise the school leaving age (ROSLA). Walker and MacDonald have judged the latter as 'a far more threatening shadow on the teachers' horizon' than America's fear of the 'red menace'.[25] Though this may overstate the case, it was plain that many teachers feared the plan and took every opportunity to criticise it. Nonetheless, in 1972 the change, originally planned for 1970, was implemented. Comprehensivisation and ROSLA drew attention to the large group of students who did not even take CSE — the 'non-examination' classes. Alongside this practical problem the ideology of mixed ability teaching also argued for the provision of more 'relevant' and 'child-centred curricula'.

The curriculum reform movement gained insight and support from the preceding movement in the USA. The decision of the Nuffield Foundation to fund school curriculum development projects was partially influenced by these American developments. The Foundation began a number of projects beginning with Nuffield 'O' level projects in physics, chemistry and biology in 1962 but covering many other subjects besides science, for instance, classics and languages. When the Schools Council for Curriculum and Examinations was established in 1964, development projects began in co-operation with Nuffield. Robert Morris, one of the first Joint Secretaries of the Council, states that its work 'was initially carried on the shoulders of Nuffield finance into a curriculum development role'.[26] Several of the early Schools Council projects grew out of Nuffield initiatives, for instance two of the science projects: Science 5–13 and Integrated Science. Other projects, like the Humanities Curriculum Project, were jointly funded by Schools Council and the Nuffield Foundation.

Rubinstein and Simon have left a summary of the climate of educational reform in 1972 following ROSLA, and the rapid growth of the comprehensive system:

The content of the curriculum is now under much discussion, and comprehensive schools are participating actively in the many curriculum reform schemes launched by the Schools Council and Nuffield. The tendency is towards the development of the interdisciplinary curricula, together with the use of the resources approach to learning, involving the substitution of much group and individual work for the more traditional forms of class teaching. For these new forms of organising and stimulating learning mixed ability grouping often provides the most appropriate method; and partly for this reason the tendency is towards the reduction of streaming and class teaching. This movement in itself promotes new relations between teachers and pupils, particularly insofar as the teacher's role is changing from that of ultimate authority to that of motivating, facilitating and structuring the pupils' own discovery and search for knowledge.[27]

The belief that rapid curriculum reform, with a range of associated political and pedagogical implications, was well under way was commonly held at this time. Professor Kerr asserted in 1968 that 'At the practical and organisational levels, the new curricula promise to revolutionise English education.'[28]

At the very time when some teachers were seeing integrated or interdisciplinary courses as the strategy for establishing new curricula, other voices were warning of the dangers inherent in curriculum reforms then being pursued. Marten Shipman read a paper before the British Sociological Association in 1969 which argued that the curriculum reforms were in danger of perpetuating the two nations approach inside the educational system, what he called a 'Curriculum for Inequality'. He spoke of the 'unintended consequences of curriculum development':

Coming less from actual content than from the introduction of new courses into a school system that is still clearly divided into two sections, one geared to a system of external examinations, the other less constrained. The former is closely tied to the universities and is within established academic traditions. The latter has a short history and is still in its formative stages. It is the consequences of innovation into these two separate sections rather than the curricula themselves which may be producing a new means of sustaining old divisions.[29]

The connecting traditions are elucidated later in the paper:

One is firmly planted in revered academic traditions, is adapted to teaching from a pool of factual knowledge and has clearly defined, if often irrelevant subject boundaries. The other is experimental, looking to America rather than our own past for inspiration, focusses on contemporary problems, groups subjects together and rejects formal teaching methods. One emphasises a schooling within a framework of external examinations, the other attempts to align school work to the environment of the children.[30]

The divisive effects of curriculum reform were not, however, the major features to gain attention. In October 1976 the Prime Minister, James Callaghan, drew together the major themes of public anxiety about curriculum in a speech he made at Ruskin College which launched the so-called 'Great Debate' on education. He was worried about what kind of curriculum pupils were being offered, about modern teaching methods, about educational standards and about the relationship between school and industry. In effect he was calling into question the whole pattern and efficiency of curriculum reform. 'No new policies were proposed but the government had now established that educational standards, and the relationship of education to the economy, were to be as much of a priority as comprehensive reform in isolation.' The concern with school-industry links touches on a recurrent and illustrative theme in curriculum history. Callaghan stated that he was concerned to find that many of 'our best trained students who have completed the higher levels of education at university or polytechnic have no desire to join industry.' He concluded that there seemed to be a need for 'a more technological bias in science teaching that will lead towards practical applications in industry rather than towards academic studies.[31] This tendency has been built upon and substantially extended since the victory of the Conservative party in 1979, not least through the new Technical and Vocational Initiative. At the time of going to press (1987) this is about to be further expanded. Thus it would seem that despite radical changes in the organisational structure of the educational system, the underlying fabric of curriculum has remained surprisingly constant.

A footnote is provided in a book by Hopkins on the 'School Debate'. He notes that 'part of the theory behind comprehensive reform was to extend the opportunities for practical study so as to favour technological advance'. But concludes 'the resulting technological advance appears to have been small (why, otherwise, a great Debate) and the status of practical subjects remains low'.[32] It would appear that, despite the unification behind comprehensivisation, despite an explicit desire to broaden the appeal of practical (and also the more pedagogic) subjects, patterns of status differentiation have been substantially sustained. It seems that it will be impossible to realise the ambitions of comprehensive educational reform unless we have a better understanding of the part played by the subjects of the curriculum in preserving a divided system in the face of organisational change. We may understand the apparent paradox more fully if we analyse the role of subject associations, sub-groups and traditions in modifying and sustaining patterns of curriculum differentiation in the era of comprehensive schooling. This will be the subject of the next chapter.

Notes

1. R. WILLIAMS, *The Long Revolution* (Harmondsworth, Penguin, 1961), pp. 156–7.
2. Report of the Royal Commission known as the Schools Inquiry Commission (the Taunton Report), 1868, Ch. 7, p. 587.

3   S. ROTHBLATT, *The Revolution of the Dons* (London, Faber and Faber, 1968).
4   R. WILLIAMS, *The Long Revolution*, p. 158.
5   J. RYDER and H. SILVER, *Modern English Society, History and Structure 1850–1970* (London, Methuen, 1970), p. 97.
6   D.V. GLASS, 'Education and social change in modern England', in R. HOOPER, (Ed.), *The Curriculum Context, Design and Development* (Edinburgh, Oliver and Boyd, 1971), p. 25.
7   RYDER and SILVER, *Modern English Society*, p. 98.
8   R. WILLIAMS, *The Long Revolution*, pp. 159–60.
9   'Joint Matriculation Board Calendar' (Manchester, 1918), pp. 41–2.
10 W.A. REID, *The University and the Sixth Form Curriculum* (London, Macmillan, 1972), p. 88.
11 A.D. EDWARDS, *The Changing Sixth Form* (London, Routledge and Kegan Paul), p. 34.
12 GLASS, in R. HOOPER (Ed.), pp. 28–29.
13 C. LACEY, *Hightown Grammar*, (Manchester University Press, 1970), p. 15.
14 *Ibid.*, p. 21.
15 THE NORWOOD REPORT, *Curriculum and Examinations in Secondary Schools*, Report of the Committee of the Secondary School Examinations Council appointed by the President of the Board of Education in 1941 (London, HMSO, 1943), p. 2.
16 *Ibid.*, p. 3.
17 *Ibid.*, p. 4.
18 GLASS, in R. HOOPER (Ed.), p. 35
19 K. GIBBERD, *No Place Like School* (London, Michael Joseph, 1962), p. 103.
20 *Ibid.*, p. 102.
21 J. PARTRIDGE, *Life in a Secondary Modern School* (Harmondsworth, Penguin, 1968), p. 68.
22 NATIONAL FOUNDATION FOR EDUCATIONAL RESEARCH, *Local Authorities Practices in the Allocation of Pupils to Secondary Schools* (Slough, NFER, 1964).
23 D. RUBINSTEIN and R. SIMON, *The Evolution of the Comprehensive School 1926–1972* (London, Routledge and Kegan Paul, 1973), p. 108.
24 *Ibid.*, pp. 110–12. The figures are completed by a 2 per cent reduction in separate 'technical schools'.
25 B. MACDONALD and R. WALKER, *Changing the Curriculum*, (London, Open Books, 1976), p. 32.
26 Interview with ROBERT MORRIS, 26.7.78.
27 RUBINSTEIN and SIMON, *Comprehensive School 1926–1972*, p. 123.
28 J. KERR, 'The problem of curriculum reform', *op. cit.*, R. HOOPER (Ed.), p. 180.
29 M. SHIPMAN, 'Curriculum for inequality', *op. cit.*, R. HOOPER (Ed.) 1976, pp. 101–2.
30 *Ibid.*, p. 104.
31 Speech by JAMES CALLAGHAN, Prime Minister 18 October 1976, Ruskin College.
32 A. HOPKINS, *The School Debate* (Harmondsworth, Penguin, 1978), p. 139.

3   Academic 'Subjects' and Curriculum Change

Introduction

The historical background presented in Chapter 2 points to the emergence of a hierarchy of high-status 'examination subjects' associated with 'revered academic traditions'. The direct connection between 'O' an 'A' level examinations and the academic tradition is one of the most enduring features of our educational system and it is normally assumed that 'able pupils' are those who can pass 'O' and 'A' level examinations. These assumptions have been faithfully reproduced in the change over from a tripartite to a comprehensive system.

The taken for granted assumption that 'O' and 'A' level examinations cover 'academic' content and are aimed at 'able' pupils, represents the culmination of a conflict that is briefly recorded in Chapter 2. In this conflict a number of alternative traditions to the academic tradition could be discerned: for instance the technical and vocational curricula promoted within the elementary schools in the late nineteenth century. These alternative traditions represent fundamental and recurrent elements in curriculum conflict. To understand their continuing subservience to the academic tradition, it is necessary to first define the major 'alternative' traditions and then to analyse the conflict over the curriculum, particularly with reference to the nature of 'examinable knowledge'. In this conflict the varying 'traditions' gain the allegiance of different sub-groups or factions among subject teachers. The academic tradition's dominance needs above all to be understood through an analysis of the nature of its appeal to these groups.

The process model developed by Bucher and Strauss for the study of professions provides valuable guidelines for those studying school subjects. Within a profession, they argue, are varied identities, values and interests, hence professions are to be seen as 'loose amalgamations of segments pursuing different objectives in different manners and more or less delicately held together under a common name at particular periods in history.'[1] The most frequent conflicts arise over the gaining of institutional footholds, over recruitment and over external relations with clients and other institutions. At times when conflicts such as these become intense professional associations may be created, or if already in existence, become more strongly institutionalised.

The Bucher and Strauss model of professions suggests that perhaps the 'subject community' should not be viewed as a homogeneous group whose members share similar values and definitions of role, common interests and identity. Rather the subject community could be seen as comprising a range of conflicting groups, segments or factions. The importance of these groups might vary considerably over time. As with professions, school subject associations often develop at particular points in time when there is an intensification of conflict over school curricula and resources and over recruitment and training.

In this book the subject community is therefore seen as comprising a shifting network of sub-groups, segments or factions. These sub-groups might, for instance, be organised around different schools of thought with different views about which knowledge should be emphasised within the subject: field work or laboratory work in biology, or regional geography as against new geography.

One of the main sources of argument between these subgroups (and indeed between subject communities) is the nature and purpose of the school curriculum. There is a long history of these arguments and it is useful to discern three major traditions: the academic, the utilitarian and the pedagogic.

Since the nineteenth century 'academic subjects' and written examinations have become closely interconnected. The alliance, whether viewed as divine or malign, was formally enshrined in the School Certificate examination defined in 1917. Since that date certain material implications have followed for those subgroups and school subjects promoting or representing the academic tradition. Questions of theoretical base or methodological perspective have often been subsumed by or channelled into the construction of acceptable written examinations. For the groups and associations promoting themselves as school subjects, and irresistibly drawn to claiming 'academic status', a central criterion has been whether the subjects' content could be tested by written examinations for an 'able' clientele. Acceptance of the criterion of examinability affects both the content and form of the knowledge presented but carries with it the guarantee of high status. The academic tradition is content-focused and typically stresses abstract and theoretical knowledge for examination.

The utilitarian tradition is conversely of low status, dealing with practical knowledge sometimes not amenable to the current 'A' level mode of written examination. Utilitarian knowledge is related to those non-professional vocations in which the majority of people work for most of their adult life. The low status of utilitarian knowledge also applies to the personal, social and commonsense knowledge stressed by those pursuing the pedagogic tradition. Whilst all school knowledge has at least an implicit pedagogy this tradition places the 'way the child learns' as the central concern in devising subject content.

School Subjects and Curriculum Change

These traditions are viewed as three 'centres of gravity' in the arguments about styles of curriculum. They do not represent a complete list of the 'traditions' in English curricula nor are they timeless entities; they simply represent three clear constellations of curriculum styles which recur in the history of the school subjects under study. In this sense they are perhaps best viewed as strategic clusters employed to help in the scrutiny of curriculum changes and conflicts.

At certain stages in their history, subjects may come to be represented by subject associations. These associations present a formal arena wherein sub-groups can promote their varied interests and where the arguments about curriculum traditions can be pursued. The range of groups involved in school subjects — sub-groups, factions, associations and communities — will be broadly referred to as subject groups.

School Subject 'Traditions' and Curriculum Change

The historical background of the English curriculum and the studies of historical elements in curriculum (notably by Layton, Williams and Banks) point to the existence of several leading traditions. Often these traditions can be related to the social class origins and occupational destinations of their pupil clienteles. Hence the curricula of public and grammar schools aimed at middle- and upper-class children preparing for professional life were primarily academic, whilst the elementary schools educating the majority stressed utilitarian training.

Writing of the 'traditions' in English primary education, Blyth discerned three different kinds: the preparatory, the elementary and the developmental. The preparatory tradition was 'almost exclusively related to what we now call grammar-school education, which developed in its turn mainly as an upper middle-class phenomenon.' Conversely the elementary tradition 'with its characteristic emphasis on the basic skills' was aimed at the lower classes. 'For those who were unfortunate, indolent or culpable enough to be poor, the minimum of education was proper and sufficient.'[2] The third tradition, the developmental, based its principles on concern with developing each child's interest in learning along the lines recommended by Rousseau and Pestalozzi. Broadly speaking Blyth's three primary traditions can be equated with three leading traditions discerned within secondary education: the preparatory with the academic, the elementary with the utilitarian and the developmental with the pedagogic traditions.

Academic, Utilitarian and Pedagogic Traditions

The definition of public and grammar school subjects in the nineteenth century which was established in the 1904 regulations and confirmed in the School

Academic 'Subjects' and Curriculum Change

Certificate examinations clearly followed the aims of education as a preparation for professional and academic life. Eggleston, commenting on the early nineteenth century, found that 'A new and important feature of the time that was to prevail, was the redefinition of high-status knowledge as that which was not immediately useful in vocation or occupation.' Hence the study of Classics 'now came to be seen as essentially a training of the mind and the fact that a boy could be spared from work long enough to experience this in full measure was in itself seen as a demonstration not only of the high status of the knowledge itself but also of the recipient — the mark of a "gentleman" rather than a worker.'[3] Eggleston's last sentence points up the contradiction: it was not so much that classical liberal education was non-vocational but that the vocations were only those fit for upper-class gentlemen. 'As educational history shows', Williams reminds us, 'the classical linguistic disciplines were primarily vocational but these particular vocations had acquired a separate traditional dignity, which was refused to vocations now of equal human relevance.'[4]

For this reason we have avoided the use of the terms vocational education or vocational knowledge. Instead we refer to the subject-based curriculum confirmed by the examination system as the 'academic' tradition, and to low-status practical knowledge as the 'utilitarian' tradition. Utilitarian knowledge thus becomes that which is related to those non-professional vocations in which the majority of people work for most of their adult life.

Despite being advocated by a number of influential government committees and commissions, neither commerical nor technical education was ever seriously considered as a new dimension of comparable status to be added to the existing classical curriculum. It was specialised training for a particular class of man, and its confinement to low-status areas of the curriculum has remained a constant feature of English curriculum conflict. For example, Layton's research on the development of science education in the nineteenth century has shown how the emphasis was increasingly placed on abstract knowledge with a consequent separation from the practical world of work.[5] Nevertheless, the alternative view of a narrowly utilitarian curriculum is still powerful, as is shown by the constant pressure for utilitarian subjects in spite of their recurrent failure to earn high status. The manpower needs of a changing industrial economy provoke continuing advocacy of utilitarian training, by industrialists although these demands are at their most shrill at times of pervasive crisis in the economic and social system. When widespread industrial failure is endemic the continuing ambivalence of educational status systems causes serious concern and pressure for change. The Great Debate was one symptom of this concern and it has been argued in 'The Times' that:

> strategies for furthering the inter-relationship between industry and the educational system need to address the complex question of status systems. The established patterns of status represent an enormously powerful historical legacy, a kind of indirect pressure group. Only if high status areas in the educational system such as the public schools

and Oxbridge are willing to remodel their value systems do current strategies stand any chance of success.[6]

The low status of utilitarian knowledge is shared by the personal, social and commonsense knowledge stressed by those pursuing a child-centred approach to education. This approach with its emphasis on the individual pupil's learning process can be characterised as the pedagogic tradition within the English curriculum. Child-centred or progressive education does not view the task of education as preparation for the 'ladder' to the professions and academia or as an apprenticeship to vocational work; rather education is seen as a way of aiding the child's own 'inquiries' or 'discoveries', a process facilitated by 'activity' methods which move the pupil away from the role of passive recipient to one of active agent in the learning process. The approach was found in the Social Studies movement of the 1930s and 1940s: 'The outlook is essentially broad and exploratory and the course is broken up into a series of correlated units of study rather than conducted as a rigid sequence of lessons. It thus offers endless opportunities for active learning; for relating the lesson to contemporary events for co-operative study by the form as a group.'[7] The pedagogic tradition often challenges the existing professional identity of teachers at two levels: (1) as a 'specialist' in a school subject, for which the teacher had normally been specifically trained; and (2) as an all-pervading authority figure within the classroom. The Interdisciplinary Enquiry (IDE) workshops run by Goldsmiths College in the sixties clarify the dual nature of the challenge. The workshops were specifically instituted as pilot courses for experienced teachers involved with those school leavers that would be staying on as a result of ROSLA.

The IDE booklets contained a series of stark messages for teachers of traditional subjects and suggested that 'the subject based curriculum has fundamental educational disadvantages'. For instance, 'the school day is fragmented into subject periods and time allocated to each subject is always regarded as insufficient by the subject specialist, as indeed it is.' Apart from the disadvantages in terms of time:

> The arbitrary division of knowledge into subject-syllabuses, encourages a didactic form of teaching with the pupils' role reduced to passive assimilation. Any enquiry resulting from a keen interest shown by children in a section of work they are doing in a subject inevitably takes them over the boundaries of the subject into another, perhaps several others. Good teachers would like to encourage this evidence of interest, but they simply cannot afford the time, especially if their syllabus is geared to external examinations.[8]

As a solution to the problems engendered by the didactic teaching of traditional subjects the Goldsmiths team advocated organising schemes of work around interdisciplinary enquiries.[9]

Another curriculum project aimed at young school leavers underlined both

Academic 'Subjects' and Curriculum Change

the need to reappraise 'subjects' and to clearly define new pedagogic relationships. The Humanities Curriculum Project (HCP) began in 1967 with Lawrence Stenhouse as its director. HCP pursued the pedagogic implications of curriculum reform through the notion of 'neutral chairmanship'. This meant: 'That the teacher accepts the need to submit his teaching in controversial areas to the criterion of neutrality ... i.e. that he regards it as part of his responsibility not to promote his own view,' and further that 'the mode of enquiry in controversial areas should have discussion, rather than instruction as its core'.[10] The pedagogic tradition has been closely allied to the so-called 'progressive' movement in education. As Shipman noted in 1969, the more progressive curricula have come to be concentrated on those sections of the pupil clientele not considered suitable for 'O' and 'A' level examinations.[11] In this way the pedagogic tradition has often suffered from the comparatively low status also accorded to the utilitarian tradition.

Examinations and Academic Subject

The connection between the subjects taught in school and external examinations was established on the present footing with the birth of the School Certificate in 1917. From this point on, the conflict over the curriculum began to resemble the contemporary situation in focusing on the definition and evaluation of examinable knowledge. The School Certificate rapidly became the major concern of grammar schools and the academic subjects it examined soon came to dominate the school timetable. Thus when the Norwood Report assessed the importance of examinations it found that

> A certain sameness in the curricula of schools seems to have resulted from the double necessity of finding a place for the many subjects competing for time in the curriculum and the need to teach these subjects in such a way and to such a standard as will ensure success in the School Certificate examination.

As a result of 'these necessities' the curriculum had 'settled down into an uneasy equilibrium, the demands of specialists and subjects and examinations being nicely adjusted and compensated'.[12] Despite these warnings, the academic subject-centred curriculum was strengthened in the period following the 1944 Education Act. The introduction of the GCE in 1951 allowed subjects to be taken separately at 'O' level (whereas the School Certificate was a 'block' exam in which a group of main subjects all had to be passed), and the introduction of 'A' level increased subject specialisation in a manner guaranteed to preserve if not enhance the largely 'academic' nature of the 'O' level examination. There was little chance that a lower-status examination such as the CSE which was introduced in 1965, would endanger the academic subject-centredness of the higher status 'O' and 'A' levels.

Indeed the CSE has proved remarkably adaptive to maintaining the status differentiation noted by Shipman and has even extended it. A recent study by Ball shows four bands within a comprehensive school allocating pupils as follows: band 1 to subject-based 'O' levels; band 2 to subject-based CSE mode 2; band 3 to 'integrated' subjects (e.g. Maths. for Living) for CSE mode 3; and band 4 to non-examined 'remedial' classes.[13]

The hegemony of the academic subject-based curriculum for 'O' level and 'A' level candidates was confirmed by the organisational structure of the Schools Council. An early role for the Council in the examinations field was advising the Beloe Committee set up to consider the proliferation of examinations in secondary modern schools. Beloe employed the subject-based framework of the Secondary Schools Examination Council, set up in the interwar years to ensure uniformity of examinations, mainly at 'O' and 'A' levels. As Robert Morris, one of the two founding joint secretaries, explained: 'You can now see why the Schools Council developed a committee structure based on subjects. It was simply logical ... we just inherited the structure of the Secondary Schools Examinations Council who had already developed a pattern for examination in academic subjects.'[14]

Accepting this structure of academic subject examinations, interest groups promoting new subjects have focused since 1917 on the pursuit of high-status examinations and qualifications. Subjects like art, woodwork and metalwork, technical studies, book-keeping, typewriting and needlework, domestic science and physical education, have consistently pursued status improvement by arguing for enhanced academic examinations and qualifications. But as we have seen, few subjects have been able to challenge the hegemony of the academic subjects incorporated in the 1904 Regulations and 1917 School Certificate. This academic tradition has successfully withstood the recent waves of comprehensive reorganisation and associated curriculum reform. The upheaval of the 'Great Debate' in the mid-1970s and the initiatives under the Thatcher government is a reminder that this survival appears to have been at the expense of certain 'dominant interests' in the economy.

Academic Subjects, Status and Resources

The strong historical connection between academic subjects and external examinations is only partly explained by 'the need to teach these subjects in such a way and to such a standard as will ensure success in the School Certificate examination'.[15] The years after 1917 saw a range of significant development in the professionalisation of teachers. Increasingly with the establishment of specialised subject training courses, secondary school teachers came to see themselves as part of a 'subject community'. The associated growth of subject associations both derived from and confirmed this trend. This increasing identification of secondary teachers with subject communities tended to separate them from each other, and as schools became larger, departmental forms of organisation arose which reinforced the separation. Thus the subject-centred curriculum developed to the point where the

Academic 'Subjects' and Curriculum Change

Norwood Report in 1943 expressed considerable concern and, in doing so, hinted at the political as well as academic side of curriculum conflict:

> Subjects have tended to become preserves belonging to specialist teachers; barriers have been erected between them, and teachers have felt unqualified or not free to trespass upon the dominions of other teachers. The specific values of each subject have been pressed to the neglect of the values common to several or all. The school course has come to resemble the 'hundred yards' course, each subject following a track marked off from the others by a tape. In the meantime we feel, the child is apt to be forgotten.

Norwood summarises the position by saying that 'subjects seem to have built themselves vested interests and rights of their own'.[16] In explaining the continuing connection between external examinations and academic subjects, the part played by the vested interests of the subject groups needs to be analysed. The dominance of academic subjects with high-status examination credentials would need to be in close harmony with the vested interests of subject groups to explain the strength of this structure over so long a period.

The 'subject' label is important at a number of levels. Obviously as school 'examination' category, but also as a title for a 'degree' or 'training course'. Perhaps most important of all the subject defines the territory of a 'department' within each school. With the important exception of administrative and pastoral work, the subject is the major reference point in the work of the contemporary secondary school: the information and knowledge transmitted in schools is formally selected and organised through subjects. The teacher is identified by the pupils and relates to them mainly through her or his subject specialism. Given the size of most comprehensive schools a number of teachers are required for each subject; and these teachers are normally organised in subject 'departments'. The departments have a range of 'graded posts' for special responsibilities and for the 'head the Department'. In this way the teacher's subject provides the means whereby salary is decided and career structure defined, and influence on school policy channelled.

Within school subjects there is a clear hierarchy of status which is based partly upon assumptions that certain subjects, the so-called 'academic' subjects, are suitable for the 'able' students whilst other subjects are not. In her study of resource allocation in schools Eileen Byrne has shown how more resources are given to these able students and hence to the academic subjects. She drew attention to two assumptions 'which might be questioned' that have been seen 'consistently to underly educational planning and the consequent resource-allocation for the more able children: First, that these necessarily need longer in school than non-grammar pupils, and secondly, that they necessarily need more staff, more highly paid staff and more money for equipment and books.'[17] Byrne's research ended in 1965 before widespread comprehensivisation, and therefore refers to the tripartite system. However, referring to the new comprehensive system she wrote in 1974 that there was 'little indication that a majority of councils or chief officers accept in principle the need for review and reassessment of the entire process of the allocation of resources in relation to the planned application, over a period of years, of an approved and progressive policy, or coherent educational development.'[18]

That comprehensive schools do place overwhelming emphasis on academic examinations, in spite of the growth of 'pastoral systems', has been recently confirmed by Ball's study of Beachside Comprehensive. He notes that 'once reorganised as a comprehensive, academic excellence was quickly established as a central tenet of the value system of the school.'[19] He provides a range of qualitative and statistical indicators to confirm this contention and concludes that 'while the division is less clear-cut and stark than in the grammar school' nonetheless it is evident that 'the teacher-resources within the comprehensive school are allocated differently according to the pupil's ability. Thus the most experienced teachers spend most of their time teaching the most able pupils. This is a reflection of the fact that the social and psychological rewards offered by the school to its pupils accrue to those who are academically successful and that academic achievement tended to be the single criterion of success in the school.'[20]

Through the study of Beachside Comprehensive considerable evidence is assembled to prove Marsden's prediction that 'if we give the new comprehensive the task of competing with selective schools for academic qualifications, the result will be remarkably little change in the selective nature of education. Selection will take place within the school and the working-class child's education will still suffer.'[21] The importance of different curriculum traditions for each ability band of pupils is central in confirming these selective patterns. After the first term we learn 'the increasing differences of syllabus and curriculum which develop between the bands mean that band 2 or band 3 pupils would have to perform exceptionally well if not brilliantly to overcome the limitations placed upon them by the organisation of the syllabus.'[22] Ball notes that the pattern of curriculum differentiation is 'not unlike that made in The Norwood Report for fourth and fifth year pupils.'[23] At the top of the hierarchy of subjects are the traditional 'O' level subjects like maths, English, the languages, sinces, history and geography? These high-status subjects have 'an academic orientation in common; they are concerned with theoretical knowledge. They are subjects for the brighter, the academic, the band 1 pupil. Below these in status come "O" levels in practical subjects like technical studies and metalwork. For band 2 and 3 pupils there are traditional C.S.E.s and lowest of all in status new Mode III C.S.E.s.'[24]

In a detailed and illuminating study of how the option system works it is possible to discern how curriculum categories and pupil clienteles (and futures) are 'matched' by the teachers. Ball shows how this works for two classes — the band 1 class 3CU and the band 2 class 3TA. After the option system has worked the '3TA pupils have been directed away from the "academic" to the practical, while the reverse has happened for the 3CU pupils'.[25] The study shows clearly that working-class pupils concentrate in bands 2 and 3 and

Academic 'Subjects' and Curriculum Change

further that the 'differentiation of access to high status knowledge with high negotiable value is crucially related to socio-economic status'. He concludes:

> Option-allocation is a point at which school careers become firmly differentiated and at which the informal differences between pupils in terms of social reputation and their experiences of the curriculum lower down the school are formalised into separate curricular routes and examination destinations. It is here that the stratified nature of the occupation structure is directly reflected in the ability stratification within the school.
>
> Both the differential status of the knowledge areas in the curriculum and the access to the sixth form that certain courses provide are aspects of the selection of pupils for further and higher education and the occupation market. The selection process and negotiation of meanings that go to make up the option-allocation procedure are part of the structural relationships within the school which label pupils with different statures and educational identities.[26]

A number of studies confirm that a status hierarchy exists for school subjects. Warwick reports that a 1968 survey showed that over 7 per cent of the male teachers who had studied within the languages and literature group (forming just over 19 per cent of the total sample), had become head teachers, compared with less than 1 per cent of those who had studied in the field of technology and handicraft (who formed just over 11 per cent of the total sample). Similarly, among male teachers 'former students of languages and literature had apparently four times as many chances as former students of music and drama, and $1\frac{1}{2}$ times the chances of former students of science and mathematics of becoming headmasters.'[27] The hierarchy of subjects is clearly derived from traditional grammar school preferences. Stevens reports that here

> 'English, science, languages and mathematics are in general the subjects in which success or lack of it is significant for the children. The fact that practical subjects come low on the scale does not in itself support an assumption that more intelligent children are weak, even comparatively, at practical subjects ... The figures are interesting rather as indicating the degree of importance with which several people, but chiefly the staff, invest subjects for the children.[28]

Also important in confirming the hierarchy of status in favour of academic subjects is the part played by university admissions policies. Reid found that the universities 'exercise almost complete control over their own admissions policies; they are seldom compelled by pressures of supply and demand, or by public policy, to revise their selection criteria; and they occupy positions of high prestige in the social structure of the disciplines.'[29] In the hierarchy of subjects no subject found complete support in its acceptability to university departments but mathematics came very close. Most of the subjects which are well established as university studies are strongly supported but 'practical and aesthetic subjects are accorded sharply lower recognition'.[30] Other subjects less well accepted were those, such as General Studies, 'which are not clearly associated with a specific discipline'. The full version of Reid's findings are presented in Table 3.1.[31]

Table 3.1: *Acceptability of 'A' Level Subject Passes to a Sample of University Departments (n = 84)*

Pure mathematics	0.92	German	0.63
Pure mathematics w. stat.	0.83	Economics	0.62
Pure mathematics w. mech.	0.82	Greek	0.62
Physics	0.81	Geology	0.61
SMP mathematics	0.78	Nuffield biology	0.60
Further mathematics	0.78	Latin	0.60
Physical science	0.71	British government	0.49
Chemistry	0.70	General studies	0.49
SMP further mathematics	0.69	Engineering science	0.46
History	0.67	Scripture knowledge	0.46
Biology	0.66	Music	0.44
Geography	0.66	Art	0.37
French	0.65	Elements of eng. design	0.27
English literature	0.64	Geom. and eng. drawing	0.24
Nuffield chemistry	0.64	Housecraft	0.15
Spanish	0.64		

The evidence presented confirms that in secondary schools the self-interest of subject teachers is closely connected with the status of the subject in terms of its examinable knowledge. Academic subjects provide the teacher with a career structure characterised by better promotion prospects and pay than less academic subjects. Seen from this viewpoint the conflict over the status of examinable knowledge is therefore essentially a battle over the material resources and career prospects available to each subject community. Of course many other arguments are mobilised in the decisions over how knowledge is defined — the utilitarian and pedagogic traditions owe their existence to radically different visions of the assumptions and intentions which underpin school subjects. Despite the recurrence of these traditions we would hypothesise that subject sub-groups or associations whose paramount concern is the material interests of their members, would over time pursue academic status. In this pursuit the aspiration to gain 'O' and 'A' level examinations in the subject is of central importance. By examining the case of a new subject contender for 'O' and 'A' level status the process of curriculum conflict and change can be analysed in detail.

Subjects in Evolution and the Case of Environmental Education

The studies in this book have been devised to test a number of hypotheses generated from previous curriculum studies and from a historical review of the

Academic 'Subjects' and Curriculum Change

changing contexts within which the curriculum is negotiated. The starting point is the belief that subjects should not be viewed as monolithic entities but as social communities containing groups with conflicting loyalties and intentions and with variable and changing boundaries. The major sub-groups or factions of subject communities often ally themselves to particular traditions and three main traditions have been tentatively discerned: the academic, the utilitarian and the pedagogic.

The material interests of teachers — their pay, promotion and conditions — are broadly interlinked with the fate of their specialist subject communities. The 'academic' subject is placed at the top of the hierarchy of subjects because resource allocation takes place on the basis of assumptions that such subjects are best suited for the able students who, it is further assumed, should receive favourable treatment. For this reason, a second hypothesis is that subject groups pursuing the material interests of their members will move progressively away from the utilitarian and pedagogic traditions and promote themselves as 'academic' subjects. The associated model of internal subject change would postulate a number of stages culminating at the point where 'the selection of subject matter is determined in large measure by the judgements and practices of the specialist scholars who lead enquiries in the field'. In the final stage the subject has its own intellectual leadership to confirm its academic character and to aid in establishing academic examinations in the subject's area of knowledge.

In order to develop a model of subject change, in Part Two three subjects have been studied in evolution: geography, biology and rural studies. Where possible, documentary evidence and the personal accounts of subject members are presented, so as to build on the existing studies in the field. The fates of the three main traditions are then traced as the subjects evolve.

Patterns of status and change do not, however, determine the curriculum solely through internal subject change. The major part of the book tries to analyse the role that the pursuit of academic status plays in the relationship between subjects. In particular the book focuses on a new contender for academic status in the form of environmental education. The main subjects involved in the aspirations of this new contender for a place in the curriculum were again geography, biology and rural studies. Curriculum conflict between subjects takes place over the issue of external examination, for if the new contender can gain high status 'O' and 'A' level examinations which are broadly accepted, then it claims academic, and therefore material and financial parity.

To analyse the nature of subject group responses it is necessary to focus on the main strategies such groups utilise to promote their members' interests. Curriculum conflict takes place against a changing background both in terms of the organisation of the educational system and the broader fabric of the national economy. Within this changing 'arena' it is possible to discern both changes in the rules of conflict and changes in the 'weaponry' employed. Certain features of the 'battlefield' have remained remarkably unchanged since 1917. The year which saw the introduction of the tank and the aeroplane heralding the modern era of warfare, also saw the birth of the School

Certificate examinations which, together with their successor the GCEs, have dominated the modern era of curriculum conflict. As we shall see, it is these examinations which have shaped the rules and weapons with which rival subject groups have contested the 'territory' of the school timetable.

Among the subject groups and communities considered in this book the power which is conferred by academic examinations means that they are drawn inexorably into playing the 'status game' concerning the nature of examinable knowledge in their subject. Such status promotion most often follows the rules of professional debate among 'associations', but the central concern is to move away from pedagogically pupil-centred or utilitarian knowledge to abstract, theoretical knowledge embodied in 'A' level examinations.

By laying claim to high-status 'academic' formulations of the subject these subject associations ensure that the special interests of their members are best served. 'Child-centred' or 'utilitarian' formulations of the subject would be at the expense of the subject communities' self-interest. This is because it is the status rather than the usefulness or relevance of each subject's examinable knowledge which ultimately takes priority. 'A' level examinations characteristically stress theoretical and 'academic' knowledge — not child-centred or basic utilitarian content; and for the subject community the establishment of an 'A' level base is crucial. It usually guarantees a subject's territory in terms of a separate 'department' or even 'faculty'; and it also ensures priority inside the school in terms of finance, rooms, furnishings, equipment, resources and graded posts. Further, 'academic' status ensures that members can claim priority in the allocation of pupil clienteles inside the school.

To develop a detailed understanding of how the conflict over examinable knowledge actually takes place, Part Three of the book concentrates on a study of an attempt to develop an 'A' level in environmental studies. Fortunately, this instance is extremely well documented, partly because the main protagonists believed publicity would further their cause. The 'A' level was promoted to establish 'a discipline of sufficient rigour as to be recognised by universities generally', and followed a Schools Council working paper which in 1969 perceived 'the need for a scholarly discipline' which would 'take the form of an integrated course of study based upon environmental experience'.

The main promoters of the 'A' level in environmental studies were the rural studies teachers: for this reason the book will focus more on the rural studies group as the instigators and pioneers in the definition of this new area of knowledge. In the early stages of the enterprise the biologists and geographers were merely unconcerned, or latently hostile, observers. The next two chapters deal with the histories of these two school subjects as a precursor to examining their reactions to the development of 'environmental studies' by rural studies teachers.

Academic 'Subjects' and Curriculum Change

Notes

1. R. Bucher and A. Strauss 'Professions in process', in M. Hammersley and P. Woods (Eds.), *The Process of Schooling* (London, Routledge and Kegan Paul, 1976), p. 19.
2. W.A.L. Blyth, *English Primary Education, A Sociological Description*, Vol. 2 (London, Routledge and Kegan Paul, 1965), p. 30 and pp. 124–5.
3. J. Eggleston, *The Sociology of the School Curriculum* (London, Routledge and Kegan Paul, 1978), p. 25.
4. R. Williams, *The Long Revolution*, 1961, p. 163.
5. D. Layton, *Science for the People* (London, George Allen and Unwin, 1973).
6. I. Goodson, 'Why Britain needs to change its image of the educated man', *The Times* 14 February 1978.
7. J. Hemming, *The Teaching of Social Studies in Secondary Schools* (London, Longmans, 1949). Quoted in D. Gleeson and G. Whitty, *Developments in Social Studies Teaching* (London, Open Books, 1976), p. 5.
8. University of London, Goldsmiths College, *The Raising of the School Leaving Age, Second Pilot Course for Experienced Teachers* (Autumn Term, 1965), p. 4.
9. *Ibid.*, p. 5.
10. The Schools Council/Nuffield Foundation *The Humanities Porject: An Introduction* (London, heinemann, 1972), p. 1.
11. Shipman, in R Hooper (Ed.), 1970.
12. The Norwood Report, *Curriculum and Examinations in Secondary Schools*, Report of the Committee of the Secondary School Examinations Council Appointed by the President of the Board of Education in 1941 (London, HMSO, 1943), p. 61.
13. S. Ball, 'Processes of Comprehensive Schooling: A Case Study' (unpublished Ph.D., Sussex University, 1978).
14. Interview with Robert Morris, 26.7.78.
15. See, p. 29.
16. Norwood Report, p. 61.
17. E.M. Byrne, *Planning and Educational Inequality* (Slough, NFER, 1974), p. 29.
18. *Ibid.*, p. 311.
19. S.J. Ball, *Beachside Comprehensive* (Cambridge University Press, 1981), p. 16.
20. *Ibid.*, p. 18
21. *Ibid.*, p. 21.
22. *Ibid.*, pp. 35–6.
23. *Ibid.*, p. 138.
24. *Ibid.*, p. 140.
25. *Ibid.*, p. 143.
26. *Ibid.*, pp. 152–3.
27. D. Warwick, 'Ideologies, integration and conflicts of meaning', in M. Flude and J. Ahier (Eds.) *Educability, Schools and Ideology* (London, Croom Helm, 1976), p. 101.
28. F. Stevens, *The Living Tradition: The Social and Educational Assumptions of the Grammar School* (London, Hutchinson, 3rd Ed. 1972), pp. 117–18.
29. W.A. Reid, *Universities and Sixth Form*, p. 61.
30. *Ibid.*, p. 49.
31. *Ibid.*, p. 50.
32. Schools Council Working Paper No. 24, *Rural Studies in Secondary Schools* (London, Evans/Methuen Education, 1969).

Part Two
School Subjects: Patterns of Internal Evolution

4 Biology: Aspects of Subject History

The Historical Background

This chapter outlines the historical background of biology with particular reference to the ensuing curriculum conflict over environmental education. As will be seen later the biologists played a far less central role than the geographers in this conflict. Hence the chapter deals only with the broad progress of biology and avoids a number of the complexities explored in the case of geography. In particular, the relationship between school biology and university biology (both teachers and courses) is not fully explored, neither are the details of 'O' and 'A' level courses, nor the full diversity of groups within the biology subject community. It will become clear, however, that biology has been subject to many of the same fears about fragmentation as those experienced by the geographers at much the same point in time. Moreover, many of the features to be discerned in the evolution of geography can also be traced in reviewing the history of biology.

In the early nineteenth century, a number of initiatives sought the inclusion of scientific subjects in secondary school curricula. Physics and chemistry were the leading science subjects, botany and zoology followed some way behind in popularity, and biology hardly existed as an identifiable discipline. Public opinion was mobilised by the advances in scientific knowledge promoted by such men as T.H. Huxley and Faraday. Advocates of science stressed not only the intrinsic value of their subject as a disciplinary training, but also the utilitarian potential.

To progress, the branches of science had therefore to exhibit these dual characteristics, and as a result we learn botany and zoology could find support 'only in so far as they contributed to useful ends, such as the extermination of insects destructive to timber in the dockyards'.[1] The teaching of these areas of science was limited throughout the nineteenth century but, significantly, whilst botany declined as a school subject, biology began to emerge in the curricula of some schools.[2]

In fact, the growth of biology in schools was extremely slow in the late nineteenth century and early decades of the twentieth century. This can be attributed to two main factors. Firstly, the more utilitarian and applied aspects of biology remained substantially undeveloped at this stage. Further, the value of the subject for 'disciplinary training' remained limited, not least because 'biological science in the nineteenth century was immature. Usually the material studied was not of any potential economic value and the subject was often considered to be more hobby or pastime of county gentlemen rather than a serious scientific study.'[3] Jenkins argues that

> a satisfactory scheme of work in biology, capable of involving pupils in both observation and experiment and self-evidently something more than an amalgam of topics drawn from the contributing sciences can be constructed only after the appropriate biological — as distinct from botanical or zoological — principles have been firmly established. Despite the advances made in the nineteenth century, it is doubtful whether such biological principles existed in sufficient number or were sufficiently clearly formulated in 1900.[4]

The changing 'image' of biology was mainly facilitated by the work of scientists in a number of emerging specialist fields. Their work both developed the utilitarian potential of the subject and its claim to 'disciplinary rigour'. For instance, following the work of Louis Pasteur, the branch of medicine and biology called bacteriology was developed; marine biology developed through studies of the nutrient bases of marine life and the biological characteristics of marine animals, particularly fishes that are used as human food; agricultural biology developed, focusing on soil studies, crop cultivation research and studies of the animal and plant breeding; physiological research broadened into the study of human function and genetics. That the establishment of the subject's utilitarian potential was an important factor determining its early progress, can be deduced by analogy with the physical sciences. Their acceptance followed closely the associated developments which may be grouped as the 'Industrial Revolution':

> The spectacular achievements of the mechanical and physical sciences during the Industrial Revolution and its aftermath appealed to the imagination of a generation immensely interested in the development of industry. The steam engine, the telegraph, the internal combustion engine and, latterly the aeroplane, all pointed to the utilitarian value of a knowledge of physics and chemistry for boys, if not for girls.[5]

The consequent chronological priority of the physical sciences was probably of considerable import for the history of biology in schools and it has been claimed that because physics and chemistry were 'first in the field' the task of establishing biology in school curricula was rendered immeasurably more difficult.

The slow growth of biology is eloquently attested to by the activities of examination boards. The Oxford and Cambridge examining board introduced biology into its examinations in 1885. Initially it attracted few candidates, but as Waring has noted, by 1904 'a new biology paper was attracting more candidates than chemistry'. She notes that 'as pressures mounted for recognition of the schools as institutions for the pre-clinical scientific training (in chemistry, physics and biology) of intending medical students going on to study for the Diploma of the Conjoint Board of the Royal College of Physicians and of Surgeons, the numbers rose.' At first only a limited number of schools were allowed to train candidates but in 1911 all public schools were granted such recognition.[6]

Following the introduction of the new School Certificate between 1918 and 1927, several boards ignored the claims of biology as a 'School Certificate subject' — notably the University of Bristol Board and the Cambridge Local Examinations Syndicate. Even the University of London, historically somewhat more flexible, ignored the subject at matriculation level. Total entries for School Certificate and matriculation in the subject in 1924 were 18 students (Universities of London and Durham) and in 1927, 175 students (London, Durham and Oxford Local). The Northern Universities Joint Matriculation Board ran an exam in 'Natural History' which covered a broadly biological field and attracted 535 School Certificate and 15 matriculation candidates in 1927. Entries for Higher Certificate exams also reflected the stunted development of the subject during these years.[7]

The figures for the Northern Board in 'Natural History' imply that this subject provided an important arena for the development of biology. As Tracey notes:

> On its initiation biology had little option but to accept the legacy of Junior School natural history, develop it further, and try to lay the foundations of the two sciences, botany and zoology. In doing so it was bound to have growing pains, for natural history is concerned with the ways of life of living creatures, and the botany and zoology which accrue to it have, until comparatively recently been more concerned with their anatomy. This inheritance has influenced its significance and acceptance in schools all along, and still influences the content of the teaching where it is governed by external examinations.[8]

The implications of the social history of biology for the teaching of the subject in school suggest further analogies with the histories of geography and rural studies. Hence:

> The teachers who taught biology in its early days were not well equipped academically to teach the subject efficiently. They did not have the experience of their own school days to fall back upon since, if they had learned any biological science then the stress had been on the botanical side. Moreover botany and zoology have been kept in watertight compartments in the universities, and very few students have gone on with both subjects in their final examinations.[9]

Besides exam board statistics, considerable evidence is available that biology was neglected in the decade or so following the First World War. In 1918, Jenkins states, 'biology in boys' secondary schools was represented almost exclusively by nature study, taught to the lower forms, and by botany and zoology taught to the few senior pupils intending to study medicine'.[10] Contemporary evidence judged that biology was 'disgracefully neglected' throughout the 1920s and a report of the Imperial Agricultural Research Conference in 1927 noted 'inadequate provision for biological teaching' in every level and type of school.[11] But rapid change was on the way and Jenkins has argued that 'it was the decade after 1930 which, more than any other, saw biology gain an established place in the secondary school curriculum'.[12] By 1931 all eight examination boards had adopted biology as a school certificate examination.

The growth in the utilitarian aspects of biology helps to explain a sudden expansion in the subject in the late 1920s and 1930s. The utilitarian function which had so facilitated the growth of physical sciences was enormously influential and Tracey argues that for biology it cleared the way for its introduction into the school as gradually there was a growing recognition in government and elsewhere that 'biology was capable of economic application and exploitation in industries such as fishing, agriculture and forestry, and also in medicine'.[13] Associated with the development of biology's applied uses was a new promotion of the subject. From the late 1920s onwards government agencies, the British Association for the Advancement of Science, the British Social Hygiene Council and the Science Masters Association promoted the cause of biology in schools.

The Prime Minister's 'Committee to enquire into the position of Natural Science in the Education System of Great Britain' began the process of interwar reappraisal of official policy in 1918. The 1926 'Education of the Adolescent' report advocated biology teaching. So too did the British Association in a report on the teaching of animal biology published in 1928 and even more importantly the Chelmsford Report in 1932 on 'Education and Supply of Biologists', the 1938 Consultative Committee on Secondary Education and finally, in 1943, the report of the Committee of the Secondary Schools Examinations Council. Significantly the last report suggested that physics, chemistry and biology should be taught in schools 'without any attempt at vocational training but on orthodox academic lines'.[14] Throughout the 1930s the issue of biological education was debated and advocated in educational journals and even in the correspondence columns of 'The Times'.[15]

These landmarks in official acceptance can be partly attributed to the work of a number of agencies promoting biology. The British Social Hygiene Council developed from the National Council for the Control of Venereal Disease and adopted the slogan 'the only sure foundation for social hygiene is a biological one'. Waring has summarised their work, often conducted through specially created sub-committees:

Biology: Aspects of Subject History

They established and sustained contact with virtually every educational institution and administrative organisation. They enlisted massive and extended support from leading biologists, psychologists, sociologists and educationists ... At a time of desperate shortage of biology teachers they organised a quite staggering programme of two and three-day conferences, of lecture series and workshops (extending over three, six or twenty sessions, and run many times over), courses and summer schools. At all of them, eminent speakers dealt with the method and content of biology teaching, in an attempt to give practical help to teachers struggling with unfamiliar materials and subject matter. Attendance figures for these meetings are very impressive indeed. Starting in the thirties, they continued throughout the war years and for some time afterwards.[16]

In 1938 the Council launched a journal for 'schools and teachers' initially called 'Biology' but after 1942 changed to 'Biology and Human Affairs'. The journal was to 'foster the development of biological teaching'.[17]

Although active in framing syllabuses, the Council allowed the Science Masters Association to handle the submission of syllabuses to the school examination boards whilst offering support and materials. In 1936 the Science Masters Association convened a conference with representatives of five of the eight examining boards to discuss biology syllabuses. A biology sub-committee was formed by the SMA to plan a biology syllabus and in 1937 this was published in a further initiative to promote the subject. One immediate reason for the increase in numbers taking biology in the 1930s was that 'many schools, particularly boys', which had taught little biology before 1930 introduced it as an examination subject, and many girls' schools replaced the study of botany by that of biology'.[18] Significantly, at the same time general science was introduced into the timetable of many shools. Since the subject was studied by less able pupils who had previously studied physics and chemistry this meant that biology's growth relative to the physical sciences was even more dramatic. The Northern Universities Joint Matriculation Board statistics, shown in Table 4.1 reflect this pattern.

Table 4.1: Percentage of Total Number of Candidates each Year Offering Biology, Chemistry and Physics, 1925–1949

	1925	1928	1934	1937	1949
Biology	2.7	4.0	13.1	23.5	31.4
Chemistry	47.1	50.4	51.1	45.8	31.9
Physics	33.4	39.7	43.0	40.1	30.3

During this period the total entries for all subjects virtually tripled from 13,474 to 34,790.[19]

The growth up until 1949 was consolidated in the subsequent decades, although there were certain continuing problems in establishing complete parity of esteem with physics and chemistry. The figures for 'O' level show biology emerging as the major scientific subject in the 1950s; 73,001 candidates in 1959 as opposed to 60,029 in physics and 53,803 in chemistry. However, at 'A' level the subject remained a poor relation: 5,086 candidates compared with 27,450 for physics and 22,188 for chemistry.[20] These figures imply that the moves to invest biology with high status still had some way to progress.

The Struggle for Recognition After 1945

The continuous struggle to establish biology after the Second World War was reflected in a number of articles in the 'School Science Review'. As early as 1942 H.P. Ramage argued the case for an expansion of biology in schools,[21] and in the same year M.L. Johnson stressed the virtues of the subject as a 'training in observation'.[22] Johnson later extended the argument to stress that if taught successfully the subject could serve as a 'training in scientific method',[23] and F.S. Russell reiterated the case for teaching the subject in a consideration of its aims and objectives.[24] In 1949 the British Social Hygiene Council held the first of a series of conferences on 'new trends in biology teaching'. A number of bodies such as the Science Masters Association, British Association and the main teacher unions were involved in the organisation which later grew into the Joint Biology Committee.[25]

Despite the growth in examination entries in the late 1940s and throughout the 1950s the overall influence of biology in the curriculum continued to be more limited than that of the physical sciences. The subject was of apparently equal importance only in the fourth and fifth year examination groups. The report on science in secondary schools compiled in the late 1950s found that biology 'makes very little impact upon the broader education with which the schools are concerned' and significantly that 'the place which is occupied by advanced biological studies in schools, especially boys' schools, at present, is unfortunately that of vocational training rather than of an instrument of education'.[26] Thus the limited number of 'A' level students noted earlier is explained because the subject was taken only by those who required it for professional qualification.

Biology appears at this stage to have been confined, not only at the upper end of the secondary school but also in the early years. This point was made by the Study Group on Education and Field Biology set up in 1960. They felt that there was a need for 'a new approach to the teaching of biology in schools. Biology is particularly well suited as an introduction to science, but it is often taught as an incompletely fused amalgam of classical botany and zoology.'[27] The solution they favoured was that biology 'should instead be treated as a comprehensive discipline in its own right, with a bearing on the teaching of geology and geography. It should involve much more field work than is customary at present. In this revised form biology should be an integral part of the junior and middle school curriculum.'[28]

The Study Group's analysis of the problem confronting biology in schools and their re-emphasis of the need for 'a comprehensive discipline' underlines the newness of biology as an intellectual synthesis. The teachers who taught the new subject in the 1940s and 1950s were by and large trained as specialists in botany and zoology. A university teacher who taught school biology at this time recalls that among the specialists 'there was an antagonism to union', and that 'specialist teachers were simply reflecting the attitudes in universities which were to stick to bot. and zoo.'[29] The stress on needing a comprehensive discipline echoes the arguments presented by Bernal in 1939. He argued that biology was waiting for 'the arrangements for greater coordination' of the various biological disciplines which might come from advances in the field of research. Until that happened biology could not move from being the cinderella of the sciences as an essentially descriptive and taxonomic study to being a 'unitary, experimental, quantitative science'.[30]

The establishment of a unitary science besides awaiting advances in research was enormously hampered by both the continuing strength of botany and zoology and the existence of separate traditions within biology. In school biology a major division arose between the medical tradition which focused on the pre-medical training role noted earlier, and the natural history or ecology tradition. 'The medical tradition in biology with its emphasis on the destructive investigation of killed specimens, contrasted sharply with the approach of the naturalists who were concerned to foster a love of nature and an interest in the activities and interests of living organisms.'[31] Although 'field work and ecological studies' tended to 'suffer the most' from the medical bias of biology 'efforts to increase their part in biology syllabuses remained very tentative.'[32] Jenkins has judged that 'the "medical problem" of sixth form biology was not to be resolved until the 1960s when grammar school biology courses were redesigned as part of a wider programme of curriculum development and there were significant changes in the structure and content of medical education.'[33] The 'redesigning' of school biology, notably through the Nuffield schemes, was related to the changes in university biology towards a more unitary science, but with a place for ecological studies within this rigorous scientific conception.

The Fieldwork and Ecology Tradition in Biology

The natural history element had been present in biology from the very beginning; the naturalist approach depended on field observation and outdoor studies. Such work within biology might clearly have led into the broadly-conceived field of environmental education. In fact field studies and ecology remained firmly defined within a conception of biology as a rigorous science. In explaining this 'containment' of the field studies tradition the role of the Study

Group on Education and Field Biology and the Nuffield Project were centrally important: both groups saw biology as a rigorous experimental science to which field studies might provide a gateway. 'I think ecology came in to biology through the notion of conservation ... not in the sense we know it now. This was conservation in the strictly limited sense of the Nature Conservancy ... we were conserving areas of natural beauty and scientific interest, that sort of thing ...' (Dowdeswell).

In 1960 the Nature Conservancy set up the highly influential Study Group on Education and Field Biology. The aim of the group was to 'examine the role of field studies and their relation to school education and to science teaching in particular: the requirements in terms of curricula and examinations, teachers and teacher training; the facilities needed ...'[34] The study group made it clear that it firmly rejected 'the view that biology in general, and field studies in particular, are less scientific or less essential in an education programme than the physical sciences. It aims to show that if their full educational potential can be realised field studies are one of the best gateways to the teaching of the sciences and one of the best bridges between biology and other sciences.'[35] In expressing this view the group made it clear which other competing views of education it was opposed to:

> there is little educational value in taking groups of children to stare uncomprehendingly and unguided at nature or to listen to sentimental, superficial, discourses by people without scientific understanding. The poverty of such teaching is only matched by that of the indoor 'parrot' learning of the correct examination answer or the so-called 'experiments' often masquerading as science teaching, not only in biology but also in physics and chemistry.[36]

The challenge to more traditional patterns of teaching was consistently pursued to the point where the divisions into scientific subjects were called into question in line with the fashion for 'interdisciplinary enquiry'. 'Field studies have been held in check by the fact that science and science teaching have become confined in arbitrary compartments. One of the main objects of a new approach must be to reduce such artificial barriers to a minimum.' To achieve this 'flexible arrangements' were needed to 'enable scientific topics to be pursued wherever they lead, thus making servants instead of masters of the disciplines involved, and never seeking to deny the altogetherness of science'.[37]

At the beginning of the 1960s field studies were being promoted by a number of prominent biologists. This development at tertiary level was of crucial importance because, when few graduates or teacher trainees were taught ecological or field studies, they in turn could teach little of the subject when they took up positions in schools. This seems to have been the case in the 1950s. According to a report issued in 1953 by a research committee of the British Association for the Advancement of Science: 'A vicious circle is in operation. Neglect of field work at universities in the past has led to neglect in training colleges (who employ biology graduates on their staff) and in schools

Biology: Aspects of Subject History

(who have graduates or training college diploma holders on their staff).' The results of this were clear for 'if members of staff neglect the subject the great majority of pupils will naturally do so, with the result that training colleges and universities then receive students whose interest in field work has not been aroused in earlier formative years.'[38] The neglect of field studies at the tertiary level was confirmed by the study group. They found that the average amount of time spent out of doors was 'a mere 130 hours in zoology departments and 225 hours in botany departments in "single subject/special honours" courses of three or four years duration'.[39]

Of course interdisciplinary constraints were only one factor limiting the growth of field studies. Other factors inhibited the growth of the approach at all educational levels. The study groups listed some of the constraints inside schools in the form of a series of questions:

> ... is the advance of field studies inhibited by lack of teachers trained to conduct them? Are the procedures of educational administration and rigidities in the school curriculum obstructing local opportunities for teaching children outside the classroom? Are teachers deterred by lack or remoteness of facilities, and generally by the sheer difficulty of coping with field studies of a higher standard on a more widespread basis? Is the examination system penalising schools which show initiative in this field as against those which stick to the indoor routine?[40]

The latter point was extended elsewhere in arguing that it was possible for a candidate who has 'never strayed outside a laboratory door and who knows no ecology whatever, nonetheless to obtain a "creditable pass" (possibly a distinction!). Schools are fully aware of this fact and many of them make the best of it.'[41] The Report of the Study Group on Education and Field Biology, whilst detailing the problems faced by ecology and field studies, remains a strongly propagandist document. Field studies were to be 'the gateway to scientific education as a whole'[42] for 'It is plain that future citizens will need a much better induction into the principles and ways of science, a deeper and more satisfying sense of values and a firmer and stronger emotional feeling of being anchored and really belonging to contemporary civilisation.'[43]

The importance of the Report was stressed by Dowdeswell who in 1962 began directing the Nuffield biology project. From the beginning he stressed the educational value of ecological studies: 'I looked upon ecology as applied natural history and I meant that that was one of the ways that one introduced children to biology ... I would reckon "science out of doors" reflected my philosophy very well.' Therefore ecology became a very important section of Nuffield biology: 'I think we were very lucky to have a go ... I was a fanatic so we decided we would go to town on ecology.' The results were less impressive than the intentions: 'In point of fact, as you probably know, that was in many ways the least successful part of the Nuffield 'O' level project ... partly because there were many teachers who still didn't accept ecology at all and it

49

failed because it was well in advance of the thinking of teachers ...' This statement gives the impression that it was mainly a conceptual problem on the part of the teachers, an impression Dowdeswell was quick to correct.

> I think there are problems of teaching methodology ... I think there is a problem of time: There's a problem of basic attitude and thinking ... It involves more of a different way of thinking than any other aspect of Nuffield and the organisational problems are great ... It meant you had to organise things and take children out of doors.[44]

The organisational prerequisites became a rallying cry for opponents of ecology and field studies: 'it was used as an excuse ... of that there was no doubt. Whether the excuse was valid or not I'm not sure but it was used as the great excuse — ecology whether we liked it or not was impractical because of the demands it made on organisation ...'[45]

In spite of the opposition and constraints evident in Dowdeswell's statements other initiatives promoted field studies in the middle of the 1960s. Ecology grew as a new intellectual synthesis within the universities. A number of the new universities established departments of ecology or 'environmental science' and there were equally significant developments in the older universities. Sir Arthur Tansley, who had been the first president of the Council for the Promotion of Field Studies, developed the subject at Oxford in line with a strongly-felt tradition at that university (Dowdeswell had studied there).

The definition of ecology as a university-based discipline within the more traditional science paradigm and the other developments in biology 'contained' the purer environmental and naturalist traditions. By and large therefore biologists stood aside from environmental education. We learn that 'the good ship "environment" was launched but not fitted out with engines or steering gear some time ago. It then proceeded to sail into uncharted sea with a very motley crew aboard. Many might feel that the Institute of Biology has been left on the shore ...'[46] In a paper on biology, Waring has written that in consequence 'as the environmental lobby gained momentum, the field studies movement grew rapidly, but the field studies biologists and the geographers ensured that the "environmentalists" remained in a subordinate position.'[47]

Biology as 'Hard Science'

Despite the broad initiatives from the study group, from the Nuffield Project, from certain university personnel and from the Keele Conference, evidence of any broad-based change in biology teaching was not forthcoming. In 1967, writing of the 'crisis' in biology, Dyer argued that the growth of 'such essentially unifying disciplines' as ecology was being ignored because of 'the unhappy separation of botany and zoology which persists in our sixth forms and so many of our universities'.[48] Even in 1971, 33 out of 44 university-taught undergraduates were in separate botany and zoology departments.[49]

Biology: Aspects of Subject History

Dyer's comment on the continuing separation of botany and zoology and his implicit plea for a 'unifying discipline' presents interesting similarities to the attempt in America in the early 1960s to produce a definition of school biology. The diversity of biology led the Biological Sciences Curriculum Study to produce three 'versions' of school biology, covering the 'biochemical', 'ecological' and 'cellular' aspects of the subject, but their reluctance to expose this apparent lack of unity led to the versions being designated 'blue', 'green' and 'yellow'. As the director later explained:

> to identify these versions as 'biochemical', 'ecological' or 'cellular' might have unintended and unfortunate implications, since some persons might then consider the versions to be courses on ecology, biochemistry or cell biology rather than as general biology programs written by groups of biologists with different backgrounds. Thus it was necessary that the versions be indicated by neutral terms ...[50]

The study also noted the difference between biology and the 'established' sciences of physics and chemistry. They argued that the absence of a clear unifying structure for biology was a result not of its immaturity but of its sophistication:

> The nature of biology itself, as a science built upon the physical sciences, is automatically of a more inclusive level of complexity and so characterisation of its structure appropriate for secondary school students may involve increased complications.

Aware of the dangerous implications of this claim it is noted that this should not be taken to imply that

> Biology represents the ultimate complexity of discipline structure remaining to be analysed by educators for presentation in curricula ... One simply needs to add to these considerations the human implications of the social sciences and the humanities to enter into still further complexities well beyond those contemplated by the biologist in confronting his science.[51]

A solution to the unstructuredness and disunity of biology came with the development of molecular biology. Here at last was the rationale for claiming parity of esteem with the physical sciences. Molecular biology provided both high prestige and an overarching theory which unified many aspects of the subject. Moreover, since plants and animals look very similar at the cellular level, the division between botany and zoology appeared far less justifiable. Jenkins summarised the development in this way: 'The enormous success of crystallographic and cytochemical studies in the field of molecular biology of which the elucidation of the structures of DNA is the best-known example led to pressure to reform the teaching of the life sciences so as to incorporate both the relevant biochemistry and the reductionist/experimental approach which had brought such triumphs.' At last the 'arrangements for greater coordination' which Bernal in 1939 had argued could come from advances in research were at hand and for a period biology could be presented as a unitary science.[52]

The breakthrough was rapidly achieved and teachers at the time noted the change: 'I remember the rise of molecular biology ... Crick and Watson and the rest ... that paved the way for the breakthrough in biology's fight to become a science. From then on there was a strong possibility that biology could become a "hard science" alongside physics and chemistry.'[53] Speaking of the late 1960s Professor Dowdeswell confirmed: 'Status followed the rise of molecular biology. The great discoveries of Crick and Watson changed everything.' Alongside these developments, however, Dowdeswell noted another theme when commenting that, 'there was a feeling that if it wasn't quantitative it wasn't science'.[54] Another university biologist explained the trend in this way: 'Biology had been ... often still is more descriptive than physical science ... in consequence weaker candidates were pushed into it ... when quantitative things were pushed it was for more respect for the subject, increased status.'[55] The twin themes of molecular biology and quantification were incorporated into school biology. The first theme on 'A' level syllabuses is now often 'the Cell' and focuses on structure, molecular organisation and functions. Similarly quantification is now a prominent feature of many 'A' level syllabuses. For example, the JMB syllabus specifically states that 'an understanding of the principles of the application of mathematics and statistics is required'.

However, school biology 'A' level courses retained elements of earlier stages in the history of biology. As was to be the case with geography there was both resistance to and a time lag in the incorporation of new versions of biology, even the hard science version. Jenkins comments that 'both the "principles" and "type" approach to constructing biology syllabuses were to survive throughout the 1960s and beyond, producing greater differences in advanced level syllabuses in biological science than at any time in the past.'[56] But both the versions Jenkins mentioned fell within the 'scientific' paradigm of biology. For the fieldwork tradition the consequences were clearer: a final result of the rise of molecular biology and quantification to dominance in biology was to finally confirm the relegation of the human and environmental aspects of ecology and field biology within the subject.

> The great problem was that the environmentalist pressures came at more or less the same time as biology was making its big push to become a hard science subject with all the status that involved ... the environmental thing came right in the middle of biology's final fight to be accepted as a hard science and was therefore pushed to the margins of the subject.[57]

By the mid-1960s biology, as a laboratory-based hard science, was being rapidly institutionalised in the expanding universities and in the schools (especially through the Nuffield project). Molecular biology, by providing high prestige and an over-arching theory, finally sealed biology's establishment as a fully-fledged, scientifically rigorous, academic discipline.

Conclusion

In the evolution of biology the subject first developed as an integrated area of knowledge which bridged certain segments of traditional botany and zoology. In the early stages, with a few exceptions, only the latter specialisms were taught in the universities. Biology developed initially in two arenas. Firstly, in the early years of the secondary school, biology built upon the already developed junior school courses in 'natural history'. Then, with the growing appreciation of the economic uses of biology in medicine and agriculture, fishing and forestry, new careers began to open up in which specialised biological training was valuable. Hence the second arena in which biology developed was in the sixth form. This development gained momentum throughout the twentieth century but increasingly from the 1930s onwards. In the 1950s it was noted that: 'The place which is occupied by advanced biological studies in schools, especially boys' schools at present, is unfortunately that of vocational training rather than of an instrument of education.' This quote confirms the low status of utilitarian elements within the status hierarchy of subjects, as does an earlier contention that biology like the other sciences should be taught 'without any attempt at vocational trend but on orthodox academic lines'.

The traditional pursuit of 'academic' status through university establishment of the subject was rendered difficult because of the hegemony of botany and zoology. In the 1950s the sixth form specialist teachers in botany and zoology reflected their training at, and the contemporary attitudes within universities which favoured the teaching of these two subjects in watertight compartments — 'there was antagonism to union'. Without establishment at the tertiary level biology was, therefore, confined to the early years of the secondary school and to vocational training at 'O' and 'A' level. In 1967 Dyer noted the consequently low popularity of the subject at sixth form level and spoke of 'the unhappy separation of botany and zoology which persists in our sixth forms and so many of our universities'.

The utilitarian and pedagogic elements in biology which so retarded its progress to high academic status were found within human biology and in certain fieldwork aspects of the subject. Hence the development of field biology sometimes ran counter to the pressures for status escalation. Status through a vision of biology as 'hard science' was increasingly pursued in the 1960s through an emphasis on laboratory investigations and mathematical techniques. In 1962, the Nuffield project confirmed the crucial importance of laboratories as status symbols and directed much of the Nuffield Foundation's money and resources towards their development. The rise of molecular biology, with the work of Crick and Watson, finally confirmed biology as a laboratory-based hard science. As a result the subject was rapidly expanded in the universities (themselves expanding apace), and, with the training of a new generation of biology graduates, the subject's incorporation as a high-status 'O' and 'A' level school subject was finally assured.

In fact, biology's establishment as a scientific discipline has been commented on by Waring. She writes that:

> The word 'biology' tends to conjure up an image of a clearly-defined body of knowledge, built up through recognisable sorts of activity and validated on the basis of agreed criteria and, indeed, this view would seem to be confirmed by the existence of the Biological Council, the Institute of Biology and a range of biology departments, courses and examinations in all types of educational institution.[58]

Yet Waring's article is concerned with whether biological science is faced by 'integration or fragmentation'. There is considerable evidence of a continuing fear of the latter: confirming the view that school subjects and academic disciplines are normally temporary coalitions. Hence we find the 'Journal of Biological Education' warning in 1975 that biology could be 'dispersed to the four winds'.[59] A year later the Biological Education Committee of the Royal Society and the Institute of Biology expressed concern over the burgeoning popularity of human biology. A working party set up to consider the problem revealed a proliferation of broadly biological courses all considerably overlapping but each with idiosyncratic features. In 1977 a discussion paper at the conference of university biology education tutors dealt with the question of teacher training.

All these committees and associated papers expressed a consensus among professional biologists that biological education must reflect, 'a rigorous, experimental science' alongside considerable 'ambivalence about the place, in biology, of the study of man, and about the implications for education of the blurring of the boundaries between biology and the social sciences.'[60] This view reflects that held by the promoters of the subject that to progress the subject needs to outgrow its pedagogic and utilitarian origins and the randomness occasioned by its concern with social and human issues. Status and resources have been achieved through promotion as a hard, experimental and rigorous science. The recurrence of pressures for more social and human biology therefore threaten the uneasy establishment of the subject as a scientific discipline which alone assure the status and resources so valued by the members of the biology subject community.

Notes

1 D. LAYTON, *Science for the People* (London, George Allen and Unwin, 1973), p. 21.
2 C.W. TRACEY, 'Biology: Its struggle for recognition in English schools during the period 1900–60', *School Science Review*, Vol. XCIII, No. 150, March 1962, p. 429.
3 *Ibid.*, p. 430.
4 E.W. JENKINS, *From Armstrong to Nuffield Studies in Twentieth Century Science Education* (London, John Murray, 1979), p. 116.
5 TRACEY, *op. cit.*, p. 429.

6. M. WARING, unpublished paper on 'History of Biology', 1980, p. 7.
7. TRACEY, op. cit., p. 429. The low status of biology is testified to in J. HUXLEY, 'Biology in schools', School Science Review Vol. 4, No. 13, 1972, pp. 5–11.
8. TRACEY, op. cit., p. 424.
9. Ibid.
10. JENKINS, op. cit., p. 119.
11. Ibid., p. 121.
12. Ibid., p. 123.
13. TRACEY, op. cit., p. 423.
14. The NORWOOD REPORT, Report of the Committee of the Secondary School Examination Council appointed by the President of the Board of Education in 1941, Curriculum and Examinations in Secondary Schools (London, HMSO, 1943), p. 112.
15. WARING, op. cit.
16. Ibid., pp. 11–12.
17. JENKINS, op. cit., p. 134.
18. TRACEY, op. cit., p. 426.
19. J.A. PETCH, Fifty Years of Examining, the Joint Matriculation Board, 1903–53 (London, 1953), p. 84.
20. TRACEY, op. cit., p. 425.
21. M.P. RAMMAGE, 'Educational Biology', School Science Review, Vol. 23, No. 91, (1943), pp. 312–19.
22. M.L. JOHNSON, 'Biology and training in observation', School Science Review Vol. 24, No. 92, 1942, pp. 56–8.
23. M.L. JOHNSON, 'Biology and training in scientific method', School Science Review, Vol. 29, No. 108, (1948), pp. 139–47.
24. F.S. RUSSELL, 'What is Biology?', School Science Review, Vol. 28, No. 104, 1946, pp. 69–79.
25. WARING, op. cit., p. 12.
26. MINISTRY OF EDUCATION, Science in Secondary Schools, Ministry of Education Pamphlet No. 38 (London, HMSO, 1960).
27. STUDY GROUP ON EDUCATION AND FIELD BIOLOGY, Science Out of Doors (Longmans, 1963), p. 196.
28. Ibid., p. 197.
29. Interview, 24.10.77.
30. JENKINS op. cit., pp. 139–40.
31. Ibid., pp. 146–7.
32. Ibid., p. 148.
33. Ibid., p. 147.
34. STUDY GROUP, op. cit., p. vi.
35. Ibid., p. 5.
36. Ibid.
37. Ibid., p. 7.
38. British Association for Advancement of Science Report, 1953.
39. STUDY GROUP, op. cit., p. 55.
40. Ibid., p. 185.
41. Ibid., p. 27.
42. Ibid., p. 10.
43. Ibid., p. viii.
44. Interview, 24.10.77.
45. Ibid.
46. See M. WARING, 'Biological science: Integration or fragmentation', History of Education Society Conference Papers, December 1978, p. 57.
47. M. WARING, op. cit., p. 20.

School Subjects and Curriculum Change

48 K.F. DYER, 'Crisis in Biology: An examination of the deficiencies in the current expansion of Biological Education', *Journal of Biological Education*, 1967, 1, 2, p. 112.
49 M. WARING, *op. cit.*, p. 51.
50 A.B. GROBMAN, *The Changing Classroom: The Role of the Biological Sciences Curriculum Study* (New York, Doubleday, 1969), p. 64.
51 *Ibid.*, p. 65.
52 JENKINS *op. cit.*, p. 153.
53 Interview with biology teacher, 15.3.77.
54 Interview 24.10.77.
55 Interview 26.10.76.
56 JENKINS *op. cit.*, p. 155. The number of 'A' level entrants is noted in JENKINS, p. 156, for 1961 and 1971.

	1961	1971	% change
Botany	4,729	1,981	−58.1
Zoology	7,409	4,428	−40.2
Biology	7,099	21,575	+204

57 Interview, 15.3.77.
58 M. WARING, *op. cit.*, p. 49.
59 J.A. BAKER, Comment *Journal of Biological Education*, 9 (1975), p. 59. Quoted *Ibid.* WARING.
60 M. WARING, *op. cit.*, p. 149.

5 *Geography: Aspects of Subject History*

Introduction

This chapter seeks to provide a historical background to the geographers' part in the curriculum conflicts surrounding the emergence of environmental studies. Hence the focus is directed to those aspects of geography's history associated with its promotion and maintenance as a subject with its own territory, status and resources. The concern is with those elements of the geographical enterprise which stress the 'survival of the discipline' rather than its intellectual advance. Whilst these cannot always be distinguished, Gregory has noted that geography has had a problem 'in so far as an exclusive concern with the survival of the discipline required a degree of pragmatism which many regarded as an abandonment of principle. The difficulty was that pragmatism was uncomfortably close to opportunism.'[1] Such opportunism has left geography with perhaps the most chameleon nature of any of the so-called 'fields of knowledge'. As a subject with a recurring crisis of identity the 'survival of the discipline' has the kind of priority among subject practitioners which sometimes seems to border on obsession.

The promotion of geography has taken place against a background of social change which has provided a range of arenas for subject advocates to react to and utilise. In the late Victorian period, a period of rapid imperial expansion, geography was promoted by strategies such as Sir George Robertson's description of it as 'the Science of Distances — the science of the merchant, the statesman and the strategist'; as Gregory notes, 'a characterisation which appeared to make a command of geography vital both for the maintenance of the Empire itself and the ascent of men to the most acclaimed positions of profit and power within it.'[2] In more recent times, geography has responded to society's needs 'for spatial efficiency and regional planning,'[3] and geographical studies have been used 'to provide an essential technical foundation for the elaboration of private and public policy'.[4] Our concern though is not with social change *per se* but with the milieu and associated opportunities such changes present to those people involved in geography's maintenance and promotion as a discipline — those concerned with its material and pragmatic, rather than intellectual, advance.

We begin with a brief historical introduction which summarises the recent background of geography in England. Certain themes are identified here, notably geographers' concern with achieving 'scientific' discipline status. The moulding of geography in pursuit of status has been commented on by Gregory in explaining that 'the early reluctance to consider man in society' was 'prompted at least in part by an important search for intellectual respectability, and a belief that by structuring human geography in terms of physical geography such a goal could be attained.'[5] Another theme picks up the evolving relationship between school geography and university geography. A third theme focuses on the promotional role of the subject association.

The 'fieldwork tradition' is then analysed for, as we shall see later, this was the tradition within the subject which was closest to 'environmental studies'.

Finally, the launching of new geography is considered and related to the aspirations and promotional strategies of geographers as they have been evidenced at work during the last century.

The Establishment of Geography in Schools and Universities

The writings of two German scholars, von Humboldt[6] and Ritter,[7] in mid-nineteenth century mark the stage at which 'modern geography is often said to begin'.[8] Because their conception of geography dominated the formative years in the evolution of the subject it has been titled 'classical geography'.[9] Classical geography sought to organise knowledge in two stages; in the first stage facts and details of geographical phenomena were collected and presented and in the second stage these were 'given coherence and made intelligible by being subsumed under a number of laws'.[10]

Towards the end of the nineteenth century in Germany, classical geography came under question from scholars like Heffner, who studied alongside Max Weber at Heidelberg, and in the early part of the twentieth century in France, notably in the work of Brunthes,[11] classical geography was attacked for its rigidity, because it encouraged notions of geographical determinism and because 'the new ideas about methodology in the social sciences made its whole approach to the understanding of social action and social change seem unrewarding'.[12] In England, in the absence of any alternative native models, classical geography remained for a time the subject 'model' to which to aspire. In 1901 in the first issue of the 'The Geography Teacher', T.C. Rooper, an HMI, noted that Britain 'awaits the birth of an epoch-making writer on geography'. The country had 'no such series of geographers as Humboldt, Ritter and Pescher, whose names add so much lustre to the fame of German learning'.[13]

In late nineteenth-century England, geography was in the process of establishing itself as a subject in schools, but had obtained only a tentative place in a few universities. The widespread comments about the teaching of the

Geography: Aspects of Subject History

subject imply that much of the knowledge that was taught remained at the first stage of classical geography's twinstage objective. Thus in 1887 when MacKinder posed the question 'Can geography be rendered a discipline instead of a mere body of information?' he noted that when 'the method of description has been adopted and still more that of enumeration, each additional fact adds an even-increasing amount to the burden to be borne by the memory.'[14]

Since at the stage MacKinder was writing geography was predominantly a school subject, his criticisms had considerable significance for its progress. In the schools, particularly the public and grammar schools, geography teachers were seeking to establish the intellectual as well as pedagogical credibility of the subject. By 1870 many public and grammar schools gave one or two periods to geography. Likewise in 1875 'elementary geography' was added to the 'class subjects' examined in elementary schools.[15] But the teaching of the subject left a good deal to be desired. In 1901 Rooper asserted that in British schools geography 'has even been a dull and uninteresting subject.' It has been, he said, 'a dreary recitation of names and statistics, of no interest to the learner, and of little use except perhaps in the sorting departments of the Post Office.'[16] Writing a decade later Holmes confirmed this view of geography teaching when he stated that the children were 'the victims of an unintelligent oral cram, which they were compelled, under pains and penalties to take in and retain till the examination was over.'[17]

The problems of geography partly stemmed from the difficulty of promoting a new intellectual synthesis in the school arena, where examinations and timetable constraints predominated. Writing in 1901 a Rochester headmaster identified two major problems. Firstly that 'the overcrowding in the school timetable makes it impossible to give more than one, at most two, lessons per week in geography', and secondly that as a school subject, geography 'suffers from the fact it generally falls into the hands of a master who takes no special interest in it and has no special knowledge of it or of the methods of teaching it.'[18]

Given the problems at university level and the limited base in the elementary and secondary school sector, the promoters of geography began to draw up plans for a subject association. In 1893 the Geographical Association was founded: 'to further the knowledge of geography and the teaching of geography in all categories of education institutions from preparatory school to university in the United Kingdom and abroad.'[19] The formation of the Association in 1893 was extremely well-timed. Two years later the Bryce Commission reported, and some of its recommendations were built into the 1902 Education Act. Furthermore, when the 1904 secondary regulations effectively defined the subjects to be offered in secondary schools, geography's inclusion in the regulations was a major staging-post in its acceptance and recognition, and in the broad-based take-up of external examinations in geography in secondary schools. As can be seen on the membership chart in Figure 1, this change was clearly reflected in the sharp increase in the Association's membership from this date.[20]

Figure 1: Geographical Association Membership 1893–1968

At this stage geography was included in many exam board regulations, both at School Certificate and Higher School Certificate, as a main subject. Certain boards, however, included geography only as a 'subsidiary subject'.[21] The founding of a subject association was only a first stage in launching the subject; what was also required was an overall plan aimed at establishing the subject in the various educational sectors mentioned in the constitution. At a discussion on geographical education at the British Association in September 1903, MacKinder outlined a four-point strategy for establishing the subject:

> Firstly, we should encourage University Schools of Geography, where geographers can be made ... Secondly, we must persuade at any rate some secondary schools to place the geographical teaching of the whole school in the hands of one geographically trained master ... Thirdly, we must thrash out by discussion and experiment what is the best progressive method for common acceptation, and upon that method we must base our schemes of examination. Lastly, the examination papers must be set by practical geography teachers.[22]

Hence the geography teacher is to set the exams and is to choose exams that are best for the 'common acceptation' of the subject — there is not even the facade that the pupils' interest should be the central criteria; the teaching of geography is to be exclusively in the hands of trained geographers and the

Geography: Aspects of Subject History

universities are to be encouraged to establish schools of geography 'where geographers can be made'.

In this sense it is clear that the crucial requirement of a university base where geographers could 'be made' can be argued for because of the need for teachers of the subject in schools. The school subject therefore provides the platform for bringing about the creation of a university base where the 'discipline' can be created by scholars. The importance of the schools in developing a well-populated university base was recently commented on by a President of the Geographical Association: 'The recognition of our subject's status among university disciplines which this gives together with the costly provision made available for its study, could never have been achieved without the remarkable stimulus and demand injected from our schools.'[23] That geography was expanding in schools was commented on by numerous writers. In 1913 W. Maclean Carey noted: 'The teaching of geography has made great strides within the last ten years.' He added, however, that it was 'now taking its place as a definite science', and went on to conclude most unhelpfully that there was a 'very strong argument in favour of geography being taught by the chemistry or physics master'.[24]

Carey notwithstanding, the number of specialist geography teachers continued to grow. In 1919 it was reported that the Geographical Association had a membership of over 2,000, which included 'practically all the recognised teachers of geography in England and many in Scotland and Ireland'.[25] The Council of the Geographical Association went on to contend that 'it was possible for this Association to issue a manifesto on the subject which has met with practically universal acceptance.'[26] This manifesto stated; 'In teaching geography in schools we seek to train future citizens to imagine accurately the interaction of human activities and their topographical conditions'; and added that 'the mind of the citizen must have a topographical background if he is to keep order in the mass of information which he accumulates in the course of his life, and in these days the background must extend over the whole world.'[27]

The benefits accruing from an expanding school geography were not however without their cost, for partly because it was labelled as a school subject, geography encountered great opposition in the universities. David Walker recently wrote of geography that 'some senior members of our ancient universities can still be found who dismiss it as a school subject'.[28]

The progress of geography in the university was severely limited due to the fierce opposition of the other subject groups. One of the first Chairs of Geography was in the Faculty of Arts at University College, London. In 1903 Professor L.W. Lynde, by basic training a historian and classical scholar, was appointed. 'He was required to give an undertaking that no instruction in physical geography (including climatology and oceanography) would be given in his department. All such teaching was given in the department of geology, and this restriction still operated even twenty years later ...'[29]

The first significant development in the university sector had been in 1887 when 'the Royal Geographical Society was successful in getting the University of Oxford to establish a readership in geography'.[30] The readership was offered to Halford John MacKinder. The role of the Royal Geographical Society at this time has been characterised as 'an organised "geographical lobby"'. It was a lobby in which from the beginning MacKinder had played a key role, seeking unsuccessfully to get the Society to sponsor a 'London School of Geography'. In the event the Society offered to help in the creation of a School of Geography at Oxford, which was opened in January 1910, with MacKinder as director. MacKinder staffed the School with A.J. Herbertson and two other lecturers and teaching of the new Oxford Diploma in Geography began. Only four candidates took the first examination but by 1914 there were 41 candidates. Summer schools in geography were also organised and in 1914 200 teachers attended such schools. At these schools the teaching of Herbertson (1865–1915) became highly influential. He wrote textbooks, of which over 1,400,000 were sold; one book, 'Man and His Work', published in 1899, was still in print in the late 1960s. Graves judges that 'his influence on what was taught in British schools was enormous and has since been unsurpassed'.[31]

Meanwhile, however, the problems of establishing geography in other universities were summarised in 1913 by MacKinder when he stated: 'Geography as a university discipline was then all but non-existent.'[32] Speaking over half a century after this difficult period for the subject, Professor Garnett reviewed some of the problems which confronted geography departments in the universities that: 'grew very slowly under a tradition of laissez-faire that strongly reflected the individualistic approaches and widely differing personalities and interests of those diverse scholars who pioneered our subject into being — no-one having received initial training in the new discipline they were professing.' Such idiosyncratic entrepreneurs produced a wide variety of initial modes of geographical training within universities that, 'if not hostile, were not over-friendly to the new upstart subject'.[33] Also speaking of the pioneering venture at University College, R.C. Honeybone recalled other problems encountered in the 1920s: 'Fieldwork was unknown, large scale maps practically non-existent, and the facilities for research severely limited.'[34] The situation at Sheffield University was markedly different. There, since 1908, for nearly 20 years the subject had received 'serious recognition only in the Faculty of Pure Science, and indeed, in the early twenties a hard battle had to be fought to gain appropriate recognition in the Faculty of Arts.' The department was directed by Dr. (later Professor) Rudmose Brown — a botanist and scientist by training 'who had come to know, and again, be much influenced by, the teaching of A.J. Herbertson. His interest lay in the development of geography as a science, and he welcomed the University's initial decision to make the Faculty of Pure Science the subject's primary home.'[35] Meanwhile at Cambridge, which has produced 'nearly 50 per cent of current holders of chairs in British universities', there were also problems in this period: the subject was not examined until 1920.

The Council of the Geographical Association explained the problems in this way: 'This relation of geography to the humanities and to the Natural

Sciences has introduced difficulties in connection with the examination of students. It does not fit easily into the examination of the Faculties of Arts or of Science, or indeed of any other group. Not one of the Faculties can claim geography as peculiarly its own. There has been a tendency to solve the difficulty by excluding it from all the Faculties.' The report added optimistically: 'It is evident from what has been said that the true solution is to include geography, pass and honours, in both Arts and Science, as has been done by the University of Wales.'[36]

By the 1920s, in spite of the problems in universities, school geography continued its expansion. The organisation of geographical knowledge was changing from 'classical' patterns towards a more 'regional' approach. Regionalism followed closely the work of the French scholar Vidal de la Blache in the previous decade. In 1927 the Hadow Report stated: 'During the last twenty-five years the method of teaching geography has noticeably changed; perhaps no subject has made a more general advance.' The Report adds that the main objective of geographical teaching was to develop 'as in the case of history, an attitude of mind and a mode of thought characteristic of the subject'.

The success of the efforts to establish geography in schools is eloquently testified to in the Committee's judgment that 'the importance of geography as a subject in the curriculum for all types of post-primary education needs little arguing'. Nonetheless the 'utilitarian reasons' are presented: 'Travel and correspondence have now become general; the British dominions are to be found in every clime; and these facts alone are sufficient to ensure that the subject shall have an important place in the school timetable.' Alongside these reasons the Committee warned of the dangers of overstressing the utilitarian rationale: 'For however useful geographical information may be its value must rest, for the purpose of our reference, on its use as an instrument of education, i.e. as a means of developing the growing interest of the pupils. In this connection it has proved itself to be a subject which, when well taught, makes a very strong appeal to them.'[37]

Nearly a quarter of a century later a Report of the Royal Geographical Society testifies to the continuing progress for the subject in schools and to its increasing 'academic status'. 'The importance of geography at all levels of education is urged not only by geographers, but by many educationists of standing and experience.' They quote Sir Cyril Norwood, who in 1943 had chaired the Board of Education's Committee which had produced the Norwood Report: 'I therefore want to make the bold claim that geography is an essential part of education whatever forms education may take, and that there can be no question of dropping it in any considered course of study.' Norwood claimed it was 'more important than a foreign language or a science, highly important as these are, for the simple reason ... that the intelligent person must understand something about the world and the country and the district in which he is set to live his life.' To fully confirm geography's acceptance, the Report notes: 'The steadily increased importance of geography in the grammar schools is reflected by the numbers of those offering the subject in public examinations.'[38]

Yet whilst Sir Cyril Norwood's position on geography in schools appears unequivocal, the Norwood Report in 1943 did point to a number of problems faced by the subject. The Report defined geography as 'the study of man and his environment from selected points of view'. The authors, however, noted that 'natural science, economics, history, the study of local conditions as regards industry and agriculture might also be concerned with environment'. They were concerned with the temptation afforded by 'the expansiveness of geography', for 'environment is a term which is easily expanded to cover every condition and every phase of activity which makes up normal everyday experience'. Hence, 'enthusiasts for geography may be inclined sometimes to extend their range so widely as to swallow up other subjects'; in doing this they 'widen their boundaries so vaguely that definition of purpose is lost, and the distinctive virtues inherent in other studies closely pursued are ignored in a general survey of wide horizons.'[39]

The results of such 'expansiveness' in school geography were later reported by Honeybone, who argued that by the thirties geography 'came more and more to be a "world citizenship" subject, with the citizens detached from their physical environment'. He explains this partly by the spread 'under American influence' of 'a methodology, proclaiming that all education must be related to the everyday experience of children'. But argued that 'when put in the hands of people untrained in geography or trained without a proper sense of geographical synthesis', this frequently meant that 'geography in school started with the life and work of man and made no real attempt to examine his physical environment'. Thus through the work of those teachers untrained or badly trained in the subject, 'by 1939 geography had become grievously out of balance; the geographical synthesis had been abandoned; and the unique educational value of the subject lost in a flurry of social and economic generalizations.'[40]

The central problem, therefore, remained the establishment of departments in universities where 'geographers could be made' and the piecemeal changes in pursuit of pupil relevance and utility controlled and directed. Tudor David maintains that the establishment of geography in the universities 'has not been achieved without a struggle and without a good deal of sotto voce hostility in "high places"'. His sources for this contention are early professors of geography, for instance Professor Frank Debenham, professor of geography at Cambridge, who asserted: 'Teachers of established subjects objected to this new omnium gatherum of a study, which threatened to invade their boundaries'.[41]

Likewise Professor Wooldridge argued that geographers were a frustrated university profession because of 'the widespread belief among our colleagues and associates that we lack academic status and intellectual respectability'. He argues that 'what has been conceded is that geography has a limited use in its lower ranges. What is implicitly denied by so many is that it has any valid claim as a higher subject.' Wooldridge, however, hints that acceptance at the lower level is the crucial threshold to cross. 'It has been conceded that if geography is

Geography: Aspects of Subject History

to be taught in schools it must be learned in the universities.'[42] The relevance of the school 'base' to university geography is well illustrated by St Catharine's College, Cambridge. The college has produced so many professors of geography for the country's universities that a conspiracy might be alleged. David Walker disagrees, saying that the reasons for the academic pattern are down to earth. 'St Catharine's was one of the first colleges to offer awards in geography: it established a network of contacts with sixth-form teachers, many of whom later were its own graduates, and with particular schools like the Royal Grammar, Newcastle.' Walker points to the personal nature of subject induction. 'Since the Second World War moreover many of the St Catharine's geographers who went on to become professors, readers and lecturers were taught by one man, Mr. A.A.L. Caesar, now the senior tutor.'[43]

The period following 1945 does seem to have been critical in geography's acceptance and consolidation within the university sector. Professor Alice Garnett explained in 1968 why this period was so important: 'Not until after the Second World War was it widely the case that departments were directed by geographers who had themselves received formal training in the discipline, by which time most of the initial marked differences and contrasts in subject personality had been blurred or obliterated.'[44] At this point, geography departments were established in most universities and the subject had a recognisable core of identity: by 1954 Honeybone could write a summary of the final acceptance and establishment of geography as a university discipline:

> In the universities, there has been an unparalleled advance in the number of staff and scope of the work in the departments of geography. In the University of London alone, there are now six chairs, four of them of relatively recent creation. Students, both graduates and undergraduates, are greater in number than ever before. Many of the training colleges and university departments of education are taking a full part in this progress; employers are realizing the value of the breadth of a university training in geography; and the Civil Service has recently raised the status of geography in its higher examinations. In fact, on all sides, we can see signs that, at long last, geography is forcing its complete acceptance as a major discipline in the universities, and that geographers are welcomed into commerce, industry and the professions, because they are well educated men and women ...[45]

The advances in university geography after the Second World War partly aided the acceptance of geography as a subject suitable for the most able children, but problems remained. In 1967 Marchant noted: 'Geography is at last attaining to intellectual respectability in the academic streams of our secondary schools.' But added, 'the battle is not quite over'; and instanced a girls' grammar school where: 'Geography is at present ... an alternative to Latin, which means that a number of girls cease to take it at the end of the third year ... there is no work available at Advanced Level'; and a boys'

School Subjects and Curriculum Change

independent school where 'In the "O" level forms, the subject is taken only by those who are neither classicists, nor modern linguists, nor scientists. The sixth form is then drawn from this rather restricted group with the addition of a few scientists who failed to live up to expectations.'[46] In 1976 the President of the Geographical Association noted that 'in some public schools geography may still be regarded as an inferior academic subject'.[47]

One of the problems of the growing reputation and intellectual rigour of university geography was that it threw the inadequacies of school geography into higher relief. This growing dichotomy between school and university geography began to be reflected in geographers' associations. The Geographical Association became the forum of school geographers (with a scattering of university scholars) whilst from the 1950s onwards the Institute of British Geographers provided the main forum for university personnel. For behind the rhetoric which sought academic legitimation and expansion for the subject, school geography often remained substantially unchanged:

> If we analyse the trends of geography teaching during this century, it appears that, although the type of memorization has changed, yet memory has always been very markedly the senior partner in the uneasy alliance of memory and understanding. At one time, there existed the much derided 'capes and bays'; at another, what we might call 'economic capes and bays', lists of products related in the flimsiest way to their environments; at another, the 'pseudo-scientific capes and bays', the era of isobars and the planetary wind system; and at the present time [1954], we seem to be overemphasizing the 'regional account capes and bays' ... Frequently, such regional accounts in school are mere feats of memory, with little or no relationship between the various parts.[48]

Two kinds of response developed to the 'capes and bays' critique. Firstly one school of geographers sought to build on the naturalist/fieldwork tradition in geography. A second response originated in the universities partly as a counter to the rapid growth of social sciences such as sociology and economics. This led to definitions of a 'new geography' stressing quantitative methods, model building and social scientific aspirations.

The Fieldwork Tradition in Geography

The fieldwork element in geography has been present since the earliest days of teaching the subject. Wise has uncovered a range of experiments in teaching geography in this manner in early nineteenth-century English schools. He summarised the methods employed in this way: 'Starting from the home or schoolroom such studies extended outwards to the neighbourhood, town, district, region, country and eventually to world studies.'[49] The intention then was to broaden out from detailed studies of the child's immediate environment

Geography: Aspects of Subject History

into studies of more extended geographical areas. The pioneering work in English schools and later in German schools influenced the Royal Geographical Society's Inspector of Geographical Education, Dr. J.S. Keltie, in the 1880s. Keltie recorded that the school boards in London, Birmingham, Edinburgh and Glasgow employed and encouraged such methods. The London boards, for instance, had 'A special map of the neighbourhood of each school, a map of the division in which the school is situated, and a map of London and its environs.'[50]

In the twentieth century school teaching of geography has continued to employ local field studies and to extend their use. Often the approach has been most favoured among classes of younger children, notably in primary and elementary schools. The Geographical Association's publication, 'Suggestions for the Teaching of Local Geography', drawn up by the Primary Schools Committee, typifies the approach in its commitment 'to the understanding of the geography of the immediate neighbourhood and ... its appropriate setting in the larger area to which it belongs.'[51] The emphasis on local geography indicates the dual reappraisal involved in developing more fieldwork in school geography: firstly, more studies out of doors; secondly, greater concentration on the child's immediate environment and neighbourhood. The head of the Geography Department at Goldsmith's College, G.J. Cons, pioneered many strategies for training pupils and students in fieldwork methods. Writing in 1938, Cons argued that: 'The classroom door is shut; in very many schools there is little relationship between what is going on in the classroom, and the busy activities of the real world.'[52] Cons therefore advocates 'the need for actuality' and in this respect the then Director of Education for Northumberland is quoted as saying: 'Geography is the most valuable key-subject of the school', for it offers 'the chance of a study of the particular environment of the schoolchild in all its details; its roads, markets, transport, cost of living, family incomes, houses, electricity, gas or the absence thereof, and so on, but from these data the geographic field moves from the locality.'[53]

The establishment of fieldwork geography in the upper ranges of the secondary school was closely allied with developments in the universities. As early as 1896 Herbertson had carried out experimental field classes with school children whilst working at Heriot-Watt College, Edinburgh. Later at Oxford, he and H.J. MacKinder, two pioneers of geography teaching, organised field courses for teachers in the years 1906–14.[54] Their work derived much from the ideas and writings of Sir Patrick Geddes (1854–1933) who had founded an 'Outlook Tower' in Edinburgh for educational scrutiny of the town's environment. In turn, Geddes' work owed much to the writings of an early French sociologist, Frederic Le Play (1806–82).[55]

The other external influence which provided a stimulus to fieldwork in geography was the work of the university field geologists at the turn of the century. 'It may be said that because much of the early fieldwork in geography was done by geologists, who had become interested in landforms, the currently accepted forms of geographical field work concentrates on the natural landscape.'[56] In an essay entitled 'Science in Education' written in 1905, Archibald Geikie advocated training in field observation so that the student would see 'more than is visible to the uninstructed man'.[57] More recently, in the period following the Second World War particularly, fieldwork has been widely advocated in university geography. The work of Wooldridge echoes many of the sentiments earlier voiced by Cons in respect of school studies: 'the ground not the map, is the primary document'[58] and again, 'over a great range of studies, reality is in the field'.[59] In 1965 the Board stated that mainly as a result of the activities of Professor Wooldridge and Geoffrey Hutching: 'fieldwork has progressed far in the last half-century, so that it is a universally respected approach to the study of geography. The generation of geographers trained by Wooldridge is today playing a major part in training yet more geographers in the same well tried methods.'[60]

The establishment of field study in university geography and the growing output of field research were associated with new demands to allow fieldwork a place in the education of academic secondary school geography pupils: 'Since people like Wooldridge at London, and others like Linton here in Sheffield were arguing for it . . . when their students went out into schools they said "can we do our fieldwork for exams"'.[61] These new initiatives towards fieldwork for academic students aimed finally to establish field geography in schools, for as the DES reported in 1972, 'In spite of constant advocacy by leading teachers for over 40 years, fieldwork held an uncertain foothold in school geography until the 1950s.'[62] From this date onwards, progress was rapid and centred around the development of new exams and new facilities. 'The fieldworking teacher needed the exams to change . . . "A" levels began to change but at first fieldwork was not compulsory. In the sixties it began to change . . . when exams changed it meant you could leave the classroom.'[63] However, to leave the classroom required an associated development of facilities in the outside environment. Professional bodies such as the Field Studies Council, Royal Geographical Society and the Geographical Association worked to establish facilities for fieldwork. The former body had in fact been formed in 1943 as the Council for the Promotion of Field Studies and involved biologists as well as geographers (c.f. Chapter 10). In 1965 it convened the first conference on field studies in London. Mr. C.A. Tinker of the Council informed delegates that the demand for places on school courses was outrunning supply by nearly 100 per cent.[64] The Geographical Association, which had established a Standing Committee on Field Studies, completed surveys of facilities beginning in 1965.

By 1969 fieldwork was clearly well established in many schools. John Everson confidently noted that: 'it is a truism to state that the campaign to put fieldwork in the mainstream of school geography is now over'. He went on to define the progress that had been made in teaching and examinations:

> Since the war, increasingly, its place has been recognised and accepted by most students and teachers. There is now a large and growing body of literature describing field techniques and areas in Great Britain and

abroad in which these techniques can be used. Examination authorities, such as Oxford and Cambridge, Cambridge and Associated Boards, put considerable emphasis on fieldwork at Advanced level. In these and other examinations questions are set which require from the student practical experience of work in the field if a satisfactory answer is to be written. The C.S.E. boards are even keener to promote this type of work and in some cases fieldwork is a compulsory part of the examination.[65]

In 1972 the DES survey of schools found that only 8 per cent of the schools did not carry out fieldwork, whereas 80 per cent regarded fieldwork as 'important or very important'.[66] The growing interest in fieldwork was also found in the universities. In 1963 Board noted that it had become fashionable 'to include references to the necessity for fieldwork in the inaugural addresses by new occupants of chairs of geography'.[67]

In spite of the widespread indicators of acceptance in the academic sectors of secondary schools and universities, a number of fundamental problems have remained unresolved. Partly, the problems of fieldwork derive from practical difficulties which as Everson has conceded are 'legion and daunting'. 'The organiser has to find time to organise and prepare for the trip; to justify to himself and, more importantly, to others, the loss of actual school teaching time, especially for classes preparing for public examinations, to find suitable staff for the work, to keep the costs down . . .'[68] The 1972 survey found that:

> In 54 per cent of the schools visited the timetable created difficulties and the problems appeared to be more severe in the grammar than in other types of school. Put in another way, fewer than half of the schools possessed sufficient flexibility in timetabling to permit educational activities widely acclaimed to be valuable for pupils of all shades of ability . . . many schools overcome their difficulties by conducting fieldwork at weekends or in school holidays.

The report adds, ominously with regard to the ensuing wave of cuts in educational expenditure, that 'about 42 per cent of the schools reported difficulties in financing fieldwork'.[69]

Such problems are also experienced at university and college level. The DES survey notes that 'many older teachers and some younger ones received little training in fieldwork techniques at university or college'.[70] The inadequacies of university fieldwork were commented on by a lecturer in a well-established department with a strong national reputation: 'they were trivial . . . aimless . . . the students took it very lightheartedly and didn't get much out of it.' Besides the practical problems of organisation and staffing, fieldwork presented epistemological and presentational difficulties. Significantly, the Presidential Address at the Geographical Association in 1976 noted that geography suffered from too many 'woolly' generalisations — there was a lack of a scientific basis. 'Nowhere is this better illustrated than in fieldwork, which has long been important in our subject ...'[71]

In recent years determined efforts have been made to develop a model of 'field research' which focuses on the process of hypothesis formulation and testing, which lead to the provision of generalisations or theories. As Everson has noted, some geographers would be worried by this approach, feeling that 'it might develop an eye for a problem, not an eye for country' and that 'children will get less thrill and less understanding than from the former approach'.[72] Similarly, the DES survey noted: 'Hypothesis testing in the field is a new venture in school geography ... it is not surprising that nearly all the work recorded was confined to older pupils.'[73] In spite of the difficulties, Everson argues that advocates of the field research approach 'would say that in this method geographers are operating in the same way as scientists (and school geographers in the same way as research geographers) and consequently providing general statements which in this form of the study are objective not subjective assessments of the answer.' In this article, Everson significantly goes on to develop an elaborate model for fieldwork titled 'a route to scientific explanation'. Hence fieldwork was seen as needing reform in a similar manner to regional geography and further as needing to present a more scientific approach. In school geography the implications of this more scientific approach was that the pupil was to be allowed 'more and more to develop the field research stage of the process as he progresses up the school and grows in appreciation and ability'.[74] But the aspiration for more scientific models of school work remained largely unfulfilled. The DES survey for instance noted that in 1972 only about 15 per cent of schools were using some hypothesis testing in the field. The most common forms of experience remained 'field teaching and "traditional" fieldwork by pupils'.[75]

The New Geography

'New geography' was a reformulated version of the subject which emerged first in the United States and Sweden. In England this new geography was effectively launched at the Madingley Lectures in 1963. Commenting on this new initiative, E.A. Wrigley contended that regional geography was 'a concept overtaken by the course of historical change'. By this view regional geography 'has been as much a victim of the Industrial Revolution as the peasant, landed society, the horse and the village community, and for the same reason'.[76] To this problem of subject anachronism Chorley and two university geographers proposed an 'immediate solution' through 'building up the neglected geometrical side of the discipline'. They noted:

> Research is already swinging strongly into this field and the problem of implementation may be more acute in the schools than in the universities. There we are continually impressed by the vigour and reforming zeal of 'ginger groups' like the School Mathematics Associa-

Geography: Aspects of Subject History

tion [n.b. this presumably refers to the School Mathematics Project] which have shared in a fundamental review of mathematics teaching in schools. There the inertia problems — established textbooks, syllabuses, examinations — are being successfully overcome and a new wave of interest is sweeping through the schools. The need in geography is just as great and we see no good reason why changes here should not yield results equally rewarding.

The messianic nature of their appeal is shown when they argue that it is 'Better that geography should explode in an excess of reform than bask in the watery sunset of its former glories':[77]

The Madingley Lectures proved a watershed in the evolution of the subject. Two years before, E.W. Gilbert, in an article on 'The Idea of the Region',[78] had stated that he 'regarded new geography in the universities as an esoteric cult'.[79] After Madingley this was no longer the case, as a college lecturer who was secretary of his local Geographical Association recalled: 'After Madingley my ideas were turned upside down ... That's where the turn-around in thinking in geography really started.'[80] But, as Walford later noted, Madingley was 'heady to some, undrinkable brew to others'.[81]

Chorley and Haggett sought to consolidate the changes they were advocating, by a new book entitled 'Models in Geography'.[82] By this time opinions were becoming progressively polarised about the 'new geography'. Slaymaker wrote in support that the book was: 'In retrospect, a turning point in the development of geographical methodology in Britain' and argued that the publication of this book demonstrated that 'the traditional classificatory paradigm is inadequate and that in the context of the "new geography" an irreversible step has been taken to push us back into the mainstream of scientific activity by way of the uncomfortable and highly-specialized process of model building'.[83] Teachers of the subject received less enthusiastic advice from their journal 'Geography' and its anonymous reviewer, 'P.R.C.': 'What ... is its object, and to whom is it addressed? These questions are avoided with perverse skill and in the absence of guidance, the conviction gradually takes root that, in fact, the authors are writing for each other! This may explain, though it does not excuse, the use in some papers of a barbarous and repulsive jargon.'[84]

A year later the President of the Geographical Association pursued a similar opposition in a more explicit statement of the fears which new geography engendered. The new systematic geography, she argued, was 'creating a problem that will increase in acuteness over the decades ahead for it leads towards subject fragmentation as fringe specialisms in systematic fields proliferate and are pursued independently to the neglect of the very core of our discipline — a core that largely justifies its existence.'

The tension between academic scholarship 'pushing back the frontiers of knowledge' and the fragmentation of the 'core' of the subject has been strongly perceived by geographers. Garnett felt that geography in the universities was in fact 'so sophisticated' and 'its numerous branches in diverse fields at times so narrowly specialised' that 'sooner or later the question must arise as to how much longer the subject can effectively be held together'.[85] Geographers' paranoia about 'holding the subject together' has been recurrent and one is reminded of the fears of the inter-war years about the so-called 'expansiveness of geography'.

The dangers of fragmentation again impinge on the university departments where 'geographers are made'. These departments, Garnet maintained had a duty to unify the subject:

> University departments have a duty to ensure that, at least at the first degree level, the core of our subject is neither forgotten nor neglected, and that the synthesis of the specialist fields and their relevance to the core are clearly appreciated by our undergraduate students. To my mind, it is only on the foundation of a first degree course structure so designed that a geographer is basically qualified either to teach in our Schools or to carry his studies further at a postgraduate research level.[86]

The relevance of new geography for the teaching of the subject was also viewed as problematic, particularly in the light of the experiences in the early twenties when as geographers 'we worked hard to free our subject from the domination of generalised concepts and principles based all too often on insecure foundations'. Moreover, 'in the hands of the inexperienced, an oversimplified model can be a most dangerous tool leading to facile and stereotyped generalisation and even into new forms of crude determinism.'[87] Garnett's fears were reiterated a year later by Professor C.A. Fisher, following an almost identical line of argument. In perusing geographical periodicals he found much which seemingly substantiates 'the familiar charge that geography lacks any central purpose to justify it being regarded as a single coherent discipline....' Hence he feared that 'The lighthearted prophecy I made in 1959 that we might soon expect to see the full 57 varieties of geography[88] had since been almost literally fulfilled, and my personal collection of different categories of geography that have seriously been put forward in professional literature now stands at well over half that number.'[89] In stark contrast to Chorley and Haggett's view of the excitement of the frontier he states:

> We appear to assume that so long as we keep repeating the magic word geography we shall all stand shoulder to shoulder, even though we have dispersed ourselves into alien territory all the way round the geographical perimeter. To speak bluntly, I believe that geography is in serious danger of doing precisely this: of over-extending its periphery at the expense of its base ... I fear that in large measure this predilection for service at the frontier reflects a lack of conviction in what the home base stands for, and a widely prevalent feeling among many of our number that the central aims which geography grew up to fulfil are hopelessly out of date if not entirely meaningless.[90]

Fisher concludes with an exhortation to return to earlier versions of geography. 'Without suggesting that the "new geography"[91] is itself a total aberration, I would urge that assessments of its contribution should be subjected to its own quantitative criteria and cut down to size. For only then it seems, will geographers as a whole return to the eminently rewarding task of cultivating their own well-favoured garden.'[92]

The coverage given to views opposing 'new geography' in the geography teachers' journal reflected the opinion of many practising teachers. Peter Hore spent a year investigating the effects of new geography in the classroom.

> Teachers are not noted for their willing acceptance of new ideas. They are essentially practical and conservative people and need to be convinced that a new trend, idea or method has classroom application before giving it their approval. Furthermore they are suspicious of persons in ivory-towered universities and colleges of education, who throw out wonderful suggestions, without testing them in the white heat of a classroom composed, say, of thirty aggressive youths from a twilight urban area. It is not surprising then, that the waves of innovation breaking over the subject are causing concern — particularly to those who have coasted along with Eskimos and Masai or the Midland Triangle and other regions of the world (assuming that they have heard the pounding surf of the new geography at all).[93]

At the same time P.R. Thomas asserted that 'the outstanding feature of established practice in geography teaching in schools' was 'the persistence of intellectual methods which academic geographers have progressively rejected'.[94] The dangers were perceived by many teachers at the time: for example, one teacher recalled that at this time, 'Geography was in a state of ferment ... it was moving too quickly ... Let alone in the schools even many of the universities didn't have new geography.'[95] Whilst another noted that, 'This new approach, however you felt about it, caused a sort of schism ... both at university and school level.'[96]

Fears of this schism were expressed in a number of contemporary books. The gap between schools and universities, of which there is much evidence in previous periods, was thought particularly worrying: 'Techniques of study are changing more rapidly in modern geography than at any previous time in the subject's history. As a result there is a great need for a dialogue between research workers and those being admitted to the mysteries of the subject.' In this respect 'Teachers provide the necessary link; and it is dangerous for the vitality and future health of geography that some teachers find current developments either incomprehensible or unacceptable.'[97] Rex Walford made a similar diagnosis, arguing that the 'need for unity within the subject' was 'more than a practical one of preparing sixth-formers for their first lectures on campus; it is, I would assert, a basic requirement for the continued existence of the subject.'[98]

In spite of the opposition of teachers and academics, many of whom saw

School Subjects and Curriculum Change

regional geography as the 'real geography', there were strong pressures working in favour of the advocates of new geography. In the introduction to the book of papers arising from the 1970 Charney Manor Conference, 'New Directions in Geography Teaching', Walford summarised the position at the time. He employed new geography as a term '... usually applied to that loose collection of ideas which revolve around models, hypotheses, quantitative techniques, concepts and percepts'. He argued the need for the change succinctly, saying that 'If geography is to survive in the school curriculum it will have to be more than a convenient examination pass for those who seek only to memorise a jumble of facts and sketch-maps.'[99] He added that 'What is in disrepute is what old geography, haunted by the spectre of fact-dominated examinations, has turned into.'[100] David Walker made a similar point in 'Geography', arguing that traditional geography courses had 'three predominant characteristics which may be considered to be unfortunate': 'firstly a large content of regional studies; secondly a lack of precision in accepted statements about inter-relationships between geographical phenomena; and thirdly, very little training in geographical techniques other than observation, recording and the attempted drawing of conclusions at an unsophisticated level.' Walker apportioned the blame for these three faults in this manner: 'The first of these characteristics seems to be very largely responsible for the presence of the other two.' Namely, 'a view of geography well expressed by Hartshorne, "that no universals need to be evolved, other than the general laws of geography, that all areas are unique".'[101]

In attacking regional geography, Walker seems to have correctly elicited one of the central targets of 'new geography'. P.R. Thomas stated this even more explicitly: 'The fundamental characteristic of the "new geography" seems not to be, as is often thought, the use of quantitative methods, but rather its changed attitude to the region within geographical studies.' Because of this change 'the study of the particular region as a unique entity has been superseded by the search for patterns common to many regions, in which the particular case is only significant as a source of data used in the process of generalization.'[102] But in the late 1960s in spite of warnings about 'the survival of geography', in many schools geography was characterised by 'the survival of the regional concept as the basis of syllabus construction, despite the progressive decline in the importance of regional geography at most universities and its virtual disappearance from some.'[103] And despite the contention that 'the quantity and scale of regional studies allowed by school syllabuses have precluded the teaching of any but the most rudimentary techniques in geography.'[104]

That fact-dominated regional geography threatened the survival of the subject could be deduced from a number of contemporary reports. In 1967 the report on 'Society and the Young School Leaver' noted that its young subjects felt 'at best apathetic, at worst resentful and rebellious to geography ... which seems to him to have nothing to do with the adult world he is soon to join.' The report adds: 'A frequent cause of failure seems to be that the course is often based on the traditional belief that there is a body of content for each separate subject which every school leaver should know.' In the least successful courses, it argued, 'this body of knowledge is written into the curriculum without any real consideration of the needs of the boys and girls and without any question of its relevance.'[105]

The threat to geography began to be appreciated at the highest level. A member of the Executive and Honorary Secretary of the Geographical Association recalls: 'Things had gone too far and geography became a too locally based regional thing ... at the same time the subject began to lose touch with reality ... geography got a bad name.'[106] A college lecturer, David Gowing, saw the problem facing the subject and argued: 'Pupils feel that present curricula have little relevance to their needs and so their level of motivation and understanding is low. Teachers are concerned that the raising of the school-leaving age and some forms of comprehensive reorganisation may exacerbate these problems.'[107]

Under these pressures new geography made considerable progress. In 1967 Marchant proclaimed: 'After the era of physical geography has come that of mathematical geography',[108] and two years later Professor P.R. Gould proclaimed: 'During the last ten years, geography ... has exploded. Geographers today are intrigued by the order and regularity they find in the patterns, structures, arrangements, and relationships of man's work on the face of the earth.'[109] More tangible proof of the change was given in the preamble to the new Oxford and Cambridge 'A' level in 1969:

> At a high level new methods and techniques are being developed, tested and retained or discarded as inappropriate. Inevitably the emphasis shifts from time to time. While we think it totally inappropriate that pupils at school should be forced to follow all the current fashions in geography, some reflection of the changing content of the subject must filter down to Advanced level pupils without upsetting the general stability of the subject. As it now stands the syllabus is not sufficiently flexible to allow this and accordingly the changes detailed (towards 'new geography') are designed to let this happen.[110]

In 1967 the Geographical Association set up a sub-committee to consider the use of models and quantitative techniques in geography teaching.

Even more substantive proof of the change is reluctantly provided in the 1976 Presidential Address to the Geographical Association. Reviewing the chart of DES courses during the years 1970–76, Sheila Jones states: 'It shows quite clearly the current trend. Obviously what some are disposed to call the "Quantitative Revolution" was infiltrating into schools from 1970 to 1973, with applicants heavily outnumbering those who could actually be accepted for the courses.'[111] Likewise the Schools Council Geography 15–18 Project, in seeking to answer the question 'Is there really a "new geography"?', concluded there had been an important general shift in approaches to the subject:

geographers have become: (a) more critical of concepts and models that had previously been taken for granted, e.g. the 'region'; the Davisian cycle, or maps themselves; and hence are less ready to rely on 'common sense' and on unquantified evaluation of how well models and concepts used in geography match the real world. (b) more enterprising in devising new models, and in borrowing ideas like systems-analysis, or methods of evaluation such as regression analyses from other subjects.[112]

In recent years fears about 'new geography' seem to have subsided and a period of consolidation has set in. Of the Cambridge base of Chorley and Haggett it was recently written, by David Walker, himself a protagonist:

> The academic revolution of quantification which has battered traditional scholarship in fields like economic history and linguistics has taken its toll in geography in recent years, but the Cambridge department, which Professor Darby took in 1966 remains on even keel. The tripos system continues to offer a fine balance of specialisation and liberal education.[113]

Perceptions of a subject in crisis have considerably mellowed. A professor, who is on the Executive Committee and past holder of a number of positions in the Geographical Association, stated: 'I see geography traditionally as a core to understand why places are as they are', but said of the present condition of geography: 'It isn't in flux ... there is no end to the subject ... of course the techniques by which you advance the subject will change ... if the present emphasis on quantitative techniques helps our preciseness who could deny that it is an advance within the subject?'[114] Ultimately the reconciliation with new geography was closely linked with geography's long aspiration to be viewed as a science. In a previous decade Professor Wooldridge had written a book on 'The Geographer as Scientist'[115] but in 1970 Fitzgerald, reviewing the implications of new geography for teaching wrote: 'The change which many think is at the heart of geography is that towards the use of the scientific method in approaching problems.'[116] Similarly, M. Yeates argued that geography can be regarded 'as a science concerned with the rational development and testing of theories that explain and predict the spatial distribution and location of various characteristics on the surface of the earth.'[117] At the 21st International Geographic Congress at New Delhi in 1968, Professor Norton Ginsburg identified social science as the 'fraternity' to aspire to. He saw

> the beginnings of a new age for human geography as a fully-fledged member of the social science fraternity ... the future of geography as a major research discipline will, I submit, be determined on the intellectual battlefields of the universities, where competition and conflict are intense; and where ideas are the hallmark of achievement.

Two presidential addresses confirmed the aspiration to 'scientific' status as a valid intention for geographical research and teaching. In 1968 Professor Garnett saw that there was a 'growing recognition of the role of geography as a space science'.[118] Whilst in 1976 Sheila Jones expressed 'a wish to develop a precision of thought and this is obviously achieved by a more scientific approach to geography ...' This was because she discerned that too often geographers 'have depended on generalisations and the lack of a scientific basis made many of our studies "woolly"'.[119]

But if by the mid-1970s the teachers of geography had accepted new geography because of its clear benefits in achieving high scientific status within the universities new dissenters were active. In 1977 Peet's 'Radical Geography' summarised some of the problems. The collection was, said Johnson, made up of the essays of scholars 'who have become disillusioned with the "scientific approach" to human geography espoused since the mid-1950s, largely because of the perceived inability of this approach to initiate major social changes.'[120] The tension between prestige and academic progress was taken up in another publication 'Change and Tradition: Geography's new Frontiers'. Butterfield, for instance, strongly reaffirms faith in new geography but argues that 'competence in purposeful, yet flexible, scientific method' is needed to hold back the 'pressures of environmental and social relevance and explanation seeking'. In summary:

> Use of quantitative methods has tended to give geography a scientific prestige by association with mathematical techniques, and has led us to believe that we are at least scientific in the techniques that we use. But not all who use a spanner may call themselves mechanics; only those who know how, when and where to use it to dismantle a problem engine may do that. Furthermore, spanners are frequently thrown into the works and to make the problems even more intractable.[121]

The answer was the adoption and teaching of scientific approaches 'not for reasons of prestige or self-justification but as a methodological construct of immense instructional as well as analytical potential for the geographer'. Although an early advocate, one of the first dissenters was David Harvey who in 1973 recognised 'a clear disparity between the sophisticated theoretical and methodological framework we are using and our ability to say anything really meaningful about events as they unfold around us'.[122] Clearly, having promoted geography as a science and having thereby earned the associated prestige, geographers were left with the problems of practically implementing what had been so eloquently promoted.

Conclusion

The establishment of geography — 'how geography was rendered a discipline' — was a protracted, painstaking and fiercely contested process. The story is not one of the translation of an academic discipline devised by ('dominant') groups of scholars in universities into a pedagogic version to be used as a school subject. Rather, the story unfolds in reverse order and can be seen as a drive from low-status groups at school level to progressively colonise areas within the university sector — thereby earning the right for scholars in the new field to define knowledge that could be viewed as a discipline. The process of evolution for school subjects can be seen not as a pattern of disciplines 'translated' down or of 'domination' downwards but very much as a process of 'aspiration' upwards.

To summarise the stages in the evolution of geography: these offer some support for Layton's tentative model although they indicate the existence of a stage preceding his stage one. In this stage, teaching was anything but 'messianic', for the subject was taught by non-specialists and comprised a 'dreary collection of geographical facts and figures'. The threshold for 'take-off' on the route to academic establishment began with MacKinder's remarkably successful and sustained recipe for the subject's promotion drawn up in 1903. In the MacKinder manifesto the geography teacher is to set the exams and is to choose exams that are best for the 'common acceptation' of the subject, the teaching of geography is to be exclusively in the hands of trained geographers and the universities are to be encouraged to establish schools of geography 'where geographers can be made'.

The strategy offered solutions for the major problems geography faced in its evolution. Most notable of these was the idiosyncratic and information-based nature of school geography. Initially the subject stressed personal, pedagogic and utilitarian arguments for its inclusion in curricula: 'We seek to train future citizens', and moreover a citizen 'must have a topographical background if he is to keep order in the mass of information which accumulates in the course of his life' (1919). Later the subject was advocated because 'travel and correspondence have now become general' (1927). But the result of these utilitarian and pedagogic emphases was that comments arose as to the 'expansiveness' of the subject and the fact that it became 'more and more to be a "world citizenship" course (1930s).

The problem was that identified by MacKinder in 1903; geographers needed to be 'made' in the universities then the piecemeal changes in pursuit of school relevance could be controlled and directed. The growth of the subject in the schools provided an overwhelming argument for the subject to be taught in the universities. As Wooldridge noted later: 'It has been conceded that if geography is to be taught in schools it must be learned in universities'. Slowly, therefore, uniformity in the subject was established to answer those who observed the chameleon nature of the subject's knowledge structure. Alice Garnett noted that it was not until after 1945 that most school departments of geography were directed by specialist-trained geographers, but as a result of this training 'most of the initial marked differences and contrasts in subject personality had been blurred or obliterated'.

The definition of geography through the universities instead of the schools began to replace the pedagogic or utilitarian bias with arguments for academic rigour: and as early as 1927 Hadow had contended that 'the main objective in good geographical teaching is to develop, as in the case of history, an attitude of mind and mode of thought characteristic of the subject'. However, for several decades university geography was plagued both by the image of the subject as essentially for school children and by the idiosyncratic interpretations of the various university departments, especially in respect to fieldwork. Thus while establishment in universities solved the status problems of the subject within schools, within universities themselves the subject's status still remained low. The launching of 'new geography' with aspirations to scientific or social scientific rigour is therefore partly to be understood as a strategy for finally establishing geography's status at the highest level. In this respect the current position of the subject in universities would seem to confirm the success of new geography's push for parity of esteem with other university disciplines.

The aspiration to become an academic subject and the successful promotion employed by geography teachers and educationists, particularly in the work of the Geographical Association, has been clearly evidenced. We know what happened in the evolution of geography: less evidence has been presented as to why this should be so. A clue can be found in Garnett's presidential address to the Geography Association in 1968: a clear link is presented between 'the recognition of our subject's status among university disciplines' and 'the costly provision made available for its study'. Plainly the drive towards higher status is accompanied by opportunities to command larger finance and resources.

Byrne's work has provided data on resource allocation within schools (see Chapter 3). The implications of the preferential treatment of academic subjects for the material self-interest of teachers are clear: better staffing ratios, higher salaries, higher capitation allowances, more graded posts, better career prospects. The link between academic status and resource allocation provides a major explanatory framework for understanding the promotion of geography. Basically, if a university base can be established the subject can be promoted as a scholarly academic discipline. In schools it follows that the subject will be 'academic', taught to abler students and provided with favourable finance and resources.

Despite its success in establishing geography as a broadly-accepted academic discipline, the fear about new geography's 'repulsive jargon' and the dangers it held of 'subject fragmentation' into 'fringe specialisms' are recorded earlier. Above all, new geography represented an attack by one group of geographers on other groups well established in schools — the regional and field geographers. David Walker states quite clearly the nature of this attack and he and Thomas confirm that regional geography survived in the majority of school courses. For a time, the identity of geography was contested by these groups but in the end new geography achieved a major place in the subject.

In this respect the current position of the subject in universities would seem to confirm the success of new geography's push for parity of esteem within universities. The direction of the subject through the new definition emanating from university scholars was throughout the period scrutinised and partly coordinated by the Geographical Association. The Association thereby acted as a mediator between geography as defined by scholars and geography as traditionally taught in schools. At stages where the glap between these two widened the Association was always at hand to warn against too rapid redefinition, to exhort teachers to change and to encourage retraining in the new definitions of the subject. Besides playing a part in defining the internal unity of the subject at the various levels the Association was alert to definitions of knowledge by those outside its territory. Environmental studies posed a particular threat because of its obvious similarity to field geography and regional geography: two traditions under attack during the launching of new geography. At this time the possibilities of a break-up of the subject threatened its survival. But the Geographical Association was on hand to challenge this low-status 'integrated subject' and to defend the integrity of its own brand of integrated knowledge that had been so fiercely promoted for 80 years.

Notes

1. D. GREGORY, *Ideology, Science and Human Geography* (London, Hutchinson, 1978), p. 21.
2. G.S. ROBERTSON, 'Political Geography and the Empire,' *Geographical Journal*, 16, pp. 447–57, Quoted *ibid.* GREGORY, p. 18.
3. R. PEET, *Radical Geography: Alternative Viewpoints on Contemporary Social Issues* (London, Methuen, 1974), p. 10.
4. GREGORY, *op. cit.*, p. 20.
5. GREGORY, *op. cit.*, p. 17.
6. A. VON HUMBOLDT, *Cosmos* (London, 1849).
7. K. RITTER, *Alloemeine Erdkunde* (Berlin, 1862).
8. E.A. WRIGLEY, 'Changes in the Philosophy of Geography', in R. CHORLEY and P. HAGGETT, (Eds.), *Frontiers in Geographical Teaching* (London, Methuen, 1967), p. 3.
9. *Ibid.*, p. 4.
10. *Ibid.*
11. J. BRUNHES, *La Geographie Humaine* (Paris, 1925).
12. WRIGLEY, *op. cit.*, p. 6.
13. T.G. ROOPER, 'On methods of teaching geography', *Geographical Teacher*, 1 (1901).
14. H.J. MACKINDER, 'On the scope and methods of geography' *Proceedings of the Royal Geographical Society*, Vol. IX (1887).
15. R.J.W. SELLECK, *The New Education: The English Background 1870–1914* (Melbourne, Pitman, 1968), p. 34.
16. ROOPER, 1901, *loc. cit.*
17. E.G.A. HOLMES, *What Is and What Might Be* (London, Constable, 1912), p. 107.
18. C. BIRD, 'Limitations and possibilities of geographical teaching in day schools', *Geographical Teacher*, 1 (1901).
19. *Ibid.* inside cover of *Geography*.
20. A. GARNETT, 'Teaching geography: Some reflections', *Geography*, 54, November 1969, p. 367.

21 For example of inclusion see Joint Matriculation Board Calendar, 1918. As a subsidiary subject see Oxford Delegacy on Local Examinations Regulations, 1925.
22 H.J. MACKINDER, 'Report of the discussion on geographical education at the British Association meeting, September 1903'. *Geographical Teacher*, 2, 1903, pp. 95–101.
23 GARNETT, *op. cit.*, p. 387.
24 W. CAREY MACLEAN, 'The correlation of instruction in physics and geography,' *Geographical Teacher*, 5, 1913.
25 COUNCIL OF GEOGRAPHICAL ASSOCIATION, 'The Position of Geography', *Geographical Teacher*, 10, 1919.
26 *Ibid.*
27 *Ibid.*
28 D. WALKER, 'The well-rounded geographers', *Times Educational Supplement*, (28.11.1975), p. 6.
29 GARNETT, *op. cit.*, p. 388.
30 N.J. GRAVES, *Geography in Education* (London, Heinemann, 1975), p. 28.
31 *Ibid.*
32 MACKINDER, 1913, *lot cit.*
33 GARNETT, *op. cit.*, pp. 387–8.
34 R.C. HONEYBONE, 'Balance in geography and education', *Geography*, 34, 184, 1954.
35 GARNETT, *op. cit.*, p. 388.
36 COUNCIL of GEOGRAPHICAL ASSOCIATION (1919).
37 BOARD OF EDUCATION, *Report of the Consultative Committee: The Education of the Adolescent* (Hadow Report) (London, HMSO, 1927).
38 ROYAL GEOGRAPHICAL SOCIETY, *Geography and 'Social Studies' in Schools*, Education Committee memorandum (1950).
39 NORWOOD REPORT, 1943, pp. 101–2.
40 HONEYBONE, 1954, *loc. cit.*
41 T. DAVID, 'Against geography', in J. BALE, N. GRAVES, and R. WALFORD, *Perspective in Geographical Education* (Edinburgh, 1973).
42 *Ibid.*, DAVID.
43 WALKER, *op. cit.*
44 GARNETT, *op. cit.*, p. 368.
45 HONEYBONE, 1954, *loc. cit.*
46 E.C. MARCHANT, 'Some responsibilities of the teacher of geography', *Geography*, 3, 1968, p. 133.
47 S.M. JONES, 'The challenge of change in geography teaching', *Geography* (Nov. 1976), p. 197.
48 HONEYBONE, 1954, *loc cit.*
49 M.J. WISE, 'An early 19th century experiment in the teaching of geography', *Geography*, 33 (1948), p. 20.
50 J. SCOTT KELTIE, 'Geographical education: Report to the Council of the Royal Geographical Society', *Royal Geographical Society Supplementary Papers*, 1 (1882–5), p. 451.
51 GEOGRAPHICAL ASSOCIATION PRIMARY SCHOOLS COMMITTEE, *Suggestions for the Teaching of Local Geography* (n.d.).
52 G.J. CONS and C. FLETCHER, *Actuality in School: An Experiment in Social Education* (London, Methuen, 1938), pp. 1–2.
53 *Ibid.*, p. 7. Quoting from the report of an address on the senior school and its curriculum by H.M. Spink, Director of Education for Northumberland.
54 J.F. ARCHER and T.H. DALTON *Fieldwork in Geography* (London, Batsford, 1968), p. 14.
55 K.S. WHEELER, 'The outlook tower: Birthplace of environmental education', *Bulletin of the Society for Environmental Education*, 2, 2, 1970, p. 26.

56 A. GEIKIE, *Landscape in History and Other Essays* (London, 1905), p. 296.
57 C. BOARD in CHORLEY and HAGGETT (Eds.), *Frontiers in Geographical Teaching*: p. 187.
58 S.W. WOOLDRIDGE and W.G. EAST, *The Spirit and Purpose of Geography* (London, Hutchinson, 2nd ed. 1958), p. 16.
59 S.W. WOOLDRIDGE, 'The spirit and significance of fieldwork', Address at the Annual Meeting of the Council for the Promotion of Field Studies (1948), p. 4.
60 BOARD, *op. cit.*, p. 186.
61 Interview, Sheffield Institute of Education, 30.6.76.
62 DEPARTMENT OF EDUCATION AND SCIENCE 'School geography in the changing curriculum', *Education Survey 19*, (London, HMSO, 1974), p. 15.
63 Interview Sheffield 30.6.76., *op. cit.*
64 ARCHER and DALTON, *op. cit.*, pp. 14–15.
65 J. EVERSON, 'Some aspects of teaching geography through fieldwork', *Geography*, 54, Part 1, January 1969, p. 64.
66 *Education Survey 19, op. cit.*, p. 15.
67 C. BOARD, *op. cit.*, p. 187.
68 J. EVERSON, 'Fieldwork in school geography', in R. WALFORD, (Ed.), *New Directions in Geography Teaching* (London, Longmans, 1973), p. 107.
69 *Education Survey No. 19*, p. 17.
70 *Ibid.*, p. 18.
71 S.M. JONES, p. 203.
72 EVERSON, *op. cit.*, p. 111.
73 *Education Survey No. 19, op. cit.*, pp. 16–17.
74 EVERSON, *op. cit.*, p. 111.
75 *Education Survey No. 19, op. cit.*, p. 16.
76 WRIGLEY, *op. cit.*, p. 13.
77 CHORLEY and HAGGETT, *op. cit.*, 'Frontier Movements and the Geographical Tradition', p. 377.
78 E.W. GILBERT, 'The idea of the region', *Geography*, 45(i), 1961.
79 D. GOWING', A fresh look at objectives', in R. WALFORD (Ed.), *New Directions in Geography Teaching* (London, Longmans, 1973), p. 153.
80 A. HORTON (5.1.77). Interview.
81 R. WALFORD, 'Models, simulations and games', WALFORD, *op. cit.*, p. 95.
82 R.J. CHORLEY and P. HAGGETT, *Models in Geography* (London, Methuen, 1967).
83 O. SLAYMAKER, 'Review of Chorley and Haggett: Frontiers in geographical teaching', *Geographical Journal*, 134, Part 2, September 1960.
84 P.R.C., 'Review of Chorley and Haggett: Frontiers in geographical teaching', *Geography*, 53, Part 4, November 1968.
85 GARNETT, *op. cit.*, pp. 388–9.
86 *Ibid.*, p. 389.
87 *Ibid.*, p. 395.
88 C.A. FISHER, 'The Compleat Geographer', Inaugural Lecture, University of Sheffield (1959), p. 6.
89 C.A. FISHER, 'Whither regional geography?' *Geography*, 55, Part 4, November 1970, pp. 373–4.
90 *Ibid.*, p. 374.
91 To distinguish it from the 'new geography' current at the turn of the century.
92 FISHER, *op. cit.*, p. 388.
93 P. HORE, 'A teacher looks at the new geography', WALFORD, *op. cit.*, p. 132.
94 P.R. THOMAS, 'Education and the new geography', *Geography*, 55, Part 3, July 1970, p. 27.
95 HORTON, *op. cit.*, Interview.
96 Interview, 14.12.76, Scraptoft College, Leicester.

Geography: Aspects of Subject History

97 R. COOKE and J.M. JOHNSON, *Trends in Geography* (London, 1969).
98 WALFORD in WALFORD (Ed.), *op. cit.*, p. 97.
99 *Ibid.*, p. 2.
100 *Ibid.*, p. 3.
101 D. WALKER, 'Teaching the new Oxford and Cambridge Board Advanced Level syllabus,' *Geography*, 54, Part 4, November 1969, p. 438.
102 THOMAS, *op. cit.*, p. 275.
103 *Ibid.*, pp. 274–5.
104 WALKER, *op. cit.*, p. 439.
105 *Society and the Young School Leaver*, Working Paper No. 11 (HMSO, 1967), p. 3.
106 ELLIS, *op. cit.*, Interview, Sheffield Institute of Education, 30.6.76.
107 GOWING, *op. cit.*, pp. 152–3.
108 MARCHANT, *op. cit.*, p. 134.
109 P. R. GOULD, 'The new geography', BALE, GRAVES and WALFORD, *op. cit.*, pp. 35–6.
110 OXFORD and CAMBRIDGE SCHOOLS EXAMINATION BOARD, *New Syllabus for Advanced Level Geography* (1969).
111 JONES, *op. cit.*, pp. 197–8.
112 SCHOOLS COUNCIL, *A New Professionalism for a Changing Geography* (London, December 1973), p. 3.
113 WALKER, *op. cit.*, p. 6.
114 Interview, Department of Geography, Leicester University, 14.12.76.
115 S.W. WOOLDRIDGE, *The Geographer as Scientist* (London, 1956).
116 B.P. FITZGERALD, 'Scientific method, quantitative techniques and the teaching of geography', WALFORD (Ed.), *op. cit.*, p. 85.
117 M.H. YEATES, *An Introduction to Quantitative Analysis in Economic Geography* (New York, McGraw Hill, 1968), p. 1.
118 GARNETT, *op. cit.*, p 391.
119 S. JONES, *op. cit.*, p. 203.
120 R. PEET, *Radical Geography* (London, Methuen, 1978).
121 G.R. BUTTERFIELD, 'The scientific method in geography' in R. LEE (Ed.), *Change and Tradition: Geography's New Frontiers* (Queen Mary College, London, 1977), p. 13.
122 D. HARVEY, *Social Justice and the City* (London, Arnold, 1973), p. 128.

6   Rural Studies: Aspects of Subject History

The origins of rural studies are both conceptually and chronologically widely spread. It is possible to distinguish two paramount themes, neither of which contributed exclusively to the development of rural studies, and parts of which were important in the development of biology and geography. Firstly were those advocates who stressed the utilitarian aspects of education allied to husbandry and agriculture. For instance, in 1651 Samuel Hartlib proposed in his 'Essay for Advancement of Husbandry Learning' that the science of husbandry should be taught to apprentices.[1] Later, alongside Britain's agricultural revolution in the eighteenth and early nineteenth centuries a number of private schools began to teach agriculture. In the early nineteenth century a school at Tulketh Hall near Preston, run by G. Edmundson, included the subject, as did A. Nesbitt's school at Lambeth, then situated in London's rural environs.[2]

The second group advocated the use of the rural environment as part of an educational method: they were concerned with the pedagogic potential of such work. Rousseau summarised the arguments in his book 'Emile', written in 1767. He believed that nature should teach the child, not the classroom teacher with his formal methods. The pedagogic implications of Rousseau's thesis were first explored practically in 1799 by Pestalozzi in his school Burgdorf in Switzerland, and later by Froebel and Herbart in Germany.

In England the major influence was seen in the elementary schools and in their curricula where the utilitarian rather than pedagogic tradition was followed. The tradition emerged in the schools of industry set up in the last decade of the eighteenth century and related to the Poor Law system.[3] The curriculum of these schools included gardening and simple agricultural operations amongst other activities, such as tailoring and cobbling for the boys and lace-making for the girls. They were seen as vocational schools for the poorer classes.[4]

The curricula of the schools of industry were partly adopted in the early monitorial schools set up by educationists like Joseph Lancaster. Utilitarian intention is evidenced in the reports of school inspectors appointed by the

Rural Studies: Aspects of Subject History

Board of Education to visit schools in receipt of grants. Mr. Tremenhearne reported in 1843 that in a Winkfield school: '... the garden work would seem to invite familiar lectures on the simple points of natural history which would lend a new interest to labour.'[5] In the later nineteenth century the use of 'nature study' in addition to school gardening was advocated by people such as T.H. Huxley and Matthew Arnold. Such advocates moved beyond utilitarian considerations and were concerned with nature study as an educational method, a separate epistemology, and drew their inspiration from German writing and practice. In 1869 T.H. Huxley said 'Let every child be instructed in those general views of the phenomena of Nature for which we have no exact English name ... "Erdkunde" — earth knowledge — that is to say a general knowledge of the earth and what is on it, in it and about it.'[6] Similarly in 1876 Matthew Arnold had remarked that he would like to see '... what the Germans call Naturkunde — knowledge of the facts and laws of nature — added as a class subject.'[7]

Both Arnold and Huxley were concerned to establish nature study as a foundation for more scientific investigation. Huxley felt that after the 'preliminary opening of the eyes to the great spectacle of the daily progress of Nature' and given familiarity with the 'three R's' the child should pass on to 'what is, in a strict sense, physical science'. Huxley saw physical science as composed of botany and physics: 'Every educational advantage which training in physical science can give is obtainable from the proper study of these two ... and I should be contented for the present if they, added to our "Erdkunde", furnished the whole of the scientific curriculum of the school'.[8] Similarly, Arnold argued that children should be taught about 'the system of nature': 'Children ... are taught something about the form and motion of the earth, about the causes of night and day and the seasons. But why are they taught nothing of the causes, for instance, of rain and dew, which are at least as easy to explain to them and not less interesting.'[9]

The arguments for nature study as a foundation for the teaching and learning of science were taken up in a number of government reports. In 1895, for instance, the Bryce Commission reported that 'Ample provision must be made in schools for scientific teaching, beginning if possible with natural history and the other sciences of observation and working up to chemistry and physics.'[10] In the last two decades of the nineteenth century the 'nature study' advocates and the utilitarian tradition of school gardening gained support from the fairly rapid conversion of agriculturalists. Selleck notes that there was 'evidence of an expectation that education might contribute to the solution of the problems of the agricultural industry in ways that were similar to those by which it had assisted other industry.' He felt that this expectation '... manifested itself in a number of ways: the introduction of nature study into the curriculum, the attempt to improve rural education, the tendency to experiment with courses in the principles of agriculture, the popularisation of the "school journey", the pressure to start school museums.'[11] Recommendations for a change in school curricula began to appear in parliamentary reports. For instance, in 1882 the Technical Instruction Commission recommended that: 'In rural schools instruction in the principles and facts of agriculture, after suitable introductory object lessons, shall be made obligatory in the upper standards.'[12] In 1883 the subject, Principles of Agriculture, appeared for the first time in official lists and seven years later the Code of the Education Department recommended 'alternative courses which could be applied to rural schools'.[13] From this point on there seems to have been rapid growth, for Hudspeth reports that in 1897 school gardening was 'introduced as part of a general education rather than being used in a purely utilitarian manner', and when in 1900 the system of block grants to replace subject grants was introduced, gardening still carried a separate grant; in 1902, for instance, this grant was earned by 4,359 children in 289 schools.[14] The expansion Hudspeth refers to was partly a result of the efforts of the Agricultural Education Committee, formed in 1899, which campaigned actively and with some success. In 1900, for instance, the Board of Education issued a circular advising teachers to: '... lose no opportunity of giving their scholars an intelligent knowledge of the surroundings of ordinary rural life and of showing them how to observe the processes of Nature for themselves.'[15] In spite of the interest shown by the Board of Education in 1904, when the secondary school curriculum was established by the issuing of the 'regulations', rural studies along with other utilitarian subjects with a working-class orientation, was omitted. Rural education though was still taken seriously within the elementary sector with emphasis on those pupils not expected to proceed to the secondary stage. In keeping with this view secondary examinations (known from 1917 as 'school certificates') did not include rural studies.

Sample courses in rural education for elementary schools were prepared. In 1905 the Board of Education's 'Handbook of Suggestions for Teachers' produced a guide to school gardening, and in 1908 a pamphlet entitled 'Suggestions of Rural Education' offered specimen courses in nature study, gardening and rural economy intended to replace earlier draft courses prepared in 1901 and 1902.

The publication of a memorandum on the Principles and Methods of Rural Education by the Board of Education in 1911 stressed that the movement to implement rural education was designed to make teaching in rural schools '... more practical, and to give it a more distinctly rural bias; to base it upon what is familiar to country children, and to direct it so that they may become handy and observant in their country surroundings.'[16] The Board of Education's statistics evidence a substantial growth in school gardens:

1904–5	551 schools
1907–8	1,171 schools
1911–12	2,458 schools

In the latter year 20 'departments' of gardening or rural education are recorded.[17] Further, some counties had appointed expert instructors to organise horticulture teaching in schools, and other counties offered help for teachers

Rural Studies: Aspects of Subject History

to go on courses of instruction at colleges and institutes of agriculture and horticulture.[18] Alongside these developments 'nature study' began to spread into many elementary schools. In 1902 a nature study exhibition in London stimulated the growth of the subject and in the same year a Nature Study Society was formed which still exists.

The pre-war growth of rural studies in school was summarised as '... an attempt to use education to further the interests of rural industry in ways similar to those in which it was being used in the city'.[19] The most obvious method of supporting rural industry was to retain the labour force that emerged at the age of 13 from the elementary schools. Many of these children joined the 'drift from the land' which seriously threatened the viability of the rural economy. Fabian Ware argued that developing an interest in his natural environment through education 'would not only make a better worker of the agriculturalist, but would strengthen him morally against, at any rate, the lower attractions of town life'.[20] The case for rural education was articulated in Parliament by Sir Carne Rasch. His concern for education was one of reluctant involvement: 'To speak plainly, I detest it so far as I am concerned. I am simply here as an agricultural member, principally to keep the rates down and particularly the rates for education.'[21] In another debate Rasch had posed the question, 'What do Honourable Members think of agricultural labourers' children? ... Do they imagine that when they leave school they turn into professors or Members of Parliament?' and answered it asserting 'They do not want your higher education: they do not want your curriculum or whatever Hon. Members choose to call it ...'[22] From here the argument leads plainly to the need for studies particularly designed for rural children.

During the 1914–18 war the country required home food to be produced wherever possible. As a result, the war gave an impetus to school gardening and the keeping of livestock. The Board of Education produced a circular called 'Public Elementary Schools and the Supply of Food in Wartime'. This circular asserted that 'Public opinion is in favour of the development in rural schools of practical interests'.[23] In the period following the war there is evidence of rural curricula being viewed and presented by the Board of Education not only as a general influence in rural schools but also as a separate subject. In 1922 the Board stated that 'teachers should regard their subject as rural science'. The circular of that year develops the linkage between rural studies and science first tentatively explored by F.E. Green's 'A First Book of Rural Science' published in 1913: 'Study of cultivated plants and the practice of their cultivation open up so many by-paths of investigation that it is very likely to produce here and there among pupils that intelligent wonder and curiosity which lie at the root of scientific research.'[24] The linkage was also developed by the Thompson Committee on 'The Position of Natural Science in the Educational System' in 1981:

> There is general agreement amongst science teachers that the best preparation for the study of science at secondary school is a course of

nature study up to the age of twelve. This course should be of as practical a character as possible and should aim at arousing an interest in natural phenomena and developing the powers of observation. Full use should be made of the opportunities afforded by the school garden to make the pupils acquainted with the spirit of scientific investigation.[25]

In the circular on 'Rural Education' of May 1925 the Board of Education again stressed links with science, asserting: 'It should be possible for the country child to learn something of the fundamental principles of mechanics, to make some study of air, water, heat and light with a view to understanding the processes of plant and animal life, and to apply simple tests in the examination of soils.' This circular, which was the precursor of a very influential board pamphlet, set out the background to the new central initiative to establish rural education:

> The Board have on previous occasions made it clear to Local Education Authorities by means of Circulars, Pamphlets, Memoranda etc. that they consider it of great importance that the teaching in rural schools should be associated closely with the environment of the children; and much has been done in the course of the last fifteen or twenty years, especially through the development of instruction in Gardening and other forms of practical work . . . it appears desirable at the present time to emphasise afresh the principle that the education given in rural schools should be ultimately related to rural conditions of life.[26]

In defining the implications for syllabus design of 'rural education' the Board followed along guidelines laid down in 1922 in a book by Gunton and Hawkes. These two rural studies teachers envisaged their subject as 'the Hub of the Curriculum Wheel'. All the subjects of the curriculum were to be taught within a rural, practical context.[27] Similarly, the Board considered the importance of a rural bias in elementary science, arithmetic, geography, history, English, manual instruction and domestic subjects.

In Hertfordshire the aims of rural education were pursued in a 'Suggested Syllabus of Rural Education' for 'Older Children of both Sexes in Public Elementary Schools'. The syllabus was approved by the County Education Committee at a meeting on 7 January 1927 and was then circulated to schools.[28] In 1929 an HMS Inspector prepared a report on the workings of the syllabus, which concluded: 'Perhaps the chief value of the "syllabus" has been the encouragement of the right outlook among rural teachers towards their special problem.' The syllabus presented '. . . a new situation which gave confidence to many Head Teachers who were in sympathy with the doctrine but were timorous of launching out.'[29] In 1929, 33 Hertfordshire elementary schools were involved in experiments related to the syllabus. The report deals with the 'Effect on Ordinary School Subjects'. Whilst all subjects were affected, in certain schools, apart from the general improvement in 'Handwork and Gardening', the most successful linkage, as in past initiatives, was with elementary science and nature study. 'This section of the syllabus is developing very well indeed, and the opportunities afforded by the farm, the garden and the countryside for observational work and simple deductions are being well utilized.' Hence the report notes: 'The school garden is being regarded more and more as a laboratory for experiments.'[30] The responsibility for contextualising the 'ordinary' subjects of the curriculum in such a rural and practical manner was seen as mainly that of the headmaster, who 'should so co-ordinate the outdoor and observational work with the ordinary subjects of the curriculum that the former becomes the starting point from which the more generalised instruction proceeds.'[31] As well as the inspector's report, the results of the Hertfordshire scheme were also commented on in the locality. At the reopening of the Merchant Taylors' School at Ashwell, the Chairman of the Education Committee made a clear statement of the Council's views which was reported in the local press: 'they particularly regretted ... the way the urban centres were growing more and more and the rural districts losing their population to the towns, and they felt that the scheme would help keep people in the rural areas.'[32] Carson records that in Hertfordshire, there was opposition to the scheme: 'There is no doubt that working people in the villages resented this attempt to keep them in their place, however good the motives, and the writer has frequently come across the deep suspicion of rural studies held by farmworking families who, above all, did not want their sons trained to stay on the land.'[33]

Nationally, opposition to the scheme was summarised in a book by Margaret Ashby on 'The Country School'. In the villages she investigated, only 40 per cent of the boys stayed on the land, and only 10 per cent of the girls worked on the land or married agricultural workers. As a doctor she especially noted the effects of poverty on rural children and posed the question, 'Is a rural bias justified morally?' and answered that 'Economic forces are infinitely stronger than school and unless we are certain that these forces favour a rural career for the children, it is plainly wrong for the school to press them in that direction.' She adds conclusively: 'If the rural labourer's child appreciated the story of his own class any tendency he might have to leave the country would be reinforced.'[34] Undoubtedly, awareness of the opposition to their schemes caused a new emphasis to be given to the Board of Education's 'Education and the Countryside' published in 1934. This time the Board argued that their pamphlet was 'not concerned primarily with the vocational training of those who will earn their livelihood in the country districts', but with the 'various ways in which schools are making the environment of their pupils contribute to the fashioning of a good general education.'[35] Besides, the pamphlet argued, rural life was improving rapidly and figures were provided to substantiate a view that the drift from the land was less significant than had been widely thought.

Significant progress in the establishment of 'rural studies organisers' in many counties is reported in the pamphlet: 'In most counties, some officer, usually well qualified in horticulture, is available to give expert advice on

School Subjects and Curriculum Change

school gardening problems. The amount of time devoted to this varies from county to county and depends largely upon the value attached by the authority to practical work in rural schools.'[36] In fact the value attached to practical rural education was subsequently changed by the 1944 Education Act and the ensuing reorganisation of the educational system. Some indications of a change in the official Board of Education view can be discerned before this date. In 1943 the Report of the Committee of the Secondary School Examinations Council appointed by the President of the Board of Education noted, with regard to natural science:

> The framing of all courses and the choice of illustrative material should in our opinion be influenced so far as may be feasible by the environment of the school. Yet that influence should not be so great as to cause the syllabus to become 'specialised'; we urge this particularly with regard to natural science in rural schools, for we do not think it in the interest of agriculture or rural industries themselves that the teaching in schools should be directed too closely to these ends.[37]

The Board's exhortations regarding specialisation were soon to prove abortive.

Rural Studies Since the 1944 Education Act

After the Second World War two influences were particularly important in redefining rural studies. Firstly, 'stimulated by the thinking that had produced the 1944 Education Act and the secondary modern schools, teachers began to search again in our rural heritage for whatever might be used educationally to advantage.'[38] Alongside this search 'the effect of the 1944 Act was to alter the school organisation so that teaching in secondary schools became largely specialist in nature.'[39] At first, the changes in secondary organisation did not radically alter the inter-war potential which rural studies had exhibited. Teachers and educationists continued in search of new educational methods of using the rural environment, and certain schools continued in focusing their whole curriculum around investigations of this environment. In 1950 A.B. Allen saw rural studies at the centre of the curriculum in country schools:

> Taking agriculture and horticulture as our foundation subjects, we see the interrelationship within the curriculum. Agriculture leads into elementary science, general biology, nature study, world history and world geography. It also leads into mathematics with its costing problems, mensuration and balance sheets. Horticulture leads into elementary science (and so is linked with agriculture), and local history.[40]

At the same time the Central Advisory Council for Education was exhorting teachers: 'The first and rather obvious point is that what a school teaches should be connected with the environment. That is, the curriculum should be so designed as to interpret the environment to the boys and girls who are growing up in it.'[41] In some of the early secondary modern schools this vision of rural studies as the 'curriculum hub' connecting school to environment and life had a marked influence. In 1949, A.J. Fuller, a keen gardener, was given the headship of Wrotham Secondary School in Kent. He appointed R. Colton to teach sciences and S. Carson to teach rural science. The new school consisted of three huts in a field. Carson taught 4F — i.e. Fourth Year Farming. There were also 4P (Practical) and 4A (Academic). However, since there were no examinations the farming class often attracted some of the brightest pupils. Recruitment often took place through the Young Farmers' Club. 'There was a less rigid division between school and community.' The agricultural apprenticeship scheme had just started: 'The best boys, the most able, who today would be in the sixth form, went into farming gladly. Good farms, good employers!' Carson built the activities of the class around the rural environment. 'I think the inspiration probably came from Fuller.' 'I had a strong feeling that education wasn't just book learning ... it involved commonsense applied to a problem.'

Carson had 4F for all subjects except science, which Colton taught, and woodwork. 'I taught them maths, English, history, etc. All tied in completely with the rural environment ... for example maths I based as much as possible on the farm activities. In fact I used a series of books which were popular then called "Rural Arithmetic".' In English: 'We were fairly poorly off for books in those days frankly, so we read a lot of literature associated with the countryside ... a lot of English was straightforwardly connected with the farm.'

As the tripartite system of education gradually emerged in the form of new school buildings and modified curricula, it became clear that rural studies and gardening were only developing in the secondary modern schools. In 1952 a questionnaire survey of gardening and rural studies teachers in Kent produced, with three exceptions, the reply from grammar and technical schools of 'subjects not taught', whilst in 63 of the 65 secondary modern schools the subject was given an important position in the curriculum.[42] (See Appendix 1)

By this time, however, secondary modern schools were increasingly concerning themselves with external examinations. The effect on Carson's scheme in Wrotham was echoed in other schools which had sought to build the curriculum around the rural environment: 'The advent of external examinations gradually prevented the more capable children from taking part and eventually led the scheme to be aimed at the less able children only.'[43] When Carson moved to Royston Secondary School in Hertfordshire in 1954 he noted the changing atmosphere in secondary modern schools. The adviser, Geoff Whitby, had run an elementary school in the 1950s at Ashwell in Hertfordshire which had epitomised the 'hub of the curriculum' vision of rural studies. However, the head of Royston, Mr. Young, had little time for such a view.

> He didn't see it as rural education in that sense because he was already thinking ahead to raising the standards of this school to what would

eventually be C.S.E. The classes were streamed. I only ever got the lowest of the three streams. While at first I could do what I liked with that bottom stream and I did the same sort of thing as in Kent, over the next few years this was whittled away from me as more specialism invaded the curriculum, and these kids eventually spent practically no time running the farm.[44]

A similar point was made in an article by Mervyn Pritchard, a St. Albans headmaster who later chaired the Schools Council Working Party on Rural Studies:

> There appear to be two extremes of thought in secondary modern schools — (a) a concentration on external examinations (b) those who won't have them at any price. In those schools where the brighter pupils are examined it is unusual to find rural science as one of the subjects taken and as the pupils concentrate more and more narrowly on their examination subjects, it is unusual to find rural science used as a social subject such as craft, art or music may be.
>
> Even where pupils are not examined there appears to be a concentration of the teaching of the subject in streams of classes of duller children.[45]

Pritchard's working party later summed up this phase: 'The old concept of the subject predominantly as gardening, often gardening for the backward boys only, did not die easily.'[46] Not only did it not easily die; subsequent events were to prove this practical version was alive and well decades later.

In 1957 the Hertfordshire Association of Teachers of Gardening and Rural Subjects, worried by the loss of status and influence of the subject, carried out a similar survey to the Kent one. This time, significantly, questionnaires were sent only to secondary modern schools. The financial treatment of rural studies showed clearly the priorities of the secondary modern headmasters: 'It is surprising to learn ... that some schools allow the rural science department no money at all while others are so small that the financial pinch entails great worry to the teacher.'[47] Of the 39 schools that returned questionnaires, 15 had no classroom allotted for rural studies.[48]

Of the 53 teachers involved, 26 were unqualified in gardening or rural studies[49] and the general 'image' of rural studies teachers is elegantly caught in the illustration opposite. Not only was the status of the rural studies teacher questionable but his isolation on the staff was often confirmed by placing the rural studies facilities in a distant corner of the school grounds.

The concern of rural studies teachers at the deteriorating status and position of their subject led to a variety of responses in the latter part of the 1950s. Mervyn Pritchard exhorted: 'As often as possible, the rural studies teacher should mix with his colleagues, even if he has to kick off muddy gum boots to drink his cup of tea. Much useful interchange of knowledge and information is carried out among the staffroom gossip. Informal discussion of

Rural Studies: Aspects of Subject History

school policy can be helped along judiciously by the rural studies teacher. Frequent contact can convince our colleagues of one's normality and value.'[50] Apart from such exhortations, some teachers were concerned to develop a 'Philosophy of rural studies'. In 1954 Carson and Colton produced a paper which appeared in the Kent Association Journal, and later in 1957, in the Lincolnshire 'Rural Science News'. It was a systematic attempt to think through a subject philosophy, a first, embryonic attempt to define a subject, and one equipped with a contemporary rationale. They argued: 'For this study to justify its inclusion in the school curriculum, it must be shown to play a vital part in developing a fully educated citizen.'[51] Carson and Colton were editors of the Kent Association of Teachers of Gardening and Rural Science Journal. The 'Rural Science' appendage was added at Carson's insistence when the Association was formed in 1949.[52] The Association was predated by an ephemeral association of rural science teachers in 1925, and by a small association in Nottingham founded in 1940, and the Manchester Teachers' Gardening Circle

"The Rural Science Teacher must take part in activities which are the heart of the organisation of the school society."

founded in 1941.[53] By 1954 the Kent Journal was beginning to define a philosophy for rural studies and soon after claimed, 'this Association has constantly sought parity of esteem with the rest of the curriculum for all rural studies'.[54]

The teachers' changing perception of their work is reflected in the changes in the name of the Kent Association: in 1958 they changed their name from 'the Kent Association of Teachers of Gardening and Rural Science' to 'The Kent Association of Teachers of Rural Science'; in 1959 this changed to 'The Kent Teachers' Rural Studies Association'. Their Journal proclaimed: 'Rural studies embraces all subjects which we know on the timetable as nature study, gardening, rural science and farming',[55] a sign that a new phase in claiming curriculum territory and promoting the subject was underway.

The Growth of Subject Associations

In February 1956, R.F. Morgan wrote in the Kent Journal that efforts were being made to contact 'similar organisations to our own with a view to exchanging ideas and one day of forming an association on a national basis'. At the time he reported that apart from Kent, only Middlesex and Nottinghamshire had flourishing associations. 'Devonshire had a Rural Science Teachers' Association but it has now been absorbed by the Science Teachers' Associaton.' Dorset, Essex, Shropshire and the West Riding of Yorkshire were all keen to form associations.[56] More significantly, R. Colton, who had just left Kent to become Rural Studies Organiser in the Holland division of Lincolnshire, was about to form an association there. S. Carson who had recently moved to Hertfordshire, formed an Association of Teachers of Gardening and Rural Subjects at a meeting in January 1957: 'The object of that [forming the association] was really to raise the status of rural studies and get the facilities for the subject which other subjects got . . . but the situation was never there to achieve any more than that it was specialism in a school and should be adequately supported.'

Carson's final sentence here summarises the situation which rural studies had come to occupy by 1957. As the Kent Journal noted, 'with the building of large secondary schools within the last few years, full-time specialists are needed.'[57] Rural studies was just one of a range of specialisms in the secondary modern schools. Moveover it was of low status and historically poorly organised.

Carson saw that rural studies had to 'adapt or perish'. In a world of examinable specialist subjects the advocation of rural studies as an all-pervasive educational approach was no longer feasible.

> By this time I'd really given up hope of getting rural studies seen in the way I'd taught it in Kent. Then I saw it as a specialist subject which had weak links.
>
> My alternative vision . . . was that a lot of kids don't learn through

paper and pencil and that we do far too much of this. A lot of kids could achieve success and use all the mental skills that we talk about in the classroom such as analysing and comparing through physical activities ... With the farm it was a completely renewing set of problems and the fact that it was a farm was incidental. You were thinking in educational terms of process with these kids.

That's the sort of dreams I was well aware of giving up and I talked about it a number of times. I've always felt dissatisfied since and I've met many teachers who'd come across the same realisation — not in such explicit terms as they'd never had the chance of doing it, whereas I had. I meet them now in schools.

In 1958 Carson took over from Geoff Whitby as the organiser for rural education in Hertfordshire. He pursued his belief that to survive, rural studies had to be defined and organised as a subject. 'I visited the secondary school teachers whom I knew through the association, and stimulated them to get themselves organised to try and get any kids other than the least able, to get them better facilities in their schools.... "If you're not given a proper classroom, refuse to teach this subject in any old place and as adviser call me in" was what I told my teachers ... If it rained, they all just sat in the bicycle shed.' The problems in raising standards in Hertfordshire convinced Carson and his Hertfordshire colleagues that Richard Morgan's tentative plans for a National Association, first mooted in 1956, represented 'a way to raise the standard and status of rural studies because we decided that unless it was raised nationally we wouldn't be able to do it in Hertfordshire.' In July 1960 Carson called a meeting of County Rural Studies Associations at High Leigh Conference Centre in Hertfordshire. The delegates were welcomed by the Hertfordshire County Education Officer, S.T. Broad. In October 1960 the Conference decided to form a National Association by affiliating County Associations at a fee of £5 per year. Six counties affiliated in this manner — Hertfordshire, Nottinghamshire, Essex, Northumberland, West Riding of Yorkshire and Middlesex. Conference saw an 'urgent need to institute an enquiry into the provision made by various counties and the drawing up of guidance on the teaching of the subject as has recently been done in their own subjects by the Maths Association and the Science Masters' Association.'[58]

In the first National Journal it was noted that the committee of the Association would 'take every opportunity to promote the teaching of rural studies'. The 1961 Journal also stated in 'The Constitution':

The aim of this association shall be 'to develop and coordinate rural studies'. Rural studies includes nature study, natural history pursuits of all kinds, the study of farming and the activities of the countryside, as taught in primary and secondary schools. Rural studies should be regarded as an art, a science and a craft; a subject as well as a method of teaching. It has unique educational, cultural and recreational significance.[59]

By 1961 eleven new County Rural Studies Associations had been formed and affiliated; the Association continued to expand throughout the decade and by 1970 had added 12 new affiliated county associations.

The Establishment of Secondary Modern Schools and the Advent of CSE

The examinations situation found in the National Associations' 1962 survey was characterised by a 'confusing variety'.[60] (See Appendix 2) A total of 188 schools took 'O' levels in such papers as biology, rural biology and agricultural science but others sat exams set by the College of Preceptors, the City and Guilds and a variety of other external bodies. Ninety-one schools entered pupils for 'area or other local teacher-controlled examinations'.[61] At this time the CSE was about to be introduced and the report speculated that 'the proportion involved in examinations will no doubt rise'.[62] However, the report added, rural studies teachers 'are by nature opposed to the competitive and restrictive aspects of examinations in schools, and for this reason have only accepted the position reluctantly. The National Association with the aid of many county associations, has spent a good deal of time and effort on experimenting with new types of evaluation designed to encourage original courses in schools.'[63] The reluctance of rural studies teachers was evident from the very beginning of the moves towards CSE. In 1959, in a report on the first year of the North Hertfordshire Certificate of Education in Rural Science, Mr. W.A. Dove mentioned the problems pupils had with the examination: 'Keeping in mind the hard fact that few "A" stream boys take gardening' he said that 'the panel decided that the exam should consist of a theory paper so compiled that weakness in the use of the English language would not be a heavy handicap.' Concluding his report, Dove commented, 'I think this exam was a successful experiment ... if we must have exams in the secondary modern school.'[64]

The spread of the CSE drew attention to the dilemma that faced advocates of rural studies. A good deal of the energies of the associations centred on gaining more facilities, time and better qualified staff for the subject. But in the increasingly exam-conscious secondary moderns little success could be hoped for in a non-examinable subject. To break out of the cycle of deprivation faced by the subject the only way forward seemed to be in defining an examinable area. By 1962 Carson had realised the cul-de-sac which the National Association's efforts had entered:

> We never forgot our aims were to see this subject get taught to *all* children ... that facilities should be better, etc. Then it became increasingly obvious to me and one or two others, that it wasn't going to get anywhere! That however many good ideals we might have and however much people like Comber[65] might stimulate us and say what good we were doing; in fact it was not going to be realised.

As a result the Association initiated a major experiment by which to test a new rural studies exam. The experiment was reported in the Herts. journal which said that following a meeting of representatives of rural study associations, the panel of HM Inspectors for rural studies and Dr. Wrigley of the Curriculum Study Group of the Ministry of Education, a joint experiment was conducted in schools in North Hertfordshire, Nottinghamshire, Staffordshire, Lincolnshire and East Sussex 'to test the validity of our examination scheme. This is being evaluated by the Ministry of Education's Study Group'.[66] Sean Carson was involved in the experiment: 'It was an attempt to find out whether exams were a good thing. We were trying to find out whether we should remain outside or whether we should have anything to do with them.'

The moves to devise an examination in the subject posed a number of problems for rural studies. For behind the rhetoric of the advocates and subject associations, and apart from a few innovatory schools and teachers, most rural studies teachers continued to base their work on gardening. The subject's essentially practical assignments were not easily evaluated by written examinations. The draft report on the experimental examinations commented that to date: 'Few examinations included much practical work and rarely was there any assessment of the candidate's practical ability and achievement over a period of time.'[67] These examinations produced 'unfavourable backwash effects in the teaching of rural studies': 'In order to produce candidates who would be successful in the written examination teachers felt that they had to concentrate on written work to the neglect of practical activities which are the essential features of rural studies.'[68] Of the new CSEs in rural studies that were being introduced in 1966 the report commented: 'Rural studies teachers were stimulated by the prospect of an external examination at fifth year level, but were concerned lest the written papers of the traditional form of examination should come to dominate examinations in rural studies and so influence detrimentally the nature of the course.'[69]

By this time it was clear that a number of rural studies teachers felt that the worst of these fears about accepting examinations were being fulfilled. A teacher at Bass Hill Secondary School in Hertfordshire wrote:

> What has been forgotten in our exuberance to thrust forward rural studies as an examinable subject is the mainspring of its very creation. This is the joy, experience, and most of all, the practical and useful scientific logic which is gained during the release from far-sighted concepts which many other subjects tend to involve themselves in.

He saw rural studies as particularly related to its main clientele in the non-examination streams of secondary moderns: 'Many will agree with me in saying that the children who gain most of all from rural studies are the academically less able.' This group were adversely affected by the kind of examinations which had been introduced: 'Once again we can see the unwanted children of lower intelligence being made servants of the juggernaut of documented evidence, the inflated examination.' He concluded:

School Subjects and Curriculum Change

> True education is not for every man the scrap of paper he leaves school with. Dare we as teachers admit this? Dare we risk our existence by forcibly expressing our views on this? While we pause after the first phase of our acceptance, are we to rely on exams for all, to prove ourselves worthy of the kindly eye of the state?[70]

The questions this teacher asked were at the time being answered by his rural studies colleagues. In 1962 Carson and Colton had written: 'To our minds, there would be very much less value in the subject if it were taught merely as an assemblage of facts concerning plants and animals.'[71] Yet reluctantly Carson ultimately accepted examinations. For him the reasons were clear:

> Sean Carson: Because if you didn't you wouldn't get any money, any status, any intelligent kids.
>
> Ivor Goodson: Did you ever think 'this is going to be a big problem, the beginning of something....'
>
> Sean Carson: No, I didn't see that as clearly as I maybe should have done. I just thought 'if you're outside this you've had it in schools'. It was already happening inside some schools. Where a [rural studies] teacher was leaving, they didn't fill the place, because they gave it to someone in the examination set up.
>
> Ivor Goodson: So you had to climb aboard that?
>
> Sean Carson: Yes, or rural studies would have definitely disappeared.

The correspondence relating to the draft report on the experimental rural studies exams implies that the overwhelming concern of those involved was with the 'existence' and status of the subject. Speaking of the publication of the draft report in bulletin form, Mervyn Pritchard wrote: 'The problem remains whether the Bulletin in its new form will enhance the prestige of rural studies';[72] and Richard Morgan, Secretary of the National Association, worried that the report '... has played down our case considerably and seems deliberately to have reduced the impact of rural studies as a subject'.[73] The concerns of Pritchard and Morgan imply that by 1966–7 rural studies teachers, having largely accepted the inevitability of an examination in their subject, were worried by the image thus presented. The Rural Studies Association had developed a definition of the subject as a broadly-based, potentially scientific discipline. When teachers came to draw up syllabuses related to their practice the predominance of gardening was clearly illustrated: 'Once you began to write a syllabus it became obvious. As soon as you enter the exam market it becomes obvious what is actually happening in school.' Yet the close scrutiny of the subject engendered by the syllabus definition required for examinations as well as illustrating that most teaching focused on horticultural training, also offered the opportunity to work out more broad-based definitions. A number of rural studies teachers, initially working with CSE began to seize this opportunity, developing new courses and questioning the horticultural tradition on which rural studies has come to be based. This initiative was to form the basis of the rural studies response to environmental education which is considered in Part Three.

The Evolution of Rural Studies

The history of rural studies, particularly in the twentieth century, indicates the close connection between the changing patterns and 'arenas' of the educational system and the way in which rural studies were defined and promoted. In the elementary schools, rural studies was often seen as a major influence pervading the curriculum, the 'hub of the curriculum wheel'. This was especially the case in those rural areas where a specific brand of rural education was promoted, with strong utilitarian or pedagogic emphases. At this stage in its development the links between rural studies, the educational system and the changing national economy were clearly exhibited.

In the period following the 1944 Education Act as the new tripartite system slowly developed the character of rural studies depended largely on local circumstances and initiatives. By the early 1950s, however, it became clear that the subject was only taking root in the secondary modern sector. The 1952 Kent questionnaire gives detailed evidence of a subject often taught only to the less able boys, inadequately equipped with toolsheds, storing space and classrooms and with substantial numbers of the teachers involved inadequately qualified or unqualified in the subject. The picture of a low-status subject was not only confirmed, but exacerbated by the growth of specialised curricula and examinations in secondary modern schools. In this new situation the subject was faced not only with status problems, but with actual survival problems. Carson talks of even the activities with the less able being 'whittled away from one as more and more specialism invaded the curriculum'. Pritchard noted how 'in those schools where the brighter pupils are examined it is unusual to find rural science as one of the subjects taken'. Increasingly as secondary modern schools became more examination conscious, rural studies disappeared or was seen as a very low priority area of the curriculum. The resources of the school were aimed at those subjects which were examinable, and through which the school could build up a record of examination successes.

In the mid-fifties, faced with status and survival problems some rural studies teachers began to appreciate the urgent need to organise themselves into a subject association — a pattern followed by those subjects successfully embodied in grammar and secondary modern curricula and examinations. The object of forming the association was seen by the prime mover, Carson, as being 'to raise the status of rural studies and get the facilities for the subject which the other subjects got' — a cry echoed by the Kent Association three years earlier: 'this association has constantly sought parity of esteem with the rest of the curriculum for all rural studies.'

School Subjects and Curriculum Change

The new subject association saw as its prime motive the development of school facilities for the subject and improved supply and training of subject teachers. The growth of CSE also ensured that the subject association had to face the need for rural studies examinations. This involved changing much of the rhetoric with which rural studies had been promoted in earlier periods and a number of dedicated subject teachers spoke out against this development.

In the early stages the oscillation between the utilitarian and pedagogic arguments for the subject was continuous, but 'academic' arguments were never seriously entertained or deployed because the subject never attained Layton's stage 2. However, the growth in importance of external examinations introduced for the first time an academic dimension. Despite opposition which recognised the threat to the utilitarian and pedagogic advantages of the subject, the association went ahead with framing examinations because as Carson said 'if you didn't you would not get any money, any status, any intelligent kids'.

The strategy involved substantial difficulties: for the first time rural studies had publicly to announce and formally define its content. Whilst opening up new risks to the subject in the fight for survival and status, new strategies and potentialities began to emerge among the more ambitious subject advocates, which led the subject away from its utilitarian and pedagogic traditions.

Notes

1. S. Hartlib, 'Essay on advancement of husbandry learning' (1651), quoted in J.W. Adamson, *Pioneers of Modern Education 1600–1700'* (Cambridge University Press, 1951), pp. 130–1.
2. W.H. Hudspeth, 'The History of the Teaching of Biological Subjects including Nature Study in English Schools since 1600' (M.Ed. thesis, University of Durham, 1962), pp. 69–70.
3. The Poor Law Act was passed in 1834.
4. Carson, MEd., 1967, p. 14.
5. Minutes of the Committee in Council on Education 1842–43, Board of Education, pp. 545–6, quoted Carson, *op. cit.*, p. 15.
6. T.H. Huxley, 'A liberal education and where to find it', in his *Collected Essays*, Vol. III (London, Macmillan, 1905), pp. 123–35.
7. M. Arnold, *Reports on Elementary Schools 1852–1882* (London, Macmillan, 1889), p. 191.
8. Huxley, *op. cit.*, pp. 123–5.
9. Arnold *op. cit.*, p. 191.
10. Board of Education, *Report of the Royal Commission on Secondary Education* (HMSO, 1895), p. 284.
11. R.J.W. Selleck, *The New Education*, (Pitman, 1968), p. 128.
12. *Second Report of the Royal Commissioners on Technical Instruction* (London, HMSO, 1884), Vol. 1, p. 537, quoted Selleck *op. cit.*, pp. 128–9.
13. Selleck, *op. cit.*, p. 129.
14. Hudspeth, *History of Biological Subjects*, p. 224.
15. Board of Education, *The Curriculum of the Rural School*, Circular 435, April 1900, quoted Selleck, *op. cit.*, p. 129.

16 BOARD of EDUCATION *Memorandum on the Principles and Methods of Rural Education* 1911, p. 7.
17 BOARD of EDUCATION, *Report for 1904–1939* (London, HMSO, 1939).
18 BOARD of EDUCATION, *Report for 1910–1911* (London, HMSO, 1911).
19 SELLECK, *op. cit.*, p. 150.
20 F. WARE, *Educational Reform* (London, Methuen, 1900), p. 62.
21 *British Parliamentary Debates*, Fourth Series, 1906, Vol. CLVI, col. 1562.
22 *British Parliamentary Debates*, Fourth Series, 1902, Vol. CVII, col. 935.
23 BOARD of EDUCATION, *Public Elementary Schools and the Supply of Food in Wartime* (London, HMSO, 1916), p. 12.
24 BOARD of EDUCATION, *Suggestions for the Consideration of Teachers and Others Concerned in the Work of Public Elementary Schools — The Teaching of Gardening*, Circular 1293 (London, HMSO, 1922).
25 BOARD of EDUCATION, *Report of the Committee on the Position of Natural Science in the Educational System of Great Britain* (London, HMSO, 1918), pp. 60–61.
26 BOARD of EDUCATION, *Rural Education*, Circular 1365, 28 May 1925 (London, HMSO), and *Rural Education: Adaptation of Instruction to the Needs of Rural Areas*, Educational Pamphlets, No. 46 (London, HMSO, 1926), p. 6.
27 H.W. GUNTON and C.W. HAWKES, *School Gardening and Handwork* (Pitman, London, 1922).
28 HERTFORDSHIRE COUNTY COUNCIL, *Suggested Syllabus for Rural Education for Older Children of Both Sexes in Public Elementary Schools*, No. 1467, C.P. 222, 1926–1927.
29 HERTFORDSHIRE COUNTY COUNCIL *HM's Inspectors' Report upon the Working of the Rural Education Syllabus in Public Elementary Schools*, No. 1581, C.P. 19, 1929–1930, p. 1.
30 *Ibid.*, p. 4.
31 HERTFORDSHIRE SYLLABUS, 1926, p. 2.
32 ASHWELL'S 'Important place in education', *Hertfordshire Express*, 18 October 1933.
33 CARSON, MEd., *op. cit.*, p. 37.
34 Dr. M.K. ASHBY *The Country School* (Oxford University Press, 1929), p. 171.
35 BOARD of EDUCATION *Education and the Countryside*, Pamphlet No. 38 (London, HMSO, 1934), p. 5.
36 *Ibid.*, p. 10.
37 NORWOOD REPORT, p. 108.
38 S. CARSON and R. COLTON, *The Teaching of Rural Studies* (London, Edward Arnold, 1962), p. 3.
39 Schools Council Working Paper 24, *Rural Studies in Secondary Schools* (London, Evans/Methuen Education, 1969), p. 5.
40 A.B. ALLEN, *Rural Education* (London, Allman and Son, 1950), p. 16.
41 Report of the Central Advisory Council for Education (England) *School and Life* (London, HMSO, 1947), p. 35.
42 *Journal of the Kent Association of Teachers of Gardening and Rural Science*, April 1953, pp. 4–6.
43 CARSON, MEd., p. 48.
44 *Journal of the Kent Teachers Rural Studies Association*, No. 17, May 1961, p. 3.
45 M. PRITCHARD, 'The rural science teacher in the school society', *Journal of the Hertfordshire Association of Gardening and Rural Subjects*, No. 2, September 1957, p. 4.
46 Schools Council Working Paper 24, p. 5.
47 PRITCHARD, *op. cit.*, p. 5.
48 *Report on Rural Subjects and Gardening in Secondary Schools in Hertfordshire*, 1957 (mimeo).
49 *Ibid.*, p. 5.

50 *Ibid.*
51 *The Kent Association of Teachers of Gardening and Rural Science Journal*, No. 4, 1954. Also appeared in *Rural Science News*, Vol. 10, No. 1, January 1957.
52 CARSON, MEd., thesis, p. 25.
53 *Ibid.*, p. 53.
54 *Kent Association of Teachers of Gardening and Rural Science Journal*, No. 10, September 1957, p. 7.
55 *Kent Journal*, No. 13, March 1959, p. 1.
56 *Kent Journal*, No. 7, February 1956, p. 22.
57 *Kent Journal*, No. 12, September 1958, p. 1.
58 S. CARSON, 'The National Rural Studies Association', *Journal of the Hertfordshire Association of Teachers of Gardening and Rural Subjects*, No. 8, October 1960, p. 21.
59 *National Rural Studies Association Journal*, 1961, p. 5.
60 *Rural Studies: A Survey of Facilities* (London, Pergamon, 1963), p. 33.
61 *Ibid.*, p. 32.
62 *Ibid.*, p. 33.
63 *Ibid.*
64 W.A. DOVE, 'Report on the North Hertfordshire Certificate of Education in Rural Science', *Journal of Hertfordshire Association of Teachers of Gardening and Rural Subjects*, No. 5, April 1959, pp. 40–41.
65 L.C. COMBER, HMI with responsibility for rural education.
66 'The Certificate of Secondary Education', *Hertfordshire Teachers' Rural Studies Association Journal*, October, 1963.
67 The Certificate of Secondary Education Experimental Examination — Rural Studies Draft Report, 1966 (not published by Schools Council).
68 *Ibid.*
69 *Ibid.*
70 P.L. QUANT, 'Rural studies and the Newsom child', *Hertfordshire Rural Studies Association Journal*, April 1967, p. 12.
71 S. CARSON and R. COLTON, *op. cit.*, p. 4.
72 M. PRITCHARD, letter to A.J. PRINCE, 7 October 1966.
73 R. MORGAN letter to M. PRITCHARD, 8 October 1966.

Part Three
Relationships Between Subjects: The Territorial Nature of Subject Conflict

7 'Climates of Opinion' with Respect to Education and the Environment, 1960–1975

As we have seen notions of 'environment' already existed in each of the three subjects whose fortunes we are following, in geography and biology through the fieldwork tradition and in rural studies if it could survive the transition to an exam-oriented curriculum. However, in the 1960s the 'environment' began to emerge as a major idea in its own right and to influence policy making in a number of ways. At this time a separate 'Department of the Environment' was designated by the government in response to a growing public concern with environmental matters; and by the end of the decade Max Nicholson was able to declare without seeming precipitous: 'It has been said that the one thing in the world which is invincible is an idea whose time has come. Such an idea in these days is the care of man's environment.'[1] In reviewing the influence of such a powerful idea it will be useful to note the different levels of the education system at which ideas can arise and be taken up and implemented. Some ideas, for instance, can influence thinking at an international level both through the activities of international agencies and through press and television. The idea of a Ministry of the Environment was not of British origin, and environmental legislation has always been influenced by international comparisons. Though the decentralised pattern of government and the language difference between countries has made it particularly difficult for educational ideas to penetrate from Europe, professional links across the Atlantic have always been significant. Curriculum development, educational technology, and more recently, accountability have all gathered strength in North America before becoming significant in Britain.

However, for ideas to be taken up and promoted at national level they have to be seen as relevant and capable of being adapted to specific national contexts. Curriculum development was transformed into a teacher-based activity when it encountered the greater power and status of the British teaching profession, and accountability may well meet a similar fate. New ideas cannot easily be implemented at national level in Britain, though as we shall see later they can be rejected if they challenge the hegemony of the subject-based examination systems. They have to be translated down to the local level

School Subjects and Curriculum Change

or school level. At the local level we meet the people who have direct contact with schools without being part of them — advisers, teacher centre wardens, college and university lecturers — and the 'cosmopolitan' heads and senior teachers who seem to share membership of the local professional community with their more specific school responsibilities. It would appear to be among such groups that the fads and fashions of the educational world are manufactured, sold and exchanged.

Then at the school level, also, ideas get invented, imported, metamorphose and die. Parlett's notion of 'ideas in currency', invented to describe the nature of policy discussions in an American college, seems equally appropriate to the English secondary school. These ideas: 'Circulate around the college and ... represent components of the informal system of college thinking. Ideas in currency are working hypotheses, constructions of reality, mini-descriptions and so forth. They represent a series of almost perceptual categories that permit ordering of experience. However, they also act as expectations and often these are self-confirming.'[2] One year political battles within a school may focus on the young school leaver, while another year it may be assessment or the pastoral system of third-year options. External ideas which suit the 'problem of the moment' may get taken up and adapted to fit the interests of the dominant coalition, while other ideas of equal validity get ignored.

This section of the book examines the fate of environmental education between 1965 and 1975; and seeks to interpret its significance for curriculum conflict in general. It therefore concerns itself with how notions of the 'environment' entered into policy discussions at all four levels — international, national, local and school — and with the interaction between these distinct but mutually influential areas.

The International Background to the Emergence of Environmental Education

The first efforts to broaden international awareness about the environment were taken by the United Nations in the favourable climate for certain aspects of world co-operation which followed the Second World War. In 1949 the United Nations convened a 'Scientific Conference on the Conservation and Utilisation of Resources'. In the same year UNESCO sponsored the foundation of the International Union for the Conservation of Nature.

In the period following these developments a series of conferences, programmes and activities was initiated, and two decades later, in 1971, the British HMI responsible for environmental education judged that for his area the most important of all the international movements was the United Nations 'with its in-built machinery of UNESCO that bears the world-wide responsibility for environmental care'.[3] UNESCO had set up a specialised Ecology and Conservation Sector in 1961 and in 1968 marked the beginning of a new wave of international activity with respect to the environment by holding the

'Biosphere Conference' in Paris. It was later claimed that at this Conference 'perhaps for the first time, world awareness of environmental education was fully evidenced'.[4] The educational programme that was advocated focused on the following needs: to develop environmental study material for educational curricula at all levels, to promote technical training and to stimulate global awareness of environmental problems.

In detail the educational programme suggested that regional surveys should be carried out; ecological components should be introduced into the present educational programmes; specialists should be trained in environmental sciences in universities and colleges of education; environmental studies in primary and secondary schools should be stimulated; national training and research centres should be set up.[5]

As a result of these recommendations the European Committee for the Conservation of Nature and Natural Resources was set up and subsequently organised the European Conference in Strasbourg in 1970. The influence of this Conference which launched 'European Conservation Year' is mentioned in 'A letter to Europeans' from the Secretary General of the Council of Europe which adequately captures the contemporary perceptions of environmental crisis:

> Pollution is here for us all to see, smell and taste. Water is often unfit to drink. Smoke and fumes attack our lungs. Our nervous systems are under severe strain from noise. Waste products, some practically indestructible, build up faster and faster. In many places soil is eroded away. Landscapes are spoiled and the variety of wildlife gets less every day. All this is happening throughout the world, but more than anywhere in our own densely populated continent. If it goes on much longer, Europe will be uninhabitable. This is not scaremongering. We are facing hard facts: facts discussed by all our nations at a conference organised in Strasbourg last February.[6]

In the same year, 1970, an International Working Meeting on Environmental Education in the School Curriculum was held in Foresta Institute, Carson City, Nevada, USA. The meeting accepted the following definition of environmental education: 'Environmental education is the process of recognising values and clarifying concepts in order to develop skills and attitudes necessary to understand and appreciate the interrelatedness among man, his culture and his biophysical surroundings'. The report suggested 'to the governments and their responsible educational authorities as well as to the national education organisations' that: 'through a reform of the total curriculum' environmental education should be introduced 'as an obligatory and integrated component of the school educational system at all levels' and further that 'national environmental legislation be used to include obligatory environmental education at all levels.'[7] Following the Nevada meeting a European working conference on Environmental Conservation Education was convened in Zurich between 15–18 December 1971. The objectives of the conference were: to assemble for the first time at a European level, specialists working in the field of environmental education, 'in order to exchange information, to clarify concepts and to formulate specific recommendations for projects and programmes related to primary and secondary education, teacher training, higher education and out of school education.'[8] In his opening address Mr. Frank Nicholls, Deputy Director General of IUCN, explained that the IUCN decided to hold the conference in the belief that education is of vital importance in the world environmental crisis, 'both in creating environmentally aware attitudes throughout the general population and in producing the environmental specialists and other professionals needed to deal with the complex problems facing mankind.'[9]

The first keynote lecture, given by Dr. Tom Pritchard of the British Nature Conservancy, reiterated the points introduced by Nicholls. Pritchard considered many of the measures taken in the name of environmental conservation to be merely palliative and attributed this to a deficiency in the system which did not allow the existing expertise to be applied by the planners and decision makers.

Thus he envisaged a dual function for environmental education both as a 'vocational training for specialists' and as a means of 'creating public awareness about environmental affairs, with the ultimate aim of realising the conservation of natural resources and stimulating enjoyment of the environment.'[10] Pritchard's comments on the incorporation of environmental education are of interest because some of the insights derive from his participation in the contemporary debate on this subject in England.

Within the formal school system, environmental education could be incorporated into existing subject areas or be taught as a subject in its own right. At the primary level, the child's interest was easily stimulated through the concept of contact with and discovery of its environment, and through the use of innovative teaching methods. This unity of approach was difficult to maintain at the secondary level since the subject areas were arbitrarily prescribed, and, at the higher secondary level, environmental education was usually available only as a specialisation. Pritchard concluded that: 'Most important of all, in the context of widespread reform of educational systems, was the recognition of environmental education as a priority area by the responsible authorities.'[11]

A second keynote lecture by Dr. J. Cerovsky raised similar questions with respect to 'Comprehensive Programmes of Environmental Education'. He argued that the most appropriate method was the promotion of interdisciplinary infiltration of environmental teaching and education in all subjects. He added that 'Introduction of a special subject of "environmental studies" should principally be accepted and encouraged, but not regarded as the only and final stage of development.'[12]

To summarise the educational strategy favoured by the Working Sector the Report adds: 'Whichever design is chosen the pedagogic methods followed in Environmental Education should require all pupils to be engaged in field work, in first hand investigation and in open discussion of problems. Teachers should act as partners rather than authorities in the learning process.'[13] The flavour of these international conferences was essentially exhortatory, and most of the currently fashionable educational ideas were hitched to the environment 'bandwagon'. Nevertheless, international interest in the environment persisted beyond the optimism of the late sixties.

Following the European Working Conference the General Assembly of the United Nations convened a conference on the Human Environment, held in June 1972. This time, significantly, the Conference was 'action-oriented' rather than limited to restating the well-known problems because by 1970 'it was clear that the world was already paying attention to the problem. In government councils, in the Press, in schools and universities, threats to the environment had become a major topic of discussion in many countries.'[14]

The National Background to the Emergence of Environmental Education

The chronology of environmental consciousness in England strongly follows that in the international community. Thus the first important development was in 1949 when the Nature Conservancy was founded. Conservation was defined as 'a philosophy for action based on ecology', and the Nature Conservancy advocated that 'we must ... guide our actions so that they are in harmony with ecological processes'. The Conservancy noted that 'Pollution is a sign of our failure to conserve properly when we produce waste beyond the capacity of nature to render it harmless.'[15] Later the Nature Conservancy became part of the National Environment Research Council which was established by Royal Charter in 1965. In its first report the Council stated that 'because the countryside and its wildlife is highly vulnerable to the impact of human pressures of many kinds, including the needs of agriculture, industry, urban development and recreation, it is important to obtain a proper understanding of the natural heritage.'[16]

In part the role of the Nature Conservancy had been adopted by the Council for Nature even before its amalgamation with the Natural Environment Research Council. The Council for Nature was founded in 1958 as a co-ordinating body for over 450 organisations and bodies representing naturalists of all interests. A year after its foundation the Council formed the Conservation Corps (now called the British Trust for Conservation Volunteers). In 1966 the Conservation Society was formed, the society considering its central aim to be: to persuade people to 'live within the renewable resources of the Earth and not beyond their limits'.[17] In 1969 the conservationist lobby was further strengthened by the forming of the Committee for Environmental Conservation. The Committee includes 14 national conservation groups and seeks to consider all matters of national importance affecting the environment.

One of the members of the Committee is the Duke of Edinburgh, who had been responsible for the most significant of all the national initiatives with respect to the environment. In 1963 it became apparent, partly as a result of the 'Observer' wild life exhibition held that year, that there was an absence of national leadership with respect to the countryside environment. This weakness was noted by the Duke of Edinburgh who initiated a study conference entitled 'The Countryside in 1970' from which it was hoped would come machinery for removing the conflicting factions in the conservation movement, and give it a common purpose for the future.[18]

The first study conference was held in 1963 and representatives from more than 90 national organisations were assembled and were encouraged to learn about one another's interests and to move towards a common understanding. Partly to facilitate this co-operation, 12 working groups were set up to concentrate on what were identified as the main issues. Jack Longland, later to become Chairman of the Council for Environmental Education, saw the catalytic role of the conference for environmental education:

> The first conference in 1963 recognised the important part that education must play in promoting an appreciation of the environment and an understanding of the problems arising from the conflicts between the many different interests concerned with the environment. Whilst it is true that the presentation of the traditional school subjects did not ignore the environment, there had by 1963 been no more than the beginnings of studies of the environment as a whole.[19]

The first study conference took a decision to call a special conference, which subsequently met at Keele University in March 1965 to: 'appraise the implications for the formal education system of the issues raised at the 1963 Student Conference'.[20]

The conference made a number of conclusions and recommendations concerning education and the environment which developed from a primary belief that: 'Positive educational methods are needed to encourage awareness and appreciation of the natural environment as well as responsibility for its trusteeship by every citizen.' And also asserted that: 'The countryside is a rich source of inspiration and teaching material which can contribute substantially to education at all levels; field studies provide a valuable means of using and developing this educational resource'.[21] The conference recommended that: 'Fundamental and operational education research, with participation by teachers, should be intensified to determine more exactly the content of environmental education and methods of teaching best suited to modern needs.'[22]

The 'Countryside in 1970' Conference undoubtedly influenced government policy, if only because of the presence of ministers at the meetings. In 1970 the Prime Minister, Edward Heath, stated that: 'The protection of our lovely countryside and our glorious coast, the prevention of pollution of our rivers and of the air we breathe, must be one of the highest priorities of the seventies.'[23] A Department of the Environment was set up to assume responsibility in England and Wales for all functions which affect the physical environment. A White Paper, 'The Protection of the Environment', was presented to Parliament in May 1970. It asserted: 'Government can and must give a lead but success will depend on an increasingly informed and active public opinion.'[24] A Royal Commission on Environmental Pollution was also set up in February 1970 and in its first report noted that 'public opinion must be mobilised'.[25]

The culmination of the environmental lobby's effort was the third 'Countryside in 1970' Conference in October of that year. The Secretary of the Standing Committee stated:

> Environmental education is variously defined ... The essentials are clear: to help individuals ... to understand the main features of their physical environment, their interrelationships with it, and the requirements for its management: to instil a sense of personal responsibility and active concern for the condition of their surroundings and to encourage enthusiasm for and enjoyment of the environment.[26]

The importance of the international initiatives described earlier for the national development of environmental education became evident in the 1970s. The National Association of Environmental Education and the Council for Environmental Education both accepted and promoted the definition of environmental education provided by the Nevada Conference.

Interestingly, in view of its influence, the United Kingdom was the only major country not officially represented. The DES refused either to grant the National Association the money to travel to the Conference or give it official representative status. However, both the National Association's Statement of Aims and the final Environmental Studies 'A' level drew widely on the working party recommendations from the Zurich Conference.

Local Developments in the Promotion of Environmental Education

Besides the conference and government agencies and reports which advocated environmental education, a number of other initiatives focused specifically on promoting its growth.

At the Keele Conference it became clear that a number of teachers, most notably the biologists, were closely scrutinising the potential use of field studies of the environment in teaching their subject. The work of these pioneers was somewhat optimistically described in a speech by Jack Longland, subsequently to become Chairman of the Council for Environmental Education: 'The windows of many classrooms have been flung wide open. Parallel with this, teaching subjects are beginning to be judged by their relevance to each other and to the world outside. The life and work of the schools have begun to flood out of doors.'[27] In the years following Keele a number of authors and advocates continued to press the case for environmental education. Garth Christian, for instance, wrote an influential article. 'Education for the environment' and a book 'Tomorrow's Countryside' in 1966, both arguing for more environmental education.[28] In the same year a grant was given to Leicester Museum by the Carnegie United Kingdom Trust to launch a research project on field studies education.

In June 1967 the Association Examining Board circulated tentative proposals to schools sitting its exams. The response indicated that 'there is a nucleus of about 30 schools interested enough seriously to consider the adoption of the proposed new subject'. The new subject reflected 'the need today for a syllabus which will enable the pupil to explore the concept of "environment", and in particular the natural or rural environment, in a way which has relevance to both the rural and urban child'. The intention was that 'the studies should lead to an understanding of the countryside as a whole, as a basic natural resource, along the lines advocated in the "Countryside in 1970" Conferences'. On the question of the title for the proposed new subject the AEB circular reported: 'Considerable discussion has already taken place regarding a title for the proposed syllabus, and the suggestion is that "Environmental Studies" is the most apt title.'[29]

Keith Wheeler puts the emergence of a climate of opinion favourable to environmental education as slightly later: 'In retrospect 1968 can be regarded as the year when the somewhat ill-defined, but potent concept of environmental education made its first real impact on the thinking of teachers'.[30] In March 1968 a co-ordinating body responsible for environmental education was established under the chairmanship of Jack Longland. This body, the Council for Environmental Education, was 'established to advance education in the importance of the environment and the status of man therein'.

At the same time a conference, held from 29–31 March 1968, was organised by G.C. Martin and a decision was taken to form a Society for Environmental Education.[31] The speaker at the conference dinner, Dr. Dyos, claimed environmental studies to be the 'most revolutionary form of educational study. It could develop an understanding and critical awareness among pupils which could lead them to care for the environment.'[32] The environmental educationists of SEE and within the Colleges of Education were overwhelmingly geographers and biologists.[33] The two prime movers of SEE, for instance, George Martin and Keith Wheeler, were both geographers. By the late 1960s it was these subject specialists who looked set to promote environmental education. However, although their arguments were beginning to carry weight they had to be translated to the school level. This meant facing questions such as 'Who will teach it?', 'To which pupils?' and 'For which exam?' It was over these issues that the respective fortunes of the subjects in schools depended and over which the ensuing battle was to be fought. Although the argument at the public level tended to be in terms of highflown aims, the realities of subject power at the school level were never far beneath the surface. Indeed the evidence presented in the chapters that follow is remarkable for the high visibility of these conflicts, which one might have expected to have been more thoroughly camouflaged.

Environmental Education at School Level

At school level a number of categories of environmental education emerged. Two main varieties can be discerned. The first was to be found in the broadly-conceived environmental studies 'faculties' which developed in the humanities and science sections of comprehensive schools. The faculties were often introduced for managerial as well as academic reasons; for in the new large-size comprehensive middle management structures offered the opportunity for delegating a range of organisational tasks. Alongside this managerial impetus contemporary curriculum initiatives like the Goldsmiths IDE course and the Humanities Curriculum Project stressed the epistemological reasons favouring new integrated departments.

Whilst new faculties were organised around integrating themes, of which the environment was a leading choice in the late sixties, the teaching personnel were composed of traditional subject specialists. In the environmental studies faculties on the humanities side, geographers predominated, and in those on the science side, biologists. But geography and biology continued to thrive and the number of traditional geography and biology departments continued to hugely outnumber the innovative faculties. Moreover very few environmental studies training courses were developed and even those that existed were training non-graduates who went largely into primary and middle schools. As a result the teachers in environmental studies faculties continued to view their careers largely in terms of their original specialist discipline: there were no reasons, other than ideological, for changing allegiance.

The second variety of environmental education was developed in a range of new environmental studies departments which originated in existing rural studies departments. The moving force in these initiatives were the rural studies teachers, most notably in Hertfordshire where the largest number of environmental studies posts and departments were created. The reasons for the concern of rural studies teachers can be fairly clearly seen for, as we showed in Chapter 6, their very survival within schools was threatened and as a result their main protagonists closely scrutinised the opportunities offered by the changing climates of educational opinion. As early as 1963, Carson had warned that rural studies must adapt to the 'changing climate' or perish. Rural studies teachers, he asserted, had two duties, 'one to their classes and one to the educational climate in which they worked'.[34] Of the latter he noted later that educationists 'were constantly saying "you should be teaching environmental studies". It was part of the climate of opinion at the time.'

Of course, Carson represented only one sub-group within rural studies, although he was also a moving force behind the Rural Studies Association. The re-definition of rural studies towards environmental studies was to be bitterly contested and the questions of teachers' livelihoods and the associated survival of the subject were to be the major considerations.

Notes

1. M. NICHOLSON, *The Environmental Revolution* (Harmondsworth, Penguin 1972), p. 17.
2. M. PARLETT, *The Wellesley Milieu* (Oxford, 1975), mimeo.
3. K. BEAL, *The Background to Environmental Education in Environmental Studies in the All Ability School*, Report of a Conference of Secondary Heads and Teachers held at Offley Place, Hertfordshire, 28th November — 2nd December, 1971, p. 34.
4. International Union for Conservation of Nature and Natural Resources, *Commission on Education: Report on Objectives, Actions, Organisation and Structures Working Programme*, August 1971, (IUCN, 1971).
5. BEAL REPORT, *op. cit.*, p. 34.
6. *A letter to Europeans from the Council of Europe*, December 1970.
7. International Union for Conservation of Nature and Natural Resources, *Final Report, International Working Meeting on Environmental Education in the School Curriculum*, September 1970, USA (IUCN, 1970).
8. International Union for Conservation of Nature and Natural Resources, *Final Report, European Working Conference on Environmental Conservation Education*, Supplementary Paper, No. 34, Switzerland 1972 (IUCN), p. 1.
9. *Ibid.*, p. 2.
10. *Ibid.*, p. 4.
11. *Ibid.*
12. *Final Report of European Working Conference*, 1972, p. 6.
13. *Ibid.*
14. *New Challenge for the United Nations*, UN Office of Public Information, 1971 (quoted in Project Environment Report, No. 2, January 1972).
15. *Twenty One Years of Conservation* (London, Nature Conservancy, 1970).
16. NATURAL ENVIRONMENT RESEARCH COUNCIL, *Report 1965–66* (London, HMSO, 1967).
17. CONSERVATION SOCIETY, *Philosophy, Aims and Proposed Action*, (London, The Conservation Society, 1970).
18. G. MARTIN and K. WHEELER (Eds.), *Insights into Environmental Education* (Edinburgh, Oliver and Boyd, 1975), pp. 7–8.
19. J. LONGLAND, 'Education and the Environment', a talk reproduced in transcript by permission of the Association of Agriculture, 78 Buckingham Gate, London SW1 (n.d.).
20. 'The Countryside in 1970, Proceedings of the Conference on Education', University of Keele, Staffordshire, 26–28 March 1965 (London, Nature Conservancy, 1965), p. 5.
21. *Ibid.*, p. 33.
22. *Ibid.*, p. 34.
23. 'Countryside in 1970, Proceedings of the Third Conference, October 1970' (London, Royal Society of Arts, 1970).
24. *The Protection of the Environment* (London, HMSO, 1970).
25. *Royal Commission on Environmental Pollution, First Report* (London, HMSO, 1971).
26. Proceedings of the Third Conference, 1970, *op. cit.*
27. Proceedings 1965, *op. cit.*, p. 10.
28. G. CHRISTIAN, 'Education for the environment', *Quarterly, Review*, April 1966; G. CHRISTIAN, *Tomorrow's Countryside* (London, Murray, 1966).
29. A.E.B. Circular to Schools, June 1967.
30. G.C. MARTIN and K. WHEELER (Ed.), *Insights into Environmental Education* (London, 1965), p. 8. Council for Environmental Constitution.

31 I.F. ROLLS, 'Environmental studies: A new synthesis', *Education for Teaching*, Spring 1969, p. 21.
32 *Society for Environmental Education Bulletin*, Vol. 1, No. 1, Autumn 1968, p. 3.
33 B. BARRET, 'The society in retrospect', *SEE*, Vol. VIII, No. 2, 1976.
34 S. CARSON, 'The changing climate', *NRSA Journal* 1963, pp. 14–15.

8 Redefining Rural Studies: The Genesis of Environmental Studies

By the second half of the 1960s, groups seeking to promote their subject or discipline and the associated interests of their membership were faced by a rapidly changing situation. The accelerating pace of comprehensive reorganisation, the growth of curriculum reform movements and the emergence of 'the environment' as a major source of concern presented a complex new arena for the subject groups to operate within.

The differing patterns of assertion, evolution and consolidation between the three groups considered herein meant that they acted in starkly different ways. The geographers had by this time, following nearly a century of assertion and change, established their subject within the secondary school curriculum. In the universities the subject was approaching final acceptance and its academic rigour was presented and promoted by new initiatives to make the subject more quantitative, theoretical and scientific. The establishment of the subject at the tertiary level represented the final consolidatory stage in Layton's three-stage model of subject evolution. In such a situation, new conditions which encouraged integration, interdisciplinarity and more environmental and local study were likely to elicit minimal adjustment rather than maximal change. Geographers were in the position of defending those strategies which had achieved the establishment of their subject and the consolidation of their own special interests.

Biologists had begun their struggle for acceptance at around the same time as the geographers and after nearly a century of assertion had made rapid progress in the fifties and sixties. The subject had become established in the universities and was near to final broad-based acceptance in the secondary schools. The major source of biology's successful promotion was the claim to be a 'hard science' with rigorous methods and theories. The new conditions encouraged those elements which biologists had progressively reduced in pursuit of hard scientific status. Environmental and field studies represented the softer, less methodical and scientific side of biology, as did initiatives towards integration and interdisciplinarity. Defence of biology's status as a science required minimal adjustment to the new conditions rather than a readiness to embrace the new possibilities.

In contrast to biology and goegraphy, rural studies remained a school subject confined within one sector of the secondary school curriculum. Rural studies was a low-status subject offered to those secondary school pupils defined as less able. In 1963 Sean Carson wrote that:

> Rural studies does not exist in a vacuum. It is influenced by what happens in other subjects and by the relative importance accorded to them, as well as by the orientation of educational programmes generally ...
>
> During the next few years considerable changes are likely, both in the framework of our school system, and in the curricula within schools, and if rural studies is to retain its influence, then those schools who believe in the subject must be clear about their aims and ready to adapt their methods to new conditions.[1]

Confined within the secondary modern school sector rural studies was especially vulnerable to comprehensive reorganisation. In 1966 the NRSA Journal carried its first report on 'The Place of Rural Studies in the Comprehensive System', produced by a working party set up at the spring 1966 Conference of Wiltshire Teachers of Rural Studies. After reviewing the rapid spread of comprehensive schools throughout the country the Wiltshire teachers proclaimed that rural studies 'has much to offer as a subject in its own right in the comprehensive system of education'.[2]

Within the report there is some evidence that the Wiltshire teachers were extremely concerned about the fate of their subject in the comprehensive school. The change to comprehensives was taking place against a background of decline in the subject which had begun in some areas in the late 1950s.[3] By the early 1960s Sean Carson saw the decline setting in in Hertfordshire in certain schools 'where a teacher was leaving, they didn't fill the place, because they gave it to someone in the examination set up'. By 1966 the Wiltshire teachers were advising: 'The urgent necessity is for us to persuade teachers and education authorities that the omission of the facilities for teaching rural studies in new schools and in buildings which are being adapted to a comprehensive form of education would be a mistake.'[4] The problem was partly explained by the fact that: 'as many of the new heads of comprehensive schools were being appointed from grammar school backgrounds these heads had little or no experience of the value of rural studies in the education of the secondary child.'[5]

The teachers themselves saw clear evidence of broad-based decline and by November 1967 one was writing of a 'general air of defeatism among rural studies teachers'.[6] A Hertfordshire teacher recalled this period:

> A few years back, rural studies was being phased out ... it was getting

itself a poor name ... it was ... you know, losing face ... it was being regarded as not the subject we want in this up-and-going day and age. And we had awful difficulty in getting examining boards and universities to accept it at 'O' level and 'A' level ... mainly because of its content ... I could see that I was going to have to phase out rural studies because the demand for it in the school was going down ... it was being squeezed out in the timetable and the demand for it at options level in the fourth year was going down.[7]

Not only was rural studies less in demand but those areas of the curriculum where the subject may have expanded were being taken over by other subject specialists. In the comprehensives rural studies was often not included or was being confined to the 'less able'. Following the Keele Conference and the Nuffield projects, biologists and geographers began to gain control of 'field studies' of the environment. At the tertiary level, as has been noted, similar specialists had begun to define 'environmental studies'.

In a position of rapidly falling demand and closing options, rural studies was faced with extinction, certainly in those counties where comprehensive education was rapidly pursued. Carson in Hertfordshire was convinced that rural studies 'would rapidly have disappeared' and Topham saw that by 1969 rural studies 'was finished'.

Faced with extinction in the emerging comprehensive schools and lacking any university base, rural studies advocates were clearly at the stage where new ideas had to be embraced and mobilised 'as a potential means of establishing a new intellectual identity and particularly a new occupational role'.[8] The new ideas available included 'integration', 'relevance' and 'team teaching' as well as 'the environment'. All were equally advocated and embraced. The 1969 rural studies teachers' annual general meeting adopted the following resolution, that: 'Vigorous steps be taken by rural studies organisations to show what their departments have to offer in the form of relevant, valuable, integrated work. Practical courses to be run with team teaching moves to dispel the inferiority complex so many rural studies teachers show ...'.[9] In a similar vein the Chairman's report advocated that: 'In the reorganisation of schools we should grasp the opportunity to assert ourselves to lead the way with team teaching and integrated courses to make sure that our subject is well established.'[10]

The adoption of the rhetoric of integration, interdisciplinarity and team teaching did little, however, to define a new intellectual and occupational identity. The major problems were the low-status image of rural studies, its inadequacy as an intellectual synthesis and the failure to provide examinations which might rectify these two deficiencies. The definition or acquisition of new intellectual content and the construction of new high-status examinations syllabuses offered a strategy which sought to transform the prospects of rural studies.

The two-pronged strategy can be analysed in detail in the period following

1965: (1) Attempts to re-define and re-direct rural studies can be clearly discerned in the conflict over the name given to the subject. (2) Attempts to increase the status and intellectual rigour of the subject can be analysed by scrutinising the new examination initiatives. Symbolically, advocates like Carson spoke of the need for a new 'discipline', thereby hinting at the high-status normally conferred through the intellectual pursuits of subject scholars in universities.

Redefining Rural Studies: 1965–9

In 1955, a lone advocate, C.C. Lewis, warned that 'for want of a name the battle might be lost'[11] in arguing for a new title for the subject. The name which Perry chose to replace rural studies was 'Lifecology', 'which I hope conveys the impression of the study of the interdependence of man and all living things with a wide variety of habitats'.[12]

The initial response of most of the members of the National Association to the arguments put forward by Perry, and to the need for reappraisal so clearly indicated at the Keele Conference in 1965, was to call for a greater promotion and consolidation of the subject. Carson argued for the exclusiveness of the subject saying that biology and geography should not deal with environmental education because 'to the teacher in secondary school the terms represent a subject with clearly defined limitations'. He concluded: 'We are left with the alternatives "environmental studies, or science" and "rural studies, or science".'[13] Having dismissed the science appendage ('nor ought there to be any magic for us in the word science') this left a clear choice between 'environmental studies' and 'rural studies'. On their relative merits Carson was firm: 'The term "environmental studies" is almost unknown outside a few colleges and has no clear definition within schools or universities.'

The case for 'rural studies' provides a useful summary of the subject's position in 1965: there were 37 county associations of teachers in Rural Studies Associations; a rural studies course existed in half the secondary moderns in England and Wales; there were CSE examinations in the subject in all boards; about 36 rural studies advisers were employed in LEAs; and five colleges of education ran three-year courses to train rural studies specialists.[14]

The rapid changes following Carson's article in 1965 led a number of rural studies teachers to begin 'redefinition' of their subject in the schools. At the same time Carson in his research at Manchester from 1966–7 was seeking to establish what certain groups and individuals thought should be taught in schools with particular reference to rural studies. He sent questionnaires to people 'widely representative of all the interests reflecting the needs of society in relation to the countryside'.[15]

Alongside his efforts to define the various countryside groups' requirements of the subject Carson also sought to establish what were the views and

School Subjects and Curriculum Change

practice of rural studies teachers. His research shows a very different perception of the subject from the two groups. The countryside groups saw the major objectives as being: 'to promote an understanding of the countryside and man's relation to his natural environment and to wild life'. Other important objectives were: 'the development of aesthetic appreciation, the encouragement of creativity, giving children a realisation of the value of a contact with nature or developing acceptable social behaviour.'[16] All these objectives were under-represented among rural studies teachers whilst one objective, 'to develop skills and standards of craftsmanship in gardening or other rural crafts', was 'heavily over-represented in schools' and in CSE syllabi. Carson noted that 'During the interviews for the validity check some teachers remarked that they had not realised that they had been paying so much attention to this objective.'[17]

Carson's research showed that the innovatory efforts of a few teachers, and his own efforts to redefine the subject, were far removed from the practice of most rural studies teachers. The National Association was faced by this basic dilemma with any strategies to change the occupational identity of the membership. This dilemma was instanced in the Council meeting of the Association held in Newark on 10 February 1968. One item referred to the proposed new AEB environmental studies 'O' level. The minutes report that Sean Carson felt that there was 'too much "sociology" in the proposed paper'[18] and there was some discussion by members of Council upon the degree of sociology which could be included and which a teacher trained for rural studies could be expected to teach. At Newark, Policy Committee considered the possibility of changing the name of the association — possibly to environmental studies, for in the next month both the Council and the Society for Environmental Education were formed. Policy Committee 'considered the question of changing the name of "rural studies" following the comments at Conference and press reports of these comments', but recommended that 'no change should be considered but that the work we do under the title of "rural studies" will determine its status.'[19] Council agreed, noting:

> that while there was some opposition to the name it would be folly to bow to it. The term was accepted by all the C.S.E. boards, many colleges of education, at least nine universities which were offering it in the BEd. context and by at least one 'A' level board. [This presumably refers to the negotiations then under way with the Northern Universities Board — see Chapter 9]. In addition it was hoped that an 'O' level board would accept the name shortly.[20]

Evidence of a volte face within weeks of the Newark decision was contained in a circular, dated 8 March, sent by Richard Morgan to all members of Policy Committee: 'Following a recent conversation with Mr. M. Pritchard I have decided that it may be to our advantage to invite him to attend our next meeting on 16th March at Tamworth.'[21] At this time Mervyn Pritchard was active as Chairman of the Schools Council Working Party on Rural Studies. The Working Party had been set up in November 1965 by the Schools Council following discussions with the National Rural Studies Association. It met eleven times under Pritchard, who was headmaster of Redbourn Secondary School, St. Albans. Its report was presented to Council in June 1968 but we can assume Pritchard had a fairly clear view of the likely conclusions by the time of the Tamworth gathering. The results of the Tamworth meeting were recorded in a confidential minute. It was decided: 'that we support Mr. Pritchard in his idea that a Standing Committee at Schools Council level ought to be set up and that the Standing Committee should be named "rural and environmental studies"', and 'that we accept the definition of rural studies in the terms: "The study of the environment in and around the school ..."'[22] The next meeting of Policy Committee in May agreed to the change of name because of 'the formation of the Council for Environmental Education, the rise in the number of environmental studies courses in Colleges of Education, the resistance of examination boards to the name rural studies, and the impression that the word that commands most respect is "environmental".'[23] In June the Schools Council Working Party report on Rural Studies was submitted and argued that: 'The realisation of the full potential of rural studies has become a matter of great educational importance. Because rural studies has such a wide bearing on many aspects of life its limits are not easy to define nor are its values so clear-cut as those of some subjects.'[24] The Working Party 'felt the need, as a prerequisite to define the subject as currently taught'. The definition is precisely the same as that adopted by the NRSA Policy Committee in March upon Pritchard's recommendation: 'Rural studies is the study of the environment in and around the school with particular reference to animals and plants important to man and leading to an understanding of man's interaction with the countryside.'[25]

The discussion on the change of name took place in the various County Associations. A letter from the West Riding branch to the General Secretary in November summarised a number of the problems which emerged. Firstly, the branch was not sure whether the change of name referred to 'the rural studies movement' or the subject of rural studies. If it was the former, 'the N.R.S.A. [should] offer a choice of either "rural studies" or "environmental studies"' presumably as subject names for secondary school courses.[26] This recommendation was subsequently accepted by Policy Committee.[27] Secondly, the branch was worried by the claim for exclusive responsibility for environmental studies which might be implied by the change of name.

In August the Association held its conference in Hertford where there were several discussions, 'often very heated', about the proposed change of name. In September, at the annual general meeting, the proposal to change the title was moved by the General Secretary and Sean Carson, who had recently changed his title in Hertfordshire to 'Adviser for Environmental Education'. The motion was passed by 12 votes to 7, with 2 abstentions.[28] Carson recalls:

'there was a bitter division at this 1969 Conference and the meetings that followed. It was the first time the spirit of comradeship had disintegrated since 1960.'

Thus the title was change to the National Rural and Environmental Studies Association. Three years later the process of transformation was completed and the National Association of Environmental Education emerged. Writing in mid-1971 in the Association Journal the Chairman, Philip Neal, had presaged the change in the editorial and hinted at the aspiration for parity with other well-established school subject associations:

> I believe we must grasp the nettle firmly — perhaps we should have had the courage to go the whole way recently — had we dropped 'rural' from our title we may well have had more members now. We are the association of teachers concerned with the environment. Let us state this clearly ... Does 'Association for Environmental Education' express exactly what we do ... Does it not parallel the Association for Science Education, the Association for Physical Education?[29]

The Need for a Discipline

Although initiatives aiming to change the National Association's name were formally distinguished from attempts to change the identity of the subject, such re-definitions were advocated in the same period. On one point, those advocating change were unanimous: what was needed was not a new 'emphasis' or 'subject' but a 'discipline'. The rhetorical requirement of 'a discipline' symbolised the dual purpose of redefinition: a new synthesis of knowledge but also one which afforded higher status and could be offered to a new clientele covering a broader ability spectrum.

Sean Carson, whose research at Manchester was particularly concerned with the new CSE, began in the autumn of 1966 to perceive the need for 'a discipline' of rural studies for the following reasons:

> The lack of a clear definition of an area of study as a discipline has often been a difficulty for local authorities in deciding what facilities to provide and more recently in having rural studies courses at colleges of education accepted for the degree of B.Ed. by some universities. It has been one of the reasons for the fact that no 'A' level course in rural studies exists at present.[30]

Further, in commenting on the Report of the Study Group on Education and Field Biology, he noted: 'Because rural studies was not recognised as a discipline at any academic level, even at 'O' level, the Group were prevented from giving it serious consideration.'[31]

Carson's judgments were passed on to the Schools Council Working Party on Rural Studies who reiterated them in the report to the Council of June 1968.

The working party perceived 'the need for a scholarly discipline'. The discipline would spread 'across the present system of specialisation' and might 'take the form of an integrated course of study based upon environmental experience in which rural studies has a part to play.'[32]

The most common pattern for defining new 'disciplines' of knowledge in the essentially hierarchical education system in England has been through the work of university scholars. Unfortunately at this time there was very little academic activity in this field for the rural studies advocates to build upon. Reviewing the university scene in 1972 Marsden noted that: 'Courses labelled "environmental studies" tend to have an individualistic flavour and a distinctly "applied" quality.'[33] The first 'environment' course was precisely of this applied kind: the School of Environmental Science at East Anglia University. The School was proposed in 1960 but had to wait seven years whilst the basic sciences of chemistry, biology, mathematics and physics were first established. Similar courses have more recently been established elsewhere by scientists at new universities, for instance the University of Ulster in Coleraine and more limited developments at Sussex. Courses have also been developed at Sheffield and at Exeter a course on 'environmental chemical engineering' has been introduced.

The idiosyncratic applied courses developed in universities offered no hope of an overarching definition of an 'environmental' discipline. The pattern was similar in the colleges of education. Paterson found that the courses were 'clearly individualistic and doubtfully defined' and to confirm this he noted the fact that environmental studies has to be discovered under a number of different names: 'Although environmental studies is the commonest title, environmental sciences, contemporary and environmental studies, social and environmental studies and environmental education itself also exist.' Paterson felt that this lack of common identity was 'not necessarily a mistake': 'If all were clearly the same the subject might be more fully recognised by the conventionally minded yet each variation in the title indicates nuances of subject matter and general ethos. These are the products of those who teach the subject and who, for the most part, actually initiated the courses.'[34]

The approach in the colleges was markedly different to developments in the schools. The first main level 'environmental studies' course was established in 1961. Three years later Leicester College opened two annexes and a Department of Environmental Studies was formed and manned by three fulltime members of staff working as a team to cover the various aspects of the course. The work at Leicester was dominated by geographers and Paterson judged the most common source of environmental courses to be 'by idealism out of geography'.[35] Biologists were a second group actively involved in many college courses on the environment. Rural studies, the background of most school pioneers, was grossly under-represented. Paterson felt that: 'It is significant to note ... the paucity of rural studies tutors whose own broad areas directly overlap and possibly include much of currently accepted environmental studies.' Few of the colleges used gardens, greenhouses or animals. One college possessed a fully equipped rural studies unit but the environmental studies department stated it 'is not much used'.[36]

In fact the developments in the colleges often followed, certainly in a chronological sense, work in secondary schools. Paterson noted that many colleges stated among the aims of their courses a desire to 'fit into the modern climate of education'. This he suggested reflected the fact 'that the schools are already calling for teachers of environmental studies, that they are educationally ahead of the colleges'.[37]

The main difference between the schools and colleges was in the position of the rural studies teachers. In the colleges they were not faced with imminent extinction because of comprehensive reorganisation (though of course there was a substantial longterm threat to their position thereby implied). In addition only five colleges specialised in rural studies in 1963.[38]

Even in those colleges which taught rural studies the overlap with practice in schools was patchy. In June 1968 Alexander and Carson, in a report on College of Education syllabuses, noted that the results of their enquiry 'showed what many in the schools have already felt to be true, that is, that college courses too often bear little relation to what is required of teachers in school and are now urgently in need of review.' Reporting on the adverse correlations between school and college courses, they state: 'If the premise is accepted that the college courses should reflect the accepted definition of rural studies then this result is important because it shows that, in fact, most courses are very different from the ideal.'[39] The confusions to which Alexander and Carson point were still evident two years later when a report by lecturers in rural studies in colleges posed the question: 'To what extent should the aims of courses in rural studies in colleges be different from those of courses in schools?' and 'what are the aims of rural studies in schools which provide the basis for the courses in colleges?'[40] The report concluded that the role of the subject in primary and scondary schools 'needs to be redefined or at least updated. The aims of the subject at school and college level could then be clarified.'[41]

Such overdue clarification has not been undertaken since 1970. In an article called 'Whither Rural Studies?' Mylechreest argued in December 1975 that 'although a definition of environmental education in the school curriculum was agreed in 1970 there is no such agreement for higher education'. He concluded: 'The continued provision of rural studies specialists is therefore of vital importance.' The argument is persuasively self-fulfilling — since no 'new specialist environmental studies teachers' are trained, 'The rural studies teacher can make a distinct contribution which is necessary for interdisciplinary environmental studies.'[42]

As a new disciplinary definition of environmental studies was not forthcoming from the scholars in the higher education sector, the process of definition had to be undertaken at the secondary level. One of the pioneers of the 'A' level syllabus later claimed that the process of curriculum development undertaken 'is schools-based and is the result of initiatives taken together by practising teachers with the support of their local authority. Such self-generated work offers a viable way of developing an area of the curriculum.'[43] Thus in the schools-based model the academic discipline is developed because classroom teachers perceive the need for a new area of knowledge and then set about involving academics in its construction.

The perception of such a need among rural studies teachers can be discerned from the beginning of 1967. In February 1967, Mervyn Pritchard, as secretary of the 'Research and Development sub-committee' of the National Rural Studies Association, reported that: 'There was some difficulty in impressing the intellectual content of the subject', and that the sub-committee: 'wanted to discover how rural studies experience can help students with gaining entry to colleges of education, and what value post "O" level qualification in rural studies would have for this purpose.' In the discussion which followed this report John Pullen, HMI, said, 'Several questions required answering', among them: 'Do we consider an "A" level course should be included in rural studies? What do we do about the reaction, "We do not want people with 'A' level in rural studies". What parts of rural studies should be treated as aspects of other disciplines?' At the same meeting policy committee reported that a sub-committee had been formed 'to find existing curricula for able children leading to at least "O" level in the rural studies field' and 'to produce evidence that there is a need for rural studies up to "O" level i.e. to show that the subject is of benefit to able pupils.'[44]

In March a 'statement of evidence' was presented by the National Association to the Schools Council Working Party on Rural Studies. The definition of rural studies advocated was almost identical to that established in Carson's Manchester research: 'The study of the landscape, its topography, geology and pedology, the ecological relationship of the plants and animals naturally present, together with the study of man's control of this natural environment through agriculture, horticulture and forestry.'[45] In advocating this definition of rural studies and adding as an objective 'The development of an awareness and appreciation of the natural surroundings' the National Association contended that there was a growing demand for examinations at 'O' and 'A' level in rural studies. 'We are certain that if such examinations are introduced they will be used increasingly.' Finally they asserted that the content which they had defined 'provides a unified and clear area of study and a valuable academic discipline'.[46]

At this time a small group of HM inspectors interested in rural studies, among them John Pullen, also saw a need for a discipline of rural studies in schools. They argued in an article published in October 1967 that, broadly interpreted, 'rural studies in school should mean that pupils will have experienced work which calls for disciplined study to acquire a structured body of knowledge about the countryside, entering into many of the familiar subjects of the curriculum.'[47] The HMIs saw such rural studies work as potentially examinable at 'A' level.

School Subjects and Curriculum Change

> Work now being attempted at many schools could justifiably claim to reach this level. It is true that some schools with strongly developed rural studies courses find, as one might expect, that older pupils turn very naturally and successfully to 'A' level courses in chemistry, biology and geography and often gain university entrance on the standards they have achieved. Nevertheless the time appears to be ripe for the introduction of 'A' level courses in agriculture, agricultural science, and in the wider field of rural studies.[48]

The changeover to comprehensives precipitated a number of teachers who had previously worked with CSE to define rural studies at 'O' level and 'A' level. The 1968 NRSA Journal noted that schools in Yorkshire, Nottinghamshire and Hertfordshire were campaigning for such exams.[49] Reporting on 'rural studies in the comprehensive school', Topham argued that 'rural studies should be so organised within the comprehensive school that no child, boy or girl, of whatever ability, is denied the opportunity to participate'.[50] The rural studies teachers in a comprehensive school should aim to offer: (a) a course leading to an 'O' level GCE; (b) a course leading to CSE; (c) an integral course; (d) to participate in a general studies course; (e) a course leading to the 'A' level GCE, and when established to a certificate of further secondary education. Consequently, 'in a large comprehensive school one can envisage generous allocation of staff to the department'.[51]

The perennial dilemma of rural studies advocates is again illustrated when having argued so cogently for a variety of examinations in the subject, Topham stated; 'I firmly believe that success in examinations is not really indicative of the value of any subject, and this is especially true of rural studies'. His opinion was anticipated by a comment from P.L. Quant in April 1967:

> There is no doubt that in our efforts to maintain our status in the looming inevitability of the comprehensive school — indeed our very existence — we have dragged the 'Science is our Leader' concept out of the cut and thrust of rural studies teaching to replace it by a syllabus of scientific detail which is chaining us down.[52]

The Schools Council Working Party on rural studies met between November 1965 and June 1968 when its report was presented to the Council (the working party's brief was 'to examine rural studies in secondary schools').[53] One of the paramount problems facing teachers of the subject was dealt with in the section on 'status':

> The position varies greatly but there is no doubt that a substantial proportion of rural studies teachers do find themselves in a difficult position because of the demanding nature of the task, the lack of ancillary help, and the attitude which regards the subject as a sublimating exercise for the less able.[54]

Elsewhere the report noted: 'The old concept of the subject predominantly as gardening, often gardening for the backward boys only, did not die easily.'[55] The remedy for this situation was clearly perceived. 'Examinations in rural studies have helped to improve the image of the subject and to give it a certain status in the eyes of the pupils and their parents. Acceptable "A" levels could raise the status still further.'[56]

The working party had produced a strong recommendation that the Schools Council 'should set up a curriculum development project to establish patterns of curricula in rural studies acceptable to all secondary schools'. The Report noted that 'the Council has agreed that a proposal for a curriculum development project in rural studies should be drawn up for its consideration'.[57] The lobbying of the Council by the working party and sympathetic HMIs seems to have ensured fairly rapid consideration of the need for a curriculum development project. What is significant is that whilst the brief of updating rural studies remained a central if implicit part of the project the title was changed in line with the new name and aspirations of the Rural Studies Association. 'Project Environment' began in April 1970 and was staffed by two leading members of the association: Ron Colton, director, and Richard Morgan, deputy director.

From the beginning the project worked very closely with representatives and agencies of the Rural Studies Association. The most significant partnership was probably with the Joint Working Party on Environmental Education. This body was convened in 1971 under the guidance of David Alexander. Alexander, an ex-rural studies teacher, was adviser in Bedfordshire and was General Secretary of the National Association at the stage of its transition from NRESA to NAEE. In a memorandum to the working party the Project Environment team posed the dilemma faced by rural studies representatives in claiming the new subject area:

> The question is, should the Joint Working Party pursue the matter of the type of updated courses in Colleges of Education which the existing rural science and rural studies departments should provide in their subject role in the wider cause of environmental education? Or should it widen its brief . . . into those physical and sociological aspects of the environment which geographers, historians, and sociologists and others might rightly claim were more central to their disciplines and look at the whole of environmental education? In a nutshell, the choice is between the up-to-date area which is succeeding rural studies and environmental education in its whole-curriculum concept.[58]

Conclusion

The position of rural studies in the mid-sixties meant that the teachers of the subject were faced with a rapid decline in its intellectual and occupational

School Subjects and Curriculum Change

acceptability. In such a situation (following Ben-David and Collins hypothesis) it can be seen from the movement to change the name of the subject just how enthusiastic some of the subject's practitioners were to embrace a new intellectual and occupational identity.

From this crisis situation advocates of a new approach to the subject were able to gain support not only for the definition of a new intellectual and occupational identity, but also for a strategy to change the status of the subject. To survive in the newly emerging comprehensive schools, the subject needed to be taught as an 'O' and 'A' level examination. By establishing such examinations, the way would be prepared for rural studies teachers to argue for more school finance and resources and to consolidate their departmental territory inside the school. It was for these reasons that a committee was set up specifically 'to produce evidence that there is a need for rural studies up to 'O' level, i.e. to show that the subject is of benefit to able pupils'.

The pursuit of academic status, however, highlighted the conflict inside the subject which had surfaced when examinations were first mooted. Topham and Quant both expressed the feelings of a substantial body of rural studies teachers that their work was ill-suited to academic examinations. The feasibility project to establish if rural studies was examinable at CSE had likewise worried about the 'unfavourable backwash effects' of written examinations for the teachers of the subject. The split over whether the subject should be titled rural studies or environmental studies was very much a split between the early emphasis on pedagogic and utilitarian traditions, and the new move to embrace the academic tradition. This conflict was reflected in the split within the subject which was evident at the meeting of 14 June. Particularly among rural studies groups in the north of England there was great 'emotional attachment' to rural studies. The 1969 Conference again showed there was a 'bitter division' and that the 'spirit of comradeship had disintegrated'. Subject association's meetings provided the area within which the various sub-groups and factions sought to promote their particular versions of the subject. The influence of examination board policy was presented as a major reason for changing the title of the subject to 'environmental studies'.

The passage to higher status followed certain aspects of Layton's model, particularly the movement away from utilitarian and child-centred aspirations. In other respects, however, the pattern was markedly different. The movement to Layton's stage 2 did not proceed as he envisaged. 'The tradition of scholarly work' could not emerge without the establishment of scholarly communities at the tertiary level. Although certain groups were established, notably in the new universities, connections with the teachers in schools only occurred in one-off events such as the Offley Conference (see Chapter 9). The central problem was that at the tertiary level the main scholars were from geographical and scientific backgrounds; although attracted to 'environmental' problems, they seldom saw 'environmental studies' as the means of establishing new intellectual and occupational identities. Indeed, in a flourishing tertiary sector there was little need for occupational redefinition.

Even with those agencies and institutions directly concerned with influencing or training personnel for the school sector, considerable differences of allegiance were evident. Project Environment's progress was enormously affected by the fact that the Director left in the middle of the three-year period to take a job in America. As a leading member of NAEE noted: 'We missed a real chance to develop a decent academic version of environmental studies ... chances like that don't come twice and I think he's got a hell of a lot to answer for'.[59] Most of the 'environmental studies' advocates in the colleges of education were actually main specialists in either geography or biology. Hence bodies like the Society for Environmental Education worked primarily in opposition to any claims from rural studies specialists that their work was synonymous with environmental education.

Notes

1. S.M. Carson *The Changing Climate*, 1963, p. 14.
2. *NRSA Journal*, 1966, pp. 31–2.
3. See, for instance, reports in the *Journal of the Kent Association of Teachers of Rural Science*, No. 12, September 1958, p. 3.
4. *NRSA Journal*, 1966, p. 36.
5. 'NRSA Policy Committee Report to Council', 17.6.67.
6. George Wing to Sean Carson, 12.11.75.
7. Interview with Gordon Battey, a Hertfordshire teacher, 8.11.75.
8. Ben-David and Collins, *op. cit.*, p. 45.
9. National Rural Studies Association Annual General Meeting Report, 6 September 1969, Resolution 2.
10. *Ibid*, Chairman's Report (W.T. Brock of Hertfordshire).
11. *Kent Association of Teachers of Gardening and Rural Science*, No. 6, June 1955, p. 22.
12. G.A. Perry 'What's in a name?', *NRSA Journal*, 1964–5, pp. 33–37.
13. S.M. Carson 'Rural studies: The case for the name', *NRSA Journal* 1964–5, pp. 32–7.
14. *Ibid*.
15. S. Carson, MEd., p. 76.
16. *Ibid.*, p. 269.
17. NRSA Council Minutes, 10.2.68.
18. *Ibid*.
19. *Ibid*.
20. *Ibid*.
21. NRSA Policy Committee Circular, 8.3.68.
22. NRSA Policy Committee Minutes, 16.3.68.
23. NRSA Policy Committee Minutes, 25.5.68.
24. Schools Council Working Paper 24, *Rural Studies in Secondary Schools*, London, 1969, p. 6.
25. *Ibid.*, p. 7.
26. Letter from West Riding Rural Studies Association to R. Morgan, 14 November 1968.
27. NRSA Policy Committee Minutes, 29.11.69.
28. NRSA Minutes of AGM, 6.9.69.
29. P. Neal 'The National Association', *Journal of the N.R. and E.S. Association*, 1971.

30 S. CARSON, MEd., p. 135.
31 *Ibid.*, p. 61.
32 Working Paper No. 24, p. 19.
33 W.E. MARSDEN, 'Environmental studies courses in colleges of education', *Journal of Curriculum Studies*, Vol. No. 2, 1971.
34 A. PATERSON 'Main courses in Environment education in college', Mimeo, 1972.
35 *Ibid.*
36 *Ibid.*
37 *Ibid.*
38 *Ibid.*
39 *Rural Studies, A Survey of Facilities 1963*, p. 36.
40 S. CARSON and D. ALEXANDER 'Analysis of some colleges of education syllabuses of courses in rural studies', NRSA Policy Committee Research Sub-Committee, June 1968.
41 'Report of the Working Party of the RES Section of the ATCDE', 1970, p. 15.
42 *Ibid.*, p. 22.
43 M MYLECHREEST, 'Whither rural studies?, *School Science Review*, December 1975, Vol. 57, No. 199, pp. 276–84.
44 S. CARSON (Ed.), NFER, 1971, p. 7–8.
45 NRSA File Minutes of Meeting on 11.2.67.
46 CARSON, MEd., p. 369.
47 *NRSA Journal*, 1968, p. 38.
48 'Rural studies in schools', *Trends in Education*, October, London, DES, 1967, p. 31.
49 *Ibid.*, pp. 30–31.
50 *NRSA Journal*, 1968, p. 44.
51 *Ibid.*, p. 45.
52 *Ibid.*, p. 46.
53 P.L. QUANT, 1967, p. 12.
54 Working Paper 24, p. 4.
55 *Ibid.*, p. 15.
56 *Ibid.*, p. 5.
57 *Ibid.*, p. 12.
58 *Ibid.*, p. 3.
59 Interview with NAEE Executive committee member, Leeds Conference, 30.8.75.

9   Construction of an 'A' Level Syllabus

Schools-based Initiatives

In the period of changeover to the comprehensive system after 1964 several schools began to offer rural studies courses in their sixth forms. As a result a number of rural studies teachers drew up courses which were potentially of 'A' level standard.[1]

The first approach to an examination board was made by the Regis School at Tettenhall in Staffordshire. The effort proved abortive and in November 1967 it was reported that 'Tettenhall submitted their "A" level syllabus to the Northern Universities Board and had it refused'.[2]

A more successful approach was made by the Shephalbury School, a school in the process of becoming a comprehensive situated in the Hertfordshire new town of Stevenage. The Head of Rural Studies at Shephalbury, Paul Topham, had trained in biology and horticulture at King Alfred's College, Winchester. His first post in 1959 was at Berkeley Secondary Modern school in the New Forest, where he was in charge of rural studies. In 1963 he moved to Shephalbury. Topham saw his work at Shephalbury up until 1966 as a 'questioning period' in considering the potential role of rural studies in the comprehensive school. By and large he considered rural studies teachers were: 'entertaining the troops because nobody else could manage them'. Apart from social control of deviant pupils he considered that the teachers of the subject 'were not getting anything out of a traditional rural studies course that you could justify if you were called to account for what you were teaching'.

Having judged traditional rural studies to be largely redundant in the comprehensive school Topham felt 'we had then to work out something we did consider a viable proposition'. In an 'all-ability' school he felt such viability was dependent on broadening the base of the subject to involve the ablest students. He began to work out a new definition of the subject in a general studies course, based on the environment, which he taught in the sixth form.

Topham's course was extremely successful in the school, where he had now become Head of Upper School. On 22 November the Head contacted an examining board to enquire about the possibility of getting Topham's course validated as an 'A' level. At this time some exam boards, notably the Associated Examining Board, were considering an 'O' level in the subject. One headmaster noted after his enquiry that he was given 'the impression that the Board would be very interested in the production of this syllabus'.[3]

As a result on 1 February 1967 Topham circulated a number of universities, colleges and professional bodies to elicit their views about content for an 'A' level in rural studies. He was particularly concerned to define the syllabus in 'the applied ecology field'. When these views were received Topham produced the first draft of an 'A' level which asserted: 'The aim of the syllabus is to provide the scientific understanding required to enable the candidate to understand man's control of his environment, and the conflicts which arise as a result of expanding requirements and the consequent need for conservation.' Significantly the draft added that 'The syllabus relates biology to physics and chemistry which it is assumed will have been studied previously or concurrently.'[4]

The 'A' level consisted of two parts: part 1 had two theory papers on the Physical Environment and the Living Environment; the second part proposed a 'submission for examination of a record of original research including fieldwork'.

In June the first draft of the 'A' level was sent round to a number of universities and examining boards for comment. A number of problems were raised. A geography professor commented: 'So much of this appears to be geography as it is now conceived that I am surprised that the word only appears once in the draft'[5]; whilst a university biologist thought that 'it would be very difficult to teach it in a genuinely scientific way at school level'.[6]

The examining board forwarded the syllabus to one of their advisers. He found the syllabus 'very difficult to evaluate since the headings are so broad and generalised'. He added 'my impression is that it may be rather thin, but I do not know exactly how far the author intends to go'.[7] He also commented on discontinuities between parts 1 and 2 and of the original research in the latter part said: 'My fear is that these projects will be simply descriptive; I suggest that they should be firmly rooted in a theoretical body of knowledge.'[8] The second draft of the syllabus replaced scientific 'understanding' with 'knowledge' in the section on aims and the reference to biology, physics and chemistry was deleted. Although the section on 'The Living Environment' was re-titled 'Biological Systems' other changes took account of the discontinuities between part 1 and 2 to which the adviser had drawn attention.[9] Once again Topham circulated his draft proposals.

This time Sean Carson, who had just completed his M. Ed. at Manchester and was again acting as adviser in Hertfordshire, was asked to comment. His work at Manchester had led to a definition of rural studies in many ways similar to Topham's, but until now they had worked independently. Carson had defined rural studies as covering 'The Study of the Landscape', 'The ecological relationship of the plants and animals naturally present' and 'the study of man's control of this natural environment through agriculture, horticulture and forestry'.[10]

Carson returned 'some suggested amendments': 'Basic biology, and geography should be omitted from this paper but instead a note should be included saying that the candidate should have sufficient basis in these subjects to develop the ecological relationships that are the concern of rural studies.'[11] He considered that the section on biological systems should be retitled: 'We are not replacing biology but extending it. Suggest "the natural environment" as this is the term used in various definitions of rural studies.'[12] Carson's experience of the 'politics' of syllabus construction acquired in his roles within the National Association were evident in two comments: 'The official definition of rural studies as used in the N.R.S.A. evidence to the Schools Council would be a better statement of aims than the one here, and would have additional validity.' And his conclusion to the letter: 'I think the above changes would give the paper a better balance, it would not tread on the toes of geography and biology but build on the same foundations as the newly defined discipline of rural studies.'[13]

Following submission of a third draft of the 'A' level to the Examining Board on 21 August, Topham was informed that the Board 'has now formally approved your proposed Advanced Level Syllabus in rural studies'. The letter added: 'You will wish to know that concern was expressed at the extensive nature of the syllabus and the question was raised as to whether or not this would lead to superficial teaching.'[14] Nonetheless the letter confirms that the 'A' level would be forwarded to Schools Council for approval.

In fact the 'A' level was not sent on to Schools Council and in July 1968 a Board official wrote in response to an enquiry from Topham that the board would prefer to consider the 'A' level in detail when it had finalised its own syllabuses.[15] In January 1969 a new Standing Advisory Committee for Environmental Subjects reviewed the syllabus and recommended it as an experimental syllabus which could not be offered with geography or biology.[16]

After submission to Schools Council by this committee six months ensued until Topham phoned the Board to request written details of the Council's response. A Board official replied:

> I attended the sub-committee at which your proposals were considered and approved in principle. This approval was subsequently confirmed in the published minutes of the sub-committee ... however, I have been told that the decision of the sub-committee is merely a recommendation to a senior committee and we are not, therefore, free to go forward.[17]

Five months later it would appear that Schools Council had referred the matter back to the Board. A board official informed Topham:

> I would now like to confirm that the Board's Advisory Committee for Environmental Subjects recently gave further consideration to your

proposed special syllabus in rural studies. The Committee confirmed their approval of the principle of an examination of rural studies at 'A' level but agreed that the current proposed syllabus was not suitable for a course leading to such an examination. They felt that the syllabus was too wide (i.e. gave details of too great a breadth of subject material) to allow a sufficient study in depth for an 'A' level examination. It is, therefore, suggested that the syllabus should now be re-drafted with a reduction in the total subject matter coverage.[18]

In preparing for a meeting with the Board to consider his redraft Topham was later offered a list of 'major points which will need consideration.'

The content of the syllabus is too extensive to allow the study in depth normally expected at 'A' level ...

The formal written examination papers should indicate the depth of treatment of the syllabus. Those submitted in January 1969 indicated an insufficient depth of study for 'A' level.

It would be advisable for the syllabus to originate from the particular environment of the school and to develop from this course.

It should be verified that success in an advanced level examination in rural studies would be acceptable as a qualification for university entrance.

The question of the degree of overlap between rural studies and other subjects must be considered. The degree of overlap would probably require the exclusion of any concurrent presentation of biological subjects and geography.[19]

The Hertfordshire 'A' Level

In August 1969 Paul Topham left Shephalbury to become an advisory teacher in environmental education under Sean Carson. Upon his joining the county staff Topham and Carson discussed the future of rural studies in the county: 'We more or less agreed that we should really do environmental studies and we would like to make a complete changeover, though be realistic and realise not everyone would join in.' The changeover to environmental studies was for two reasons: firstly, the National Association, in dialogue with Mervyn Pritchard of the Schools Council Rural Studies Group, had already advised that environmental studies should be recognised and promoted by rural studies teachers; secondly in circulating his draft 'A' level in rural studies, Topham had: 'taken advice from various people, biologists, geographers and so on in universities and basically they were saying we were talking about a broader aspect and that perhaps we should use the word "environment".' Carson and Topham decided upon a strategy to implement the changeover to environmental studies in the Hertfordshire secondary schools. They concluded that: 'probably the best way to establish environmental studies would be at the highest academic level that could be established in schools.'

Paul Topham was somewhat ambivalent about the new undertaking which inevitably superceded his Shephalbury initiatives: 'I would like to have seen this piece of work as a school-based "A" level, if only to show that a school can put an "A" level up and get it accepted.' He felt that what was particularly significant about the Shephalbury scheme 'was the fact that we were trying to tailor a course to the needs of the kids and not have to meet the requirements of other people's courses.' The Hertfordshire initiatives began in the final months of 1969 with a series of evening meetings with teachers to discuss the possibilities for teaching the new subject. By now Topham thought: 'that we had got to prove that environmental studies was something that the most able of students could achieve and to do something with it ... if you started off there all the expertise and finance that you put into it will benefit the rest — your teaching ratio goes up, etc. and everyone else benefits — the side effects that people don't mention sometimes.'

Sean Carson adds a number of reasons for the founding of the working party of Hertfordshire teachers:

> In talking to Paul, we decided that the only way to make progress was ... to draw up an examination even though it meant entering the examination racket ... We decided that the exam was essential because otherwise you couldn't be equal with any other subject. Another thing was that comprehensive education was coming in. Once that came in, no teacher who didn't teach in the fifth or sixth form was going to count for twopence. So you had to have an 'A' level for teachers to aim at.

Initially, the working party consisted of a group of headmasters and sixth form teachers drawn almost exclusively from 12 Hertfordshire schools interested in teaching environmental studies at 'A' level. In early 1970 the group met to redraft Topham's 'A' level which had recently been rejected for the third time by the Examining Board. On 23 February, Carson began a new set of negotiations with the Board: submitting the new syllabus 'on behalf of a consortium of schools in Hertfordshire ...'

Carson explained that as a result of the working party's deliberations, Topham's syllabus had been 'completely redesigned'. It was divided into four sections: (i) physical environment; (ii) biological systems; (iii) productive systems; and (iv) the changing environment. It was to be taught in 'an integrated manner with practical studies throughout' with '40 per cent of the marks given for records of fieldwork throughout the course.' Carson concluded hopefully that 'as the content of the syllabus has not been appreciably changed and we understand that the previous paper was agreed in principle by at least one of the Schools Council Committees we look forward to this paper being adopted as early as possible.'[20]

The Associated Examining Board rapidly judged the new submission and it would appear that on 10 March Carson was unofficially informed that the

School Subjects and Curriculum Change

submission was unsuccessful. On 3 June he informed his Chief Education Officer that he was writing to the Examining Board to try to elicit the basis for their comments on 10 March.

At this point the County Education Officer decided to call a conference to which were invited university teachers, representatives of the examination boards, colleges of education, professional bodies, HMI, the Schools Council, the representatives of the Hertfordshire head teachers and sixth form teachers who had started to meet as a working party to reconsider the syllabus.[21] The initiator of the conference idea was Sean Carson:

> I went to see our County Education Officer ... said what we'd like to do ... that we couldn't get any satisfactory answer from exam boards about things we put up ... universities wouldn't accept rural studies, and didn't know what they were supposed to accept.
>
> Could we have a conference, I would write to universities, head teachers etc. and try to get from them what sort of thing we should be doing and the okay to do it. So that is what we did, we set the conference up.

The Offley Conference

Aims and objectives

The conference met at Offley in Hertfordshire from 23 to 25 October 1970. In convening the conference it is clear that the advocates of environmental studies in Hertfordshire followed Carson in hoping that the sponsorship of the universities and other professional groups could be engaged to overcome opposition to the new subject. A local head stated: 'This may possibly be an historic occasion. It is not very often that a new discipline is injected into the English system of education.'[22] Another headmaster felt that 'There was those who are themselves regarded as academically acceptable who might produce an acceptable syllabus'.[23] The aims of the conference were outlined by its convenor, Mr. S.T. Broad, the Hertfordshire County Education Officer: 'This conference has been called to do a job of work. We hope, as a result, to have an area of study called environmental studies or environmental science, clearly outlined, that will have the authority of this conference behind it and which we can present with confidence to schools and examination boards.'[24] The source of the 'authority of this conference' was hinted at later: 'Some agreed core is essential to any further advance ... it must lead to an "A" level examination acceptable for university entrance.'[25] The power which universities had in determining 'A' level acceptability was dealt with in Carson's introductory speech; referring to earlier pioneers of 'A' levels in rural studies, he stated:

> Often they were asked 'what evidence have you that universities would accept candidates with this sort of "A" level', and on making enquiries to universities the reply was 'show us the successful

candidates and we will tell you'. A chicken and egg situation. Finally it was decided to contact the universities direct and see whether there was sufficient interest and agreement on the subject for an attempt to be made to break the deadlock. Hence this conference.[26]

A later speaker was even more explicit about this perception of who controlled the content of the 'A' level when he said 'In crude terms we must consult the customer and get his ideas of what the product should look like in detail.'[27] The reasons for schools accepting the universities' hegemony were clearly enunciated by Mr. Broad. 'It is essential for schools now that there should be "A" level courses acceptable for university entrance. For courses to succeed in sixth forms it is important for them to have academic respectability and validity and this is often represented by examinations.'[28]

Later in the discussion Professor Hunter, using a broadened concept of 'the customer', dealt with some of the potential problems:

> I am convinced of the value of environmental studies on educational grounds but there is the difficulty of convincing the customer. The problem is that the customers, and in particular the Civil Service, are specialists. They don't want people with a general picture except for a very few at the top and these normally arrive there in the course of their professional experience.[29]

M.H. Edwin of the DES commented that: 'What is coming out of our discussion is the familiar tension between school courses based on pupils' needs and courses which meet university requirements';[30] and developing this theme, Mr. Hartrop of Durham University Education Department then reminded the conference 'that the real customers are the pupils who will take this course'.[31]

In summarising one of the group discussions Professor Hunter alluded to an emerging dichotomy:

> We must decide whether we are aiming in the schools at a syllabus to satisfy university entrance requirements or one on educational grounds. Although a course aimed mainly at educational value may be highly desirable, there is a danger of environmental sciences being put in a similar category as general studies. If this then has to serve as a university entrance requirement, I think university selection committees will be reluctant to accept it in assessing a student's ability for a university place.[32]

Syllabus discussion

The Offley Conference, having begun with the introductions by Mr. S.T. Broad and Sean Carson and the report of the Hertfordshire teachers' working party, was organised around a series of papers and study groups, each followed by group discussions. Dr. R. Best spoke on 'Problems of the Countryside', Professor Newbould on 'World Conservation Problems', and J.D. Fladmark on

'The Urban and Social Environment'. Study groups considered 'A Sociological Approach', 'A Biological Approach', 'World Conservation Problems' and 'Man and his Environment'. The idea of the specialist papers and study groups was to focus discussion on specific themes, but the original transcripts indicate that the participants were mainly concerned with certain fundamental issues. One group leader reported: 'I have no guidelines for a syllabus to offer' because 'members obstinately insisted that far more fundamental questions had to be answered before you could get down to an actual syllabus.'[33] Two recurrent features in the discussions were firstly, the concern for the boundaries of the knowledge to be defined and secondly, the search for unifying themes or concepts for the new 'A' level subject. Sean Carson had in fact exhorted the conference to consider these questions in the first session: 'Definition of the concepts is important, and delineation of the boundaries. This will be your main task at this conference. Some things must finish up outside our boundaries if only for reasons of the limited time available in schools.'[34] Before the study groups he added: 'The Chairmen of the groups will bring you up against the hard facts and I draw attention to the necessity for establishing boundaries early in the conference.'[35]

The participants who gave most consideration to boundary problems at the conference were the representatives of the university science and geography departments. In his introduction, Mr. P. Jackson, a Hertfordshire headmaster, had referred to the biologists and geographers as 'the heavy-weight group'! Their comments bear elegant testimony to Esland's perspective on 'subject communities': 'They are exponents of English, Maths, or whatever; they have been initiated into the problems and procedures of a community which appear to them as plausible and self-evident.'[36]

Professor Newbould discussed the entry requirements of his School of Biological Studies at Ulster with regard to boundaries: 'Will "A" level environmental studies substitute for biology?' he asked. 'I am not clear about this. Biology and geography "A" levels will continue to be the main intake, but how will this new subject adjust to existing subjects? It might be necessary to adjust the boundaries between subjects.'[37] The following speaker, Dr. Healey of King's College Zoology Department, added: 'I assume a course with a geographical basis with biology included. I agree that boundaries need careful definition.'[38] Later Newbould hinted that when boundary negotiations were completed a new subject community might emerge: 'We would also hope to produce teachers who would teach environmental studies in schools, and thus that the circle would be completed.'[39] Geographers were also very concerned about the boundaries of the proposed new subject. A number of speakers were evidently worried about the degree of 'overlap', but a solution was proposed by Dr. Douglas of Hull University, who stated: 'To have a scheme of environmental studies which is different from geography, such as wide-ranging environmental studies of the local area or part of your immediate school hinterland would create a new field of study which doesn't overlap too much with geography.'[40] Mr. Hartrop of Durham University Education Department asserted that: 'The way in which geography is developing now includes almost everything now suggested in the environmental studies syllabus. Parts of geography could be expanded to consume almost everything.'[41]

Another speaker, Mr. Pritchard, who had chaired the Schools Council working party on rural studies, commented on the problem posed by subject representatives on exam. board committees: 'the Boards analyse such a syllabus only in geographical content, or they go before a biological committee and they examine them only for biological content. Each of these complains that there is not sufficient for their own discipline'.[42] Professor Newbould, in conceding that 'we have to draw boundaries', saw that 'the one essential is to have lines drawn logically'.[43] As a partial solution to the problem of 'the breadth and depth implicit in the subject of environmental studies',[44] he suggested that 'a strong unifying theme'[45] was needed. (Newbould recommended that the theme should be 'Energy'.)

The search for a unifying criterion was connected with the procedures of examination construction. Jackson commented somewhat invertedly:

> To develop a subject for which the present examination system is not structured, requires both naive students and irresponsible teachers. As long as examinations are the status symbol in the sixth form, we must make it possible to pursue their (environmental) studies without handicap.[46]

Miss B. Hopkins of the University of London Schools Examination Board asserted: 'We must look for unity in construction in the syllabus',[47] and Mr. G.J. Neal of Schools Council added: 'This criterion is one by which acceptance is governed. The elements of unity and of depth of study are regarded as important. You cannot take one particular subject in isolation from the examination as a whole, they must have some degree of comparability.'[48] That the 'essential unity' of environmental studies as a new 'A' level subject was regarded as problematic by some was implied in the final discussion. The confrontation between Mr. Lucia of the Associated Examining Board and Mr. Broad of Hertfordshire was to prove prophetic:

> Mr. Lucia: We have had a syllabus put forward to us, as you know, for environmental studies and have approved it at 'O(A)' level. I think, however, that we must look carefully at some of the reasons for examining environmental studies. I did not find impressive the arguments that, say history and mathematics are available at both 'A' and 'O' levels. These are subjects which are taught in infant, primary and secondary schools and they take on very different aspects in these different areas. I think I am right in saying that the problem is one of definition. This conference must ask itself the question — what is it that we see as fundamentally an 'A' level discipline and does the subject 'environmental studies' satisfy our criteria? I understand the London, Oxford, N.J.M.B. and Cambridge Boards have 'O' level

syllabuses either for general use or as special papers. Our problem here is concerned with the paper of an 'A' level syllabus. We find ourselves, as did the Chairman of one of the four groups, referring to the fact that an 'A' level syllabus should be $\frac{2}{3}$ science — is this generally acceptable? We shall not be able to decide whether environmental studies is appropriate for 'A' level examining until we have sorted out our aims and objectives and decided what part of the sixth form is likely to be involved and why they want this particular examination.

Mr. Broad: Yes, perhaps because you have not been here during the Conference you have missed some of the explanations. The way in which we started off was to say that none of the company here was unaware of the need for conservation. We accepted that as a nation we have almost the entire mass of the people in positions of authority, superbly ignorant in these fields and yet wielding enormous power. We thought that it would be a good idea that these people should not be so ignorant and that in fact the people who were going out from our schools and universities should not be without any knowledge of the problem of environmental control at all. We realised that the supply of teachers either from universities or colleges of education who should be basically knowledgeable in these matters was essential. Everybody here accepts the need for the 'A' level course, without which we cannot begin to deal with the problems. If Britain isn't able to deal with the problem what other country can? It is urgent that something should be done and that we ought not to be choking over gnats at this stage.[49]

Significant in this discussion is Mr. Lucia's comment which introduces the link between the search for boundaries and unifying criteria and the need for an 'A' level examination to be 'a discipline': 'What is it that we see as fundamentally an "A" level discipline and does the subject "environmental studies" satisfy our criteria?' Once again this reaffirmed the sort of criteria used by examining boards and the need for an overarching definition of a 'discipline'. This would have most academic acceptability if developed by university scholars, but in Hertfordshire it was to be developed in detail largely by practising teachers.

The Hertfordshire Working Party

The maintenance of the momentum after the Offley Conference was provided by an initiative in Hertfordshire promoted by Sean Carson. Clearly the local follow-up to Offley had to take place rapidly so as to maximise the prestige and status afforded by such a large gathering of academics and educationists. Carson decided the best way to follow up Offley was by convening a working party composed of a range of teachers whose specialist subject reflected the main content areas of the envisaged syllabus. The group met in December 1970 with a clear brief 'to prepare an "A" level syllabus, based on the views of the conference, for submission to a number of examination boards'. This objective was pursued in the hope that an examination board would adopt the syllabus and thus make it possible for schools everywhere to devote sixth form time and teaching to environmental studies. The working party was made up of specialists in those disciplines Carson and Topham adjudged relevant; notably biology, physics, geography, history and social anthropology. The participants were all practising teachers freed from their teaching duties on the relevant days to work at the Hertford Teaching Centre. They were aided by Dr. J. Kitching of Durham University, Miss B. Hopkins of the University of London Schools Examinations Department, Dr. Healey of King's College, London, Mrs. J. Riley of Manchester University and Mr. J. Sykes of the Town Planning Institute.

The teachers were expected to develop the sections of the syllabus where their specialist disciplines contributed. But 'Sean laid it down at the beginning of the working party that all comments by separate subject specialists on their subject must be phrased in ways understood by the full team ... and the relationships between subjects had to be developed.'

Other requirements for an 'A' level syllabus were clarified in the early period of the working party's meetings. A telephone memo which seems to be from an examination board exists for early February 1971.[50] This memo and other information, much of it gathered at Offley, allowed Carson to define in March 'a number of clear functions' for an 'A' level syllabus. He claimed 'the working party have had these in mind throughout':

> First, the examination must be recognised by a number of university faculties as a qualification for entry.
> Secondly, universities generally must recognise the course as a discipline of sufficient rigour to indicate intellectual quality of the successful candidate ...
> Thirdly, an 'A' level pass must offer career opportunities at non-graduate level ...
> Fourthly, an 'A' level syllabus must offer a course that is relevant to modern needs, educationally worthwhile and which has a logical unity of purpose ...
> Fifthly, the introduction of a new course at this level must offer new educational methods (which will involve students deeply) and new examination methods which will assess achievements in these activities if it is to justify its inclusion as distinct from (and not instead of traditional subjects) ...
> Finally, the course has to be a practical possibility in schools ...[51]

The requirements that the course 'has to be a practical possibility in schools' seems weakest when viewed in terms of who would teach the course.

As we have noted, the main constituency among teachers was likely to be the rural studies teachers — a group of teachers largely trained for, and associated with, 'non-academic' pupils. Carson and Topham set out with a predilection for geography and biology and consequently asked geographers and biologists to join the working group. These specialists tended to see the exercise in terms of the 'gains and losses' for their specialist subject. Hence the factual content derived from these traditional disciplines was actively promoted. As a result the 'A' level emerged with a strong bias in favour of the more 'academic' geographical and biological content. As a result viability of the course within schools depended heavily on the involvement of these specialists in teaching the course. As we have seen, the self-interest of such specialists often ran counter to involvement in such integrated courses. Carson's syllabus, whilst intellectually justifiable, faced major problems of political viability.

Conclusion

The Hertfordshire initiatives promoted by Carson and Topham followed from their belief that 'the best way to establish environmental studies would be at the highest academic level'. The practical appeal of this strategy was that teaching ratios and resources would both improve if the able students were to be offered an academic examination. Both Carson and Topham believed that 'the only way to make progress was to get in on the examination racket' and with the emergence of comprehensive schools they saw that 'no teacher who didn't teach in the fifth and sixth form was going to count for tuppence!'

The initial negotiations with examination boards having proved abortive, Carson decided to organise a conference of academics and headmasters to 'try to get from them what sort of things we should be doing', and the 'okay to do it'. The plan 'to gain the consent and sponsorship of the universities' was supported by the Hertfordshire Chief Education Officer and by local headmasters. One of the latter noted that 'there are those who are themselves regarded as academically acceptable who might produce an acceptable syllabus'. The nature of university influence over 'A' level examinations is clearly evidenced, although the tension between the academic tradition and pupil needs is signified in the comments of Edwin, Hartrop and Hunter.

What is, however, very clear is that university personnel were far from unanimous in their response to this new area of knowledge. Following Young, one would expect that the dominant interest groups within universities would firmly reject the initiative as indeed many of them did. But the significant point is that Carson was able to select a range of supporters from within the universities who were willing to act as promoters of the new subject. In this way the conference represented an attempt to reverse the normal hierarchical control of examination syllabuses by the universities in selecting university personnel who were actively on the side of this new contender for academic status. At the same time, the concern with 'boundaries' at the conference

Construction of an 'A' Level Syllabus

implicitly conceded the territorial concerns of most geographers and biologists (evidenced best in the early reactions to Topham's syllabus). Such opposition was normally channelled into contesting the claim of environmental studies to be a discipline, thereby fighting on ground where traditional academic subjects were strongest. Similarly the opposition of the examination boards was based on the sort of points raised by Lucia about whether environmental studies was 'fundamentally an "A' level discipline'. By invoking the academic tradition in this manner, Lucia was contesting Carson's strategy of establishing academic credibility by an organised display of university support.

Notes

1 Speaking of these courses a group of HMIs felt they could 'justifiably claim' 'A' level status, *Trends in Education*, October 1967, *op. cit.*, p. 30.
2 George Wing letter to Sean Carson, 27.11.67.
3 Internal memo, Shephalbury School.
4 Rural Studies 'A' level: First Draft, Shephalbury County Secondary School.
5 Letter, 27.7.67, personal file.
6 Letter, 6.2.67, personal file.
7 Letter, 20.7.67, personal file.
8 *Ibid.*
9 Rural Studies 'A' level, Second Draft, Shephalbury County Secondary School.
10 CARSON, MEd., *op. cit.*, p. 369.
11 Letter, August 1967.
12 *Ibid.*
13 *Ibid.*
14 Letter, 20.11.67.
15 Letter, 26.7.68.
16 Letter, 18.2.69.
17 Letter, 4.11.69.
19 Letter, 12.1.70.
20 S. Carson to P.D. Neale, Secretary to the Board, 23.2.70.
21 S. Carson to S.T. Broad, Internal memo, 3.6.70.
22 S. CARSON (Ed.), *Environmental Studies, The Construction of an 'A' level Syllabus* (Slough, NFER, 1971), p. 6.
23 *A level Environmental Studies*, Report on a Conference held in Hertfordshire on 23rd–25th October 1970 (Hertfordshire County Council, mimeo), 1970, p. 12.
24 *Ibid.*, p. 54.
25 *Ibid.*, p. 3.
26 *Ibid.*, p. 4.
27 *Ibid.*, p. 8.
28 *Ibid.*, p. 11.
29 *Ibid.*, p. 3.
30 *Ibid.*, p. 14.
31 *Ibid.*, p. 15.
32 *Ibid.*, p. 16.
33 *Ibid.*, p. 56.
34 OFFLEY REPORT, p. 55.
35 *Ibid.*, p. 29.
36 *Ibid.*, p. 50.

37 *Ibid.*, p. 9.
38 Course E282, Unit 2, p. 7 (section written by G. ESLAND).
39 OFFLEY REPORT, p.13.
40 *Ibid.*
41 *Ibid.*, p. 15.
42 *Ibid.*, p. 29.
43 *Ibid.*, p. 17.
44 *Ibid.*, p. 29.
45 *Ibid.*, p. 40.
46 *Ibid.*, p. 31.
47 *Ibid.*, p. 32.
48 *Ibid.*, p. 11.
49 *Ibid.*, p. 30.
50 Hertfordshire 'A' level file.
51 CARSON, *op. cit.*, pp. 76–7.

10 The Defence of Geography and Biology

Geography and 'Integrated Studies': Historical Background

As was recounted in Chapter 6 since its early beginnings in the nineteenth century geographers in England have been preoccupied with finding an answer to MacKinder's (1887) question, 'Can Geography be rendered a discipline?'. The quest has been continuous, and more recently Honeybone has noted: 'The question of internal balance in geography is ... one which must, of necessity, be always with us. A discipline which recruits its students from the sciences and the humanities alike has continually to keep its synthesis under review'.[1] This continuing identity crisis at the heart of geography is accentuated by the relationship between university geography and 'school geography', and most of all by the relationship between geography and other subjects. As Williams (1976) has noted, these problems are interlinked for, 'if geographers divide over definitions of "geography" and "school geography", it is not surprising that when geography is allied with other subjects the problem of definition of terms is almost insoluble'[2].

The relationship between geography and integrated studies has been historically difficult, notably because 'complication arises from the nature of geography itself'[3]. But the fears relating to geography's identity which integrated studies evoke have been compounded by the complex historical relationship between geography and other subjects. Crucially, geography itself was created by specialists from other disciplines whose studies were integrated by concentration on problems perceived as geographical. As Kirk (1963) has stated, 'modern geography was created by scholars, trained in other disciplines, asking themselves, geographical questions'[4]. At the level of scholarship, therefore, geography was one of the earlier 'integrated studies', but this was also true in schools. To tentatively establish a position in schools, geography was initially presented as an ingredient of integrated courses, as Williams has noted; 'The early attempts at introducing integrated courses stemmed from the struggle to introduce geography into secondary schools ... often as an ingredient of courses integrated with history but also sometimes with the sciences, notably physics.'[5]

As a result, any new versions of 'integrated studies' stand as a dual reminder to geographers of the prolonged and continuing quest for a stable subject identity through a process of internal 'integration' and of the early days when the subject itself was a low status ingredient of integrated courses. Once geography was established as a separate subject in its own right in the early years of the twentieth century, geographers began to obsessively patrol their subject borders. They sought to ensure that no other integrated subjects could follow their route to separate subject status.

The first opportunity to scrutinize this symbiotic relationship is in the period before the First World War for 'no sooner had geography taken its place as an accepted part of school curricula than it was subjected to pressure to be related more closely to other subjects'[6]. The main pressure group at this time was concerned with 'Education for Citizenship' and, as a result, attempts were made to link history and geography. One of the leading protagonists was H.J. MacKinder, who advocated 'a combined subject' in 1913 in an address to the Geographical Association[7]. He was mindful of the vested interests of those who taught history (by then a well-established school subject) and recalled the fears of geologists twenty years before that geographers would 'make inroads upon their classes' and that their careers would thus be limited as fewer posts became available. He added: 'Well, even scientific folk are human, and such ideas must be taken into account'. Thus he assured historians: 'There need be no question of vested interests in connection with the two subjects ... There is no idea of attacking the teaching of history as such in training colleges and in similar institutions'. He was concerned only with the 'upper half of elementary education and the lower tiers of secondary education': 'There what I suggest is the teaching of single subject, geography and history. In those stages of education, let us have one subject, but let that subject be taught by a teacher who has learnt both geography and history, and learnt them separately'. MacKinder's arguments in favour of integration were clearly linked to a view about geography's aspirations as a school 'subject':

> How are children going to use their curiosity? By taking up a 'subject'? That is an academic idea. A special subject will be taken up by a few scattered people as a hobby, but the vast majority will increase their knowledge not by the study of any definite subject, but by reading this and that cheap book, by reading the newspapers, by talking with friends and by seeing what they can when travelling.

This leads MacKinder to argue that for the vast majority

> ... what is important is not to send them out with the rudiments of history as such and the rudiments of geography as such in their minds, but to send them out with some sort of orderly conception of the world around them. Whether a fact is historical or whether it is geographical matters not one straw to them.

Significantly, MacKinder adds that:

> It does, perhaps, matter to those who are going to increase the knowledge of geography, or who are to be specialized teachers of those subjects, and who are going to prepare for examinations in those subjects.[8]

In fact, the specialist teachers of geography reacted to MacKinder's suggestions in a manner which confirmed his last point. Thus, in the discussions which followed MacKinder's address a school teacher, Miss Spalding, argued that the most effective way of achieving the better citizenship desired by MacKinder was to train pupils 'to love one or two subjects so much that they really go on and study them by themselves'[9]. Dr. J.F. Unstead, a university geographer and textbook author, agreed and offered an alternative view of geography as a school subject:

> What is a subject? It is an organized body of knowledge, the different parts of which naturally hang together, and I think in practical teaching it is well to develop it as a whole ..., in geography, the facts do hang together; children can see relations, they may get the sense of proportion if they have the thing treated as a whole ...[10].

A few years later the Council of the Geographical Association issued a statement since 'the question of the position of geography in the curricula of schools and universities is a fundamental one at the present time':

> It is first necessary to understand what is meant by geography and the reasons why it is studied. Among many of those who have not followed closely the recent development of geographical study, an impression prevails that there are important divergencies of opinion on these points, that different authorities hold different and conflicting conceptions even of the subject. But a more careful scrutiny reveals the fact that a close agreement is being steadily reached.[11]

The statement then refers to the growth of the Geographical Association and to a recent manifesto on the subject 'which has met with practically universal acceptance'. Geography, they argue, is a unique combination, 'a balanced subject with a unity of its own', and may claim '... to contribute in a unique fashion to an education which aims at the appreciative interpretation of the modern world'[12].

Alongside the group pursuing a combined subject of history and geography was another group which felt that geography was 'rapidly taking its place as a definite science'. The dangers of scientific aspiration were that taken to its logical conclusion it presented 'a very strong argument in favour of geography being taught by the chemistry or physics master'[13].

In the inter-war period, geography was confronted with a new integrationist initiative in the form of the growing social studies movement. Thus in 1935, Happold argued for a reconstructed curriculum to take account of the fact that 'a boy comes to school not to learn geography or history or English, but to be

School Subjects and Curriculum Change

trained how to live'. With a sexism characteristic of the period, he replaced these subject divisions by social studies, '... a unified course designed to give the boy a knowledge and understanding of his own age, considered not in isolation, but in relation to its origin — that is, a picture both of his environment and his heritage'[14].

After the war the moves towards social studies continued to be linked with the Association for Education in Citizenship and were seen primarily as courses in civic education. In 1949 the Ministry of Education, reporting on 'Citizens Growing Up', saw geography and history as the most relevant of the traditional subjects:

> The question which teachers of these subjects have to ask themselves today is how far they will make this civic value their sole value and criterion in their syllabus and presentation. Many history and geography teachers have taken up advanced positions in this respect, and the older subject names have sometimes in such cases given place to 'social studies' — an indication of the change in point of view. But others are reluctant to allow the illumination of the contemporary scene to become the sole purpose in this range of work, and hold to the more traditional approach which proceeds historically through the centuries and geographically through the regions of the world.[15]

The position of these traditional geographers who were reluctant to embrace social studies was eloquently summarized in a memorandum prepared in 1950 by the Royal Geographical Society's Education Committee. The committee stated frankly that social studies would 'destroy the value of geography as an important medium of education' and hence was 'concerned at its spread in the schools'[16]. The comments of the committee indicate considerable fear that geography might be replaced by social studies especially, it was noted, in secondary modern schools:

> It is difficult to estimate precisely how far this elimination of geography as an ordered study has proceeded. There is, however, much evidence of a strong tendency to 'break down the barriers between subjects' (an explanation given for the change) and to teach an amorphous hotch-potch of geography, history and civics under the heading of social studies.[17]

The report conceded that the nature of these amorphous hotch-potches varied considerably between schools, and that most contained some geography 'but in a disjointed and attenuated form, insufficient to preserve the characteristic outlook and discipline of the subject (p. 81).[18] Above all, the report sees any integration of subjects as likely to impair 'standards of instruction' in geography.

> An attempt to study a group of subjects together introduces such complexity that children cannot see any general pattern or gain a clear

The Defence of Geography and Biology

and memorable educational experience. The geographer is well aware that knowledge is whole, but makes no apology for dividing it into separate subjects for the purpose of learning. History and geography, for example, are distinct branches of study, and each is recognized as having a unique contribution to make to the intellectual equipment of the educated citizen of today. But these contributions are different and cannot be made unless the recognized content and characteristic method of presentation of each subject are preserved.[19]

Thus the integrationist perspective of social studies is presented as wholly undesirable: 'The result is exactly what happens when the lemon is squeezed: the juice is removed, and only the useless rind and fibres remain'[20].

Geography and Environmental Studies

The Emergence of Environmental Studies

The first reactions to the emergence of environmental studies from geographers came in 1950. At the time, the Royal Geographical Society was preoccupied with the threat of social studies, but in the memorandum on that subject attention was drawn to the associated dangers of environmental studies. Concern focused on the growth of environmental studies in training colleges, though the report noted: 'Under the name of "social studies" this new subject is being increasingly taught in schools.' In the colleges, environmental studies were replacing geography courses and '... as a result, the number of teachers in training who study geography beyond the stage they reached at school is reduced to the small percentage taking "advanced" geography.' The report recognised a further danger, that: 'Student teachers may misunderstand the special purpose of this course of "environmental studies" in their own training, and regard it as another "subject" suitable for the primary or secondary modern school.'[21]

In fact geographers' fears that trainee teachers would not be successfully socialised into their subject proved premature. The advance of environmental studies really began in the second half of the 1960s and for a time geographers remained more concerned with successors to social studies such as 'IDE' and 'humanities'.[22] In the presidential address to the Geographical Association in 1967, E.C. Marchant typified the normal response of geographers to such integrated work. '"We geographers", they say, "have built up our subject into a discipline which is at last treated with academic respect: now we are asked to undermine it with superficiality, propaganda — and pictures of water taps"'.[23] A year later, the President, Alice Garnett, criticised geographers' responses:

> We rightly acclaim our discipline as a unique 'bridging subject' and as a keystone in educational curricula, so concerned within itself with the integration of knowledge that, surely, geographers should be the first

to express interest in taking a lead in such interdisciplinary trends. Yet at times I have gained an impression that the reverse seems to be the case.[24]

The uncertainty about responses to IDE and humanities integrated courses was discussed by the Executive Committee in 1969, but new worries were voiced: 'at the omission or exclusion of geography from some current integrations of subjects in secondary schools'. The minutes then noted that 'there were no specific findings to report back' but that in the meantime 'correspondence with members has shown their fears concerning the threat to geography involved in the growth of environmental studies in schools, colleges and universities. There was a matter worthy of deeper consideration.'[25] Some members felt that even discussing this would be: 'tantamount to admitting the validity of environmental studies or would indicate a measure of approval.'[26]

In addition to the legacy of geographers' responses to the 'threat' of integrated studies stretching back half a century, the reaction to environmental studies was complicated by a further factor. In earlier sections the internal dissent among geographers with reference to 'new geography' is recorded. In large measure the opposition came from those with a 'regional' or 'fieldwork' orientation in their training and practice. The close relationship of regional geography and the fieldwork tradition was reflected in the work of Professor S.W. Wooldridge. He argued that the aim of geographical fieldwork is 'regional synthesis',[27] and in his obituary in 'Geography' it was recorded by M.J. Wise, later an advocate of close links with environmental studies, that: 'Above all, geography was for him regional geography.'[28]

In 1966 Professor C.A. Fisher read a paper to the Research Committee of the Royal Geographical Society — it was later published in extended form under the title 'Whither Regional Geography?' Fisher argued that geographical research was in serious danger of 'over-extending its periphery at the expense of neglecting its base'.[29] For Fisher the 'traditional core of geography' was regional study as against the 'new', systematic geography, but he noted: 'While systematic geography now flourishes like the Biblical bay tree, regional geography (however defined) appears to be declining and even withering away.' Fisher added some details of this decline of regional geography: '... not only has there been a noticeable decrease in the importance attached to it in the university syllabus, but this process is apparently also spreading to the schools'. He noted the announcement that the Southern Universities Joint Board 'O' level geography examination for 1970 would include no paper in regional geography.[30]

The increasingly threatened supporters of regional geography were therefore faced with the pervasive challenge of new geography alongside the more traditional challenge of integrated studies currently epitomised by environmental studies. For once the internal threat seems to have been deemed greater than the external dangers represented by the emergence of environmental studies. The obituary of Professor P.W. Bryan, an eminent regionalist,

The Defence of Geography and Biology

records that in 1967: 'Only twelve months before his death and already a sick man' he attended a 'strenuous full-day conference at Leicester University on environmental studies. He probably felt that this term expressed more clearly his own life's work and ambitions as a geographer.'[31] Similarly, in 1970, P.R. Thomas asserted in 'Geography' that:

> The tendency towards an environmentalist approach to explanation in school geography is at least partly due to the survival of the regional concept as the basis for syllabus construction, despite the progressive decline in the importance of regional geography at most universities and its virtual disappearance from some.[32]

But the alliance between regional geography and environmental studies was not to last. Partly this was because after 1970 the 'new geography' tradition began to lose impetus and became increasingly assimilated into traditional patterns of geography. A college lecturer felt 'the new geographers became less violent . . . they flushed regions out but then accepted regionalism back in not as facts . . . but as a spirit and concept.' He noted a further conclusive reason for ending the alliance: 'The crisis in geography caused traditional geographers to flee into environmental studies . . . they wanted a refuge to go on teaching as they were teaching . . . but they were overtaken by the environmental crisis and the rapid growth in environmental studies that followed it . . .'[33] The increasing convergence of new, systematic geography and regional and field geography, together with the rapid growth of the new subject environmental studies, once again helped unite geographers in their opposition to the perceived external challenge.

The Geographers' Reaction 1970–75

The initiatives from Hertfordshire, led by rural studies teachers, to promote environmental studies as a new school subject and 'scholarly discipline', culminated in the Offley Conference of 1970. The spokesmen for geography at the conference reflected the growing concern. Dr. Douglas, for instance, sought to define environmental studies in a way that would not 'overlap too much' with geography.[34] Indeed speaking of the claims the geographers made, Mr. Hartrop, in a manner reminiscent of the Norwood Report's complaints at the 'expansiveness of geography' nearly 30 years before, commented that 'parts of geography could be expanded to consume almost everything'.[35]

The reasons for the geographers' reaction can partly be deduced from the evidence of a sample survey of secondary schools carried out by HM inspectors in 1971/2.[36] They found that whilst in grammar schools only one 'combined studies' course had replaced geography (one out of 44 schools), in secondary modern schools 40 schools out of 104 had replaced geography by such courses, and in comprehensive schools 20 out of 59 schools.[37]

That the geographers were intensely worried by the threat of Hertfordshire teachers defining an 'A' level in environmental studies was illustrated when Sean Carson went to speak to the Geographical Association at this time.

> I was invited to go and speak on environmental studies ... There was a really good start when the chairman and 'I'm Chairman of this meeting but I can't adopt a neutral attitude on something I feel so strongly about ...'
>
> Then I made my spiel about geography not being God-given religion, but a range of knowledge we had assembled to our convenience and there was no reason why we shouldn't reassemble it in any other form. This (i.e. environmental studies) was another form in which it might be reassembled and just because you had learnt things in a different tradition, there's no reason why you should go on repeating so other people repeat it after you ...'

After his speech 'There broke out shouting and rude remarks and the Chairman made very little effort to control it ... they said I was out to destroy geography. I remember thinking "it's like facing a Congressional Inquiry".'

The geographers' official reaction to environmental studies was summarised in a presidential address to the Geographical Assoication on January 1973 by Mr. A.D. Nicholls. His speech began by asserting, somewhat wishfully: 'It is not surprising that in the minds of most teachers, environmental studies should be associated with geography'. Having thereby hinted at the thrust of his argument, he later stated: 'The definitions given by well-known geographers to provide answers to the question "What is geography?" might equally well be used to answer the question "What are environmental studies?".' And similarly, with a sideswipe at 'new geography': 'In the first decade of this century the founding fathers of the then "new" geography came from many and varied disciplines. Their original choice of discipline would make an admirable list of environmental studies.'[38] Nicholls' views were undoubtedly shared by most geographers; one college of education lecturer remembers that at this time: 'At an early environmental studies meeting we felt that geography had been doing it for years and we said so ...'[39] Tony Fyson also claimed that: 'On a pragmatic level a new subject dealing with the environment is still going to leave a lot of geography teachers claiming that their traditional fare is the true way to approach the topic'; and that 'on an academic level it is possible to argue that geography ... can develop to include the aims of the environmental studies lobby'.[40]

Nicholls' second argument turned on the need for 'a subject'; again he drew on a long tradition. In 1913 Dr. J.F. Unstead had argued against MacKinder's advocation of a combined subject, saying that a subject is an organised body of knowledge and that: 'in geography, the facts do hang together.'[41] Unstead's argument was again used in the 1960s when there were fears about school geography: 'No subject can claim a place on the school curriculum unless it has a clear structure, a precise theme and a worthwhile purpose ... if geography is to survive in school it, too, must be a scholarly

The Defence of Geography and Biology

discipline with a clearly defined purpose and a carefully organised structure.'[42] Nicholls began by conceding that environmental studies were generally accepted as useful in teaching 'young children' but then argued that: 'As the width and depth of knowledge acquired increase so does the need to specialise; subject divisions appear and the need for subject disciplines arises. These codes of study are the framework or basic principles which are necessary for specialised learning and understanding.'[43]

The role of geography as a subject discipline ordering and unifying the 'unrelated facts' of environmental studies was widely promoted by geographers at this time. 'Geography because it is an integrated discipline at the heart of environmental studies is better placed than any of the other constituent nuclei to coordinate and unify the larger body of studies of which it is the core'.[44] The implicit hierarchy contained in this statement is clarified by another geographer exploring the same relationship: 'To put it in terms of a model, geography may be likened to a pyramid the base of which is environmental studies, but the apex is the sharp intellectual discipline fashioned in the university.'[45] A university professor confirmed this view, and explained the implications for school geography: 'You need high level theoretical development first of all ... then you break it down in digestible level in school.'[46]

The third strand of Nicholls' argument, undoubtedly the most convincing aspect for the many teachers in the audience, dealt with the 'practical realities' for 'practising teachers'. Crucial to this argument was the recognition that:

> It is likely, but by no means certain, that if environmental studies or environmental education is considered as a subject in its own right, some, but not all, of the time previously devoted to constituent subjects will be made available to the new omnibus subject. With constant pressure on teaching time, headmasters are ever searching for new space into which additional prestige subjects can be fitted, and the total loss of teaching time to environmental subjects may be considerable. Nor, in my experience, have I found departments very eager to surrender previous teaching time, particularly with the more able classes, to make good other departments' losses.

Nicholls stressed a further practicality: 'If undifferentiated environmental studies of an omnibus nature are to be introduced into the school curriculum, which of the academic disciplines is going to cater for suitably qualified men and women to take charge of them?'[47]

A publication prepared by the Environmental Education Standing Committee of the Geographical Association, which included Mr. Nicholls, clarifies the nature of the fears over such 'wrangling'. They assert that 'The concerns of environmental education render the presence of a person with geographical training in each team quite essential'; and similarly: '... that a team which lacked a geographer would be handicapped; a team with one would have a wider range of possible activities.'[48]

Nicholls explored this theme in considerable detail in his address:

'Qualified men and women of academic stature have selected their subjects because of their interest in them and the importance they consider them to have. They also like to see the inspiration of their teaching reflected in their pupils' "advancement".' The relationship between subject expertise and pupil advancement is later elucidated:

> A shallow approach to any subject inevitably becomes less satisfying, and finally utterly boring both to teacher and class. Not every question from a class calls for an immediate answer in depth, but when the teacher's ignorance of the subject becomes evident to the class the pupils lose confidence in their teacher, and more pitifully, the teacher loses confidence in himself, and confusion becomes chaos. The teacher must know his subject ...[49]

The relationship between the status of a 'subejct' and the pupils which traditional subjects attract, is alluded to by Nicholls in discussing a DES survey's findings with regard to environmental studies: four varieties were distinguished: (a) one comprehensive school used environmental studies for all first-year pupils and thereafter separate subjects were taught. (b) two schools have environmental studies for slow learners in years 1, 2 and 3 only; the average and able pupils did ordinary subjects. (c) two schools gave environmental studies in year 4 only for fourth-year leavers. These were non-examination pupils. The rest did ordinary subjects. (d) one school gave environmental studies for able fifth-year pupils for 'O' level as option against other subjects. From these findings Nicholls concludes:

> First, average and above average pupils are considered to be able to cope with ordinary subjects, though it might be unsafe to assume they would rather not spread their abilities. Secondly, environmental studies are thought to be easier or can be made more attractive to less able scholars. Thirdly, separate subjects may be easier to teach successfully. Cynics might suggest that combined studies provide a more successful opiate to potentially rowdy classes. You as teachers, may reach other equally valid conclusions.[50]

The last sentence confirms that the message, despite its philosophical and logical shortcomings, aims to focus on the teachers' perception of the practical realities of their work.

The final strand of Nicholls' argument concentrates on the need to keep geography as a unified discipline. An earlier President had touched on the socialising role of the university. Geography departments which 'have a duty to ensure that, at least at the first degree level, the core of our subject is neither forgotten nor neglected and that the synthesis of the specialist fields and their relevance to that core are clearly appreciated by our undergraduate students.'[51] The symbiotic relationship between the university geography and school geography is explored:

The Defence of Geography and Biology

> There is now an intake from sixth forms, into our university departments of at least one thousand students each year to read geography. The recognition of our subject's status among university disciplines which this gives, together with the now costly provision made available for its study, could never have been achieved without this remarkable stimulus and demand injected from our schools.[52]

Nicholls argued from a similar position about what is required of geography as a subject:

> At sixth form level it must ... provide a challenge to the young men and women who may have ambitions for the future and wish to carry their studies further and go to a university. They will become, in the best sense, students. Some of these will furnish the university schools of geography with young men and women who will expect to have some knowledge with sound and deep foundations so that understanding between them and their lecturers, readers and professors is mutual. We should be wise not to stray too far from the recognised routes — the frontiers of the subject are alluring, but not all are worth extending, at least in School. If we provide the universities with undergraduates who have a wide but shallow acquaintance with many subjects, will they prefer these students before those with a sound foundation in fewer relevant subjects?[53]

Nicholls' conclusion stressed the need for staying within 'the recognised routes':

> Ten years ago, almost to the day and from this platform, Professor Kirk said 'Modern geography was created by scholars, trained in other disciplines, asking themselves geographical questions and moving inwards in a community of problems; it could die by a reversal of the process whereby trained geographers moved outwards in a fragmentation of interests seeking solutions to non-geographical problems'. Might not this be prophetic for us today? Could it not all too soon prove disastrous if the trained teachers of geography moved outwards as teachers of environmental studies seeking solutions to non-geographical problems?[54]

Nicholls' conclusion is as explicit a statement of the geographers' 'party line' as it is possible to make: in effect he is saying we must not allow the process which created geography to be repeated.

Negotiations for Environmental Studies as a Subject

Nicholls' only allusion to the Hertfordshire initiatives was obscure,[55] but support for environmental studies was actually voiced in the address which followed Nicholls'. Professor Wise, a university geographer schooled in regional geography and the fieldwork tradition, echoed the schism in the geographers' ranks noted earlier, when he said: 'we sometimes tend to assume that "geography" and "environmental studies" are synonymous. The theme of this paper is that, while they are not, geography has an essential contribution to make.'[56]

Following Nicholls' argument we can see why such an assertion was a dangerous heresy. The extent of this heresy was made clear later in the paper when he recommended the growing tendency to think in terms of replacing subject-oriented courses with the problem- or concept-oriented courses centred on aspects of the environment appropriate to inter-disciplinary attack. He added later that 'Clearly, the field is too wide to be the property of one or even a small number of academic disciplines.'[57]

Sean Carson, who concedes that Professor Wise 'has always been supportive' consulted a number of sympathetic geographers at about this time in the course of the negotiations for the London 'A' level. His reply to the geographers stressed a number of common assumptions in the arguments they deployed. Notably the tendency to argue that 'everything is geography' or that 'parts of geography can be expanded to comprise almost everything'. This he noted was in fact 'to say that geography is not in any way a specialism'.[58]

At an ATO DES course in March 1973, Carson offered a defence of his whole strategy:

> If environmental education is to lead to the study of the problems I have outlined then a discipline of some recognisable sort must exist. For this reason I do not agree with those that suggest that existing subject definitions should suffice to cover these problems by an adjustment of their syllabuses. That is not in my view a practical proposition. A main subject in this area of curriculum is geography, but developments in geography are in another direction ...[59]

Later he developed this last point:

> I had thought ... that in geography they have introduced very much more the statistical approach and the idea of patterns ... Therefore they don't any more do geology, the landscape and the rocks underneath. Well, this is good environmental stuff, understanding the landscape. So I said to the geographers, 'you don't want to do that any more — our people do! If you're worried about the technical barrier being drawn between us, we'll do the landscape appreciation.'[60]

Though factually dubious, in that many geography teachers continued to teach physical and regional geography, Carson's strategy was a masterly way of exploiting the schism among geographers, and serves to explain the passion with which his initiatives were thereby greeted.

The answer provided by the Geographical Association to Carson's strategy of defining a new discipline was to argue against the feasibility of such a definition. A discussion paper prepared by the Standing Committee on Environmental Education in December 1974 argued that: 'There has been a growth of environmental studies in schools which merely utilizes a wide range of inter-disciplinary material as stimuli in the classroom. This method lacks any real integration of the material, though it does not create any new subject boundaries.'[61] In this way the lines were drawn up for the negotiations inside Schools Council, following a strategy of denying that geography and environmental studies were sufficiently distinguishable for the latter to be a separate discipline.[62]

Later, in 1975, a paper circulated to the Schools Council Working Party on Environmental Studies noted that:

> At present, students taking environmental studies at G.C.E. 'A' level are not allowed to combine this choice with geography. Subject compatibility is frequently a source of discord but it is important to prevent the perfectly legitimate misgivings of academics about subject demarcations being turned into obstacles unfairly placed in the path of students.[63]

In the event, the delaying tactics pursued by the geographers have now produced a positive strategy along the traditional lines of subject re-definition. Recently a number of syllabuses entitled Environmental Geography have appeared and a new 'Handbook for Teachers' of this emerging synthesis produced. The title Environmental Geography was used 'to emphasise our aim of helping to restore the study of school geography to a central role in the understanding of the human habitat ... we contend that geography, along with ecology, offers an important way of comprehending environmental problems.'[64]

Conclusion

The historical background of the relationship between geography and integrated studies confirms the existence of a series of sub-groups within the subject. In the early twentieth century those geographers arguing for an 'integrated subject', notably MacKinder, were opposed by those aspiring to an 'academic' subject. In the latter group Unstead characterised geography as 'an organised body of knowledge, the different parts of which naturally hang together' and the Geographical Association as 'a balanced subject with a unity of its own'. The process thereby initiated was later described by Marchant who noted that 'we geographers have built up our subject into a discipline which is at least treated with academic respect'.

Marchant was writing in 1967, but new schisms lay ahead. Most significant of these was the struggle between groups with allegiance to regional and field geography and those promoting new geography. Carson exploited this schism in promoting his version of 'environmental studies' and in doing so won a number of supporters within geography (e.g. Professor Bryan and Professor Wise). In the long run, however, new geography established a major place within the subject which could now claim to be a fully-fledged academic discipline. The role of university scholars in defining geography is noted in the phrase which portrays a subject whose 'apex is the sharp intellectual discipline fashioned in the university'.

The practical realities of academic status are clearly enunciated by Nicholls' speech. Hence 'average and above average pupils are considered to be able to cope with ordinary academic subjects' and these pupils at present are taught geography. Environmental studies 'are thought to be easier or can be made more attractive to less able scholars'. If, however, environmental studies were to be considered an 'academic subject in its own right', the 'total loss of teaching time to environmental subjects may be considerable'. Nicholls adds 'Nor, in my experience have I found departments very eager to surrender precious teaching time, particularly with the more able classes.' The threat of losing able students and departmental resources is thereby made real if academic parity is conceded to environmental studies. By placing the threat to resources and career at the centre of the debate about geography's future the implicit exhortation is to subjugate the claims of intellectual scholarship to those of subject self-interest.

Biology and the Promotion of Field Studies

Biology and the emergence of Environmental Studies

In the fifties and sixties rural studies was viewed condescendingly by biologists — as courses of applied biology for the less able. The Report of the Study Group on Education and Field Biology reflects the manner in which biologists kept rural studies at arm's length: 'In their present rather fluid state, rural studies are not at all easy to assess critically and realistically.'[65] Following the Keele Conference and later, the Hertfordshire Conference at Offley, some biologists began to consider the emerging 'environmental studies' more seriously. The 1960s and early 1970s were, as noted before, a time of rapid change and redefinition in the field of science education. Inevitably some of these reformist efforts overlapped into the domain of rural and environmental studies.

At this time a number of boards were reconsidering their science papers at 'O' level and 'A' level, particularly in subjects like 'rural biology'. This reconsideration coincided with efforts by rural studies advocates to redefine their subject and occasionally the two initiatives converged. For instance in June 1970 Carson reported to the Hertfordshire working party that Paul Topham: 'has been invited to be a member of the Biology Advisory Panel of the London University Examination Board. This panel are producing an "O" level syllabus which we expect will closely follow the Hertfordshire ideas (as does the Oxford Local Boards "O" level paper). The panel have raised the possibility of an "A" level and we have sent them our syllabus.'[66] The fraternisation of rural studies teachers and biologists was not all one way, however, for a number of prominent biologists became involved in new 'environmental' initiatives. A working party set up by the Joint Matriculation Board Examination Council to define an environmental studies science 'A' level included several prominent biologists, notably Professor D.H. Jennings of the Hartley Botanical Laboratories. The working party was weighted with other 'science advocates', lecturers and teachers. Not surprisingly the group finally agreed to title the syllabus they drew up 'environmental science'.[67]

The manner in which biologists who became involved in new 'environmental' syllabuses still retained their affiliation to their parent discipline, is eloquently testified to by John Price. Price became Chief Examiner to the Associated Examining Board's new 'O' level in environmental studies. At a conference called by the Board to discuss the paper he had drawn up, he had this to say:

> The apparent biology weighting throughout was mentioned several times. I could justify this by claiming that Environmental Studies really is the ecology of man and to that extent is a biological subject but if you look at the syllabus you do in fact find that a lot of it could be described as biological. It may be the technology of agriculture or horticulture but it can still be called biology.[68]

The biologists who became involved with new environmental studies syllabi were mainly advocates of ecology and field studies. As we have noted the major developments in biology were at this time antagonistic to such approaches. W.H. Dowdeswell became involved with the Wiltshire working party on Rural and Environmental Studies, whilst Dr. Perrot, the other major advocate of field biology, became involved in producing pamphlets for the National Association of Environmental Education. Yet the involvement with rural studies was always restrained and 'loyalty' to biology, even if in fundamental disagreement with the direction the subject was taking, was always paramount.

This paramount loyalty meant that rural studies teachers were left to dominate the emerging field of environmental studies, for developments in biology were clearly leading elsewhere. Dowdeswell saw this with remarkable clarity:

> Rural Studies, of course, was always the depressed area, they were always the underdogs, generally underqualified, they were always looked down upon by school staff . . . they always got the wrong end of the bone and all that. Through developing 'O' levels and 'A' levels in Environmental Studies they had a chance of finally achieving academic responsibility.

However rural studies and biology were viewed as very close in terms of content if not in terms of status: 'Rural Studies always looked to me like Biology

School Subjects and Curriculum Change

... some of it is applied Biology in the sense that you get into the gardening and cultivation area. My students who go out to teach Rural Studies always end up teaching Biology.'[69]

The rapid expansion and final establishment of biology as a high-status school subject in the 1960s left the subject more or less unhindered by the challenge of rural and environment studies. The only exception was in the combining specialist development of ecology and field biology. Hence the main challenge to biology was deflected from the mainstream hard science laboratory core of the subject towards the fieldwork elements which the subject was anyway concerned to play down. In the battle for control of 'field studies' the biology (and geography) fieldwork advocates were able to maintain a dominant influence over field studies, in spite of being only minority groups within their own subjects.[70]

Field Studies

The use of the rural environment as an educational resource, which had been traditionally advocated by rural studies teachers, was also promoted from 1946 onwards by the Field Studies Council (initially called the Council for the Promotion of Field Studies). The Council made very slow progress and in 1960 had only six centres in England and Wales (which existed alongside the rural studies centres run by three local education authorities). Even at this stage traditional disciplines seem to have dominated in the provision of courses in the centres. We are told they were: 'designed mostly for sixth-form pupils from grammar schools, and for student teachers and university undergraduates in biology, geography and geology.'[71]

In 1960 to overcome 'the shortage of data about the existing situation, results and trends within the education system and the consequent difficulties in directing field studies along lines likely to achieve desirable educational objectives',[72] the Nature Conservancy established the Study Group on Education and Field Biology. The Study Group's establishment marked the beginning of an effort to promote field studies work through close liaison with the traditional disciplines in the school curriculum, notably biology.

The Report of the Study Group in 1965, as the title 'Science out of doors' indicates, began to define ways in which the science teacher, particularly the biologist, could use field studies. Also at this time the Nuffield Foundation Science Teaching project were considering ways of utilising field study techniques.[73] The 1965 Education Conference sponsored by the 'Countryside in 1970 movement' confirmed that field studies and science were coming to be seen as closely related in school curricula. In his opening address to the Keele Conference, Lord Bowden assumed that studies of the countryside in schools would be the responsibility of the science teacher. After referring to the Nuffield initiatives, 'at this moment, as you probably know, the whole processes of organising and teaching science in schools are being completely transformed',[74] he went on to comment on the potential of this curriculum reform.

> To a certain extent physics is bound to be a formal subject, best taught in the lab. But this is not at all true of Biology, and I think it is extremely important that children should have opportunities of going out into the field and realising for themselves what the scientific method is.[75]

The synonymity of field studies of the natural environment and science is confirmed later: 'There is an immense merit for the whole of the future of science in the great development of a type of experimental work which children can do in the natural environment.'[76] In a similar vein Dr. Pritchard of the Nature Conservancy, who acted as 'Scientific Secretary' to the Study Group on Education and Field Biology, argued that: 'Environmental Studies must be firmly anchored to Scientific disciplines because the problems created by the intermingling of natural and human forces can neither be understood nor interpreted without the use of science'.[77] Dr. D.E. Perrot submitted a paper to Conference on 'Research on the Teaching of Field Biology' which reported a programme carried out at Keele University in 1964.[78] The programme indicated that field studies was

> a better stimulus to the recall of factual information than other types of work for pupils of 12–15 of all kinds of ability, but by mental age 16 pupils engaged in field problems showed the greatest gains in recall ... At that stage pupils engaged in field problems showed greater increases in problem-solving skills than those engaged in laboratory problem-solving and other types of work.[79]

Following the Keele Conference, geography teachers also became active, and the Geographical Association established a standing committee of field studies. In 1965 and 1966 the committee completed surveys of facilities for field studies and in 1969 a further survey was completed by the Geographical Association, covering local authority field centres and other sorts of centres for field study work. The interest of the Geographical Association was reflected in the growing use made by geography teachers of field studies to teach their subject.

The promotion of field studies was essentially linked to the traditional disciplines of biology and geography, and throughout left rural studies firmly outside the dialogue. From the beginning Carson had protested that field studies were being linked with only subjects recognised as academic disciplines. Speaking of the Study Group on Education and Field Biology he wrote: 'Because rural studies was not recognised as a discipline at any academic level, even at "O" level, the Group was prevented from giving it serious attention.'[80] And at the Keele Conference he twice protested at the apparent hegemony of the biologists: 'In spite of all that has been said about broadening the outlook, we still seem[ed] to be talking in the narrow context of biology.'[81] He asserted: 'The approach of biologists in schools, colleges and universities was too narrow and formally scientific and took insufficient account of agriculture and other land uses.'[82]

Carson wanted a more interdisciplinary conception of field studies of the environment. At Keele he said: 'We must break down the barriers between academic disciplines. In Secondary Modern Schools this [is] particularly important'.[83] His later writings confirm this vision: 'When it came down to terms it was unfortunate that the educationists present were so concerned to present their separate cases that there was no time for them to come together and agree.'[84] In another article, written under a pseudonym, Carson wrote that at Keele: 'A major weakness that still plagues efforts to establish Environmental Studies became evident. This was the inability of teachers representing school subjects to appreciate the interdisciplinary nature of environmental problems and to move from entrenched positions defending their own interests.'[85]

The degree to which biology and geography had come to dominate field study work can be seen in a survey carried out in 1965. Of the total number of centres doing field study work, 120 covered geography and biology as subjects, 53 'general environmental studies' and 40 agriculture, horticulture and forestry. (These figures and later figures partially confuse the issue by including rural studies under 'agriculture, horticulture and forestry', but also some rural studies teachers would have been involved in 'general environmental studies'.) In the Field Studies Council centres only: 14 covered the two traditional disciplines, 6 general environmental studies and 3 agriculture, horticulture and forestry. By 1969 the number of centres having grown: 332 now covered geography and biology, 167 general environmental studies, and 123 agriculture, horticulture and forestry (including rural studies). In the Field Studies Council and school centres it was reported 'a distinct pattern of emphasis on rather more specialised subject treatment is available'. In the Field Studies Council centres 18 covered geography/biology, 5 general environmental studies and 5 agriculture, horticulture and forestry (including Rural Studies). In School Centres the corresponding figures were 32, 14 and 13.[86]

The figures from the 1965 and 1969 surveys show clearly that biology and geography were established as the main subjects using field studies of the natural environment. In this situation, claims that rural studies were uniquely concerned with the natural environmental were rapidly losing credibility. Carson was clearly very worried and in January 1968 wrote to the General Secretary of the National Association, Richard Morgan, on the matter. Morgan replied that the Field Studies Association

> cover a wider range of people than those interested in Rural Studies and we have no hope of carrying out the whole function they stand for. In this area, we have come to the conclusion that to fend them off our territory of study will only get us a poor name.... However, this does not prevent us existing — or being a strong voice in our own field. But I think that we shall be more effective in co-operation than in resisting

and claiming that we already provide the service which they are trying to provide. Because this claim is not true; they are catering for a much wider range of environmental interest than we are.

Morgan's statement reflects the acceptance of the domination of field studies by groups largely drawn from biologists and geography. His comments provide an epitaph to the frustration of Carson's hopes for rural studies in this area by the existing field studies groups because 'they reach a wider membership than we can ever hope to reach they are bound to be stronger financially and in every other way than we are'.[87] In this manner rural studies was once again frustrated in colonising a viable area of curriculum activity.

Conclusion

In Chapter 4 we described how the competition in the 1960s within biology between the sub-groups representing field biology and ecology and those promoting a hard-science, laboratory-based version had ended with the subject dominated by the latter group. The field biologists for a time developed connections with environmental studies, rather in the manner of the geography sub-group that was on the defensive in the 1960s, the regional geographers. But in biology these connections were never very strong: the subject was rapidly expanding and about to achieve final establishment as a high-status school subject. Apart from this the field biologists secured a strong position inside the field studies movement and together with the geographers managed to control most of the field studies centres. In this position there was little reason to fraternise with rural studies.

Any challenge from the new environmental studies to the growing subject of biology was thereby deflected to and successfully managed by the 'field studies' group within the subject. For mainstream biology with its 'hard-science' image, and its rapidly growing number of departments (and associated laboratories) within schools and universities, the challenge of the new environmental subject was hardly worthy of consideration.

Notes

1. R.C. HONEYBONE 'Balance in geography and education', *Geography* 34, 184 (1954), p. 70.
2. M. WILLIAMS (Ed.) *Geography and the Integrated Curriculum*, London, Heinemann, 1976, p. 8.
3. *Ibid.*
4. W. KIRK 'Problems of geography', *Geography*, 48, p. 357.
5. WILLIAMS, *op. cit.*, p. 8.
6. *Ibid.*
7. H.J. MACKINDER 'The teaching of geography and history as a combined subject', *The Geographical Teacher*, 7 (1913).

School Subjects and Curriculum Change

8 H.K. MacKinder 1913 in M. Williams (Ed.) 1976, pp. 5–6.
9 *Ibid.*, p. 10.
10 J. Unstead, Discussion of MacKinder paper, *The Geographical Teacher*, 7 (1913).
11 Council of the Geographical Association 1919 in M. Williams (Ed.) 1976, pp. 15–16.
12 *Ibid.*, p. 18.
13 W.M. Carey 'The correlation of instruction in physics and geography', *The Geographical Teacher* 5 (1913).
14 F.C. Happild *Citizens in the Making* London, Christophers 1935, p. 67.
15 Ministry of Education, 1949, in M. Williams (Ed.) 1976, pp. 62–63.
16 Royal Geographic Society 1950 in M. Williams (Ed.) 1976, p. 81.
17 *Ibid.*, p. 10.
18 *Ibid.*, p. 81.
19 *Ibid.*, p. 82.
20 *Ibid.*, pp. 80–81.
21 Royal Geographical Society (1950).
22 C.B.G. Bull, 'I.D.E.: A geography teacher's assessment', first printed in *Geography* 53 (1968), pp. 381–6, reprinted Bale, Graves and Walford, *op. cit.*, p. 259.
23 E.O. Marchant, *op. cit.*, p. 139.
24 A. Garnett, 'Teaching geography: Some reflections', *Geography*, Vol. 54, 4 November 1969, p. 396.
25 Geographical Association Notes of Meeting of Chairmen of Section/Standing Committee (28.9.70).
26 *Ibid.*, p. 2.
27 S.W. Wooldridge and G.E. Huntchings *London's Countryside*, Geographical Field Work for Students and Teachers of Geography (London, Methuen, 1957), p. xi.
28 M.J. Wise 'Obituary: Prof. S.W. Wooldridge', *Geography*, Vol. XLVIII, Part 3, July 1963, p. 330.
29 C.A. Fisher, *Whither Regional Geography?*, 1970, p. 374.
30 *Ibid.*, pp. 375–6.
31 R. Millward, 'Obituary: Patrick Walter Bryan', *Geography* Vol. 54, Part 1, January 1969, p. 93.
32 P.R. Thomas, *Education and the New Geography*, pp. 274–5.
33 Interview, 14.12.76.
34 Offley transcript, p. 29.
35 *Ibid.*, p. 27.
36 Department of Education and Science, Education Survey 19, *School Geography in the Changing Curriculum* (London, HMSO, 1974).
37 *Ibid.*, p. 6.
38 A.D. Nicholls, 'Environmental studies in schools', *Geography*, Vol. 58, Part 3, July 1973, p. 197.
39 Interview, 14.12.76.
40 C. Ward and A. Fyson, *Streetwork — The Exploding School*, (London, Routledge and Kegan Paul, 1973), p. 106.
41 *Geographical Teacher*, 1913.
42 N.V. Scarfe, 'Depth and breadth in school geography', *Journal of Geography*, Vol. XXIV, No. 4, April 1965.
43 Nicholls, *op. cit.*, p. 200.
44 I. Thomas, 'Rural studies and environmental studies', *SEE*, Vol. 2, No. 1, Autumn 1969.
45 K.S. Wheeler 'Review of D.G. Watts' *Environmental Studies*, (London, Routledge and Kegan Paul, 1969), *Journal of Curriculum Studies*, Vol. 3, No. 1, May 1971, p. 87.
46 Interview, Leicester University, 14.12.76.
47 Nicholls, *op. cit.*, p. 200.
48 'Environmental Studies; A Discussion Paper for teachers and lecturers prepared by

the Environmental Education Standing Committee of the Geographical Association', draft edition (January 1972).
49 NICHOLLS, op. cit., pp. 200–1.
50 Ibid., pp. 204–5.
51 GARNETT, op. cit, p. 389.
52 Ibid., p. 387.
53 NICHOLLS, op. cit., p. 201.
54 Ibid., p. 206.
55 Ibid., p. 198.
56 M.J. WISE, 'Environmental studies: Geographical objectives', Geography, Vol. 58, Part 4, November 1973, p. 293.
57 Ibid., p. 296.
58 S. CARSON, Review of 'Streetwork', Environmental Education (Summer 1974), pp. 56–7.
59 S. CARSON, ATO/DES Course, Paper No. 2, Environmental Education: Design for the Future (March 1973).
60 CARSON interview.
61 'The Role of Geography in Environmental Education. A discussion paper presented by the Standing Committee for Environmental Education to the Geographical Association Executive' (December 1974), pp. 1–2.
62 CARSON, memo to BROAD (16.3.73).
63 University of London GCE 'A' level Environmental Studies, Paper presented to Schools Council Working Party on Environmental Education.
64 K. WHEELER and B. WAITES (Eds.), Environmental Geography: A Handbook for Teachers (London, Hart-Davis Educational, 1976), p. 9.
65 Science Out of Doors, p. viii.
66 S. CARSON at Hertfordshire Working Party, Hertfordshire File, 3.6.70.
67 'Joint Matriculation Board Proposals for the Introduction of a Syllabus in Environmental Science (Advanced)', (mimeo, n.d.).
68 'Associated Examining Board Environmental Studies: Report of a Conference' 23, October 1971, p. 46.
69 DOWDESWELL interview, 24.10.77.
70 Study Group on Education and Field Biology, Science Out of Doors (London, 1963), pp. 94–5.
71 Ibid., p. 83.
72 A. HERBERT, P. M. OSWALD and C.A. SURKES, 'Centres for Field Studies in England and Wales, the Results of a Questionnaire Survey in 1969', Field Studies, Vol. 3, No. 4, 1972, p. 658.
73 Proceedings of the Conference on Education, 'The Countryside in 1970', Keele, 1965 (London, Nature Conservancy, 1965), p. 20.
74 Ibid., p. 7.
75 Ibid., p. 8.
76 Ibid.
77 Ibid., p. 11.
78 Ibid., p. 20.
79 Ibid.
80 CARSON MEd., op. cit., p. 61.
81 Proceedings of the Conference on Education, op. cit., 1965.
82 Ibid., p. 16.
83 Ibid., p. 22.
84 S. CARSON, NRSA Journal 1964–5, p. 33.
85 W.P. FENWICK, 'Education and environment', The Ecologist, August 1972, p. 8.
86 HERBERT, OSWALD and SURKES, Centres for Field Studies, p. 676.
87 Letter from R. MORGAN to S. CARSON, 19.1.68.

11   *The Negotiation of Environmental Studies*

Negotiations with the Examining Boards

In the period during which the Hertfordshire working party were completing their final draft of the 'A' level, from late 1970 into the early months of 1971, only two examining boards were actively involved. As has been noted, one board, the Associated Examining Board, had been scrutinising the various proposals ever since Topham's first submission in 1967. A second board, London University, had allowed an examinations officer to attend the working party meetings, but had stressed that she was attending only in 'a private capacity'.[1]

In January 1971, Carson received two detailed replies from the first board to his letter enclosing the working party's draft. The first letter noted[2] that the secretary of the Board had 'shown the preliminary draft syllabus to a number of colleagues and it has been generally well received'. The main objections were to the fieldwork-oriented Section 2 of the syllabus. The secretary stated that there was a 'need to know a lot more about how to teach Section 2 in the schools', and added that this would also 'resolve part of the examination problem. I doubt if the large volume of fieldwork suggested is possible from the examiner's point of view.' The uncertainties about Section 2 were amplified later in the letter; the secretary perceived two main problems. The first was whether it could 'measure up to the criteria for an "advanced level" study'. In other words 'can it be made explicit that the studies undertaken will be equivalent in intellectual demands made upon the pupils to studies undertaken as parts of other established courses leading to examination certification at G.C.E. Advanced level?' In answer to this question the secretary added 'my view is that it can, but that more detail is required, perhaps in the form of notes for guidance, to make this clear'.

The second problem referred to assessment, and again the secretary noted: 'I do not believe that this problem is as great as the authors appear to fear': 'Any assessment method which is proposed must be capable of producing reliable results: this is essential for the sake of the pupils.' After listing 'a wide range of organisations they must consult before embarking upon this task' —

The Negotiation of Environmental Studies

for instance, the NFER, the secretary thought that 'the Schools Council might provide relevant information or be prepared to help themselves'.

In a further letter, sent the following day,[3] the Board's apparent optimism seems severely tempered:

> I have today received another commentary on your draft syllabus which is so detailed and obviously carefully thought out that I felt you would wish to see it even if it does arrive too late for your working party. The author indicates in a private letter to me that he is conscious of the blunt, destructive nature of some of his comments but, as he is a man intimately concerned with environmental studies as such I feel sure you would welcome a verbatim transcription, especially at the preliminary draft stage of your syllabus.

His memorandum began with a series of detailed criticisms of the sub-sections. In his more general comments which follow he began by conceding 'that the time is right to regard environmental studies as a suitable medium to promote the intellectual development expected of "A" level students.'

But in his reasons for his opposition to the Hertfordshire proposals he elucidated points which had first surfaced at Offley:

> My essential dissatisfaction with the proposals of Hertfordshire is that, like several other attempts at a syllabus for environmental studies, I cannot see it as a coherent discipline ... The study must be a 'discipline' — a coherent body of fact and concept demanding an ordered mind for its appreciation and furtherance. It must be recognisable as such even by the student. The student must feel he is going somewhere, getting somewhere; and must feel he has accomplished something definable at the end of the course. The course must not be a collection of bits and pieces from other subjects — pursued by a hotchpotch of their disciplines. That is not sustaining food for a developing mind.

He then referred specifically to the Hertfordshire efforts to define a discipline for 'A' level study.

> The Hertfordshire Conference was in part concerned to find some unifying theme which would serve as a backbone to the course. Hence the Energy Flow and Land Use ideas. But to my mind the only appropriate central theme to environmental studies is the organism that, in a sense, defines the environment — man. The core of the proper study of man's environment is man himself. Everything has a relevance and the whole has a coherence if man is consistently seen to be at the centre. This may seem to be a platitude, but it cannot have the unifying functions, cannot provide coherence and backbone for a discipline, if it is taken for granted — as it is in the Hertfordshire syllabus.

Later in the memorandum he notes that most recent publications derived from curriculum development work also devote considerable attention to the specification of teaching objectives. A clear statement of the anticipated outcome of the proposed course in environmental studies would '... prevent many of the difficulties which might otherwise arise when the final version of the syllabus is formally considered by examining boards and the Schools Council.'

The latter prophecy was to prove, perhaps not surprisingly, remarkably accurate. In fact as far back as June 1970, in reply to a memo inquiring what the major problem was in getting the 'A' level accepted, Carson noted: 'It has proved very difficult to get any information, but somewhere between the Board and the Schools Council things are constantly stuck.'[4] The problem continued throughout 1971. In March, in reply to Carson's despatch of the final Hertfordshire draft, he was informed: 'In recent weeks brief consultations have taken place but I have to inform you that the general opinion is that your revised draft does not meet the majority of the comments forwarded to you from the Board in early January.'[5] In September, in a discussion at the standing panel which Hertfordshire had set up to implement the 'A' level, it was minuted that the secretary of the Board had 'turned down the proposals immediately on the argument that the method of examining was not suitable'.[6] In December, S.T. Board wrote to Mr. C. Mellowes at the Council for Environmental Education, who was on the Board panel:

> I understand that Sean Carson has spoken to you about our 'A' level syllabus which had been turned down without its having reached your Education Committee, and I wonder if you could let me know what the position is. We are making some progress with other boards but a number of schools would still like to use the Board and to feel that the syllabus is receiving consideration by your Board also.[7]

Mellowes replied that he had 'already registered my opposition to the ruling about the environmental studies "A" level proposals'.[8] In blocking the Hertfordshire proposals the Board seemed to be in accord with the opinions of most of the examining boards. Other boards had been sent the proposals and had reacted with similar dissent. In December 1970 the senior assistant secretary of another examining board approached by Carson wrote,[9] somewhat increduously, about the first draft of the syllabus prepared after Offley:

> The first reaction is that the syllabus is awesome in its demands. No proposals have been put forward in the conference report or in the preliminary draft of the syllabus regarding the recording of examination results, but the allocation of time suggested under the heading Problems on the first page suggests that it is envisaged that the course is intended to be regarded as a single Advanced level subject.

He felt that:

The Negotiation of Environmental Studies

If this is the case then I fear that there is a serious danger that the approach to many of the topics included in the syllabus will inevitably be superficial. If the topics are to be dealt with in the depth implied by the draft, the syllabus is likely to be regarded as being far too overloaded and demanding.

Later in the letter this view was elucidated following a statement that the 'thematic approach of the syllabus is appreciated'. 'If an attempt were to be made to devise a syllabus without a consistent, identified theme there would be a serious danger of the subject matter being fragmented for both the teacher and pupil.'

Some of the assistant secretary's fears appeared to be related to notions about the 'new' clientele for 'A' levels which were growing with the spread of comprehensivation. He argued that some care would need to be taken to ensure that the 'A' level proposals 'do not founder because they have been made with too optimistic a view of what the sixth form pupil is capable of achieving in one-part of his sixth form studies.' Again the assistant secretary envisaged problems over the fieldwork: '... the external assessment of such work is a difficult and expensive operation and with the methods available the reliability of such external assessments may be in doubt.'

By October 1971 with one board having turned the proposals down and other boards plainly uneasy, Carson was beginning to fear that no board would accept the Hertfordshire syllabus. As a result new initiatives were taken and Carson attempted to raise the matter with the secretaries of GCE examining bodies. He received replies which made plain most boards' opposition to the new syllabus.[10]

The opposition from the boards was reflected in the slow progress with the London Board. Following the meeting of GCE secretaries, the London Board had contacted Carson. The original letter cannot be traced but Carson referred to it in another letter written on 21 October to C.L. Mellowes: 'I have received a letter from a secretary of London University Examining Board saying he has become aware that it is being suggested that his Board are going to service the "A" level examination for everyone, but that this is not so. He seems rather incensed by the suggestion.'[11] In spite of these fears the London Board continued to follow the Hertfordshire developments closely and in December, after an invitation from Carson,[12] sent a representative to a meeting of the Standing Panel of Hertfordshire Schools set up to aid in the 'A' level's acceptance. By January C.L. Mellowes was writing: 'I think there are grounds for being hopeful about the response of the London Board.'[13]

The Hertfordshire Standing Panel

The Standing Panel was first mooted by Carson, after gaining the support of C.T. Broad, in July 1971. On 27 July the idea was put to Hertfordshire heads in a circular[14] saying there had been a number of suggestions that it might be appropriate for the schools intending to undertake the 'A' level environmental studies course to set up a Standing Panel so that mutual problems could be looked at as they arose. The Standing Panel representing the heads of schools and colleges was set up in order to keep an eye on the progress of the syllabus. It was hoped that official recognition by the Schools Council might be obtained by about March 1972 in time for schools to organise courses beginning in September 1972.[15]

The first meeting of the Standing Panel was on 27 September and the minutes[16] record that Mr. Carson reminded members that all the work that had been done to have the syllabus accepted and all the publicity that had been received 'would count for nothing if in fact schools and teachers did not make arrangements to start the course and teachers did not take this opportunity'. At the second meeting of the panel on 15 December, attended by Miss Hopkins of the London Board, it was noted[17] that a meeting had been arranged for December 20. Miss Hopkins suggested 'that we did not push the board too quickly'. Carson reported to the heads on the London meeting:[18]

> The syllabus has been considered by four advisers of the London Board and their comments made no serious criticisms so the Board will be setting up a Subject Panel very shortly. It is hoped that this Panel will meet in January and that they will ask your representatives to meet them in February. As a result of this meeting a finally agreed syllabus will be put before the London University Council for approval on 2nd March. If they approve it will then be forwarded to the Schools Council for their May round of Committees and it is hoped that a result will be known in June 1972.

Carson then speculated on the implications for Hertfordshire schools:

> Although at this stage I cannot say anything definite I am very optimistic that we will have an examination available for students starting in September 1972 and I hope that you will feel confident enough to make your plans accordingly.

On 19 January a newly constituted 'ad hoc committee in environmental studies' of the London Board met in Gower Street, London, under the chairmanship of Professor Brown. The minutes noted that: 'The Hertfordshire Advanced level syllabus was discussed and there was a general agreement that it should be considered as a London G.C.E. syllabus.' The syllabus was considered in detail. Two main categories of revision were suggested. Firstly, that in some sections 'syllabus content could be considerably reduced, together with associated teaching notes'. In some cases such reduction was suggested by subject specialists on the panel: 'nothing is known about energy flow in parasites — suggest this be removed from syllabus.' Secondly, in Sections 2 and 3 particularly, there was a demand for more consideration of the urban situation. In Section 2 the question was posed: 'In this whole section, in the

The Negotiation of Environmental Studies

teaching notes, could more guidance be given to the urban school?' In Section 3 'Urbanization should receive an earlier mention', 'notes should include urbanization not being restricted to Britain'.[19]

On 4 February the ad hoc committee met the official representatives of the Hertfordshire Standing Panel: Mr. Smith, Mr. Gwenlan and a biology teacher, Mr. Lord. It was reported[20] that the delegation agreed with the Board's committee that they would recommend the syllabus to be put forward as a Mode II 'A' level syllabus in environmental studies which may be taken by any school, either in Hertfordshire or outside on application.

At this stage Carson circularised[21] all those people who had applied for information about the 'A' level. In the period after the NFER publication many headmasters had written asking if they could take the 'A' level.

> The syllabus is now ready to go forward as a Mode II syllabus, that is to say it will be limited to schools who have applied to take it rather than be available in the general circular. I have agreed with the London Board Environmental Studies 'A' level committee that membership of the Standing Panel of Heads concerned with environmental studies at 'A' level, which has been the negotiating body so far, may now be widened to include Heads from schools anywhere in the United Kingdom and that this would be the appropriate channel for application to take the examination.
>
> I am, therefore, inviting Headteachers to join the Standing Panel. Obviously it will not be necessary for their Heads to attend meetings although they would be welcome to do so, either personally or by sending a representative from the school. All the information will be centralised through this arrangement.

In advising the Hertfordshire schools to complete plans to begin the 'A' level and the following year and in encouraging schools from all parts of England to join the Standing Panel, Carson was clearly anticipating a successful outcome at Schools Council. In fact the negotiations with the university dragged on until late May. On 10 May the Schools Council Geography Subject Committee saw the syllabus and on 22 May the Science Committee. On 7 June Carson circulated[22] members of Standing Panel:

> The representations to the Schools Council by the London Board, on behalf of our 'A' level submissions, have not so far proved successful and it is now likely that there will be further discussions in the Autumn.
>
> I regret to advise you that in the circumstances it seems most unlikely that an examination will be available before June 1975, in other words students beginning the course in September 1973.
>
> This is a major setback but there appears to be no way round it at the moment.

Carson reported the implication of the setback:[23]

> We have suffered a setback from the Schools Council and it does not appear possible for schools to take this examination in 1974. That means that schools setting up courses this September will have to aim them at alternative and less demanding examinations. At the meeting of the Standing Panel yesterday, some agreed that they would do this and others thought they might follow the 'A' level syllabus even if they had only their own certificate to award at the end.
>
> I hope we can still make grants this year to those schools beginning sixth form courses in spite of this setback ...

Negotiations with Schools Council

The Standing Panel first received reports of the abortive Schools Council negotiations on 21 June:[24]

> On 10th May, Mr. Topham had attended the Geography Subject Committee of the Schools Council. The syllabus was discussed in detail, questions were particularly asked about the Section on 'entropy'.
>
> On 27th May he had attended the Science Committee. This committee had consisted of eight members only out of twenty-four, of whom most seemed to be physicists and only one a serving teacher. They had studied the first section of the syllabus only and asked no questions about any other area.

The minutes add that Sean Carson reported that on 24 May 'we were informed by 'phone from London University that the syllabus had not been approved by either committee'. The opinions of the geography and science sub-committees were later detailed in a letter from Schools Council to the London Board:[25] 'It was felt that the syllabus was too extensive, not only because it would lead to the superficial treatment of many topics, but also because a number of sections appeared irrelevant to the central concern of environmental studies.'

The letter gives as an example of superficiality the case of entropy: 'Members felt that this was a difficult concept and that it should not be studied in isolation. It would be necessary to know the difference between enthalpy and free energy before entropy could be understood.' The judgment as to the superficiality of topic coverage was quite clearly based on the specialists' knowledge of their own subject. The letter notes that a significant criticism was that: 'The depth of treatment of the science in the syllabus was not comparable with that of similar topics in an "A" level physics or chemistry syllabus.' If an interdisciplinary syllabus is judged for superficiality only from 'single subject' perspectives, the judgment is virtually self-fulfilling. Similarly with the criticisms as to the irrelevance of certain topics:

The Negotiation of Environmental Studies

The parts of the syllabus that seem to be quite removed from the core interests of the subject include (a) most of the work on geology, e.g. theories of the origin of land masses, plate tectonics, isostasy, (b) man as a heterotrophic organism, and (c) the historical evolution of man.

Following these judgements the letter proclaims in paragraph V (see later note 32).

If such irrelevant topics were envisaged as removed, the effect would be to reveal how close the resulting syllabus would be to existing syllabuses in geography. Concern was expressed at the heavy overlap between this syllabus and syllabuses in both geography and biology. For example it was thought that a candidate prepared for geography would have little difficulty in answering many of the questions. The suggestion was therefore made that there should be some restriction on the subjects that could be offered at 'A' level along with environmental studies.

Two other criticisms were noted: firstly, that there was a clear feeling that by 'trying to make an umbrella for everything that might excite sixth-formers they were trying to do the impossible'. To some extent linked to this was concern 'at the view put forward during discussion in support of the syllabus that the syllabus was designed for the new sixth form, and not necessarily aimed at the pupil requiring an academic "A" level with a view to going on to university.'

A participant recalled the meetings with the two subcommittees representing geography and science. 'It was a territorial response ... fair enough — it's a natural response. I think it was taken to extremes.'

He commented on the general 'climate of opinion' at the time of the meetings: 'What worried me is that the Schools Council at the point in time our syllabus was going up, was calling out for integrated approaches and types of syllabuses. This was the first one that came up and they didn't know how to manage it.' He described how he considered Schools Council had reacted to the Hertfordshire initiative:

They brought together a bunch of geographers and scientists, who were orientated to their own subjects and couldn't see outside. That's the way they'd been educated and it's the way they see their disciplines ... and it's not their fault ... Those aren't the right people to get to comment on it.

Carson was particularly incensed by the science sub-committee's position on entropy:

The Chairman said 'you can't mention Entropy unless you quote the two laws of thermodynamics and then you must do the supporting experiments.' Well, this would have taken two terms and would have been so much physics it would have unbalanced the whole thing. We had great arguments about this, went back to the university — the university science people said 'how ridiculous'.[26]

Ivor Goodson: How do you explain the scientists' reaction to that?

Sean Carson: In my opinion the scientists' view was 'we're not having these people teaching that.' They're not doing it properly ... in science you don't make a statement, you arrive at a conclusion based on experimental data — they would say. I would say, they make experiments to fit the answer they want ... 'This is the scientific method ... if you're not using that method we don't want you making these statements.'

The point we were making is that you're not teaching physics, you're using certain scientific information. You cannot go through the process of building up each time you want to use scientific or biological information.

Ivor Goodson: In which case you don't need a scientist to teach.

Sean Carson: No ... we'd already said 'you don't need a physical scientist'. A confident broadminded geographer or biologist could teach it. We're already teaching combined sciences in schools ...

With the geography sub-committee Carson felt 'they were anti the whole thing — more so than the scientists':

> People would say 'there is nothing in this that couldn't be taught in an "A" level geography syllabus.' We'd say 'no, it isn't' and itemise how it was quite different ... Some would say silly things, for example, 'you won't get geographers to teach this, so you won't be able to manage it' ... I said 'we have geographers to teach it now' ... They didn't want to know that. They continually said we wouldn't get it accepted by universities. So I said, 'until I've got it finally prepared I can't submit it to find out what universities would accept it, but in fact here is the conference, here are these people, some geographers, who have said they will accept it' ...

A Hertfordshire teacher commented on the immediate response to the Schools Council rejection: 'We were furious about it ... Sean started a press campaign ... the university were absolutely livid ... So was Broad.' Carson recalled his reaction: 'At first I was lost ... But I'm very stubborn, I became determined to get it through Schools Council ... even at the expense of my health.' In a letter to Standing Panel members Carson commented on the letter received from Schools Council. Referring to the geography sub-committee's exhortation to remove 'irrelevant topics', he noted: 'Obviously if everything else is removed there would be nothing left but geography. Their suggestion shows clearly that they do not understand what we are after.'[27]

The first protests to the Schools Council came from the London Board. An assistant secretary informed Carson:[28] 'I am very disturbed at the slow progress of this business and have been in frequent communication with Schools Council to try to hasten the process.' A detailed letter from Hertfordshire to Schools Council expressed the dismay at the rejection:

The Negotiation of Environmental Studies

> Of our twenty-four schools, twelve have planned to start courses in September 1972 for examination in June 1974 and the authority has been generous in allocating funds for this development. I believe that it now appears unlikely that the one hundred and twenty students concerned will be able to begin the course after all. Already after a series of curriculum development workshops at teachers' centres, environmental studies courses at C.S.E. and 'O' level are running in many of our secondary schools and we have a pilot environmental studies scheme for examination at C.E.E. level. Both the regional C.S.E. Board and the London University Schools Examinations Department have established environmental studies panels composed of people practising in the field of environmental education to reflect the needs of our schools.[29]

The letter ended with an offer of help which indicated his desire for a speedy response and saying that he understood 'that you may be setting up an environmental studies panel, and if this is the case we would be glad to offer the services of some of our experienced environmentalists ... ' A week after this letter the Standing Panel met to consider their response. They 'unanimously agreed to ask the Chairman to prepare a letter to the Schools Council'[30]

> asking them in what ways the syllabus was unsatisfactory; to set up an interdisciplinary committee; reminding them of their recent publication, *Growth and Response* on sixth-form work which very much supported our approach, and pointing out the urgency necessary if agreement is to be reached this Autumn and another year is not to be lost.

The response of the University Examination Board was similar to the reaction in Hertfordshire, as a Hertfordshire adviser recalled: 'The University were absolutely livid that it had come back ... especially those who had steered the whole thing through.' The university's letter to Schools Council followed closely the conclusion of the Standing Panel at a meeting on 12 September. Carson summarised their conclusions in a letter to Barbara Hopkins. He began by listing changes in the syllabus. Besides some changes in title the panel were willing[31] 'to accept the criticisms about Entropy and omit it, and also to omit much of the geographical material ... we have also included some detail on the statistics required.' (The Schools Council letter of 13 July had stated 'In statistics it was felt more guidance should be given.') Carson then noted, 'I must report that they objected to Paragraph V[32] of the Schools Council's letter to Mr. Stephenson and we have not made any major change in principle in the coverage of the syllabus.' Following several meetings between the university's advisers and Carson and Topham, Barbara Hopkins wrote to Schools Council.[33] The letter reiterates the changes listed by Carson and also notes:

The comments in V caused some surprise. It would seem that the objectives of the syllabus have been misunderstood by the subject committees. The syllabus is considered to be a demanding one for any sixth former to study. It is felt that the views recorded in the last sentence of V did not accord with the tenor of the Schools Council Working Paper 45, 16–19 'Growth and Response' 1. 'Curricular Bases'.

A further section requested 'that the modified syllabus may be discussed with a single Schools Council representative body which includes experts with a professional concern for environmental studies'. One concession that the university had agreed with Carson and Topham was noted:

The possible overlap with other London examination syllabuses[34] was discussed in some detail. The University advisors finally decided, with some reluctance, to recommend that candidates taking the syllabus should not be allowed to sit geography at the same examination.

The university representatives met the Schools Council committee on 17 January 1973. They were Professor E.M. Brown, Department of Geography, University College, London, and Moderator in Environmental Studies; Professor G.W. Dimbleby, Professor of Human Environment, Institute of Archaeology; Sean Carson and Paul Topham. Carson reported the results of the meeting in a memo:

The Panel was a more representative one and included people prominent in the environmental studies field, as well as representatives of all the G.C.E. Examining Boards and the Chairman of the Science and Geography Committee. The Panel was chaired by Mr. Sibson, Secretary of the Schools Council. We had an hour and a half's interrogation and then had to leave. I understand from my sources that the Panel then agreed to recommend the syllabus almost unanimously. It has to go to the Geography and Science Panels for their final approval which it will do in the next few weeks, but I am assured, privately, that this time there will be no trouble. As soon as we get official confirmation of its acceptance, schools will be able to begin to organise courses for September 1973, to be examined in June 1975. There are likely to be two restrictions on the syllabus — (1) it may not be taken with geography at the same examination, and (2) it will be limited to schools in the Standing Panel although how flexible this will be remains to be seen.

Everything seems to be over now, bar the shouting, and the next job will be to encourage schools to develop their courses.

The acceptance by the Schools Council's ad hoc committee on environmental studies was confirmed by letter on 21 February 1973.[35] The syllabus was to be offered 'on an experimental basis for a period of five years'. The

The Negotiation of Environmental Studies

general tenor of the remarks is markedly different from those received from the science and geography sub-committees the year before. For instance: 'Commenting on the way in which assessment and moderation were to be carried out the plea was made that in the initial stages these operations should be as complex as time and money would allow.' In several cases previous exhortations were reversed: 'The suggestion was made that less emphasis should be put on the mathematical treatment of statistics. Instead students should be encouraged to use the laboratory approach in the recording of data.'

The schools taking the examination were now organised by the University Examinations Board into a 'consortium'. In the final list of schools submitted to Schools Council on 5 July 1973 there were 24 schools and colleges from Hertfordshire and 16 from other parts of the country.[36] These schools began the course in September 1973.

Fittingly, the last word in the negotiations with Schools Council came from the science and geography sub-committees. The assistant secretary had written on 18 February and 11 April to ask about the general availability of the syllabus. In reply, on 23 April, the Sixth Form Curriculum and Examinations Officer stated:[37]

> I put the question of general availability of this syllabus to our Science and Geography 'A' level committees and as you know they were most unhappy about its being generally available and wished me to say just this.
>
> In order to be as helpful as possible, I did, however, circulate the syllabus in its revised form to members of the ad hoc group and asked that they assess the syllabus pointing out where they felt it unsuitable.
>
> In the light of the comments received, the Chairman of the Geography 'A' level sub-committee has now been through the revised syllabus and made the comments which are attached ...

In many ways the Chairman's comments resemble unrepentant reiterations of the sub-committee's earlier position. This is made clear in the first comment: 'It was noted with approval that candidates could not take this examination together with Geography'. The major concerns were again

> about the breadth of coverage that may lead to a consequent superficiality of treatment. There was concern also about the continued inclusion of aspects that seem to have no direct relevance to the main objective of the syllabus and it was felt that certain parts of it could be reduced or omitted thereby achieving greater focus on the main aims of the syllabus.

The final point was again familiar:

> There is as yet no indication that universities would be prepared to accept a pass in this subject as an entry qualification for degree courses and in order to gain acceptance by the Council it may be necessary for

a statement to this effect to be a preface to the syllabus.

Sean Carson's recollection of the negotiations with Schools Council is inevitably somewhat bitter. Of the detail of the negotiations, he remembers disconcerting factors related to the 'architecture' of committee meetings, which he found intimidating:

> A big room ... right round the chairman. You're under fire in a sort of desk situation. They will have considered it already ... and will put their points to you and you can reply. The other people will support them. The whole thing lasts less than ... maybe an hour ... They're polite but hostile.

He felt that

> The Schools Council finally cracked through too much pressure ... What can you say? This was a school-based piece of work. This is what schools and teachers wanted — not what the hell the Council wanted ... This is the fundamental point about it that really got under my skin ... Curriculum development should not be done by Schools Council, then be imposed on schools. I'm not decrying them but it should be the other way round. This is the first piece of curriculum development from schools and teachers in the history of English education to reach Advanced Level. If the needs are there what right have Schools Council ... All right, tell us about standards, advise us about content and where we might be falling short on skills and abilities. All right ... but they're not right to put down the syllabus ...

In a letter to a leading advocate of environmental education. Carson confirmed these opinions:

> The problems are enormous, but although there has been considerable support from the universities the group [Hertfordshire Working Party] are not happy about the reaction of Schools Council, who have the final say in allowing schools to take the syllabus. In their opinion the fact that the Schools Council is organised in subject committees means that these committees jealously guard the preserves of their subject. There is no environmental studies committee, but after considerable pressure the Schools Council set up an Ad Hoc Environmental Studies Committee to vet the syllabus. Unfortunately this consists of the chairman or representatives of other subject committees, who are more concerned to obstruct rather than to encourage the development of a cross-disciplinary subject such as this is (it is true there is one environmentalist co-opted to the committee). By their constitution, the Schools Council's committees should have a majority of serving teachers ... This committee, however, has to the best of my knowledge no serving teachers at all and certainly none representing environmental studies as such although we have asked for this a number of times.[38]

Conclusion

The negotiations for the Hertfordshire 'A' level show clearly how the process was dominated at key points by the academic subject tradition. The comments made by the representative from the examining board strongly reiterate points raised at Offley. He wrote: 'The study must be a discipline — a coherent body of facts and concepts demanding an ordered mind for its appreciation.' The thorough renunciation of the pedagogic tradition was implicit in the statement that the syllabus should be a discipline and must be recognisable as such, 'even by the student'.

The dominance of the academic subject tradition was confirmed not only by ideology but by the organisational structure through which the Hertfordshire 'A' level had to pass before recommendation. The 'A' level, an avowedly interdisciplinary scheme, was perused at Schools Council by traditional subject committees who made comments which reflected a profound misunderstanding, or wilful disregard of the 'A' level's interdisciplinary intentions. Thus the science sub-committee found to its apparent amazement that 'the depth of treatment of the science in the syllabus was not comparable with that of similar topics in an "A" level physics or chemistry syllabus.' When an interdisciplinary syllabus combining academic, utilitarian and pedagogic intentions is appraised by such committees only in terms of the academic content of existing disciplines the judgment is merely self-fulfilling and serves to duplicate the traditional academic content of existing disciplines within the new subjects. This renders the subject committee's second line of defence similarly inevitable. Since 'irrelevant topics' have to be removed so that the main (academic) topics can be covered in single subject 'depth', it follows that the effect is 'to reveal how close the resulting syllabus would be to existing syllabuses'.

The intransigence of the subject sub-committees seems to have caused embarrassment inside the Schools Council and fury among those involved at the London Examining Board. The Schools Council responded by forming a new panel to sidetrack the subject committees, the Examination Board reacted by sending two well-known professors to argue the syllabus's case. Even then the subject committees responded with evident resistance, still being 'unhappy' at the syllabus being 'generally available'. As a result the syllabus was limited to a five-year experiment within schools in the Standing Panel and was not to be offered with geography. These conditions, which express the continuing power of the traditional academic subject committees, were enough to ensure the syllabus would not gain many recruits. Carsons's judgment of the Subject Committees reflected his disappointment. In 1974 he wrote: 'The fact that the Schools Council is organised in subject committees means that these committees jealously guard the preserves of their subject.' These committees he thought come from 'the descendants of the old Schools Council, which was called the Examination Council'. He saw them as 'the status quo, what they call "standards" and all that', and felt they were made up of the 'most conservative academics' in universities and the 'uncommitted and conservative elements among teachers'.

Certainly the judgment that the subject committees 'jealously guard the preserves of their subject' seems to be substantiated by the record of events, although this was true for the 'middle of the road' subject specialists as well as the conservative elements which Carson, probably unduly, draws attention to. The range of limitations put on the new 'A' level and especially the one-year delay must have substantially affected its progress. The 'A' level has in fact been adopted in only the small minority of schools associated with the Standing Panel, and they base the 'A' level within their old rural studies departments. In 1972 there were 28 schools preparing for the examination, 19 of them in Hertfordshire. By 1975 this had increased to 35 schools, 20 in Hertfordshire. Only in Hertfordshire has there been encouragement at county level to provide graded posts for heads of environmental studies departments.

Since 1975 the pattern of financial retrenchment has adversely affected the prospects even for those dedicated schools taking the 'A' level. This will have an influence on the Hertfordshire 'stronghold' as Carson recently noted: 'The economic cuts will no doubt affect the spread of the "A" level, as will the present attention given to a core curriculum. Already several schools and F.E. colleges have packed up because they could not get enough candidates ... and I hear that more plan to drop out.'[39] The recent examination board figures for June 1979 record that in secondary schools 168 candidates took the examination.[40] As one footnote, in 1979 Sean Carson retired. Without its leading advocate in Hertfordshire and the NAEE the 'A' level plainly faces a very difficult future. The prolonged 'filibuster' engaged in at examination board and School Council level together with the restrictions initially placed on who could take the 'A' level may have ultimately blocked the aspirations of environmental studies not only to broad-based acceptance but to actual survival at 'A' level. A final footnote: the Schools Council was itself closed down by the Conservative Government in 1983.

Notes

1. Hopkins to Carson, 4.1.71.
2. Letter to S. Carson, 7.1.71.
3. Letter to S. Carson, 9.1.71.
4. Memo 5048 SMC.BC/RS/01/2, S. Carson to S.T. Broad, 17.12.70.
5. Letter to S. Carson, 26.3.71.
6. Minutes of the meeting of the Standing Panel held at Offley Place on Monday 17 September, Hertfordshire File 07/2.7.
7. S.T. Broad to C.L. Mellowes, 13.12.71.
8. C.L. Mellowes to S.T. Broad, 4.1.72.
9. Letter to S.T. Broad, 14.12.70.
10. W.G. Bott to S. Carson, 15.11.71.
11. S. Carson to C.L. Mellowes, 21.10.71.
12. S. Carson to Miss B. Hopkins, 25.11.71.
13. C.L. Mellowes to C.T. Broad, 4.1.72.
14. S. Carson to all Heads, 27.7.71, Hertfordshire File SMC. BC/RW/01/2.

The Negotiation of Environmental Studies

15 S. Carson to Heads, undated, Hertfordshire File SMC. BC/RW/07/2.7.
16 Minutes of Standing Panel, Hertfordshire File 07.27, 27.8.71.
17 Minutes of Standing Panel, Hertfordshire File 07.2.7, 13.12.71.
18 S. Carson to all Heads, 3.1.72, Hertfordshire File SMC. BC/RW/07.2.7.
19 University of London School Examinations Department Ad Hoc Committee in Environmental Studies. Notes from first meeting on 19 January 1972.
20 Report to Standing Panel, Hertfordshire File, 8.2.72.
21 S. Carson to past applicants, undated, Hertfordshire File SMC.BC/RW/07.2.7.
22 S. Carson to Standing Panel, 7.6.72, Hertfordshire File, SMC.BC/CCR.
23 S.Carson to S.T. Broad (and Mr. Carter and Mr. Barr), 20.6.72, Hertfordshire File SMC.BC/MMD/07.2.7.
24 Members of Standing Panel, 21.6.72, Hertfordshire File, SMC.BC/MMD/07.2.7.
25 Letter, 13.7.72, Schools Council, Sr/L/G/191.
26 Interview, 30.10.75.
27 S. Carson to members of Standing Panel, 21.7.72, Hertfordshire File, SMC.BC/DP/07/27.
28 E.B. Champkin to S. Carson, 10.7.72.
29 S.T. Broad to R. Sibson, 14.6.72, Hertfordshire File, B/SMC.BC/CCK/07.2.2.
30 Minutes of Standing Panel, 19.6.72, Hertfordshire File, SMC.BC/MMD/07.2.7.
31 S. Carson to B. Hopkins, undated, Hertfordshire File, SMC.BC/CAS/07.2.
32 Schools Council letter to Mr. Stephanson, 13.7.72.
33 B. Hopkins to F.T. Naylor, University of London Examinations Department, 2.11.72, 21.2.73, GC/BMA/PC.
34 Letter Schools Council, 21.2.73, SS/L/G/191.
35 Letter Schools Council, 21.2.73, SS/L/G/191.
36 Appendix 2, List of Consortia submitted to Schools Council by London University 5 July 1973.
37 Schools Council, 23.4.74, SC/72)225(322/0/SS/1/G/191.
38 Letter, 2.7.74, Hertfordshire File SMC.BC/DS/07.2.
39 Letter from S. Carson, 5.11.76.
40 University of London, General Certificate of Education Examination Statistics (University of London, 1970).
41 See M. PLASKOW, *The Life and Death of the Schools Council* (Falmer Press, Lewes, 1985).

Part Four
Conclusions

12 Conclusions, Complexities and Conjectures

Conclusions

In summarising the research reported in this book it is perhaps appropriate to begin by re-examining our original hypotheses. Firstly, the book provides support for the initial hypothesis that subjects, far from being monolithic entities, are comprised of shifting sets of sub-groups, 'delicately held together under a common name at particular periods in history'.

Obviously this pattern would appear most strongly in subjects representing 'fields' rather than 'forms' of knowledge. The history of geography, for instance, shows that in the early stages the subject was made up of a variety of idiosyncratic local versions devised or taught by specialists from other disciplines. During the period in curriculum history that is the concern of this book, the battle over environmental education in the late sixties and early seventies, the sub-groups within geography can be seen 'pursuing different objectives in different manners'. So much so that in 1970 Professor Fisher wrote that 'The light-hearted prophecy I made in 1959 that we might soon expect to see the full 57 varieties of geography has been almost literally fulfilled, and my personal collection of different categories of geography that have seriously been put forward in professional literature now stands at well over half that number.' At about the same time, the President of the Geographical Association was warning that new geography created a problem because 'it leads towards subject fragmentation', so that ultimately 'the question must arise as to how much longer the subject can effectively be held together.' The potential danger of new versions of geography was touched on by Walford who argued that 'unity within the subject' was 'a basic requirement for the continued existence of the subject'.

The tendency to fragmentation in geography through the proliferation of sub-groups and sub-versions is a recurrent feature of the subject's history (see Chapters 5 and 10), and was echoed by the Norwood Report's fear about the 'expansiveness of geography'. At this earlier stage, 1943, they saw geography as 'The study of man and his environment from selected points of view' — a

184

Conclusions, Complexities and Conjectures

definition at that time leading to fears that through its expansiveness geography was becoming 'a "world citizenship" subject, with the citizens detached from their physical environment'. As a result at this time 'geography had become grievously out of balance; the geographical synthesis had been abandoned'. The problem was rapidly addressed and a decade later Garnett claimed that most school departments were headed by specialists so that 'The initial marked differences and contrasts in subject personality had been blurred or obliterated.'

The means by which the fragmentary sub-groups were monitored, controlled and periodically unified will be dealt with later. However, in the period of the battle over 'environmental education', two, or more accurately three, major sub-groups within the subject were actively concerned: the regional geographers, the field geographers and, the fastest-growing sub-group, the new geographers. The first two groups represented strong traditions within the subject and had large support among school geography teachers. The latter group was largely derived from new developments in the subject within the universities. As related in Chapter 10 the first two sub-groups were considerably more sympathetic to environmental initiatives than the new geographers. This was because the environmental lobby offered aid and sustenance to the field and regional geographers. Hence we find eminent regional geographers like Professor Bryan promoting conferences in environmental studies because this expressed more clearly than new geography 'his own life's work and ambitions as a geographer'. P.R. Thomas explained the affection for environmental approaches entirely in terms of the struggle for survival of the regional sub-group and a college lecturer in geography judged that the new crisis among geography sub-groups 'caused traditional (i.e. regional and field) geographers to flee into environmental studies' for a time. This flirtation proved a short-run phenomenon because of the overwhelming desire for fully-fledged academic status among all geographers; because new geography carried within it the seeds of this final acceptance; and because the activities of the Royal Geographical Society, the Geographical Association and the university schools of geography helped to direct and manage the change towards a new 'geographical synthesis' where once again the sub-groups were 'delicately held together'.

The pattern discerned among geography sub-groups in the period of environmental education's emergence is partly echoed when considering biology. Again the subject began with a variety of idiosyncratic versions and groupings devised and taught by specialists from other disciplines, in botany and zoology. By the 1960s biology had also developed a major sub-group whose concern with ecology and field biology bordered on the new environmental approaches. For a time this sub-group gained considerable momentum from initiatives like the Keele Conference which saw this version of biology as promoting environmental awareness.

Alongside field biology a sub-group promoting biology as a 'hard science' based in laboratories gained increasing adherents. The rise of molecular biology with the work of Crick and Watson in the 1950s gave a changed impetus to the work of this group. In the new universities opening up in the 1960s and in schools following the Nuffield project, this group managed to dominate the versions of biology that were accepted. Hence the 'hard science' version was embodied in the new laboratories that were then being built and in the departments that were set up.

So dominant did the 'hard science' group become in biology, that for a time the ecology and field biology sub-group developed defensive connections with environmental studies. As with geography a number of professors associated with the sub-group appeared at events or in publications sponsored by the National Association for Environmental Education. However, although only a sub-group on the defensive within biology, the field biologists secured a dominant position (along with the field geographers) in the field studies movement which grew rapidly as the 'environmental lobby' gained momentum. The field biology sub-group was thereby able to develop important new 'territory' inside the growth area of field studies which partly compensated for losing the battle for mainstream biology to the hard-science sub-group. By securing this leading role in field studies any permanent collusion with the rural studies groups promoting environmental studies was rendered both unnecessary and undesirable.

In both geography and biology the sub-groups allied to distinctive versions of the subject often gathered very different degrees of support according to whether school or university groups were being considered. Sometimes this reflected a time-lag effect as the new versions of the subject only slowly worked their way into the schools with new graduates taking up teaching posts in them. This was for instance the case in the battle between the regional geography and new geography groups: a long time after new geography was well established in universities, regional geography retained the allegiance of the majority of school teachers.

In rural studies the varying support according to whether one concentrates attention on school or university groups, was never an issue as the subject was not taught in universities. The sub-groups within rural studies therefore concentrated on particular versions of the subject within schools. In the period when environmental studies was launched, the two main groups were those who wanted to quickly attach rural studies to a new examination subject with some connections in the tertiary sector and those who wanted to retain traditional rural studies as a subject of outstanding appeal to the more 'practical' pupil. The battle over the name of the subject association and the new subject recorded in Chapter 8 was essentially a battle between these two sub-groups and ended in resounding victory for the first group.

The second hypothesis examined within the book relates to three major traditions discerned in school subjects: the academic, the utilitarian and the pedagogic. It was thought that an evolutionary profile of the school subjects under study would show a progressive movement away from stressing utilitarian and pedagogic versions of the subjects towards increasing promotion

Conclusions, Complexities and Conjectures

of more academic versions. We have already seen when discussing the nature of school subjects that sub-groups representing new geography, 'hard science' biology and examinable environmental studies, had come to be leading promoters of their subjects by the early 1970s. The process and rationale behind this outcome require fairly detailed understanding, representing as they do the culmination of a contest between a range of well-supported alternative definitions within each of the subjects.

The model of subject establishment towards a culminating 'academic' discipline was found to be closely applicable to both geography and biology. Once successfully promoted as an academic discipline the selection of the subject content is clearly considerably influenced 'by the judgment and practices of the specialist scholars in the field'. Subjects defined in this way, require a base of 'specialist scholars' working in universities to continue the definition and legitimation of disciplinary content.

The strategy for achieving this third stage received early recognition in geography. MacKinder's 1903 four-point plan provides an explicit statement of a subject aspiring to academic acceptance. The key to the strategy was the first point, the establishment of 'university Schools of Geographers where Geographers can be made'. To complete the control of the subject's identity, geography teaching and examination construction was to be placed in the hands only of teachers 'made' in the universities. The mediation between university and school was in geography, placed in the hands of the Geographical Association. The Association, founded in 1893, played a central role in the promotion of geography, since in its early days the subject was confined to idiosyncratic schools-based versions and had obtained a tentative place in only a few universities.

The close linkage between the growth in schools and the establishment of the subject elicits regular comment in the pages of 'Geography'. The President of the Geographical Association paid homage to 'fruits of inspired teaching' which have led to the 'intense and remarkable upsurge in the demand to read our subject in the universities'. The result has been 'the recognition of our subject's status among university disciplines ... together with the costly provision made available for its study'. The latter point shows the direct link between academic status and resources in our educational system: the triumph of the 'academic' tradition over the utilitarian and pedagogic traditions which played such a prominent part in geography's early days is to be partly understood in these terms.

The establishment of 'discipline' status inside the universities which had been so systematically pursued since MacKinder's 1903 proclamation provided a range of material improvements in the subject's place within schools. In 1954 Honeybone could claim that 'at long last, geography is forcing its complete acceptance as a major discipline in universities, and that geographers are welcomed in to commerce, industry and the professions, because they are well educated men and women.' Acceptance as a major vocational qualification finally meant that geography could claim its place in educating the most able children, and thereby become established as a well-funded department inside schools staffed with trained specialists on graded posts. By 1967 Marchant noted that geography was 'at last attaining to intellectual respectability in the academic streams of our secondary schools'. But he noted that the battle was not quite over and gave the instances where the subject was still undesirably taught as a 'less able' option. With the launching of new geography the subject finally attained total acceptance as an academic discipline in universities and as a fully-fledged 'A' level subject in all schools, with the resources and 'costly provisions' which such status attracts.

In biology the evolution of the subject is distinguishable from geography because from the beginning there was an associated and well-established university base in the form of botany and zoology. For this reason and also because from the outset the subject benefited from the side-effects of the influential science lobby the task of subject promotion never totally resembled geography's 'beginning from scratch'. Biology's task was more to present a case for inclusion within the, by then well-established (and consequently well-resourced) science area of the curriculum. This task was often pursued within the overall arena of the Science Masters Association, who from the 1930s onwards played an active role in promoting biology. In 1936 an influential biology sub-committee was formed to promote biology syllabuses, and many articles in the Association's 'School Science Review' argued the case for biology's recognition as an examination subject for the able student. The problem was best voiced by the Ministry of Education in 1960: 'The place which is occupied by advanced biological studies in schools . . . is unfortunately that of vocational training rather than of an instrument of education.' The need to be seen as an 'instrument of education' meant that the promoters of the subject needed to move away from the utilitarian towards more academic versions — only then could an 'A' level subject command sufficient pupil numbers to warrant 'departmental' status and resources in schools. Hence we find the common theme being advocated: biology must be treated 'as a comprehensive discipline in its own right'.

In the final stages in the promotion of biology as an 'academic discipline', the two main initiatives stressed the subject as a hard science needing 'laboratories and equipment'. In the rapidly expanding universities it was this version of the subject which was widely introduced, thereby establishing the academic discipline base; likewise the Nuffield Biology Project for Schools centred on 'a crusade in terms of equipment and laboratory staff'. With the new generation of biology graduates trained in this hard science at universities, the establishment of the subject as a fully fledged academic 'O' and 'A' level subject was finally assured.

Unlike biology and geography, rural studies remained for generations a low-status enclave, stressing highly utilitarian or pedagogic values. Confirming Ben-David and Collins' contention, the move to a change in intellectual and occupational identity came at the time when the subject was faced with survival problems in a reorganising educational system stressing the academic

Conclusions, Complexities and Conjectures

tradition. The pervasive influence of this tradition can clearly be seen in the following quote: 'The lack of a clear definition of an area of study as a discipline has often been a difficulty for local authorities in deciding what facilities to provide ... It has been one of the reasons for the fact that no "A" level course in rural studies exists at present.' The Schools Council working party in 1968 confirmed this with the broad hint that there was the 'need for a scholarly discipline'.

With no tertiary base and hence no specialist scholars involved, except random specialists from other disciplines, the Hertfordshire strategy was to develop an 'A' level syllabus from groups working in the secondary schools. This offered the promise of tailoring 'a course to the needs of the kids' and not to 'have to meet the requirements of other people's courses'. But the crucial reason in terms of the subject teachers' material self interest was often frankly admitted: 'I think we had got to prove that environmental studies was something that the most able of students could achieve and do something with ... if you started off there all the expertise and finance that you put into it will benefit the rest — your teaching ratio goes up etc. and everyone else benefits.' Likewise, another leading advocate admitted that they had seen that 'the only way to make progress was to get in on the examination racket ... the exam. was essential, otherwise you couldn't be equal with any other subject. Another thing was that comprehensive education was coming in. Once that came in, no teacher who didn't teach in the fifth or sixth form was going to count for twopence. So you had to have an "A" level for teachers to aim at'. The survival rationale was always a strong factor: 'I just thought if you're outside this you've had it in schools: it was already happening in some schools where a [rural studies] teacher was leaving, they didn't fill the place, because they gave it to someone in the examination set up.' And beyond survival the reasons for an academic 'A' level were simply 'because if you didn't you wouldn't get any money, any status, any intelligent kids'.

The 'A' level in environmental studies is a recognition of the factors defining the aspirations and efforts of these rural studies teachers. What has subsequently been denied is not that environmental studies represents a valid area of curriculum, but that it can thereby claim to be an academic discipline. Such claims it would appear are best validated through university scholarship and without a university base status passage to acceptance as an academic subject has been denied. As Carson noted at Offley, new contenders for academic status are often placed in an impossible situation since they are asked 'What evidence have you that universities would accept this sort of "A" level?' On making enquiries to universities, the reply was 'show us the successful candidates and we will tell you'. A chicken and egg situation!

The third hypothesis in the book follows on from consideration of the patterns of internal evolution in school subjects to investigate the role that the pursuit of academic status plays in the relationship between subjects. In continuity with the second hypothesis we would expect established subjects to defend their own academic status at the same time as denying such status to any new subject contenders, particularly in the battle over new 'A' level examinations.

In the struggle to launch environmental studies as an 'A' level subject, the geographers' reaction strongly, and the biologists' much more mildly, followed the lines of the hypothesis. MacKinder, the founding father of geography's road to academic establishment, would have understood this. In explaining the geologists' opposition to geography he saw their fear of the new subject making 'inroads in their classes' as the reason for their response and noted that 'even scientific folk are human, and such ideas must be taken into account'. In continuity with this the geographers strongly opposed social studies, an integrated package that predated environmental studies by several decades. The geographers, it was claimed, 'saw the new proposals as a threat to the integrity and status of their own subject'.

The growth of environmental studies was treated in similar manner by the geographers. The discussion of the Executive Committee of the Geographical Association show precious little concern with the intellectual or epistemological arguments for environmental studies. The discussion focused on 'the threat to geography involved in the growth of environmental studies'. Indeed, when the possibility of a dialogue with environmental studies teachers was suggested 'some members felt that to do so would be tantamount to admitting the validity of environmental studies'. Carson's reminiscences of his talk to the Geographers' Conference tends to confirm the spirit in which new contenders for academic status were viewed if they were at all adjacent to geography's broad and shifting frontiers. The response was patently directed towards territorial defence — not academic dialogue. The most overt plea for defence rather than dialogue came in the Presidential Address to the Geographical Association in 1973. Mr. A.D. Nicholls laid great emphasis on the 'practical realities' for 'practising teachers'. 'With constant pressure on teaching time, headmasters are ever searching for new space into which additional prestige subjects can be fitted, and the total loss of teaching time to environmental subjects may be considerable.' Beyond these practical fears about the material interests of geography teachers, environmental studies evoked a particularly emotional response among geographers because of its proximity to geography's continuing identity crisis. Nicholls provides an unusually frank admission of the need for territorial defence being placed above any intellectual imperatives:

> Ten years ago almost to the day and from this platform, Professor Kirk said 'modern geography was created by scholars, trained in other disciplines, asking themselves geographical questions and moving inwards in a community of problems; it could die by a reversal of the process whereby trained geographers moved outwards in a fragmentation of interests seeking solutions to non-geographical problems.' Might not this be prophetic for us today? Could it not all too soon prove disastrous if the trained teachers of geography moved outwards as teachers of environmental studies seeking solutions to non-geographical problems?

Conclusions, Complexities and Conjectures

The fears which geographers expressed so strongly and emotionally about the emergence of environmental studies were not shared to the same degree by biologists. As we have seen only the field biology sub-group was threatened and they managed to expand into the growing territory of field studies. However in the negotiations at Schools Council the science sub-committee, which included a number of biologists, joined forces with the geographers in their opposition to the environmental studies 'A' level. In both sub-committees 'concern was expressed at the heavy overlap between this syllabus and syllabuses in both geography and biology.' The alleged overlap was coupled with exhortations to remove those 'irrelevant topics' not related to geography and biology. The result was the self-fulfilling indictment 'if irrelevant topics were envisaged as removed, the effect would be to reveal how close the resulting syllabus would be to existing syllabuses in geography'.

The judgment quoted by Carson that the Schools Council sub-committees 'jealously guarded the preserves of their subject' was confirmed by the comments from the geography sub-committee when the decision on the 'A' level was finally announced. They were plainly fairly satisfied with their territorial defence and 'noted with approval that candidates could not take this examination together with geography'. A final point was added that there was 'as yet no indication that universities would be prepared to accept a pass in this subject as an entry qualification for degree courses'. The restriction on environmental studies being offered with geography, together with the initial restriction to a five-year period and to only the Standing Panel schools, placed enormous practical obstacles in the way of any widespread adoption of the subject. By ensuring these obstacles faced the new subject in the early years when the momentum for change was strong, the opponents to the new subject effectively extinguished the chances of its establishment in the school curriculum.

The book provides evidence of three subject communities in evolution and in conflict. It shows a range of conflicting sub-groups within the subjects and that these often concentrated around the three major 'traditions' discerned. The pursuit of material self-interest ultimately ensured that the sub-groups attached to the academic tradition came to dominate the subjects. This was because the flow of resources, finance and recognition of 'departmental' territory and needs has been linked especially to 'scholarly disciplines' that can be taught to 'able' students. We have seen how the promotion of a subject as a scholarly discipline was systematically co-ordinated by subject associations and by groups of university scholars. Once the academic base of the scholarly discipline was established within the universities the dominance of the academic tradition within the subject was firmly wedded to the vested interests of the university scholars. The university departments then played a major role in defining the subject (though often with significant time-lags) through their control of the training of the school teachers of the subjects; through their role in the major influential committees, such as the Schools Council Subject Sub-Committees, and within examination boards; and through their role in decisions about which 'A' levels are acceptable qualifications for their degree courses. The subject communities and associations representing the school teachers accepted, indeed at points conspired to produce, this dominant university role because the teacher's career was so crucially dependent on the flow of resources linked to the subject's continuing status as a scholarly discipline for 'O' and 'A' level students.

In the battle to promote environmental studies we have seen how the rural studies advocates were barred from following the route to academic establishment. With no prospects of a scholarly discipline of environmental studies coming from the universities, the Hertfordshire advocates were forced into attempting to define 'a discipline' from the school level. This allowed opponents of the new subject, whilst broadly conceding its value to young and less able students, consistently to deny that it could be viewed as in any sense 'a scholarly discipline'. With a few exceptions school subject groups and university scholars of geography and, to a much lesser extent, biology, stuck firmly to the defence of subject integrity epitomised in Nicholls' speech to the Geographical Association. Considerations of an intellectual sort were thereby subordinated to the defence of subject territory which ensured that scholars and teachers of the subject would continue to benefit in terms of resources and career prospects.

Complexities

In summarising the studies undertaken in this book it is important to examine whether the patterns of control discerned add up to 'domination' by powerful high-status groups as has been contended by M.F.D. Young *et al* in 'Knowledge and Control'.[1] The role of dominant groups shows perhaps most clearly in the victory of the academic tradition in the early years of the twentieth century. This victory was embodied in the influential 1904 Regulations and most significantly, the 1917 School Certificate. Once established, however, these curricular patterns (and their associated financial and resource implications) were retained and defended in a much more complex way and by a wider range of agencies. It is therefore correct to assume that initially the rules for high-status knowledge reflected the values of dominant interest groups at that time. But it is quite another issue to assume that this is inevitably still the case or that it is dominant interest groups themselves who actively defend high-status curricula. It is perhaps useful to distinguish between domination and structure and mechanism and mediation.

By focusing on subjects in evolution and the conflict over 'A' level examinable knowledge the studies in this book clearly indicate the central role played by school subject groups. The most powerful of these agencies are those school subject groups promoting the academic tradition. Successfully in geography and biology, but unsuccessfully in environmental studies, these groups demanded the creation of an academic discipline based in the univer-

Conclusions, Complexities and Conjectures

sities. The 'academic tradition' sub-groups act in this way because of the legacy of curricular, financial and resource structures inherited from the early twentieth century (when dominant interests were actively defended). Because of this legacy able pupils and academic examinations are linked and consequently resources, graded posts and career prospects are maximised for those who can claim academic status for their subject.

The evidence indicates not so much domination by dominant forces as solicitous surrender by subordinate groups. Far from teacher socialisation in dominant institutions being the major factor creating the patterns discerned it was much more considerations of teachers' material self-interest in their working lives. Since the misconception is purveyed by sociologists who exhort us 'to understand the teacher's real world', they should really know better. High-status knowledge gains its school subject adherents and aspirants less through the control of the curricula which socialise than through well-established connection with patterns of resource allocation and the associated work and career prospects these ensure. The studies in this book argue that we must replace crude notions of domination with patterns of control in which subordinate groups can be seen actively at work.

But if domination by the universities fails to characterise a complex process correctly, the activities of 'academic' sub-groups in school subjects clearly do conspire to increase the control over the definition and direction of subjects by university scholars. The conflict then focuses on the alliance between the universities and the academic school subject groups and those other subject traditions, notably the pedagogic and utilitarian, which often express internal school needs. In this continuing contest the academic tradition holds all the cards. Reid contended that within schools a

> major area of conflict is ... between the external constraints arising from university requirements and the internal pressures which have their origin in the school. Schools are, however, poorly equipped to resist university pressures. To a large extent they allow the legitimacy of university demands, and have evolved an authority structure which is linked to them ... They are, by contrast much better placed to deal with internal demands, and have a variety of means at their disposal for clamping down pressures which conflict with the responses stimulated by university influence.[2]

The existence of academic, pedagogic and utilitarian traditions in school curricula has its origins in the separate sectors of the educational system which preceded the comprehensive era. The continuance of these traditions and the continuing dominance of the academic tradition bear testimony that the fundamental structures of curriculum have withstood comprehensive reorganisation. As in the tripartite system so in the comprehensive system, academic subjects for able pupils are accorded the highest status and resources. The triple alliance between academic subjects, academic examinations and able pupils ensures that comprehensive schools provide similar patterns of curriculum differentiation to previous school systems. For the teachers who have to cater for all kinds of pupils this concentration on a particular kind of pupil and a particular kind of educational success poses the same dilemma voiced by the rural studies teacher in response to the promotion of academic examinations in his subject; 'Once again we can see the unwanted children of lower intelligence being made servants of the juggernaut of documented evidence, the inflated examination.' This conclusion summarises the continuing choice:

> True education is not for every man the scrap of paper he leaves school with. Dare we as teachers admit this? Dare we risk our existence by forcibly expressing our views on this? While we pause after the first phase of our acceptance are we to rely on exams for all to prove ourselves worthy of the kindly eye of the state?[3]

The deep structures of curriculum differentiation are historically linked to different educational sectors, to different social class clienteles and occupational destinations, to different status hierarchies. Differentiated curricula and the social structure are matched on very firm foundations: by building on these foundations comprehensive reorganisation has had to accept the antecedent structures which contradict its stated ideal.

Conjectures and Current Debates

Beyond the specific conclusions and complexities noted there seems some evidence for suggesting that the embryonic theoretical framework of this study provides a useful starting point for other studies. Such studies, by extending the focus and the analysis, will test the generalisability of some of the broader conjectures contained herein.

In considering future studies it is perhaps worth re-examining the limitations of the current study. Firstly the research focused on the promotion of only three school subjects and the detailed negotiation of just one examination syllabus. Clearly then studies are needed to elucidate further the detailed connection between promotional strategies and 'rhetorics' and the 'reality' of the curriculum content and classroom practice. There are a number of levels within the educational system each with varying degrees of autonomy. Hence whilst we have seen that the academic tradition is most commonly used to promote school subjects far more detailed study is required of how far this promotional activity affects the 'small print' of curriculum content, both within the range of examination syllabuses, in the associated but by no means directly related examination question papers and within school classrooms. Above all, in following up the studies in this book, such detailed investigation of the relationships between these complex arenas and levels of curriculum negotiation must be undertaken. With rural studies we know that promotional rhetoric substantially affected the curriculum 'reality' of a new 'A' level

Conclusions, Complexities and Conjectures

syllabus in environmental studies. We also know that this process of translation from rhetoric to notional reality was deeply contested by groups inside and outside the subject community.

Secondly the study was specific to a particular period of time in the evolution of three school subjects. The concern was with subjects during the period when academic establishment was the primary pursuit. For geography and biology we have not investigated whether the patterns were modified after broad-based acceptance and for rural and environmental studies this remains a hypothetical issue. Certainly there seem grounds for believing that the periods when subjects pursue and achieve academic establishment (with the associated status and resources) may be times of particular concern with, and acceptance of, unity within the subject. Nonetheless comparison between the subjects studied illuminates a number of important and suggestive differences. The description of the evolution of geography, for instance, shows that here was a subject with a profound and continuing identity problem. In such a situation a firm alliance was moulded between academic geographers and the school teachers who were organised in the Geographical Association. The case of biology, however, shows that other subjects do not necessarily share to the same degree either the geographers' paranoia nor their strong sense of alliance in the face of new contenders for academic status. It is therefore possible that subjects with higher academic self-confidence would not act in the starkly territorial manner discerned in this book.

In considering other subjects, classics would seem to offer an interesting study of an 'academic' subject representing powerful interest groups which has nonetheless declined. Perhaps this indicates a paradox: that although subjects must grow out of their utilitarian origins to become 'academic' they need to continue to be generally accepted as 'vocational' qualifications in order to survive. Likewise once accepted as 'academic' subjects, they must continue to appeal at a pedagogic level to learners. Hence in the era following academic acceptance such issues sometimes receive considerable attention as was the case with the Nuffield projects in science subjects.

Some subjects have successfully followed the route to academic acceptance so hopefully pursued by environmental studies advocates but still encountered barriers to total entry into the secondary school curriculum. For instance politics, economics and psychology have developed as disciplines in universities and been broadly accepted at 'A' level yet are still rarely found in the general curriculum of secondary schools. This could again illustrate the negative territorial power of school subject groups.

Whilst certain aspects of curriculum control and 'territorial' response therefore seem complex and difficult to generalise about, other issues are less so. The general nature of subject communities and the pervasive direction of subject definition and promotion can be clearly discerned. Subject sub-groups (and versions of the subject) may focus on issues such as pedagogy and utility as well as intellectual worth. In the long run, however, the sub-group and the version of the subject which is likely to be successfully promoted is that most in harmony with the material interests of the subject's scholars and teachers. Given the link between knowledge status and resources, subjects can best promote themselves through the academic tradition.

The legacy of differentiated status for the academic, utilitarian and pedagogic traditions draws on tripartite patterns of educational organisation. In considering curriculum change it is vital to understand that this tripartite hierarchy of status has been reproduced not only in the respective parity of esteem *between* different categories of subject but also to kinds of knowledge *within* subjects. At the latter level, scrutiny of 'what counts as education' is necessary. For instance, much of the debate about teaching craft and technology as a way of reinstating practical curricula has missed this point. Given the status patterns discerned one might expect that even if technology were to achieve high status and acceptance the version which would 'count as education' would be academic and theoretical and therefore stand in contradiction to more practical objectives. The differentiated status of academic, utilitarian and pedagogic traditions pervades both the type of subject and the internal form of each subject. Curriculum reform needs to address both of these levels of differentiation.

The differentiated status of the three curriculum traditions discerned and their link with the way finance and resources are allocated and pursued is confirmed by a number of studies already undertaken.

Banks' study of parity and prestige in the English secondary system ends by stressing 'the persistence of the academic tradition' throughout that period of the system's existence.[4] Hanson's study of art education and Dodd's work on technology offer similar evidence.[5] The latter speaking of the Crowther Report noted that they had shown how 'an alternative route to knowledge' lay through practical subjects which did not destroy the intellectual curiosity of the pupil in the way associated with the 'academic' ones. Dodd notes that 'the problems lay in the status of practical subjects by tradition second class ... Discussion on its own is insufficient and it requires legitimization by those institutions who hold this facility (universities, examination boards, employers and society at large).[6]

As we have seen, the legitimising institutions together with established and indeed aspiring subject groups share the vested interest in the belief that 'a scholarly discipline' is needed if a school subject is to be granted high status. The stranglehold of the academic tradition has seldom been seriously threatened by its overwhelming need to shun 'practical utility'. The theme which Dodd points to was just as common when the 1904 regulations were established. A contemporary noted that the school curriculum was 'subordinated to that literary instruction which makes for academic culture, but is of no practical utility, to the classes for whom the local authorities should principally cater.'[7]

The dominance of the academic tradition is patently supported by the major vested interest groups within education and the broader society. Yet the very need for academic subjects to escape from the allegations of 'practical utility' may yet lead to irresistible pressure for change in the period of economic malaise which we currently confront.

Conclusions, Complexities and Conjectures

The studies in this book show clearly that school subject groups tend to move progressively away from concerns with 'utilitarian' or 'relevant' knowledge. High status in the secondary school curriculum is reserved for abstract theoretical knowledge divorced from the working world of industry and the everyday world of the learner. As we have seen this is not coincidental. The very price of success in achieving high status in an academic discipline is to renounce practical connections and relevance to the personal and to the industrial and commercial world. To these high-status academic subjects go the main resources in our educational system: the better qualified teachers, the favourable sixth form ratios and the pupils that are deemed most able. Hence the main flow of financial support in our school curriculum is invested in those subjects which have promoted themselves as academic disciplines. In short the politics of curriculum, the process of becoming a high-status subject and discipline, ensures that most money in education is invested in subjects which stress their divorce from practical and social relevance. As a formula for economic decline such a pattern of curriculum negotiation and investment could hardly be perfected.

Economic dysfunctionality is, however, not the only indictment. As a formula for the education of a mass clientele the system is similarly diametrical in its misdirection. We have noted that Layton sees the academic tradition as the prelude to disenchantment for most pupils. Hemmings has likewise inveighed against the 'academic illusion', which he says 'bristles with anti-educational consequences'.[8] There is indeed a good deal of evidence that the academic subject is profoundly unsuitable for many pupils, specifically those from working-class backgrounds. For instance Witkin has shown how working-class pupils actively prefer and choose lessons they can relate to the everyday world.[9] The teachers of such pupils constantly confirm this view; their mode 3 CSE syllabuses devised for these pupils provide documentary proof that they judge practical relevance to be in the best motivational material for 'average' and 'below average' pupils. Unfortunately school teachers have career interests as well as classroom interests. As we have seen the former may subjugate the latter: the pursuit of academic status whilst providing the gateway to career success for the teacher simultaneously inaugurates the prelude to disenchantment for his pupils.

In summary the politics of the school curriculum and the predominance of the academic tradition present the dominant interests in our society with a classic contradiction. The academic subject curriculum undoubtedly works smoothly to educate a meritocratic minority although meanwhile disenchanting the majority. The social class status quo is thereby preserved along with the requisite ratio of managers and workers. But the price to be paid is high for managers as well as workers. The academic curriculum renounces practical relevance and industrial and technical skills. To succeed in the educational system our future managers must share this renunciation. Not surprisingly our educational priorities are reflected in our management teams: most are high-status academic specialists, few have technical or engineering skills. A recent report, after noting the large numbers of engineers among West German and French managers, commented that in England 'too few of our graduates go into industry and those that do tend to have an irrelevant educational discipline.'[10]

Given the academic curriculum to which managers owe their success this industrial illiteracy is an inevitable corollary. The academic curriculum produces industrial illiteracy for its successful minority, pervasive disenchantment for the majority. How much longer such an educational recipe will be deemed suitable in a country on the verge of economic crisis and social conflict remains to be seen.

Notes

1 M.F.D. YOUNG (Ed.), *Knowledge and Control* (Collier Macmillan, 1971).
2 W.A. REID, *Sixth Form*, p. 106.
3 P.L. QUANT, see Chapter 6, p. 163.
4 See BANKS, *Parity and Prestige*.
5 See Chapter 1, notes 12 and 13.
6 DODD, *Design and Technology*.
7 Quoted in BANKS, *op. cit.*, p. 41.
8 J. HEMMINGS *The Betrayal of Youth* (London, Marion Boyars, 1980).
9 B.W. WITKIN 'Social class influence on the amount and type of positive evaluation of school lessons', *Sociology*, Vol. 5, No. 2, 1971.
10 *The Times*, 14 February 1978.

Appendices

APPENDIX 1

Analysis of the Questionnaire circulated to Schools — February 1952

Grammar and Technical Schools
With the exception of one boys' and one girls' grammar school and one boys' technical school, the questionnaire form was returned marked 'subjects not taught'.

Secondary Schools
65 replies were received, but at two schools the subjects were not taught. In most schools the subject taught is gardening.

Replies received:

Division		Boys	Girls	Mixed	Total
			Schools		
1.	Penge	–	–	–	–
2.	Chislehurst	3	1	1	5
3.	North-west Kent	5	1	1	7
4.	Thames–side	1	2	1	4
5.	West Kent	4	1	2	7
6.	Maidstone	1	–	5	6
7.	Medway	4	1	1	6
8.	North-east Kent	3	3	1	7
9.	St. Augustine	–	–	1	1
10.	Ashford	1	2	2	5
11.	Folkestone	1	1	–	2
12.	Dover	1	1	4	6
13.	Thanet	1°	1	1	3
14.	Beckenham	–	1°	–	1
15.	Bexley	2	–	–	2
16.	Bromley	1	1	–	1
17.	Gillingham	1	–	–	1
	Totals	29	16	20	65

°Subjects not taught

Appendices

			Boys	Girls	Schools Mixed	Total
A.	(a)	No. on roll	13,194	6,099	8,502	27,295
	(b)	No. receiving gardening instruction	7,791	3,079	4,028	14,898

In mixed schools chiefly boys take gardening.

   (c)   In 7 boys' schools gardening taken by all pupils
         In 2 girls' schools gardening taken by all pupils
         In 1 mixed school gardening taken by all pupils
         In 25 schools gardening taken by boys in 1st year
         In 3 schools gardening taken by girls in 1st year
         In 34 schools gardening taken by boys in 2nd year
         In 9 schools gardening taken by girls in 2nd year
         In most schools gardening taken in 3rd and 4th years.
         In 17 schools gardening not taken by 'A' forms.
         In almost every school gardening taken by retarded pupils.

   (d)   Time allowed for gardening in many schools is two periods per week, varying from 35–40–45 minutes per period. In some schools half a day is devoted to gardening. In other schools time allowed varies according to 1st, 2nd, 3rd or 4th years, and whether A, B or C forms.

   (e)   In 18 schools there were over 20 in a boys' gardening class.
         In 3 schools there were over 20 in a girls' gardening class.

   (f)   18 pupils from 7 schools attend part-time courses in agriculture or horticulture at Technical Institutes.

B. (a)   34 schools (26 boys' and mixed, 8 girls') have a classroom allocated for the teaching of gardening or rural science.

   (b)   12 schools have this room suitably equipped.

   (c)   Where there is no room allocated indoor lessons are taken in:

room shared with another class	air-raid shelter
any available classroom	corridors
Headmaster's room	cloakrooms
any odd corner	dining hall
Assembly Hall	canteen
showers, dressing room	

   (d)   No. of schools possessing:

	Adequate	Inadequate
54 tool sheds	32	22
43 storage spaces	22	21
40 frames	30	10
15 potting sheds	13	2
4 Dutch lights	3	1
14 cloches	11	3
17 glass houses, cold	14	3
4 glass houses, heated	3	1
32 lawn mowers	25	7

Appendices

        3 other machinery — auto culto, rotary hoe, Howard Bantam
        At 8 schools tool shed built by pupils
        At 14 schools frames built by pupils
        At 3 school potting shed built by pupils
        At 2 schools Dutch lights built by pupils
        At 8 schools cold glasshouse built by pupils
        In many cases school funds have been used for purchase of garden equipment.
        In many cases the lawn mower possessed by schools is for the use of ground staff only.

C. (a) 15 schools have over 2 acres of land cultivated by children
        17 schools have 1–2 acres of land cultivated by children
        31 schools have up to 1 acre of land cultivated by children
   (b) At 17 schools decorative grounds maintained by children
        At 17 schools decorative grounds maintained by groundstaff
        At all others part maintained by pupils, part by groundstaff

D. (a) Livestock:
        9 schools keep poultry   13 schools keep rabbits
        5 schools keep pigs   19 schools keep bees
        2 schools keep goats   1 school keeps a calf
   (b) At 3 schools there is adequate accommodation for the storage and preparation of food.

E. 10 schools have services of groundstaff, gardener-stockman or gardener-groundsman at weekends and holidays. Other schools dependent upon enthusiasm of teacher and pupils.

F. (a) 139 teachers take gardening in the 63 schools that have completed the questionnaire.
   (b) 114 teachers are qualified or have experience
        In 21 schools Gardening/Rural Science taken by one teacher
        In 26 schools Gardening/Rural Science taken by two teachers
        In 7 schools Gardening/Rural Science taken by three teachers
        In 5 schools Gardening/Rural Science taken by four teachers
        In 4 schools Gardening/Rural Science taken by five teachers
        In 39 schools all teachers taking these subjects are qualified or have experience.
        In 18 schools not all teachers are qualified or have experience.
        In 6 schools there are more teachers on the staff who are qualified or who have experience than are required for these subjects.

G. 21 schools would welcome a course on the keeping of livestock.

H. 19 schools operate scheme 'B'; the rest scheme 'A'.

Observations
Chiefly (a) Holiday difficulties — need of assistance
        (b) Lack of accommodation

Appendices

APPENDIX 2

Extracts from Rural Studies. A Survey of facilities in Secondary Schools in England and Wales, July 1962, (London, Pergamon).

The Actual Figures Returned and the Adjusted Totals
Figures were received from 54 counties, 3 County Boroughs (and the L.C.C., whose figures were not included).
(a) Adjustment made for those 5 English and 3 Welsh Counties that did not make any Returns.
       3088   Schools in counties surveyed.
        360   Schools in counties to be assessed.
       1387   Positive replies.
        163   Replies to be expected from assessed counties.
(b) Adjustment for those schools teaching Rural Studies but which did not return their Questionnaires.

In 19 cases, where returns were collated by County Education Officers, the number failing to return their forms was very small. Where we were able to check it was around 5%.

In 38 cases where returns were made to our own collators the number failing to return their forms varied from 10% to 15% in those counties where the figure was known to us from other sources. An average of 12.5% was taken.

On the assumption that the numbers of schools in each collator's area averaged out equally an adjustment of 10% or 155 schools was therefore made to the total on this account.
(c) Schools in the L.C.C. and County Boroughs not covered by this Survey.

As we have no evidence for the County Boroughs no figure is included for the small number of schools that we know teach Rural Studies in these authorities.

Final Adjustment
The totals of (a) and (b) above is 318 schools, or 23% of the 1387 schools returning figures. This gives the total number of schools teaching Rural Studies as 1387 + 318 = 1705. An adjustment of +23% has therefore been made to assess the figures for the whole of England and Wales. Throughout the report the actual returns are given in parenthesis. A further adjustment has had to be made in a few cases where a particular collator was unable to offer figures for a section of the survey. A note has been made in each such case.

It will be seen from the tables that Rural Studies is taught in 1705 schools (1387) in England and Wales (plus a small number in the County Boroughs not included, and the L.C.C.). 1601 (1302) of these schools are Secondary Modern Schools, 63 (52) are Grammar or Technical Schools, 27 (22) are Comprehensive Schools and 14 (11) are other types of Secondary schools.

These figures represent 41.35% of the Secondary Modern Schools (and

Appendices

equivalents) in England and Wales and 5.4% of the selective secondary schools (Grammar, Technical multilateral) and Comprehensive Schools.

Comments by the Committee of the Association are included wherever appropriate.

The report was approved by the National Executive Committee on 11th December 1962 which enabled us to publish this survey in its present from.

S. McB. Carson
Hon. Policy Secretary
A.H. Mallinson
Chairman

1st January 1963

Table I
Schools teaching Rural Studies

Grammar, Comprehensive and other types of schools.
Secondary Modern Schools and equivalents

Gram.	Sec.		
1948	3782	a.	Total in England and Wales
827	2261	b.	Total in Counties covered (not 3 County Boroughs)
82	278	c.	Schools in Assessed Counties
909	2539		Total b and c.
84	1302		Positive replies received.
+20	+299		Adjustment + 23%
104	1601		Final Adjusted Figure
5.4%	41.35%		% of schools in England and Wales teaching Rural Studies
11.4%	63%		% of schools in the areas covered by the Rural Studies Survey

Table IV

Classes taking Rural Studies total 11,444 (9304), of these

101 (82)	are in Grammar streams
2560(2081)	in bright streams in Secondary Modern Schools
5128(4169)	are in average streams
3655(2972)	are in below average streams

Classes divided into years

2550(2073)	1st year
3082(2506)	2nd year
3121(2537)	3rd year
2551(2074)	4th year
140 (114)	5th year

Size of classes

7843(6376)	20 and under
2490(2024)	20–30
1082 (879)	30–40
31 (25)	Over 40

Appendices

Table VII

Staff engaged in Rural Studies
The equivalent of 1726 (1403) full time teachers are engaged in rural studies.
Women	Men	
49 (40)	153(124)	Grammar and other selective schools
330(268)	1194(971)	Secondary Modern and equivalent schools

To maintain this figure in the schools one-twentieth have to be replaced annually, to allow for normal retirement, that is 86 new full time teachers.

Table IX

Qualifications
Women	Men	
75(61)	316(257)	Graduates
11 (9)	57 (46)	Holders of National Diplomas
13.4%	20.5%	National average in Secondary Modern Schools
18.6%	16.4%	Average amongst rural studies teachers (including Grammar schools)
21.3%	19.3%	If we include as equivalents the qualifications of N.D.A., N.D.H.

The R.H.S. Teacher's Diploma in School Gardening has been recognized as a valuable if restricted qualification, obtained after three years part time study, and demanding both a good level of craftsmanship and a good appreciation of the educational uses of school gardens. It is held by 11 (9) women and 169 (137) men.

Rural Studies was taken as a supplementary third year course (before the introduction of general three year training courses) by 23 (19) women and 166 (135) men, and as a main college subject in a two year course by 68 (55) women and 438 (356) men.

We may regard all the above as having some specialist rural studies qualifications.

Women	Men
188(153)	1146(931)

The number of qualified teachers with no special rural studies training:

Women	Men
214(175)	780(638)

Shown as percentages:

Women	Men	Total	
46.6%	59.5%	57.2%	Specialist
53.4%	40.5%	42.8%	Non-specialist training

Notes
Training Colleges
There are five teachers' Training Colleges where students receive a three-year

Appendices

course to equip them as specialist teachers of rural studies. These colleges are:
 City of Bath Training College
 Culham College, Abingdon
 Trinity College, Carmarthen
 St. John's College, York
 City of Worcester Training College

In some other colleges students are given the opportunity to take rural studies as a main subject or as one of a group of subjects in a three-year course for secondary or primary school teaching. It is difficult to know exactly which colleges are concerned.

Advisory Staff
The following authorities (according to our information) include amongst their staff Advisers or Organizers of Rural Studies (under a variety of titles).

Bedfordshire	Northumberland
Buckinghamshire	Nottinghamshire
Cumberland & Westmorland	Oxfordshire
Cheshire	Somerset
Dorset	Staffordshire
Essex	East Sussex
Hertfordshire	East Suffolk
Kent	Warwickshire
Leicestershire	Worcestershire
Lindsey, Lincs	East Riding, Yorks
Manchester	West Riding, Yorks
Middlesex	

Appendices

APPENDIX 3

Shephalbury County Secondary School, First Draft
Rural Studies — 'A' level

The aim of the syllabus is to provide the scientific understanding required to enable the candidate to understand man's control of his environment, and the conflicts which arise as a result of expanding requirements and the consequent needs for conservation. The syllabus relates Biology to Physics and Chemistry which it is assumed will have been studied previously or concurrently.

Part I   Two theory papers of 3 hours each will be set.

Physical Environment:
>The earth as a planet: the seasons, cyclical variations; sun spots. Effect of these on plant and animal life. Air masses: zones of change; pressures and winds, circulation of winds. Local factors affecting weather.
>Effect of weather on plants and animals.
>Structure and constitution of the earth.
>Strata —
>Geomorphology and landform; geology and landscape.
>Outline study of the geology of Great Britain with more detailed study of a selected area.
>Recognition of common rocks and minerals.
>Soil as the source of life on land; soil and plant relationships.
>Processes of soil formation illustrated by selected area.
>Soil structures and chemistry.
>Soil fertility.
>Study of soil profiles in the field and recognition of soil types occurring locally.
>Elementary study of atomic fall-out, mutations, irridation.

Living Environment:
>The plant and animal kingdoms,
>Structure and function in plants and animals — stress to be laid on the ecological relationship.
>The specialised structures of crops and livestock in relation to their agricultural uses: cereals, roots, potatoes, brassicas, legumes; cow, horse, sheep, hen, pig, wood pigeon and pheasant or grouse.
>Pests and Diseases, emphasising their ecological relationships examples to be drawn from each of the following groups:
>Diseases — virus, bacterial, fungal.
>Pests — insects, spiders, nematoids, molluscs, birds, also squirrel, fox and rabbit.

Appendices

Weeds — characters and importance of:
Control of pests, diseases and weeds by chemical and biological methods. Effects on environment. Inheritance of characteristics of structure and function in plants and animals. Genetics in plant and animal breeding.
Physiology — metabolism of plants and animals of economic importance. Enzyme systems. Carbohydrates, proteins and lipids in relation to the nutrition and energy needs of plants and animals.

Part II The submission for examination of a record of original research including fieldwork.

Select one:
1. A study to include historical, geographical, social, economic and industrial development of a rural settlement.
2. Development of the English Garden.
3. Development of Agriculture in the 18th Century to the present day.
4. Study of an English Country Craft.
5. The landscaping of New Towns.
6. The Common Market.
   A General Study of European Farming Methods and comparison with our own.
7. Biological Field Study — The candidate must satisfy the examiners that he has attended an approved course in Field Studies and submit original course account and Field Book.

Appendices

APPENDIX 4

Draft 16.12.70

'A' Level Environmental Studies Syllabus — Hertfordshire Working Party

The syllabus is constructed in two equally weighted sections:-
  Section 1 — Processes and Systems of the Natural Environment and the limits of the Resources Base
  Section 2 — Man's Impact on the Environment

In Section 1 the theme of 'energy flow' is followed from solar energy to animal life through six sub-sections. We would like sub-section 1.6. to be approached through field-work in a defined habitat.

Section 2 is related to the theme of 'land use' and involve two studies both in the field.

Problems
Section 1 should not account for more than 50% of the course time (or under 200 hours) and for this reason will require further pruning of any material which is not strictly relevant to the theme. Your suggestions on this would be valuable.

Section 2 — We have been advised that examination boards will have great difficulty in accepting the submission of so much fieldwork because of the problem of examining it reliably. So many universities have stressed the need to develop good attitudes in students that we are loath to rewrite this section in a form that can be presented as a theoretical study even if this were possible. We would like to know whether you support this attitude or not.

Draft as at 10.12.70
'A' Level Syllabus
Environmental Studies

Section 1 — Processes and Systems of the Natural Environment and the limits of the Resources Base

Content only
The theme of 'energy flow' is followed from solar energy to animal life.
Sub sections — 1.1. The Solar System
               1.2. The Atmosphere
               1.3. The Hydrosphere
               1.4. The Lithosphere
               1.5. The Biosphere
               1.6. Ecology

Appendices

1.1. *The Solar System*
Brief outline — sun, moon, earth.
Revolution, rotation, orbits, gravity.
Sun as a source of energy — nature, size and distance, temperature, nature and motion of sun spots, effect on climate.
The nature of fission and fusion.
The Transport of Energy
Radiation — radio waves, light, X-rays, cosmic rays.

Earth Reception of Energy
Reflection, refraction, absorbtion (see °Rigg, Chap. 4.3. for detail)

1.2. *The Atmosphere*
Atmospheric layers and filtering effects
Ionosphere — presence of Allen's layer
Troposphere — presence (see Kay Gresswell 'Physical Geography' page 36 etseq.) Physical Composition, insolation.
Insolation — definition, seasonal and diurnal variations over the world.
Principles of the solar energy circulation between the earth and the atmosphere (see diagram page 57 of Scientific American or Rigg)
Air Masses — The general circulation of the atmosphere. Pressure systems, wind, jet streams and upper air movements (see Rigg)
Weather Systems and Climate — depressions and anti-cyclones, location, occurrence, formation. Cloud formation and types. Climate — recognise main divisions. Weather phenomena — humidity, super saturation, condensation.

1.3. *The Hydrosphere*
The Water Cycle (see Scientific American page 102)
Distribution of world's water, precipitation — variation in distribution (link to climate), evaporation. Ocean currents, circulation. River discharge. Groundwater. Tides and the moon and sun. (Link hydro-electric power).
(Link with biosphere)

1.4. *The Lithosphere*
World distribution of natural resources
Basic classification of rocks — minerals, fossil fuels. Sedimentary, igneous, metamorphic, structure of rocks — relation of fossil fuels to geological and evolutionary periods, ability to interpret topographical and geological maps. An outline of the appreciation of effect of geology on soil types. Appreciation of geological time scale, earth movements — continental drift, folding, faulting, vulcanicity, effects on biological distribution and on mineral resources.
The Soil
Weathering and the formation of soil — physical and chemical processes of weathering, soil constituents, particles, sizes and structure, mechanical analysis and chemical reactions (pHO, colloids and electrolysis, pore space, water

---

°Rigg J., A Textbook on Environmental Study, Constable, 1968.

Appendices

movement and capillary action. Soil water — mineral salts and trace elements. Soil atmosphere — Presence of O_2, CO_2, N. Soil profile — horizons, leaching, flushing, podzols, hardpans.
(Link with biosphere)

1.5. *The Biosphere*
The origin and nature of life — organisation of organic matter by energy.
The biosphere — definition — area occupied by living things.
Realms — The Sea
           The Land
           The Air
The physical and chemical factors that affect life in these realms.
Problems for life forms in the major realms.
Conception of Circulation of Elements
Oxygen cycle
Nitrogen cycle
Methods of obtaining energy — autotrophic and heterotrophic nutrition
Autotrophic Nutrition of Green Plants
Photosynthesis as a means of conversion of light energy to chemical energy. Chloroplasts, pigments — light and dark reactions energy transfer, translocation, transpiration, mineral uptake, outline of synthesis of carbohydrate, fats and proteins.
Structure and Adaptation of Plants in relation to these functions
Single cell plants. Root, tissues, leaf, stem of higher plants (to cell structure level).

Heterotrophic Nutrition of other Organisms — animals, fungi, viruses, bacteria.
Food as a source of energy, carbohydrates, fats, proteins, vitamins and minerals. The absorbtion, conversion and use of food energy by plants and animals.
   Adaptations of heterotrophic organisms for obtaining food.

1.6. *The Ecosystem*
This section will be studied through fieldwork in a defined habitat chosen from the following list (List A).
List A.
Habitats for study — The habitat selected should be one suitable for the wide and unspecialised study

   1. A wood
   2. A grass field
   3. A pond
   4. A hedge and a verge
   5. An area of waste land

The Ecosystem — pyramid of numbers and energy
Food webs — Examples and principles
Gross and net primary production — (plant respiration)

Appendices

Primary consumption — herbivores
Secondary consumption — carnivores
Decomposers and parasites
Energy flow through food webs.
Community and population ecology
Ecology of Population
Factors affecting distribution and dispersion of plants and animals.
Reproduction — sexual, asexual, vegetative propagation
Parthenogenesis
Reproductive capacity
Reproduction at cellular level, cell division.
Mitosis and Meiosis
The chromosomes and heredity in outline, diploid, haploid, and polyploid conditions.
Mutation and variability, natural selection.
Diversity of organisms. (Outline classifications).
Dispersions and migrations.
Climatic and edaphic factors.
> Air temperature, rainfall, wind velocity and direction, aspect situation, height above sea level, pH, soil type, minerals, humus, water content, structure of soil (related to Section 1.5.)

Biotic factors
> Food, predators and competitors

Population growth and its natural regulation
Ecology of Communities
Colonisations — substrates by plants and animals
Successional processes in ecosystems — seres
sub-seres and climax communities.
Brief account of major biomes and of world vegetation types.

Section 2 — Man's Impact on the Environment
Content Only
The theme of 'land use' is followed in this section
Sub sections — 1. Man as an animal
               2. Man's economic activities
               3. Man's social activities

2.1. *Man as an Animal*
    2.1.1. An appreciation of his basic needs, and how these are supplied in different societies today (peasant, industrial ...)
    2.1.2. An outline of human social structure
    2.1.3. An outline of the development of the use of tools and effects on human society of such inventions as iron axes, the plough, steam power; electricity; recent developments in mechanism, and the computer.
    2.1.4. Land use pressures — causes and effects in historical perspective (particularly in relation to Europe)

Appendices

2.2. *Man's economic activities*

The student will choose a topic from the following list (List B.) The study will be concerned *ONLY* with the impact of this example of man's economic activity on the total environment. In each case an operational establishment will be studied in detail in the field and related to a real pattern of the industry and extended to the national and world situation. Each study dealt with under the following headings.

- 2.2.1. Resource base — limitations — rate of exploitation. Site, geology, relief.
- 2.2.2. Sources of energy used — dispersal of energy.
- 2.2.3. Historical development where this has an effect on the present situation and implications for the future.
- 2.2.4. Methods of management of the operational establishment and relation to general practices in the industry — ownership, capital source, labour and organisation, degree and effect of mechanisation.
- 2.2.5. External influences — communications, markets, technological change, legislation affecting the establishment or industry.
- 2.2.6. Identification of environmental conflicts.
- 2.2.7. Planning — management of resources, objectives and management policies of establishment (or industry); planning objectives and legislation of national and local government affecting the establishment (or industry) determination of how the identified conflicts might be resolved by planning.
- 2.2.8. Impact on the environment — an assessment of the impact of the establishment (or industry) on the total environment, its effect on soils, wild life, human social conditions — pollution problems and conservation.

List B. Standard industrial classification

- 001 Agriculture or horticulture
- 002 Forestry
- 003 Fishing
- 101 Coal Mining
- 102 Stone or slate quarrying and mining
- 103 (1) Chalk, limestone and cement manufacturing
  - (2) Clay extraction and pottery or brick manufacturing
  - (3) Sand and gravel extraction
- 104 Petroleum and natural gas
- 105 Other mining and quarrying
- 311 Iron and steel
- 500 Construction
- 601 Gas
- 602 Electricity
- 603 Water

Appendices

The candidate will make his choice and agree them with the Board at an early stage.

2.3. *Man's Social Activities*

The student will choose one defined community from the following list (List C) and will study this in detail in the field. The study will be concerned ONLY with land use, the conflicting claims on land and resources and their resolution, problems of pollution and conservation. The study will be dealt with under the following headings:
1. Residing — description of the housing, density, organisation, services provided, relation to standards set by local government.
2. Social institutions — description of provision for education, health welfare and social services, the arts, amusement, sport, leisure and recreation, public administration, religious; political.
2.1. Retail trade — shopping facilities.
3. Industry — description, classified broadly as in Standard Industrial structure, mapping of land use.
4. Infra structure — transport, communications, including pipelines, transmission of energy.
5. Environmental open space (largely non productive open spaces) common, SSSI, nature reserves.
6. Vacant unused land, building or channels.
7. Identification of environmental conflicts.
8. Planning — study of local or national planning legislation and policies affecting the community, recognition of attempts to resolve the environmental conflicts identified.
Investigation and evaluation of differing viewpoints.
9. Impact on the environment — an assessment of the impact of the community on the total environment — land use, effects on wild life, soils, pollution problems and conservation.

List C. Communities

Note: The Community must be a unit with defined boundaries, the size should be such as to provide the candidate with the opportunities to study it in full in the field and to use available source material for statistics and maps.
1. Village or town
2. Rural area
3. Neighbourhood
4. Redevelopment area
5. Town centre
6. National park
7. Country park

Appendices

APPENDIX 5

Draft as at 14.1.71

Environmental Studies — Content only (Total — 360 hours)

Section 1 — *Processes and Systems of the Natural Environment and the limits of the Resources Base (100 hours)*
The theme of 'energy flow' is followed from solar energy to animal life.
Sub sections — 1.1. The Solar System (10 hours)
                1.2. The Atmosphere and Hydrosphere (35 hours)
                1.3. The Lithosphere (20 hours)
                1.4. The Biosphere (35 hours)

1.1. *The Solar System*
Brief outline — sun, moon, earth
Revolution, rotation, orbits, gravity
    1.1.1. *Sun as a source of energy*
Nature size and distance, temperature, effect on climate.
The nature of fission and fusion.
The laws of thermodynamics
    1.1.2. *The Transport of Energy*
The nature of solar radiation
    1.1.3. *Earth Reception of Energy*
Reflection, refraction, absorbtion

1.2. *The Atmosphere and Hydrosphere*
    1.2.1. *Atmospheric layers and filtering effects*
Ionosphere — presence of Allen's layer
Troposhere — presence, Physical and Chemical
composition, insolation, tropopause.
    1.2.2. *Insolation*
Definition, seasonal and diurnal variations over the world, temperature variations.
Principles of the solar energy circulation between the earth and the atmosphere.
    1.2.3. *Weather systems, air masses and climate*
Evaporation, humidity, condensation, super saturation, precipitation, air stability and instability.
The general circulation of the atmosphere.
Pressure systems, winds, depressions and anti-cyclones, location, occurrence, formation.
Recognition of main climatic regions.
    1.2.4. *Water cycle*
Distribution and redistribution of the world's water.

1.3. The Lithosphere

Earth structure, internal energy flow and its relation to continental drift, associated effects on biological distribution, earth quakes, vulcanicity, folding, mountain building.

Formation of igneous sedimentary and metomorphic rocks, mineral resources. Appreciation of geological time scale.

Weathering processes leading to soil formation.

Land forms — aspect, drainage and slopes as features of land surfaces and soils, classification of soil types.

1.3.1. The Soil

Weathering and the formation of soil — physical and chemical processes of weathering, soil constituents, particles, sizes and structure, mechanical anaylsis and chemical reactions (pHO, colloids and electrolysis.

Soil water — mineral salts and trace elements.

Soil atmosphere — presence of O_2, CO_2, N. Living constituents of the soil (link with biosphere).

Soil profile — horizons, leaching, flushing, podzols, hardpans.

Soil management — fertility, conservation and erosion — salination, irrigation.

1.4. The Biosphere

The origin and nature of life — organisation of organic matter by energy. The biosphere — definition — area occupied by living things. The physical and chemical factors that determine the forms of life in the sea, the land, the air. Problems for life forms in these major realms.

1.4.1 Conception of the circulation of elements

Taking as examples:
- Oxygen cycle
- Carbon cycle
- Nitrogen cycle

Link with Lithosphere, Atmosphere

1.4.2. Methods of obtaining energy

The significance of autotrophic and heterotrophic nutrition. The conversion and use of food energy by plants and animals. Adaptations of heterotrophic organisms for obtaining food. Food as a source of energy, carbohydrates, fats, proteins, vitamins and minerals.

Section 2 — The Ecosystem (80 hours)

The student will carry out an ecological study in the field in connection with this section to illustrate the theme of energy flow, through the following topics:

2.1. Climatic and edaphic factors

Air and ground temperatures, rainfall, humidity, wind velocity and direction, aspect, situation, drainage, height above sea level.

Rock type, soil type, minerals, humus, pH, water content, structure of soil

Appendices

2.2. *Pyramids of numbers*
Populations.
Energy flow and nutritional relationships.

2.3. *Food Webs*
Examples and principles.
Gross and net primary production — (plant respiration).
Primary consumption — herbivores.
Secondary consumption — carnivores.
Decomposers and parasites.
Energy flow through food webs.

2.4. *Ecology of Population*
Factors affecting distribution and dispersion of plants and animals.

2.5. *Population, control mechanisms*
Reproductive capacity.
Diversity of organisms.
Dispersions and migrations.
Population growth and its natural regulation.
Competition, food and predators.

2.6. *Ecology of Communities*
Colonisations — substrates by plants and animals.
Successional processes in ecosystems — seres, sub-seres and biotic or climatic climax communities.

Section 3 — The interaction of Man and the Environment (60 hours)

3.1. *Man as a heterotrophic organism* (2 hours)
The satisfaction of his fundamental requirements (food, oxygen, warmth, shelter).
Reproductive capacity and historical outline of world population figures.

3.2. *Evolution of modern man as a tool using, rational creature* (16 hours)
Man's domestication of plants and animals.
Man's acquisition of energy exploiting techniques and their applications to his evolutionary success as illustrated by:
  (i) simple tools
  (ii) power sources (animal, wind and water, fire, internal combustion engines, electricity, atomic fuels)
Man's use of mineral resources.

3.3. *Human Societies* (10 hours)
A consideration of hunter, pastoral, agricultural and industrial societies.

3.4. *Pressures on the environment* (26 hours)
The identification of pressures; conservation and management policies.

Appendices

The relationship between available land, efficiency of use and population levels.
The effects of urbanisation.
The conflict with the natural environment — deforestation, effects of monoculture, erosion and salination.
The use of chemical fertilisers and pesticides and the pollution of land, air, water, by pesticides, sewage effluents, garbage, industrial pollutants.
Conservation measures.

3.5. *Special Study* (10 hours)
A study in depth to illustrate relevant parts of sections 3.1. to 3.4. chosen from one of the following topics:
    Coal mining
    Social and economic influence of the potato
    Development of modern strains of wheat/rice/maize
    Mechanisation of modern agriculture
    Effects of modern fishing techniques
    A world conservation problem
    World population

Section 4 — Environmental Conflicts and Planning — A Field Study (120 hours)
The student will select one topic from the list shown at the end of this section and submit it to the board for agreement at an early stage of the course. The study will be concerned with the interaction of man and the natural or built environment, i.e.
    (a) The influence of man's social and economic activities on land use, natural resources, townscape and buildings, and the balance of living things.
    (b) The effect of change in the natural environment and the ecosystem on man's activities.

The student will be expected to draw on material from all previous sections where this is relevant to the aim of the study. Similarly the headings listed below are to be regarded as a check list and should be brought into the study only where relevant to its objectives.

The emphasis should be on the inter-relationship of all processes and activities outlined in the syllabus rather than the internal workings of these activities where they are not inter-related with each other.

The study will also be a test of the student's familiarity with the techniques of analysis and evaluation, his grasp of content, handling of sources, ability in communication and presentation.
(Various criteria to be listed in teaching notes later.)

4.1. *Resources Base*
Limitations — rate of exploitation.
Situation, geological formations, relief and soil.

Appendices

4.2. *Sources of fuel and energy*

4.3. *Historical Development*
Where this has had an effect on the present situation. To include factors affecting siting of the community and of the enterprise in the community.

4.4. *Man's social and economic activities and their expression in physical form as listed below:*

    4.4.1. *Residing*
Description of the housing, density, household structure, layout and relation to design standards.

    4.4.2. *Social facilities and activities*
Provision for education, social services, leisure and recreation, shopping facilities.

    4.4.3. *Industry*
(use the classification list in the Standard Industrial Classification as a guide to the type of industrial activities carried on in the community).

        4.4.3.1. *Methods of Management*
Methods of management of the enterprise and relation to general practices in the industry — ownership, capital sources, labour and organisation, degree and effect of technological change.

        4.4.3.2. *External Influences*
Communications, markets, technological change, legislation affecting the establishment or industry.

4.5. *Environmental Conflicts*
Identification and assessment.

4.6. *Planning*
Management of resources, objectives and management policies adopted by the community or individual enterprises; determination of whether the identified conflicts have been, or need be, resolved by planning and intervention and how this has been or might be achieved.

    4.6.1 Particularise on the management policies that have been or might be introduced e.g. land zoning, control of siting of buildings, structures, roads, traffic control, land management, landscaping, aesthetic considerations; design of buildings and structures in relation to their surroundings, conservation policies.

4.7. *Effects*
Effect of this management policy on the environment and consideration of any further conflicts which might arise.

APPENDIX 6

University of London Schools Examination Department Hertfordshire Mode Two Syllabus in Environmental Studies at the Advanced Level

The aims and objectives of the two-year course are that the student should be better able:

(a) to identify and appreciate the inter-relationships of the physical and biological factors that make up the environment;

(b) to analyse and synthesize the ways in which man may control his environmental impact and to recognise the values by which such control may be guided;

(c) to evaluate and establish a set of personal values towards the place of man in the environment, and the impact of human society on its biophysical surroundings.

The working party felt that these objectives would be better advanced by placing the student in a situation of personal involvement, and contributing to his own studies as far as possible through extensive activities in the field and laboratory rather than by too much authoritative teaching.

The examination will consist of two theory papers and the teacher's assessment of project and field work which will be weighted as follows:

Paper 1 (3 hours) 30% } 70%
Paper 2 (3 hours) 40% }
Teacher assessment of field work of Section 2   10% } 30%
Teacher assessment of field study of Section 4 20% }

Both theory papers will be externally set and examined.

Paper 1 will normally consist of approximately 10–12 compulsory questions of a structured format with the answers to be written or drawn in spaces provided in the question booklets. The questions will cover Sections 1, 2 and 3 of the syllabus and will be of approximately equal weighting and the mark allocation will be indicated on the paper. The questions will be designed to test the candidate's familiarity with the contents of Section 1, 2 and 3, his ability to interpret and apply relevant data, draw conclusions, state them effectively, recognise the limitations of data and draw accurate inferences.

Candidates should be able to present their answers in diagrammatic and graphical form where appropriate.

Paper 2 will consist of approximately ten questions. Candidates may answer question one and any other three questions. The mark allocation will be higher for question one than each of the other three questions and will be indicated on the question paper. Candidates will be allowed to bring in their field notes for reference purposes.

Paper 2 is designed to test the candidate's ability:

(a) to apply knowledge of basic principles gained in syllabus Sections 1, 2 and 3;

Appendices

    (b) to use skills developed in the field study in Section 4;
    (c) to integrate the above in the analysis of new situations.

The field work of Section 2 and the field study of Section 4 will be assessed by the teacher (an outline scheme for marking the field study is included at the end of the syllabus) and externally moderated. Further information on the moderation of the field study is given in the appendices to the syllabus.

Candidates must satisfy the examiners in both the field and theory work.

The syllabus is designed and teaching notes have been drawn up to fit a situation where the course is taken by a single teacher (eight periods a week) or by two teachers (four periods a week each). A suggested timetable is included in the appendices. Training courses for sixth-form teachers of environmental studies in Hertfordshire have been held and further courses for teachers, to cover the background of different parts of the syllabus, are planned.

Synopsis of Syllabus Headings and Appendices

1.1 *The Source of Energy: The Solar System*
    1.1.1. Sun as a source of energy

1.2. *The Transport of Energy: Radiation*
    1.2.1. Atmospheric layers and filtering effects
    1.2.2. Insolation
    1.2.3. Weather systems, air masses and climate
    1.2.4. Water cycle

1.3. *The Lithosphere*
    1.3.1. Energy and mineral resources in the lithosphere
    1.3.2. The soil

1.4. *Transference of Energy in the Biosphere*
    1.4.1. Conception of the circulation of elements
    1.4.2. Methods of obtaining energy

Section Two: The Ecosystem

2.1. *Climatic and Edaphic Factors*
2.2. *Pyramids of Numbers and Energy*
2.3. *Food Webs*
2.4. *Ecology of Population*
2.5. *Population Control Mechanisms*
2.6. *Ecology of Communities*

Section Three: Man as an Organism within the Environment

3.1. *The Satisfaction of his Fundamental Requirements (Food, Oxygen, Warmth, Shelter)*

Appendices

3.2 *The Evolution of Modern Man as a Tool-Using Rational Creature*
3.2.1   A consideration of the effects on the environment of hunter, pastoral and agricultural societies.
   3.2.2. Man's domestication of plants and animals.
   3.2.3. Man's use of mineral resources.
   3.2.4. Man's acquisition of energy exploiting techniques and their application to his evolutionary success.
   3.2.5. Urbanization and industrialization.

3.3 *Pressures on the Environment*
   3.3.1. Population structure.
   3.3.2. The pressure of urban growth.
   3.3.3. Environmental problems in rural areas in an age of industrialism.
   3.3.4. Further illustrations of pressure on the environment resulting in degradiation.

Section Four: Environmental Conflicts and Planning: A Field Study

4.1. *The Enterprise*
   4.1.1. Identification.
   4.1.2. Historical development.
   4.1.3. Management and its aims.
   4.1.4. External influences.
   4.1.5. Resources base

4.2. *Associated Needs*
   4.2.1. Housing and special facilities.
   4.2.2. Infrastructure

4.3. *Identification of Environmental Effects*

4.4. *Evaluation and Planning*
   4.4.1. Evaluation of impacts.
   4.4.2. Planning.
   4.4.3. Judgements.

Appendices
A. List of enterprises for submission as a field study (Section Four)
B. Assessment of Field Study in Section Four
C. Timetabling Suggestions
D. Specimen Questions

Note: An extensive resources list of over 800 references and an equipment list are available but have not been included with these appendices.

Index

academic achievement 32
academic subjects 5, 10, 24–36
  examinations and 25, 29–31
  see also school subjects
academic tradition 3, 24–9, 143, 179, 186–7, 189, 191
  subjects' promotion through 24–5, 187, 193, 194, 196
  unsuitability of 197–8
Agricultural Education Committee 86
'A' level exams
  academic nature of 24–5, 29–30
  functions of 141
  see also environmental studies 'A' level
Alexander, D. 124, 127
Allen, A.B. 90
Arnold, M. 85
Ashby, Margaret 89
Associated Examining Board
  environmental studies and 112, 120, 132–4, 135–6, 139–40, 159
Association of Teachers of Gardening and Rural Subjects 94

bacteriology 42
Ball, S. 30, 32
Banks, D. 9, 26, 196
Beloe Committee 19, 30
Ben-David, T. and Collins, R. 10, 128, 188
Bernal, J.D. 47, 52
Bernstein, B. 5–6, 7
Best, R. 137
Biological Sciences Curriculum Study 51
biologists
  see biology teachers

biology 41–54, 116–17, 185–6, 188, 195
  after 1945 46–7
  as hard science 50–4, 116, 163, 185–6, 188
  before 1945 44–6
  environmental studies and 52, 158–63, 185–6, 188
  fieldwork in 46, 47, 53, 160–3
  growth of 41, 42–3, 45, 188
  molecular 51, 52, 185–6
  status of 52–4, 116–17, 159
  syllabuses 42, 52
  teaching methods 48, 51
  university 47, 53, 116
  utilitarian value of 42, 44, 52–3
  see also fieldwork; Nuffield biology
'Biology and Human Affairs' 45
biology teachers 43, 47
  environmental studies and 142
  field studies and 111–12
  training of 54
Blache, V. de la 63
Blyth, W. 26
Board of Education 15, 63
  rural studies and 85, 86, 88, 90
botany 43, 47, 50, 51, 53
Bourdieu, P. 6–7
Bowden, Lord 160
British Association for the Advancement of Science 44, 46, 48, 60
British Social Hygiene Council 44–5, 46
Broad, S.T. 95, 136–40 passim, 168, 169, 174
Brown, E.M. 170, 176
Brown, R. 62
Brunthes, J. 58
Bryan, P.W. 150, 185

Bryce Commission (1895) 14, 15, 16, 59, 85
Bucher, R. 24–5
Butterfield, G.R. 77
Byrne, E. 31, 79

Caesar, A.A.L. 65
Callaghan, J. 22
Cambridge University
  geography at 62, 64–5, 76
  in nineteenth century 8
Campbell, F. 7
Carey, W.M. 61
Carson, S. 89–99 passim, 113–24 passim, 132–43 passim, 152, 156–7, 158, 161–3 166–80 passim, 189–91
Cerovsky, J. 108
Certificate of Secondary Education
  see CSE
Chelmsford Report (1932) 44
child-centred education 28, 36
Chorley, R. 70
Chorley, R. and Haggett, P. 71, 72, 76
Christian, G. 111
classical education 7–8, 14, 15, 27, 195
colleges of education
  see teacher training
Collins, R.
  see Ben-David and Collins
Colton, R. 91, 93, 94, 98, 127
Committee for Environmental Conservation 109
Committee of the Secondary Schools Examination Council (1943) 44
Committee to enquire into the position of Natural Science ... (1918) 44
comprehensive reorganization 4, 19–22, 116, 169, 194
  rural studies and 117–18, 126
comprehensive schools vi, 4, 19–22, 24
  exams in 19, 32–3
conflict 36
  between subjects 3, 192
  political nature of 31
  whitin subjects 25, 128
Confucian education 7
Cons, G.J. 67, 68
Conservation Corps (now British Trust for Conservation Volunteers) 109
Conservation Society 109
Consultative Committee on Secondary Education (1938) 44
Council for Environmental Education 110, 111, 112, 121, 168

Council for Nature 109
Countesthorpe School vii
'Countryside in 1970' conference 110, 112, 160
craft
  see design education
Crick and Watson, 52, 186
Crowther Report (1959) 196
CSE 19, 29–30, 96–100
  in geography 69
  in rural studies 97–9, 100, 119, 122, 128
curriculum
  content vi, 192
  lack of change in vi–vii, 17
  traditions 25–34, 124–5
curriculum differentiation 4, 17, 22, 194
  ability and 32–3
curriculum reform movement 20–1, 116, 196

David, T. 64
Davie, G.E. 8
Debenham, F. 64
DES 19, 68, 69, 70, 75, 111, 137
design education 8–9
Dimbleby, G.W. 176
Dodd, T. 8, 196
dominant groups 6, 11, 192–3, 197–8
Douglas, Dr. 138, 151
Dove, W.A. 96
Dowdeswell, W.H. 48, 49, 50, 52, 159
Dyer, K.F. 50–1, 53
Dyos, H.J. 112

ecological studies 47, 49–50
  university courses 50
  see also fieldword and field studies
Edinburgh, Duke of 109–10
Edmundson, G. 84
Education Act 1870 13, 14
Education Act 1902 14–15, 59
Education Act 1944 18, 29, 90
'Education of the Adolescent' report (1926) 44
Edwin, M.H. 137, 142
Eggleston, J. 5, 8, 9, 27
elementary schools 14–15, 26
  geography in 59, 67
  rural studies in 84
eleven-plus exam 19
elite education 7–8, 14
environment, the 105–13
  government departments for 105, 110–11

Index

ideas about 105-6
UN conference on (1972) 106-7
environmental studies 50, 105-13, 166-80, 192
  as a discipline 122-7, 139-40, 167, 179
  at school level 107, 112-13, 124
  European conference on (1971) 107-8
  genesis of 116-29
  geography and 57, 149-55, 156-7
  international background to 106-9
  International Meeting (Nevada) 107, 111
  Keele conference (1965) 50, 110, 111, 118, 119, 160-2 passim
  local promotion of 111-12
  national background to 109-11
  new departments of 113, 123
  university course 123, 177
environmental studies 'A' level 36, 111, 131-43, 166-80, 189, 208-9, 210-19, 220-2
  accepted 176
  assessment of 166-7
  fieldwork in 135, 166, 167
  Hertfordshire's proposals 134-43, 151-2, 166-80 passim, 208-9, 220-2
  overlap with other subjects 132, 133-4, 138-9, 173-4, 191
  requirements 141
  school based initiatives 131-6, 178, 192
  scientists' views of 172-4
Everson, J. 68-9, 70
examination boards
  environmental studies and 120-1, 132, 158, 166-9
  geography and 69
  introduction of biology by 42-3, 44
  power of 15-17
  see also specific boards
examinations
  academic subjects and 25, 29-31
  in biology 44, 45-6, 53
  in comprehensive schools 32, 189
  in geography 59, 60, 68, 74, 75
  in rural and environmental studies 96-8, 112, 124-9
  secondary modern schools and 18-19, 30
  status and 24, 33-4, 36, 189-90

Faraday 41
Field Studies Association 162
Field Studies Council 68, 160, 162

fieldwork and field studies 48-9, 118, 159, 160-3, 186, 191
  in biology 46-7, 48-50, 53, 111, 161-3
  in environmental studies 110, 162-3
  in geography 66-70, 79, 118, 150, 157, 161-3
Fisher, C.A. 72-3, 150, 184
Fitzgerald, B.P. 76
Fladmark, J.D. 137
Froebel, F. 84
Fuller, A.J. 91
Fyson, A. 152

gardening 85-6, 87, 127,199-201
  see also rural studies
Garnett, A. 62, 65, 71-2, 77, 78, 79, 149, 185
GCE 29
  in secondary moderns 18-19
  see also examinations
Geddes, Sir P. 67
Geikie, A. 68
General Certificate of Education
  see GCE
geographers
  see geography teachers
Geographical Association 59-60, 61, 70, 80, 146, 147, 184-7 passim, 195
  environmental studies and 80, 152, 156-8, 190
  field studies and 67, 68, 69-70, 161
  membership 59-60
  new geography and 75, 152, 184
  promotional role of 59, 79, 80, 187
  university geography and 62-3, 187
geography 57-80, 184-8
  as a science 58, 61, 76-7,147
  classical 58-9
  environmental studies and 57, 149-55, 156-7
  establishment of 57, 58-66, 77, 116
  expansiveness of 64, 72, 78, 184-5
  fieldwork in 66-70, 79, 118, 150, 157, 161-3
  fragmentation of 72, 155, 184-5
  and integrated studies 145-9, 150, 157
  new geography 66, 70-7, 79, 150-1, 152, 157-8, 184-5, 186
  regional 63, 74, 150-1, 157, 184-5, 186
  school and university gap 61, 64-5, 66, 145, 154-5
  and social studies 148-9
  threatened 150, 190

224

Index

university 58, 59, 61-3 64-5, 68, 116, 155
geography teachers 60, 64, 78
 environmental studies and 112, 151-5, 190
geology 67
Gibberd, K. 18
Gilbert, E.W. 71
Ginsburg, N. 76
Glass, D.V. 18
Goody, J. and Watts 7
Gould, P.R. 75
Gowing, D. 75
grammar schools 13, 15, 26
 comprehensivization and 20
 geography in 59, 63, 69
Graves, N.J. 62
'Great Debate' 22, 27, 30
Green, F.E. 87
Gregory, D. 57-8
Gunton, H.W. and Hawkes, C.W. 88

Hadow Report (1927) 63, 79
Haggett, P.
 see Chorley and Haggett
Hanson, D. 8, 196
Hartlib, S. 84
Hartrop. B.B. 137, 138, 142, 151
Hartshorne, R. 74
Harvey, D. 77
Hawkes, C.W.
 see Gunton and Hawkes
Hawkins, D. vii
Healey, Dr 138, 141
Heath, E. 110
Hemmings, J. 197
Herbart, H.F. 84
Herbertson, A.J. 62, 67
Herfordshire
 'A' level proposals 134-43, 208-9, 220-2
 Association of Teachers of Gardening and Rural Subjects 92, 94
 environmental studies posts 113
 rural studies in 88-9, 91, 95, 96-7, 117-18
 Standing Panel 169-72
Hirst, P.M. 4, 5
Holmes, E.G.A. 59
Honeybone, R.C. 62, 64, 65, 145, 187
Hopkins, A. 22
Hopkins, B. 139, 141, 170, 175
Hore, P. 73
Hudspeth, W.H. 86

Humanities Curriculum Project 20, 29, 113
Hunt, A. vii-viii
Hunter, Prof. 137, 142
Hutching, G. 68
Huxley, T.H. 41, 85

IDE
 see Interdisciplinary Enquiry
industry 8, 13, 70, 197-8
 links with 22, 42
 rural 87-90
Institute of British Geographers 66
interdisciplinary curricula 21, 28-9, 48-9, 149-50, 162
Interdisciplinary Enquiry workshops 28
IUCN 108

Jackson, P. 138
Jenkins, E.W. 42, 44, 51, 52
Jennings, D.H. 159
Johnson, M.L. 46
Johnson, R. 77
Joint Biology Committee 46
Joint Matriculation Board (JMB) 15, 52, 159
 Northern Universities 45, 131
Joint Working Party on Environmental Education 127
Jones, S. 75, 77
'Journal of Biological Education' 54

Keltie, J.S. 67
Kent Association of Teachers of Rural Science 92, 93-4, 99
Kerr, J. 21
Kirk, L. 145, 155
Kitching, J. 141
knowledge, definitions of 4

labour government 19
Lacey, C. 16
Lancaster, J. 84
Layton 8, 10, 26, 27, 116, 128, 197
Le Play, F. 67
Lewis, C.C. 119
literate culture 7
London University Examination Board 158, 166, 170, 174-7, 179
Longland, J. 110, 111, 112
Lucia, Mr 139-43 passim
Lynde, L.W. 61

Macdonald, B. 20

225

Index

MacKinder, H.J. 59, 60, 62, 67, 78, 145–7 passim, 152, 157, 187, 190
Madingley lectures 70–1
Marchant, E.C. 65, 75, 149, 157, 188
Marsden, W.E. 32, 123
Martin, G.C. 112
medical education 47
Mellowes, C. 168–9 passim
Morgan, R.F. 94, 98, 127, 162–3
Morris, R. 20, 30
Musgrave, P.W. 7
Musgrove, F. 5
Mylechreest, M. 124

National Association of Environmental Education 111, 122, 159, 186
National Environmental Research Council 109
National Rural Studies Association (NRSA) 95–6, 98, 117, 120, 121, 125, 126, 133
natural history 43, 47, 53
Nature Conservancy 48, 108, 109–10, 160–1
nature study 85
Nature Study Society 87
Neal, G.J. 139
Neal, P. 122
Nesbitt, A. 84
Newbould, Prof, 137–9 passim
Nicholls, A.D. 152–6 passim, 158, 190, 192
Nicholls, F. 108
Nicholson, M. 105
Northern Universities ... Borad
  see under Joint Matriculation Board
Norwood, Sir C. 63–4
Norwood Report (1943) 17–18, 29, 31, 32, 63–4, 151, 185–6
Nuffield biology 47, 49–50, 160, 188
Nuffield curriculum projects 20–1, 48, 118, 195

Offley conference (1970) 136–40, 151, 158, 167–8, 189
'O' level exams 29
  high status 29, 34, 35
option system 32–3
Oxford University
  biology at 50
  geography at 62

Parlett, M. 106
Partridge, J. 18

Pasteur, L. 42
Paterson, A. 123–4
pedagogic tradition 3, 25, 28, 29, 34, 128, 179, 186–7
  movement away from 35
Peet, R. 77
Perrot, D.E. 159, 161
Perry, G.A. 119
Pestalozzi, J.H. 26, 84
Peters, R.S. 4
Phenix, P.S. 4–5
physical sciences 42, 51
pollution 107, 109, 111
Poor Law 84
Price, J. 159
primary education 13, 26
  geography in 67
Pritchard, M. 92–3, 98, 99, 120–1, 134, 139, 161
Pritchard, T. 108
professions 24–5
'Project Environment' 127, 129
psychology 10
public schools 14, 26
  comprehensivization and 20
  curriculum broadened 14
  geography in 59, 66
  in the nineteenth century 7, 13
Pullen, J. 125

Quant, R.L. 126, 128
quantification 52, 75–6
questionnaire, analysis of (1952) 199

Ramage, M.P. 46
Rasch, Sir C. 87
Reid, W.A. 33–4, 193
resources
  for academic and utilitarian subjects 35, 79, 196–7
  for rural studies 92, 142, 158, 202–5
  status and 35, 79, 187, 188, 191–2, 196
Riley, J. 141
Ritter, K. 58
Robertson, Sir G. 57
Rooper, T.C. 58, 59
Rothblatt, S. 8, 14
Rousseau, J.J. 26, 84
Royal Commission on Environmental Pollution 111
Royal Geographical Society 61–2, 63, 67, 68, 148, 149, 150, 185
Rubinstein, D. 20
rural studies 84–100

Index

after 1944 Act 90–4
'A' level (Shephalbury School) 206–7
associations 94–6, 96–7, 98, 99–100, 119
evolution of 84–90, 99–100, 186
examinations in 91, 96–8, 118, 125–7
philosophy of 93
redefined 90, 113, 119–27
status of 92, 95, 99, 117, 118, 122, 126–8, 159, 188
utilitarian value of 84, 100
see also environmental studies
rural studies teachers 36, 92–4, 97, 99, 113, 118, 124–5, 201, 204–5
Russell, F.S. 46
Ryder, J. 14

School Certificate 25, 26–7, 29, 30, 192
introduction of 15, 29, 35–6, 43
school leaving age 18–19, 35–6, 43
'School Science Review' 46, 188
Schools Council 20–1, 30
environmental studies 'A' level and 157, 166–80
Geography 15–18 Project 75–6
Geography Subject Committee 171, 172
Science Subject Committee 171, 177
Working Party on Environmental Studies 157
Working Party on Rural Studies 92, 121, 122–3, 125, 126, 134
school subjects, 184, 192–3
acceptability of, to pupils vii–vii, 195
evolution of 3, 10–11, 34–5, 78
explanations of 4–7
groups within 3, 24–5
hierarchy of, 33, 53
social history of 4, 5, 7–11
status of 4, 8, 30–4, 53
science 7, 10, 27
evolution of 10
utilitarian value of 41
Science Masters' Association 44, 45, 46, 95, 188
secondary modern schools 17–18
comprehensivization and 19–20
examinations and 18–19, 30, 92
rural studies in 91, 92, 99, 117
Selleck, R.T.W. 85
Sheffield University 62
Shephalbury School 131, 134–5, 206–7
rural studies 'A' level 206–7
Shipman, M. 21, 29, 30

Silver, H. 14
Simon, 20
Slaymaker, O. 71
social class 9, 13–14, 16, 18, 26, 194, 197
social sciences 66, 76, 145
Social Studies movement 28
'Society and the Young School Leaver' report (1967) 74
Society for Environmental Education 112, 120, 129
Society of Art Masters 8
sociology
in rural studies 120
status 4, 8–9, 196–7
attraction of pupils and 154
differentiation 29–30, 196–7
examination subjects and 24, 33–4, 36, 189–90
of biology 52–3, 116–17, 159
of geography 58, 64, 79, 116
of rural studies 92, 95, 99, 117, 118, 122, 126–8, 159, 188
of utilitarian subjects 27–9, 53, 197–8
status improvement 30
Stenhouse, L. 29
Stevens, F. 33
Strauss, A. 24–5
Study Group on Education and Field Biology 46–7, 48, 160–2
report 49, 158, 160
subject associations 8, 17, 25, 26, 30, 192
growth of 94–5
in rural studies 94–6, 99–100
subjects
see school subjects; university subjects
Sussex University vi, viii
Sykes, J. 141

Tansley, Sir A. 50
Taunton Commission (1868) 13–14, 16, 18
teachers
material interests of 34–5, 79, 189, 191, 196, 197
professionalization of 30
socialization of 6
teacher training 48–9
for environmental studies 112–3, 123–4, 204–5
Technical Instruction Commission (1882) 86
Tettenhall school 131
Thomas, P.R. 73, 74, 79, 150, 185
Thompson Committee (1918) 87

227

Index

Tinker, C.A. 68
Topham P. 118, 126, 128, 131–43 passim, 158, 166, 175, 176
Tracey, C.W. 43, 44
tripartite system 18–19, 91

UNESCO 106
universities
  acceptability of school subjects to 33–4, 191
  environmental studies in 123, 128, 177
  geography in 58, 59, 61–3, 64–5, 68, 116, 155
  influence of, on curricula 6, 14, 21, 136, 142, 191–2, 193
  new subjects and 11, 122, 187, 189, 193
university subjects 5, 187
  not in secondary curriculum 195–6
Unstead, J.F. 147, 152
utilitarian knowledge 25, 26–7, 197–8
utilitarian tradition 3, 25, 26, 28, 29, 34, 128, 186–7
  movement away from 35, 188
  rural studies and 84, 86

vocational curricula vii, 9, 15, 18, 195–6
  and social class, 9, 84

vocational needs 9
von Humboldt, A. 58

Walford, R. 71, 73, 74, 184
Walker, D. 61, 65, 74, 76, 79
Walker, R. 20
Ware, F. 87
Waring, M. 43, 44, 50, 54
Warwick, D. 33
Watson
  see Crick and Watson
Weber, M. 7, 58
Wheeler, K. 112
Whitby, G. 91, 95
Wilkinson, R. 7
Williams, R. 9, 13, 14, 26, 27, 145
Wiltshire and rural studies 117
Wise, M.J. 66, 150, 156
Witkin, B.W. 197
Wooldridge, S.W. 64, 68, 76, 78, 150
working class children vii, 13, 32, 197
Wrigley, E.A. 70, 97
Wrotham Secondary School 91

Yeates, M. 76
Young, M.F.D. 5–6, 142, 192

zoology 43, 47, 50, 51, 53

Renovating the Ivory Tower

Canadian Universities and the Knowledge Economy

edited by

David Laidler

Policy Study 37

C.D. Howe Institute

C.D. Howe Institute publications are available from:
Renouf Publishing Company Limited, 5369 Canotek Road, Unit 1,
Ottawa, Ontario K1J 9J3
phone: (613) 745-2665; fax: (613) 745-7660;
Internet: www.renoufbooks.com

and from Renouf's store at:
71½ Sparks Street, Ottawa (613) 238-8985

Institute publications are also available in microform from:
Micromedia Limited, 20 Victoria Street,
Toronto, Ontario M5C 2N8

This book is printed on recycled, acid-free paper.

National Library of Canada Cataloguing in Publication Data

Main entry under title:

   Renovating the ivory tower : Canadian universities and the knowledge economy

(Policy study ; 37)
Includes papers presented at the annual meetings of the Canadian
   Economics Association.
Includes bibliographical references.
ISBN 0-88806-537-X

   1. Education, Higher — Economic aspects — Canada. I. Laidler, David, 1938– II. Canadian Economics Association. III. C.D. Howe Institute. IV. Series: Policy study (C.D. Howe Institute) ; 37.

LA417.5.R46 2002   338.4'337871   C2002-900520-5

© C.D. Howe Institute, Toronto.
Quotation with appropriate credit is permissible.
Cover design by Leroux Design Inc.
Printed in Canada by Printcrafters Inc., Winnipeg, Manitoba
April 2002.

Contents

Foreword vii

Renovating the Ivory Tower:
 An Introductory Essay, by *David Laidler* 1
Outline of This Essay 2
Canadian Universities: Some Historical Background 3
The Standard of Living and the Knowledge Economy 6
What These Studies Establish 12
Interpreting the Evidence 19
Directions for Policy 28
Concluding Comment 35

Universities and the Knowledge Economy, by *Paul Davenport* 39
The Challenge of Accessibility and Quality 39
University Education and the Knowledge Economy 44
University Research, Innovation, and Globalization 49
Meeting the Challenge of Accessibility and Quality 54

Do We Have a Problem Yet? Women and
 Men in Higher Education, by *Stephen T. Easton* 60
Where Have the Boys Gone? 64
Demand: The Rate of Return on a Degree 67
Supply: The Number of University-Ready Students 75
Conclusion 78

The Global Talent Hunt and the Growth of
 e-Recruiting in Canada, by *Alice Nakamura and Joel Bruneau* 80
How e-Recruiting Works 81
Commercial e-Recruiting Services 86
Nonprofit e-Recruitment Services 89
A Private, Nonprofit Complement to e-Recruitment Services 92
The Evolution of Campus Career Placement Services 94
Questions Raised 96
Recommendations 98
Appendix: Canadian Postsecondary Institutions
 Partnered with Campus WorkLink 100

Comments on Davenport, Easton, and
Nakamura and Bruneau,
by Melville L. McMillan 105

Quantity or Quality?
Research at Canadian Universities,
by John Chant and William Gibson..125
Indicators of Research Performance..127
Research Performance, 1994–98 131
Performance Over Time 135
A Focus on Institutions 142
Conclusions 146
Appendix Tables 150

A Matter of Discipline:
Early Career Outcomes of Recent
Canadian University Graduates, by Ross Finnie 169
The Data 171
Setting the Stage: Distributions, Evaluations, Unemployment 175
Earnings 183
Conclusions 202
Appendix: The Earnings Models 209

The Returns to University Education
in Canada, 1990 and 1995,
by François Vaillancourt and Sandrine Bourdeau-Primeau 215
Literature Review 216
Methodology 216
Returns to Education 224
Conclusion 228
Appendix Tables 229

Returns to University Education in Canada
Using New Estimates of Program Costs,
by Kelly Ann Rathje and J.C. Herbert Emery...241
Benefits of Total Education 242
Costs 244
Total Rates of Return to University Education.......................................245
Externalities 247
Private Rates of Return 249

Implications for Tuition Policy 252
Conclusions 252
Appendix A: Regression Results for
    Canadian University Graduates 255
Appendix B: Costs..258

Comments on Chant and Gibson, Finnie,
    Vaillancourt and Bourdeau-Primeau,
    and Rathje and Emery,
    by *Jeffrey Smith* 265

The Contributors 281

Members of the C.D. Howe Institute 285

Foreword

Change is the order of the day in the Canadian economy. The nature of many of the goods we consume and the technology used to produce them is in constant flux. Increasingly, too, the competition that Canadians face and the shocks to which our economy is exposed are international, rather than local, in scope and origin. Coping with this new economic environment and taking advantage of the opportunities it presents are a major preoccupation. Phrases such as "new economy" and "knowledge economy" have become commonplace in discussions of economic policy. Moreover, the welfare of Canadians is more than merely material, and our political and social institutions, and the values they embody, are also under constant pressure to evolve.

In such an environment, new ideas — and a highly skilled, adaptable, and creative labor force to implement them — are crucial to Canada's economic progress. A well-educated and thoughtful citizenry will ensure that economic prosperity underpins the growth of more general social and political well-being. Canada's universities are a major source of all these things, and policymakers concerned with designing measures to raise Canadians' quality of life must pay careful attention to them for that reason alone.

It is quite natural, therefore, that the C.D. Howe Institute, whose basic task is to provide well-informed and policy-relevant analysis of economic, political, and social issues, should pay attention to the current state of affairs in Canadian universities. To that end, the Institute organized two sessions dealing with these issues at the July 2001 meetings of the Canadian Economics Association held at McGill University in Montreal. This volume brings together the papers presented at those sessions in a more permanent form. Together, they provide an overview of the current state of play in Canada's universities. They discuss some the challenges these institutions now face and their success in meeting them, and they also offer suggestions about public policies that might make their contributions to Canadian life more effective.

These essays build on an already well-established academic literature, and it is hoped that, in their turn, they will become the basis for further research. But, as is always the case with C.D. Howe Institute publications, their authors have taken particular care to make their work accessible to a wider audience. Some of the essays deal with universities as producers of new ideas in their research function and as creators of educated and productive graduates in their teaching role; others take up certain quite specific problems they now face, created by the male/female balance of their student bodies, to give one example, or of managing aspects of the transition of their graduates to the labor force, to give another; still others discuss the extreme economic pressures Canadian universities have faced in recent years, and propose some remedies for the difficulties these have created.

In bringing this work to the attention of a broader audience than is usually reached by academic researchers, the C.D. Howe Institute hopes to promote a better understanding of the role of universities in the knowledge economy, and the way they are responding to the challenges it poses. It also hopes to promote discussion of how best to provide the resources needed for these institutions to remain efficient contributors to Canada's economic, social, and political life.

The book was copy edited by Ruth Crow, Elizabeth d'Anjou, Lenore d'Anjou, and Ron Edwards, and prepared for publication by Marie Hubbs and Barry A. Norris. As with all C.D. Howe Institute publications, the analysis and opinions presented here are the responsibility of the authors, and do not necessarily reflect the views of the Institute's members or Board of Directors.

Jack M. Mintz
Preseident and
Chief Executive Officer

Renovating the Ivory Tower:
An Introductory Essay

David Laidler

This volume derives from two conference sessions that took place at the Annual Meetings of the Canadian Economics Association in Montreal on July 2, 2001. At each session, three papers were presented and then subjected to critical commentary by a single discussant.

The first session dealt with aspects of the broader debate about universities: their role in the economy, including their influence on economic growth and their current funding problems (Paul Davenport); that long-standing cause for concern, the question of equal access for men and women to higher education (Stephen Easton); and the effects of technology on graduates' transition from university to the job market, including some implications of these effects for the "brain drain" (Alice Nakamura and Joel Bruneau). Melville McMillan acted as discussant.

The second session dealt more directly with Canadian universities' productivity both in research (John Chant and William Gibson) and in the creation of human capital (papers by Ross Finnie and by François Vaillancourt and Sandrine Bourdeau-Primeau). To these three papers has been added a fourth on the creation of human capital, by Kelly-Ann Rathje and Herbert Emery, based on work carried out by the former in the course of her graduate studies at the University of Calgary, which came to the editor's attention shortly after the conference. Jeff Smith provides a critical commentary on this group of essays.

I am grateful to Clark Leith, Melville McMillan, Bill Robson, Jeff Smith, and François Vaillancourt for comments on an earlier draft.

All these papers take an economic approach to describing the activities of Canadian universities. The appropriateness of doing so derives from the simple and unquestionable fact that these institutions use scarce inputs to generate valuable outputs. From the economist's viewpoint, the university sector is a capital-goods-producing industry, and is appropriately analyzed as such. Its output consists of knowledge and of people who comprehend that knowledge and are able to put it to use. Universities produce ideas, sometimes given the label *knowledge capital*, and they also impart skills to people, creating in the process what is usually called *human capital*. Economic analysis is not capable of providing a comprehensive treatment of universities' complex role in society, but the economic approach is helpful as far as it goes — and, in many respects, it goes a long way, as I hope this volume demonstrates. As we shall see, the picture that emerges is one of a system that, while still functioning rather well, is nevertheless showing some signs of stress.

Outline of This Essay

In this introductory essay, I first outline the historical and institutional factors that frame current debates about the place of universities in Canadian life. I then turn to a brief survey of their role in what has come to be known as "the knowledge economy," including some important caveats about certain currently fashionable ways of looking at this matter. I proceed to discuss the substantive findings of the studies in this volume, paying particular attention to what they reveal about the factual background that ought to inform public policy towards universities. Finally, I offer some suggestions of my own about the directions that policy in this area might take. They are not meant to be definitive but to provoke further debate about some vitally important questions.

Specifically, I argue the following:

- The currently healthy rates of return yielded by undergraduate education permit a significant shift toward tuition fee revenue as a source of finance for the sector.

- Such a move would force universities to become more responsive to students' own assessments of their often diverse needs, making them less reliant on funding from the government and business sectors, which seem to be taking a dangerously narrow view of the way in which these institutions contribute to Canada's well being.
- Any such move must be accompanied by measures to ensure that financial markets provide adequate access to funding for the accumulation of human capital.
- Such a change would not preclude government and business from continuing to support both the teaching and research functions of the university sector — indeed, a strong case can still be made for such support.

My suggestions have the practical aims of increasing the overall level of funding available to universities and reducing their reliance on any one sector for support.

Canadian Universities: Some Historical Background

Historians of the university have often told us that the institution's current complexity is the outcome of a number of tendencies that have long co-existed uneasily with one another. In some times and places, the creation, preservation, and transmission of cultural and, particularly, religious understanding have been the prime function of the university; in others, pure scientific research has taken pride of place. It is these traditional activities, both of which involve the pursuit of knowledge for its own sake, that underlie the metaphor of the ivory tower.

But universities have never operated in total isolation from the economy. They have provided not just pure research but useful knowledge that allows the community at large to enhance its material well-being, and they have trained young people in productive and marketable skills. In the 1960s, the word "multiversity" came into fashion (see, for example, Kerr 1963), characterizing what many seemed to think was a newly emerging complexity in the activities expected of such institutions. But it is worth recalling that, even in the Canada of 1836, Victoria College (now part of the University of Toronto, but then in Cobourg, Ontario) was teaching surveying and navigation in addition to divinity, and that in so doing it was following an already well-established, nonconformist, and mainly US model (Cameron 1991, 12).

What is new about modern universities and has put them in need of renovation is neither the complexity of their offerings nor the potential for conflict among the constituencies they are expected to serve, but the sheer scale of their activities as both creators and purveyors of knowledge of all kinds. Populist impulses to broaden and expand their activities under government auspices were already at work in the nineteenth century, most notably, but by no means uniquely, in the United States, when the land grant universities, which now form the backbone of the state university system, were created by the *Morrill Act of 1862*.

World War II marked another major turning point in the development of the modern university. As Franklin (2000) notes, the war itself led to a huge expansion of government support for university research in science and engineering, not least where it might lead to military applications. The war's end saw student bodies expanded dramatically as ex-servicemen reentered civilian life. Thereafter, the Cold War in general, and US–Soviet competition in the wake of the 1957 Sputnik launch in particular, provided the motive for further expansion on all fronts. Canada, like virtually every other Western country, followed the United States' lead, with governments providing most of the necessary funds.

The Economic and Political Background to Current Debates

The rapid secular postwar growth in productivity that made all this university expansion, and much else, seem affordable slowed suddenly around 1973, but this fact was not obvious until a decade or more later. Canada, like other countries, is still living with the consequences of this slowdown and of the fiscal exuberance that preceded it and persisted for awhile even after its recognition.

These consequences extend far beyond the university sectors of all the countries affected, of course, but certain features of the Canadian landscape have made the pressures on universities here particularly acute, especially compared with those experienced by post-secondary institutions in the United States.

First, the resources needed to create, maintain, and expand Canadian universities have, from the outset, come predominantly from government. There are no Canadian equivalents of the great privately endowed US research universities such as Harvard, Chicago, and Stanford, or indeed of such smaller private institutions as Oberlin or Swarthmore, which tend to specialize in undergraduate teaching. In Canada, when governments feel short of funds (for good or bad reasons is not relevant to this point) and cut back on university spending, the reduction impinges on the whole sector, not just one segment of it. Furthermore, the existence of private universities in the United States not only cushions the effects of government cutbacks on the sector as a whole, it also provides competitive pressures that constrain the extent to which it is politically prudent to cut support to publicly funded universities.[1]

Second, as a direct, though surely unintended, outcome of the division of functions between the federal government and the provinces, and between the public and private sectors of the economy, Canadian universities compete directly and visibly with health care for public funding. Provincial governments are responsible for both services and, since 1977, funding in aid of these activities from Ottawa has been bundled into a single block grant. For any provincial treasurer, then, the opportunity cost of each dollar spent on universities is a dollar of health care expenditure. Given

---

1 Studies of the factors that systematically motivate university boards and administrations have mainly been concerned with US experience. This work strongly suggests that enhancing the prestige of the institution for which they are responsible, both absolutely and relative to that of others, ranks high among their goals (Winston 1999). Administrators of the major state universities are thus sensitive to competition emanating from their privately funded rivals, and respond to it. To some extent, they can influence politicians whose policies might undermine their ability to maintain their standing. Even so, many of the pressures currently being felt in Canada are also affecting US state universities. (See "Land Grant Universities" 2001).

the Canadian electorate's commitment to the public provision of health care and the fact that this sector directly serves the whole population rather than just one segment of it, not to mention the high political profile of its current financial difficulties, it is hardly surprising that higher education in general, and universities in particular, have come under increasing financial pressure.

Finally, the Canadian electorate remembers the fiscal excesses of the 1970s and 1980s and the measures that were needed to turn things around in the 1990s. It is in no mood to sanction any wholesale loosening of government purse strings without compelling arguments — an attitude unlikely to change in the near future. On the other hand, that same electorate seems unwilling to sanction any reduction in access to university education for young people.

As a consequence of these three factors, government funding has failed to grow in line with enrollments and there has been only a partial easing of restrictions on tuition fees, so that universities increasingly depend on funds raised from the business community to fill the resulting gap. Some may regret these facts and wish them different, and others may welcome them; but facts they are, and any practical discussion about policies toward universities must recognize them. Canadian universities are certainly under considerable financial pressure, as Davenport convincingly argues, but if they are to receive more resources, it must be shown that the money would be well spent. And if the resources are to come from government, it must be shown that there are good reasons the private sector cannot be expected to provide them.

The Standard of Living and the Knowledge Economy

A salient fact of North American economic life in the 1990s was that gross domestic product (GDP) per head of population grew faster in the United States than in Canada. It is a commonplace that this measure is not the be-all and end-all of economic and social well-being, but it is remarkable how much more attention people seem able and willing to pay to cultural and spiritual matters when their material comfort is well taken care of. So let us agree that "standard of living" as measured by this imperfect indicator does matter and that when it tells us Canada has been falling behind its nearest neighbor and has begun to catch up only in the past two or three years, this is a cause for concern.

Productivity and Its Rate of Growth

Any country's GDP per head is, as a matter of arithmetic, the consequence of two factors: the proportion of the population that works, and the amount of output that each working person produces on average. In turn, the level and the rate of growth of GDP per head depend on the performance of the labor market and on the level and rate of growth of the productivity of labor. Sharpe (2001) demonstrates that both these factors (the labor market and productivity) contributed to Canada's failure to keep pace with the United States in the 1990s. In the first part of the decade, poor labor market performance, reflecting the depth of the 1991–92 recession and the slowness of the subsequent recovery, was the dominant factor at work; thereafter, labor productivity was the main culprit. As, for example, Davenport's Figure 11 shows, output per person-hour grew more slowly in Canada up until 1998, particularly in manufacturing.[2]

Within manufacturing, however, the productivity growth differential between the two countries has been concentrated in the machinery and electrical equipment sectors. The popular notion that the spectacular US economic performance of the 1990s was the result of developments in high-technology activities, is well grounded in fact (see Rao and Tang 2001). And because these activities involve using highly educated workers to exploit new developments in science and engineering, it is understandable that another popular notion has developed — namely, that the key to securing a rising standard of living at the turn of the millennium lies in the creation and dissemination of knowledge, particularly technologi-

---

[2] As Davenport also tells us, recently revised data show that, since 1998, Canada's GDP and growth of GDP per capita have actually surpassed those in the Unites States. Productivity growth, however, as measured by output per person hour, has continued to lag. (See Little 2001.)

cal knowledge. The "new economy" is said to be a "knowledge economy," and within it, universities are often presented as having special roles to play as creators of new ideas in their research function and as producers of human capital capable of exploiting those ideas in their teaching function. In this way of looking at things, the output of universities is a vital input into the material progress of the market economy.

A Role for Universities

This vision of universities as primarily handmaids to material growth in a capitalist economy is quite horrifying to many within the Canadian academic community (see Turk 2000) — not entirely without cause, as we shall see in due course. It is important to recognize that some of the ideas universities produce do turn out to be valuable in the world outside their gates, that their graduates do possess superior productive powers acquired in the course of their education, that these ideas and powers do have value in the marketplace, and that the university sector's performance is likely to be judged by taxpayers according to these criteria. But it is equally important to insist that Canadian universities cannot simply be turned into engines of economic growth, nor should they seek political support by pretending they can be.

In order to clarify the issues at stake here, it is important first to distinguish between the factors influencing the economy's *level of productivity* and those influencing the rate at which that level *grows* over time. To the extent that a more educated and better trained labor force is able to produce more output because it embodies more human capital, the proportion of the economy's labor force that has received higher education affects the *level* of the economy's productivity as measured by output per person-hour of work. An increase in that proportion, therefore, will increase the level of the economy's productivity. Such an increase will enhance the *ongoing rate of growth of productivity*, however, only if this more educated labor force also turns out to be better at generating new ideas, each of which in turn enables more output to be wrung from a given level of inputs (including human capital). This latter possibility also provides the main economic justification for universities' involvement in research and development (R&D) activity, as opposed to the mere transmission of already-existing knowledge.

Second, even if these possibilities are realizable in fact, they do not in themselves make a case for government involvement in promoting the knowledge economy by way of public expenditure on universities. As long as those who embody human capital obtained through university education can capture the returns this yields in the form of enhanced market incomes — including enhancements generated by new productive ideas that the possession of such capital enables them to create — and as long as there are no barriers to people investing in their own education in the first place, then the usual marketplace mechanisms should ensure that both the highly educated labor force and the font of new ideas are adequately supplied without public subsidies.

The Economic Case for Public Subsidies

In order to justify public intervention designed to increase expenditures on education and research beyond the levels private market activity would supply, the *social* returns to such intervention — particularly as they involve the effects of the creation and dissemination of ideas on the level of well-being generated by the economy and on the rate of growth of that well-being — must exceed the market incomes of those directly involved in these activities. Advocates of such intervention rest their case mainly on the claim that, once created, productive ideas become generally — and, to all practical purposes, freely — available to the economy at large, and can therefore be profitably exploited without any compensation for the original creators of those ideas.

If the *spillover effects* — often called *external benefits* or *positive externalities* — of education and research are indeed empirically significant, an economy that relies on market incentives alone to bring about investment in such activities will be inefficiently underprovided with them. To the extent that these education and research activities are located in universities, the case for supporting those institutions with public funds is made.

In recent years, proponents of so-called *endogenous growth theory* have argued that spillover effects are a significant engine of economic growth and that they have been at work in, among other times and places, the United States in the 1990s.[3] It is easy to argue further that this mechanism for promoting growth can be imitated in Canada, to the great benefit of our living standards, if only government will provide the incentives for the acquisition of human capital, and its subsequent devotion to R&D activities, that market mechanisms are now failing to deliver in adequate amounts.

Some Caveats

These arguments seem to be plausible, particularly when applied to science and technology. But a few caveats are in order before anyone jumps to conclusions about the likely desirable impact on Canada's economic prospects of further investment of funds in universities in general, and in their science and technology programs in particular.

To begin with, there is the idea that statisticians call the *regression fallacy*. In the current context, it suggests that, among any group of countries at any time, the one that is performing best is probably performing above potential as a result of transitory factors quite beyond any policymaker's control. It is therefore likely to perform less well in future. Consistent with this idea is evidence that formulas for economic success seem to be extraordinarily difficult to transfer across national boundaries or even to sustain in working order at home for very long. Over the past 40 years or so, there have been periods when the Swedish, French, and Japanese "models" seemed to be just the thing for any economically ambitious country to imitate, but we do not hear much about these anymore. It might well turn out, therefore, that the US model of productivity growth based on scientific and technological education and research will prove no more durable.[4] If the United States has been performing

---

3   For a comprehensive, albeit highly technical, account of this area, see Aghion and Howitt (1997).

4   François Vaillancourt reminds me that, in recent Canadian discussion, the US model has run into some competition from the Irish model. The same warning applies to the latter.

above its potential over the past decade, then the results of Canada's seeking to reproduce that level of economic growth by making large investments in the production of scientific knowledge and technically skilled human capital might turn out to be disappointing. (Then again, Canada itself could be the lucky recipient of a random boost to economic growth!)

Furthermore, when economists look behind national data on productivity growth rates to information gathered at the level of individual industries, they find a great deal of diversity. This result is completely consistent with what we know about the narrow industrial base of US productivity growth in the 1990s, and at first sight there is nothing particularly disturbing about it. It is, however, less widely known and much more discomfiting that even more specific research, at the level of individual firms or even individual plants, finds that this huge diversity in productivity performance persists. That is why Harberger (1998) likens the appearance of productivity growth — to which he prefers to give the more down-to-earth label "real cost reduction" — to the isolated sprouting of mushrooms as opposed to the generalized rising brought about by yeast. This striking simile captures the fact that, rather than having an across-the-board effect on all aspects of an economy's performance, the ideas that drive productivity growth seem to raise output by very different amounts at different times, often in widely scattered places. Interspersed among the expanding plants and firms in industries where productivity is improving rapidly on average are to be found many where it is stagnant or even declining.

These facts suggest that the implementation of productivity-enhancing and, hence, real-cost-reducing, measures is very much a scattered and localized activity rather than one whose effects involve the general application of new ideas that radiate out from specialized "knowledge factories" to the economy at large. Those who bring about such cost reductions may well be exploiting knowledge created outside of their own establishments, but there is clearly a large element of local insight and ingenuity involved in discovering and exploiting their productive potential. It is hard to interpret the facts of real-world productivity growth as corresponding to the generalized productivity-growth spillovers that variables with names such as "knowledge" or "education" bring about in modern endogenous growth models. They suggest, indeed, that these models, for all their *a priori* appeal, are intellectual artifacts that fail to explain some key properties of productivity growth data as we are beginning to understand them.[5] This does not, of course, imply that knowledge and education are unimportant to economic well-being, or that universities do not create valuable ideas and educate productive graduates. It does, however, warn us that no one has yet shown that these mechanisms generate general external benefits on any significant scale. In our current state of knowledge, we ought to be extremely skeptical of popular arguments for the public subsidization of scientific and technological research in universities as a sure-fire method of raising Canadians' standard of living.

What These Studies Establish

These important caveats notwithstanding, the studies in this volume clearly demonstrate that Canadian universities are productive institutions on even the narrowest of economic criteria. If there are good reasons to question their capacity to act as engines of material growth, there can be little doubt about three other matters: that they make a major contribution to sustaining the level of Canadians' living standards; that the right policies can enhance this contribution; and that the wrong policies can undermine it.

Returns to Human Capital

The concept of human capital has been central to the economic analysis of education for about 40 years now (Teixera 2000), so the papers by Finnie, Vaillancourt and Bourdeau-Primeau, and Rathje

---

5 As Mark Blaug, a leading expert in the economics of education, recently remarked:

> Where is the evidence that human capital generates externalities that makes growth endogenous? While the new growth theory has raised a lot of interesting technical ideas relating to the influence of economies of scale, externalities, R&D and so on, none of these are ever pinned down very precisely. (1999.)

and Emery are additions to an already well-established tradition in economic research, in Canada as elsewhere. All three investigate the returns to investment in university education, all three are particularly interesting in that they do so on a discipline-by-discipline basis, and, as Smith points out, none yields any major surprises to anyone already familiar with this line of work. But when matters of economic policy are at issue, it is critical to get, and keep, the facts straight, and the facts that emerge from these studies, or that are confirmed by them, throw important light on some currently contentious issues, and considerably strengthen our faith in the factual basis that ought to underlie any serious discussion of them.

To begin with, as Davenport points out, there has recently been a tendency for some commentators to argue that the economic value of university education in general, and of undergraduate education in the social science and humanities in particular, has been declining. It might be added that such views may also have influenced some Canadian politicians in their decisions about university funding, though Davenport offers no conjectures about this. The results presented by both Finnie and Vaillancourt and Bourdeau-Primeau suggest that there was no serious evidence to support these views, at least down to the mid-1990s. Whether one considers the private returns — measured purely in terms of subsequent wages and salaries — students realize on their own investment of time and money in education, or the broader social returns that also take account of the public subsidies they receive while in university and the taxes they pay when working (and that, hence, are particularly relevant to policymakers), undergraduate education seems to have been a profitable undertaking for both the individuals receiving it and for society in general in those years.

Rathje and Emery's results complicate this picture, however, with rather lower estimates of the returns to education than those of Vaillancourt and Bourdeau-Primeau. The differences here stem from two main sources. First, Rathje and Emery's estimates for the private returns to university education are based on more up-to-date measures (tuition fee data for 1998) of the costs students incur in undertaking education. It is evident from their results that the increase in tuition fees that had then recently taken place had a notable impact on reducing the private returns to education. Second, their estimates for the total returns exclude income from self-employment in measuring the incomes of graduates, whereas Vaillancourt and Bourdeau-Primeau include income from this source. For reasons that both sets of authors explain, excluding such income completely probably leads to a downward bias in rate-of-return estimates, while including it creates an upward bias. Thus, between them, these studies provide lower and upper bounds to the range within which such returns probably lie.

It is significant that all three studies show that the returns, both private and total, realized by educating women are distinctly higher than those accruing to the education of men. In certain areas, in fact, notably fine arts and the humanities, the returns to men seem to fall below any reasonable benchmark that might be applied in any market test of whether the investment is worthwhile. It also seems to be the case that the returns realized in the early years of employment are higher on average, for both men and women, in certain "harder" (that is, more mathematically demanding), disciplines, such as engineering and natural sciences, and in professional areas, particularly those in commerce and health sciences, than they are in the arts and humanities. In addition, as Finnie's work shows, graduates in some subjects at the "softer" end of the spectrum take longer to get established in the labor market. Since it is often argued that university education would be of more social value were it more directly aimed at preparing its recipients for the job market, these results are of considerable interest.

On the other hand, Finnie also shows that labor market disadvantages for humanities graduates seem to disappear within a few years of graduation, and, crucially, that there is no sign that graduates' satisfaction with their studies is lower among those educated in the humanities and social sciences than in other fields. Moreover, Davenport presents data on student loan default rates that show these to be much lower for university students than for college or private vocational school students, whose education is, on average, much more directly aimed at preparing them for the labor market. And it is worth noting that even Rathje and Emery's results show that, when sex differences are averaged out, rates of return to undergraduate education in all fields (except fine arts), whether private or total, remain attractively high. Taken overall, these considerations argue against jumping to the conclusion that the return to an education more narrowly directed to preparation for the job market is so much higher than the return to other courses of study that a major reallocation of resources is called for.

None of these results will come as a surprise to anyone familiar with earlier work on the economics of universities. Nor will it be a surprise that both Vaillancourt and Bourdeau-Primeau and Rathje and Emery conclude that the returns to graduate work (again as measured purely by salaries) are in most areas, particularly at the PhD level, on the low side or even negative. It is a necessary implication of the productivity of undergraduate education that the costs of graduate study are very high in terms of forgone earnings, and it is this fact that largely drives the results in question. Furthermore, many PhDs work in universities, where salary levels are relatively low but the *equalizing differences* (as economists call them) that arise from the working environment are widely agreed to be quite attractive. There is, however, some disagreement about just what these differences are. Outside universities, one sometimes encounters disparaging comments about professors who use the protection afforded by academic tenure as a means of consuming more leisure than other, less fortunate, members of the labor force. Within universities, the talk is more likely to be of the opportunities afforded for research and scholarship.

Research Productivity

The essay by Chant and Gibson throws some light on this vexatious issue, for it is a path-breaking attempt to compare the research productivity of the best-performing Canadian universities, mainly in science and technology, with their US counterparts. Its results are easy to summarize, but perhaps a little harder to interpret.

The most productive Canadian universities compare very well indeed with their US counterparts as far as the quantity of research (as measured by numbers of papers published in learned journals) is concerned. But when it comes to the impact of that research, as measured by the frequency with which those papers are subsequently cited, they compare less well. Since the data used in this study mainly derive from scientific and technological disciplines, the biases that naturally arise from the lack of interest of the US academic community in many issues in the humanities and social sciences that concern Canadians — and, hence, the infrequent citation by US researchers of Canadian work in those disciplines — are likely to be minimal. The main difficulty in interpreting these results arises from the fact that the US universities whose research is widely cited are overwhelmingly those large, well-endowed private institutions to which there is no Canadian counterpart. It is a commonplace of the anecdotal evidence on these matters that Canada has neither universities as good as the best nor as bad as the worst in the United States, so it comes as no surprise that the University of Toronto, which ranks at the top among Canadian institutions, fares relatively poorly compared with, say, Stanford, as far as the impact of its research is concerned.

Some Problems in the Sector

Even so, it would be a mistake to conclude that all is well with Canadian universities and that the ever-shrinking budgets Davenport describes have had no effect on their performance. The data analyzed by Finnie, Vaillancourt and Bourdeau-Primeau, Rathje and Emery, and Chant and Gibson are inevitably backward looking. In the main, they tell us about how well the sector was performing up to the mid- to late 1990s, and although budgets had been tightening for some time even then, they have tightened still further in subsequent years. It is therefore important to be alert to any signs of current stress revealed, or even hinted at, in the studies collected together here.

Attention has already been drawn to the significant disparities in the returns to university education earned by men and by women; Stephen Easton deals with material bearing on this matter. He presents compelling evidence that universities now admit significantly more women than men, whereas 25 years ago men were in the majority. Just as the shortfall in women's enrollment levels a quarter-century ago perhaps implied that they were failing to achieve their full educational, and, therefore, economic potential (among other things), so the shortfall among men now has the same implications. Given that these tendencies are at work in an economy that, as

Davenport shows, already educates a significantly smaller proportion of its population to university level than does the United States, they are disturbing — and all the more so because the missing men are not going into the college sector but seem to be moving straight out of high school into segments of the labor force where rewards are already low and still declining.

Easton suggests that women university graduates earn a labor market premium over high school graduates that exceeds the one accruing to men, that this premium has been increasing, and that the increase in the university enrollment rate of women relative to that of men, therefore, may reflect a relative growth in demand for university-educated women. This conjecture is certainly consistent with the results discussed earlier. McMillan, however, citing work by Riddell and Sweetman (2000), questions whether the premium accruing to women has indeed been rising, and suggests that what we are seeing here might better be interpreted as a supply-side shift. Easton does provide some preliminary information on one factor that might be at work on the supply side in the shape of data he interprets as suggesting that high schools are currently doing a better job of preparing women for further education than they are of preparing men for it. But if this is indeed the case, then this fact, in turn, needs to be explained. It is hard, therefore, not to sympathize with McMillan's view that the facts about women's increasing enrollment in universities, and their relative success once enrolled, may have altogether deeper social causes that lie well outside of the educational system. There is a major puzzle here that requires further investigation.

Things are more clear-cut in the case of the labor market problem that Nakamura and Bruneau document. They argue that the technical properties of the electronic systems now widely used by US-based employers in the process of recruiting university graduates entail economies of scale that give these recruiters advantages over their Canadian counterparts, and that these advantages in turn accrue to potential US employers of high-caliber Canadian graduates, thus making a contribution to the "brain-drain." To summarize their case at some risk of oversimplifying it, US recruiters can add the résumés of Canadian job seekers to the lists their US clients search at a low marginal cost, which their Canadian competitors cannot match for their Canadian clients. Hence, information about Canadian job seekers becomes more cheaply available to potential US employers than to Canadian employers, particularly to smaller firms.[6]

As McMillan suggests, it is easy to dismiss the concerns that Nakamura and Bruneau express with phrases such as "welcome to the market." In the increasingly integrated North American economy, big "buyers" of highly trained graduates are more likely to be found in the United States. It thus pays recruiting services to cater to them, and it is understandable that Canadian graduates respond to the incentives that result from these facts. But as McMillan also notes, there is a little more to it than that.

Nakamura and Bruneau suggest that the problems they document have arisen as unintended consequences of the withdrawal of the Canada Manpower agency from university campuses and its replacement by local placement services that, because of universities' funding problems, are often supported on a cost-recovery basis. It goes without saying that there should be no barriers to emigration in a free country, but it is surely anomalous that Canadian firms, whose taxes help to support Canadian universities, are at a disadvantage *vis-à-vis* their US competitors when it comes to recruiting their own country's graduates. How large and significant this problem might be is hard to say on the basis of currently available information, but it would surely be worth further study.

One other notable hint of stress in the Canadian university system emerges. Although the public perception has long been that there exists a large oversupply of well-educated PhDs ready and willing to fill any university teaching vacancies that might occur in

---

6 As Nakamura and Bruneau tell us, systematic evidence on the extent of this problem is not available. For what it is worth, conversations with the placement service at my own university reveal that an increase in the number of US firms approaching graduating students whose résumés they had found while scanning electronic databases has been noted in recent years. This activity, which was described as "low level" relative to the overall scale of the placement service's operations, seemed to be concentrated in the high-tech sector and had become less frequent in 2001, when that sector was contracting. This anecdotal evidence is consistent with Nakamura and Bruneau's fears of a "selective brain drain."

Canada, there is overwhelming anecdotal evidence that this is not in fact the case. Certain disciplines are under considerable competitive pressure when it comes to faculty recruitment and retention as a result of the interaction of budgetary stringency with a strong demand for their practitioners in the United States. This has been the case for many years in areas such as computer science and economics, not to mention in certain specialities, notably finance, that find their home in business schools. It has, however, been hard to say whether these pressures have had seriously adverse effects on standards of research and teaching. Although business schools are not singled out for special attention in the studies in this volume, Chant and Gibson do document an apparent relative decline in the quantity and quality of research emanating from Canadian universities in computer science and economics, and Finnie finds evidence of a significant decline in satisfaction with their education among economics graduates (particularly women). One cannot help but wonder whether we are seeing the first signs of declining academic standards in Canadian universities that will spread further across the system with time as their budgets get ever tighter relative to those of their US counterparts.

Interpreting the Evidence

At first glance, the results on returns to university education presented in this book seem to support popular conceptions about the role of universities as contributors to productivity growth in a knowledge economy. At the undergraduate level, these returns, however they are measured, seem quite respectable in all but a few cases, and they are higher in, for example, science, engineering, health sciences, and commerce than in other areas. Three points, however, need to be considered before jumping to any conclusions about the desirability of encouraging further expansion in these and related fields.

Human Capital and Productivity

As was argued above, it is important to distinguish between the effects of higher education on the *level of productivity*, and those on its *rate of growth*. There is no reasonable doubt that university education in most areas significantly increases the level of its recipients' productivity and, hence, indirectly the level of Canadians' standard of living. This is the effect that Finnie, Vaillancourt and Bourdeau-Primeau, and Rathje and Emery all measure. But none of these studies seeks or provides evidence that university education endows its recipients with human capital that enables them to contribute to the generation of economy-wide productivity growth over time. It might do that, but we do not have any hard evidence that it does. There is some empirical basis for arguing that the provision of university education in Canada on a larger scale than exists now might create a step-up in the level of labor productivity in the economy. The evidence — presented by Vaillancourt and Bourdeau-Primeau and by Rathje and Emery — that undergraduate education yields high rates of return in most areas, combined with two facts Davenport documents — the relatively high number of Canadians receiving college as opposed to university education, and the lower returns accruing to the former — are highly suggestive here. However, we do not have any evidence that such a change would contribute to the economy's ability to grow at a faster rate.

In any event, the returns to university education to which the evidence in this volume pertains are those captured as income by the individuals who received that education. Where the returns to human capital accrue solely to the individuals in which that capital is embodied, then one should presume that those individuals are intelligent enough to respond appropriately to the investment incentives they provide without the aid or encouragement of government. The fact that returns are, on balance, higher in science and technology fields and in professional programs than in arts and humanities in no way changes this conclusion. If there is any validity to the widely held perception that mathematical abilities differ among potential university students, then it is likely, as Smith wisely points out, that students who are relatively well endowed with them will choose areas of study where those abilities can be exploited. The returns to those who have already chosen such disciplines might indeed be higher, perhaps substantially so, than those observed elsewhere; but, crucially, those returns will also be higher than the returns that would be realized by any less mathematically adept people who shifted into these areas. Indeed, since there is no evidence of a general shortage of university places in these high-return areas, the presumption must be that the students who currently could, but do not, enter them, must perceive the expected returns that face them as being no more, and perhaps less, than those in the fields they do indeed enter.

The evidence on the productivity of human capital presented in this book is, then, at least as supportive of the case for setting undergraduate tuition fees at levels that would cover all the costs of providing teaching services and then letting potential students make their own choices about whether and what to study, as it is of the argument for expanding the level of public funding of such institutions. Indeed, Auld (1996), among others, has already made a case along just these lines for permitting private universities to operate in Canada. To point this out, however, is by no means to argue for a complete withdrawal of government from the university sector. Quite apart from these institutions' research functions, not to mention the provision of postgraduate education, there is still the question of how best to enable undergraduates to pay the costs of their education. I discuss these matters below.

The Social Returns to University Education

The studies in this volume do not specify, let alone quantify, any returns to human capital that accrue to society at large over and above the market incomes earned by the individuals in whom it is embodied, But this fact does not mean that such returns do not exist — indeed, the case for public subsidies to university education rests heavily on the claim that such returns do exist. Subsidies are indeed ubiquitous in Canada. This matter therefore requires further discussion.

Here, it is worth recalling at the outset that Canada, as with every other advanced country, makes lower levels of education compulsory up to a certain age and provides education free to all recipients up to the end of high school. That these arrangements are utterly uncontroversial surely suggests that the value to society of having all its members educated up to a certain level is so high, and is so generally perceived to be high, that we are willing to set aside the rights of families to make unconstrained choices in these matters. It also suggests that education beyond the compulsory minimum is perceived to yield external returns that are large enough to warrant society at large bearing a significant fraction of its cost.[7] Two points follow from this. First, it is extremely unlikely that the apparently large external benefits education is so widely believed to yield disappear entirely as the transition between the secondary and postsecondary sectors is made; second, it is, therefore, understandable that society by and large seems to take for granted a large public sector role in postsecondary education — indeed, to support it.

Nevertheless, to apply economists' standard cost-benefit calculus to the design of an economically efficient scheme of subsidies to university education that takes account of these external benefits, it would be necessary to quantify and put a cash value on them. The prospect of even attempting to do this has long made economists acutely uncomfortable. Vaillancourt and Bourdeau-Primeau follow Stager (1996) in noting that the external benefits to society flowing from university education, whose nature they leave undefined, might be quite large, but that, because those benefits seem to be unmeasurable, there is nothing more to be said on the matter. In this, they follow a long tradition among economists. West (1988), for example, suggests that arguments in this area tend to be about "atmospheric effects" on such things as social cohesion, and concludes that they ought to be downplayed, while Blaug reports that "no one has ever been able to quantify the externalities from higher education in Britain, or for that matter anywhere else" (1999, 331).

Smith (in this volume) conjectures, however, that economists find externalities in this area hard to discuss simply because they have not paid much attention to investigating them systematically. After all, the externality economists call "pollution" was once hard to discuss, before a research literature developed to deal with its

---

[7] The reader is reminded that forgone income is an important component of the cost of education; therefore, providing tuition-free education does not render it costless to its recipient.

quantification and the design of mechanisms to cope with it. The fact that economists have yet to undertake serious work on a problem does not necessarily mean that it is unimportant. We simply will not know how economically important are the external benefits flowing from university education until some serious work on the question is done.[8] In this respect, Rathje and Emery's approach to the issue is of particular interest. Instead of trying to measure external effects directly, they ask how large these effects would have to be to bring rates of return in areas of study where the pecuniary benefits are low up to a benchmark level. They then speculate as to whether the subsidies implicit in these estimates seem "reasonable." There is, of course, a strong subjective element to the final step of this exercise, and readers will have to make up their own minds about whether or not they agree with Rathje and Emery's particular judgments. But the authors' approach to this issue is, to my knowledge, original, and it is surely useful as a way of organizing further thinking about these matters.

I suspect, however, that, once they venture beyond the narrow field of productivity spillovers, economists need help from other disciplines to advance their understanding of the wider social benefits of education in general, and of university education in particular. Such matters as the nature of the society in which we want to live, our relationships with fellow citizens, the obligations we feel toward them, and the ethical importance we attach to various features of societal arrangements are all at stake here. It is sometimes claimed by, for example, university teachers of the humanities and social sciences that important general benefits are conferred on a democratic society by those who can think critically about and discuss coherently competing value systems and their implications for social and political issues. The trouble with trying to subject claims of this type to conventional economic analysis is that the toolkit economics uses to evaluate externalities measures costs and benefits in

---

8 Smith has drawn my attention to a study by Barth (2001), who, using Norwegian data, looks at the influence on individuals' productivity, as measured by wages, of the average level of educational attainment of the workers in the establishments where those individuals are employed. Barth finds that influence to be significantly positive.

terms of given "tastes" on the part of the population. It is hard to see how such a metric can be used to put a value on activities whose purpose, in part, is to examine and perhaps modify those very tastes, particularly in a society where diversity in such matters is itself accorded a significantly positive value. But to say that the issue is beyond the scope of economic analysis is not to deny its social importance.

Research, Productivity, and Spillovers

Universities create knowledge as well as educate students, and the type of knowledge they create is often said to be, by its very nature, a public good, the entire benefit of which is available freely to all, and for which there is no feasible way of charging. Such a good confers all of its benefits on the whole of society, and it may be usefully thought of as representing a limiting case of a positive externality. Furthermore, such a good would not be produced by a private, for-profit enterprise. Hence, so the argument goes, there is a straightforward case for public subsidies to those who engage in the search for knowledge for its own sake.

The archetypical example of a public good, much used in the economics textbook literature, is national defense, and to have persuaded US legislators in the late 1950s that universities contributed so much to its production that they would be worthy beneficiaries of a *National Defense Education Act* was a stroke of opportunistic genius on someone's part. Nowadays, there is little mileage to be had from this particular argument, even in the United States, let alone Canada. It has, as we have seen, been replaced by the claim that knowledge, scientific and technical knowledge in particular, is the key to increasing national prosperity, and, therefore, that its generation by researchers must have government support. It has already been pointed out that there is room for skepticism in the face of this argument.

Recall, first of all, Harberger's (1998) study, discussed above, which looks for, but does not find, signs of economy-wide spillover effects on productivity growth, emanating perhaps from the general expansion of knowledge. Here too, it is also worth drawing attention to such work as that of Zucker, Darby, and Armstrong (1998) on more localized spillover effects. They study the interaction between research carried out in California universities and the activities of nearby firms in the biotechnology sector. That such interaction has been important is beyond question, but apparently it has not involved generalized spillover effects. The results of university-based research in this area were not public goods available for anyone in the vicinity of their creation to exploit. Rather, there were collaborative efforts between identifiable university researchers and specific firms, with these firms rewarding the researchers in question for their efforts with private income.[9] These findings confirm the theory that basic science yields economically productive applications, but they provide no support for its public subsidization. On the contrary, they suggest that private markets provide adequate incentives to get basic science done and then applied.[10]

On the other hand, the evidence just cited comes from one particular industry, and it may be that, in other areas, there are indeed significant scientific and technical ideas of great productive potential that do quickly become common knowledge and generate spillovers. In that case, public subsidies to their production would seem to be justified. There is, however, a trap in this argument. As we are so often told, Canada operates in a "global" economy, and shares a border with the most productive economy in the world. If Canada is ambitious about improving its productivity performance by exploiting new ideas that really do generate substantial external effects on productivity growth, it has a cheaper alternative to subsidizing the production of such ideas at home. It can simply take a free ride on research results produced in the United States, which, by common consent, already has the most intellectually fertile university system the world has ever known.

---

9   This paper is not an isolated effort, but a recent product of an ongoing research agenda. Its results are typical of those its authors and various associates have obtained in other studies, many of which are listed in its bibliography.

10 This result should not perhaps be surprising, because it has long been understood that, to the extent ideas can be protected as trade secrets, or patented, the returns they yield can be captured by their originators. There is no reason those who can establish rights to exploit the fruits of research in this way should expect anyone else to pay for it.

Externalities and Current Policies

Recent initiatives at the federal level in Canada, notably the Centres of Excellence and Canada Research Chairs programs, suggest that the argument outlined above has not been accepted in policy-making circles; and perhaps there are, after all, other external effects that would justify these programs.

For example, it is sometimes suggested that externalities arise not just from university research itself, but also from public confidence in the independence and integrity of those who carry it out. From this perspective, even knowledge that *can* be patented and privately exploited confers more benefits if it is the outcome of disinterested research and remains in the public domain. James Turk, clearly intending his argument to apply well beyond the bounds of research in science and technology, puts the matter as follows:

> [T]he university's mission is the unqualified pursuit and public dissemination of knowledge and truth. The university serves the broad public interest by treasuring informed analysis and uncompromising standards of intellectual integrity. (2000, 3.)

This statement has considerable merit as a justification for disinterested public participation in the funding of research, but the operative word here is *disinterested*. Governments, no more willing than any other agents to remain at arm's length from the activities they fund, increasingly seek to influence the direction those research activities take.

It is worth noting, furthermore, that governments themselves nowadays often encourage the formation of "partnerships" between universities and private sector agents with a view to producing and then sharing the revenue generated by commercially exploitable ideas. Turk (ibid.) and his associates are particularly critical of such arrangements — rightly so, in view of the criteria they bring to bear on the matter. But they perhaps pay insufficient attention to the general threat to the integrity of universities that is bound to arise whenever they become too dependent on any single source of revenue, be it public or private. It is not clear to me that the integrity of the research activities of a university sector that attracts a significant proportion of its funding from multiple partnerships with private agents is under greater threat than one that relies for its support on public expenditures for strategic initiatives designed by politicians and bureaucrats. These considerations suggest that arm's-length arrangements are just as important for ensuring the integrity of government funding of research as they are in the case of the private sector.

A second argument about the external benefits created by the public funding of universities reveals an apparent contradiction in certain current policies. That argument has it that such benefits are generated not just by ideas, but also by the presence in a community of the individuals who generate them. People capable of excellence in research (as in other endeavors), so the argument goes, are a desirable ornament to any self-respecting community, and Canada is poorer if they do their work elsewhere, even if its results take the form of an immediately available public good whose material benefits Canadian free riders can readily exploit. If this argument is compelling, however, it suggests that we ought not to tolerate (as Smith notes) restrictive salary agreements in our universities, particularly those that are unionized, that make it impossible for them to compete with their US counterparts for truly excellent personnel. It also suggests that immigration restrictions that give privileges in the academic job market to merely competent citizens and landed immigrants over outstanding foreigners are damaging to Canada. Excellence, like misery, loves company, and if we restrict immigration so as to discourage the employment of excellent foreign researchers in Canada, we should not be surprised to find that excellent Canadians emigrate to the United States to work with them there. It is, therefore, a small step in the right direction that such restrictions have been relaxed a little.

Note finally, however, that some of the above arguments, notably those about opportunities for free riding on research done in other countries, apply best to technical and scientific subjects. It is one thing to take a free ride on scientific and technical research done elsewhere, but another altogether to try the same trick with the outcome of scholarly work in the humanities and social sciences. Scientific and technical truths do not change at national borders, but a country that relies on another jurisdiction to do its critical thinking for it on matters of values, and of their application to social questions, will in due course end up with no values or distinctive policies of its own, and will cease to be a distinct entity. As with the creation of human capital, so too with the generation of new ideas: the case for public subsidies to Canadian universities is at least as strong in the humanities and social sciences as it is in science and technology. Here, too, the fact that conventional cost-benefit analysis seems not to apply implies a great deal about the limitations of that technique but nothing at all about the intrinsic significance of the problem.

Directions for Policy

Current policy toward universities in Canada seeks to provide broad access to undergraduate education by imposing stringent limits on fees. Against this background, it seems to favor scientific, technical, and professional fields over others when it comes to funding research and postgraduate study. At the same time, Canada's postsecondary education policy actively encourages a deeper involvement of business in the work of universities as a means of funding both research and teaching. Overall, this policy stance is not well justified by what we know about the economics of the matter, and I now turn to making some suggestions for change. Let it be clear that, in doing so, I do not intend to implicate the authors of subsequent essays in this volume as advocates of specific measures. These authors can and do speak for themselves on the issues raised by their own studies.

Tuition Fees and Loan Guarantees

First and foremost, note that the returns accruing to recipients of undergraduate university education in Canada are comfortably positive in most areas, even when full account is taken of the subsidies students currently receive. Vaillancourt and Bourdeau-Primeau argue on the basis of 1995 data that there was then room for a significant increase in tuition fees, a conclusuion that, as Rathje and Emery show, still holds in light of 1998 data. The only area of undergraduate study where a significant increase in tuition fees could not be absorbed by students is fine arts.[11]

There is no reason to believe, therefore, that the system could not continue to function even if all restrictions on the fees universities charge were removed and courses of study were priced, along lines suggested by Davenport (1996), to reflect the costs of providing them. Such a step would make undergraduate students, rather than government and business, the principal source of funding for universities. They would, therefore, become the principal arbiters of what programs are offered, on what scale, and at what levels. The demand for well-educated workers seems to be still growing in Canada, and some catching up to the United States remains to be done in terms of the proportion of the population receiving university education, despite the fact that such training is already a good deal more costly to obtain south of the border. It is therefore doubtful that the increases in Canadian tuition fees implicit in this proposal would lead to an absolute shrinkage in the demand for university places. It might well lead to some significant reallocations of resources within universities, however, as students began to take more careful note than they do now of the relationship between the resource costs of various programs and the returns they can be expected to yield. It is hard to believe that the overall outcome would be anything other than an improvement in the university sector's efficiency as a producer of human capital.[12]

One important condition must be satisfied to make any such deregulation of tuition fees desirable, a condition called for by considerations both of economic efficiency and of equity. Government

---

11 Note however, that their calculations involve rates of return in which sex differences have been averaged out. This is appropriate, for universities could hardly charge different fees to men and women. At the same time, a move to tuition fees based on the costs of education would likely lead to some movement of men among disciplines, and perhaps out of university education altogether.

12 To the extent that students themselves were paying for undergraduate education, the potential, noted by Nakamura and Bruneau, for electronic placement services inadvertently to transfer resources from Canadian taxpayers to US employers would be reduced or even removed altogether. I am grateful to François Vaillancourt for this point.

must ensure that lack of access to funds for education does not shut any otherwise qualified and willing applicant out of the university system. Potential students who are already in possession of sufficient resources could use them to buy an education offered at its market price, but in the absence of some sort of intervention, the less wealthy would face a serious barrier arising from the simple fact that private sector financial institutions do not usually make loans without collateral. Since indentured labor is, with good reason, illegal, any loans in aid of the purchase of higher education that they would be likely to offer in the absence of government intervention would go only to those who do not need them.

There is an obvious case for repairing this important gap in the private capital market by, at a minimum, having government provide guarantees in lieu of collateral to institutions making educational loans. The reader who wonders whether this has not already been tried and found wanting is reminded that what is being advocated here is support for *university* education, and Davenport's evidence shows that the default rate in this area has been low under current arrangements. Advocacy of the general principle of making student loans readily available should not be read as support for any specific program. This is an area where many devils lurk in the details, and there is not space here to deal with them.[13]

The Role of Subsidies

Those who believe there are important social payoffs to university education will continue to favor its further support by outright public subsidies. The considerations that would justify such measures involve, as has already been noted, fundamental social and political values not amenable to economic analysis. They must, then, be debated and dealt with through political processes — and, since

---

13 Here the reader's attention is drawn to Finnie (2001), who provides a careful analysis of the advantages of loans over grants as means of making postsecondary education accessible, and of the virtues (of which there are many) and shortcomings of the system currently in place, together with suggestions for improving it.

the questions at stake are of national significance, there is a clear role for the federal government in coping with them.

If the outcome of these deliberations is, however, a decision in favor of tuition subsidies, the arguments advanced above for giving market power to individual students still stand, suggesting that subsidies should be given directly to those individual students rather than to provincial governments or university administrations to be spent on their behalf. They could, for example, take the form of cash grants or of interest subsidies for student loans; the tax subsidies currently offered in registered educational savings plans (RESPs) also conform to this principle.[14]

Since we know so little about how the value of the external benefits that would justify public subsidies varies across areas of study, it would probably be best to distribute them in proportion to student enrollments in various disciplines, thus ensuring that public support for universities does not become a covert means whereby governments divert their activities away from the mix that their customers desire. This would happen automatically if federal subsidies were given to individual students by way of vouchers, independent of their chosen fields of study. However, other donors, including individuals, firms, and industry associations, not to mention provincial and local governments, should be left free to endow scholarships and to offer other support in particular areas as they see fit, subject only to the willingness of the university in question to accept what is offered. In this way, organizations that believe certain lines of study produce human capital of a type that yields particular benefits to them can pay for its production if that seems to be in their self-interest. And universities, ever mindful of the need to attract paying students, can be expected to be vigilant against gifts that arrive with conditions attached whose implementation would undermine the integrity of their programs of study.

---

14 One form of subsidy that seems to have much popular support would make the repayment schedules for student loans contingent on income earned after graduation. See, however, Smith's penetrating discussion in this volume of the perverse incentives implicit in such schemes.

Graduate study presents a no more complicated set of issues. For most professional programs, arrangements similar to those suggested for undergraduates should work without problems.[15] For those closer to the purely academic end of the spectrum, there might be more difficulties, but to the extent that the low material returns revealed by the Vaillancourt and Bourdeau-Primeau and Rathje and Emery studies are compensated for by intangible rewards, this would not be the case. Besides, if most PhD recipients go into university teaching, and if university revenues are to be mainly driven by undergraduate fees, then market mechanisms will work to ensure a level of reward necessary to maintain a supply of suitably qualified teachers. Even so, in the current state of knowledge, we should not rule out the possibility canvassed by Rathje and Emery that there are substantial externalities to be realized at this level that would justify the public provision of postgraduate scholarships and other forms of support.

Research Funding

Chant and Gibson suggest that universities use their research performance as a means of signaling to potential students the quality of the education they offer. To that extent, there is a case for funding research expenditures out of tuition revenue. By and large, university teachers enjoy research and other scholarly activities, and will choose to work at institutions that provide them with the time and resources to engage in them, through such means as lighter teaching loads and access to research assistants (who are usually drawn from the graduate student body).

---

15 Rathje and Emery's results on rates of return to medical education present a special problem in this context. To the extent that the low returns they estimate simply reflect a measurement bias stemming from the omission of self-employment income, they can be ignored. To the extent, however, that they reflect the effects of the organization of Canada's health care system, they suggest either that changes need to be made to that organization with a view to increasing the incomes of medical practitioners, or that the education of those practitioners requires subsidies. This issue raises questions far too complex to be addressed here.

If these benefits have to be paid for out of undergraduate tuition revenues, the ultimate judges of which academics will enjoy them will be their students. Professors who neglect undergraduate teaching in order to pursue research will not last long in such a system, and there can surely be no complaint about that. It might be objected that such arrangements would prove difficult to implement in institutions where faculty are unionized, and that universities constrained by such arrangements would be hard put to compete with those that are not subject to them. One can only respond that, if this does turn out to be the case, unionized institutions will be forced to contract, to charge lower fees for the services of lesser teachers, or to change their ways. It is hard to see why such an outcome would be anything other than desirable.

As with the creation of human capital, particularly at the postgraduate level, there are strong arguments that pure research and scholarship yield important social benefits. But, as I have argued, in this realm conventional economic analysis is, by its very nature, of only limited help in providing quantitative estimates of their value. Furthermore, policies regarding public funding of university-based research and its scale are also political matters of national importance, and similarly need to be debated and settled in the federal political arena. Current economic knowledge nevertheless yields two important lessons for such decisions. First, it would be unwise to premise them on productivity-growth spillover effects, the existence of which is extremely dubious. Second, if research productivity in universities is, like productivity elsewhere, a matter of "mushrooms" rather than "yeast," then public support for research would be better concentrated on researcher-initiated and curiosity-driven projects than, as at present, on centrally designed strategic initiatives.

Philanthropic private sector support ought, of course, to be part of the picture here, too. It ought to continue to be possible for firms and industries to pay for research that will be beneficial and profitable to them, subject to whatever restrictions the universities themselves see fit to place on such arrangements. Universities that come to rely more heavily than they now do on tuition fees paid by students, who will be concerned about the integrity of the institutions they attend, can be expected to take care to defend that integrity. To this end, it would be a matter of simple self-interest for universities to ensure that all research contracts, whether with government or the private sector, be open to public scrutiny, and that no restrictions be placed on the publication of results generated under their auspices.

The Political Context

Universities are currently a provincial responsibility, but the forgoing arguments lead to the suggestion that provincial financing take on a secondary role in supporting a system that draws its basic revenue from tuition fees, supported by federal government guarantees — and perhaps subsidies — in a student loan market, as well as from subsidies to research that emanate from both the federal government and the private sector. Something, therefore, needs to be said about the political feasibility of such a rearrangement of financial responsibilities.

Note first of all that there is no suggestion here that the provinces surrender their statutory authority over universities or the right to continue subsidizing them if they see fit. The major change advocated is that they stop using their regulatory powers to hold down fees below the levels that universities themselves would like to set. Given that there is immense pressure on governments at all levels to increase health care spending, that universities compete directly with health care in provincial budgets, and that Ottawa's grants in aid of these two sectors are bundled together into the Canada Health and Social Transfer, there is perhaps room for a federal-provincial agreement that would see the provinces deregulate university fees in exchange for the creation of a federal loan guarantee system, with the resulting public expenditure savings being partly devoted to health care funding. In this way, overall government expenditures at both levels could be cut, spending on a popular program could be increased, and a new and more secure tuition revenue base could be provided for the funding of the important, but not so politically popular, university sector. The matter is surely worth some further thought along these lines.

Finally, it would do no harm if there were freedom of entry, subject to a minimum level of oversight designed to prevent outright fraud, into the provision of university education. This again is an area where the provinces could use their powers without incurring expenditure obligations. In this case, there is no need for federal-provincial or interprovincial cooperation. Each province can experiment with what it does and does not approve. The recent and continuing growth of online universities in Canada has, in fact, already moved us a long way toward freedom of entry in this sector, at least as far as its teaching function is concerned. In saying that this is a positive step, I should not be read as approving of the specific programs offered by particular institutions, some of which, to judge from their websites, are heirs apparent to the organizations that used to advertise on matchbooks in the days when more people smoked.[16] I only mean to express the belief that the weaker ones among them will soon be weeded out by market forces, while the stronger ones will prevent the exploitation of monopoly power by existing institutions over particularly lucrative lines of business.

Concluding Comment

In this essay, I have highlighted the major results presented in the papers that follow, and tried to extract a coherent policy message from them as a whole. The main thrust of this message is easily summarized.

First, Canadian universities are productive institutions, but they have problems that need addressing. Some of these — the relative dearth of male undergraduates, and their relatively poorer performance — are probably not of their making; others — the influence of e-recruiting on their job-placement efforts — are quite specific and can be addressed in isolation. Still others, however, stemming both from methods and levels of funding, are system wide, and

---

16 Thus, I have considerable sympathy with Noble's (2000) opinions on the merits of these institutions. His comparison of modern internet-based "distance learning" initiatives to earlier efforts in this area that involved correspondence courses is revealing and, in many respects, compelling. I differ from him in having more faith in the capacity of prospective students to make informed choices among the better, worse, and downright fraudulent courses that are offered.

attract considerable attention because of the presumed importance of both education and research to the rise of Canadians' standard of living. Universities are undoubtedly major players in the knowledge economy, but their role stems from two facts: the majority of their graduates have useful skills that command high salaries; and the universities produce ideas that sometimes have social importance, including the potential to contribute to the economy's output.

Current public policies toward universities seem to be premised on the belief that their activities in teaching and research, in addition to the private benefits they confer, also spin off public goods capable of enhancing the economy's rate of productivity growth, the supply of which can be increased by government subsidies to a subset of their activities. This subset is concentrated in the science and technology area, where government encouragement of cooperation with the private sector is also being touted as a source of such spillovers. Unfortunately, the empirical basis for this belief is weak, and the thrust of current policies may well be misplaced.

A more realistic perception of the role of universities focuses on their well-established capacity to produce both human and knowledge capital that yields significant private returns. It follows that making use of the incentives implicit in this role would bring about an enhancement of their performance. To harness these incentives, universities must become more responsive, not to government but to their students, and the way to do that is to make those students the universities' principal source of revenue. A national educational loan program that eliminates capital market impediments to the implementation of such a change ought, therefore, to be a high priority. It may prove impossible to move policy all the way in the directions suggested in this essay. Nonetheless, current policies, some of which seem to be moving in the opposite direction, are probably rendering Canadian universities less, rather than more, efficient contributors to the knowledge economy.

References

Aghion, P., and P.W. Howitt. 1998. *Endogenous Growth Theory*. Cambridge, Mass.: Massachusetts Institute of Technology Press.

Auld, D. 1996. *Expanding Horizons: Privatizing Universities*. Toronto: University of Toronto Press.

Barth, E. 2001. "External Effects of Education? Evidence from the Wage Structure." Paper presented at a Workshop on Skill Needs and Labour Market Dynamics, Wissenschaftszentrum, Berlin, November 8–9. Oslo: Institute for Social Research. Mimeographed.

Blaug, M. 1999. "Mark Blaug." In B. Snowden and H.R. Vane, eds., *Conversations with Leading Economists: Interpreting Modern Macroeconomics*. Cheltenham, UK: Edward Elgar.

Cameron, D. 1992. *More than an Academic Question: Universities, Government, and Public Policy in Canada*. Montreal: Institute for Research on Public Policy.

Davenport, P. 1996. "Deregulation and Restructuring in Ontario's University System." *Canadian Business Economics* 4 (July–September): 27–36.

Finnie, R. 2001. "Measuring the Load, Easing the Burden: Canada's Student Loan Programs and the Revitalization of Canadian Postsecondary Education." *C.D. Howe Institute Commentary* 153. Toronto: C.D. Howe Institute.

Franklin, U. 2000. "What Is at Stake." In J.L. Turk, ed., *The Corporate Campus: Commercialization and the Dangers to Canada's Colleges and Universities*. Toronto: James Lorimer.

Harberger, A.C. 1998. "A Vision of the Growth Process." *American Economic Review* 98 (March): 1–23.

Kerr, C. 1963. *The Uses of a University*. Cambridge, Mass.: Harvard University Press.

"Land Grant Universities: An Old Dream in Trouble." 2001. *The Economist*, June 2–6, pp. 29–30.

Little, B. 2001. "Canada plays catchup despite solid growth." *Globe and Mail* (Toronto), August 13, p. B6.

Noble, D.F. 2000. "Digital Diploma Mills: Rehearsal for the Revolution." In J.L. Turk, ed., *The Corporate Campus: Commercialization and the Dangers to Canada's Colleges and Universities*. Toronto: James Lorimer.

Rao, S., and J. Tang. 2001. "The Contribution of ICTs to Productivity Growth in Canada and the United States in the 1990s." *International Productivity Monitor* 3 (Fall): 3–8.

Riddell, W.C., and A. Sweetman. 2000. "Human Capital Formation in a Period of Rapid Change." In W.C. Riddell and F. St-Hilaire, eds., *Adapting Public Policy to a Labour Market in Transition*. Montreal: Institute for Research on Public Policy.

Sharpe, A. 2001. "Determinants of Trends in Living Standards in Canada and the United States, 1982–2000." *International Productivity Monitor* 2 (Spring): 3–10.

Stager, D. 1996. "Returns to Investment in Ontario University Education 1960–1990, and Implications for Tuition Fee Policy." *Canadian Journal of Higher Education* 26 (2): 1–22.

Teixera, P.N. 1999. "A Portrait of the Economics of Education, 1960–1999." In R.E. Backhouse and J. Biddle, eds., *Towards a History of Applied Economics*, annual supplement to *History of Political Economy* 32. Durham, NC: Duke University Press.

Turk, J.L., ed. 2000. *The Corporate Campus: Commercialization and the Dangers to Canada's Colleges and Universities*. Toronto: James Lorimer.

West, E. 1988. *Higher Education in Canada*. Vancouver: Fraser Institute.

Winston, G.C. 1999. "Subsidies, Hierarchy and Peers: The Awkward Economics of Higher Education." *Journal of Economic Perspectives* 13 (Winter): 13–36.

Zucher, L.G., M.R. Darby, and J. Armstrong. 1998. "Geographically Localized Knowledge: Spillovers or Markets?" *Economic Inquiry* 36 (January): 65–86.

Universities and the Knowledge Economy

Paul Davenport

One of the striking attributes of the advanced economies during the past three decades has been the strong growth in demand outside universities for university graduates and university research. This long-term trend reflects the transition toward a knowledge economy, in which formal education, lifelong learning, and fundamental research are central to economic progress. All levels of education are important to the knowledge economy, and Canada's public schools and extensive community college systems all are worthy of our attention and support. My focus here is on universities, which, through advanced education and research, have a special role in allowing Canadians to take full advantage of the new economy.

The Challenge of Accessibility and Quality

Canadian universities will face an extraordinary challenge with respect to accessibility and quality over the next decade as the children of the postwar baby boomers reach university age, producing the third great surge in university enrollments since 1945. The first surge involved the returning veterans in the late 1940s and early 1950s. The second was the baby boom itself in the 1960s. In Ontario, for example, university enrollments increased by nearly 100,000 from 1961 to 1971. For the 1998–2010 period, current forecasts indicate an increase of some 80,000 (see Figure 1). The increase in the 1960s was associated with a significant investment of public funds, much of it for massive increases in faculty and staff, believed to be

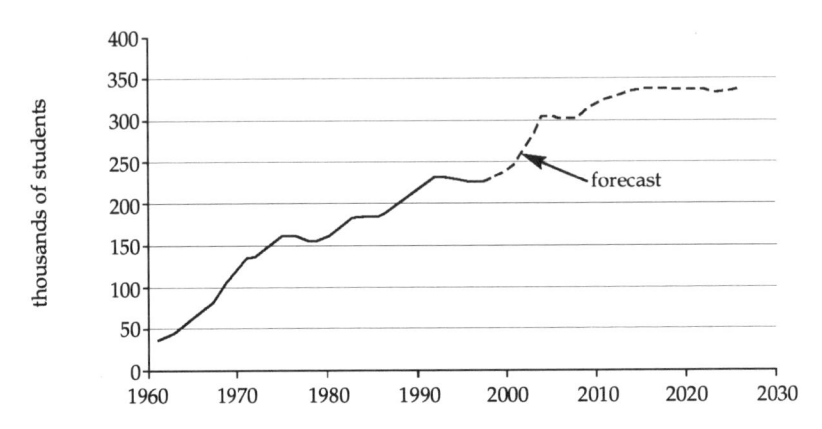

Figure 1: *Full-Time University Enrollment, Ontario, 1961–2026*

Source: Council of Ontario Universities.

essential to maintaining quality as enrollments rose. Are we ready to maintain quality in the same fashion in Canada during the coming decade?

Judging by the policies of the past decade, there is no reason for confidence in our ability to meet the accessibility challenge. In Ontario, for example, recent years have seen severe cuts in real university operating funding (see Figure 2). University budgets have declined throughout Canada, while US states have increased their funding of state universities, creating a growing divergence in the funding of public universities in the two countries. As Figure 3 shows, during the past two decades, real public operating funding per student in public universities has fallen by 30 percent in Canada and increased by 20 percent in the United States. Revenue per student is nearly 40 percent greater in US public universities than in Ontario, with core public funding, tuition, and fees per student all significantly higher in the United States (Figure 4). The comparison is done with a purchasing power parity rate for the Canadian dollar of 82 cents US, well above the official exchange rate.[1] An

---

1 Note that in Figures 3, 4, and 5 I compare Canadian universities to such US state universities as Ohio State and Rutgers, not to the elite private universities such as Harvard or Stanford, which would have resources per student many times those in the public universities.

Figure 2: Provincial Operating Grants to Ontario Universities, fiscal years 1987/88 to 2000/01

Source: Council of Ontario Universities.

Figure 3: Real per Student Public Funding of Public Universities, Canada and the United States, 1980–98

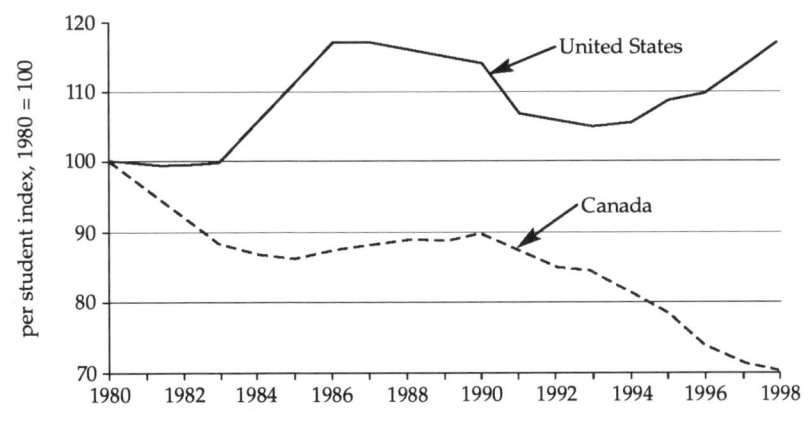

Note: Data for 1998 are estimates.
Source: Council of Ontario Universities.

immediate result of these differences is the growing inability of Canadian universities to compete for faculty with US universities. The competition is most intense in areas where private demand for faculty is also high, such as business and economics, electrical engineering and computer science, and certain areas of medical research.

Figure 4: Revenue per Student in US Public Universities relative to Ontario Unversities, by Funding Category, fiscal year 1997/98

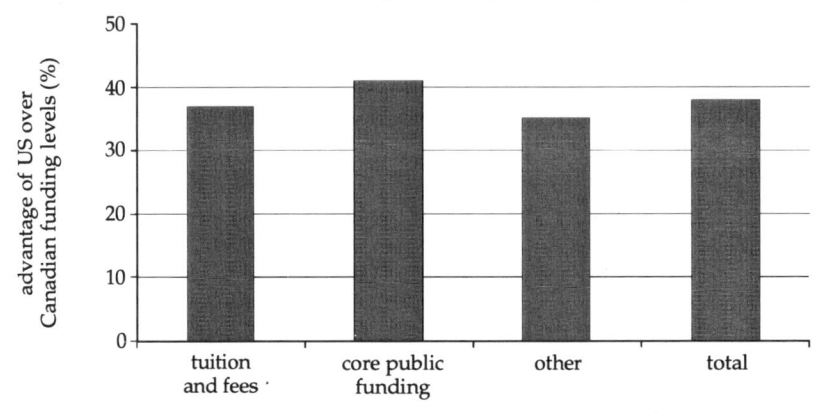

Note: Assumes purchasing power parity for the Canadian dollar equal to 82 cents US. US data are from 11 states.

Source: Council of Ontario Universities.

Figure 5: Ratio of Full-Time Students to Full-Time Faculty, Ontario Universities, school years 1987-88 to 1999-2000

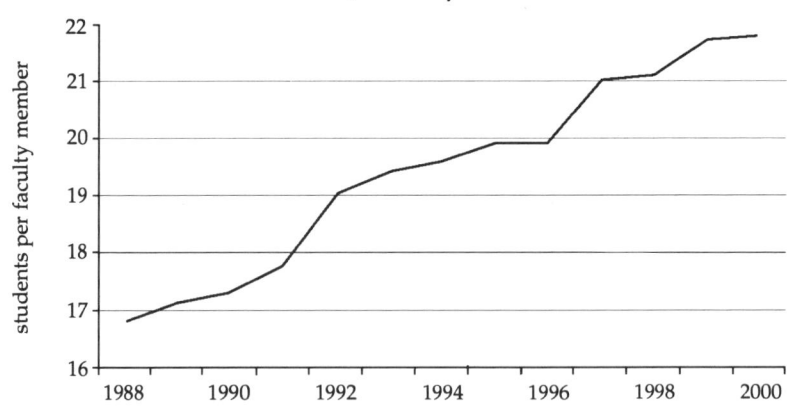

Source: Council of Ontario Universities.

The cuts in real operating funds have led to a growing student-faculty ratio in Canadian universities. Figure 5 shows the situation in Ontario, where the student-faculty ratio has increased by some 25 percent since the 1987–88 school year, an extraordinary change in just over a decade. The result has been larger classes, less contact between faculty and students, and what both students and faculty

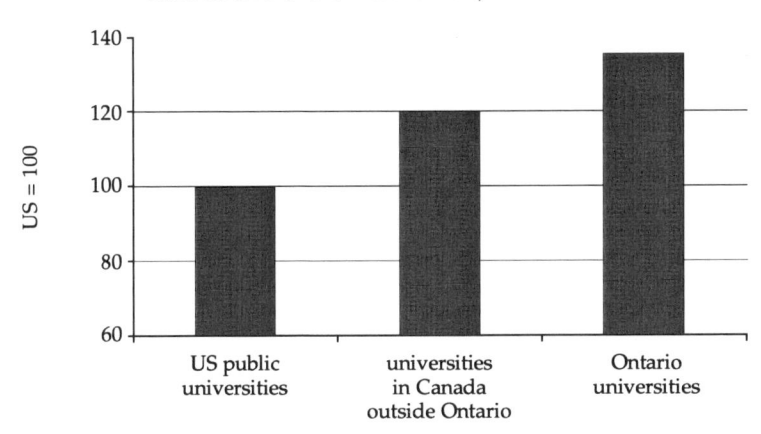

Figure 6: Relative Student-Faculty Ratios, Public Universities, Canada and the United States, 1998

[Bar chart with y-axis labeled "US = 100", ranging from 60 to 140:
- US public universities: 100
- universities in Canada outside Ontario: ~120
- Ontario universities: ~135]

Source: Council of Ontario Universities.

experience as a decline in educational quality. Again, the comparison with US public universities is instructive. Figure 6 shows that the student-faculty ratio is some 30 percent higher in Ontario than in the United States, and some 20 percent higher in the rest of Canada. The superior funding in US public universities allows for a higher quality of education for students and better salaries and working conditions for faculty, thus contributing to the brain drain of outstanding academics to the United States.

One approach to the accessibility challenge in Canada over the coming decade would be simply to allow the student-faculty ratio to continue to increase. In Ontario, for example, where it has increased by 25 percent, there has been no great public outcry. Larger class sizes, unlike dramatic crowds at emergency wards or growing waiting lists for surgery, do not dominate our political debates or provide leading stories for the evening news or the morning paper. Who really cares if the student-faculty ratio goes up another 25 percent in the next decade? Canada could adopt what might be termed the "barn model" of university accessibility. As long as you get in the barn and eventually get a degree, you receive all the benefits of university education — what goes on in the barn is not really very important.

I believe that the barn model is wrong — wrong for students and wrong for society. Students do need a high-quality education if they are to compete effectively in the knowledge economy, and quality does require the student-faculty interchanges that are reduced as the student-faculty ratio grows. Moreover, all in our society benefit from the innovation and productivity that well-educated university graduates help to create. To explore these themes, we need to review the role of university education in the knowledge economy.

University Education and the Knowledge Economy

Evidence of the growing importance of the knowledge economy comes in large part from the relative growth and superior remuneration of highly educated persons in the workforce. The number and proportion of university graduates in the labor force has risen dramatically over the past four decades, with no corresponding decline in their relative income. If the nineteenth century was marked by a strong demand for physical capital in the form of buildings and machines, the twentieth century saw a growing demand for the intangible capital represented by education and research. In the words of two distinguished US economic historians, in the twentieth century "the bias of technological innovation has been intangible capital-using, and, in particular has increased the relative demand for human capital formed through investments in education" (Abramovitz and David 1996, 44). This is a broad definition of the importance of education in the economy, not limited to any particular sector of economic activity. Finance Minister Paul Martin made this point very clearly in a January 17, 2001, speech to the Canadian Society of New York: "The volatility of the dot-com craze notwithstanding, the spread of technological change will continue to drive economic growth in all sectors.... [T]his is where the true new economy is to be found."

Too often, however, reference to the knowledge economy is given an overly technological definition — as meaning that the economy is now almost entirely driven by the changes in information technology that have occurred during the past three decades.

I do not hold that view, although I think that changes in such technology have been crucial to the development of the knowledge economy.² Rather, I believe that, to understand the knowledge economy, we must focus first on people and organizations, not on technology, still less on a particular technology. Learning in organizations has two fundamental characteristics — it involves the ability to learn and the ability to interact with and learn from others. These abilities are at the heart of an individual's success in the knowledge economy.³

With regard to teaching and learning, the knowledge economy generates a strong demand for university graduates because of the very nature of scholarly activity in a university. Universities are special places because learning takes place in an environment of research and scholarly innovation. Non-university institutions may well play a growing role in conveying facts and basic skills to young people after high school. As important as facts and basic skills are, however, the knowledge economy sets a higher premium on the ability to learn continuously, to take risks, and to work in teams — the very abilities universities cultivate because of their special position of teaching in a research setting.

For a decade, the Conference Board of Canada has asked its members to describe the skills they seek in university graduates. The skills they identify do not focus on information technology but instead are those of the knowledge economy. Canadian companies are looking for graduates with the ability to communicate clearly both orally and in writing, work effectively in teams, think critical-

---

2 On information technology and productivity, see Davenport (1997); a shortened, English version of that article is in Davenport (1998). Taking a 60-year perspective from 1970 to 2030, new materials and biotechnology may prove to be as important to the economy as information technology. On new materials, see Ball (1997); on biotechnology, see Thackray (1997).

3 P. Senge, founder of the Center for Organizational Learning at MIT's Sloan School of Management, demonstrates the importance of learning with numerous company case studies (see Senge 1990). My view of the knowledge economy follows that of the business writer who popularized the term, Peter F. Drucker (1993). Thirty years before Drucker, Machlup (1962) set out some of the key issues.

ly and creatively, solve problems, and exercise leadership. Learning these skills requires the debate and discussion typical of small classes. Students who spend virtually all their time in very large classes will be shortchanged on this crucial part of their learning experience. The "barn model" of accessibility just does not work for the real needs of students in the knowledge economy. Thus, as we discuss the accessibility of university education, we need at the same time to ensure quality — and that must involve stopping the steady climb in the student-faculty ratio.

The high return to university education, for the individual and for society, is a central tenet of belief in the United States but is still poorly understood by some in Canada. Writing in the *Financial Post* in 1998, Diane Francis asserted that "[t]he public is beginning to realize a technical education at a college or vocational school is considerably more valuable than more university degrees." While Ms. Francis refers to an opinion survey conducted in Ontario in 1998, she does not examine any real data on employment and income, and with good reason: all the official data we have for decades show the superior labor market performance of university graduates. Using her comparison of college and university graduates, the data show that university graduates have lower unemployment rates (Figure 7), higher incomes (Figure 8), and lower rates of default on student loans (Figure 9). As Figure 9 shows, the 1999 default rate for private vocational schools in Ontario — institutions whose only purpose is their presumed close connection to the labor market — was 31 percent, nearly four times the university rate of 8 percent.

Those holding Ms. Francis' view of universities often retreat into one of three positions when confronted with the data on the economic outcomes for university graduates. Some claim that, although the average economic returns of university graduates may be superior to returns of colleges and vocational school graduates, those with degrees in the humanities and social sciences have inferior economic outcomes. In fact, liberal arts graduates do better than college and vocational school graduates, as the work of Allen (1998) and others has demonstrated. A second defensive position holds that, whatever the rates of return, we already have a higher rate of university participation in Canada than in the Unit-

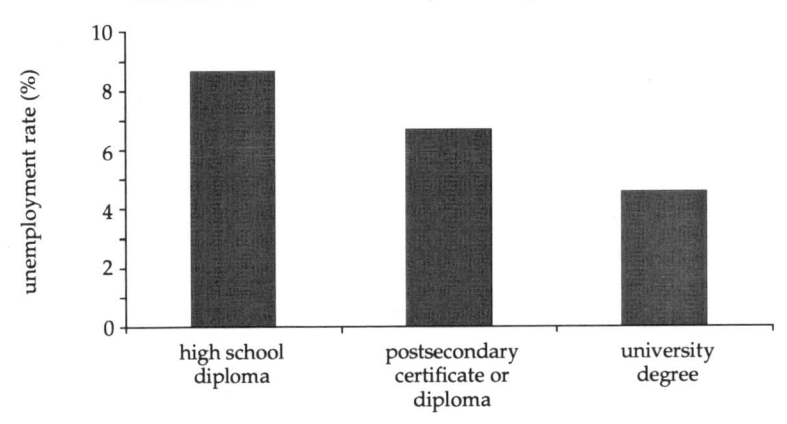

Figure 7: *Unemployment Rate, by Educational Level Attained, Canada, 1997*

[Bar chart showing unemployment rate (%) on y-axis from 0 to 10. Bars: high school diploma ~8.7%, postsecondary certificate or diploma ~6.7%, university degree ~4.5%.]

Source: Council of Ontario Universities.

ed States.[4] This common misunderstanding arises from data from the Organisation for Economic Co-operation and Development (OECD) on "tertiary education," which lump all postsecondary education into one category. While university education has a certain similarity among countries, non-university tertiary education varies widely among countries. As Figure 10 shows, Canada lags well behind the United States in the percentage of the labor force with a university degree, with the major European countries a bit behind Canada. This country is alone, however, in the extraordinary investment it makes in non-university postsecondary education, much of it training that is undertaken in the private sector elsewhere.

A third position is sometimes suggested, often by specialists in the area — that increased schooling is undertaken by those with

---

4 Riddell and Sweetman (2000, 86) refer to this as the "over-education/under-employment" view of higher education, which "implies that the rising educational attainment of many Canadians is a waste of their and society's time and money." The notion here is that we already have too many university graduates and that they are generally working in jobs that do not require higher education. Riddell and Sweetman find (p. 135) that their evidence contradicts this view and is more consistent with a growing demand in the economy for highly educated workers.

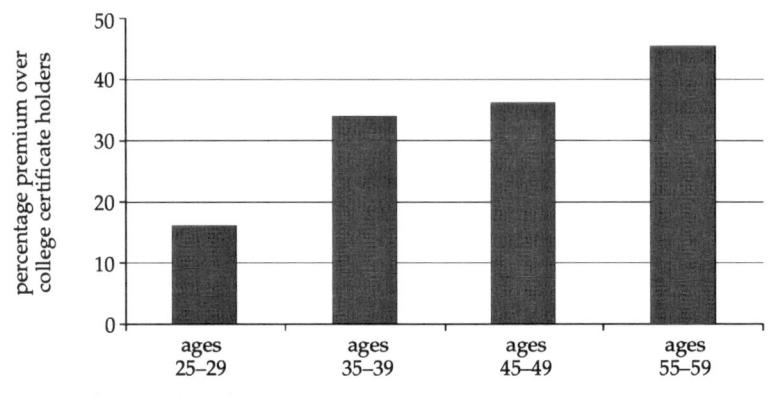

Figure 8: Income Premium for University Graduates, by Age Group, Canada, 1998

Source: Statistics Canada.

Figure 9: Student Loan Default Rate, by Type of Postsecondary Institution, Ontario, 1996 and 1999

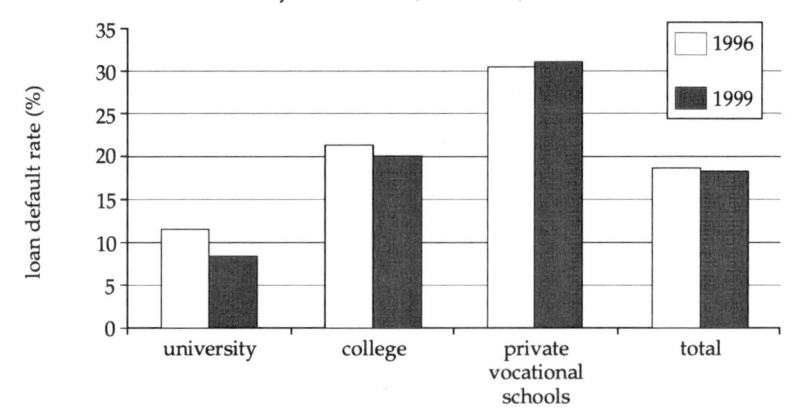

Note: Loans are those provided under the Ontario Student Assistance Program.
Source: Council of Ontario Universities.

greater innate ability, and it is the ability and not the schooling that explains their higher incomes. Ashenfelter and Krueger (1994) confront this position with evidence on schooling and income for identical (monozygotic) twins, and conclude not only that schooling is an important determinant of income, but that past studies may actually have underestimated the economic returns to schooling.

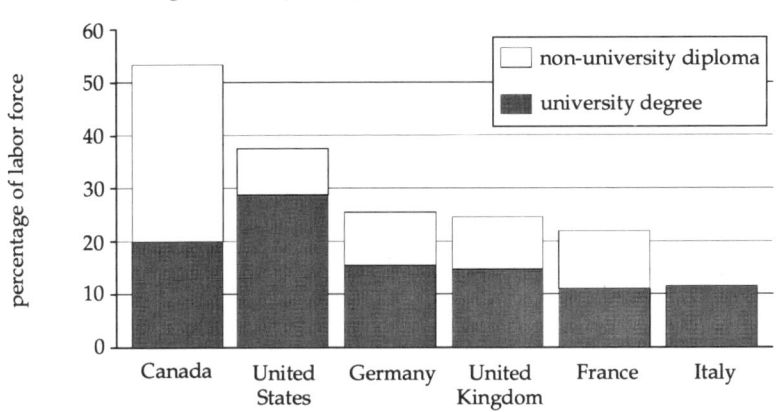

Figure 10: *Share of the Labor Force with a Postsecondary Degree or Diploma, Selected Countries, 1996*

[Bar chart showing percentage of labor force with non-university diploma and university degree for Canada, United States, Germany, United Kingdom, France, and Italy]

Source: Organisation for Economic Co-operation and Development.

In the event, parents and high school students in Canada have not been much affected by the gloom and doom of those skeptical of university education. They are aware of the high rate of return to university education, and have continued to drive up university enrollments over the past decade despite significant increases in tuition.[5]

University Research, Innovation, and Globalization

Growth in the knowledge economy is founded on discovery and innovation, in which university research has a central role. There will continue to be debate in all advanced countries about the balance between fundamental and applied research in universities and the appropriate degree of public funding for each. It is vital to understand, however, that it is precisely the distance of universities from the market which makes them such valuable collaborators with competitive firms in the knowledge economy. When the dis-

---

5 During the past decade in Ontario, tuition as a proportion of operating expenditures has risen from about 10 percent to about 33 percent, a figure similar to that of the early 1950s.

coveries of fundamental research run dry, the innovative companies of the private sector have no fuel in their pipelines. While technology transfer and industrial collaboration are important, if universities ever lose the focus on basic, fundamental research, the knowledge economy as a whole will suffer.

In his New York speech, Mr. Martin listed with pride the massive federal investments in recent years in support of university and hospital research, citing the Canada Foundation for Innovation, the Canada Research Chairs, the Canadian Institutes for Health Research, and Genome Canada. The provinces have also supported research. Ontario, for example, has invested hundreds of millions of dollars through the Ontario Research and Development Challenge Fund, the Ontario Investment Trust, and the Premier's Research Excellence Awards. These investments have made a profound impact on our ability to undertake research in Canada, to retain some of our best faculty, and to keep the innovation pipeline full of discoveries from fundamental science.

Mr. Martin made his speech, however, in the context of a continuing gap between productivity in the United States and Canada. Figure 11 shows labor productivity in Canada has stayed about 15 percent below the US level since 1980. In the manufacturing sector, the gap has generally been greater and has grown in recent years. Figure 12 shows the difference in income per capita in 1998, with the US level 25 percent above the Canadian level. The first figure focuses on output per hour worked, while the second shows national income divided by the total population. Thus, in translating productivity into the standard of living, the percentage of the population of working age, the labor force participation ratio, and the unemployment rate will all effect the standard of living for a given level of productivity. Sharpe (2001) brings these relationships out clearly. There is no cause for complacency in Canada, however, with regard to our relative performance in either productivity or standard of living compared with the United States.

The significant public investments in university research have created a strangely bifurcated pattern of funding in Canada's major universities. Growing volumes of research funding contrast with a penury of operating funds. Programs begun since 1997 — including the Canada Foundation for Innovation, the Ontario Research

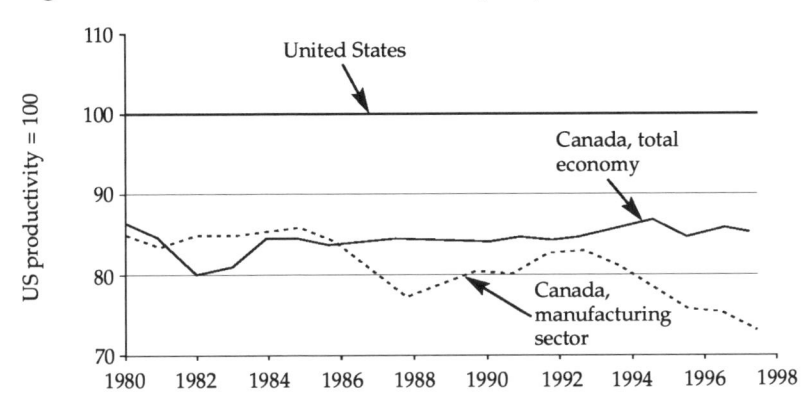

Figure 11: *The Canadian-US Productivity Gap, 1980–98*

[Line graph: US productivity = 100 on y-axis (70–110), years 1980–1998 on x-axis. United States line at 100. Canada, total economy around 85. Canada, manufacturing sector declining dashed line.]

Source: Statistics Canada.

Figure 12: *The Canadian-US Standard of Living Gap, 1998*

[Bar chart: income per capita in 1998 C$. Canada approximately 29,000; United States approximately 37,000.]

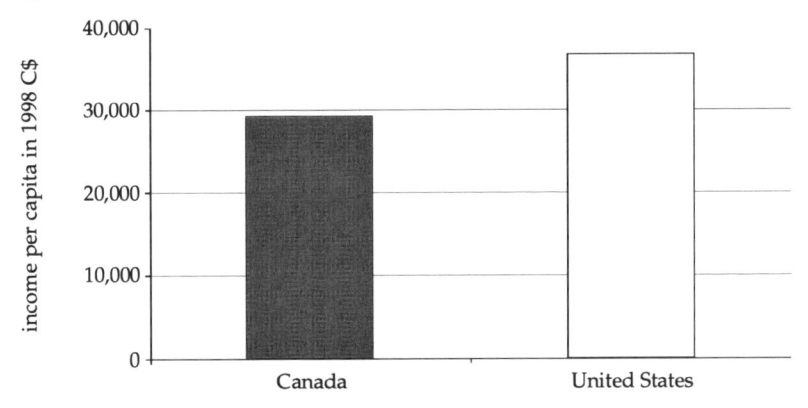

Note: US income per capita is converted at Purchasing Power Parity (C$1.00 = US$0.82).
Source: Statistics Canada.

and Development Challenge Fund, the Ontario Investment Trust, and associated private matching funds — have led to a remarkable increase in research funding, illustrated for the University of Western Ontario in Figure 13. Those who associate the regular announcements of new research funding at Western with general prosperity at the institution are often startled to hear that over the past decade faculty positions have fallen by 12 percent and staff by 16 percent, while enrollments have increased by 8 percent.

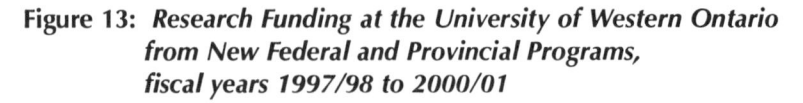

Figure 13: *Research Funding at the University of Western Ontario from New Federal and Provincial Programs, fiscal years 1997/98 to 2000/01*

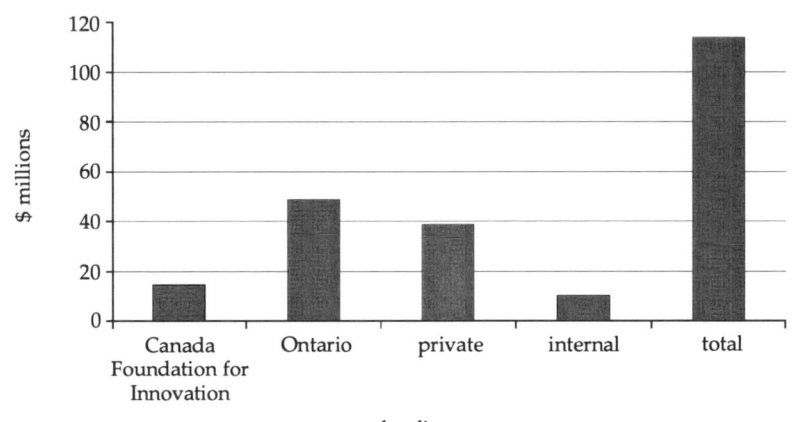

Note: Private includes other external funding.
Source: University of Western Ontario.

The reductions in real operating funds have forced Western to lay off staff and close faculty positions on a regular basis. Research funding, which is focused on equipment, laboratory renovations, and research assistants, generally does not allow for the payment of faculty salaries and indeed diverts operating funds away from teaching to the support of space and other infrastructure requirements of modern research. Hiring in Canadian universities over the past decade has generally been insufficient even to replace departing professors, at a time when we should be preparing for the enrollment boom of the coming years and anticipating the growing tightness of the faculty labor market.

Looking at the bifurcated approach to funding, one might think that Canada's national strategy for universities in the knowledge economy is to maintain a small nucleus of very well supported research professors in a limited number of fields and let the general education and research capacity of Canadian universities continue to decline. Such a strategy would fail, because the knowledge economy is broadly based — it is present "in all sectors," to use Mr. Martin's words — and is thus creating a growing demand for well-educated university graduates in all fields. Our current approach to university funding will not allow that broad demand to be met at a high quality of education, and will drive economic opportunities and talented people from Canada.

In this context, it may be helpful to use the distinction between *frontier knowledge* and *transferable knowledge* that Lloyd-Ellis and Roberts (2000) make. They conceive of frontier, or new, knowledge as knowledge produced in an innovation or research and development sector, in contrast to transferable knowledge, which is knowledge embodied in humans and transferred from one generation to the next by education. Sustained growth[6] requires both kinds of knowledge. Frontier knowledge alone will encounter diminishing returns without a complementary investment in education and transferable knowledge. The strategy of significant increases in research funding and reductions in real university operating funding per student employed over the past five years in Ontario and some other Canadian provinces can be viewed in these terms as a strategy that focuses on frontier knowledge alone. To get the full benefit of the investments in frontier knowledge, we need to invest also in the operating funds that support broad university education.

One way to think about the funding problem is in terms of faculty recruitment. Faculty retirements will be unusually high during the next decade, as the cohort hired for the first baby boom retires. To replace them and stabilize our current student-faculty ratio will require that we hire nearly as many new faculty over the next decade as we currently have in Canada (Figure 14). Put differently, annual levels of hiring over the next decade would have to be more than twice the average level of the 1990s (Figure 15). This will be difficult for three reasons. First, the United States will be experiencing the same combination of heavy faculty retirements and expanding student numbers. Second, PhD enrollments have not expanded in proportion to the need for new faculty in either country. Third, in many sectors the demand for PhDs outside the universities is expanding in response to the needs of the knowledge economy. Without very significant increases in university operating funds, we should expect the student-faculty ratio to continue rising.

---

6 In a constant elasticity of substitution production function.

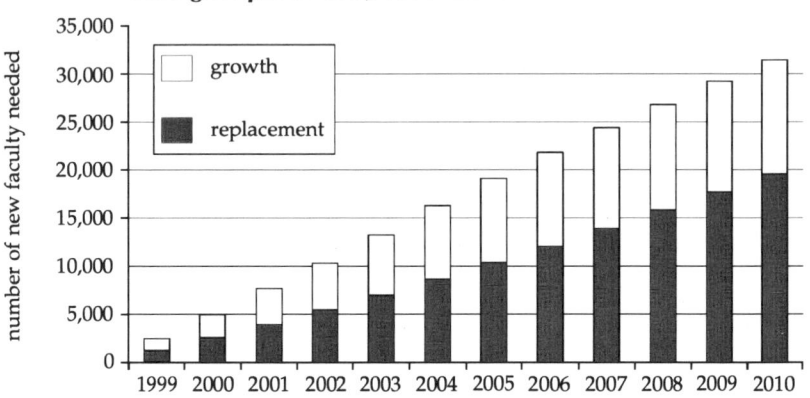

Figure 14: *Canadian University Faculty Hiring Requirements, 1999–2010*

[Bar chart showing number of new faculty needed from 1999 to 2010, with bars divided into "growth" and "replacement" components, rising from about 2,000 in 1999 to about 32,000 in 2010.]

Source: Association of Universities and Colleges of Canada.

Meeting the Challenge of Accessibility and Quality

To meet the coming enrollment surge, we need to build on the investments in research of recent years with a similar substantial commitment to operating funds. The glass is half-full now. We need to fill it if we are to remain competitive in the North American knowledge economy. Fortunately, the challenges facing Canadian universities can be met if we focus on four policy initiatives: reducing the student-faculty ratio; funding the indirect costs of research; extending the growth in direct research funds; and building more income contingency into the repayment plans for student loans.

Reducing the Student-Faculty Ratio

A modest goal for the next ten years would be to reduce the average student-faculty ratio in Canadian universities by 10 percent, thereby narrowing the large gap with the United States. This will require sufficient increases in operating grants to achieve two objectives: to accommodate the surge in university enrollment while reducing the student-faculty ratio by 10 percent; and to ensure that Canadian faculty salaries do not become less competi-

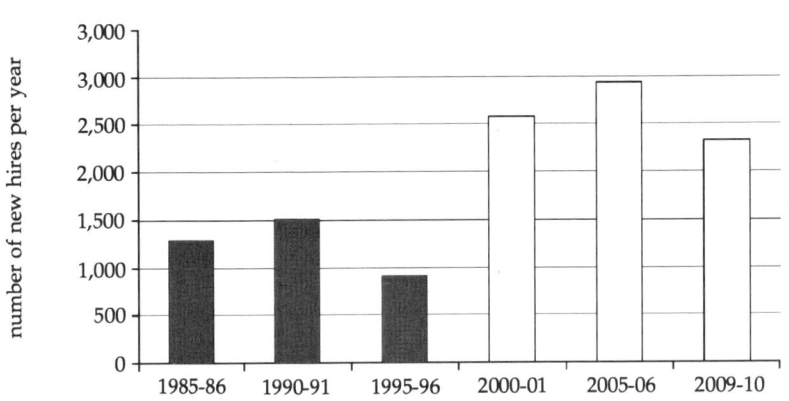

Figure 15: *Canadian University Faculty Annual Hiring Requirements, Selected Academic Years, 1985-86 to 2009-10*

Source: Association of Universities and Colleges of Canada.

tive with those in US public universities. The challenge will be a great one because, as noted above, the need for additional faculty will come at a time of record retirements.

In Ontario, for example, it is estimated that, over the next decade, universities will need to hire 13,500 new faculty — 7,500 to replace retirements and other departures, 4,200 to meet the enrollment expansion, and 1,800 to reduce the student-faculty ratio by 10 percent (Council of Ontario Universities 2000). This total is greater than the current level of 12,000 full-time faculty. By the 2005–06 academic year, additional provincial operating funding of some $600 million a year will be needed, along with the additional tuition revenue from higher enrollment, to enable all Ontario universities to accommodate most students and reduce the student-faculty ratio by 10 percent.[7] Without such a commitment of public

---

7 See Council of Ontario Universities (2000, 15). My total consists of the $456 million shown in that document and an additional $144 million to recruit 1,800 additional faculty to bring down the student-faculty ratio. In its spring 2000 budget, Ontario announced that tuition fees in regulated programs would be limited to increases of 2 percent per year for the next five years, a decision that underscores the need for public funds to meet the accessibility challenge. In its spring 2001 budget, the province committed funding of...

funds, we will not maintain an affordable university system of high quality. Graduate programs in Canada have not been expanding at a rate sufficient to meet this challenge, and we can expect severe competition, both in hiring and in salary levels, from the United States (Smith 2000).

Funding the Indirect Costs of Research

For years, Canada's universities have called on the federal government to fund the indirect costs of the research on its direct research grants. These indirect costs are costs assumed by the university, not by the individual research grant holder, in such areas as the capital and operating costs of space, information technology, library, and accounting. In its spring 2000 budget, the Ontario government announced such funding for its own research grants. The generally accepted rate of indirect cost, and the one adopted by Ontario, is 40 percent of the direct grants. Provision of these funds by the federal government would help in building world-class centers of research excellence, by allowing universities to use the funding of indirect costs to build on their strengths.

In its December 2001 budget, the federal government announced funding for the indirect costs of research on federal grants for one year at a rate of about 20 percent, and signaled its intention to consider funding the indirect costs on a permanent basis. This breakthrough on the issue was immediately celebrated by Canada's research community. It is to be hoped that future federal budgets will raise the indirect cost rate to 40 percent and make the policy permanent. Provision of the indirect costs of research would help Canadian universities build on their strengths and create world-class centers of excellence. The funds would be allocated among universities on the basis of peer-reviewed grant competition, thereby fostering competitive excellence and providing an incentive to institutions to make difficult selective choices in support of outstanding research.

Note 7 - cont'd.

...$220 million for expanding university enrollments to 2003–04. This can be seen as a first payment on the $600 million suggested here.

Extending the Growth of Direct Research Funds

While direct support for research in Canadian universities has grown significantly over the past five years, the average size of grants, measured per faculty and the percentage of faculty receiving grants, is still only a fraction of that in the United States. We need to continue the upward trend and extend new funding to the social sciences and humanities. New government research funding programs have for the most part focused on science, engineering, and medicine. It is now time to expand the opportunities for outstanding faculty in the social sciences and humanities, whose work is vital to the guidance of private decisions and public policy in such areas as economic regulation, immigration, bioethics, and support of Canadian culture.[8]

Building an Income-Contingent Loan Repayment System

Maintaining accessibility requires not only that the faculty and staff are in place to teach and serve students, but that the resulting education is affordable. Rising tuition over the past decade has led to growing debt loads for students. While default rates have declined slightly in Ontario in recent years (look back at Figure 9), there is nonetheless a growing concern among students and parents with regard to student debt and potential default. During the later 1990s, the federal and Ontario governments increased support for student aid significantly, with programs for interest relief, interest deductibility, and new scholarships, as loans outstanding increased steadily. There is, in my view, one very desirable policy that has been discussed at some length but that has yet to be implemented: a full-fledged income-contingent loan repayment plan coordinated between the two levels of government, involving both interest relief and debt reduction.

---

8 On the importance of university research in the humanities and social sciences, see Davenport (2000).

Such a comprehensive plan would involve society sharing the risk involved in student borrowing, and providing sufficient help to those with very limited incomes to keep them from defaulting. This would increase accessibility, especially for students from low-income families who might hesitate to take out a student loan because of the potential for default. Such a plan would also be beneficial to society as a whole, as it reaps the productivity and tax benefits of the majority of university graduates who are very successful on the labor market, at the relatively minor cost of helping those who are not.

While the knowledge economy, with globalization and rapid technological change, is opening up tremendous opportunities for Canadians, we must make the necessary public investments to prepare our workforce to compete in that economy. Although Canada lags behind the United States in the percentage of the labor force with a university degree, it is ahead of major European countries. Canada has thus been doing a fairly good job in encouraging university participation, but that accessibility has been bought at an unacceptable rate of increase in the student-faculty ratio. As we look ahead to the echo of the baby boom, we need a commitment to increase public funding in a manner that will accommodate large numbers of additional students while reducing the student-faculty ratio. With sufficient public funding for operating budgets and student aid, complemented by private giving and tuition, we can increase the quality of our universities and keep them affordable.

References

Abramovitz, Moses, and Paul David. 1996. "Technological Change and the Rise of Intangible Investments: The US Economy's Growth-Path in the Twentieth Century." In D. Foray and B.A. Lundvall, eds., *Employment and Growth in the Knowledge-Based Economy*. Paris: Organisation for Economic Co-operation and Development.

Allen, Robert G. 1998. "The Employability of University Graduates in the Humanities, Social Sciences, and Education: Recent Statistical Evidence." Ottawa: Social Sciences and Humanities Research Council of Canada. August. Mimeo.

Ashenfelter, Orley, and Alan Krueger. 1994. "Estimates of the Economic Return to Schooling from a New Sample of Twins." *American Economic Review* 84 (December): 1157–1173.

Ball, Philip. 1997. *Made to Measure: New Materials for the 21st Century*. Princeton, NJ: Princeton University Press.

Council of Ontario Universities. 2000. *Access to Excellence*. Toronto: COU.

Davenport, Paul. 1997. "Le paradoxe de la productivité et la gestion des technologies de l'information." In M.C. Monnoyer, ed., *L'entreprise et l'outil informationnel*. Paris: L'Harmattan.

——. 1998. "The Productivity Paradox and the Management of Information Technology." *Europe Productivity Ideas* 3: 1–3.

——. 2000. "The Liberal Arts in the Knowledge Society." University of Toronto Convocation Address. Available from Internet website: www.uwo.ca/pvp/honors/faculty/hondegrees/pres1.htm.

Drucker, Peter F. 1993. *Post-Capitalist Society*. New York: HarperCollins.

Francis, Diane. 1998. "Universities grabbing too big a slice of the education pie." *Financial Post*. September 22.

Lloyd-Ellis, Huw, and Joanne Roberts. 2000. "Twin Engines of Growth." Canadian Institute for Advanced Research, Program in Economic Growth and Policy Working Paper 143. Toronto.

Machlup, F. 1962. *The Production and Distribution of Knowledge in the United States*. Princeton, NJ: Princeton University Press.

Martin, Paul. 2001. "Winning the World Over." Available from Internet website: www.fin.gc.ca.

Riddell, W. Craig, and Arthur Sweetman. 2000. "Human Capital Formation in a Period of Rapid Change." In W. Craig Riddell and France St-Hilaire, eds., *Adapting Public Policy to a Labour Market in Transition*. Montreal: Institute for Research on Public Policy.

Senge, P. 1990. *The Fifth Discipline: The Art and Practice of Learning*. New York: Doubleday.

Sharpe, Andrew. 2001. "Determinants of Trends in Living Standards in Canada and the United States, 1989–2000." *International Productivity Monitor* 2 (Spring): 3–10.

Smith, David C. 2000. "Will There Be Enough Excellent Profs? Report on Prospective Demand and Supply Conditions for University Faculty in Ontario." Toronto: Council of Ontario Universities.

Thackray, Arnold, ed. 1997. *Private Science: Biotechnology and the Rise of the Molecular Sciences*. Philadelphia: University of Pennsylvania Press.

Do We Have a Problem Yet?
Women and Men in Higher Education

Stephen T. Easton

The last decade of the twentieth century saw a profound change in the enrollment structure of Canadian higher education. From 1987 to 1997, total university enrollment increased from 486,009 to 573,099. At the same time, the ratio of women to men on campus increased from rough parity in 1987 to 1.2 women for every man in 1997. This shift may be a boon for the men that have arrived, but the disparity is as much a cause for concern today as it was when the numbers were reversed — long ago in 1979.

Should we care? If this disparity in enrollment rates simply reflects a difference in the tastes of young people of the two sexes, then we might say, *laissez-faire*. But if it is a result of policy, we may want to redress the balance. There is little reason to believe that a Canadian university education should be directed primarily at either men or women. The parents of both are taxed at the same rates to pay for it. Both pay the same fees. Clearly, both should have equal opportunity for access. Do Canadians benefit from having one sex less well educated than another? Nobody wants to see an underclass of undereducated men or women. Higher education may not be for all, but a child's sex is not, obviously, the way to make the decision about schooling. Most educators and education specialists in this day and age presume that a rough equality should be present among our most well-educated citizens.[1] Yet no such equality exists in Canada today and the gap appears to be growing.

---

1 As long as women have a primary role in child production and early child-raising there will always be an incentive to have different educational levels...

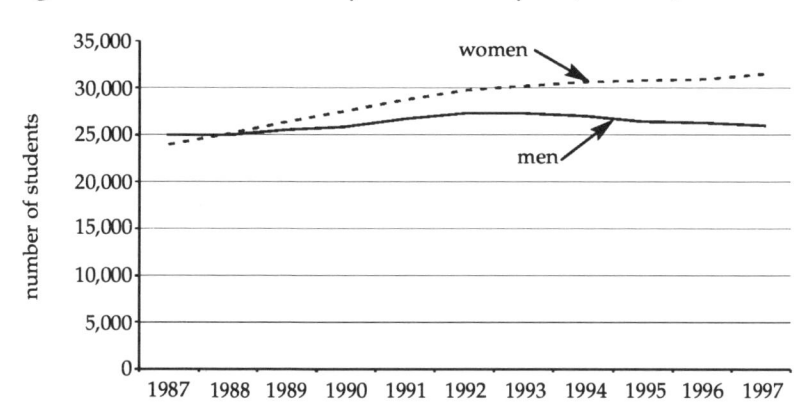

Figure 1: Full-Time University Enrollment by Sex, Canada, 1987–97

Source: Statistics Canada, CANSIM database.

Do we have a problem yet? If so, why? Any statement about the reasons for the relative increase in university enrollments by Canadian women is bound to be speculative. Nonetheless, looking at the most simple measures may prove useful — albeit brave.

Figure 1 shows the number of full-time students enrolled in Canadian universities from 1987 to 1997. The divergence between the rates of attendance for men and women is immediately striking.

A Clear Pattern

The total number of Canadians likely to seek higher education in any given year may be driven by demographic factors, but there is nothing in the demography to explain the increasingly unequal attendance rates. If there were more women than men for a particular age group, then we would find more women than men to be

---

Note 1 - cont'd.

...than men. On the one hand, with a potentially shorter market labor force experience, women will tend to have less time to recoup any investment in education. On the other hand, they will want to substitute education for experience as a way to raise lifetime income. Although these competing forces suggest that equality of education between men and women is not implied by basic theory, since they tend to offset, differences in desired average education levels are likely to be small.

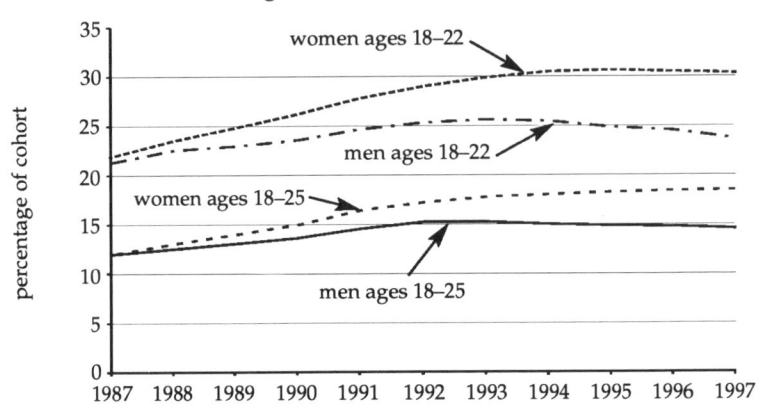

Figure 2: Full-Time University Enrollment by Sex, Relative to Age Cohorts, Canada, 1987–97

Sources: Statistics Canada, CANSIM database; and data from Figure 1.

in school even if their attendance rates were identical. But a look at the relevant age-sex cohorts belies this possible explanation.

Figure 2 plots the number of men and women in university relative to the number of men and women at specific ages in the general population. We assume that those ages 18 to 22 are most likely to attend university; the top two lines in the figure report the shares of women and men of that cohort attending university full time. Notice that since 1993 the line representing the share of university-going men in that age group has declined. Women in the corresponding age cohort increased their proportion of university-goers from 1993 to 1997; that rate has stabilized in the past four years.

The second pair of lines shows that the same pattern persists in the larger 18-to-25-year-old cohort, providing additional evidence that the decline in the number of university men relative to university women is not some short-term blip, but a definite pattern.

Table 1 describes the relative numbers of men and women enrolled as undergraduates in university for the most recent decade for which data are available from Statistics Canada.[2] The second column presents total enrollment in Canadian universities and the

---

[2] A quick perusal of provincial government education websites will confirm that the trends are not changing.

Table 1: *Ratio of Women to Men in Full-Time University Enrollment, Canada, 1987–97*

	Total Enrollment	Ratio of Women to Men
1987	486,009	0.97
1988	499,520	0.99
1989	515,025	1.03
1990	532,131	1.05
1991	553,954	1.07
1992	569,480	1.09
1993	574,320	1.11
1994	575,713	1.13
1995	573,194	1.16
1996	573,635	1.17
1997	573,099	1.20

Source: Statistics Canada, CANSIM database.

third indicates the ratio of women to men in university. In the 11 years included in the table, the fraction of students who were women has risen steadily. The patterns in Table 1 show that the growth in the number of students has been steady throughout the early 1990s. There is no reason to believe that the changing ratio of women to men is due to rapidly fluctuating total enrollments. There are currently more than 1.2 women per man in universities across the country.

The same trend is present in the ratio of women to men receiving university degrees, as shown in Figure 3. Women have tended to receive more degrees for the past decade, not surprisingly given the numbers in Table 1; their share of total degrees granted is increasing as well.

A National Trend

The remarkable thing about the numbers presented in Table 1, which are national averages, is how faithfully they are reflected at

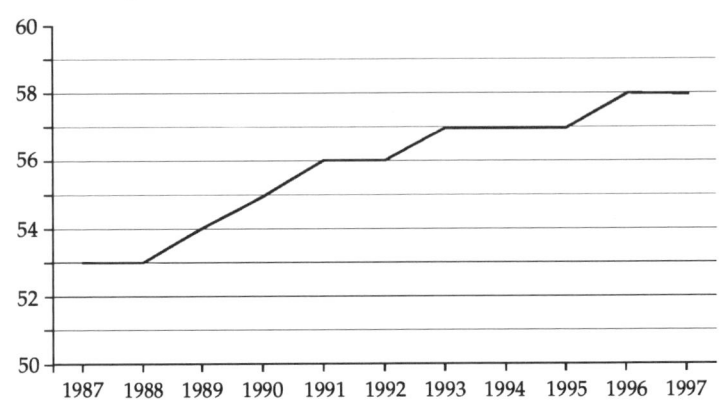

Figure 3: *Percentage of All Degrees Granted Going to Women, Canada, 1987–97*

Source: Statistics Canada, CANSIM database.

the provincial level. Each of the provinces shows the ratio of women to men attending university growing, albeit at differing rates. Table 2 lays it out with the first and last years highlighted to emphasize the significance of the growth in each of the provinces over the whole period. The average increase in the provincial ratios of women to men is about 2.3 percentage points per year. This is consistent with the national trend of higher university women to men ratios.

History Reversed

Historically, these ratios have been weighted toward men. In 1939 about 13 percent of Canadian university graduates were women — a ratio of 0.15 women per man. In 1946 the figure was 22 percent, or a ratio of 0.28 women per man. By 1960/61, the ratio had grown to 0.35, and by 1970 it reached 0.62 women per man. The sexes reached equality in terms of first university degrees in the early 1980s.

Where Have the Boys Gone?

If fewer young men, proportionally, are attending university full time, what are they doing instead? Are more males deciding to go to university on a part-time basis? Are they choosing college over

Table 2: Ratio of Women to Men in Full-Time University Enrollment, by Province, 1987–97

	Newfound-land	P.E.I.	Nova Scotia	New Brunswick	Quebec	Ontario	Manitoba	Sask-atchewan	Alberta	British Columbia
1987	1.13	1.18	1.03	0.97	0.99	0.97	0.91	0.94	0.94	0.88
1988	1.17	1.24	1.10	1.01	0.99	1.00	0.96	0.94	0.97	0.93
1989	1.18	1.25	1.14	1.06	1.04	1.03	0.99	0.98	1.00	0.96
1990	1.20	1.22	1.15	1.09	1.06	1.05	1.00	1.02	1.03	1.00
1991	1.19	1.22	1.16	1.12	1.08	1.06	1.02	1.06	1.07	1.01
1992	1.24	1.21	1.15	1.12	1.10	1.07	1.03	1.08	1.09	1.05
1993	1.23	1.32	1.17	1.14	1.12	1.09	1.05	1.11	1.12	1.08
1994	1.24	1.45	1.22	1.13	1.16	1.10	1.08	1.12	1.15	1.10
1995	1.28	1.56	1.25	1.19	1.19	1.13	1.12	1.16	1.16	1.14
1996	1.27	1.58	1.25	1.19	1.20	1.15	1.18	1.21	1.16	1.12
1997	1.31	1.59	1.28	1.21	1.22	1.17	1.19	1.26	1.17	1.18

Source: Statistics Canada, CANSIM database.

university? Or are they simply not opting for higher education as often as women?

Part-Time Enrollment

The possibility that more men are turning from full-time to part-time university turns out not to be the case. While the number of part-time students in Canadian universities is decreasing, there is only the slightest tendency for part-time studies to be frequented increasingly by men. From 1987 to 1997 the ratio of women to men in part time university studies fell from 1.6 women per man to 1.55 women per man. The number of students taking their university education part time fell from 300,000 to 250,000, or about 15 percent. This is particularly interesting because the number of full-time university students actually *increased* from 480,000 to 570,000 (or about 18 percent) during the same period. It would be unreasonable, therefore, to believe that men are substituting part-time for full-time higher education.

The College Alternative

If men are not moving to part-time studies, are they turning more frequently to colleges? Here, too, the answer appears to be no. As Figure 4 shows, at the usual 5 percent confidence level, there is no tendency for the fraction of men enrolling in Canadian colleges to increase. Over the past decade, the share of men in the college system has increased not a whit, although that observation masks a series of statistically insignificant fluctuations about this level.

There is no evidence of a significant shift from university to college among young men, and certainly not relative to the number of women. If men are increasingly substituting college for university, the change is a modest one.

An Economist's View

It seems, therefore, that young men are not switching to part-time studies, or to college, in droves; why then are they enrolling in university in smaller proportions than their female peers? I cannot

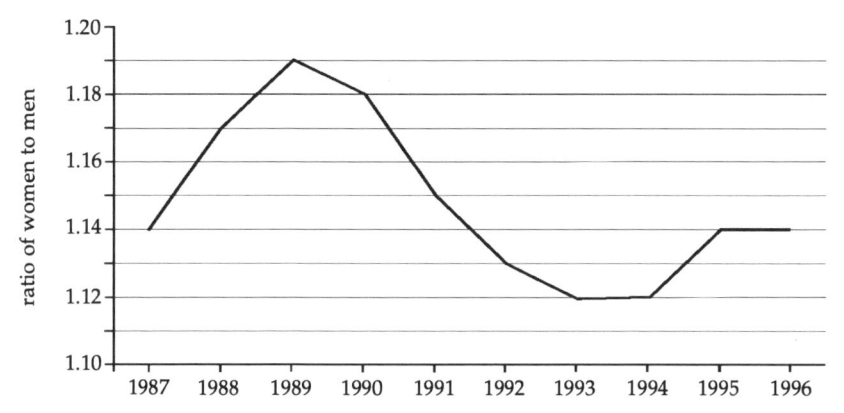

Figure 4: *Ratio of Women to Men in Colleges, Canada, 1987–96*

Source: Statistics Canada, CANSIM database.

give a definitive answer, but I can offer some insight into the issue from the economist's traditional two boxes of supply and demand. Let us examine each in turn.[3]

Demand: The Rate of Return on a Degree

First, let us think of what could be termed the demand side of the framework: the rate of return to a university education — that is,

---

3 I have committed a slight abuse of the nomenclature of demand and supply — call it poetic license. Usually we think of the university as *supplying* an education and students *demanding* it. My argument assumes that students *demand* an education as directed by incentives. The issue of who goes to university from high school is more complex, of course. Although students may demand university preparation in their high-school courses, the process that prepares them — supplies the education to students who wish to go to university — involves more than a simple choice by students. If we were to insist on a precise characterization of supply and demand, I would claim that the student *demands* the university education in the usual way, but that the *opportunity* to go to university is supplied by the secondary school. Shocks that hit the high-schooling process are different from demand-related shocks facing the student arising from the opportunities to use a university education. Of course, in all of this I am ignoring the traditional "supply" of university places and how they are determined. But these must be secondary in looking at the relative numbers of male and female students.

the amount by which someone can expect his or her income to rise as a result of having a degree, relative to the cost of obtaining the degree. Has this rate changed for men, women, or both? Does it pay relatively better for women to receive higher education today than it did in the past? Or is the return on higher education falling for young men?

Either way, the key is the return expected relative to the next best alternative — presumably a high school diploma, a trade, and/or a college certificate, for the most part. In our approach, the individual student makes demands on the university system guided by the rate of return each expects.

The Available Data

To investigate this incentive-based explanation, we need to know what has happened to the rates of return on university education for men and women. Ideally, we would have measures of the expected rates of return on university education facing students of each sex for each year as they prepared to enter. Even more than that, in an ideal world, or at least in a data-rich world, we would have the rates of return that students could anticipate for *all* types of education. Given their talents and resources and interests, students would choose the kind of education that maximized their individual rates of return. We do not, however, live in this data-rich environment. There are relatively few estimates of the returns to university education in Canada. Fewer still are broken down by sex, and none reports those returns as a time series over the past century.

Even without formal rates of return, however, we can still find some information about the potential rewards to a university degree. Recent work by Statistics Canada (1999), for example, calculates the ratio of earnings between men and women by (some measures of) education level since 1971, and with consistent data shows that, in the past decade, the ratio of women's to men's income rose by 10 percent. Figure 5 illustrates the average earnings of full-time male and female employees as well as their ratio. The topmost line is the ratio of women's to men's income.

Figure 5: Earnings of Men and Women in Full-Time Employment, Canada, 1967–97

Source: Statistics Canada 1999, table 1.

Although more awkwardly linked, data by education level are also available.[4] But this point raises a question as to exactly what approach to forecasting is appropriate for a student of today looking to the future to gauge returns (and, of course, anticipating the costs of education and the like).[5] I do not have a very good answer to this question. My strategy, however, is to take the most simple framework and see if there is any merit in what would surely be one variable that is related to the decision process, however imperfectly. To these ends, we need a calculation of the wages of men and women associated with a university degree and those associated with finishing high school. I focus on these two groups because the evidence from the past few decades suggests relatively little substitution into college or part-time university studies.

Recent work by Beaudry and Green (1997) gives us a framework to impute the wage rates to different groups, ignoring short-

---

4 Some of the education levels are not entirely consistent over the period.

5 There are many ways to forecast the future! We could assume that we have perfect foresight, we could assume that we are correct in our forecasts on average, or we could assume that the future looks exactly like the past. These are a few of the possible forecasts.

run phenomena such as unemployment. In their study, they construct a model of the earnings of men and women who have university as their highest level of education, and of those whose highest level of education is high school. Their model draws data from Statistics Canada's Survey of Consumer Finances from 1971 to 1993.[6]

Changes in the financial reward offered by more education are expected to guide the amount of education a person demands. An ideal construction would separate changes in the observed return that result from additional people obtaining an education, which would tend to drive the average return down, from shifts in the return that result from changes in technology or other factors. This approach, however, would entail a great deal of confidence in the underlying model of production. As an alternative to discovering the time shifts in the marginal product of education function, what I have done is to use the model of returns to education for men and women estimated by Beaudry and Green to impute a wage to education based solely on men's or women's experience, proxied by their age (and age squared), the cohort in which they were born, and some interactions.

The details of the formula are displayed in Table 3; the dependent variable is the log of earnings (adjusted for inflation). I have not included what I take to be short-run variables, such as the rate of unemployment.

Figure 6 displays a plot of the pattern of earnings associated with the different levels of education. The data are in logs and should be thought of as indexes. They are internally consistent, but not benchmarked to wages, since short-term variables such as the unemployment rate are left out.

The high degree of correlation inherent in the construction of the measures of wages to each of the four groups, and the tendency for enrollments to follow a rolling average of entrances, ensures a complex time series structure. The smoothness of the income indexes as forecasts of the gross return to different levels of educa-

---

6 Several other recent studies also produce returns to men's and womens' education, but they are not as easily adapted to our purposes. See, for example, Drolet 2001; and Baker and Fortin 2000. Beaudry and Green (1997) also list many of the recent studies.

Table 3: *Estimating Equations for Earnings of Males and Females with High School or University Education, Canada, 1971–96*

	High School Education		University Education	
	Males	Females	Males	Females
Intercept	5.81	5.33	6.18	5.95
Cohort	0.04	0.032	–0.012	–0.024
Cohort^2	–0.0028	–0.0019	–0.0001	0.0008
Cohort*age	–0.0021	–0.0008	–0.0004	0.0021
Age	0.04	0.01	0.065	0.004
Age^2	–0.0015	–0.00008	–0.0027	0.00009
Age^3	0.00002	–0.000002	0.00003	–0.000005

Source: Beaudry and Green 1997, tables 1–4.

tion is probably appropriate as forecasts of future values are likely to be weighted averages of anticipated future values.

From the figure, it is apparent that the income received by full-time female university graduates is increasing but declining modestly for men. (The income return from a high school education is falling for both men and women, with men's income falling faster in this category.)

The Responsiveness of Enrollment to Wage Changes

The simplest approach to measuring how responsive enrollment levels are to changes in wages — the heart of the "demand" explanation — is to regress the relative number of female university students (the female-to-male ratio) on their opportunity costs and the relative number of female and male students who are enrolled in grades 12 and 13.

Table 4 shows the results of this regression. The dependent variable is (the log of) the ratio of female to male undergraduates. The relevant opportunity cost measures are the difference between

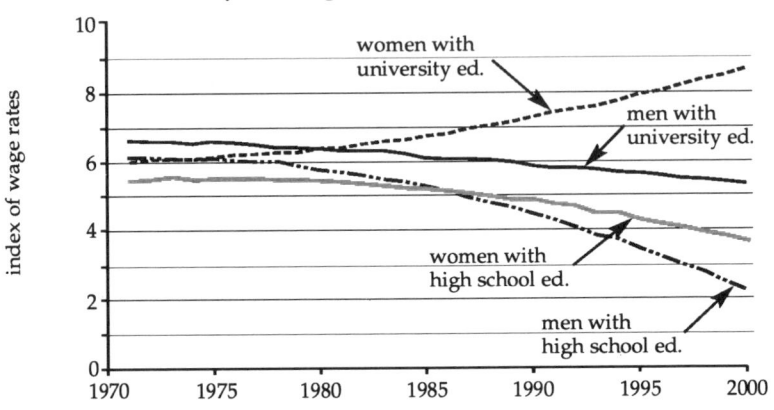

Figure 6: *Indexes of Wages for Men and Women with University and High School Education, Canada, 1971–2000*

[Line chart showing index of wage rates from 1970 to 2000 for four groups: women with university ed. (rising from ~6 to ~9), men with university ed. (slightly declining from ~7 to ~7), women with high school ed. (declining from ~6 to ~4), and men with high school ed. (declining from ~6 to ~3.5).]

Source: Author's calculations from the data in Table 3.

the (log of the) wages received by university women, UW, the wages received by women with high school as their highest level of education, HSW, and the same difference for men, UM-HSM.

In addition, the lagged value of high school graduates, identified in the table as the (log of the) ratio GRADEF(-1)/GRADEM(-1), is potentially relevant. High school graduates constitute, at least nominally, the largest readily identifiable pool eligible for entry to university.[7] The ratio is lagged, since the entering class this year depends most directly on the number of high school graduates from the previous year. Unfortunately, high school graduates are not reported by sex, so we have had to use the actual numbers of male and female students in grades 12 and 13 as indicators of potential readiness for university.[8] In the table, the variable QM is

---

[7] The problem is more complex, since in reality not all students who go to university do so immediately after high school. It would be desirable to distinguish those who enter university from each high school each year, but what we have are all students in the upper grades and the total enrollment of the universities. At some point, we could refine the measure to include only first-year students, but students who transfer from colleges and life-long learners will always make this a more complex issue with a range of opportunity costs not easily characterized.

[8] From 1975, one has to distinguish between CEGEP and high school in Quebec.

Table 4: *Ratio of Female to Male Undergraduates, 1972–94*

(as measured by the dependent variable LOG((UGFCAN)/UGMCAN))

Variable	Coefficient	t-Statistic	Coefficient	t-Statistic
C	–0.35	–15.6	–0.28	–5.97
UW-HSW	0.76	10.2	0.69	2.48
UM-HSM	–1.01	–7.7	–0.92	–2.02
LOG(GRADEF(–1)/ GRADEM(–1))	0.79	2.5	0.19	0.66
QM	1.36E-06	3.73	3.14E-07	0.94
AR(1)			0.76	5.84
R-squared	0.99		R-squared	0.996
Adjusted R-squared	0.99		Adjusted R-squared	0.995
Standard error of regression	0.016		Standard error of regression	0.013
Durbin-Watson statistic	1.74		Durbin-Watson statistic	2.04

Note: Shaded figures are corrected for autocorrelation.

Sources: Wage data from Figure 6; grade 12 data for 1972–75 from Statistics Canada 1978; for 1976–79, from Statistics Canada 1979; for 1980–94, from Statistics Canada, cat. 81-229, various issues.

a (0,1) dummy that identifies Quebec's move away from grade 12 and 13 to a format of grade 11 graduation followed by CEGEP. It has little role to play in our analysis as its coefficient is very small.

There are two regressions reported in the table. The first is written without shading and the second is shaded. Both report a regression for the same set of variables; the only difference between the two is a correction for autocorrelation. Fortunately, little of substance changes.[9]

The most interesting result is the magnitude and the sign of relative incomes. I will confine my remarks to the first two columns

---

9 Autocorrelation in the residuals tends to make results appear to be more statistically significant than they really are. The correction ensures that the levels of statistical significance are appropriate. I present both uncorrected and corrected data, as is common practice, to show that the coefficients are consistent.

for the moment and comment on the difference between the simple regression and the corrected one below.

I begin by baldly interpreting the coefficients in the table. In the first column of coefficients, the impact of an increase in the relative return to university education over high school is positive. That is, more women will tend to be in university when the relative wage received by women with higher education increases. Recall that the measures are of the difference between the (log of the) wage that is received by a university graduate and that received by a high school graduate. The coefficient is positive and statistically significantly different from zero at the usual 5 percent confidence level.

Further, a 10 percent increase in the relative wage received by female university graduates over their high-school-educated counterparts induces a 7.6 percent increase in the male-to-female ratio of undergraduates. Although we have little theory to guide us, it is interesting (and possibly suspicious) that the result appears so prompt and so strong.

A similar finding is also relevant for men. In this case, the result is effectively proportional. That is, a 10 percent increase in the relative wage rate of university men leads to a 10 percent fall in the ratio of women to men in university. This is interesting insofar as the coefficient is statistically different from zero, but the proportional response is not particularly revealing, as one does not have strong prior beliefs about what the appropriate magnitude of the coefficient should be.

There is a difference between the coefficients associated with the two sexes. That is, statistically, the response of men to changes in the wage of the university-educated relative to the wage of the high-school-educated differs from the response of women. Men appear to respond more elastically to the reward changes than do women. If this finding is confirmed — and recall the many caveats along the way in this study — it would be an interesting result. Usually, in labor supply studies, women tend to be the higher-elasticity participants. That is rationalized by their more complex labor market behavior — balancing childbearing and family with labor force participation. However, these data suggest the opposite — that men have the higher elasticity of response to wage incentives.

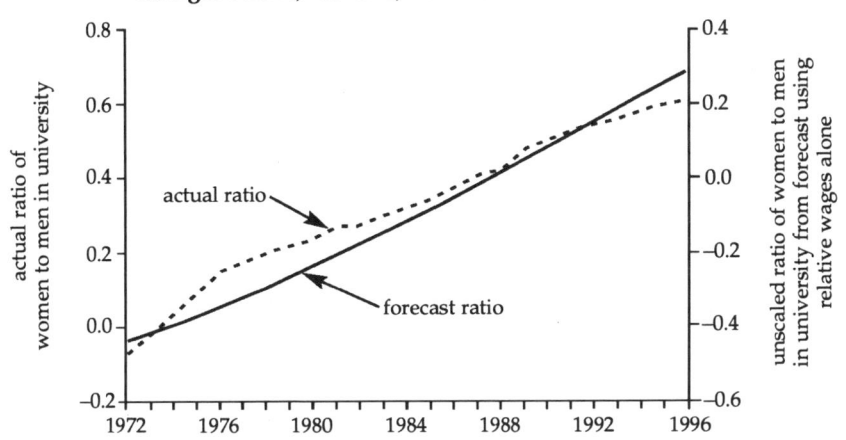

Figure 7: Predictions by Relative Wage Rate Changes Alone, Canada, 1972–96

The different rate of response by men and women (to the income differentials) gives the correct magnitude of changes in the proportions of university students. This tells us that both play a role in determining changes in the ratio of men and women in university. Although there are any number of ways to display the information, if one plots the impact of the wage rate differential changes multiplied by their coefficients, one can superimpose the net effect on the actual growth rate of the ratio of men to women in university. This is done in Figure 7.

Although there is clearly much left to explain in the pattern of enrollments by men and women, the relative wage story is at least one credible component, since it picks up some of the changes.

Supply: The Number of University-Ready Students

The flip side of the possible explanation focuses on what I would like to call the "supply" of students: the university readiness of students coming from high school. If women are better prepared than men by high schools, and if universities are sex-blind and do not admit men differentially, then women will tend to be accepted in relatively greater proportion. This aspect of the problem is even less well studied, but I think it worth investigating

What factors in the educational process that takes place before university — at high school and even earlier — might prepare boys and girls in increasingly different proportions for university-level work? One likely candidate is the proportion of assessment that is based on classroom work versus that based on province-wide exams.

In British Columbia, for example, as Peter Cowley and I report (1999), while boys may, on average, do better or worse than girls on the province-wide final exams depending on the subject, they always received poorer marks on average than girls in their school-based assessment. Since school-based assessment provides 60 percent of the final grade in provincially examinable grade 12 classes, it has the potential to have a significant impact on the ability of different students to graduate or otherwise qualify for university.[10]

Figure 8 illustrates the class-based and exam-based assessments for British Columbia's 1996/97 marks. For each of the most popular subjects in the province, the figure displays the average differential in marks received by boys and girls in their school-based assessment (the dark bar) and their exam-based assessment (the light bar). The subjects are arrayed in the order of the frequency with which they were taken.

For example, in English (the most frequently written exam), girls perform better than boys on both their school-based assessment (by nearly 6 percentage points) and their provincial exam results (4 percentage points better). In math, girls' school-based assessment is 2 percentage points better, although their exam-based results are marginally poorer. The same pattern is true in biology, and chemistry, and is most dramatic in geography and history. Women have better school assessment and exam scores in physics and French.

As suggested above, what stands out from the figure is the tendency for girls always to receive higher marks in the school-based assessment. Such a picture raises a host of questions. If university

---

10 Recall that hundreds of thousands of students take exams. Although I do not do the arithmetic to calculate how the number of boys versus girls would change with a different weighting of the school and exam marks, the reader will appreciate that there are many students who are marginal and for whom small differences in the total grade mean "go" or "no go."

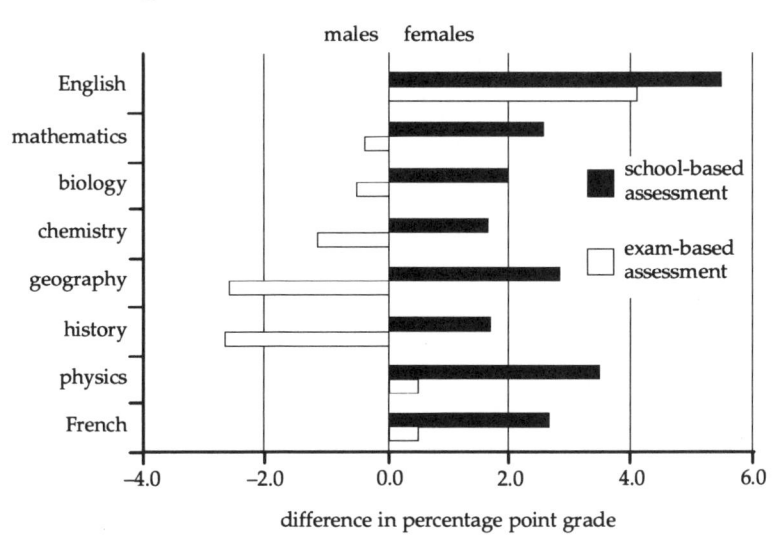

Figure 8: *School-Based versus Exam-Based Assessments by High School Course, British Columbia, 1996/97 School Year*

Source: Cowley and Easton 1999, figure 2.

eligibility was historically more heavily exam weighted than school-assessment weighted, then our increasingly school-based assessment process may provide some explanation for a growing pool of female university-eligible high school graduates.

Are these patterns mirrored in other provinces? Since I am not aware of other studies that track Canadian school-based versus exam-based performance, and ours deals exclusively with British Columbia, such a supply-based approach will have to wait until appropriate data are available to assess the usefulness of the hypothesis.

It may not be the case that everything we learn is learned in kindergarten, but it is surely the case that the sex disparity phenomenon that is overtaking the universities is a process that started long before. We need to assess why boys are relatively less successful than girls in the classroom, regardless of how well their external exam scores suggest they know the material. Is it exclusively a matter of weighting? Or are boys performing less well because of something that is being done differently, either at home or at school?

Conclusion

We do not know why university enrollment proportions are changing so dramatically. Perhaps men simply make more money in computer technologies and sports, for which university education is less of a prerequisite. I have looked at the issues from the economist's traditional two points of view, demand and supply, and have argued that there are reasons to believe that both have some ability to explain the phenomenon. Although the evidence is far from conclusive, the increase in the average woman's wage relative to the cost of her university education may explain some of the demand side of the story, since the actual income received by university men appears to be falling gradually.

On the supply side of the ledger, the importance of young women going to university has been emphasized for years. Institutionally, increasing weight has been placed on areas of secondary school performance in which women are relatively more successful (Cowley and Easton, 1999). There is, however, no quantitative assessment of the consequences of these changes.

Is the sex-related change in university enrollment a good thing? That is a debate worth having. In the meantime, the reasons behind the change should continue to be investigated. It would be unfortunate if, in a world in which we expect jobs to increasingly emphasize the accumulation of knowledge, we did not understand why it is that fewer men are turning to university.

References

Baker, Michael, and Nicole Fortin. 2000. "The Gender Composition and Wages: Why Is Canada Different from the United States?" Analytical Studies Branch research paper. Cat. 11F0019MPE140. Ottawa: Statistics Canada.

Beaudry, Paul, and David Green. 1997. "Cohort Patterns in Canadian Earnings: Assessing the Role of Skill Premia in Inequality Trends." NBER Working Paper 6132. Cambridge, Mass.: National Bureau of Economic Research.

Cowley, Peter, and Stephen Easton. 1999. "Boys, Girls, and Grades: Academic Gender Balance in British Columbia's Secondary Schools." *Public Policy Sources* 26. Vancouver: Fraser Institute.

Drolet, Marie. 2001 "The Persistent Gap: New Evidence on the Canadian Gender Wage Gap." Analytical Studies Branch research paper. Cat. 11F0019MPE157. Ottawa: Statistics Canada.

Statistics Canada. 1978. *Historical Compendium of Education Statistics: From Confederation to 1975.* Cat. 81-568. Ottawa.

———. 1979. *Education Statistics for the Seventies.* Cat. 81-569. Ottawa.

———. 1999. Consumer Income and Expenditure Division. *Earnings of Men and Women.* Cat. 13-217-XIB. Ottawa. June.

———. *Advanced Statistics of Education.* Cat. 81-220. Various issues. Ottawa.

———. *Education in Canada.* Cat. 81-229. Various issues. Ottawa.

———, and the Canadian Education Statistics Council. 2000. *Education Indicators in Canada: Report of the Pan-Canadian Education Indicators Program 1999.* Cat. 81-582-XPE. Ottawa.

The Global Talent Hunt and the Growth of e-Recruiting in Canada

Alice Nakamura and Joel Bruneau

Thomas Courchene states that economic policy should strive toward "developing, enhancing and employing-in-Canada the human capital of Canadians" (2001, 12). Canadian universities are committed to developing and enhancing Canadian human capital, but who is responsible for attending to Courchene's third point of employing the human capital of Canadians in this country? Success in that area must go hand in hand with the first two items to benefit Canada as a whole, and the importance of retaining educated human capital (Courchene's third item) will grow in importance.

An educated workforce is the critical resource for success in the new knowledge-based economy. The traditionally high quality of Canadian universities has made Canadian university-trained talent attractive to US and other foreign recruiters. The increased use of the Internet for recruiting — e-recruiting — poses a selective brain drain threat to Canada, and the problem is becoming more

---

The authors thank economists Mel McMillan, Emi Nakamura, and especially David Laidler, as well as Ken Nakamura, a medical doctor, for helpful comments on this and an original version of the paper titled "Post-Secondary Funding, Admissions and Job Placement." The original version was presented on June 2, 2001, in Montreal at the C.D. Howe Institute session, "Universities and the Canadian Economy," at the 35th Annual Meetings of the Canadian Economics Association. The authors bear sole responsibility for any errors of fact or interpretation.

serious due to Canadian progress in getting students on-line, coupled with the growth of e-recruiting. US dominance in the industry gives the largest recruiters, which are often US-based, the advantage in recruiting Canadian talent.[1] The human capital that Canada produces and then loses to foreign competitors may, quite literally, work against the future prosperity of this country, though Canada does, of course, gain workers educated in other countries as well.[2]

In this paper, we first describe e-recruiting and then examine three of the leading commercial e-recruiting services operating in Canada. We discuss their business operations and look at the many ways they earn profits. We next introduce two nonprofit e-recruiting services: one government operated and one private. These two e-recruiting services were developed to help Canadian-trained individuals find work with Canadian employers and thus realize greater returns to Canadian investments in postsecondary education. Unfortunately, the potential of these services has thus far been only partially realized, and we suggest some reasons why this is so. We conclude with some suggestions for corrective measures that universities, the federal and provincial governments, business and political leaders, and individual Canadians might consider.

How e-Recruiting Works

E-recruiting services operate quite simply. The recruiting companies post job advertisements on their websites, which attract individuals who are looking for employment. Job seekers must register in order to use the full services of the site.[3] This registration infor-

---

1 For a list of e-recruiting sites, the vast majority of which are headquartered in the United States, see www.internetpost.com/internetpost/AlphaList.html.

2 This is a country-level counterpart of the often discussed problem firms face of investing education and training in workers who may then be recruited by other employers that can offer better wages for experienced workers trained elsewhere because they did not have to pay for the education and training of those workers.

3 This is true for open as well as closed e-recruiting services. Passwords are assigned as part of the registration process. One purpose of passwords is to enable the service provider to control access to user information stored on the...

mation can then be used by a commercial e-recruiting service or its owner for its business purposes, including selling selected excerpts to interested employers. Some e-recruiting services go beyond simply displaying job postings and job-seeker information by offering electronic matching and screening assistance for employers, job seekers, or both.[4] For example, many services give job seekers the option of being notified by e-mail when ads matching their stated job preferences are posted on the system. Also, most of the commercial services will sell employers access to electronic files of job-seeker qualifications and contact information.

Most e-recruiting services are free to those looking for work, but employers are charged a fee for posting job ads and another, higher fee for access to résumé files. These pricing policies have implications, especially for Canada, where a limited number of firms recruit large enough numbers for it to be in their interests to pay commercial fees for access to job-seeker qualifications and contact information. These access fees are reasonable for firms seeking hundreds of employees, not just a few.

The largest and most successful firms are those most willing and able to pay the highest prices for job-seeker information, and many of these are foreign. Thus, an e-recruiting service operating in Canada may choose to display mostly Canadian job postings while selling job-seeker information primarily to large foreign-

---

Note 3 - cont'd.

...site. That is, the passwords are utilized in much the same way that personal identification numbers help banks appropriately control access to account information and funds.

4 David Autor notes:

The reasons that job boards have proliferated are clear. They offer more information, are easier to search, and are potentially more up to date than their textual counterpart, newspaper help wanted ads. In addition, job boards allow individuals to advertise their skills to employers as well as the reverse. Given the costs of online publishing relative to printing, job boards are also comparatively cheap. Placing a 30-day job advertisement on the largest job board, Monster.com, costs less than 5 percent of the price of running a help wanted advertisement in the Sunday *New York Times*. Estimates indicate that it also reaches potentially more visitors. (2001, 2.)

based companies because they are the ones willing to pay top dollar. In effect, the brain drain threat posed by e-recruiting services is a result of several factors. One is e-recruiters' ability to make money by obtaining job-seeker information in exchange for free access to job postings. Another reason is that most job seekers do not object to being considered by employers outside Canada, even if they themselves would not actively have sought foreign employment opportunities. A third factor is the economic reality that some global employers are willing — and able — to pay substantial amounts for information about skilled people looking for work. Finally, many workers in Canada are registered with, and give their qualifications and contact information to, these services, even though they are actually searching for other work opportunities at the time.

Most e-recruiting services have open websites that allow free access to all job searchers. Others, such as the e-recruiting sites of most university career centers and some of the services that were built with tax dollars, are "closed" — that is, restricted to those belonging to authorized groups.[5]

To understand e-recruiting, it is important to appreciate how these services fit into the whole recruiting process and to realize that they are not a replacement for most of what traditional employment services, including campus career centers, provide. In fact, no one should even consider cutting back on the funding of campus career centers because of the growth of e-recruiting. Indeed, as we will see, e-recruiting is undercutting the revenues from employer job postings that have been a financial mainstay for some campus career centers, which may necessitate increases in the levels of funding provided by universities to their campus career centers.

---

5 Some of these campus career centers will not even help the spouses of current students if those spouses were educated elsewhere, despite the fact that spouses often need help locating local employment in order to pay the tuition and living costs of their partners. Also, many spouses have postsecondary educational credentials and would be well suited for some of the jobs listed with the campus career centers. Nevertheless, the refusal to assist spouses educated elsewhere is reasonable considering how campus career centers are funded.

The process of finding a job, or filling one, can be broken down into eight steps for job seekers and employers, ranging from deciding to go to the job market to starting the new job (see Table 1).[6] To date, e-recruiting has revolutionized only the third step — finding work opportunities for job seekers and filling job openings for employers (steps JS3 and E3 in the table). Traditional employment services, such as campus career centers, continue to provide essential assistance to job seekers and employers in all areas, including steps JS3 and E3. For example, campus career centers schedule on-campus employer interviews for students and run cooperative education (co-op) programs.

Many people in both government and industry would like to know who is using e-recruiting, how much it is being used, and with what results. However, reliable information is not available at present due largely to the way e-recruiting operates. These services are communication providers that enable job seekers and employers to locate each other. Unlike the full-service personnel agencies, the e-recruiting services do not arrange employment matches. Those who use these services are not required — and in many cases would probably be unwilling — to report employment success resulting from their use of e-recruiting services. Thus, the e-recruiting services themselves have no direct way of knowing how many of those who visited their sites found employment or hired someone. What these services directly observe are things such as the numbers of people registered, the amounts of job postings and other services paid for by employers, and the numbers of visits to the site by various users.

Every e-recruiting service makes claims about their rising numbers of users,[7] but these should be taken with a grain of salt since

---

6 See Autor (2001) and Kuhn (2000) for analysis and evidence on how e-recruiting fits with and is affecting job search and employer recruiting in different types of labor markets.

7 All e-recruiting providers have an obvious interest in showing statistics that indicate high and rising use and high success rates. Some independent commercial agencies also claim to be able to provide traffic and other usage information for e-recruiting sites, but these agencies also have client-related vested interests in this information. In addition, a variety of technical and user...

Table 1: The Eight Steps of the Job Search and Recruitment Process

Job Seekers	Employers
JS1. The decision to look for a job	E1. The decision to look for an employee
JS2. Making a qualifications dossier	E2. Making a job description
JS3. Finding job openings to apply to	E3. Spreading information about the job opening
JS4. Assessing interested employers	E4. Examining applications from job seekers
JS5. Preparing and going for interviews	E5. Conducting interviews
JS6. Bargaining; assessing job offers	E6. Choosing among candidates; making offers
JS7. Accepting an offer	E7. Hiring a new worker
JS8. Starting work	E8. Having the new employee start work

these services are likely to report only statistics that are favorable to them. These organizations also control aspects of the services they operate that can greatly affect measures of site usage, which are collected using various accepted methods of monitoring. Even disinterested third-party providers of data on the e-recruiting industry may have difficulty collecting accurate information.

Even in the absence of good data, it seems obvious that the thousands of job postings now available on-line represent an important expansion in the information available to job seekers about employment opportunities. It is important to note, however, that most of the job postings on the main commercial e-recruiting services in both Canada and the United States are for big companies. Perhaps this is because they are best prepared to take advan-

---

Note 7 - cont'd.

...behavioral reasons make it difficult for anyone to collect accurate information about e-recruiting usage and success rates. We believe it is a mistake to treat most of the currently available information as reliable until more is known about the specifics of how the information was collected and processed, and until more thought has been given to the likely problems with the data. Statistics Canada recently began a data collection program covering limited aspects of e-recruiting and e-commerce. This is a much-needed development.

tage of the new e-recruiting technology, having had previous experience with their own electronic intranet systems for internal competitions for positions. In addition, big companies enjoy economies of scale in using e-recruiting services even for simple job postings. A single posting by a large corporation on an e-recruiting service for, say, an accountant can actually be an advertisement for dozens or even hundreds of open accounting positions.

The cost of posting job ads on a commercial e-recruiting site is much lower than the cost of gaining access to job-seeker data files. These fees are set so that they are reasonable for large employers trying to fill large numbers of positions, but they are probably prohibitively high for many smaller employers that have only one or two job openings at a time to fill. Being able to search job-seeker information files has important advantages over just posting job ads. Searching those files can, for example, help a recruiter find students nearing the completion of training programs in areas of high demand and identify those who are no longer actively seeking employment because they have already found jobs but who might be tempted by direct contact to consider a new job.

In summary, commercial e-recruiting services tend to charge prices that only larger companies are willing to pay because of the economies of scale they enjoy in making use of these services. From the point of view of e-recruiting companies, it is easier to deal with a few big employers with a large number of postings than with many smaller employers, each with just a few job ads.

Commercial e-Recruiting Services

In this section, we examine three of the most important commercial e-recruiting services operating in Canada, focusing on their corporate connections and business models for commercial services. In addition to selling job postings and electronic access to job-seeker information files, for-profit e-recruiting services exhibit important commercial complementarities with certain other sorts of businesses. Some of the associated commercial activities can increase the likelihood that job seekers who start out looking for work in Canada may end up considering jobs with large US or global companies instead.

The two largest commercial e-recruiters headquartered and operating only in Canada are Workopolis and CareerClick. Although both services help connect Canadian job seekers with mainly Canadian employers, both also belong to businesses with global interests. Workopolis is the result of an alliance between Globe Information Services (part of The Thomson Corporation) and Toronto Star Newspapers Ltd. As a result of business amalgamations, CareerClick came to be owned, along with the *National Post* and other newspapers, by Winnipeg-based CanWest Global Communications Corp., another company with global corporate affiliations and interests.

The dominant foreign-based e-recruiting service operating in Canada is Monster.ca, the Canadian site of Monster.com.[8] The Monster family of sites is controlled by TMP Worldwide, a long established US-based personnel and marketing agency network. As a Monster.ca newswire release explains:

> Monster is the flagship brand of the Interactive Division of TMP Worldwide Inc.....Founded in 1967, TMP Worldwide...is the online recruitment leader, the world's largest recruitment advertising agency network, and one of the world's largest search and selection agencies. TMP Worldwide, headquartered in New York, is also the world's largest Yellow Pages advertising agency and a provider of direct marketing services. The company's clients include more than 90 of the Fortune 100 and more than 480 of the Fortune 500 companies. (Monster.ca, Press release, February 27, 2001.)

As already noted, commercial e-recruiting services are typically free for job seekers but charge employers hundreds of dollars to post a job ad and thousands for access to files of job-seeker qualifications and contact information. Price information for Workopolis, CareerClick, and Monster for a single job posting and for access to job-seeker qualifications and contact information files is summarized in Table 2.[9]

---

8 As of August 2000, Monster.com contained 3.9 million résumés and 430,000 jobs (Autor 2001, 35).

9 The fees that employers must pay are not usually displayed to job seekers on the e-recruiting sites. In fact, some e-recruiting services do not display this information on their sites even in the employer information sections; instead, employers are instructed to call for information about fees.

Table 2: *Charges for Selected Major For-Profit e-Recruiting Services Operating in Canada*

	Cost	Corporate Affiliation
Workopolis (www.workopolis.com)	$500 for a single job posting for 21 days $1,500 per month, or $4,500 for one year, to search the résumé database	Globe Interactive, part of The Thomson Corporation
CareerClick (www.careerclick.com)	$500 for a single job posting for 21 days $450 per month, or $5,400 for one year, to search the résumé database	CanWest Global Communications Corp.
The Monster Board (www.monster.ca; www.monster.com)	$295 for a single job posting for 60 days for a single location and job category; $225 for each additional location or category $1,450 to search the résumé database for three months	TMP Worldwide

Note: Information collected during the first week of September 2000.

The revenues from the fees employers pay for job postings and for access to résumé files are only part of the economic benefits a parent company can potentially reap from owning an e-recruiting service. As already noted, e-recruiting services are a potential complement to certain other business activities. For instance, Workopolis and CareerClick are helping to protect the viability of newspaper classified ads in an Internet era. Both also have associations with full-service recruiting agencies with large corporate clients headquartered outside as well as in Canada (that is, they have associations with global headhunters). The Monster Board enhances TMP Worldwide's established full-service personnel agency network, its Yellow Pages business, and its direct marketing operations. The high value of the Monster-TMP Worldwide complementarities may be part of the reason Monster.ca is able to charge lower fees for some of its e-recruiting services than Workopolis or CareerClick.

There is no public information on the extent to which these obvious sorts of complementarities are financially important for commercial e-recruiting services, but the possibilities are clear. For instance, a full-service global headhunter operating in conjunction with an e-recruiting service could identify and skim off the most commercially valuable job seekers who register with the e-recruiter. This skimming off could occur even before the employers paying to search job-seeker qualifications and contact information files have had a chance to find and contact job seekers.[10]

Nonprofit e-Recruitment Services

E-recruiting services can complement not only other established for-profit business activities, but government services as well. As

---

10 JobShark, another commercial e-recruiting service operating in Canada, appears to recognize this skimming practice. In November 2001, its website stated:

> Through its proprietary matching technology, called JAWS, jobshark.com matches on skill sets and then notifies prospective candidates by email of matching job postings directly to qualified candidates. The principal is based on sourcing local people for local jobs, but with JobShark's growing global network of countries, international searches have become very much the reality. Globally, JobShark has the largest skill set profile database in the industry, with over 750,000 résumés and profiles of job seekers, with over 430,000 in Canada and over 250,000 in Latin America and over 60,000 in the UK. By pre-screening applicants through the matching process, jobshark.com provides higher quality candidates for recruiters, and an effortless way for job seekers to find out about exciting new opportunities. Because jobshark.com's database is private and nonsearchable, job seekers are assured of 100% confidentiality, and *recruiters can be sure that the cream of the crop has not been skimmed* [italics added]. JobShark has over 1,000 corporate clients.

JobShark thus used to claim, in effect, that all employers who paid to use their JAWS search capabilities would receive the same good value because JobShark did not have a full-service headhunter operating in the background and did not sell direct access to their job-seeker registration information to anyone.

Nakamura and Lawrence (1993) and Nakamura (1995) suggested when Internet use was first starting to accelerate, e-recruiting services could enhance the return on public investments in postsecondary education by making it cheaper and easier for Canadian employers to locate and communicate with Canadian-trained postsecondary students and alumni.[11]

The labor markets for advanced skills are highly fragmented, which forces those with specialized skills to conduct wide searches for a suitable employer.[12] For example, in most smaller Canadian cities and towns, there are job openings for retail clerks or laborers, but not for brain surgeons or theoretical physicists.[13] Thus, Canadian university students need access to career placement services that are national or even global in scope. E-recruiting technology enables wide, low-cost searches for both job seekers and employers.

In the early 1990s, most university campus career centers did not have websites or e-recruiting services, and the anticipated cost of building these at each school was high and viewed by some as a wasteful duplication of effort. But with the encouragement of several university presidents, the federal ministers of Industry and Human Resources Development committed funds to building a postsecondary-level e-recruiting service. That service, inaugurated by Industry Canada in 1995, is now known as Campus WorkLink.[14] Currently, the service charges employers between $20 and $449 for a single job posting, depending on the number of postsecondary institution job-seeker groups the employer wants the posting to be

---

11 Including those who had received a degree as well as those who had taken university courses but had left before graduating.

12 Economists have been making this argument for a long time. Diewert (2001) provides references and thoughtful commentary on this point.

13 It should, however, be noted that, although people tend to assume a general shortage of employment opportunities also means an absence of job openings for highly specialized workers, this is not always the case. Openings for medical and other specialists sometimes exist in parts of the country where unemployment in general is high.

14 For more on the development of www.campusworklink.com, see Nakamura, Wong, and Diewert (1999), and Nakamura and Pugh (2001).

displayed to and the length of time it will be on the system. Many employers, ranging from large institutions such as the Bank of Canada, to small volunteer operations, report success using Campus WorkLink.

Campus WorkLink has, however, faced constraints resulting from the fact that it was built with tax dollars. While it was still being developed, a private sector e-recruiting company brought charges of unfair government competition. Since university-educated workers are the premium market for private sector recruiters and since they usually have below-average unemployment rates, it is difficult to justify government intervention in postsecondary labor markets on the grounds of market failure.

In the United States, the federal government did not develop e-recruiting services for postsecondary recruiting but instead allowed commercial providers to fill this need. The dominant commercial e-recruiting service for US universities and colleges is JOBTRAK.COM, which provides résumé database and interview scheduling software support as well as e-recruiting services for more than 1,100 US university and college campus career centers. In November 2000, JOBTRAK was acquired by Monster.com and became a talent feeder system for it. This alliance demonstrates that there can also be interesting complementarities among different sorts of e-recruiting services as well as between e-recruiting services and other sorts of businesses.

In Canada, the private sector challenge to Campus WorkLink was resolved by an agreement that limited use of its services to students and recent alumni of Canadian postsecondary institutions that agreed to participate. "Recent alumni" are defined as those who have ended their postsecondary studies within the previous three years. Under the terms of the agreement, directors at each campus career center had the right to opt out of the Campus WorkLink system, and almost all of them did at first. University participation remained poor in the first years after the service went on-line. By now, however, most Canadian postsecondary institutions have signed Campus WorkLink partnership agreements through their campus career placement offices. (See the Appendix for a list of partnered institutions.)

A Private, Nonprofit Complement to e-Recruitment Services

Campus WorkLink now provides thousands of Canadian employers affordable access to the students and alumni of Canadian postsecondary institutions, a success that confirms the forecast by Nakamura and Lawrence (1993) that employers and postsecondary level job seekers would avail themselves of this sort of low-cost e-recruiting service if it were available to them.

As of 1998, however, large numbers of Canadian postsecondary students and graduates still could not access job postings through Campus WorkLink because the campus career centers of several institutions, including the universities of Alberta and Western Ontario, had not agreed to participate. And even at those institutions that were part of Campus WorkLink, relatively small fractions of the students had bothered to get their Campus WorkLink passwords. Also, anyone, whether Canadian-born or an immigrant, who had graduated more than three years earlier or who had taken their postsecondary training outside the country, was ineligible to receive targeted job postings through the Campus WorkLink system.[15] This situation motivated Nakamura and others to set up a new e-recruiting service to complement the coverage of Campus WorkLink.

Faculty members across the country volunteered time and money to create the nonprofit CareerOwl e-recruiting service, which was built with private donations, not university funds or tax dollars, to avoid the problems of Campus WorkLink.[16] CareerOwl

---

15 Although this part of the agreement was not enforced, it nevertheless served to forestall active initiatives to sign up the alumni at large for universities that partnered with Campus WorkLink. This constraint will become more serious if structural changes in the economy mean that growing numbers of experienced workers with postsecondary credentials must change jobs many times over the course of their careers. See Picot, Heisz, and Nakamura (2000) for empirical evidence on this point.

16 For background on CareerOwl, including the way in which some of the key ideas and collaborative relationships grew out of funded research provided by the Social Sciences and Humanities Research Council of Canada, see Nakamura et al. (1999). There is also a French-language Owl (www.chouettecarriere.ca). The CareerOwl system, both English and French, is managed by the CareerOwl...

went on-line in September 1999 and became fully operational in March 2000. The service has special features to facilitate job search and employer recruiting, such as confidential direct messaging. In addition, CareerOwl is open to all: anyone can sign up and receive a password. Users choose their own passwords on-line, which are used solely to allow job seekers to maintain control over who can access or change personal information stored on the system.

Regular job postings for Canadian jobs can be advertised on CareerOwl for up to eight weeks for a flat fee of $25 each. Ads for jobs in other countries can be posted by both domestic and foreign companies, but at a cost of $100 each. A unique feature of CareerOwl is the ability of employers to search job candidates' qualification profiles on-line at any time for free or a nominal $25 fee, which allows smaller and medium-size Canadian businesses to use this search option.[17]

More than 75,000 Canadian students and graduates from more than 500 postsecondary institutions — including more than 200 that are not part of the Campus WorkLink system — now use CareerOwl.[18] Canadians who went to foreign postsecondary insti-

---

Note 16 - cont'd.

...Institute, a Canadian nonprofit, noncharitable organization. As a noncharitable organization, CareerOwl claimed no tax writeoffs for the start-up funds donated to create it.

17 We believe that small companies potentially have at least as much to gain from using e-recruiting as big companies do in terms of help with finding needed talent, provided, of course, that they can afford to use such services. Small companies typically lack large personnel offices and budgets for advertising widely and for sending recruiters far afield in search of promising candidates for open positions, all of which is standard for big companies. Helping small companies with their personnel problems is important for ensuring this country's future prosperity.

18 CareerOwl users include more than 10,000 students and alumni of the universities of Alberta and Western Ontario, the two largest postsecondary institutions that have not joined Campus WorkLink. The presidents of both the University of Alberta and the University of Western Ontario have been part of the faculty volunteer support base for CareerOwl from the start. Their statement of support, which is also signed by the president of the University of British Columbia, can be found on the CareerOwl website.

tutions, which are not eligible to partner with Campus WorkLink, are also using CareerOwl in rising numbers.[19]

Resistance to Campus WorkLink and CareerOwl

Both Campus WorkLink and CareerOwl are now being used regularly by large numbers of Canadian job seekers and employers, but there are still many who have not even heard of either one, implying that the value of these services for Canadian employers is less than it could be. One reason is that some university career centers do not take the trouble to tell students and graduates about these e-recruiting services, favoring instead other commercial e-recruiting services such as Monster.ca and Monster.com.

We are not arguing that campus career centers should ignore commercial e-recruiting services, which many postsecondary students and alumni likely find useful. But it seems unreasonable to us for campus career centers to give such prominence to expensive (for employers) commercial services while ignoring or downplaying government and nonprofit sites. We suspect the reason they do so relates to the way in which many campus offices are set up and paid for, as well as to the nature of the funding and performance measurement arrangements of the universities themselves. A little history about the evolution of career services on Canadian university campuses is helpful for understanding this point.

The Evolution of Campus Career Placement Services

In the 1970s, Canada was ahead of the United States in providing accessible, nationwide job placement services for university-trained

---

19 For students and alumni who are eligible to use Campus WorkLink, information on this service and a direct link to Campus WorkLink are provided on the CareerOwl website. In fact, the website has a job-seeker resources section with links to hundreds of federal and provincial government, nonprofit, and commercial e-recruiting, and other employment information websites that may be useful to Canadian job seekers.

talent. Canada Manpower offices on Canadian university campuses were open to anyone eligible to work in this country. However, these offices were closed in the 1980s as a federal cost-cutting measure and were replaced by university-run campus career centers. Then, as now, these came in two varieties — one serving the whole campus, and the other for the business faculty only. In most cases, neither type of career center assists students or alumni from other postsecondary institutions.

From the start, universities provided little direct funding for their main career centers, many of which, as a result, came to rely heavily on the fees they charged employers for posting their job ads.[20] In contrast, career centers run by business faculties typically had base operating budgets, which is probably why most still do not charge employers for displaying their job postings.[21] Most business faculties regard their career centers as giving them a competitive edge in attracting top students and building relationships with potential donors.

Funding arrangements for the two types of career centers invite noncooperation between them. To their credit, most directors of career centers manage to rise above the dictates of the underlying economic signals, but incentives for noncooperation with other career centers, even at the same university, are strong. In addition, universities, colleges, and technical schools compete with each other for their public budget allocations. Real and rumored information about employment opportunities for students of the various institutions plays a role in this budgetary process in most provinces. This institutional funding situation reinforces the territorial incentives of career center funding arrangements, and might be part of the reason senior administrators at some postsecondary institutions have failed to act on complaints from the business community and recruiters about the territoriality of some campus career centers.

---

20 These career centers have, however, usually been provided with in-kind support, such as space. In addition, some have been given shares of the student union or other student activity fees.

21 Some business faculty career centers raise funds from employers or students by, for example, running cooperative education programs or collecting a portion of what employers pay as remuneration for co-op students.

Until e-recruiting became widely available, most campus career centers had a virtual monopoly on the provision of local career services, and employers who wanted university-trained employees could not avoid dealing with them. E-recruiting has, however, disrupted this monopoly. In private discussions with the authors of this paper, some career center directors have explained that, from their perspective, the higher-priced commercial e-recruiting services do not pose a competitive threat, partly because they charge fees that are substantially above those of the main campus career centers. Nonetheless, government and nonprofit services that charge employers nominal fees have been treated as a threat on some campuses, and they have reacted by trying to partner with US-based Monster, a move that could give them a more secure revenue base while reducing their job-posting costs.

In February 2001, Monster.ca announced it would be "offering free software that is focused on the needs of the career centers as well as co-op programs, and a split-revenue solution" (Monster.ca, Press release, February 27, 2001). This offer would almost surely be more financially rewarding for many campus offices than anything Campus WorkLink or CareerOwl could provide. The latter services aim to hold down the costs of recruiting for Canadian employers and hence cannot provide revenue to campus career centers in the amounts Monster is now offering. Already, Montreal's Concordia University has said it would take up Monster's offer, and unless university administrators or provincial or federal governments move quickly, many other campus career centers could follow Concordia's example.

Questions Raised

E-recruiting has made it easier and cheaper for all employers to find and communicate with Canadian job seekers. In the past, foreign recruiters were always able to entice away some of Canada's most accomplished university graduates,[22] although they had to mount expensive recruiting campaigns to collect information about

---

22 For information on the brain drain and references to the related literature on this topic, see Kesselman (2001).

and attract available Canadian job seekers. E-recruiting is, however, eroding still further the home-country advantage of Canadian employers in finding and contacting Canadian talent. The candidate search phase of recruiting can now be conducted almost as cheaply from Silicon Valley or Wall Street as from Ottawa, Toronto, or Vancouver. We are concerned that, with better access to information through e-recruiting services, US and other foreign companies may become quicker and better at locating valuable Canadian postsecondary graduates with the scarce skills everyone seeks.

What, then, are the broad questions about e-recruiting in Canada that need to be addressed? For example, how should information about the various e-recruiting sites be presented to Canadians? Some materials put out by governments and campus career centers seem to favor the largest e-recruiting websites.[23] Is this strategy in the best interest of Canada if it results in preferential advertising for US-dominated e-recruiting sites? Is global or even national size what matters most? Some employers that use e-recruiting report that the presence of candidates with the qualifications they require is more important than size.[24] Does it matter that firms heavily engaged in direct marketing for foreign clients own or have close

---

23 See, for example, Canada (2001). This booklet, sponsored by Human Resources Development Canada and distributed Canada-wide, lists Monster.ca ahead of the Canadian for-profit sites Workopolis and CareerClick and well ahead of the nonprofit CareerOwl.ca and Canadian-government-sponsored sites such as Campus WorkLink. In an updated, online version of an article that appeared in CAREER OPTIONS, another publication widely distributed to Canadian university students and campus career centers, Sara Newton-Smith, writing for the Canadian Association of Career Educators and Employers (CACEE), lists the 40 sites as the "Top Websites for Your Job Search." Her list is alphabetical; hence, Monster.ca appears after Campus WorkLink and Careerclick, but CareerOwl.ca is not listed, although numerous commercial sites are. Her introductory remarks single out Monster.ca along with the Industry Canada/CACEE-run CampusWorkLink.com e-recruiting service for special mention. On Monster.ca, she writes that it provides "job matching services that let you create your own job search agent and have job prospects e-mailed directly to you!" The latter is a service that CareerOwl has been providing since 1999, as a technological leader at that time. See www.cacee.com/co2000/2007.html.

24 Warburton and Warburton (2001) make this point for a Canadian recruiting example.

business associations with some of the e-recruiting sites being promoted to Canadian job seekers?

Will the qualifications and contact information that Canadian job seekers enter when registering to use e-recruiting sites such as Monster.ca be equally available to Canadian and US companies for hiring and direct marketing purposes? Monster reports that the clients of its parent, TMP Worldwide, "include more than 90 of the Fortune 100 and more than 480 of the Fortune 500 companies" (Monster.ca. Press release, February 27, 2001). How many Canadian companies can afford such services? More generally, will foreign-based e-recruiting services be knowledgeable about and responsive to the special circumstances of Canadian job seekers and employers?[25]

Job seekers incur no dollar costs for using most e-recruiting services, but employers usually pay, and the fees charged for commercial services are usually higher than they are for nonprofits such as Campus WorkLink or CareerOwl. Perhaps more Canadians would register with noncommercial services if they realized that doing so could translate into cost savings for Canadian companies, which could then be used for better wages and market development. Should campus career centers do more to help Canadian job seekers and employers learn about such lower-cost e-recruiting services? Who, on campuses, is answerable for choices that affect the costs to employers of contacting the students their tax dollars helped to educate?

Recommendations

Since Canadian postsecondary institutions are partially supported by taxes, is it in the economic best interest of Canadian taxpayers when those trained at Canadian schools take jobs with foreign companies in other countries? Because freedom of information and of

---

25 The press release just cited claims, incorrectly, that "Monster.ca is the first and only national bilingual recruiting services Web site in Canada." In fact, virtually all government and private sector for-profit and nonprofit e-recruiting services operating in Canada offer bilingual services.

movement are important rights, we do not believe Canadian graduates should be discouraged from exploring foreign job opportunities. We do, however, recommend that campus career centers do more to help Canadians find out about e-recruiting services that are designed and operated first and foremost to help connect Canadian employers with Canadian-trained talent.

We also recommend that the schools and provincial governments review the funding, reporting, and performance assessment arrangements for campus career centers, and that the centers be given guidelines and incentives to participate in the Campus WorkLink system and to display relevant information for other e-recruiting websites, particularly those with a mission to connect Canadian employers with Canadian job seekers.

The current mechanisms for delivering financial support to schools and for judging the success of the graduates of these institutions encourage these institutions and their career centers to be territorial about their role in job placement. In this regard, we recommend careful consideration of alternative funding arrangements for universities, such as those considered by Davenport (in this volume), Diewert (2001), and Morck (1995).

A key goal should be to better align the interests of those who foot the bills for Canadian educational institutions with those who design the services offered by their campus career placement offices. The rules and incentives under which these centers operate should encourage them to ensure that human capital developed at the expense of Canadian taxpayers is at least as accessible to Canadian employers as it is to their foreign competitors.

Appendix:
Canadian Postsecondary Institutions Partnered with Campus WorkLink*

Acadia University
Alberta College of Art and Design
Algoma University College
Algonquin College
Assiniboine Community College
Athabasca University
Bishop's University
Brandon University
British Columbia Institute of Technology
Brock University
Cambrian College
Camosun College
Canadian Information Technology College
Canadore College
Cape Breton Business College
Capilano College
Carleton University
CDI College — Laval
CDI College — Nepean
CDI College — Ottawa
Cégep de Chicoutimi
Cégep de Gaspésie et des Iles
Cégep de Jonquière
Cégep de l'Abitibi-Témiscamingue
Cégep de Rimouski
Cégep de Rivière-du-Loup
Cégep de Sainte-Foy
Cégep de Saint-Laurent
Cégep de Sept-Iles
Cégep de Trois-Rivières
Cégep du Vieux-Montréal
Cégep Heritage College
Centennial College

Champlain Regional College — St-Lambert
Champlain St.Lawrence
Champlain — Lennoxville
Collège Ahuntsic
Collège Boréal
Collège communautaire du Nouveau-Brunswick — Bathurst
Collège communautaire du Nouveau-Brunswick — Campbellton
Collège communautaire du Nouveau-Brunswick — Dieppe
Collège communautaire du Nouveau-Brunswick — Edmunston
Collège d'Alma
Collège de Bois-de-Boulogne
Collège de l'Acadie
Collège de l'Outaouais
Collège de Maisonneuve
Collège de Sherbrooke
Collège des Grands Lacs
Collège Édouard-Montpetit
Collège Laflèche
Collège Lionel-Groulx
Collège Montmorency
Collège MultiHexa Ste-Foy
College of New Caledonia
College of the North Atlantic — Bonavista
College of the North Atlantic — Cornerbrook
College of the North Atlantic — Gander
College of the North Atlantic — Grand Falls
College of the North Atlantic — Labrador City
College of the North Atlantic — Ridge Road
College of the North Atlantic — St. John's

---

* Information current as of July 14, 2001.

- College of the North Atlantic — Stephenville
- College of the Rockies
- CompuCollege School of Business — New Brunswick
- CompuCollege School of Business — Prince Edward Island
- Concordia University
- Conestoga College
- Confederation College
- Dalhousie University
- DALTECH
- Dawson College
- Devry Institute of Technology — Calgary
- Douglas College
- Durham College
- École de Technologie Supérieure
- École des Hautes Études Commerciales
- École nationale d'administration publique
- Emily Carr College of Art and Design
- Fanshawe College
- George Brown College
- Georgian College
- Grant MacEwan Community College
- Holland College
- Humber College
- Information Technology Institute — Calgary
- Information Technology Institute — Halifax
- Information Technology Institute — Ontario
- The Institute for Computer Studies — Ottawa
- The Institute for Computer Studies — North York
- John Abbott College
- Justice Institute of British Columbia
- Kemptville College of Agricultural Technology
- Keyano College
- Kwantlen University College
- La Cité collegialé
- Lakehead University
- Lambton College
- Langara College
- Laurentian University
- Lethbridge Community College
- Loyalist College
- McGill University (including MacDonald Campus)
- McMaster University
- Malaspina University-College
- Medicine Hat College
- Memorial University of Newfoundland
- The Michener Institute of Applied Arts
- Mohawk College
- Mount Allison University
- Mount Royal College
- Mount St. Vincent University
- New Brunswick Community College — Moncton
- New Brunswick Community College — Saint John
- New Brunswick Community College — St. Andrew's
- New Brunswick Community College — Woodstock
- Niagara College
- Nicola Valley Institute of Technology
- Nipissing University
- NorQuest College
- North Island College
- Northern College of Applied Arts and Technology
- Northern Lakes College
- Nova Scotia Agricultural College
- Nova Scotia College of Art and Design
- Nova Scotia Community College — Annapolis Valley Campus and Pictou Campus
- Olds College
- Ontario College of Art and Design
- Ontario Institute of Information Technology
- Queen's University
- Red Deer College
- Red River College
- Royal Roads University
- Ryerson University
- St. Clair College
- St. Francis Xavier University

St. Lawrence College
Saint Mary's University
Saskatchewan Institute of Applied Science and Technology — Kelsey Campus and Woodland Campus
Sault College of Applied Arts & Technology
Seneca College
Sheridan College
Simon Fraser University
Sir Sandford Fleming College — Frost Campus and Sutherland Campus
Technical University of British Columbia
Toronto School of Business/Compu College (General)
Trent University
Trinity Western University
Université de Moncton
Université de Montréal
Université de Sherbrooke
Université du Québec à Chicoutimi
Université du Québec à Hull
Université du Québec à Montréal
Université du Québec à Rimouski
Université du Québec à Trois-Rivières
Université du Québec en Abitibi-Témiscamingue
Université Laval
University College of Cape Breton
University College of the Cariboo
University College of the Fraser Valley
University of British Columbia
University of Calgary
University of Guelph
University of Lethbridge
University of Manitoba
University of New Brunswick — Fredericton
University of New Brunswick — Saint John
University of Northern B.C.
University of Ottawa
University of Prince Edward Island
University of Regina
University of Saskatchewan
University of Toronto
University of Victoria
University of Waterloo
University of Windsor
University of Winnipeg
Wilfrid Laurier University
York University

References

Autor, David. 2001. "Wiring the Labor Market." *Journal of Economic Perspectives* 15 (Winter): 35–40.

Canada. 2001. Department of Human Resources Development. "Top 100 Internet Sites for Learning and Employment." Ottawa.

Courchene, Thomas J. 2001. *A State of Minds: Toward a Human Capital Future for Canadians*. Montreal: Institute for Research on Public Policy.

Diewert, W. Erwin. 2001. "Productivity Growth and the Role of Government." Discussion Paper 01-13. Vancouver: University of British Columbia, Department of Economics. Available from Internet website: www.econ.ubc.ca/diewert/hmpgdie.htm.

Kesselman, Jonathan R. 2001. "Policies to Stem the Brain Drain — Without Americanizing Canada." *Canadian Public Policy* 27 (1): 77–94.

Kuhn, Peter. 2000. "Policies for an Internet Labour Market." *Policy Options* 21 (8): 42–47.

Morck, Randall K. 1995. "A Plan for Making Public Universities Financially Independent." Working Paper. Edmonton: University of Alberta, Faculty of Business.

Nakamura, Alice O. 1995. "New Directions for UI, Social Assistance, and Vocational Education and Training." Presidential Address delivered to the annual meetings of the Canadian Economics Association, Université du Québec à Montréal, June 3, 1995; published in *Canadian Journal of Economics* 28 (November): 731–754.

———, et al. 1999. "The Genesis of CareerOwl: The Story of How SSHRC Funded University Research Led to an On-Line Electronic Hiring Hall for Canadian Post Secondary Students and Alumni." Available from Internet website: www.CareerOwl.ca.

———, and Peter Lawrence. 1993. "Education, Training and Prosperity." PEER Group Working Paper 93-12-1, 1-50. Subsequently published in revised form in Thomas J. Courchene, ed., *Stabilization, Growth and Distribution: Linkages in the Knowledge Era*. Kingston, Ont.: Queen's University, John Deutsch Institute for the Study of Economic Policy.

———, and T. Pugh. 2001. "Our Governments Should Stop Freezing Out Smaller Canadian e-Recruiters." *Policy Options* 21 (8): 48–52.

———, G. Wong, and W.E. Diewert. 1999. "New Approaches to Public Income Support in Canada." In Organisation for Economic Co-operation and Development, *The Local Dimension of Welfare-to-Work: An International Survey*. Paris: OECD.

Picot, Garnett, Andrew Heisz, and Alice Nakamura. 2000. "Were 1990s Labour Markets Really Different?" *Policy Options* 21 (6): 15–26.

Warburton, R.N., and W.P. Warburton. 2001. "Canadian-Made e-Solution Proves Cheap and Effective." *Canadian Business Economics* 8 (3): 37–39.

Comments on Davenport, Easton, and Nakamura and Bruneau

Melville L. McMillan

The papers that I comment on address three important aspects of university education: Paul Davenport examines the production process students are exposed to while in Canadian universities; Stephen Easton looks at who is going to them; and Alice Nakamura and Joel Bruneau consider how students subsequently make the transition from university to work — that is, get jobs — in the world of e-recruiting.[1] While the papers constitute a natural package with a fairly consistent outlook, there is little overlap among them. Hence, I discuss each paper independently in the order just mentioned.

Paul Davenport on University Resources, Knowledge Transfer, and Production: What's Going On in the "Barn"?

Paul Davenport presents an excellent overview of what has happened at Canadian universities over the past couple of decades, where they are at today, and what the issues of the future are. Davenport's message is clear: First, there is a strong demand for university graduates. Second, there has been a major and serious erosion of university resources, which a shift to more tied but

---

1 The other four papers focus more on the output of universities in terms of research and labor market experience, paying particular attention to indicators of quality and value.

incomplete research funding has exacerbated for the general university budget. Third, concern exists as to whether or not we can maintain, let alone improve upon, our already eroded institutional quality over the next decade in the face of another surge in enrollments, substantial retirements, and strong competition for faculty from the United States and elsewhere. As steps toward solving these problems, Davenport recommends pursuing a 10 percent reduction in the student-to-faculty ratio through extra recruitment, increased direct and indirect research support, and the establishment of an income-contingent student loan system to facilitate student access.

One cannot argue with Davenport's assessment of the situation nor take exception to the recommendations. More can be said, however, especially about the recommendations. Before following that line of thought, however, I will insert a comment on the strong demand for university graduates. It is this strong demand that has maintained the earnings of university graduates despite the rapid expansion in their numbers, and especially in the number of women graduates. Also, in support of Davenport's position on the education needs of the knowledge economy, I point to Robert Allen's observations that there is demand for both builders and users (Allen 1999). That is, while the new information economy requires — and universities are called on to supply — those capable of conceptualizing, designing, and building infrastructure, there is a parallel demand created for the people who understand, know how to use, and can exploit the potential of those systems and the information that they deliver. Hence, and as other contributors have indicated, the strong demand for university graduates will continue to be broadly based, not simply focused on computer scientists and engineers.

Davenport's recommendations are definitely a step in the right direction, but they suggest some need for further study and even research. The case for reducing the student-faculty ratio is based on an assumption about educational quality: that a 10 percent reduction in this ratio will partially restore the quality of undergraduate education that a 25 percent increase over recent years has undermined. Universities have little objective evidence, however, on which to say with confidence what improvement in quality would result from such a change, or even what might be optimal ratios on average, let alone for a particular year or faculty. Nor is there much evidence about what instruction methods are superior. We might benefit from more investigation into university teaching. While the results that could be obtained from formal analysis in this matter may be limited, universities do have lots of experience with teaching. There should be a healthy respect for the lessons learned and the intuition gained in practice. The management of university teaching resources may be quite good at realizing results for the same reasons that good business managers can succeed in their markets despite being unfamiliar with the theory of marginal revenue and marginal cost.

There is some evidence that students are willing to pay significant premiums for "quality" programs involving smaller class sizes. Those premiums may not reflect well the improved quality of either the university inputs or of the students enrolled, but rather, at least in part, the willingness to pay for the exclusivity, prestige, and recognition associated with such programs, which is effective in propelling those students to the forefront in the job market competition.[2] Universities, and the governments supporting them, must ensure that preferred learning environments are made available not only to those able to pay a premium but also to those best able to benefit; at the same time, they must provide quality education to all university students. Doing so is a challenge in an environment of limited resources, retiring faculty, and increasing student numbers.

Canada devotes considerable resources to postsecondary education. As Davenport takes care to point out, relative to other countries, an extraordinary share of that goes to nonuniversity programs. The promotion of these programs and the pressures to expand them have been substantial and have challenged universities (see, for example, Allen 1999). Has this emphasis served Canada well, or might the country better consider other options for producing those skills and reallocate public funding to university education, which demonstrates attractive rates of return?

---

2 Convenience can be another valuable attribute of these programs, especially those catering to employed students.

Davenport makes the point that the low level of university research funding in Canada, especially relative to comparable programs in the United States, argues for increased funding, especially if leading researchers are to be retained. Given the shortage of research funding available, it would be helpful to investigate how existing and new funds could be used most effectively to enhance research productivity — by affecting, for example, the kinds of indicators that Chant and Gibson explore in their paper in this volume. Where should new money go? Where would it have the greatest impact? Is the current allocation among and within funding councils, among disciplines and programs, the most effective? Are the many specific-purpose and "strings-attached" programs effective or constraining? There seems to have been little research into research and research funding.

Income-contingent loans for students are a reasonable suggestion. The idea has been discussed for some time, and such loans do exist in some countries (such as Australia). Davenport does not outline the income-contingent program he foresees. This is unfortunate, because this is clearly a program for which "the devil is in the details." What role and what impact would the loan program have? Would it be a backstop option for a few or a mainstream program for most? Would the distribution of the burden differ much from that of the existing tax system? Would it promote better decision making by students, the universities, or government? Might it promote further student indebtedness? Would it prompt further tuition increases?[3] Essentially, would this contingent loan program enhance access, or would it primarily modify university finance? the idea of income-contingent loans for university students clearly deserves further investigation.

So far, my comments have been the academic's usual fallback: tossing out caveats and calling for more research. I change direc-

---

3 The scope for further tuition increases may be limited in some programs where tuition already approaches instruction costs. Thus, increasing tuition raises the possibility of further differentiating tuition fees, as Rathje and Emery suggest in their essay. This prospect has various pros and cons. See Smith's comments on the topic elsewhere in this volume and Litten (1984) and Stager (1989) for other perspectives.

tion here to extend somewhat the analysis of Davenport's paper. I reflect on three issues: student input into the knowledge production process, the potential federal role in university finance and, the resulting implications for the provinces.

Davenport is concerned about the decline in university funding and the impact, especially through the increasing student-faculty ratio, that it has on quality education. I call attention here to another resource of the education production process that appears to be declining: student input. I refer here not to the *number* of students, which continues to increase, but to the *time* that students devote to their university education. In 1991, the Smith Commission reported that a survey of arts and science undergraduates revealed that 45 percent were employed either on or off campus (Smith 1991). It also reported that, between 1975 and 1990, the percentage of full-time university students who were employed increased from 26 to 38 percent, with less than one-third of these working fewer than 10 hours per week.[4] I do not have comparable data for the 1990s, but the Labour Force Survey reports that, although student labor force participation rates have declined sharply since 1989, for students in the 20-to-24 age range (that is, the typical postsecondary range), it has remained relatively constant.[5] While this information does not refer specifically to university students, casual observation and anecdotal evidence certainly give no indication of any abatement. The growth in the employment of *full-time* students, plus their longer hours, suggests that there is less time available for — and hence less time devoted to — university studies. I am sure that many academics can testify to observing this trend and to the impact that it has had on their classes and on student learning. Also, because teaching methods may be modified in the face of this trend — for example, fewer assignments — and competition among

---

4 About 40 percent of those employed work 10–19 hours per week. The largest increases were in the groups of students working 10–19 and 20–29 hours per week.

5 For example, see Jennings (1998). In a recent survey (1,407 responses), the University of Calgary Students' Union found that students were, on average, working 17.5 hours per week during the school year.

students reduced, the whole class, not just those working, may be affected.

Thus, the quality of university education may be being eroded by reduced input not only from the university, but from the student. Universities need to consider that they may have accommodated this trend by adjusting their performance expectations for full-time students.[6] Any attention paid to concerns about the quality of university undergraduate education needs to address student employment: the extent that it detracts from university studies and the pressures underlying it.

Davenport has legitimate reasons to lament the underfunding of research at Canadian universities and to call for a larger federal contribution. An expanded federal role for research support is logical. The products of research are highly mobile and the benefits spread widely. Hence, provinces may be reluctant to invest as heavily in research as the federal government, which can internalize more of the benefits. There has been some expansion of federal research funding lately, but the new funds are focused on the direct costs of research, such as equipment, supplies, technical support, and some student support. Indirect or overhead costs have been neglected — the space, services, utilities, and libraries that provide necessary support.[7] When the funding does not cover all the costs associated with a research effort, operating funds end up being diverted from other parts of the university. One result is less money to hire faculty. Ironically, faculty are the key ingredient of research. Yet the federal government does not share in the salary expenses of university faculty, although they devote a considerable portion of their time to research. Federal research funding, like most other kinds, covers only those "extras" that faculty must have to do research. This approach distorts the university's allocation of resources and may make the object of more and better research more difficult to achieve. Thus, both the level and the kind of federal research funding are problematic.

---

6 The related concern of grade inflation has garnered more attention.

7 The programs carry with them a variety of conditions and requirements that complicate and often distort the funding of university research.

The distortions imposed by direct-cost only research funding, together with the benefit spillovers from research, make a strong case for more comprehensive federal research support. Research is a major function of Canadian universities, and gains would result from the federal government contributing significantly — at a level corresponding to the associated national benefits — to the full costs of academic research. As an illustration, let me suggest that, in support of research, the federal government contribute an overall 25 percent toward the operating costs of Canadian universities.[8] Added to existing funding, this amount might move us halfway toward closing the funding gap with major public universities in the United States, judging from Davenport's figures.[9] More senior readers will recognize that this proposal resembles the old Established Programs Financing (EPF) program that existed when the federal and provincial governments shared university costs roughly 50–50. To avoid one of the major problems contributing to the demise of that program, the funding could be capped so that provinces would, at the margin, be spending entirely their own money on university research.

This additional federal funding for universities is not intended as relief to the provinces. It should be conditional on the provinces maintaining their own support to universities. The intention is, rather, to upgrade Canadian universities, making them better and more competitive, especially in research.[10] Doing so would make our

---

8 Based on fiscal year 1998/99 figures, 25 percent would amount to $3.15 billion. Including existing federal research funding in that 25 percent would reduce the additional outlay to $1.85 billion. The 25 percent share is smaller than the one-third share that is implied by Allen's (1999) view that about two-thirds of university costs are for teaching (including graduate instruction).

9 The federal government, through the tax system, is a major beneficiary of the productivity and income increases resulting from university education. This fiscal spillover is another reason for enhanced federal support to university education but it is an argument not pursued here.

10 The added federal funds would not go entirely, or even necessarily, mostly, to research in the narrow sense. In part, the funds are to compensate universities for the research that they are doing already and to help strike a better balance between research and other activities. Thus, some of the funds could be expected to be spent on hiring faculty, a move that, while adding to universities' capacity to do research, would also help to improve the student-faculty ratio. Part of the funding would also go to indirect research costs.

universities better able to contribute to society both through the undertaking of research and through the preparation of Canadians for the knowledge economy. A federal contribution such as I describe here could also address other concerns among those Davenport mentions.

Davenport mentions the difficulties for universities that result from the failure of the federal government to finance the indirect costs of research that are associated with its direct research grants. I am sure that he and many others were delighted by the December 2001 federal budget's provision of $200 million to partially fund those costs. Even if only at half the normal rate and committed for only one year, the initiative is a breakthrough. While the amount is a helpful step, at 1.6 percent of university operating budgets it is a small but notable contribution toward solving the significant problems confronting Canadian universities. Their pressing concerns have developed over a generation, so quick solutions are unlikely. However, we are more likely to resolve them eventually if we establish and follow a comprehensive plan for the federal government to support a significant portion of all university research costs.

Davenport's essay relates to the production processes of universities. As a final comment, I suggest that we study their production methods more intensively in the hope of improving on our techniques and resource utilization — that is, on efforts to become more effective in getting output out of the "barn." Although plagued by measurement problems, investigation of the production processes in units of higher education have attracted considerable attention in both the United Kingdom and the United States (see, for example, Izadi et al. 2002; and Koshal and Koshal 1999) while Canadians have only scratched the surface.

Stephen Easton on Enrollments and the Male/Female Balance

Easton looks at the dramatic increases in female university enrollment in Canada, particularly relative to male enrollment, and seeks an explanation. Not finding answers in the changes to part-time enrollments or to college enrollments, he explores causes of changes

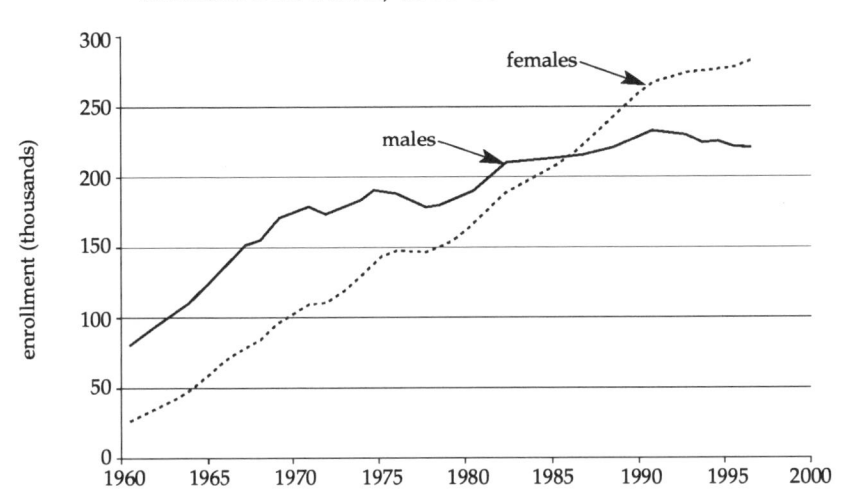

Figure 1: *Full-Time Undergraduate Enrollment in Canadian Universities, 1960–98*

Sources: Statistics Canada, cat. 81-568, 1978; idem, cat. 81-229, various issues.

in the demand for university education and in the supply of potential students. Changes over time in the relative earnings premiums that a university education provides for women and men appear to be important determinants of the female-to-male undergraduates ratio. Shifts in the ratio of female and male high school graduates — the supply of potential students — have had an ambiguous impact, but Easton sees high school grading practices as contributing to university enrollment patterns.

Because some of Easton's analysis extends back to the early 1970s but the data presented only goes back to 1987, it is useful to look at the enrollment data for an extended period, even if only for emphasis. Figure 1 shows male and female undergraduate enrollments since 1960. In that year, the proportion of female undergraduates broke out of the 21-to-23.5 percent range that it had occupied for 35 years. The relatively steady growth in female enrollments thereafter, getting stronger after 1970 and reaching 56 percent in 1998, is obvious.

Part-time enrollments have diminished since the early 1990s. While it is true, as Easton argues, that males have not shifted from full- to part-time studies, because of the disproportionate number of women in part-time studies (1.6 females for each male), the move of more students generally to full-time studies reinforces the growing share of full-time university undergraduates who are women. If all of the 50,000-student decline in part-time enrollments that Easton notes occurred between 1987 and 1997 represented a shift to full-time studies, it would have contributed almost 31,000 of the 73,000-student increase in the full-time enrollments of women over that period. In fact, the decline in the number of males enrolled in part-time studies (19,000) exceeded the increase in the number of males enrolled full-time (14,000). Nonetheless, the decline in part-time enrollment should not be dismissed, because it could account for about one-sixth of the 0.23 increase in the female-to-male ratio — from 0.97 to 1.20 — noted. But this is a minor point.

At the heart of Easton's paper are the regressions in his Table 4. Those regressions seek to explain the (log of the) ratio of female-to-male undergraduate enrollments using variables of demand for university education and supply of potential students.

Consider the demand variables first. The demand for university education is expected to increase as the labor income reward for a university degree increases. That reward is defined as the amount by which the earnings of a university-educated person exceed the earnings of one who only went to high school — that is, the university earnings premium. Women are expected to respond to the premium for women, and so to affect the numerator of the dependent variable, and men to the premium for men, affecting the denominator of the dependent variable. The higher-education premiums for women and men are calculated using the results of regressions from Beaudry and Green (1997), who estimate real weekly earnings-age profiles for birth cohorts for women and men, both university and high school educated.

The variable for supply of students is the (log of the) ratio of lagged female high school graduates to male high school graduates (as approximated).

The regression results are strikingly strong, even though the coefficient for the supply ratio is not significantly different from zero once the correction for autocorrelation is imposed. The two demand variables, however, are quite robust, and the R^2 value is high at 0.99. Easton states that a 10 percent increase in the female education premium generates a 7.6 percent increase in the female-to-male enrollment ratio. A 10 percent increase in men's education premium generates a 10 percent fall in the enrollment ratio — that is, leads to an 11 percent increase in male enrollment if female enrollment is unaffected.

Easton's results are so good as to be somewhat puzzling; in addition, some of his data appear to need reconciliation with other data. Riddell and Sweetman (2000), who also study earnings and education, report education premiums for male and female Canadian workers in 1970, 1980, and 1990. They find that, typically, women holding bachelor's degrees have earned 1.5 to 2.0 times the earnings of high-school-educated women of the same age. Men's education premium has been consistently lower, typically about 1.5 or somewhat less.[11] A more interesting point in this context is that the education premium has been steady (for those ages 21 to 30) or declining (for those ages 31 to 40 and 41 to 50) over the decades from 1970 to 1990, for both men and women.[12] This downward trend in the education premium is consistent with the growing proportion of university educated workers in the labor market. However, the decline in the premium for women over time is not consistent with the positive response Easton finds in the female-to-

---

11 These values are for full-time, full-year employment. See Riddell and Sweetman (2000), table 7 and figure 3. Allen (1999) also provides age-earnings profiles, but for 1995 only. The high economic rewards that women realize from obtaining a university education are also reflected in rate-of-return studies. For 1985, Vaillancourt (1995) reports private rates of return for bachelor's degrees as being 8.3 percent for men and 18.8 percent for women. Subsequent work reported in this volume for 1990 and 1995 suggests that the differential has narrowed to 2 or 3 percent, as a result of increases in the estimated rates of return to university education for men. Allen (1999) also estimates rates of return, but only social, not private, ones. His results are quite comparable to the 11 percent social rates estimated by Vaillancourt and Bourdeau-Primeau for 1995 for bachelor's degrees. For graduate education, Allen's estimates are notably higher than theirs.

12 Although not without exception, the declines have been absolute as well as relative.

male enrollment ratio. That is, the education premium for women, while large, has been steady or declining, while more women have been going to university and women have been becoming a larger share of the undergraduate student population. One suspects that Easton's data (unlike Riddell and Sweetman's) must show a rising education premium for women to have the positive association with a rising enrollment share.[13]

The actual education premiums that Easton uses as data for his regressions and their time patterns are not obvious. He plots indexes of men's and women's — weekly, I believe — wages for university and high school education in his Figure 6. That figure shows the wages of university-educated women rising while those of high-school-educated women decline. This figure suggests that the education premium is widening, as required for Easton's econometric results, but I am uncertain whether or not the premium can be determined from the relative positions of the two lines; are they consistently scaled? In contrast, the figure shows the real wages of university-educated men declining over time, but those of high-school-trained men declining even faster.

If Riddell and Sweetman (2000), using census data, show education premiums for women of a specific age declining or remaining steady over time (like men's), how does Easton obtain a growing education premium for women? Turning to Beaudry and Green (1997), from which Easton obtains the wage regressions used to calculate age-earnings profiles and education premiums, one notes that, for university-educated females the (year of birth) cohort intercepts of the age-earnings profiles drop — although the decline for females is less than that for males, and, unlike the men's, those declines are offset by increases in the slope of the profiles over time. In other words, there has been an increase in the returns to experience in the labor market for women. In addition, Beaudry and Green's estimates of the gains to women from experience are largest for the most recent entrants; that is, they find "very large age slopes for the

---

13 It is assumed that controlling for the male premium controls male enrollments and that there is no significant interrelationship between male premiums and female enrollment or vice versa.

most recent cohorts." They go on to note, "since the high earnings levels predicted for the most recent cohorts later in life correspond to age ranges that are well out of sample, such extrapolation should be interpreted with caution" (p. 17). I am speculating here, but I suspect that it is the relatively large predicted gains to experience for women, and especially those for the latest labor market entrants, that provides the education premiums that are driving the results for women in Easton's model. The smoothly growing estimates of the education premium for women that are suggested by Easton's Figure 6 and that might be implied by his use of the Beaudry and Green results, in combination with the steady growth of the female-to-male enrollment ratio, could generate the kind of excellent fit and significant coefficient he finds. It would have been interesting and informative if Easton had reported the education premium data used for his estimates and compared them to the data of other observers such as Riddell and Sweetman.

A growing share of Canada's young women is attending university. The enrollment rate — undergraduate women as a percentage of 18-to-24-year-old women — began to increase in the 1970s, and doubled between 1980 and 1995 (from 9 to 19 percent).[14] This dramatic growth occurred during a period in which there was a hefty education premium for women, but also one in which that premium seems to have been compressed. Growth in female university enrollment during a period in which the education premium has diminished somewhat is at odds with Easton's model. While I have no doubt that the economic rewards for university education, and changes in those rewards, do influence people's decisions to pursue higher education, I also believe that there are more factors determining the growth, and the relative growth, in female university enrollment. That is, I suspect that a variety of factors have caused women to respond more to the continuing large education premiums in recent years than they did in the past. That the growing share of women in universities began in the 1960s, just as effective contraception became widely available to them, is not a coinci-

---

14 The male enrollment rate declined during the 1970s, rose slowly during the 1980s, and leveled off in the 1990s. See Riddell and Sweetman (2000).

dence. Changes in divorce laws, trends in marriage and family size, and new child-rearing patterns, including the increased availability of day care (and changes to the tax treatment of child care costs), all of which have extended women's projected work force lives, have probably had an impact on the numbers of women who choose university. Broad changes in social attitudes toward women both in the home and in the workplace have also contributed. The stagnating returns to male earners, partly the result of a growing labor force, may have induced still more women into both the labor market and universities. These are only some suggestions of other contributing factors; readers can add their own.

In short, a broad range of social and economic factors, often interrelated, has contributed to the growth of the share of women attending universities in Canada. These factors are overlooked in Easton's analysis, which singles out the education premium and, I suspect, attributes to this factor too strong an explanatory power. I have already suggested checking the education premium data as one cautious response to Easton's statement. Another alternative would be attempting to explain female and male enrollment separately — that is, estimating two equations and, ideally, trying to include variables reflecting some of the other possible factors contributing to the trends in women's employment and education decisions. Combining economic and social forces acting on education decisions could provide a much more powerful explanation and offer even more interesting insights.

Easton also points out that the high school graduation grading system may be affecting the relative supplies of female and male university students. In British Columbia, final high school grades are a combination of the provincial exam grade and a school-based assessment. On average, females consistently perform better than males in the school-based assessments, unlike in the exam performance. Easton speculates that moves to include school-based assessments may contribute to the increasing portion of women in universities. That may be so, but, after allowing for an adjustment period, it should only cause a one-time shift, unless there is a progressive expansion of the weight given to school-based assessments. It would be interesting to investigate whether or not the inclusion of school-based grades better predicts university performance.

Alice Nakamura and
Joel Bruneau on e-Recruiting

Most readers will find the Nakamura and Bruneau paper an eye-opening update on the recruiting of university graduates. Many of us, including those on staff in the universities, have not kept fully abreast of how this process has evolved. E-recruiting has created a cost-effective national, even international, recruiting system overlayering the university placement offices, which continue to exist like islands in an archipelago. E-recruiting is expanding the amount and kind of information available, broadening search horizons, speeding the process, and lowering the costs of recruiting on both sides of the market. It has the potential to enhance job market performance, but the incentives facing campus placement offices and the market dominance (partly by US-owned firms) in the e-recruiting industry is hampering the realization of those gains for Canadians. Organizations that should be working together for the benefit of our university graduates and employers are at odds. This lack of cooperation frustrates especially the efforts of CareerOwl, a small player (of which Alice Nakamura is a founder) in the e-recruiting world, despite the advantages it offers especially to smaller employers.

E-recruiting does not replace traditional recruiting methods, according to Nakamura and Bruneau, but supplements them. While some aspects of that role are clear enough from their analysis, it would be informative if we had been told more about the place that e-recruiting now occupies in the larger recruiting picture, especially with regard to new university graduates. How quickly has it evolved? What kinds of employees recruited by this method? What portion of those jobs appear on the Internet? To what extent do employers use e-recruiting exclusively? How extensively do new graduates rely on it? For what share of placements made is e-recruiting responsible? Are campus recruiting offices becoming less relevant in the placement of new graduates, or is their role in the process still as important, but changing?

This kind of basic information is missing from Nakamura and Bruneau's paper. Perhaps it is not readily available. An article in a human resources magazine reports that "almost half of Fortune Global 500 companies actively recruit on the Internet," that a survey of Workopolis.com users shows that 69 percent applied for a job listed on the site, that 40 percent of applicants were contacted for an interview, and that 94 percent of college graduates use corporate websites to gather information on potential employers (Altass 2001). Warburton and Warburton (2001), reporting on a British Columbia government experience in e-recruiting, state that, at the time of the search they studied, Monster.ca had more than 200,000 registered job seekers, CareerMosaic had 90,000, and CareerOwl 40,000. (Currently, CareerOwl has 59,000, a fact that demonstrates the rapid growth of e-recruiting.)

The Warburtons' report is positive on the subject of e-recruiting; they also briefly review several alternatives that were considered. Monster and CareerMosaic are branches of large US operations; those two and CareerOwl offered the lowest costs for posting positions, well below the rates of the two large Canadian commercial e-recruiters, Workopolis and CareerClick. Among the three used in that search, CareerOwl stood out in terms of low cost, convenience, affordable options, technical quality, and search categories. The job seekers listed there came primarily from the major English-speaking Canadian universities. Despite its current small size, CareerOwl appears to be a credible player in the e-recruiting marketplace.

The difficulties facing CareerOwl, despite the advantages it offers, appear to result from its being a small player, and from competition in e-recruiting with university placement services. The glib and simplistic response to this situation is "welcome to the market." Real markets are not perfect; there is not perfect information, and the outcomes are not necessarily fair. In some ways, e-recruiting resembles the world of Microsoft and operating systems; the dominant service may not be the best or have the most desirable features, but it is very hard for customers to avoid using it. The result is a difficult market for minor competitors.

The more serious and thoughtful response to this situation is that there is evidence that market imperfection is limiting the potential of e-recruiting in Canada and tilting the playing field against Canadian employers, especially small ones, as Nakamura and Bruneau argue. That US e-recruiters could be dominating the market (we do not know whether or to what extent this is the case) and exposing Canadian job seekers to US employers is not, in itself, the issue. This exposure to a broader range of potential employers expands the job choices available to Canadian graduates. A problem arises if Canadian employers — and, in turn, potential employees — are not well served by the available options, or have difficulty gaining access to them — or if pure market power squeezes Canadian based e-recruiters out of the marketplace altogether.

There would be advantages for university placement services in linking with national and international e-recruiters. E-recruiters also can gain from such links, especially if an individual operation can dominate a university's connections. Favored-party arrangements can be expected to develop. One could speculate that these arrangements might take the form of exclusive marketing deals, similar to those that soft-drink manufacturers have been offering universities. Such incentives will look good to resource-short, self-funded campus career offices, but the limitations they would place on choice might be problematic. Limited choice in soft drinks on campus is one thing; limited choice (or even preferential direction) in job placement services is another. The exclusivity or preferences of "Coca-Cola"-type arrangements could work to the disadvantage of graduates, employers, and the country. By instituting inappropriate incentives, being slow to respond to the revolution in recruiting by creating guidelines, and failing to consider the long-run consequences of self-financing placement offices, universities may easily lead themselves, and all of us, into a less than desirable outcome.

Markets work most effectively in a context of competition and information. Students and employers should be aware of the full range of e-recruiting options. University placement offices are more likely to be serving both their constituents (students) and employers well if they inform them about and link them to the whole spectrum of e-recruiters. Current incentives do not push in this direction, however.

Unfortunately, Nakamura and Bruneau do not offer — at least in the original draft of the paper — explicit recommendations for modifying those incentives. Universities might reconsider whether or not the existing arrangements with their placement offices — including funding and oversight — are, or will be, the best way to serve their students in the e-recruiting world. Governments might consider their influence as major employers, as e-recruiters (Campusworklink.com), and as market information providers.

Each player in the placement market, whether an e-recruiter or a university placement office, would gain from better linkages. Arrangements to share the charges for services based on the number and type of connections made by users would go some way toward rewarding each recruiter for its contribution and for achieving broad access. Broad access, competition and fair distribution of revenues, however, are not likely to be the common objectives, especially of dominant players. While low-cost e-recruiters may have little revenue to share, the jobs and the additional recruits that they add to the pool can be expected to have value to other market participants. Hence, some concerted action, ideally initiated by the major universities, seems essential if improvements are to be made to the developing market structure.

E-recruiting offers many advantages for the labor market, and it is growing rapidly. It is important that a highly effective, open, and competitive e-recruiting market evolves.[15] For this goal to be realized, it seems that some policy initiative will be required, especially at the university level. In any case, if CareerOwl continues to receive positive reviews such as that of Warburton and Warburton, its prospects for surviving and making an important contribution in the long term are encouraging.

Conclusion

The papers by Davenport, Easton, and Nakamura and Bruneau are individually insightful pieces; collectively, they provide a valuable broad overview of many important issues facing Canadian universities today. The Easton and the Nakamura and Bruneau papers in particular raise more obscure, often neglected matters. Each of the papers is excellent reading: informative and stimulating.

---

15 Success in the selection of a person's first job is an important determinant of his or her career path. For example, see Finnie in this volume.

References

Allen, Robert C. 1999. "Education and the Technological Revolutions: The Role of the Social Sciences and Humanities in the Knowledge Based Economy." Vancouver: University of British Columbia, Department of Economics. November.

Altass, Angela. 2001. "E-Cruiting: Changing the HR Landscape." *Network* 3 (2): 12–14.

Baudry, Paul, and David Green. 1997. "Cohort Patterns in Canadian Earnings: Assessing the Role of Skill Premia in Inequality Trends." NBER Working Paper 6132. Cambridge, Mass.: National Bureau of Economic Research. (Also published in 2000 in *Canadian Journal of Economics* 33 (4): 907–936.)

Izadi, Hooshang, et al. 2002. "Stochastic Frontier Estimation of a CES Cost Function: The Case of Higher Education in Britain." *Economics of Education Review* 21: 63–71.

Koshal, Rajindar, and Manjulika Koshal. 1999. "Economies of Scale and Scope in Higher Education: A Case of Comprehensive Universities." *Economics of Education Review* 18: 269–277.

Jennings, Phillip. 1998. "School Enrolment and the Declining Youth Participation Rate." *Policy Options* 19 (3): 10–14.

Litten, Larry H. 1984. *Issues in Pricing Undergraduate Education*. San Francisco: Jossey-Bass.

Riddell, W. Craig, and Arthur Sweetman. 2000. "Human Capital Formation in a Period of Rapid Change." In W. Craig Riddell and France St-Hillaire, eds., *Adapting Public Policy to a Labour Market in Transition*. Montreal: Institute for Research on Public Policy.

Smith, Stuart L. 1991. *Report of the Commission of Inquiry on Canadian University Education*. Ottawa: Association of Universities and Colleges of Canada.

Stager, D.A.A. 1989. *Focus on Fees: Alterative Policies for University Tuition Fees*. Toronto: Council of Ontario Universities.

Statistics Canada. 1978. *Historical Compendium of Educational Statistics from Confederation to 1975*. Cat. 81-568.

———. Various years. *Education in Canada*. Cat. 81-229.

Vaillancourt, François. 1995. "The Private and Total Returns to Education in Canada, 1985." *Canadian Journal of Economics* 28 (3): 532–554.

Warburton, Rebecca, and William Warburton. 2001. "Canadian-Made E-Solution Proves Cheap and Effective." *Canadian Business Economics* 8 (3): 37–39.

Quantity or Quality?
Research at Canadian Universities

*John Chant and
William Gibson*

Universities provide many different services to their students. The most obvious one is the transfer of knowledge through classroom teaching. Universities also filter, or sort, their students according to their abilities. But these roles alone would make institutions of higher learning little more than extensions of primary and secondary schools. Recent approaches to higher education focus on another important function of universities: providing their students with signals. Some of these signals relate to individual students — for example, indications of their performance relative to other students through grades or personal recommendations from professors. Others are collective signals based on a university's overall reputation. A degree from a particular university tells the outside world that the student has met that institution's standards. These collective signals may be shaped by many factors, such as the historical performance of alumni and the grandeur of a university's campus. But one crucial component in the signal sent by a university's reputation is the research performance of its academic staff.

In this essay, we examine the research performance in science and social science of top Canadian universities relative to those in the United States. We believe this is important for several reasons.

The authors thank Steve Easton, Jack Knetsch, David Laidler, John Polanyi, and Jeff Smith for their helpful comments, and Elizabeth d'Anjou for her superb editing.

Some argue that a professor's research contributes to his or her effectiveness as a classroom teacher.[1] It also makes a contribution to our collective knowledge and, for that reason, benefits society. Without discounting these arguments, we emphasize the positive impact research has on a university's reputation and hence on the signals it sends. Even undergraduate and professional students benefit from research if it enhances the reputation of a university in the minds of the general public, especially employers. For high school students selecting a university to attend, for graduates choosing a graduate school, or for employers evaluating résumés, reputations are important substitutes for first-hand experience.

We believe that the research performance of Canadian universities matters. Strong performance will enhance their reputation for quality and benefit Canadian students, whether they seek employment or continue their studies after graduation, in or outside Canada. Employers will pay more to hire students from universities that are prominent and well-known for their research. Similarly, top graduate and professional schools are selective with respect to the institutions from which they draw their students. And an enhanced reputation for a graduate school leads to a larger applicant pool, allowing the university to be more selective in its admissions. This perceived increased difficulty of entry, in turn, serves to enhance the university's reputation further in the eyes of the public.

This paper is organized as follows. We begin by describing the data we use to analyze the comparative research performance of Canadian and US universities. In the second section, we compare the recent research performances of Canadian and US universities in 21 disciplines. In the third section, we examine trends in relative performance from the early 1980s to the present. We then shift our attention away from individual disciplines to the overall performance of universities. Finally, we conclude with some reflections on the significance of our results.

---

1 While we accept the validity of this view, we would not push it very far. It must deal with the evidence that there is an inverse relation among professors between their effectiveness as researchers and the amount of their time devoted to teaching undergraduates. The argument appears more valid at the graduate level.

Indicators of Research Performance

In this study, we use the two data sets collected by the Institute for Scientific Information (ISI) that are based on their well-known citation indexes.[2] These data sets provide information on both the number of papers published and the citations these papers received in more than 23 disciplines for a broad sample of Canadian and US universities over the 1981–98 period (see Tables A-1 and A-2 in the Appendix). The data sets we used do not include information for the arts and humanities. They are based on papers published and citations received in some 5,500 journals in science and 1,800 in the social sciences. The Canadian and US data sets differed somewhat in their coverage. The 111 universities included in the US data set consist primarily of research universities. In contrast, the 67 universities in the Canadian set include many institutions that emphasize teaching.[3]

We use two parts of the data collected by ISI: the number of papers and the number of citations per paper — the "paper impact" — identified with a particular discipline at the universities that we study. The number of papers, in our view, is a measure of research *quantity*, or the level of research activity at an institution. The paper impact measures the recognition that the research gains from other scholars on a paper-by-paper basis, which to us is a measure of research *quality*.

Although we believe that both the number of papers and paper impact contribute to the value of a university's overall reputation, we do not know the relative contribution of each. Moreover, each measure has shortcomings. Clearly, the size of an institution will be a major factor contributing to the number of papers identified with it. Although we lack the information to correct for size, we do discuss

---

2 The Canadian data have been analyzed in two *Science Watch* papers (1992; 1995), and summarized by Strauss (1995).

3 Only 17 of the US institutions published fewer than 10,000 papers and none had fewer than 1,000. In contrast, 48 Canadian institutions (almost 70 percent of them) published fewer than 10,000 papers. Of these, 7 published fewer than 100 papers.

how university size relates to our results.[4] Similarly, the paper impact measure treats all citations to a paper equally regardless of whether they occur in well-regarded or lesser journals, and whether they are laudatory or critical. Although these considerations may be important in judging the impact of any particular paper, we believe they will be less significant when examining the impact of a university's papers over an entire discipline in the longer term. A premium citation will beget further citations. Over time, therefore, the "quality" of citations will be captured by the number.

We used only 21 of the 23 fields surveyed by ISI in our study. In most fields, national differences in research content are unlikely to make much difference, but we chose not to use law because it is the field most likely to feature work that is specific to the country in which the research takes place. Articles on Canadian law topics are less likely to be cited by US scholars than articles by their compatriots. Given the relative size of the two countries, comparisons of article impact in this field would not be an adequate measure of research quality. We also did not consider the field ISI calls "other social sciences" because it is not clear that the content of this category is comparable across institutions.

The fields covered in our study differ substantially with respect to the number of papers published, the number of per paper citations, and the distribution of these, as shown in Table 1. The number of papers identified with the top-ranked university over the 1994–98 period in a particular discipline ranged from a low of 215 for education to a high of more than 15,000 for clinical medicine. Similarly, the citations per paper identified with the top-ranked university ranged from more than 39 for molecular biology to just 3.1 for engineering. In addition, the differences among institutions varied across disciplines. In two disciplines, the second-ranked institution published fewer than half as many papers as the top-ranked institution; in some other disciplines, more than 20 institu-

---

[4] To correct for size, we would need the number of researchers in each discipline at each institution. Such a measure would be complicated by the fact that many of the disciplines do not correspond closely to one or even several well-identified departments. For example, one institution that ranks in the top ten in physics does not actually have a department in that discipline.

Table 1: Maximum Citation Rates and Number of Papers Published, by Discipline, Canadian and US Universities, 1994–98

Discipline	Maximum No. of Citations per Paper	Rank of Institution with 50% of Maximum Citation Rate	Maximum No. of Papers Published	Rank of Institution Publishing 50% of Maximum No. of Papers
Agricultural sciences	8.3	8	834	15
Astrophysics	13.5	38	1,810	3
Biology and biochemistry	16.4	38	4,577	2
Chemistry	10.1	48	2,471	14
Clinical medicine	9.4	49	15,056	4
Computer science	3.2	33	305	22
Ecology and environment	6.0	50	809	14
Economics	4.7	30	980	12
Education	3.2	38	215	18
Engineering	3.1	42	2,326	13
Geosciences	8.7	31	1,364	8
Immunology	22.9	20	1,733	1[a]
Mathematics	3.3	26	597	23
Materials sciences	6.6	13	838	12
Microbiology	21.9	22	842	10
Molecular biology	39.1	19	3,252	1[a]
Neurosciences	13.4	44	2,560	11
Pharmacology	11.5	22	528	24
Physics	9.2	47	3,821	12
Plant and animal sciences	6.7	22	2,941	9
Psychology	7.1	44	1,732	7
Maximum	39.1	50	15,056	23
Minimum	3.1	8	215	1

[a] The second-ranked institution published fewer than half the number of papers of the first-ranked institution.

Sources: Institute for Scientific Information 1981–98a; 1981–98b.

tions published at least half that number of papers. Differences in the patterns of citations per paper were less pronounced; in every case, at least eight institutions gained half the citation rate of the leading institution, and in one case more than 50 institutions received at least that many citations.

These differences in patterns served to limit the types of comparisons among disciplines that we could make in this study. Comparing institutions by total papers or by citations per paper over all fields would not be meaningful. An institution specializing in clinical medicine might appear to be much more productive than one specializing in mathematics; in fact, the differences would arise almost entirely from the differences among fields. Similarly, a university with a concentration of strength in economics — in which the maximum per paper citation rate at any institution was 4.7 — would appear to have lower-quality research than a university that concentrated on microbiology, where even the twentieth-ranked institution received more than ten citations per paper published. For these reasons, we do not present any university-by-university measures with respect to total papers published or average citations rates to papers published.

We also took discipline differences into account in setting our standards for comparing Canadian and US institutions. The more comprehensive coverage of Canadian universities in our sample raises problems for comparing the number of citations. If, in some fields, Canadian institutions that have relatively little research output nevertheless gain high citation rates, the overall performance of Canadian institutions would be overstated for these fields. Moreover, it is not clear that a high citation rate for a very small number of articles contributes significantly to the reputation of an institution. To overcome this problem, we introduced thresholds for including institutions in the comparisons of article impact. In all cases, we included the top 50 institutions in the combined Canadian-US sample to ensure a broad representation. We also added institutions beyond the fiftieth ranking when necessary to include all institutions that accounted for publications at a level of at least 20 percent of the institution with the most publications in the discipline. The purpose of this second dimension of the threshold was to ensure that small differences among institutions with respect to papers published did not skew the results with respect to either papers published or paper impact.

Research Performance, 1994-98

By what standards should the research performance of Canadian universities be judged relative to their US counterparts? Both countries have many universities with different missions that cater to different groups of students. In focusing our attention on the top performers with respect to research in both countries, we have used the "rule of ten," a common yardstick for quantitative comparisons between Canada and the United States. If the distribution of Canadian universities by their research performance were comparable to that of US universities, in the combined sample one Canadian university would be expected in the top ten and the top three Canadian universities overall could be expected to fall between tenth and twentieth. While this expectation (based on the fact that the United States' population is about ten times Canada's) is clearly a rough-and-ready standard, we believe it provides a good starting point.

The Quantity of Papers

Canadian research measures up quite well with respect to the number of papers published by discipline, as Table 2 shows. The leading Canadian institution was ranked in the top ten for 12 of the 21 disciplines considered. In only two fields (economics and physics) did the top-ranked Canadian institution fall outside the top 20 from the combined sample. The top ranking in Canada for the number of papers published was, for all disciplines, one of just five institutions — Toronto, Guelph, McGill, the University of British Columbia (UBC), and Waterloo — with Toronto accounting for the top Canadian ranking in 15 fields. The performance of the top three Canadian institutions in the various disciplines also meets the expectations of our "rule of ten" yardstick: the average of the top three ranks came in between tenth and twentieth in 12 of the disciplines.

Table 2: *Relative Performance of Canadian Universities, by Number of Papers Published, 1994–98*

Discipline	Number of Papers Published — Average of Top 3 Canadian Universities	Number of Papers Published — Average of Top 3 Canadian and US Universities	Rank by Number of Papers Published — Average of Top 3 Canadian Universities	Rank by Number of Papers Published — Top-Ranked Canadian University
Agricultural sciences	418	729	16	7
Astrophysics	230	1,342	33	18
Biology and biochemistry	1,775	3,084[a]	13	3
Chemistry	1,209	1,972	17	10
Clinical medicine	6,182	10,985[a]	13	2
Computer science	185	290	16	8
Ecology/environment	400	677	17	12
Economics	271	771	34	22
Education	118	192	16	5
Engineering	943	2,124	21	15
Geosciences	511	1,127	21	19
Immunology	405	1,105	30	7
Materials sciences	388	717	15	8
Mathematics	326	566	19	14
Microbiology	342	680	21	14
Molecular biology	1,046	2,056	13	4
Neurosciences	1,349	2,061	12	4
Pharmacology	423	505[a]	7	2
Physics	1,313	3,495	29	28
Plant and animal sciences	1,226	3,281	17	8
Psychology/psychiatry	886	1,458[a]	42	3

[a] A Canadian institution is included in the top three.

Source: Table A-3 of this paper.

Quality of Papers

The research performance of Canadian universities, as shown in Table 3, is weaker with respect to its impact on, or recognition from, other scholars than it is with respect to the number of papers published, according to our measures. In only three disciplines (astrophysics, education, and materials sciences) did the rate of citations per paper of the top-ranked Canadian institution fall within the top ten of the combined Canadian-US sample. Moreover, the top-ranked Canadian institution in 12 of the disciplines failed to rank within the top 20 institutions in the combined group.

The top rankings for citations per paper within a discipline were less highly concentrated than those for total number of papers. Ten different institutions received the top ranking in Canada for one or more fields. While the University of Toronto received the largest number of first rankings, it earned only seven top rankings for paper impact, compared with its 15 with respect to the number of papers published.

Canada's lower success rate with respect to paper impact, or quality, is also seen in the average ranking of the top three Canadian institutions. In only four disciplines (agricultural sciences, astrophysics, materials sciences, and plant and animal sciences) did the average rank of the top three meet our yardstick of falling within the top 20, and in three it was not even within the top 40.

Conclusions

Overall, it appears that the research performance of Canadian universities is better with respect to the quantity of papers they produce than to the impact those papers have. Although Canadian universities hold their own alongside their US counterparts in the number of papers published, they rank well below the top US universities in the recognition their research receives from their peers.

Our results with respect to paper impact could be challenged on the grounds that some research is of interest primarily to Canadians and is therefore unlikely to be cited heavily by researchers outside Canada. As mentioned earlier, we left out law out of our

Table 3: *Relative Performance of Canadian Universities, by Citation Rate, 1994–98*

Discipline	Average of Top 3 Canadian Universities	Average of Top 3 Canadian and US Universities	Average of Top 3 Canadian Universities	Top-Ranked Canadian University
	Average Number of Citations per Paper		Rank by Number of Citations per Paper	
Agricultural sciences	2.8	4.6	13	10
Astrophysics	9.3	12.8	17	7
Biology and biochemistry	8.6	16.7	37	31
Chemistry	5.7	9.5	42	29
Clinical medicine	6.3	9.2	36	32
Computer science	1.3	2.5	38	47
Ecology/environment	4.6	6.0	22	13
Economics and business	1.8	4.3	42	37
Education	2.0	2.6[a]	24	1
Engineering	1.8	3.1	36	28
Geosciences	4.0	8.7	39	37
Immunology	10.9	25.4	25	18
Materials sciences	3.1	6.8	19	8
Mathematics	1.6	3.2	37	27
Microbiology	6.5	17.5	54	48
Molecular biology	14.0	35.4	36	28
Neurosciences	8.1	17.5	35	31
Pharmacology	6.5	11.6	25	20
Physics	6.3	11.8	31	19
Plant and animal sciences	3.6	6.2	19	13
Psychology/psychiatry	3.9	7.4	37	28

[a] A Canadian institution is included in the top three.

Source: Table A-4 of this paper.

list of disciplines on the assumption that it was likely to be particularly country-specific. To varying degrees, national cultural differences may affect the citation rates of papers in some other disciplines as well. Of the disciplines in our study, those where the peculiarities of Canadian research seem likely to be the greatest include agricultural sciences, economics, and plant and animal sciences. It is less likely that there would be a distinctly Canadian approach to such fields as astrophysics, mathematics, neuroscience, or physics. As Table 3 shows, however, Canadian institutions' performance in those fields displays no relationship between the expected degree of a field's specificity to Canada and its rank in terms of paper impact. The top three Canadian institutions in the fields most relevant to Canada have an average rank of fourteenth, nineteenth, and forty-second (the average across all fields is thirty-second). Of the four fields in which the Canadian top three did worse than fortieth, only one, economics, seems likely to be specific to Canada to some degree.

Performance Over Time

The fact that the ISI data set extends over nearly two decades allows us to examine, to some extent, how Canadian universities' research performance has changed over time. Once again we look at both the number of papers (quantity) and the rate at which they are cited (quality).

Changes in Papers

Table 4 shows how the relative performance of Canadian universities has changed with respect to the number of papers published by disciplines across four periods: 1981–85, 1984–88, 1989–93, and 1994–98.[5] Panel A gives the position of the top-ranked Canadian university in the overall sample for each discipline in each period;

---

5 The table compares four five-year periods for the 19 years of the data set. This period necessitates some overlap of periods for five-year comparisons. We chose to overlap the first two periods.

Table 4: *Changes in Rankings of Canadian Universities, by Number of Papers Published, 1981–98*

	Rank				Change Relative to 1994–98		
Discipline	1981–85	1984–88	1989–93	1994–98	1981–85	1984–88	1989–93
A. Position of Top-Ranked Canadian University							
Ecology/environment	23	17	18	12	–11	–5	–6
Mathematics	25	19	20	14	–11	–5	–6
Education	15	9	6	5	–10	–4	–1
Molecular biology	14	6	5	4	–10	–2	–1
Agricultural sciences	16	14	8	7	–9	–7	–1
Economics	29	26	28	22	–7	–4	–6
Materials sciences	14	12	14	8	–6	–4	–6
Biology and biochemistry	8	6	5	3	–5	–3	–2
Immunology	10	7	9	7	–3	0	–2
Astrophysics	21	17	14	18	–3	+1	+4
Clinical medicine	4	4	2	2	–2	–2	0
Psychology	4	3	3	3	–1	0	0
Chemistry	11	13	12	10	–1	–3	–2
Neurosciences	4	3	4	4	0	+1	0
Engineering	14	17	18	15	+1	–2	–3
Microbiology	13	16	23	14	+1	–2	–9
Pharmacology	1	1	1	2	+1	+1	+1
Plant and animal sciences	5	5	5	8	+3	+3	+3
Computer science	5	8	18	8	+3	0	–10
Geosciences	12	9	12	19	+7	+10	+7
Physics	19	22	18	28	+9	+6	+10
Average	12.7	11.1	11.6	10.1	–2.6	–1.0	–1.4

Source: Table A-5 of this paper.

Table 4 - continued

Discipline	Rank 1981–85	Rank 1984–88	Rank 1989–93	Rank 1994–98	Change Relative to 1994–98 1981–85	1984–88	1989–93
B. Average Position of Top Three Canadian Universities							
Molecular biology	27	18	18	13	−14	−5	−5
Agricultural sciences	27	23	17	16	−11	−7	−1
Ecology/environment	28	24	21	17	−11	−7	−4
Clinical medicine	23	20	16	13	−10	−7	−3
Psychology	22	18	17	13	−9	−5	−4
Biology and biochemistry	21	19	17	13	−8	−6	−4
Mathematics	27	24	22	19	−8	−5	−3
Education	23	18	20	16	−7	−2	−4
Immunology	26	25	22	19	−7	−6	−3
Microbiology	27	24	25	21	−6	−3	−4
Pharmacology	13	11	10	7	−6	−4	−3
Neurosciences	14	10	9	12	−2	+2	+3
Materials sciences	16	17	19	15	−1	−2	−4
Astrophysics	33	28	23	32	−1	+4	+9
Plant and animal sciences	17	16	16	17	0	+1	+1
Engineering	20	22	21	21	+1	−1	0
Chemistry	15	15	21	17	+2	+2	−4
Physics	26	29	23	29	+3	0	+6
Economics	30	28	36	34	+4	+6	−2
Geosciences	17	15	18	21	+4	+6	+3
Computer science	14	20	29	24	+10	+4	−5
Average	22.1	20.2	20.0	18.5	−3.7	−1.7	−1.5

Source: Table A-5 of this paper.

panel B does the same for the average of the top three. Both show an overall improvement in the rankings of Canadian institutions over the period. The average of the first ranks improved between 1981–85 and 1994–98 by more than two places (from 12.7 to 10.1), while the average rank of the top three institutions by discipline improved by more than three places (from 22.1 to 18.5).

This improvement was not, however, uniform over fields. The top rankings improved in 13 of the 21 fields, and the average of the top three rankings improved in 14. In both cases, one field showed no change, but Canadian universities slipped in the ranking in all the other fields.

Changes in Impact

Any analysis of how the rank of the Canadian universities in our sample changed over time with respect to paper impact is more complicated, these rankings can change in a number of ways. The most straightforward situation is when the same institution holds the top rank — or the top three schools hold the top three ranks — across all four time periods. In this case, any change in the ranking reflects changes in the performance of the school (or group of schools). The analysis becomes more complicated when different institutions make up the top group from period to period. When an institution moves up the ranks and replaces one of the previous leaders, changes in the performance of the earlier leaders are tempered by the replacement of one of them by another institution. The most difficult case to analyze is when an institution meets the threshold for inclusion in the sample in one period and fails to meet it in another. In this case, the overall ranking of Canadian institutions in a discipline can change substantially without any significant change in the performance of any institutions in that discipline.[6] Moreover, such a change in ranking can occur as a result

---

6 For example, consider a discipline where Canadian institutions rank tenth, twentieth, and thirtieth in one period, to average twentieth over the top three. Assume also that, during the period, a Canadian institution that failed to meet the threshold for inclusion with respect to the number of articles published...

of only a minor change in an institution's performance with respect to the threshold criterion.[7]

Table 5 summarizes the changes in the ranking of both the top-ranked Canadian institution (panel A) and the average of the top three (Panel B) with respect to the impact of articles over the same time period used in Table 4. Here, the evidence is mixed. The standing of the top-ranked institutions improved by 0.8 of a place over the period as a whole. Part of this change is, however, accounted for by the inclusion of Simon Fraser University as the top-rated university in education for the final period even though it failed to qualify for inclusion during the 1984–88 and 1989–93 periods. When the analysis is restricted to institutions qualifying in all periods, the average rank of the top-rated institutions deteriorated by 0.8 of a place.

Table 5 also shows that the differences among disciplines with respect to the change in first-ranked Canadian institutions are substantial. The split was quite even: 10 first-ranked institutions moved up and 11 moved down. At the extremes, education and astrophysics each improved by almost 30 places, while the top institution in computing fell by 37 places.

Panel B of the table shows how the average rank in the overall sample of the top three Canadian institutions in each discipline changed. Over the entire period, these rankings slipped on average by more than two places — from 30.1 in the initial period to 32.3 in the final period. The final three columns show that this decline

---

Note 6 - cont'd.

...would have ranked first in terms of impact if it had been included. If, in another period, this institution had qualified and the institutions did not change their rankings, the top three Canadian institutions would have ranked first, tenth, and twentieth, for an an average of tenth. This change would have taken place without the ranking of any Canadian institution changing. The same phenomenon also works in reverse when an institution that had previously met the threshold no longer does so.

7 For example, an institution could be excluded from the impact comparison in one period if it published 49 articles and included the next if it published 50. If it had a high ranking on paper impact, such a change could substantially affect the impact performance of the top-ranking institutions.

Table 5: *Changes in Rankings of Canadian Universities, by Citations per Paper, 1981–98*

Discipline	Rank 1981–85	Rank 1984–88	Rank 1989–93	Rank 1994–98	Change Relative to 1994–98 1981–85	Change Relative to 1994–98 1984–88	Change Relative to 1994–98 1989–93
A. Position of Top-Ranked Canadian University							
Education	29	10	19	1	–28	–9	–18
Astrophysics	34	21	9	7	–27	–14	–2
Physics	39	39	30	19	–20	–20	–11
Materials sciences	23	21	32	8	–15	–13	–24
Biology and biochemistry	44	10	29	31	–13	+21	+2
Immunology	30	13	15	18	–12	+5	+3
Clinical medicine	42	37	39	32	–10	–5	–7
Molecular biology	36	29	17	28	–8	–1	+11
Ecology/environment	20	23	15	13	–7	–10	–2
Chemistry	31	43	54	29	–2	–14	–25
Engineering	19	11	18	20	+1	+9	+2
Plant and animal science	11	6	14	13	+2	+7	–1
Agricultural science	6	5	16	10	+4	+5	–6
Geosciences	32	35	28	37	+5	+2	+9
Psychology	23	30	15	28	+5	–2	+13
Neurosciences	24	37	25	31	+7	–6	+6
Mathematics	19	35	28	27	+8	–8	–1
Pharmacology	6	10	5	20	+14	+10	+15
Microbiology	33	36	37	48	+15	+12	+11
Economics	10	18	31	37	+27	+19	+6
Computer science	10	10	11	47	+37	+37	+38
Average	24.8	22.8	23.2	24.0	—0.8	+1.2	+1.0

Source: Table A-6 of this paper.

Table 5 - continued

Discipline	Rank 1981–85	1984–88	1989–93	1994–98	Change Relative to 1994–98 1981–85	1984–88	1989–93
B. Average Position of Top Three Canadian Universities							
Astrophysics	37	34	21	17	–20	–17	–4
Immunology	39	31	24	25	–14	–6	+1
Physics	42	40	38	31	–11	–9	–7
Materials sciences	29	25	38	19	–10	–6	–19
Biology and biochemistry	46	27	39	37	–9	+10	–2
Clinical medicine	44	43	41	36	–8	–7	–5
Ecology/environment	30	27	16	22	–8	–5	+6
Education	35	21	29	29	–6	+8	0
Molecular biology	40	39	34	36	–4	–3	+2
Plant and animal science	17	12	18	19	+2	+7	+1
Chemistry	39	46	60	42	+3	–4	–18
Geosciences	34	36	34	39	+5	+3	+5
Neurology	30	40	33	35	+5	–5	+2
Agricultural sciences	8	13	20	13	+5	0	–7
Mathematics	27	37	30	37	+10	0	+7
Engineering	22	19	21	33	+11	+14	+12
Pharmacology	14	31	25	25	+11	–6	0
Psychology	26	29	28	37	+11	+8	+9
Microbiology	39	47	41	54	+15	+7	+13
Economics	19	20	36	42	+23	+22	+6
Computer science	14	21	23	49	+35	+28	+26
Average	30.0	30.4	30.9	32.2	+2.2	+1.9	+1.3

Source: Table A-6 of this paper.

accelerated over time. Here, too, the situation differed substantially, depending on the discipline. In astrophysics, for example, the average of the three leaders improved by 20 places, while in both economics and computing it slipped by more than 20 places.

A Focus on Institutions

So far, we have analyzed the record of Canadian higher education solely through the accomplishments of Canadian institutions and their scholars on a field-by-field basis. In this section, we shift the to the overall accomplishments of institutions.

At the top tier of US institutions of higher education is a group of universities with brand names recognized throughout the world. This group includes both private universities — Harvard, Yale, Massachusetts Institute of Technology, Princeton, Duke, Chicago, and Stanford, among others — and public universities — such as the University of California at Berkeley, the University of California at Los Angeles, Michigan, and Wisconsin. To what extent is the prominence of such institutions attributable to their perceived excellence across many fields? How well do Canadian institutions fare in our Canadian-US sample in terms of their overall performance across disciplines? Is the strength of the Canadian performance the result of occasional strength in fields by a variety of different institutions, or do some Canadian institutions perform well across a range of areas? As in the previous analysis, we consider performance with respect to both the number of papers a university's faculty publishes and the impact of these papers as indicated by the frequency with which they are cited.

Institutions and Papers

Table 6 shows how often universities from our sample ranked in the top ten institutions across 21 disciplines covered by our study in terms of the number of papers they published from 1994 to 1998. In general, these data reveal a substantial concentration of high rankings among relatively few institutions. The top 11 institutions

Table 6: **Top US and Canadian Universities, by Number of Papers Published, 1994–98**

	Papers		Citations	
Institution	Rank by Disciplines in Top 10	Number of Disciplines in Top 10	Rank by Disciplines in Top 10	Number of Disciplines in Top 10
University of Toronto	1	10	27T	2
Harvard University	2T	9	1T	16
Massachusetts Institute of Technology	2T	9	4T	8
University of California at Berkeley	2T	9	27	2
University of Michigan	2T	9	16T	4
University of Minnesota	2T	9	27T	2
University of Wisconsin	2T	9	27T	2
Stanford University	7T	8	2	13
Univ. of California at San Francisco	7T	8	3	11
Johns Hopkins University	9T	7	20T	3
University of Washington	9T	7	20T	3
Univ. of California at Los Angeles	9T	7	27T	2
McGill University	17T	4		0
University of Guelph	32T	2		0
Université de Montréal	38T	1		0

Note: Ranks are reported as the best ranking of a group that is tied (T).
Sources: Derived from Institute for Scientific Information 1981–98a; 1981–98b.

— there was a tie for tenth place — of the 177 in the two data sets account for 48 percent of the possible 210 top-ten rankings over the fields surveyed. Overall, the composition of this list of top-ranked institutions is not surprising in that it includes mainly institutions with well-recognized reputations. It also features a mix of private and public institutions: seven of the top 11 US institutions by this measure are publicly funded.

Most illustrative for the Canadian-US comparisons that are the central concern of this paper is the position of University of Toronto: it had more top-ten rankings with respect to papers published than any other institution in the two countries. Other Canadian institutions also fared well: McGill ranked 17th, and both Guelph and Université de Montréal ranked in the 30s with two and one top-ten finish, respectively. On this basis, top Canadian institutions appear to compare favorably with top US institutions in demonstrating strength across a number of fields.

Institutions and Impact

A very different picture emerges, however, when one looks at the impact of published papers (see Table 7). The US rankings are dominated by private institutions, which accounted for nine of the top 11 positions. And while the top 11 institutions accounted for a share similar to that for the top institutions by papers published, there was a much greater concentration among the most highly ranked institutions. The top three — Harvard, Stanford, and the University of California at San Francisco — accounted for 40 top-ten ranks with respect to paper impact; the top three schools in Table 6 supplied just 28 top-ten ranks for papers published. Interestingly, the three institutions at the head of Table 7 are the only ones that appear in the top ten of both rankings.

The differences discussed earlier between measures of performance by the number of papers published per discipline and their impact are even more pronounced in these university-wide comparisons. The University of Toronto, the top-ranked Canadian institution with respect to article impact, features in the top ten in only two fields, giving it a tie for twenty-eighth place, compared with its first-place finish in terms of the number of papers published. Indeed, Simon Fraser is the only other Canadian university to rank in the top ten in any discipline with respect to article impact.

Size and Performance

As discussed earlier, an institution's size can be expected to be an important determinant of the number of papers it publishes, but it is less likely to affect performance with respect to paper impact. Table 8 shows that, on average, the top ten institutions by number of papers published had more than twice the level of enrollments

Table 7: *Top US and Canadian Universities, by Citations per Paper, 1994–98*

	Citations		Papers	
Institution	Rank by Disciplines in Top 10	Number of Disciplines in Top 10	Rank by Discipline in Top 10	Number of Disciplines in Top 10
Harvard University	1	16	2T	9
Stanford University	2	13	8T	8
Univ. of California at San Francisco	3	11	8T	8
Massachusetts Institute of Technology	4T	8	2T	9
University of California at San Diego	4T	8	17	4
Princeton University	6T	7		0
University of Pennsylvania	6T	7	13T	6
Duke University	6T	7		0
University of Chicago	9T	6		0
Columbia University	9T	6	17	4
Yale University	9T	6	26T	3
University of Toronto	27T	2	1	10
Simon Fraser University	55T	1		0

Note: Ranks are reported as the best ranking of a group that is tied (T).
Sources: Derived from Institute for Scientific Information 1981–98a; 1981–98b.

of the top ten institutions ranked by paper impact. This finding suggests that the good performance of Canadian institutions with respect to the number of papers published may be due to their relatively large size.[8]

Institutions Overall

The analysis of how Canadian universities fared relative to their US counterparts with respect to papers published and citations over the 1994–98 period offers some insights about their research

---

8 Enrollment at the University of Guelph is, however, lower than all but two of the top ten universities by number of papers published.

Table 8: *Size of Top Ten Canadian and US Universities, by Citations per Paper and Number of Papers Published*

Enrollment	Number in Top Ten by Citations per Paper	Number in Top Ten by Papers Published
More than 30,000	7	0
20,000–30,000	1	3
10,000–20,000	2	5
Less than 10,000	1	3
Average enrollment	30,697	14,278

Note: The number of institutions in each case is 11 to take account of ties.

Sources: US universities: United States, Department of Education, National Center for Education Statistics, *Integrated Postsecondary Education Data System (IPEDS), Fall Enrollment 1997*; Canadian universities: Association of Universities and Colleges of Canada, *Full-Time and Part-Time Enrollment by Institution and Level*; available from Internet website www.aucc.ca/en/research/enr_inst2.htm.

performance over the period. In terms of number of papers published, the rankings suggest that there is no difference in research productivity between top Canadian and US universities in this respect. Indeed, one Canadian university ranked in the top ten in this area in more fields than did any US university.

Canadian universities performed less well with respect to citations per paper, a measure of the quality of research. No Canadian university ranked in the top 20, only one was in the top 30, and one other with at least one top-ten ranking in a particular discipline managed only a share of fifty-fifth place overall. By this measure, private US universities, which tend to be smaller than state-supported research universities, dominated both Canadian and US public institutions, accounting for all but three of the top 11 rankings.

Conclusions

Our analysis provides new results about the research performance of Canadian universities relative to universities in the United

States. Our approach is quite rudimentary and takes into account neither the relative size of Canadian universities nor the resources available to them for research. Given these limits, the analysis suggests a striking finding about Canadian research efforts. The top Canadian universities perform reasonably well with respect to the volume of their publications in the fields surveyed, but lag substantially behind the top US universities in terms of the recognition their research garners from scholars, a widely agreed-on measure of the quality of research. We conclude that the quality of research at top Canadian universities falls substantially short of that found in the top US institutions.

We can only speculate about the cause of the lower quality of Canadian university research. Several possible causes are well known: Canada lacks the well-funded private research universities that exist in the United States; Canada is also poorer than its southern neighbor and the provinces provide a lower level of financial support for their universities than do many US states. The level of research funding from the federal government also falls short of that available in the United States.

We raise the possibility of a further relevant factor: differences in the approach to funding university research in the two countries. Canadian policy appears to stress criteria other than the excellence of the research itself. Surprisingly, excellence seems to play a relatively minor role in the National Research Council's (NRC's) process for choosing among research projects.

Canadian chemist and Nobel laureate John Polanyi characterizes the role of excellence in Canadian criteria for research funding as follows:

> I have beside me...the guidelines for participation in what is called a Canadian Centre of Excellence. These exist...primarily to foster university research. The reference to "excellence" acknowledges...that it is the vision (the free enterprise, if that is your line of business) of a small number of researchers that lead to new ideas that matter. So pick the best scientists (excellent, you know) and give them freedom — just so long as they remain the best. This is how it should be done.

But it's not what we do. In our hunger for payoff, our Centres of Excellence give a miserable 20 percent weight to excellence. The remaining 80 percent of the marks in the selection process are for such voguish things as interdisciplinarity, inter-institutional relations, management structure, relevance, training and socio-economic impact. (That was easy to write; I copied it from the form.)

Applications for funding must address these criteria. They are then sent for evaluation to the scientific peers of the applicant, who pretend to judge worth on this absurd basis. It is absurd, since university research is performed (or should be) in the marketplace for ideas, and not that for devices. (Polanyi 2000.)

In the United States, in contrast, the merit review process under which the National Science Foundation (NSF) allocates research funds has two main criteria: what is the intellectual merit of the proposed activity? what are the broader impacts of the proposed research?

The NSF, like the NRC, also considers criteria other than excellence in making its funding decisions. Its guidelines stress that criteria related to the broader impacts be "considered and addressed in both proposals and reviews," and that staff will give careful consideration to the "integration of research and education" and "integrating diversity into NSF programs, projects and activities" (NSF 2000, 1). But its emphasis appears different. The NSF mentions neither interdisciplinarity nor inter-institutional relations. Moreover, its guidelines do not prescribe the weights the various elements should receive. To the contrary, they suggest that reviewers "be asked to address only those that are relevant to the proposal." Scholars familiar with practice in the two countries assure us that criteria other than simple intellectual excellence are taken much more seriously in Canada.

Polanyi's discussion suggests that those who set the criteria for success used in Canadian research funding policy might consider our concerns to be largely irrelevant. They might argue that research in the two countries should not be compared solely in terms of excellence, and that other criterial should also be taken into account. We do not accept this view. We agree with Polanyi that excellence should be the predominant goal. Greater emphasis on excellence in research will benefit Canadians. Success in research is important for the students going through university. It is part of the way they signal their quality to top graduate schools when they apply for further studies, and it is part of the way they signal to employers that they are qualified for jobs requiring scholastic accomplishment and skill.

Canadian policymakers do not appear to accept the view that support for science research should be concerned solely with fostering new ideas that matter. Possibly they believe that the other values they factor into funding decisions — interdisciplinarity, inter-institutional relations, relevance, training and socio-economic impact — can be achieved with little cost in terms of the pursuit of excellence. Our work suggests, however, that these add-ons may come at a cost. Our top research universities lag well behind their counterparts in the United States in creating ideas that other scholars notice. We believe these differences in national research policies may be a factor. Still, any definite conclusion about the sources of the differences in performance requires further work.

References

Institute for Scientific Information. 1981–98a. *Canadian University Science Indicators*. Philadelphia: ISI Thomson Scientific. Diskette.

———. 1981–98b. *U.S. University Science Indicators*. Philadelphia: ISI Thomson Scientific. Diskette.

National Science Foundation. 2000. *Grant Proposal Guide*. Washington, DC: NSF.

Polanyi, J. 2000. "Review: The equation that rocked the planet." *Globe and Mail* (Toronto), November 4, p. D6.

Science Watch. 1992. "If Quebec Separates, Will Canadian Science Suffer?" June/July, pp. 1–2, 7–8.

———. 1995. "University of Toronto Triumphs in Tally of Canada's Tip-Top Talent." November/December, pp. 1–2.

Strauss, S. 1995. "Bigger not always better in academic publishing." *Globe and Mail* (Toronto), October 27, p. 6.

Appendix Tables

Table A-1: *Universities in the Canadian Data Set*

Acadia University
Bishop's University
Brandon University
Brock University
Carleton University
Concordia University
Dalhousie University
Daltech
École de Technologie Supérieure
École des Hautes Études Commerciales
École Nationale d'Administration Publique
École Polytechnique de Montréal
Institut Armand-Frappier
Institut National de la Recherche Scientifique
Lakehead University
Laurentian University
McGill University
McMaster University
Memorial University of Newfoundland
Mount Allison University
Mount Saint Vincent University
Ontario Institute of Education
Queen's University
Royal Military College of Canada
St. Francis Xavier University
Saint Mary's University
St. Michael's College
St. Paul University
Simon Fraser University
Trent University
Trinity College
Trinity Western University

Université de Moncton
Université de Montréal
Université de Sherbrooke
Université du Québec
Université du Québec à Chicoutimi
Université du Québec à Hull
Université du Québec à Montréal
Université du Québec à Rimouski
Université du Québec à Trois-Rivières
Université du Québec en Abitibi-Témiscamingue
Université Laval
University of Alberta
University of British Columbia
University of Calgary
University of Guelph
University of Lethbridge
University of Manitoba
University of New Brunswick
University of Northern British Columbia
University of Ottawa
University of Prince Edward Island
University of Regina
University of Saskatchewan
University of Toronto
University of Victoria
University of Waterloo
University of Western Ontario
University of Windsor
University of Winnipeg
Victoria University
Wilfrid Laurier University
York University

Table A-2: *Universities in the US Data Set*

Arizona State University
Baylor College of Medicine
Boston University
Brandeis University
Brown University
California Institute of Technology
Carnegie-Mellon University
Case Western Reserve University
City University of New York
Colorado State University
Columbia University
Cornell University
Dartmouth College
Duke University
Emory University
Florida State University
Georgetown University
Georgia Institute of Technology
Harvard University
Indiana University
Iowa State University
Johns Hopkins University
Lehigh University
Louisiana State University
Loyola University
Massachusetts Institute of Technology
Michigan State University
New Mexico State University
New York University
North Carolina State University
Northwestern University
Ohio State University
Oregon Health Science University
Oregon State University
Pennsylvania State University
Princeton University
Purdue University
Rice University
Rockefeller University
Rutgers State University
Stanford University
State University of New York at Buffalo
State University of New York atStony Brook
Syracuse University
Texas A&M University
Tufts University
Tulane University
University of Alabama
University of Alaska
University of Arizona
University of California at Berkeley
University of California at Davis
University of California at Irvine
University of California at Los Angeles
University of California at Riverside
University of California at San Diego
University of California at San Francisco
University of California at Santa Barbara
University of California at Santa Cruz
University of Chicago
University of Cincinnati
University of Colorado
University of Connecticut
University of Delaware
University of Florida
University of Georgia
University of Hawaii
University of Illinois at Chicago
University of Illinois at Urbana
University of Iowa
University of Kansas
University of Kentucky
University of Maryland at Baltimore
University of Maryland at College Park

Table A-2 - continued

University of Massachusetts
University of Massachusetts at Amherst
University of Massachusetts at Worcester
University of Miami
University of Michigan
University of Minnesota
University of Missouri
University of Nebraska
University of New Hampshire
University of New Mexico
University of North Carolina at Chapel Hill
University of Oregon
University of Pennsylvania
University of Pittsburgh
University of Rochester
University of Southern California
University of Tennessee
University of Texas at Austin
University of Texas at Dallas
University of Texas at Houston
University of Texas at San Antonio Health Science Center
University of Utah
University of Vermont
University of Virginia
University of Washington
University of Wisconsin at Madison
Utah State University
Vanderbilt University
Virginia Commonwealth University
Virginia Polytechnic Institute
Wake Forest University
Washington State University
Washington University
Wayne State University
West Virginia University
Woods Hole Oceanographic Institute
Yale University
Yeshiva University

Table A-3: **Research Performance of Canadian Universities, by Number of Papers Published, 1994–98**

			Average Number of Papers Published			Average Rank of Top 3 Canadian Universities
Discipline	Top 3 Canadian Universities	Number of Papers Published	By Top 3 Canadian Universities	By Top 3 US and Canadian Universities	Rank	
Agricultural sciences	U. of Guelph McGill U. U. of Alberta	589 399 267	418	729	7 17 24	16
Astrophysics	U. of Toronto U. de Montréal U. of British Columbia	358 189 143	230	1,342	18 35 43	33
Biology and biochemistry*	U. of Toronto McGill U. U. of Alberta	2,278 1,863 1,186	1,775	3,084	3 8 27	13
Chemistry	U. of Toronto U. of British Columbia McGill U.	1,331 1,202 1,096	1,209	1,972	10 23 29	17
Clinical medicine	U. of Toronto McGill U. McMaster U.	9,454 5,442 3,651	6,182	10,985	2 13 24	13

Field	University				
Computer science	U. of Toronto	215	185	290	8	16
	U. of Waterloo	213			10	
	U. of British Columbia	128			29	
Ecology/environment	U. of British Columbia	464	400	677	12	17
	U. of Alberta	387			16	
	U. of Waterloo	348			24	
Economics and business	U. of British Columbia	349	271	771	22	34
	U. of Toronto	274			32	
	U. of Western Ontario	189			48	
Education	U. of Toronto	151	118	192	5	16
	U. of Alberta	115			17	
	U. of British Columbia	90			27	
Engineering	U. of Toronto	1,089			15	21
	U. of Waterloo	946			20	
	U. of British Columbia	793			29	
Geosciences	U. of Toronto	543	511	1,127	19	21
	U. of British Columbia	511			21	
	McGill U.	479			22	
Immunology	U. of Toronto	559	405	1,105	30	
	McGill U.	359			7	
	U. of British Columbia	296			20	
					29	
Materials sciences	U. of Toronto	466	388	717	8	15
	McGill U.	393			15	
	U. of British Columbia	305			21	

Table A-3 - continued

Discipline	Top 3 Canadian Universities	Number of Papers Published	Average Number of Papers Published By Top 3 Canadian Universities	Average Number of Papers Published By Top 3 US and Canadian Universities	Rank	Average Rank of Top 3 Canadian Universities
Mathematics	U. of Waterloo U. of Toronto U. of Alberta	363 327 289	326	566	14 19 25	19
Microbiology*	McGill U. U. of British Columbia U. of Toronto	381 354 290	342	680	14 17 31	21
Molecular biology	U. of Toronto McGill U. McMaster U.	1,308 1,242 587	1,046	2,056	4 5 30	13
Neurosciences	U. of Toronto McGill U. U. of British Columbia	1,650 1,648 749	1,349	2,061	4 5 28	12
Pharmacology*	U. of Toronto McGill U. U. de Montréal	499 397 374	423	505*	2 9 10	7

Physics	U. of Toronto	1,367	1,313	3,495	29
	U. of British Columbia	1,287			28
	McGill U.	1,286			29
					30
Plant and animal sciences	U. of Guelph	1,674	1,226	3,281	17
	U. of British Columbia	1,079			8
	U. of Saskatchewan	929			19
					24
Psychology and psychiatry	U. of Toronto	1,294	886	1,458	42
	McGill U.	708			3
	U. of British Columbia	657			16
					21

* A Canadian university ranks in the top three overall in this discipline.

Sources: Institute for Scientific Information 1981–98a; 1981–98b.

Table A-4: Research Performance of Canadian Universities, by Number of Citations per Published Paper, 1994–98

Discipline	Top 3 Canadian Universities	Number of Citations per Paper Published	Average Number of Citations per Paper — By Top 3 Canadian Universities	Average Number of Citations per Paper — By Top 3 US and Canadian Universities	Rank	Average Rank of Top 3 Canadian Universities
Agricultural sciences	U. of Toronto	2.84	2.8	4.6	10	13
	McMaster U.	2.83			11	
	U. of British Columbia	2.66			17	
Astrophysics	U. of Toronto	11.11	9.3	12.8	7	17
	U. of British Columbia	8.80			20	
	U. de Montréal	8.12			25	
Biology and biochemistry	U. of Toronto	9.47	8.6	16.7	31	37
	U. of Alberta	8.56			38	
	McGill U.	7.74			41	
Chemistry	U. de Montréal	6.34	5.7	9.5	29	42
	U. of Toronto	5.29			46	
	U. of Calgary	5.02			51	
Clinical medicine	McMaster U.	6.78	6.3	9.2	32	36
	U. of British Columbia	6.08			37	
	U. of Western Ontario	5.92			38	

Field	Institution				
Computer science					38
	U. of Victoria	1.38	1.4	2.8	47
	McMaster U.	1.37			49
	U. de Québec à Montréal	1.35			52
Ecology/environment					22
	U. of Waterloo	4.69	4.6	6	13
	U. of Toronto	3.97			24
	U. of British Columbia	3.71			280
Economics and business					42
	U. of British Columbia	1.99	1.8	3.9	37
	U. of Western Ontario	1.66			43
	U. of Toronto	1.62			45
Education					24
	Simon Fraser U.	3.18	2	2.6	1
	Ontario Inst. for Studies in Education	1.59			24
	U. of Toronto	1.10			43
Engineering					36
	U. of Waterloo	2.13	1.8	3.1	28
	McGill U.	1.66			39
	U. of Toronto	1.63			40
Geosciences					39
	Dalhousie U.	4.14	4.0	8.7	37
	U. de Québec à Montréal	3.9			40
	U. of Toronto	3.89			41
Immunology					25
	U. of Toronto	11.85	10.9	25.4	18
	McMaster U.	10.79			27
	U. de Montréal	10.56			29
Materials sciences					19
	U. of Toronto	3.58	3.1	6.8	8
	U. de Laval	2.93			23
	McMaster U.	2.93			26

Table A-4 - continued

Discipline	Top 3 Canadian Universities	Number of Citations per Paper Published	Average Number of Citations per Paper — By Top 3 Canadian Universities	Average Number of Citations per Paper — By Top 3 US and Canadian Universities	Rank	Average Rank of Top 3 Canadian Universities
Mathematics	Simon Fraser U.	1.74	1.6	3.2	27	37
	U. of Toronto	1.66			35	
	U. of British Columbia	1.48			49	
Microbiology	McGill U.	7.36	6.5	17.5	48	54
	U. of Alberta	6.99			53	
	U. of British Columbia	6.05			61	
Molecular biology	U. of Toronto	16.16	13.8	35.4	28	36
	McGill U.	13.92			37	
	McMaster U.	11.85			42	
Neurosciences	U. of British Columbia	8.69	8.1	17.5	31	35
	McGill U.	7.78			37	
	U. of Toronto	7.68			38	
Pharmacology	U. of Western Ontario	7.01	6.5	1.6	20	25
	U. de Sherbrooke	6.2			27	
	McGill U.	6.19			28	

Physics	McGill U.	6.99	6.3	11.8	19	31
	U. of Toronto	6.42			32	
	U. of British Columbia	5.41			41	
Plant and animal sciences	U. of Toronto	3.89	3.6	6.2	13	19
	McGill U.	3.7			18	
	U. of British Columbia	3.13			26	
Psychology/psychiatry	McMaster U.	4.25	3.9	7.4	28	37
	McGill U.	3.75			40	
	U. of Toronto	3.65			43	

Sources: Institute for Scientific Information 1981–98a; 1981–98b.

Table A-5: Changes in Rankings of Canadian Universities, by Number of Papers Published, 1981–98

Discipline		\multicolumn{4}{c}{Rank}	Change from 1981–84 to 1994–98
		1981–85	1984–88	1989–93	1994–98	
Agricultural sciences	average of top 3	27	23	17	16	–11
	1st ranked	16	14	8	7	
	2nd ranked	32	24	21	17	
	3rd ranked	33	30	23	24	
Astrophysics	average of top 3	33	28	23	32	0
	1st ranked	21	17	14	18	
	2nd ranked	36	30	24	35	
	3rd ranked	42	38	32	43	
Biology and biochemistry	average of top 3	21	19	17	13	–8
	1st ranked	8	6	5	3	
	2nd ranked	19	18	20	8	
	3rd ranked	36	32	25	27	
Chemistry	Average of top 3	15	15	21	17	+2
	1st ranked	11	13	12	10	
	2nd ranked	14	15	22	17	
	3rd ranked	20	18	30	23	
Clinical medicine	average of top 3	23	20	16	13	–10
	1st ranked	4	4	2	2	
	2nd ranked	23	22	22	13	
	3rd ranked	42	34	25	24	
Computer science	average of top 3	14	20	29	16	2
	1st ranked	5	8	18	8	
	2nd ranked	9	13	27	10	
	3rd ranked	29	38	41	29	
Ecology/ environment	average of top 3	28	24	21	17	–11
	1st ranked	23	17	18	12	
	2nd ranked	35	26	19	16	
	3rd ranked	36	29	25	24	
Economics	average of top 3	30	28	36	34	+4
	1st ranked	29	26	28	22	
	2nd ranked	30	28	36	32	
	3rd ranked	32	30	45	48	

Table A-5 - continued

Discipline		Rank 1981–85	Rank 1984–88	Rank 1989–93	Rank 1994–98	Change from 1981–84 to 1994–98
Education	average of top 3	23	18	20	16	−7
	1st ranked	15	9	6	5	
	2nd ranked	25	16	18	17	
	3rd ranked	28	28	37	27	
Engineering	average of top 3	20	22	21	21	+1
	1st ranked	14	17	18	15	
	2nd ranked	20	20	19	20	
	3rd ranked	27	28	25	28	
Geosciences	average of top 3	17	15	18	21	+4
	1st ranked	12	9	12	19	
	2nd ranked	17	15	20	21	
	3rd ranked	21	21	21	22	
Immunology	average of top 3	26	25	22	19	−7
	1st ranked	10	7	9	7	
	2nd ranked	28	27	26	20	
	3rd ranked	40	41	32	29	
Mathematics	average of top 3	27	24	22	19	−8
	1st ranked	25	19	20	14	
	2nd ranked	26	22	21	19	
	3rd ranked	30	32	24	25	
Materials sciences	average of top 3	16	17	19	15	−1
	1st ranked	14	12	14	8	
	2nd ranked	15	15	20	15	
	3rd ranked	18	23	24	21	
Microbiology	average of top 3	27	24	25	21	−6
	1st ranked	13	16	23	14	
	2nd ranked	31	22	25	17	
	3rd ranked	34	35	27	31	
Molecular biology	average of top 3	27	18	18	13	−14
	1st ranked	14	6	5	4	
	2nd ranked	33	24	20	5	
	3rd ranked	34	25	28	30	

Table A-5 - continued

Discipline		Rank 1981–85	Rank 1984–88	Rank 1989–93	Rank 1994–98	Change from 1981–84 to 1994–98
Neurosciences	average of top 3	14	10	9	12	–2
	1st ranked	4	3	4	4	
	2nd ranked	11	7	5	5	
	3rd ranked	28	21	19	28	
Pharmacology	average of top 3	13	11	10	7	–6
	1st ranked	1	1	1	2	
	2nd ranked	15	15	12	9	
	3rd ranked	22	17	18	10	
Physics	average of top 3	26	29	23	29	+3
	1st ranked	19	22	18	28	
	2nd ranked	23	27	21	29	
	3rd ranked	35	39	31	30	
Plant and animal sciences	average of top 3	17	16	16	17	0
	1st ranked	5	5	5	8	
	2nd ranked	23	19	20	19	
	3rd ranked	24	24	22	24	
Psychology	average of top 3	22	18	17	13	–9
	1st ranked	4	3	3	3	
	2nd ranked	29	25	22	16	
	3rd ranked	34	26	27	21	
All disciplines	average of top 3	22.1	20.2	20.0	18.5	–3.6
	1st ranked	12.7	11.1	11.6	10.1	–2.6

Sources: Institute for Scientific Information 1981–98a; 1981–98b.

Table A-6: **Changes in Rankings of Canadian Universities, by Citations per Paper, 1981–98**

Discipline		Rank 1981–85	Rank 1984–88	Rank 1989–93	Rank 1994–98	Change from 1981–84 to 1994–98
Agricultural sciences	average of top 3	8	13	20	13	+5
	1st ranked	6	5	16	10	
	2nd ranked	8	16	18	11	
	3rd ranked	10	19	26	17	
Astrophysics	average of top 3	37	34	21	17	−20
	1st ranked	34	21	9	7	
	2nd ranked	37	39	23	20	
	3rd ranked	39	43	32	25	
Biology and biochemistry	average of top 3	46	27	39	37	−9
	1st ranked	44	10	29	31	
	2nd ranked	47	31	43	38	
	3rd ranked	48	39	44	41	
Chemistry	average of top 3	39	46	60	42	+3
	1st ranked	31	43	54	29	
	2nd ranked	38	46	58	46	
	3rd ranked	49	48	67	51	
Clinical medicine	average of top 3	44	43	41	36	−8
	1st ranked	42	37	39	32	
	2nd ranked	43	45	42	37	
	3rd ranked	47	47	43	38	
Computer science	average of top 3	17	25	23	49	+31
	1st ranked	10	10	9	47	
	2nd ranked	13	30	29	49	
	3rd ranked	29	34	32	52	
Ecology/ environment	average of top 3	30	27	16	22	−8
	1st ranked	20	23	15	13	
	2nd ranked	34	27	16	24	
	3rd ranked	36	31	17	28	
Economics	average of top 3	19	20	36	42	+23
	1st ranked	10	18	31	37	
	2nd ranked	21	21	35	43	
	3rd ranked	27	22	43	45	

Table A-6 - continued

Discipline		Rank 1981–85	Rank 1984–88	Rank 1989–93	Rank 1994–98	Change from 1981–84 to 1994–98
Education	average of top 3	35	21	29	29	−6
	1st ranked	27	10	18	1	
	2nd ranked	30	26	24	34	
	3rd ranked	48	37	40	43	
Engineering	average of top 3	22	19	21	33	+11
	1st ranked	19	11	18	20	
	2nd ranked	21	22	19	39	
	3rd ranked	26	25	25	40	
Geosciences	average of top 3	34	36	34	39	+5
	1st ranked	32	35	28	37	
	2nd ranked	35	36	36	40	
	3rd ranked	36	37	38	41	
Immunology	average of top 3	39	31	24	25	−14
	1st ranked	30	13	15	18	
	2nd ranked	39	37	23	27	
	3rd ranked	48	42	33	29	
Mathematics	average of top 3	27	37	30	37	+10
	1st ranked	19	35	28	27	
	2nd ranked	23	36	29	35	
	3rd ranked	40	41	32	49	
Materials sciences	average of top 3	29	25	38	19	−10
	1st ranked	23	21	32	8	
	2nd ranked	31	26	40	23	
	3rd ranked	34		28	42	26
Microbiology	average of top 3	39	47	41	54	+15
	1st ranked	33	36	37	48	
	2nd ranked	38	51	41	53	
	3rd ranked	46	52	44	61	
Molecular biology	average of top 3	40	39	34	36	−4
	1st ranked	36	29	17	28	
	2nd ranked	40	42	41	37	
	3rd ranked	44	47	44	42	

Table A-6 - continued

Discipline		1981–85	1984–88	1989–93	1994–98	Change from 1981–84 to 1994–98
Neurosciences	average of top 3	30	40	33	35	+5
	1st ranked	24	37	25	31	
	2nd ranked	30	40	29	37	
	3rd ranked	37	44	45	38	
Pharmacology	average of top 3	14	31	25	25	+11
	1st ranked	6	10	5	20	
	2nd ranked	10	25	32	27	
	3rd ranked	25	39	37	28	
Physics	average of top 3	42	40	38	27	−11
	1st ranked	39	39	30	19	
	2nd ranked	41	40	35	32	
	3rd ranked	45	42	49	41	
Plant and animal sciences	average of top 3	17	12	18	19	+2
	1st ranked	11	6	14	13	
	2nd ranked	18	15	18	18	
	3rd ranked	21	16	23	26	
Psychology and psychiatry	average of top 3	26	29	28	37	+11
	1st ranked	23	30	15	28	
	2nd ranked	24	33	38	40	
	3rd ranked	31	34	40	43	
All disciplines	average of top 3	30.0	30.4	30.9	32.3	2.3
	1st ranked	24.8	22.8	23.2	24.0	−0.8

Sources: Institute for Scientific Information 1981–98a; 1981–98b.

A Matter of Discipline:
Early Career Outcomes of Recent Canadian University Graduates

Ross Finnie

It is obvious that the career outcomes of university graduates vary to a great degree according to their fields of study, but the empirical evidence on the extent of these differences in Canada is actually quite scant.[1] And yet the issue is as important as it is intriguing.

The principal contribution of this paper is thus to exploit the unique National Graduates Survey (NGS) databases in order to present new evidence on earnings differences by discipline among three cohorts of recent Canadian university graduates.

Financial support received from the Applied Research Branch of Human Resources Development Canada and the Social Sciences and Humanities Research Council of Canada is gratefully acknowledged, as are the helpful comments received from Doug Giddings, Philip Jennings, David Laidler, John Myles, Garnett Picot, Ted Wannell, and participants in the C.D. Howe Institute-sponsored session at the June 2001 meetings of the Canadian Economics Association, where this paper was first presented. The detailed suggestions provided by Jeffrey Smith are particularly appreciated. The participation of Marc Frenette in this research, including his co-authorship of a related paper (Finnie and Frechette forthcoming), is noted with pleasure. The copy editing of Elizabeth d'Anjou was beneficial and instructive. Barry Norris shepherded the paper through all stages of production with skill and grace.

1   The literature includes Cohn (1997); Côté and Sweetman (1997); Dodge and Stager (1972); Finnie (1995); Mehmet (1977); Stager (1996); and Vaillancourt (1995). In some of these papers, earnings patterns by discipline are used principally as inputs for calculating rates of return to education along this dimension; in others, they are the focus.

A second contribution of the paper is to develop a simple index of the conditional variability of earnings (that is, their variability after controlling for various personal attributes) within given disciplines, and to determine whether or not intradisciplinary earnings inequality has increased over the period covered by the analysis, a time when labor market inequality, as measured in more conventional fashions, has generally increased.

Finally, the paper also includes an analysis of the distribution of graduates by field of study and the male-female splits in each field, of unemployment rates, and of students' overall evaluations of their choice of discipline, all as a run-in to the analysis of earnings differences that makes up the bulk of this paper.[2]

These results should be of interest for a number of reasons. First, subject to some important caveats, they provide new information on the relative returns to different types of human capital represented by the various disciplines.[3] And recent graduates are an especially interesting group in this regard because, as new labor market entrants, they may be harbingers of future trends and because recent evidence indicates that the major portion of real lifetime earnings growth occurs during the early years of individuals' careers (Murphy and Welch 1990).

Policymakers should find such evidence pertinent to their thinking about differences in the value of different kinds of postsecondary

---

2 Companion papers include Finnie (2001), which reports a range of other outcomes using simpler (non-econometric) techniques; Betts, Ferrall, and Finnie (1999), which includes field-of-study variables in an econometric analysis of school quality on graduates' earnings; and Lavoie and Finnie (1999), which compares the outcomes of science and engineering students with others over a range of outcomes. Finnie (1999) uses the same data to look at earnings and other labor-market outcomes for graduates by level of education (college, bachelor's, master's and doctorate) and by sex, but not by field of study, while Finnie (2000a) more fully exploits the longitudinal aspect of the NGS data to look at the evolution of various labor market outcomes in the years following graduation.

3 It should be noted that this paper does not present any sort of formal rate-of-return analysis in this regard. See the paper by Vaillancourt and Bourdeau-Primeau in this volume for such an exercise.

education and in setting priorities in terms of expanding enrollments and educational resource allocation in general.

The results should also be relevant to a variety of other post-secondary education policy issues. For example, they could be useful in determining the different shares of education costs that students of different disciplines might be expected to bear if a policy of differential fees were introduced, and would help in designing or estimating the effects of an income-contingent loan repayment system or other student assistance programs.

The findings could also be useful for young people about to make choices regarding what field of study to enter, since better decisions should result from an improved understanding of the earnings patterns — as well as employment rates and overall evaluations — associated with each option, while graduates who have already been through the system might be interested in comparing their own experiences to those of others.

For readers with a more academic bent, the analysis should cast in a new light previous studies of this type carried out both in Canada and in other countries. It groups disciplines differently from some of these earlier studies, with sometimes surprising findings. It offers more precise tracking of outcomes over time than most, both from one cohort to another and over the years following graduation within each group. And it provides some distinctive measures not available in other studies, such as graduates' overall evaluation of their chosen programs.

Finally, it is very interesting to compare these results to those found elsewhere, notably the United States, thus leading to some very important questions pertaining to differences in labor markets and the university system.

The Data

First, a look at the data — its source, the selection of the samples, and the choice of discipline groups.[4]

---

4 See Finnie (2000b) for more detailed discussion of the material covered in this section.

The National Graduates Surveys

This analysis employs the data from the NGS and associated Follow-Up surveys. This unique series of databases, developed by Statistics Canada in conjunction with Human Resources Development Canada, comprise large, representative samples of those who successfully completed programs at Canadian colleges and universities in 1982, 1986, and 1990. For each group of graduates, information was gathered during interviews carried out two years and then five years after graduation (that is, in 1984 and 1987; 1988, and 1991; and 1992 and 1995).

These databases have numerous strengths for a study of this type. First, the fact that data were gathered at two interviews for each cohort allows for tracking the evolution of differences in earnings and the other outcomes considered in the years following graduation — and in a very precise fashion. Furthermore, the five-year interviews, which were conducted at a point where the average age of the graduates was over 30, provide a longer-run perspective on earnings patterns.

Second, the availability of data for three different cohorts of graduates permits the separation of the more stable patterns from those that have been more volatile, as well as the identification of trends. This perspective is of particular interest because the period under study (the early 1980s through the mid-1990s) was characterized by important labor market changes, especially for younger workers.

Third, the large sample sizes (30,000 to 35,000 observations per survey) and the representative nature of the NGS data mean that the analysis can be conducted at the desired level of detail, and that the results should generalize to the full population of graduates.[5]

---

5 The NGS databases are based on a stratified sampling scheme (by province, level of education, and field of study). All results reported below reflect the appropriate sample weights and should be representative of the relevant underlying populations of graduates in each year. The databases also include graduates of colleges, trade schools, and vocational schools, as well as university graduates at the master's and PhD levels; those groups are not, however, included in the current analysis.

Finally, sufficient control variables are included in the databases to permit the estimation of the sort of earnings models that are standard in this literature.

In summary, the three NGS databases facilitate a focused, detailed, and dynamic analysis of the earnings patterns and other outcomes by field of study of Canadian bachelor's-level graduates in the critical five years following graduation from the early 1980s into the mid-1990s. These data are not only valuable in a Canadian context, but unique at the international level.

Selection of the Working Samples

The analysis was carried out using bachelor's-level graduates who were under age 35 and had fewer than five years of full-time work experience at the time of graduation. The analysis thus focuses on graduates with "normal" career profiles, who had finished their studies and were at the point of entering the labor market. Individuals were excluded if they obtained an additional degree over the period observed — except in the initial part of the analysis, which looks at individuals' overall evaluations of their programs — or were part-time workers who cited school as the reason for having only partial involvement in the labor market, since such people clearly had not finished their studies and entered the labor market in full as of the year of graduation in question (1982, 1986, 1990).[6] The relatively small number of individuals who were neither regular wage earners nor self-employed workers (for example,

---

6   An argument could be made for including individuals who went on to a graduate degree in the analysis, but this approach was not followed here. One reason is that students in this category mix school and work after the original graduation date, and the results would reflect this combination of activities, thus deviating from the clean two- and five-year postgraduation profiles provided for non-continuers. Second, the interdiscipline differences in earnings at the graduate level may well differ from those at the bachelor's level; the results would, therefore, mix the effects that hold at the different levels, yet in a non-complete fashion (since only those who went on to graduate school and finished within the two- or five-year windows provided here would be included in the group of graduate students).

volunteers or family workers), who failed to provide the information required for any part of the analysis, or who were deemed to have unreasonably low earnings (less than $5,000 at annualized rates for full-time workers), were also excluded; these criteria eliminated just 1 to 2 percent of the sample in each period.

The Discipline Groupings Employed

For the most part, the field-of-study categorizations used here reflect the major discipline groups employed in standard classification schemes and other analyses of this type. Some fine-tuning of these categorizations was, however, carried out according to a preliminary analysis of earnings patterns to ensure that like disciplines were grouped together and that those with distinctly different earnings profiles were kept separated. Thus, natural sciences and engineering, which are typically grouped into a single broad category (especially the pure and applied sciences), are here split into three separate categories; economics is separated from other social sciences. Engineering and computer science are, however, safely grouped together.

The field categorizations used in this analysis are thus as follows:

- education (includes elementary/secondary teaching and other education);
- fine arts and humanities;
- commerce (includes business administration and related fields);
- economics;
- other social sciences;
- agricultural and biological sciences;
- engineering and computer science (includes architecture);
- other health and life sciences (includes nursing and other health professions but excludes medicine and dentistry);
- mathematics and physical sciences; and
- other fields/no specialization.[7]

---

[7] This category represents those who truly had no specialization as well as those who had one too general to fit into the other categories and too small to be put on its own, such as general social sciences.

Setting the Stage: Distributions, Evaluations, Unemployment

The presentation of the empirical results begins with a look at the distribution of graduates by discipline, their own overall evaluations of their programs, and unemployment rates. These results are interesting on their own, but they also nicely set the stage for the earnings analysis that follows.

The Distribution of Graduates by Field of Study

The distribution of graduates by field of study and the male-female composition of each discipline are shown in Table 1. The field-of-study distributions are quite different for men and women. Female graduates have been much more likely than men to graduate with degrees in education, fine arts and humanities, and other health fields, and, to a lesser degree, commerce and other social sciences. Conversely, the shares of female graduates in economics, engineering and computer science, and mathematics and physical sciences have been much lower than for men. The shares of male and female graduates in the agricultural and biological sciences have been quite similar.

Contrary to what might have been expected given a period of significant economic change, particularly in labor markets — including the emergence of the "knowledge-based economy" and a widely reported general rise in the importance of science and technology — the distributions of graduates by discipline have been quite stable. For men, there was an increase in the percentage of graduates in technical and scientific fields from the first cohort to the second (from 36 percent to 41 percent), but this share dropped back again (to 35 percent) in the third cohort, driven by the declines in engineering and computer science and in mathematics and physical sciences. These shifts were offset by mirror-image trends in the other social science category (which had 15, 12, and 15 percent of the graduates in the three cohorts). None of the other fields varied by more than one percentage point over time. As a result, the distribution of male graduates in the third cohort was generally quite similar to that in the first.

The overall share of graduates in the four scientific and technical disciplines was even more stable across cohorts for women than for men, but at much lower rates (22, 22, and 21 percent), with engineering and computer science remaining the most glaring discrepancy in this regard (23, 24, and 20 percent for men, versus 3, 5, and 3 percent for women). More significant, perhaps, are the declines in the percentage of female graduates with degrees in education and in fine arts and humanities, and the offsetting increases in commerce and in other social sciences.

Thus, although there was no general shift of female graduates toward engineering and the sciences (as many would like to see, for various reasons) and the splits between men and women in most disciplines were quite stable, there was something of a shift in female enrollment away from certain fields they have dominated in the past and toward the slightly "harder" social sciences and business.

This change presumably reflects the growing commitment of women to the labor market, steadier job attachment, and a generally greater orientation toward careers in general — a finding consistent with the results of any number of other studies.[8]

The relative stability of the distribution of graduates, males in particular, is particularly surprising when contrasted with the shifts that have been found in the United States, where the most marked changes have been increased numbers of graduates in the more technical disciplines, especially in the case of women. These shifts have generally been interpreted as stemming from the relatively higher earnings levels that graduates in these areas have enjoyed.[9] The US literature covers a somewhat different period (the 1970s through the 1980s rather than the 1980s to 1990 as reported here for Canada). However, the findings raise a number of questions. In

---

8 The role of field of study in the earnings gap between male and female bachelor's-level graduates, as well as other outcomes by sex, are analyzed in Finnie and Wannell (1999).

9 See, for example, Eide 1994; Rumberger and Thomas 1993; Grogger and Eide 1995; and Turner and Bowen 1999.

Table 1: *Distribution of Graduates by Field of Study and Sex, 1982, 1986, and 1990 Cohorts*

	Field of Study Distribution by Cohort			Sex Distribution by Cohort		
	1982	1986	1990	1982	1986	1990
	(percent)					
Males						
Education	9	9	10	26	30	31
Fine arts and humanities	13	12	13	37	37	39
Commerce	16	16	16	62	56	53
Economics	7	6	7	79	67	72
Other social sciences	15	12	15	42	33	36
Agricultural and biological sciences	6	7	7	47	48	42
Engineering and computer science	23	24	20	87	82	84
Other health and life sciences	1	2	2	14	14	19
Mathematics and other physical sciences	6	8	6	71	70	64
Other fields	3	5	4	56	50	49
Total	100	100	100	49	47	46
Females						
Education	24	19	20	74	70	69
Fine arts and humanities	20	18	18	63	63	61
Commerce	10	12	12	38	44	47
Economics	2	3	2	21	33	28
Other social sciences	21	22	23	58	67	64
Agricultural and biological sciences	7	6	8	53	52	58
Engineering and computer science	3	5	3	13	18	16
Other health and life sciences	9	8	7	86	86	81
Mathematics and other physical sciences	3	3	3	29	30	36
Other fields	2	4	4	44	50	51
Total	100	100	100	51	53	54

Note: In this and subsequent tables, the samples exclude those who were older than age 35 or who had more than five years of full-time experience by the date of graduation.

Source: Author's analysis of National Graduates Survey data, as described in the text.

particular, is this stability primarily due to demand-side or supply-side factors with respect to the education system? — that is, do the patterns reflect students' preferences or simply the spots available at universities? Has the "production" of graduates in different fields been as flexible and responsive to shifts in employment opportunities (and employers' needs) as it should be? Should the general lack of any secular shifts in the distribution of graduates by field of study be cause for worry as the economy moves in directions that seem to favor certain types of graduates over others?

Overall Evaluation of the Educational Program

The figures on graduates' overall evaluations of their choice of major (Table 2) represent the percentage of graduates who said that, given the chance, they would choose the same field of study again.[10]

Averaging over all graduates (including those who continued with their studies and are therefore excluded from the other results reported in this paper), the results indicate that approximately three-quarters of all bachelor's-level graduates were satisfied with their choices, with female graduates' scores running slightly lower than males' scores in all years. While this fraction seems high, the fact that approximately one-quarter of all graduates were not content with their choices should perhaps be cause for concern, given the importance of this decision to an individual's career.

The fields where satisfaction is generally highest include the professions and related programs: education (especially for women), commerce (although a little less so for females than for males, especially in the most recent cohort), engineering and computer science, and other health and life sciences. The next tier of disciplines with medium or more mixed levels of satisfaction includes fine arts

---

10 The results, except for those from 1984, when it was not asked, are based on the question, "Given your experience...would you have taken the same field of study or specialization?" The answer options were Yes or No. The responses were then built into an index by the author by assigning scores of 100 (for a Yes answer) or 0 (for a No answer). See Finnie (2001; 2000b) for further details.

Table 2: Index of Overall Evaluations of Fields of Study, 1982, 1986, and 1990 Cohorts

	1982 Cohort	1986 Cohort		1990 Cohort	
	1987	1988	1991	1992	1995
	(percent)				
All graduates	71	77	74	72	69
Males					
All fields	73	77	76	74	71
Education	70	78	79	82	76
Fine arts and humanities	74	81	78	72	70
Commerce	82	83	80	77	77
Economics	64	69	64	64	64
Other social sciences	67	64	60	61	55
Agricultural and biological sciences	68	68	69	70	69
Engineering and computer science	76	85	83	84	81
Other health and life sciences	81	90	87	84	80
Mathematics and other physical sciences	69	68	73	67	65
Other fields	83	77	74	71	63
Females					
All fields	69	76	73	71	68
Education	70	83	78	84	77
Fine arts and humanities	71	77	74	68	62
Commerce	78	81	77	73	71
Economics	51	63	61	44	37
Other social sciences	61	68	65	62	61
Agricultural and biological sciences	66	68	65	61	62
Engineering and computer science	78	82	83	82	79
Other health and life sciences	80	82	82	82	79
Mathematics and other physical sciences	71	76	71	69	71
Other fields	72	66	69	69	65

Source: Author's analysis of National Graduates Survey data, as described in the text.

and humanities (except among females in the 1995 cohort), and mathematics and physical sciences in the case of women (but not men). The lowest levels of satisfaction have been for graduates in economics, other social sciences, agricultural and biological sciences, and mathematics and physical sciences — the last of these in the case of men only.

Although the highest approval ratings thus generally went to the disciplines most directly connected to labor market skill sets and relatively clear career paths, the fine arts and humanities graduates, whose fields of study are presumably the polar opposite in this respect, scored in the middle rank, placing them almost uniformly ahead of graduates in the social and the pure and applied sciences. Thus, satisfaction with the educational program is clearly more than a matter of job market preparation — at least for some groups of graduates.

One particularly noteworthy finding is that female economics graduates had the lowest approval scores in all periods; the last cohort in particular had the astoundingly low ratings of just 44 and 37 percent for the two interview dates.[11] That is, almost two-thirds of these graduates said that, given the chance, they would have chosen another field of study. These results give the economics discipline reason to consider their meaning, their underlying causes, and what might be done to improve matters, especially since enrollments in economics have been falling at many institutions in recent years. It is worth noting, meanwhile, that male economics graduates have generally expressed levels of satisfaction similar to those in the other social sciences — although this is not setting the bar particularly high.

The relatively low levels of satisfaction among graduates in the pure and applied sciences might be cause for concern at a broader social level, since the science and technology sectors are critical to the wealth of nations in the new "knowledge-based economy". In particular, these results lead to questions regarding the available career opportunities in these areas (are graduates finding the inter-

---

11 Standard errors for a comparable set of figures are reported in Finnie (2001).

esting and rewarding jobs they hope for and expect?), as well as the means by which more individuals could be attracted to them.[12]

No clear trends appear in the scores from the first interview to the second for the given cohorts, perhaps implying that graduates have not generally been surprised by how their careers have evolved (at least in relation to their chosen fields of study) subsequent to their initial postgraduation experiences, even though their job outcomes have changed to a considerable degree over this interval (see below).

Neither were there any general shifts in the scores across cohorts (the first and third groups in particular are most directly comparable because they faced similar labor market conditions and rates of further education). These relatively stable satisfaction levels contrast with the popularly held belief that conditions have become increasingly difficult for succeeding cohorts of young people entering the labor market and that opportunities are more limited. While the survey question underlying these evaluation scores is obviously a subjective one, it is quite clearly worded, and any general increases in the dissatisfaction of graduates should probably have shown up in this variable.

Unemployment Rates

Unemployment rates for all graduates taken together have generally been quite low, ranging from 3 to 10 percent across the different interview periods, with similar rates for men and women (see Table 3). Within this range, the rates generally declined quite significantly from two to five years following graduation, from the 8 to 11 percent level down to 3 to 6 percent. The rates again show no clear trend across cohorts; those for the first set of graduates are similar to those for the last.[13]

---

12 These issues are focused on in Lavoie and Finnie (1999).

13 See Finnie (1999) for further discussion of employment and earnings patterns among graduates by sex and level of education (college, bachelor's, master's, doctorate).

Table 3: *Unemployment Rates of Graduates by Field of Study, 1982, 1986, and 1990 Cohorts*

	1982 Cohort		1986 Cohort		1990 Cohort	
	1984	1987	1988	1991	1992	1995
			(percent)			
All graduates	9	4	10	6	9	3
Males						
All fields	8	3	11	6	10	3
Education	7	3	5	5	7	3
Fine arts and humanities	15	5	20	5	13	3
Commerce	6	3	7	7	9	3
Economics	9	7	15	9	10	5
Other social sciences	9	4	23	6	13	6
Agricultural and biological sciences	13	6	16	13	15	2
Engineering and computer science	7	2	7	5	6	2
Other health and life sciences	—	0	—	3	7	2
Mathematics and other physical sciences	9	8	7	12	10	4
Other fields	7	—	14	4	10	3
Females						
All fields	9	4	10	6	9	3
Education	11	3	6	7	10	2
Fine arts and humanities	12	5	14	11	10	8
Commerce	6	0	8	5	8	4
Economics	1	0	4	10	6	5
Other social sciences	10	5	13	5	10	3
Agricultural and biological sciences	14	3	17	5	12	3
Engineering and computer science	5	4	4	4	9	0
Other health and life sciences	3	3	2	2	2	2
Mathematics and other physical sciences	6	5	12	3	14	4
Other fields	20	7	16	0	12	7

Note: In this and subsequent tables and figures, the samples also exclude those who had obtained a new diploma by the relevant interview or who were identified as being part-time workers because they were students.

Source: Author's analysis of National Graduates Survey data, as described in the text.

There is significant variation in unemployment rates by discipline, but the patterns are also quite mixed across cohorts, interview years, and sexes, thus making general categorizations rather difficult. Fine arts and humanities graduates experienced rather high unemployment rates as of the first interviews, but, interestingly, much more average rates by the second (especially men). The medium-to-high rates for the pure and applied sciences, as with the program satisfaction measures reported above, are perhaps surprising; the low-to-medium rates among engineering and computer science and other health and life sciences graduates are more as anticipated. The other disciplines are characterized by more mixed rates.

Earnings

The discussion here focuses on the following themes:

- the identification of generally low-, medium- and high-earnings disciplines;
- the evolution of the earnings patterns from two to five years following graduation;
- cross-cohort patterns;
- comparisons of results for males and females;
- the role of intermediary influences (such as labor market experience and personal characteristics) in the discipline effects; and
- differences in the variability of earnings around the regression-based predicted values.

One point worth noting here is that the earnings variable represents the individual's annualized rate of pay. This approach is somewhat unconventional but is appropriate for the purposes of this study as it adjusts for irregular work patterns. (See the Appendix for further details.)

Raw Earnings Patterns

Let us begin with a look at mean earnings by discipline as of each of the two interview dates (also the percentage change in mean earnings over time) for the three cohorts of male and female graduates (Table 4), and the results of a set of regression models that include only an intercept and the field variables — thus putting the same patterns in a more formal econometric framework (Table 5). (For details on the models presented here and below, see the Appendix.) The field coefficients for this simple model (Model 1) are plotted in Figure 1. Due to the nature of the specifications employed, the coefficient estimates represent the earnings level of each field relative to the average level across all fields (the coefficients sum to unity).

For men, the highest-earnings fields are, in order, other health and life sciences, engineering and computer science, commerce, and mathematics and physical sciences. The low-earnings fields are, from the bottom up, fine arts and humanities, agricultural and biological sciences, and other social sciences. Education and economics have mixed records, but generally lie in the middle of the earnings distribution.

The relative consistency of this ordering across cohorts is interesting — although it is also worth noting that the estimated effects do, in fact, vary to a significant degree from one year to another. For example, the coefficient for engineering and computer science graduates ranges from a low of 0.09 (1988) to a high of 0.21 (1984 and 1992). Thus, the general categorization of the disciplines into those having low, medium, and high earnings is quite consistent, but there is substantial interview-to-interview variation within these broad tendencies.

The earnings patterns for female graduates are relatively similar to those for male graduates, but show some moderate differences in the details. Thus, while the high earnings fields are the same four, their relative standings are somewhat different, with engineering and computer science graduates generally performing even more strongly than was true for men, mathematics and physical sciences graduates also typically doing a little better (except in 1992), and other health and life sciences graduates not doing as well as in the male group. (In this context, recall from Table 1 the very different distributions across these fields between men and women.)

Table 4: Mean Earnings of Graduates, by Field of Study, 1982 and 1986 Cohorts

	1982 Cohort			1986 Cohort		
	1984	1987	% Change	1988	1991	% Change
	(constant 1995 $)			(constant 1995 $)		
All graduates	31,100	39,100	26	31,200	38,400	23
Males						
All fields	34,000	43,800	29	33,700	42,100	25
Education	31,100	36,600	18	33,400	38,100	14
Fine arts and humanities	25,900	38,600	49	28,300	35,100	24
Commerce	33,900	44,800	32	34,900	44,400	27
Economics	32,100	45,300	41	32,800	39,600	21
Other social sciences	30,400	41,300	36	29,800	36,200	21
Agricultural and biological sciences	29,400	41,400	41	27,500	39,800	45
Engineering and computer science	38,900	47,000	21	36,200	44,800	24
Other health and life sciences	45,100	62,600	39	47,400	56,700	20
Mathematics and other physical sciences	35,000	46,100	32	33,900	44,700	32
Other fields	30,400	42,600	40	35,100	45,600	30
Females						
All fields	28,300	34,300	21	28,800	34,700	20
Education	27,600	31,900	16	28,700	32,700	14
Fine arts and humanities	23,900	31,000	30	24,200	29,400	21
Commerce	29,400	37,600	28	30,600	39,100	28
Economics	29,100	—	—	32,800	33,700	3
Other social sciences	24,900	31,900	28	26,300	33,200	26
Agricultural and biological sciences	26,500	33,000	25	25,000	32,200	29
Engineering and computer science	36,700	43,600	19	33,600	41,500	24
Other health and life sciences	35,700	38,800	9	35,000	38,000	9
Mathematics and other physical sciences	33,500	42,800	28	32,000	39,700	24
Other fields	26,200	—	—	29,800	35,800	20

Source: Author's analysis of National Graduates Survey data, as described in the text.

Table 5: Model 1 — Field Variables Only, 1982, 1986, and 1990 Cohorts

	1982 Cohort				1986 Cohort				1990 Cohort			
	1984		1987		1988		1991		1992		1995	
	Coeff.	Std. Error	Coeff.	Std. Error	Coeff.	Std. Error	Coeff.	Std. Error	Coeff.	Std. Error	Coeff.	Std. Error
Males												
Education	−0.03	0.02	−0.09**	0.03	0.02	0.02	−0.06**	0.02	0.05*	0.03	−0.04	0.02
Fine arts and humanities	−0.26**	0.03	−0.22**	0.03	−0.13**	0.03	−0.21**	0.02	−0.35**	0.03	−0.22**	0.02
Commerce	0.05**	0.02	0.08**	0.02	0.09**	0.02	0.07**	0.02	0.04	0.02	0.05*	0.02
Economics	0.00	0.03	0.09**	0.04	−0.07*	0.03	−0.02	0.03	0.04	0.04	0.05	0.03
Other social sciences	−0.09**	0.02	−0.06*	0.03	−0.05	0.03	−0.08**	0.03	−0.13**	0.02	−0.12**	0.02
Agricultural and biological sciences	−0.12**	0.03	−0.11**	0.04	−0.18**	0.03	−0.11**	0.04	−0.20**	0.04	−0.15**	0.04
Engineering and computer science	0.21**	0.02	0.14**	0.02	0.09**	0.02	0.11**	0.02	0.21**	0.02	0.15**	0.02
Other health and life sciences	0.30**	0.06	0.18**	0.07	0.23**	0.05	0.18**	0.05	0.36**	0.06	0.25**	0.05
Mathematics and physical sciences	0.06*	0.03	0.06	0.03	0.01	0.03	0.07*	0.03	0.02	0.04	0.04	0.04
Other fields	−0.12**	0.05	−0.06	0.07	−0.01	0.04	0.06	0.04	−0.04	0.05	−0.03	0.04
R^2	0.13		0.09		0.06		0.09		0.14		0.09	
Number of observations	2,370		1,904		2,143		2,005		2,235		2,193	

Females

Education	−0.07**	0.02	−0.10**	0.02	−0.01	0.02	−0.05*	0.02	0.04	0.02	−0.05*	0.02
Fine arts and humanities	−0.24**	0.02	−0.20**	0.03	−0.23**	0.02	−0.16**	0.02	−0.17**	0.03	−0.15**	0.02
Commerce	0.05	0.03	0.07*	0.03	0.06**	0.02	0.12**	0.02	0.08**	0.03	0.04	0.02
Economics	0.00	0.06	0.00	0.06	0.06	0.04	−0.06	0.05	−0.05	0.06	−0.03	0.06
Other social sciences	−0.17**	0.02	−0.05*	0.03	−0.11**	0.02	−0.04	0.02	−0.10**	0.02	−0.10**	0.02
Agricultural and biological sciences	−0.08*	0.04	−0.10*	0.04	−0.18**	0.04	−0.13**	0.05	−0.11**	0.04	−0.09*	0.03
Engineering and computer science	0.26**	0.04	0.22**	0.05	0.13**	0.03	0.20**	0.04	0.21**	0.05	0.19**	0.04
Other health and life sciences	0.24**	0.03	0.07*	0.03	0.18**	0.02	0.09**	0.03	0.26**	0.03	0.13**	0.03
Mathematics and physical sciences	0.15**	0.05	0.18**	0.06	0.07	0.05	0.07	0.06	−0.03	0.05	0.08	0.05
Other fields	−0.14*	0.06	−0.08	0.07	0.03	0.04	0.03	0.05	−0.13**	0.05	−0.02	0.04
R^2	0.12		0.06		0.10		0.05		0.07		0.04	
Number of observations	2,253		1,884		2,432		2,182		2,567		2,545	

Note: The samples exclude those who were older than age 35 or who had more than five years of full-time experience by the date of graduation.

* Indicates significance at the 0.05 confidence level.

** Indicates significance at the 0.01 confidence level.

Source: Author's analysis of National Graduates Survey data, as described in the text.

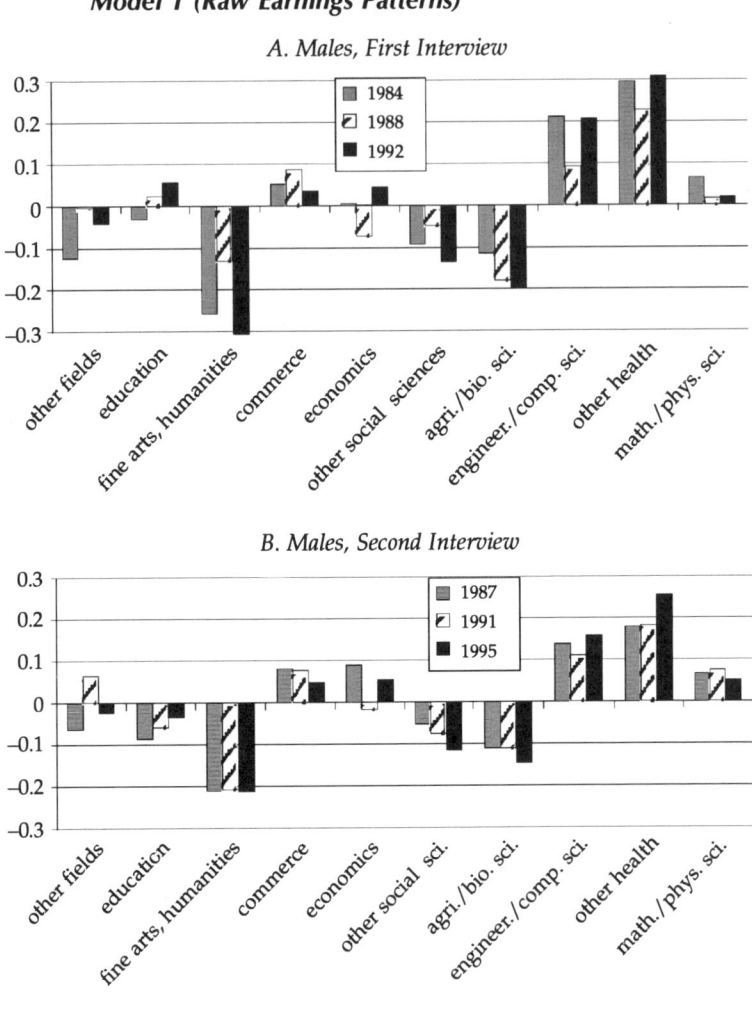

Figure 1: Coefficient Estimates — Model 1 (Raw Earnings Patterns)

A. Males, First Interview

B. Males, Second Interview

Adjusted Earnings Pattern

The Standard Models

The discipline coefficients generated by the second set of regressions (Model 2), which include a more or less standard set of control variables representing labor market experience, personal

Figure 1 - continued

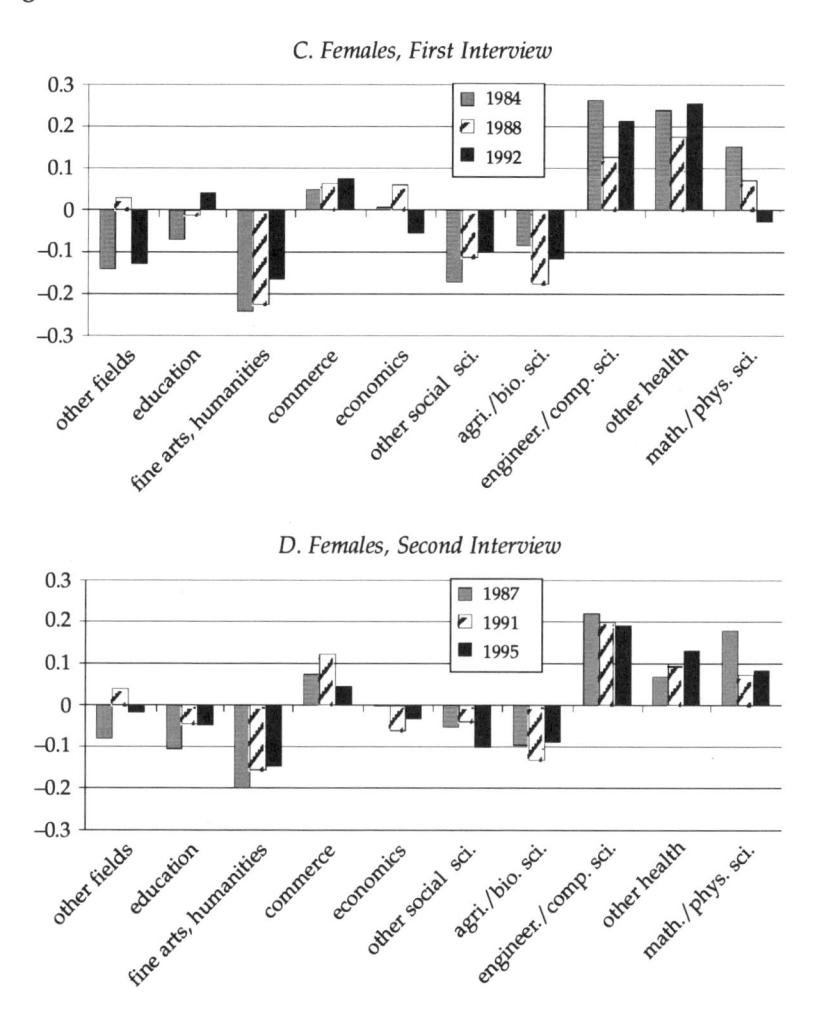

C. Females, First Interview

D. Females, Second Interview

characteristics, and so on (Table 6 and Figure 2), represent the relevant earnings differences net of any influences that operate through these other variables (for example, certain fields lead to greater full-time employment opportunities).[14]

---

14 The full model results are reported in Finnie (2000b). See Daymont and Andrisani (1984) for a discussion of the potential endogeneity of certain regressors in such models.

The general ordering of the adjusted field effects is the same for unadjusted earnings: once again, the high-earnings fields are other health and life sciences, engineering and computer science, mathematics and physical sciences, and commerce; the low-earnings fields are fine arts and humanities, other social sciences, and agricultural and biological sciences; education and economics are generally in the middle rank.

Although the effects are smaller than those found in the simple field-only models, they remain quite large — as found by others for the US situation (see, for example, Rumberger and Thomas 1993; Grogger and Eide 1995). The earnings differences typically vary from 30 to 40 log points between the lowest and highest fields, and soar as high as 59 points for male fine arts and humanities versus other health and life sciences graduates in 1992 (coefficients of −30 and .29 respectively). In short, large differences in earnings by field of study remain after controlling for certain standard labor market characteristics and personal attributes.

The two-year versus five-year patterns allow us to plot the evolution of field effects over at least the early part of an individual's career and to begin to identify longer-term profiles. In general, graduates with degrees in education (both males and females) saw their relative earnings levels decline between the two interview dates, falling from around the middle of the pack at two years after graduation to decidedly below average at five years after graduation. Other health and life sciences graduates also saw relative declines; their earnings were among the very highest at the first interview point but they had only a moderate advantage three years later. The initially higher, but subsequently flatter earnings profiles observed for these two groups presumably reflect the effects of these graduates' typically finding employment in highly unionized public and semi-public sectors. (Union status is not, unfortunately, indicated directly in the NGS data.)

Conversely, fine arts and humanities graduates generally experienced relative gains over time, and although they remained among the lowest paid at the five-year point, they were typically not so far behind as they had been two years after graduation (males in the middle cohort are an exception in this regard). This tendency seems to suggest that these typically more generalist graduates face a more dynamic labor market, with individuals finding interesting job opportunities, gaining promotions, and generally moving ahead in the workplace in the years following graduation. The other disciplines generally showed no consistent change over the interval from two to five years following graduation.

The clearest cross-cohort pattern is that the latest cohort of graduates in the other health and life sciences disciplines enjoyed higher relative earnings than did their earlier counterparts. The other technical and scientific disciplines showed no such improvement; in fact, the cross-cohort movement in many cases was downward. More specifically, both male and female graduates in the third cohort of agricultural and biological sciences and in mathematics and physical sciences had lower relative earnings than those in the first, except for female agricultural and biological sciences graduates at the five-year point, whose earnings held steady. Male engineering and computer science graduates did a little better in the latest cohort (after dipping somewhat in the second), but this was another area of relative decline for female graduates. Overall, there have been no general gains in the more technically and scientifically oriented fields, contrary to what many might have expected.

Other fields that experienced relative earnings gains in the later cohorts were education (both males and females) and fine arts and humanities (females, but not males). General declines occurred for male graduates in other social sciences. For the other disciplines, there are no clear trends across the three cohorts.

Adding Occupation and Industry to the Models

Occupation and industry are fairly highly correlated with, and capture some of the effects of, discipline, and thus these coefficients generate a generally less interesting set of findings. They are, however, worth looking at for the light they cast on how the discipline effects play out in the labor market. Figure 3 plots the coefficients estimated for each of three models (Model 1, including just the field variables; Model 2, including the standard control variables as discussed above; and Model 3, including the occupation and industry variables) averaged over all three cohorts. These graphs

Table 6: **Model 2 — Adding Basic Control Variables, 1982, 1986, and 1990 Cohorts**

	1982 Cohort					1986 Cohort					1990 Cohort			
	1984		1987		1988		1991		1992		1995	
	Coeff.	Std. Error	Coeff.	Std. Error	Coeff.	Std. Error	Coeff.	Std. Error	Coeff.	Std. Error	Coeff.	Std. Error
Males												
Education	0.01	0.02	-0.08**	0.02	0.03	0.02	-0.05*	0.02	0.04	0.02	-0.01	0.02
Fine arts and humanities	-0.20**	0.02	-0.15**	0.03	-0.12**	0.02	-0.14**	0.02	-0.30**	0.02	-0.16**	0.02
Commerce	0.01	0.02	0.06**	0.02	0.07**	0.02	0.06**	0.02	0.03	0.02	0.05**	0.02
Economics	0.00	0.03	0.05	0.03	-0.08**	0.03	-0.06*	0.03	0.02	0.03	0.03	0.03
Other social sciences	-0.07**	0.02	-0.04	0.02	-0.05	0.02	-0.08**	0.02	-0.11**	0.02	-0.13**	0.02
Agricultural and biological sciences	-0.09**	0.03	-0.08*	0.03	-0.15**	0.03	-0.10**	0.03	-0.14**	0.03	-0.14**	0.03
Engineering and computer science	0.15**	0.02	0.10**	0.02	0.08**	0.02	0.09**	0.02	0.17**	0.02	0.14**	0.02
Other health and life sciences	0.20**	0.05	0.13*	0.06	0.20**	0.05	0.17**	0.05	0.29**	0.05	0.21**	0.05
Mathematics and physical sciences	0.07*	0.03	0.07*	0.03	0.03	0.03	0.06*	0.03	0.03	0.03	0.05	0.03
Other fields	-0.08	0.04	-0.05	0.06	0.00	0.03	0.05	0.03	-0.02	0.04	-0.04	0.04
R^2	0.35		0.29		0.24		0.29		0.36		0.30	
Number of observations	2,370		1,904		2,143		2,005		2,235		2,193	

Females

Education	-0.01	0.02	-0.05*	0.02	0.02	0.02	-0.01	0.02	0.04*	0.02	-0.03	0.02
Fine arts and humanities	-0.19**	0.02	-0.17**	0.02	-0.19**	0.02	-0.14**	0.02	-0.13**	0.02	-0.09**	0.02
Commerce	0.00	0.02	0.04	0.03	0.03	0.02	0.09**	0.02	0.04	0.02	0.01	0.02
Economics	-0.02	0.05	-0.02	0.05	0.06	0.04	-0.12**	0.04	-0.06	0.05	-0.10*	0.05
Other social sciences	-0.16**	0.02	-0.06**	0.02	-0.12**	0.02	-0.04*	0.02	-0.07**	0.02	-0.07**	0.02
Agricultural and biological sciences	-0.03	0.03	-0.08*	0.04	-0.15**	0.03	-0.10**	0.04	-0.13**	0.03	-0.07*	0.03
Engineering and computer science	0.18**	0.04	0.17**	0.04	0.09**	0.03	0.15**	0.03	0.15**	0.04	0.13**	0.04
Other health and life sciences	0.17**	0.02	0.08**	0.03	0.17**	0.02	0.13**	0.02	0.24**	0.03	0.16**	0.02
Mathematics and physical sciences	0.12**	0.04	0.12**	0.05	0.06	0.04	0.05	0.05	-0.01	0.05	0.06	0.04
Other fields	-0.05	0.05	-0.03	0.06	0.02	0.04	0.06	0.05	-0.09*	0.04	0.01	0.04
R^2	0.38		0.35		0.31		0.38		0.33		0.36	
Number of observations	2,253		1,884		2,432		2,182		2,567		2,545	

Note: The samples exclude those who were older than age 35 or who had more than five years of full-time experience by the date of graduation. The model includes controls for pre-program educational level, age, postgraduation experience, self-employment status, marriage/children, region, and language.

* Indicates significance at the 0.05 confidence level.

** Indicates significance at the 0.01 confidence level.

Source: Author's analysis of National Graduates Survey data, as described in the text.

Figure 2: *Coefficient Estimates — Model 2 (Adding Basic Control Variables)*

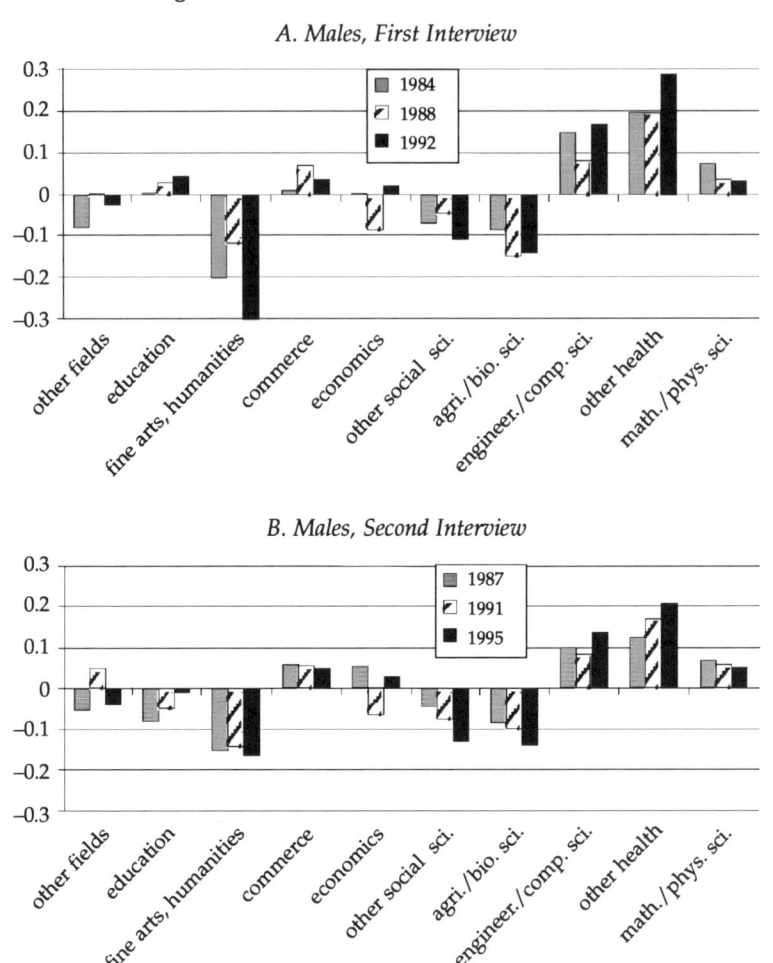

A. Males, First Interview

B. Males, Second Interview

thus show the average effects (across all the cohorts) on the discipline coefficients of adding the two groups of control variables to the specification — which, in fact, accurately represent the findings for the three models for each of the cohorts individually, as reported in Finnie (2000b).[15]

---

15 That is, the coefficients shown in Figure 3 represent the arithmetic means of the estimated coefficients of the simple fields-only earnings models across the...

Figure 2 - continued

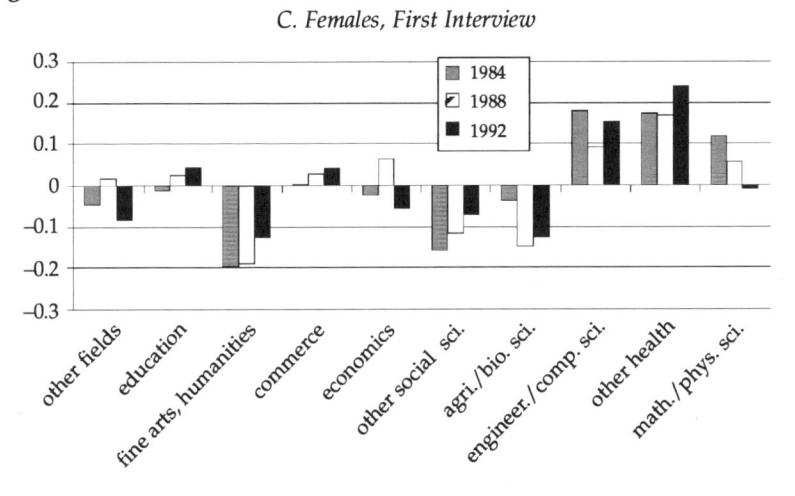

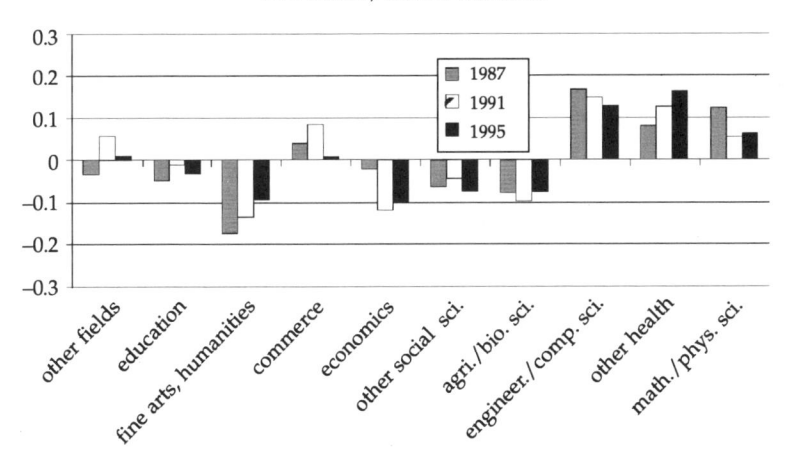

C. Females, First Interview

[Bar chart with legend: 1984, 1988, 1992. X-axis categories: other fields, education, fine arts/humanities, commerce, economics, other social sci., agri./bio. sci., engineer./comp. sci., other health, math./phys. sci. Y-axis from -0.3 to 0.3]

D. Females, Second Interview

[Bar chart with legend: 1987, 1991, 1995. X-axis categories: other fields, education, fine arts/humanities, commerce, economics, other social sci., agri./bio. sci., engineer./comp. sci., other health, math./phys. sci. Y-axis from -0.3 to 0.3]

Adding the additional control variables is seen to generally — but not uniformly — reduce the (net) field effects in the case of both men and women. That is, the high-earnings disciplines are

---

Note 15 - cont'd.

three cohorts (Model 1), the means of the models with the basic set of controls included (Model 2) across the three cohorts, and the means of the coefficients generated by the models that include occupation and industry (Model 3) across the three cohorts.

196　Ross Finnie

Figure 3: Means Coefficient (All Three Cohorts), by Model

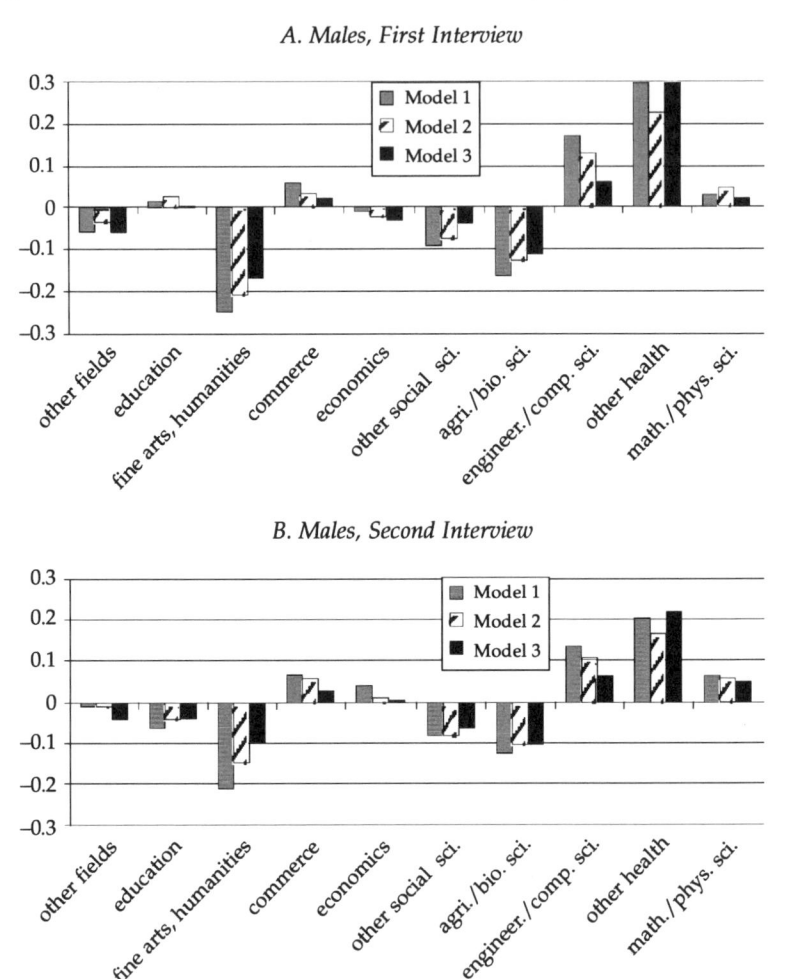

A. Males, First Interview

B. Males, Second Interview

not quite as high when the controls are added, the low-earnings fields are not as low, and so on. The only really notable exception is the other health and life sciences category in the case of men, where adding occupation and industry to the models actually increases its net advantage, suggesting that such graduates have tended to find employment in occupations and industries that are generally lower paying (for men). Economics is also of some interest since, in three of the four cases (excepting only female gradu-

Figure 3 - continued

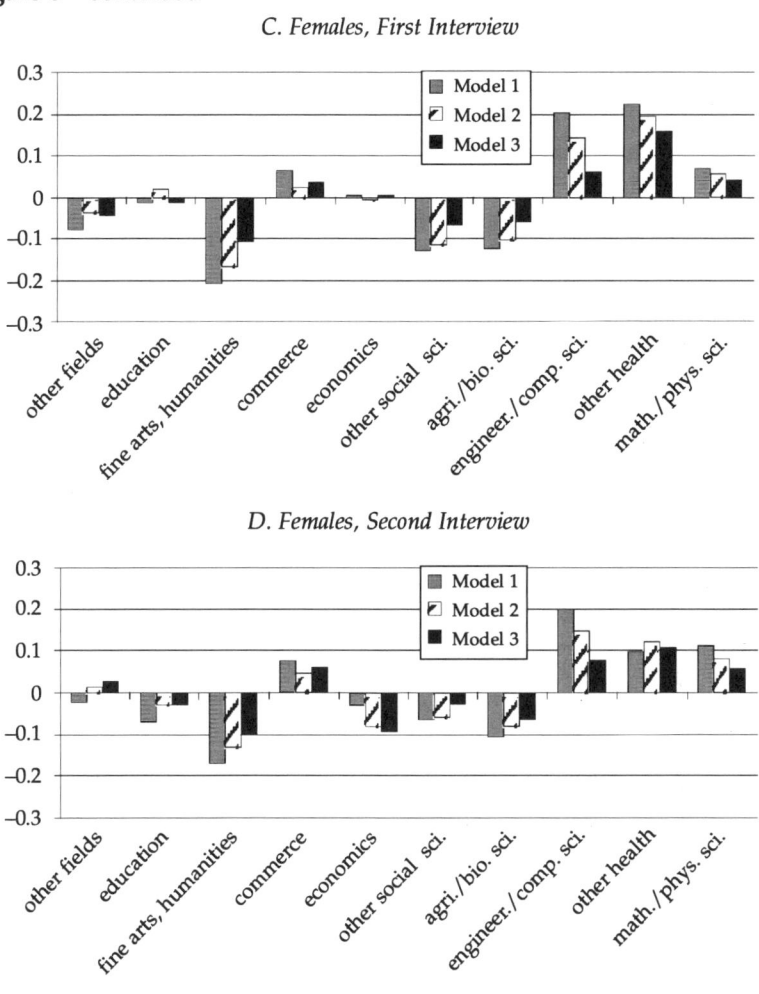

C. Females, First Interview

D. Females, Second Interview

ates two years after graduation), the coefficients become moderately less positive or more negative when the extra controls are added. This result indicates that the middle-rank earnings levels of economics graduates are due to their having moderately "high-earning" labor market and personal attributes (especially in terms of the broad occupational and industrial groups in which they find employment), as seen in the fact that their earnings were actually below average once such factors are taken into account. An economics degree thus appears to get graduates into well-paying occupational environments but in which they are the somewhat poorer cousins.

The (Unexplained) Variation in Earnings by Discipline

We now look at the intradiscipline variance of earnings based on the difference between individuals' predicted and actual levels. The mean absolute differences by discipline based on the Model 2 regression specifications reported in Table 7 and Figure 4 thus represent the (approximate) "average error" by discipline in percentage terms.[16] To the degree that the regression models reflect individuals' estimates of their future earnings, this measure also represents the extent of uncertainty of future earnings for a typical graduate entering a given discipline.[17]

Whereas we would expect some disciplines to have smaller deviations from their predicted values simply because they represent more narrowly defined fields (for example, economics and perhaps agricultural and biological sciences), other comparisons can be made across categories representing discipline groups that are more evenly defined in terms of the different number and varying nature of the fields included. It is also interesting to note where the small-versus-large comparisons do not appear to follow a simple "aggregation rule."

Over all disciplines, actual earnings deviate from the regression-predicted levels by averages of 21 to 26 percent across the different survey years for men, and by 23 to 27 percent in the case of women. Interestingly, there are no clear trends in the extent of these errors from two to five years following graduation or in the cross-cohort patterns, except that the second-cohort errors are slightly smaller

---

16 The results for the models with occupation and industry included are reported in Finnie (2000b).

17 Other measures of variability could, of course, have been employed, but this "average error" has a nice intuitive interpretation while generally serving the purposes of the analysis.

Table 7: **Model 2 — Mean Absolute Errors, by Field of Study**

	1982 Cohort		1986 Cohort		1990 Cohort	
	1984	1987	1988	1991	1992	1995
	(dollars)					
Males						
All fields	0.24	0.24	0.22	0.21	0.26	0.24
Education	0.21	0.19	0.18	0.18	0.20	0.18
Fine arts and humanities	0.33	0.36	0.27	0.30	0.38	0.27
Commerce	0.24	0.24	0.25	0.23	0.24	0.25
Economics	0.23	0.29	0.22	0.19	0.23	0.28
Other social sciences	0.29	0.29	0.25	0.20	0.34	0.28
Agricultural and biological sciences	0.31	0.27*	0.31	0.23	0.34	0.34
Engineering and computer science	0.18	0.17	0.18	0.17	0.17	0.18
Other health and life sciences	0.26*	0.24*	0.24*	0.17	0.23*	0.18
Mathematics and physical sciences	0.24	0.23	0.23	0.21	0.32	0.25
Other fields	0.31*	0.32*	0.24	0.31*	0.33*	0.26
Females						
All fields	0.26	0.26	0.23	0.24	0.27	0.24
Education	0.29	0.27	0.23	0.23	0.23	0.23
Fine arts and humanities	0.32	0.32	0.26	0.30	0.32	0.27
Commerce	0.20	0.23	0.18	0.23	0.23	0.23
Economics	0.24*	0.24	0.28*	0.27	0.30*	0.33*
Other social sciences	0.28	0.26	0.28	0.26	0.30	0.26
Agricultural and biological sciences	0.26	0.24	0.26	0.27	0.32	0.27
Engineering and computer science	0.20	0.21	0.22	0.15	0.22	0.20
Other health and life sciences	0.15	0.21	0.17	0.20	0.20	0.19
Mathematics and physical sciences	0.23	0.25*	0.22	0.28*	0.32*	0.24
Other fields	0.25*	0.25*	0.19	0.23*	0.37*	0.28

Note: Mean absolute errors are calculated as the mean absolute difference between actual log earnings and their predicted values (based on the regression estimates) for the individuals of each field.

* Indicates a standard error between 0.01 and 0.02. Other means have standard errors below 0.1.

Source: Author's analysis of National Graduates Survey data, as described in the text.

Figure 4: *Mean Absolute Errors, by Field of Study — Model 2*

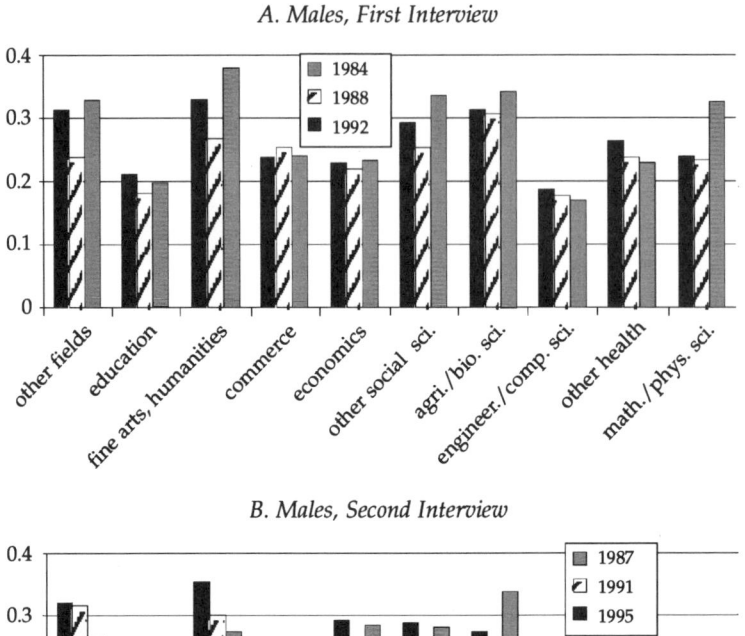

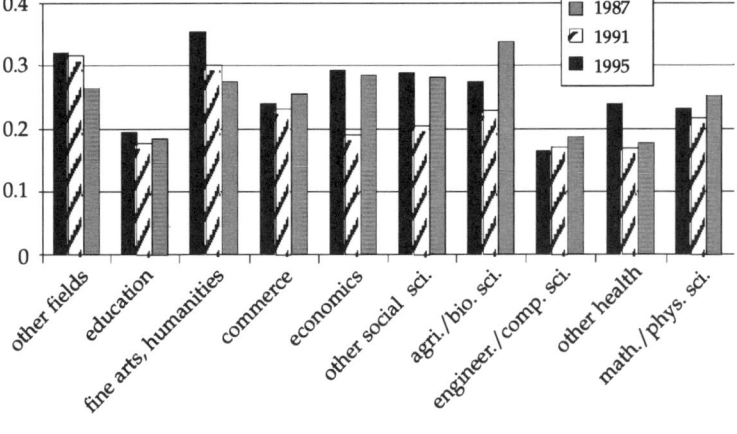

A. Males, First Interview

B. Males, Second Interview

than those of the first and last. Thus, while many observers talk of labor markets having become more uncertain and outcomes more polarized, the numbers do not seem to support this hypothesis in the case of bachelor's-level graduates — at least as measured in this manner.

The most notable outcome in terms of disciplines is probably the relatively low percentage errors that characterize engineering and computer science graduates, especially for men. These low

Figure 4 - continued

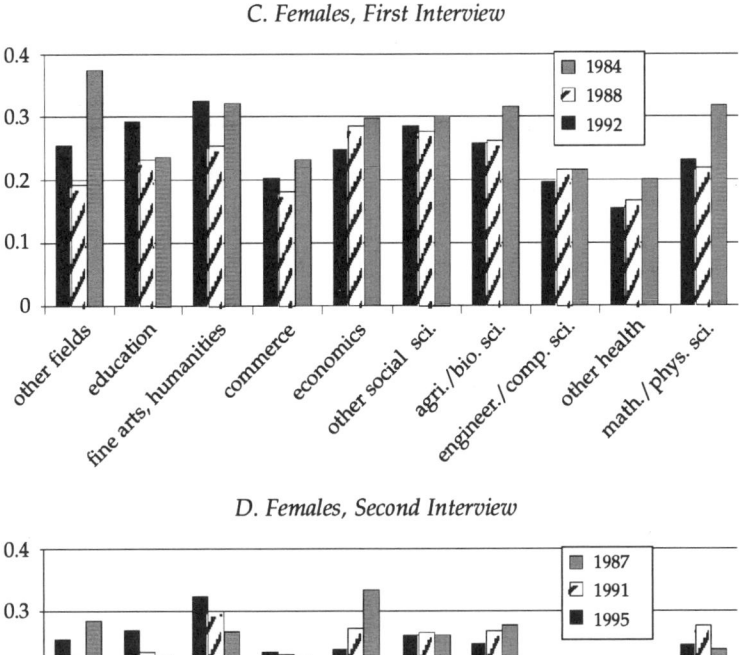

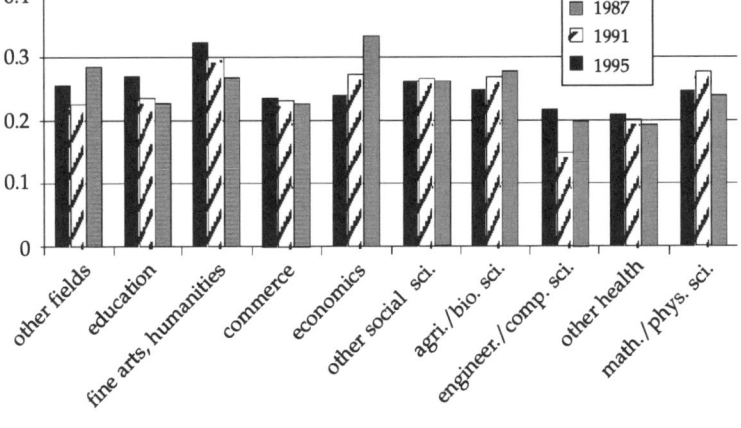

C. Females, First Interview

D. Females, Second Interview

errors presumably indicate that these disciplines boast relatively homogenous groups of graduates who face well-structured job markets. Other health and life sciences disciplines, especially in the case of women, also have relatively well-predicted earnings values, as do male education graduates — again, presumably reflecting a relative homogeneity of graduates and their typically finding jobs in highly unionized sectors with standardized wage scales. At the other extreme, fine arts and humanities graduates tend to have the greatest variation in earnings around the regression-based predicted values — presumably reflecting the heterogeneity of graduates characterizing this broad area and the commensurate variation in earnings opportunities and preferences. Of perhaps greater surprise is the fact that the single field of economics is characterized by prediction errors in the middle rank, whereas one might have expected smaller errors from such a relatively uniform group of graduates; the wide range of labor opportunities realized by economics graduates (from Bay Street to bank clerks) is apparent in these numbers.

Conclusions

The principal findings of this analysis of differences in earnings by discipline among bachelor's-level university graduates in Canada may be summarized as follows.

First, there are still significant differences in the distribution of graduates by sex, and there was surprisingly little change in the distribution of graduates across disciplines for either sex for the three cohorts that finished their schooling in 1982, 1986, and 1990.

Second, there are important differences in earnings by discipline, consistent over time and, in many cases, large. The highest-earnings fields are other health and life sciences, engineering and computer science, commerce, and mathematics and physical sciences; the low-earnings fields are fine arts and humanities, agricultural and biological sciences, and other social sciences. Education and economics are generally in the middle of the earnings distribution.

Adding two different sets of control variables to the models typically reduces the (net) field effects, but the general ordering persists across the various specifications. The effects of discipline on earnings thus appear to operate to some degree through the accumulation of greater labor market experience and other work-related characteristics (including occupation and industry), and are also perhaps associated with certain personal attributes that affect earnings; significant discipline effects remain, however, even after controlling for these influences.

The general ordering of the earnings differences by discipline is relatively consistent for both male and female graduates for the two-year and five-year interview points and for the three cohorts of graduates, although tests not shown indicate that the differences are, in fact, statistically significant along all these dimensions — hence the estimation of the different models shown.

One finding particularly worth mentioning is that there was no general improvement in the earnings of science and technology graduates (the exception being other health and life sciences workers) — a somewhat surprising result, since these fields are typically cited as being critical to the knowledge-based economy and students are often urged to enter these areas for the benefit of their own careers, as well as the sake of the country's economic performance. The general, though moderate, declines in the relative earnings of pure and applied science graduates over this period are especially noteworthy in this regard, as are the continued (relative) low earnings levels of graduates in the applied sciences.

Finally, the measure of the difference between individuals' actual earnings levels and those predicted by the regression models indicates that, overall, these "average errors" were relatively constant across cohorts, suggesting that labor market outcomes have not necessarily become more variable or uncertain among bachelor's-level university graduates over the period covered by this analysis. Graduates in engineering and computer science as well as in other health and life sciences tended to have earnings levels that are more accurately predicted by the regression models, while the greatest (conditional) variation in earnings — that is, earnings uncertainty — has been among fine arts and humanities graduates.

Implications of the Findings

There are various reasons earnings might differ by field of study. First, exogenous shifts in demand or supply (driven by factors such as changes in technology or the greater opening of the economy to global forces, or demographic shifts) will have at least short-run effects on relative earnings patterns, and such effects should be greatest for those, such as recent graduates, who are just entering the labor market and thus at its margins. Second, compensating differentials generate more enduring earnings differences by discipline; the underlying factors include the time and effort required at school and on the job, the degree of stress or level of responsibility, the uncertainty of outcomes, offsetting perquisites, and so on. Third (and related), longer-term ("equilibrium") earnings differences tend to arise in the face of any general scarcity of skills — for example, engineers and other more technically oriented workers might be higher paid if there are a limited number of individuals with the technical abilities required to enter the discipline. Fourth, more artificial supply-side constraints could exist, perhaps reflecting the structure and behavior of the postsecondary system itself (for example, limited admission to certain programs), the actions of associated professional associations (such as the exams required for certification in certain professions), and other institutional influences. Finally, a wide range of government policies could affect earnings patterns by discipline, including those relating to education (for example, subsidies to enter some fields and not others), the labor market (measures that shift the relative costs or benefits associated with different occupations), and others.

One interesting aspect of the findings is the lack of change in the distribution of majors despite the large earnings differences between them. One potential explanation is that the observed mean differences in returns reflect differences in average ability and that the marginal earnings for a person of a given ability are, in fact, the same across majors. If this is the case, the unchanging distribution of persons across majors is not a puzzle because, at the margin, no one has an incentive to move, and the earnings differences represent the sort of skill premiums described above. A similar conclusion would hold in the face of other "equilibrium" explanations, such as compensating differentials.

Alternatively, the stability of the distribution of graduates could stem from rigidities on the supply side. Universities, in particular, have perhaps not been responsive to the need for different types of graduates (as reflected in the observed earnings differentials by discipline). In short, universities may not have been meeting students' preferences and the underlying (relative) demand for graduates of different disciplines, instead continuing to produce the same types of graduates as in the past. Any such rigidities could be the result of blockages in the university system, where, for example, each institution is stuck with a given number of tenured professors, or where interdepartmental "turf battles" for resources are based on internal power structures rather than on the number of students queuing up.

From another perspective, the relative stability of earnings patterns by discipline across the different cohorts of graduates reported above suggests that the forces that determine these patterns have been relatively steady over time in Canada, at least as they apply to the recent bachelor's-level graduates treated here. For all the talk of the manner in which the Canadian economy is generally reorienting toward science and technology, of "globalization," of the emergence of the "knowledge-based economy," of the "polarization" of earnings levels, and so on, earnings patterns have, in fact, remained remarkably stable — as has the distribution of graduates. Furthermore, these two patterns are presumably related — if individuals are, in fact, able to move toward disciplines with higher and/or increasing earnings. Interestingly, the shifts that are observed — declines in the relative earnings of certain science graduates, in particular — seem to go in the opposite direction of what one might have predicted. Furthermore, these dynamics differ from the US experience.[18]

One interpretation of these findings is, therefore, that the underlying forces of supply and demand have been remarkably — indeed, surprisingly — stable over this period. This would, in turn, suggest that the Canadian labor market has, in fact, not been moving as strongly in the suspected directions as many think. That is, neither relative earnings patterns nor numbers of graduates have shifted because the economic forces that tend to drive such adjustments simply have not been present.

---

18 In some US studies (for example, Berger 1988; Eide 1994; Grubb 1992; and Hecker 1995), earnings and enrollment differences by major — as well as the effects of these differences on male/female earnings patterns, the rate of return to college, or shifts in earnings patterns over time — are the particular focus of the analysis. In others (for example, Daniel, Black, and Smith 1999; Datcher Loury and Garman 1995; Daymont and Andrisani 1984; Grogger and Eide 1995; Grubb 1993; Jones and Jackson 1990; and Rumberger and Thomas 1993), discipline effects are considered along with other education-related factors, such as school quality/selection, performance (grades), curriculum (specific courses taken), and ability (test scores), that affect earnings.

An alternative interpretation is that the Canadian economy might indeed be evolving as suspected, but that this change has not resulted in any significant shifts in earnings patterns (at least for recent graduates) or, correspondingly, in the relative numbers of graduates. Such wage rigidity would be surprising, and certainly worthy of further investigation, as would the lack of much response on the part of universities to such changing economic circumstances.

In short, the observed stability of the relative earnings of graduates of different disciplines and the numbers of graduates is surprising, especially as it contrasts with US experience. Has the Canadian economy simply been more stable? Does the Canadian experience reflect greater labor market rigidities? Is Canada's university system less responsive to changing job opportunities (and students' preferences) than it should be? Answering such questions would be a natural path for future research.

The relative consistency of earnings by discipline from the first to the second interviews is also interesting, as it suggests that the above-mentioned forces are fairly constant: high- (and low-) earnings fields tend to be so throughout at least the early part of graduates' careers. Nonetheless, the observed shifts point to the existence of some significant differences in the slope of graduates' age-earnings profiles by discipline, and the discipline effects are generally statistically different at the two interview points.

In fact, these findings point, first of all, to the need to look beyond initial postgraduation outcomes to get a proper understanding of how earnings compare in the longer run. In particular, fine arts and humanities graduates did some significant catching up to the better-paying disciplines from two to five years following graduation, indicating that they face a generally more dynamic labor market, characterized by more improved job opportunities and greater earnings growth than other graduates. This might, furthermore, help explain the finding that fine arts and humanities students are relatively satisfied with their choice of discipline — beyond what might have been expected from looking at initial labor market outcomes alone.

These results also have direct implications for the interpretation of previous studies in which the differences in earnings by discipline are estimated across all age cohorts, or at different points in time following graduation; there are important differences in earnings patterns along these dimensions that such studies miss.

The general similarity of the earnings patterns by discipline for the two sexes is also noteworthy, although there are some moderate differences in this regard. Meanwhile, the very large differences in the distribution of graduates across disciplines by sex, which are largely unchanged across the three cohorts of graduates, remain an intriguing aspect of earnings patterns and labor market behavior more generally — especially, perhaps, when the relative earnings patterns are similar.

Unobserved Ability

Unobserved ability clearly plays an important role in the earnings patterns analyzed here. The higher-earnings disciplines unquestionably are capturing innate characteristics such as general intelligence, specific skills, perseverance, and so on, as well as the effects of the chosen field of study *per se*.

While the patterns reported here are still of interest for the reasons cited at the beginning of this paper, one important implication of the missing ability factor is that "extra" or marginal graduates would not necessarily be expected to have the earnings levels reported here. For example, while one might argue that it is good public policy to increase enrollment in engineering and computer science programs, the additional places created presumably would be filled by individuals with lower average ability than past graduates in these disciplines, and earnings — and the labor market productivity those earnings are usually assumed to represent — of these marginal graduates would be commensurately lower as well.

This is the classic problem characterizing the literature on earnings patterns by discipline, and this paper offers no special treatment in this respect; in fact, it suffers from the lack of any sort of ability measures at all, including those of the types that have been used in US work. Future Canadian databases, including the Youth in Transition Survey (which will track various waves of young people from their middle and late teens and early twenties over time), might offer some interesting opportunities in this regard.

Other Paths for Future Research

One promising possibility for future research is a similar analysis at a more detailed level for selected disciplines, to see if the aggregate-level findings reported here — relative stability of the patterns by cohort, by year relative to graduation, by sex, and so on — hold up. It might also be interesting to see how the "average error" measure behaves at a more detailed level, and if there are the sorts of tradeoffs across disciplines in terms of the average level and variance of earnings that theory predicts.

Another potential avenue of research is to look at earnings at a later point in time following graduation to see how patterns evolve over the longer run. But work of this type would have to await another follow-up survey of one of the NGS cohorts already interviewed, which Statistics Canada is not currently planning, or other data.

Finally, building from the preceding discussion of unobserved ability, it would be extremely interesting to model the choice of discipline, both for its own sake and as the first stage of a broader model that controlled for the related selection dynamics and associated omitted heterogeneity in the estimation of differences in earnings by discipline. This task, however, would not only be fairly complex from a theoretical econometric perspective, but on a practical level it would probably lie beyond the capacity of at least the NGS data used here, which suffer from a relative paucity of the sorts of background variables that could be used to identify the necessary structural relationships (that is, variables that affect the choice of discipline but have no direct effect on earnings).[19]

In the meantime, the estimates reported here represent a useful descriptive analysis of earnings differences by discipline, providing a set of benchmark estimates of the earnings differences by field of study that have existed for Canadian graduates over the past decade and a half and an empirical footing for various policy discussions.

---

19 See Altonji (1993) for a model of the choice of the number of years of study with certain endogenous regressors, including discipline; Garen (1984) for an earlier piece in the same spirit; and Coté and Sweetman (1997) for an attempt to model the differences in earnings by discipline with the choice of discipline treated as a choice outcome, but with limited success due to the questionable nature of the instruments employed.

Appendix: The Earnings Models

The primary objective of this paper is to estimate the differences in labor market earnings by field of study of recent postsecondary graduates at two specific points in time after leaving school corresponding to the interview dates of the National Graduates Survey data. The standard approach is to estimate earnings models that include indicators of a graduate's discipline while controlling for various other influences. The models used here conform to these conventions as adapted to the postgraduation period covered and the information available in the NGS databases. The specific variables included in the models are described below.

One innovation offered here is the imposition of restrictions on the parameter estimates that force the field-of-study coefficients to be expressed relative to the (conditional) mean. In the more usual approach, one discipline is used as the (omitted) baseline against which other field effects are measured, meaning that various pairwise comparisons are required to gauge the effects of any specific discipline relative to the others. Furthermore, the estimated effects shift with the earnings of the baseline group, rendering cross-year and cross-sex comparisons particularly complex — for example, a decrease in the relative earnings of the baseline group will cause all other coefficients to rise. The approach adopted here thus allows for a more straightforward and robust "relative to the average" interpretation of the estimated field effects.

The models are estimated separately for men and women for each of the six interview dates (two and five years following graduation for each of three cohorts). This disaggregated approach was adopted after conventional tests indicated that the structure of earnings was sufficiently different for the two interview points within a given cohort, for the three different cohorts, and for both sexes to require the estimation of separate models along each of these dimensions. The same logic holds for the discipline effects themselves: pooling was rejected even after allowing all nondiscipline parameters to vary freely across interview dates (and sex), indicating in a formal fashion that the differences in earnings by field of study vary significantly between the two interview points, across cohorts, and by sex — an interesting result to begin with, and one with potential relevance for other studies where such poolings are imposed.

The earnings variable available on the NGS databases is based on the question: "Working your usual number of hours, approximately what would be your annual earnings before taxes and deductions at that job?" It thus represents what the graduate would earn (before deductions) on an annual basis if the job he or she held at the time of the interview lasted the full year, regardless of the actual number of weeks worked. In adjusting for irregular work patterns in this manner, the measure represents the individual's rate of pay on an annual basis rather than the amount earned. It is a somewhat unconventional measure but embodies a relatively well-defined and analytically appropriate concept and suits the purposes of this study. All earnings values are expressed here in constant 1995 dollars, and in the NGS data are rounded to the nearest thousand and capped at the $99,000 upper limit that characterizes the 1984 data (the lowest bound in the six databases), or $143,035 in constant 1995 dollars.

Standard practice is followed by using the natural log of earnings as the dependent variable, thus allowing the coefficient estimates to be interpreted in (approximate) percentage terms. Three models are specified: Model 1 includes no regressors except for the field-of-study indicators, and thus reveals the "raw" earnings differentials by discipline in a formal regression framework. Model 2 includes the variables listed below representing labor market experience, previously held degrees, and personal characteristics, thereby yielding the earnings differences by field that hold after controlling for these factors. Model 3 adds dummy variables representing the individual's occupation and industry, but since these variables are fairly strongly correlated with field of study and undoubtedly pick up some of the discipline effects, the discussion of these findings is relatively brief.

The variables included in Models 2 and 3 are:

- other degrees — a dummy variable indicating that the individual held a higher degree (master's or doctorate) before entering the bachelor's program;

- age and age squared — note also the sample restriction to individuals under age 35 at graduation (as discussed in the text);
- postgraduation work experience — proxied in the first interview regressions with part-time and full-time employment status as of two specific dates between graduation and the first interview (the October in the following year and the January after that), and in the second interview regressions with the addition of employment status as of the first interview (more conventional experience variables reflecting the total time working are not available in the NGS databases); tenure with the current employer was excluded on the grounds that it could capture some of the effects that properly belong to the discipline studied;
- part-time work — the standard definition (30 hours), to control for individuals' labor supply decisions;
- self-employment — a standard dummy variable indicator (as opposed to being a paid worker);
- marital status/presence of children — standard indicators that, in this case, allow for the effects of children to vary by marital status: single (never married) with/without children; married with/without children; and widowed, separated, or divorced with/without children;
- province/language — allows for provincial and regional effects (the Atlantic provinces, Quebec, Ontario, Manitoba and Saskatchewan, Alberta, British Columbia, and the territories) plus minority language effects (anglophone in Quebec, francophone outside of Quebec, other language);
- industry — 13 standard industrial sectors;
- occupation — 15 standard occupational groups

See Finnie (2000b) for further discussion of the data and the econometric approach employed here.

References

Altonji, Joseph G. 1993. "The Demand for and Return to Education When Outcomes Are Uncertain." *Journal of Labor Economics* 11 (1): 48–83.

———. 1995. "The Effects of High School Curriculum on Educational and Labor Market Outcomes." *Journal of Human Resources* 30 (3): 39–44.

Berger, Mark C. 1988. "Cohort Size Effects on Earnings: Differences by College Major." *Economics of Education Review* 7 (4): 375–383.

Betts, Julian, Chris Ferrall, and Ross Finnie. 1999. "The Effects of School Quality on Bachelor's Graduates' Earnings." Paper presented at the American Education Research Association Meetings, Montreal, April.

Cohn, Elchanan. 1997. "Rates of Return to Schooling in Canada." *Journal of Education Finance* 23 (2): 193–206.

Côté, Sylvain, and Arthur Sweetman. 1997. "Does It Matter What I Study? Post-Secondary Field of Study and Labor Market Outcomes in Canada." University of Victoria. Unpublished.

Daniel, Kermit, Dan Black, and Jeffrey Smith. 1999. "College Quality and the Wages of Young Men." Paper presented at the American Education Research Association Meetings, Montreal, April.

Datcher Loury, Linda, and David Garman. 1995. "College Selectivity and Earnings." *Journal of Labor Economics* 13 (2): 289–308.

Daymont, Thomas A., and Paul J. Andrisani. 1984. "Job Preferences, College Major, and the Gender Gap in Earnings." *Journal of Human Resources* 19 (3): 408–428.

Dodge, David, and David A.A. Stager. 1972. "Economic Returns to Graduate Study in Science, Engineering and Business." *Canadian Journal of Economics* 5 (2): 182–198.

Eide, Eric. 1994. "College Major Choice and Changes in the Gender Wage Gap." *Contemporary Economic Policy* 12 (April): 55–64.

Finnie, Ross. 1995. "Steppin' Out: An Analysis of Recent University Graduates into the Labour Market." Industry Canada Working Paper 5. Ottawa: Industry Canada.

———. 1999. "Holding Their Own [1999]: Recent Trends in the Employment Rates and Earnings Levels of Post-Secondary Graduates." *Canadian Business Economics* 7 (4): 48–64.

———. 2000a. "From School to Work: The Evolution of Early Labour Market Outcomes of Canadian Post-Secondary Graduates." *Canadian Public Policy* 26 (2): 197–224.

———. 2000b. "What You Study Matters: An Econometric Analysis of Earnings Differences by Field of Study amongst Recent Canadian Bachelor's Level University Graduates." Human Resources Development Canada working paper. Ottawa: Human Resources Development Canada, Applied Research Branch.

———. 2001. "Fields of Plenty, Fields of Lean: the Early Labour Market Outcomes of Canadian University Graduates." *Canadian Journal of Higher Education* 31 (1): 141–176.

———, and Marc Frenette. Forthcoming. "Earnings Differences by Major Field of Study: Evidence from Three Cohorts of Recent Canadian Graduates." *Economics of Education Review*.

———, and Ted Wannell. 1999. "The Gender Earnings Gap amongst Canadian Bachelor's Level University Graduates: A Cross-Cohort, Longitudinal Analysis." In Richard Chaykowski and Lisa Powell, eds., *Women and Work*. Kingston, Ont.; Montreal: McGill/Queen's University Press.

Garen, John. 1984. "The Returns to Schooling: A Selectivity Bias Approach with a Continuous Choice Variable." *Econometrica* 52 (5): 1199–1218.

Grogger, Jeff, and Eric Eide. 1995. "Changes in the College Skills and the Rise in the College Wage Premium." *Journal of Human Resources* 30 (2): 280–310.

Grubb, W. Norton. 1992 "The Economic Returns to Baccalaureate Degrees: New Evidence from the Class of 1972." *Review of Higher Education* 15 (2): 213–231.

———. 1993. "The Varied Economic Returns to Postsecondary Education: New Evidence from the Class of 1972." *Journal of Human Resources* 28 (2): 365–381.

Hecker, Daniel E. 1995. "Earnings of College Graduates, 1993." *Monthly Labor Review*, December, pp. 3–16.

Jones, Ethel B., and John D. Jackson. 1990. "College Grades and Labor Market Rewards." *Journal of Human Resources* 25 (2): 253–266.

Lavoie, Marie, and Ross Finnie. 1999. "Is It Worth Doing a Science or Technology Degree in Canada? Empirical Evidence and Policy Implications." *Canadian Public Policy* 25 (1): 101–121.

Mehmet, Ozay. 1977. "Economic Returns on Undergraduate Fields of Study in Canadian Universities: 1961 to 1972." *Industrial Relations* 32 (3): 321–339.

Murphy, Kevin M., and Finis Welch. 1990. "Empirical Age-Earnings Profiles." *Journal of Labor Economics* 8 (April): 202–229.

Rumberger, Russell, and Scott L. Thomas. 1993. "The Economic Returns to College Major, Quality and Performance: A Multilevel Analysis of Graduates." *Economics of Education Review* 12 (1): 1–19.

Stager, David. 1996. "Returns to Investment in Ontario University Education, 1960–1990, and Implications for Tuition Fee Policy." *Canadian Journal of Education* 26 (2): 1–21.

Turner, Sarah E., and William G. Bowen. 1999. "Choice of Major: The Changing (Unchanging) Gender Gap." *Industrial and Labor Relations Review* 52 (2): 289–313.

Vaillancourt, François. 1995. "The Private and Total Returns to Education in Canada, 1985." *Canadian Journal of Economics* 28 (3): 532–553.

The Returns to University Education in Canada, 1990 and 1995

François Vaillancourt and Sandrine Bourdeau-Primeau

The purpose of this paper is to present new, comparable estimates of the 1990 and 1995 private and total rates of return to university education in Canada. The calculation is by level of schooling and, for bachelor's degrees, by field of study.

These findings should be of interest to those working in higher education because the rates of return to schooling are used, at least implicitly, in allocating resources. Private decisionmakers — individuals faced with the choice of pursuing further education, such as college or university level studies (or funding such studies as parents) or of entering the labor force — want to know if further studies are associated with monetary returns. Public decisionmakers, who face competing demands for scarce funds from the education sector and other sectors of society and, within the education sector, from various postsecondary programs, may want to use total rates of return to guide, in part, their spending decisions.

The paper is divided into three parts. The first one reviews the recent literature, and the second presents an analytical framework, assumptions, data sources, and the calculations made with them. The third analyzes the results and draws some conclusions.

Research results reported in this paper were prepared using funding from the Social Sciences and Humanities Research Council of Canada and Human Resources Development Canada. We thank David Laidler, conference organizer, and Jeffrey Smith, conference commentator, for their comments on the conference version of this paper.

Literature Review

Vaillancourt (1995) reviews the Canadian literature on the rates of return to education. In Table 1, we list the seven studies published since that survey. All these studies use data from the 1991 or 1996 census. The main differences among them are their use of mean earnings or of individual observations to calculate earnings profiles and the type of rate of return estimated. If we limit ourselves to the most comparable sets of numbers — private rates of return for a bachelor's degree by sex (four studies) — we find a remarkable degree of agreement with rates for men in the 14 to 17 percent range and for women in the 15 to 19 percent range.

Note that we limit our list to studies on the rates of return and omit studies on the returns to education. The latter studies examine the effect education has on labor income (wages, earnings, and so on), measured using either a continuous years-of-schooling variable, which is assumed to have a linear or quadratic impact on labor income, or a set of dichotomous variables related to the level of schooling attained. Such studies, although quite useful for labor market analysis, do not link the costs of schooling to its impact on labor income; they are thus not comparable to our study.

Methodology

This section presents our analytical framework and the assumptions used, and then explains the data sources and the calculations themselves.

Analytical Framework

We apply the standard analytical framework to calculate rates of return. We use pre- and post-investment earnings profiles to measure benefits, while up-front costs include forgone earnings and overall out-of-pocket expenses.

Table 1: Rates of Return to Education Studies for Canada, 1996–2000

Study: Data Year and Area	Type of Rate of Return	Income Data, Methodology[a]	Tax Issues	Rates of Return
Stager (1996): 1990, Ontario	Private and total rates for men and women, BA/BSc., all and by field of study	Mean earnings by age group, 1991 census	Yes, using taxation statistics data by income class	Private rates are 13.8% (men) and 17.8% (women); total rates are 10.7% (men) and 11.9% (women) for a bachelor's degree; return varies by field of study
Dickson, Milne, and Murrell (1996): 1990, New Brunswick	Total private and fiscal (provincial and federal), men and women separate, rates for university degrees	1991 census, OLS	Yes, using simulations	Fiscal rates between 4.3% and 5.1% overall; private rates between 7.6% and 11.6%; social rates between 6.1% and 8.5%
Stager (1998): 1995, Ontario	Total and private rates, men and women separate, bachelor's degree, all and by field of study	Mean earnings by age group, 1996 census	Yes, using taxation statistics by income class	Private rates are 13.1% (men) and 19.0% (women); total rates are 9.7% (men) and 10.7% (women) for a bachelor's degree[b]
Vaillancourt (1997): 1990, Canada	Private and total rates, men and women separate, BA/BSc., MA/MSc./PhD and Health, plus field of study for undergraduates	1991 census, OLS	Yes, using simulations	Private rates are 15% (men) and 18% (women); total rates are 9% (men) and 8% (women) for a bachelor's degree. Returns vary by field of study
Demers (2000): 1990 and 1995, Quebec	Private rate, bachelor's degree; 75% of difference in rate of return attributed to schooling	Mean earnings by age group, 1991 and 1996 censuses	Yes, using Fraser Institute data on personal, payroll, corporate, sales, and property taxes	Private rate is 11.1% in 1990 and 9.5% in 1995 for a bachelor's degree
Demers (1999): 1990 and 1995, Quebec	Fiscal rate, bachelor's degree	Mean earnings by age group, 1991 and 1996 censuses	Yes, using Fraser Institute data on personal, payroll, corporate, sales, and property taxes	Fiscal rate is 8.7% in 1990 and 10.5% in 1995
Bourdeau-Primeau (1999): 1995, Canada	Private and total rates, men and women separate, BA/BSc., MA/MSc./PhD and Health plus field of study BA/BSc.	1996 census, OLS	Yes, using simulations	Private rates are 17% (men) and 15% (women); total rates are 10% (men) and 10% (women) for a bachelor's degree

[a] Statistics Canada is the source for the cost data in all these studies except Demers (1999; 2000), who uses data from the Quebec government.
[b] Stager's returns are reported in Table A-11 of this paper.

We then solve the following regression for a rate of return, r, such that the present value of the income stream associated with schooling is given by:

$$0 = \sum_{i=1}^{N} \frac{(A_i - B_i)}{(1 + r)^i} - C,$$

where N denotes the number of years of earnings after the investment, A and B the <u>a</u>fter and <u>b</u>efore investment earnings profiles, and C the up-front costs.

Such a calculation may yield a positive, zero, or negative rate of return, depending on the relative size of the differences in earnings and the costs of the investment.

Assumptions

The standard analytical framework contains a set of more or less explicit assumptions. The following list presents them and, for most, indicates their effect on calculated rates of return as a bias that is positive (overestimation) or negative (underestimation).

1. Benefits are measured only by earnings. Fringe benefits from employment are excluded. Because these fringe benefits normally increase as a percentage of wages and salaries when wages and salaries increase, this simplifying assumption gives a negative bias to the model.
2. All monetary costs are included and assumed to be incurred in the year immediately preceding graduation; thus they are not discounted. Nonmonetary benefits, such as civic participation and child-rearing skills, are omitted.
3. No correction is made for differences in the abilities of individuals with and without higher levels of schooling. This assumption likely has a positive bias since the impact of abilities is captured by schooling differences (more able individuals go on to higher levels of schooling).
4. Individuals with no employment income are excluded — to allow the computation of the natural logarithm (ln) of earnings. This has a positive bias, since lack of employment income is not entirely explained by level of university schooling.

5. Earnings are defined as wages plus self-employment income. The consequent inclusion of the returns to the nonhuman capital used by the self-employed has a slight positive bias.
6. The same retirement age is used for everyone, and no correction is made for differential mortality rates by level of schooling. This assumption has a negative bias, but it is small because discounting reduces the impact of earnings received 30 or 40 years after graduation.
7. The income tax is fully indexed, and no excess burden of taxes is taken into account. This assumption has a positive bias for private rates of return, because the income tax has historically been less than fully indexed to inflation, and for public rates of return, because omitting the excess burden underestimates the costs of public support to university education.
8. No productivity growth occurs. This simplifying assumption has a negative bias; allowing productivity to rise would increase earnings.
9. A single year represents the life cycle. This common assumption undoubtedly has some effect on the calculated rates of return, but its direction is uncertain.

The two crucial assumptions, in our opinion, are the omission of nonmonetary benefits, such as better child-rearing skills, and more societal implication through volunteerism or greater participation in the political process, and the lack of correction for differences in abilities between individuals with different levels of schooling.

On the former point, one can do little except to note that it may be quite important (Stager 1996) or that more systematic research should be carried out.[1] Because of the latter point, some authors use information extraneous to their study to correct their rates of return to account for this. Constantatos and West (2000) reduce them on the basis of their reading of the literature; thus, their social rate of return to university education goes from 9.9 percent to 7.6 percent. By presenting uncorrected rates, we leave readers free to carry out whatever modification they deem appropriate.

---

1 As Jeffrey Smith argues persuasively elsewhere in this volume.

Fields of Study

Because we present rates of return for various levels of university education and various fields of study, we must specify the programs to which each field corresponds.[2] We used the following groupings:

Education:	primary and secondary, general and specialized (physical education and so on), counselling
Humanities:	fine and applied arts, music, drama, classics, languages, philosophy, communications, history, library science
Social sciences:	geography, anthropology, sociology, economics, political science, psychology, social work, law
Commerce:	management, business
Pure sciences:	agriculture, biological, pure and mathematical sciences
Engineering:	engineering and applied sciences
Health sciences:	nursing, health professions (speech therapy, physiotherapy and so on)

Notice that some of the groupings are quite wide; the social sciences, for example, include law.

Data and Calculations

The formula given above requires us to know the lifetime earnings of individuals, with and without the level of schooling, for which a rate of return is being calculated — A and B — and the costs, C. We first explain how we obtain A and B and then turn to C.

After and Before Investment Earnings (A and B)

We take data on earnings from the public use microdata files of the 1991 and 1996 Canadian censuses. These files comprise, respectively,

---

2 We constructed this list with microdata file code books. The census variables and codes are presented in Appendix Table A-1.

a 3.0 percent sample from all 1991 census respondents and a 2.8 percent sample from 1996 (drawn from long-form respondents). The number of individuals used in the analysis appears in Appendix Tables A-3 and A-4.

Earnings profiles by degree were obtained by using the following equation:

$$\ln(\text{earnings}) = B_0 + (B_1 \times \text{Age}) + (B_2 \times \text{Age}^2) + \left[\sum_{i=1}^{7} (B_{i3} \times \text{Fields}) + \sum_{i=2}^{7} (B_{i4} \times \text{Fields} \times \text{Age})\right].$$

We use the standard semi-logarithmic relation between earnings and age/age^2 and ordinary least squares (OLS) regressions to estimate returns by level of education. In other words, we relate the natural logarithm of earnings, not earnings *per se*, to the age and field-of-studies variables. The statistical technique of OLS allows us to find the set of coefficients that best represents the relationship between the variable to be explained (earnings) and the factors that explain it (age and fields of studies). When we take fields of study into account, we add the terms in square brackets to modify the intercept and the slope of the equation. Appendix Tables A-3 through A-6 report our regression results for 1990 and 1995.

With these equations, we calculate each individual's earnings for each year in the labor market. To do this, we make assumptions about age at attaining various levels of education and at retirement. Students are assumed to graduate from high school and start university studies at age 18, to end their BA or BSc studies at age 22. If they continue in school, they finish their MA or MSc or health degree studies at age 24 (after receiving a BA or BSc) and their PhD at age 28 (after receiving an MA or MSc). They then enter the work force and work until they retire at age 63.

For example, to calculate the rate of return for a man who received a BComm in 1995, we compute for each age from 22 to 62 — that is, for 41 years — the earnings of a BComm holder and, in contrast, those of a high school graduate. Thus, for a 30-year-old:

BComm earnings = 6.8369 + (0.1661 × 30) + (− 0.0018 × 900) + (−0.0140) + (0.0047 × 30) = 10.3269, of which the exponential value (antilog) is $30,543;

high school earnings = 6.1765 + (0.1797 × 30) + (−0.0019 × 900)
= 9.8575,

of which the exponential value (antilog) is $19,101.

For total rates of return, we calculate for each of the 41 years the difference between the higher level and the lower level of education to obtain the difference between A and B. In our example, the difference at age 30 is

$30,543 − $19,101 = $11,442.

For private rates of return, we must find the individual's after-tax income — gross income minus personal income tax. We calculated it for a single individual who claims the personal exemption, employment insurance (EI) and Canada (or Quebec) Pension Plan (CPP/QPP) credits, and the allowable registered retirement savings plan (RRSP) deduction of 18 percent of earnings to a maximum of $13,500). For both years, we use the federal income tax schedule and the Ontario tax-on-tax rate as a proxy for the provincial rates (see Table 2).

In our example, according to the parameters of the tax table, $30,053 becomes $25,993 and $19,101, $16,896. We then subtract these amounts to obtain the difference between A and B for private rates of return:

$24,987 − $16,896 = $8,091.

Up-Front Costs (C)

For our basic equation, we need the up-front costs of an individual's investment in education. These costs are tuition, other out-of-pocket expenses (textbooks, and so on), and forgone earnings.

The amounts that we used for tuition and other out-of-pocket expenses are set out in Table 3 (the sources and methods of calculation are listed in Appendix Table A-2). To obtain a total for a particular level of education, we added the two amounts and multiplied the result by the appropriate number of years of study.

Table 2: Tax Parameters Used in the Simulation of Private Income

Parameter	1990	1995
Personal exemption	$6,169	$6,456
First tax bracket: 17% rate	$0–$28,275 taxable income	$0–$29,590 taxable income
Second tax bracket: 26% rate	$28,276–$56,550 taxable income	$29,591–$59,180 taxable income
Third tax bracket: 29% rate	More than $56,550 taxable income	More than $59,180 taxable income
Ontario tax rate	53% of federal tax	58% of federal tax
EI contribution rate	1.95%	3.0%
EI maximum taxable earnings (weekly)	$640	$815
CPP/QPP contribution rate	2.2%	2.7%
CPP/QPP minimum taxable earnings (annual)	$2,800	$3,400
CPP/QPP maximum taxable earnings (annual)	$28,900	$34,900
RRSP contribution rate	18% of earnings	18% of earnings
RRSP maximum contribution	$13,500	$13,500

Source: Authors, drawing on Canadian Tax Foundation 1990; 1995.

For example, we calculated the up-front private costs of a bachelor's degree obtained in 1995 as follows:

Out-of-pocket expenses $1,753 + Tuition $2,633 = $4,386 per year × 4 = $17,544.

Then we calculated forgone earnings, using the equation associated with the B income stream. Because postsecondary students usually attend classes only eight months a year (and spend the other four working), we assumed they forgo two-thirds of the annual earnings of high school graduates of the appropriate age. For example, we calculate the earnings forgone by a man who completed a BComm in 1995 as two-thirds of the sum of the earnings of a male high school graduate over the ages of 18, 19, 20, and 21. Those annual forgone amounts were $20,735 (private) and $20,818 (total).

Table 3: Annual Cost Data, 1990 and 1995

	1990	1995
	(current dollars)	
	Private Costs	
Tuition		
University		
Undergraduate, all fields	1,687	2,633
Graduate, all levels	1,547	2,688
Other out of pocket		
University, all levels	1,139	1,753
	Public Costs	
University		
Undergraduate, all fields	17,797	17,386
Graduate		
Master's level	29,663	28,977
PhD level	71,190	69,545

Note: For both tuition and other out-of-pocket expenses, annual costs are added up for the relevant number of years, without present value calculations: bachelor's degree, four years (after high school); master's degree, two years (after a bachelor's); and a PhD, four years (after a master's).

These earnings were calculated on an annual basis using the relevant equations of Appendix Tables A-3 and A-4. Thus, the earnings of a woman age 18 used in the calculations of the 1990 rates of return were:

$$7.3944 + (0.0966 \times 180 + (-0.0011 \times 324) = 8{,}7768,$$

with the antilog yielding $6,482 for a full year and thus $4,317 for eight months.

The results of our calculations are set out in Tables A-7 through A-10. We then combine A, B, and C using the internal rate of return (IRR) function of the Excel spreadsheet program.

Returns to Education

In this part of the paper, we present our result, by levels of education and, for bachelor's degrees, by fields of study.

Results by Levels of Education

Table 4 sets out our results by level of postsecondary education. Our key findings here are as follows:

- Private rates of return for bachelor's degrees are high in absolute and relative terms, ranging between 16 and 20 percent in 1990 and 1995. Recall that these are *real after-tax rates of return*. To obtain a similar rate of return on a financial asset would require at least a 30 percent before-tax rate of return. In 1990, the nominal yield on a 10-year government of Canada bond was 10.3 percent, and in 1995, it was 7.1 percent.
- The total rates of return for bachelor's degrees are only about half the private rates of return. The reason for the difference is the high level of subsidies to higher education in Canada; tuition fees represent only about a quarter to a third of the cost of an undergraduate degree (the exact proportion varies across provinces). Notice, however, that the rates of return are still high. They show, for example, that the amount spent on producing one extra bachelor's degree earned 10 percent in real terms in 1995 in the labor market. (And recall that we are neglecting nonpecuniary returns.)
- Rates of return for master's and PhD degrees are substantially lower than those for bachelor's degrees. This result is found in studies of returns to education across the world. The main reason is the fact that the high returns associated with a bachelor's degree elevate the opportunity cost of graduate studies. Their relatively low rates of monetary returns may be misleading as a guide for funding purposes if their other benefits, such as growth-generating externalities (Martin and Trudeau 1998), increase with schooling.

Results by Field of Study

Turning to Table 5, we find that rates of return vary across fields of university studies. The lowest returns are from humanities, while

Table 4: *Private and Total Rates of Return by Level of University Education, 1990 and 1995*

	Bachelor's[a]	Master's[b]	PhD[c]
		(percent)	
		1990	
Men			
Private	16	9	7
Total	8	4	1
Women			
Private	19	10	8
Total	8	4	−2
		1995	
Men			
Private	17	< 0*	3
Total	10	< 0*	−2
Women			
Private	20	5	12
Total	10	0	2

Note: Some rates of return could not be calculated because of technical issues, such as the A and B earnings profiles crossing each other twice, or because of high initial negative values. In such a case, we examined the profiles involved and indicate here by 0* if the rate of return was close to zero and < 0* if it was negative.

[a] Compared with completed secondary schooling.
[b] Compared with a bachelor's degree.
[c] Compared with a master's degree.

Source: Authors' calculations, using data in Tables A-3 through A-10.

the highest are obtained from fields that demand some mastery of science or mathematics, such as engineering or commerce.

This result may, in part, reflect the objective difficulty of mastering mathematics and science as opposed to less-demanding subjects. Or it may come from young peoples' belief that science is more difficult, a belief that leads some capable students to shy away from these fields. One cannot sort out these two influences, although we suspect that both are present.

Table 5: Private and Total Rates of Return to a Bachelor's Degree, by Field of Study, 1990 and 1995

	Education	Humanities	Social Sciences[a]	Commerce	Natural Sciences	Engineering	Health Sciences
				(percent)			
				1990			
Men							
Private	19	1	12	15	14	20	8
Total	6	< 0*	9	10	7	9	< 0*
Women							
Private	19	13	19	27	22	37	26
Total	11	7	11	16	9	11	3
				1995			
Men							
Private	14	−3	15	20	19	24	18
Total	11	< 0*	12	15	8	12	4
Women							
Private	19	13	18	25	22	25	28
Total	13	8	12	17	8	8	5

Notes: Calculations are made in comparison to completed secondary schooling. Only coefficients significantly different from zero ($t > 1.65$) are used.

Some rates of return could not be calculated because of technical issues, such as the A and B earnings profiles crossing each other twice, or because of high initial negative values. In such a case, we examined the profiles involved and indicate here by 0* if the rate of return was close to zero and < 0* if it was negative.

[a] Includes law degrees.

Source: Calculations by the authors using data in Tables A-3 through A-10.

Here, again, it may be useful to take into account the externalities associated with scientific research in allocating funds between fields of studies.

The Robustness of Results

Before concluding, we find it useful to consider the robustness of our findings. First, our rates of return are very stable over a five-year interval. The single exception is men's returns to education in the health field. This outlier may reflect the relatively small number of men in the field (nursing, speech therapy, and so on), which makes estimates of the earnings functions less stable.

Second, a comparison with the results of Stager (1998) for Ontario for 1995 (see Table A-11) is also reassuring. He finds rates of return of the same order as ours. Finally, Finnie obtains results (reported elsewhere in this volume), that agree with ours as to the relative value of various fields of study even though he was using a different database and methodology.

Conclusion

This paper presents a set of rates of return to schooling in Canada for 1990 and 1995. Our main conclusion is that investing in human capital yields high real rates of return, both privately and for society as a whole, with significant differences between fields of studies. This finding holds for results calculated with data associated with a recession year (1990) and an expansion year (1995). Given the size of these returns, increasing tuition fees significantly (doubling them, for example) would not make investing in a bachelor's degree unprofitable from a private perspective.

Appendix Tables

Table A-1: *Definitions of Level of Schooling and Field of Study, Earnings Regressions, 1990 and 1995*

Level of Schooling	1991–96 Census Data File Variables and Codes	
	(DGREE)	(HLOSP)
Bachelor's degree	6	11
Master's degree	9	13
PhD	10	14
Field of study	(DGMES)	
Education	1	
Humanities	2 or 3	
Social Sciences	4	
Commerce	1991: 5 or 6; 1996: 5–9	
Pure sciences	1991: 7 or 12; 1996: 10 or 18	
Engineering	1991: 8 or 9; 1996: 11–15	
Health sciences	1991: 10 or 11; 1996: 16 or 17	

Note: See the main text for the programs included in each field of study listed here.

Source: Authors, from microdata file codebooks, 1991 and 1996 censuses.

Table A-2: *Annual Cost Data Used, 1990 and 1995*

	Method of Calculation	1990	1995
		(current dollars)	

Private Costs

Tuition

University, all levels — Fees for university students were calculated as the unweighted means of fees of major universities in each region. Fees for undergraduate commerce, education, engineering, and science studies and for graduate (MSc, PhD) studies were taken directly from the source. Fees for humanities and social sciences were for arts degrees. Canadian fees were an unweighted mean of provincial fees for the appropriate field of study.

The source is Statistics Canada, cat. 81-219, table 1, 1990/91 and 1993/94, corrected by the Canadian consumer price index tuition fees subindex. In terms of line items (universities) of that table, Atlantic Canada corresponds to lines 1–3, 5, 11, 13–17, Quebec to lines 19–24, Ontario to lines 25–26 and 28–41, the Prairies to lines 43, 44, 46–48, and 53, and British Columbia to lines 54, 56, and 58 (1990 line numbers).

		1990	1995
Undergraduate			
All fields		1,687	2,633
Education		1,564	2,570
Humanities		1,554	2,500
Social sciences		1,554	2,500
Commerce		1,566	2,510
Pure sciences		1,561	2,544
Engineering		1,696	2,708
Health		2,317	3,099
Graduate, all fields		1,547	2,688

Other out of pocket

University, all levels — Porter and Jasmin 1987, p. 35, table 14, sum of columns 3 and 6. An unweighted sum of the amounts is used to compute the expenses for Canada as a whole. The data are converted to 1990 and 1995 dollars using the consumer price index. — 1,139   1,753

Table A-2 - continued

	Method of Calculation	1990	1995
		(current dollars)	
	Public Costs		
University	We use data on enrollments taken from Statistics Canada, 81-204, 1991 and 1996. 1991 data for bachelor's enrollments are from table 7, master's from table 9, and PhD from table 10. Part-time enrollment is converted to full time by multiplying it by one-third. Bachelor's enrollments in education, humanities, commerce, social sciences, and mathematical and natural sciences are obtained by summing lines 2, 3, 4, 5, and 29 minus 35, enrollments in engineering by summing lines 38 and 55, and enrollments in health by summing lines 48 and 35 from table 7. Master's enrollments in education, humanities, commerce, and social sciences are obtained by summing lines 2, 3, 4, 5, and 15 from table 9, while master's enrollments in mathematical and pure sciences, engineering, and health are obtained by subtracting the previous total from line 1 of that table. Similar calculations are made for 1996. Total costs were from Statistics Canada, cat. 81-229, tables 42 through 58, postsecondary – universities column.		
	Breakdowns by Program and Level		
Undergraduate (bachelor's)	Education, humanities, social sciences, commerce, mathematics (1: reference point); pure sciences (1.5); engineering (2); health (3.33; two-thirds of health degrees).	All: 17,797 Ref. point: 11,865	All: 17,386 Ref. point: 11,591
Graduate			
Master's	Education, humanities, social sciences, commerce (2); mathematics and pure sciences, engineering, health (3).	All: 29,663	All: 28,977
PhD	All disciplines (6).	71,190	69,545

Note: For both forgone earnings and out-of-pocket expenses, annual costs are added for the relevant number of years, without present value calculations: bachelor's degree, four years (after high school); master's degree, two years (after a bachelor's); health degree, six years (after high school), and PhD, four years (after a master's).

To calculate the public cost of a bachelor's or master's degree, one multiplies the reference point value by the appropriate factor (1 to 6). For example, the public cost of a bachelor's degree in engineering in 1995 was $11,591 × 2 = $23,182 × 4 years, which yields $92,728 (see Table A-10).

Table A-3: *Regression Results, by Level of Education, OLS, ln (Employment Income), 1990 (1991 Census)*

	Secondary School	Bachelor's Degree	Master's Degree	PhD
		Men		
Constant	6.7734*	7.2457*	6.5514*	6.4381*
	(154.46)	(105.62)	(40.02)	(19.89)
Age	0.1545*	0.1473*	0.1847*	0.1831*
	(67.69)	(44.98)	(25.32)	(14.09)
Age^2	−0.0017*	−0.0016*	−0.0020*	−0.0018*
	(−60.07)	(−41.74)	(−25.04)	(−14.32)
R^2	0.1588	0.1002	0.0949	0.1137
F	2,907.12	1,130.10	320.62	102.67
N	30,793	20,309	6,118	1,602
		Women		
Constant	7.3944*	8.0324*	7.0066*	5.3196*
	(143.17)	(88.44)	(27.97)	(6.53)
Age	0.0966*	0.0938*	0.1498*	0.2346*
	(36.51)	(20.43)	(13.01)	(6.80)
Age^2	−0.0011*	−0.0011*	−0.0017*	−0.0026*
	(−32.95)	(−19.19)	(−12.91)	(−7.21)
R^2	0.0452	0.0249	0.0473	0.1578
F	787.60	224.37	84.73	28.95
N	33,283	17,575	3,412	311

Note: An asterisk indicates that $|T| > 1.96$; T-statistics are in parentheses.

Source: Authors' calculations, based on individual microdata file, 1991 census.

Table A-4: Regression Results by Level of Education, OLS, ln (Employment Income), 1995 (1996 Census)

	Secondary School	Bachelor's Degree	Master's Degree	PhD
		Men		
Constant	6.1765*	6.7681*	6.2867*	6.3183*
	(120.16)	(86.08)	(34.98)	(17.97)
Age	0.1797*	0.1707*	0.1959*	0.1930*
	(67.95)	(45.51)	(24.66)	(13.59)
Age^2	−0.0019*	−0.0018*	−0.0021*	−0.0020*
	(−60.50)	(−42.94)	(−24.49)	(−14.25)
R^2	0.1670	0.0933	0.0858	0.1059
F	2,866.83	1,107.01	304.16	107.80
N	28,600	21,516	6,481	1,822
		Women		
Constant	6.4428*	7.2277*	6.2542*	5.9519*
	(106.58)	(78.39)	(24.84)	(7.70)
Age	0.1389*	0.1340*	0.1859*	0.2017*
	(46.03)	(28.44)	(16.09)	(6.07)
Age^2	−0.0015*	−0.0015*	−0.0021*	−0.0021*
	(−41.05)	(−25.91)	(−15.88)	(−6.16)
R^2	0.0807	0.0464	0.0572	0.0724
F	1,301.36	508.29	129.41	19.01
N	29,648	20,911	4,271	489

Note: An asterisk indicates that |T| > 1.96; T-statistics are in parentheses.

Source: Authors' calculations, based on individual microdata file, 1996 census.

Table A-5: *Regression Results, Bachelor's Level, by Field of Study, ln (Employment Income), 1990 (1991 Census)*

	Men	Women
Constant	7.1333*	7.8455*
	(73.93)	(72.04)
Age	0.1461*	0.0996*
	(39.80)	(20.37)
Age^2	0.0016*	−0.0011*
	(−43.05)	(−19.29)
Field of study[a]		
Arts, humanities	−0.6655*	−0.0305
	(−6.81)	(−0.34)
Social sciences	−0.4224*	−0.0402
	(−4.74)	(−0.44)
Commerce, management	0.0405	0.3605*
	(0.46)	(3.36)
Pure and biological sciences	0.0050	0.3633*
	(0.05)	(3.32)
Engineering, applied science and technology	0.1283	0.9904*
	(1.49)	(4.05)
Health sciences, techniques	−0.5742*	0.4580*
	(−3.87)	(4.29)
Field of study × age[a]		
Arts, humanities × age	0.0120*	−0.0042*
	(5.09)	(−1.88)
Social sciences × age	0.0149*	0.0013
	(6.86)	(0.52)
Commerce, management × age	0.0028	−0.0064*
	(1.30)	(−2.10)
Pure and biological sciences × age	0.0029	−0.0105*
	(1.24)	(−3.59)
Engineering, applied sciences and technology × age	0.0038	−0.0235*
	(1.84)	(−3.21)
Health sciences, techniques × age	0.0158*	−0.0087*
	(4.56)	(−3.17)
R^2	0.1284	0.0378
F	213.92	49.24
N	20,309	17,575

Note: An asterisk indicates that |T| > 1.96; T-statistics are in parentheses.

[a] Results are calculated with respect to the educational field (the omitted dichotomous variable in the regression).

Source: Authors' calculations, based on individual microdata file, 1991 census.

Table A-6: **Regression Results, Bachelor's Level, by Field of Study, ln (Employment Income), 1995 (1996 Census)**

	Men	Women
Constant	6.8369*	7.1369*
	(62.45)	(67.10)
Age	0.1661*	0.1354*
	(40.20)	(27.43)
Age^2	0.0018*	−0.0015*
	(−42.57)	(−25.32)
Field of study[a]		
Arts, humanities	−0.5084*	−0.0877
	(−4.72)	(−1.01)
Social sciences	−0.3292*	−0.0623
	(−3.36)	(−0.75)
Commerce, management	0.0140	0.3066*
	(−0.14)	(3.18)
Pure and biological sciences	0.2364*	0.2928*
	(2.27)	(2.78)
Engineering, applied science and technology	0.2547*	0.7955*
	(2.64)	(3.99)
Health sciences, techniques	−0.0078*	0.4273*
	(−0.04)	(4.12)
Field of study × age[a]		
Arts, humanities × age	0.0059*	−0.0030
	(2.31)	(−1.41)
Social sciences × age	0.0110*	0.0013
	(4.75)	(0.59)
Commerce, management × age	0.0047*	−0.0051
	(2.02)	(−1.94)
Pure and biological sciences × age	−0.0044	−0.0073*
	(−1.75)	(−2.69)
Engineering, applied sciences and technology × age	−0.0007	−0.0231*
	(−0.31)	(−4.02)
Health sciences, techniques × age	0.0036	−0.0058
	(0.86)	(−2.26)
R^2	0.1172	0.0599
F	203.81	95.07
N	21,516	20,911

Note: An asterisk indicates that |T| > 1.96; T-statistics are in parentheses.

[a] Results are calculated with respect to the educational field (the omitted dichotomous variable in the regression).

Source: Authors' calculations, based on individual microdata file, 1996 census.

Table A-7: Private and Public Costs for Various Levels of Education, 1990

	Direct Costs[a]	Forgone Earnings[b] Men	Forgone Earnings[b] Women	Total[c] Men	Total[c] Women
		(current dollars)			
		Private Costs			
Bachelor's degree	11,304	24,150	18,790	35,454	30,094
Master's degree	5,372	20,385	17,621	25,757	22,993
PhD	10,744	49,399	39,733	60,143	50,477
		Public Costs			
Bachelor's degree	71,188	24,916	18,790	96,104	89,978
Master's degree	59,326	22,878	19,413	82,204	78,739
PhD	284,760	56,576	44,456	341,336	329,216

[a] Total private or public costs found in Table 3 × the number of years of education necessary.

[b] Two-thirds (portion of the year spent studying) × the annual earnings that would have been gained if the person had worked instead.

[c] Direct costs + forgone earnings.

Source: Authors' calculations.

Table A-8: Private and Public Costs for Various Levels of Education, 1995

	Direct Costs[a]	Forgone Earnings[b] Men	Forgone Earnings[b] Women	Total[c] Men	Total[c] Women
		(current dollars)			
		Private Costs			
Bachelor's degree	17,544	20,735	14,242	38,279	31,786
Master's degree	8,882	19,578	16,243	28,460	25,125
PhD	17,764	47,687	36,893	65,451	54,657
		Public Costs			
Bachelor's degree	69,544	20,818	14,242	90,362	83,786
Master's degree	57,954	21,717	17,522	79,671	75,476
PhD	278,180	54,163	40,587	332,343	318,767

[a] Total private or public costs found in Table 3 × the number of years of education necessary.

[b] Two-thirds (portion of the year spent studying) × the annual earnings that would have been gained if the person had worked instead.

[c] Direct costs + forgone earnings.

Source: Authors' calculations.

Table A-9: Private and Public Costs, Bachelor's Degree, by Field of Study, Compared with Completed Secondary Education, 1990

	Direct Costs[a]	Forgone Earnings[b] Men	Forgone Earnings[b] Women	Total[c] Men	Total[c] Women
		(current dollars)			
		Private Costs			
Education	10,811	24,150	18,790	34,961	29,601
Humanities	10,772	24,150	18,790	34,922	29,562
Social sciences	10,772	24,150	18,790	34,922	29,562
Commerce	10,819	24,150	18,790	34,969	29,609
Pure sciences	10,801	24,150	18,790	34,951	29,591
Engineering	11,340	24,150	18,790	35,490	30,130
Health sciences	13,826	24,150	18,790	37,976	32,616
		Public Costs			
Education	47,460	24,216	18,790	71,676	66,250
Humanities	47,460	24,216	18,790	71,676	66,250
Social sciences	47,460	24,216	18,790	71,676	66,250
Commerce	47,460	24,216	18,790	71,676	66,250
Pure sciences	47,460	24,216	18,790	95,406	89,980
Engineering	94,920	24,216	18,790	119,136	113,710
Health sciences	237,300	24,216	18,790	261,516	256,090

[a] Total private or public costs found in Table 3 × the number of years of education necessary.

[b] Two-thirds (portion of the year spent studying) × the annual earnings that would have been gained if the person had worked instead.

[c] Direct costs + forgone earnings.

Source: Authors' calculations.

Table A-10: *Private and Public Costs, Bachelor's Degree, by Field of Study, Compared with Completed Secondary Education, Canada, 1995*

	Direct Costs[a]	Forgone Earnings[b] Men	Forgone Earnings[b] Women	Total[c] Men	Total[c] Women
		(current dollars)			
		Private Costs			
Education	17,295	20,735	14,242	38,030	31,537
Humanities	17,011	20,735	14,242	37,746	31,253
Social sciences	17,011	20,735	14,242	37,746	31,253
Commerce	17,054	20,735	14,242	37,789	31,296
Pure sciences	17,187	20,735	14,242	37,922	31,429
Engineering	17,844	20,735	14,242	38,579	32,086
Health sciences	19,410	20,735	14,242	40,145	33,652
		Public Costs			
Education	46,364	20,818	14,242	67,182	60,606
Humanities	46,364	20,818	14,242	67,182	60,606
Social sciences	46,364	20,818	14,242	67,182	60,606
Commerce	46,364	20,818	14,242	67,182	60,606
Pure sciences	69,546	20,818	14,242	90,364	83,788
Engineering	92,728	20,818	14,242	113,546	106,970
Health sciences	231,820	20,818	14,242	252,638	246,062

[a] Total private or public costs found in Table 3 × the number of years of education necessary.

[b] Two-thirds (portion of the year spent studying) × the annual earnings that would have been gained if the person had worked instead.

[c] Direct costs + forgone earnings.

Source: Authors' calculations.

Table A-11: *Private and Total Rates of Return, Bachelor's and First Professional Degree Programs, Ontario, 1995*

	Men Total	Men Private	Women Total	Women
	(percent)			
Humanities, fine arts	4.4	5.6	9.8	15.1
Social sciences[a]	9.4	11.4	11.3	17.5
Biological sciences[b]	5.0	7.1	8.5	16.1
Mathematics, physical sciences	11.3	15.6	13.2	22.2
Health professions[c]	9.8	14.5	12.4	23.9
Commerce	13.6	16.9	14.5	23.2
Engineering[d]	10.5	15.1	11.0	21.7
Law	13.0	14.6	13.6	17.7
Medicine[e]	13.9	20.2	11.6	20.6
All bachelor's degrees[f]	9.7	13.1	10.7	9.0

[a] Excludes commerce, social work, law.
[b] Includes agriculture.
[c] Includes nursing, pharmacy, rehabilitation medicine.
[d] Includes architecture.
[e] Includes dentistry, veterinary medicine, optometry.
[f] Includes LLB, BEd, BSW, and so on.
Source: Stager 1998, tables 1 and 2.

References

Bourdeau-Primeau, Sandrine. 1999. "Les taux de rendement privés et sociaux de l'éducation au Canada." Montreal: Université de Montréal.

Canadian Tax Foundation. 1990. *The National Finances*. Toronto: CTF.

―――. 1995. *The Finances of the Nation*. Toronto: CTF.

Constantatos, Christos, and Edwin G. West. 1991. "Measuring Returns from Education — Some Neglected Factors." *Canadian Public Policy* 17 (2): 127–138.

Demers, Marius. 1999. "La rentabilité du diplôme." *Bulletin Statistique de l'éducation* 8. Québec: Ministère de l'Éducation.

―――. 2000. "L'éducation..., oui c'est payant!" *Bulletin Statistique de l'éducation* 16. Québec: Ministère de l'Éducation.

Dickson, Vaughan, William Milne, and David Murrell. 1996. "Who Should Pay for University Education: Some Net Benefit Results by Funding Source for New Brunswick." *Canadian Public Policy* 22 (4): 315–329.

Martin, Fernand, and Marc Trudeau. 1998. "L'impact économique de la recherche universitaire." *Dossier de recherche* 2 (3). Ottawa: Association of Colleges and Universities of Canada.

Porter, Marion, and Gilles Jasmin. 1987. *Profile des étudiants du niveau postsecondaire au Canada*. Ottawa: Secrétariat d'État and Statistics Canada.

Statistics Canada. 81-204. *Universities, Enrolment and Degrees*, 1991 and 1996. Ottawa: Statistics Canada.

―――. 81-219. *Tuition Fees and Living Accommodation Costs at Canadian Universities*. 1990/91 and 1993/94. Ottawa: Statistics Canada.

―――. 81-229. *Education in Canada: A Statistical Review*, 1990/91 and 1995/96. Ottawa: Statistics Canada.

Stager, David. 1996. "Returns to Investment in Ontario University Education, 1960–1990, and Implications for Tuition Fee Policy." *Canadian Journal of Higher Education* 26 (2): 1–22.

―――. 1998. "Returns to Investment in University Education in Ontario, 1995." University of Toronto. Mimeographed.

Vaillancourt, François. 1995. "The Private and Total Returns to Education in Canada, 1986." *Canadian Journal of Economics* 28 (3): 532–554.

―――. 1997. "The Private and Total Returns to Education in Canada, 1990: A Note." Montreal: Université de Montréal. Mimeographed.

Returns to University Education in Canada Using New Estimates of Program Costs

*Kelly Ann Rathje and
J.C. Herbert Emery*

This study of the private and total rates of return to university education in Canada differs from others in the area in four ways. First, we use a novel method of calculating the operating costs of providing education by field of study, based on data from the actual budgets of a sample of Canadian universities (see Rathje 2000). The cost figures routinely used in studies of this type arbitrarily account for assumed differences in the intensity of resource use across programs; this method, however, yields direct estimates of the costs in question, and thus more accurately represents the social costs of education in the fields under consideration.

Second, we address the arguments that social investment in programs with low rates of return may still be warranted on the grounds that the returns to university education accrue not just to its recipients, but also to society at large. Specifically, we provide estimates of how large these external benefits of university education would have to be to justify current total expenditures on education in fields where the returns, when measured solely by the incomes of graduates, currently fail to meet a reasonable benchmark.

Third, in calculating private rates of return to university education, we use tuition fee data for 1998; most other existing studies

---

We thank David Laidler for comments.

are based on less recent figures. This use of more current data has a significant effect on our findings, since, by 1998, fees were on average significantly higher in Canada than they had been earlier in the decade.

Fourth and finally, we discuss the possibility of instituting differential fee levels for different disciplines, offering estimates of the amounts by which fees could be raised (or, in one case, lowered) in order to bring private rates of return down (or up) to the same reasonable benchmark used in analyzing externalities.

In this study, we use what has become standard methodology for measuring the total rates of return to education. We refer the reader to the work by Vaillancourt and Bourdeau-Primeau (in this volume) for a full discussion of the formula, assumptions, and other details of the relevant internal rate of return (IRR) calculations. As our work adopts the same approach as theirs in many essentials, the discussion below highlights only the key ways that our calculations of the returns to education differ from those of Vaillancourt and Bourdeau-Primeau.

Benefits of Total Education

As in other studies that examine the rates of return to higher education, we assume here that earnings reflect a worker's productivity, and measure the benefits of obtaining a given level of education both to society and to the individual, using the incremental increase before-tax and after-tax in earnings, respectively. Nonpecuniary benefits, such as the effects of advanced education in encouraging political involvement, informed decisionmaking, and the bettering of communities, are not included.

To estimate the benefits of university education, we use the following model:

$$\ln(\text{income}) = \beta_0 + \beta_1 \text{age} + \beta_2 \text{age}^2 + \beta_3 \text{bach} + \beta_4 \text{mast} + \beta_5 \text{phd} + \beta_6 \text{medical} + [\sum_{I=1} \beta_{7i} \text{degree}^* \text{field of study}] + \beta_8 D91 + \beta_9 D96 + \epsilon.$$

Using dummy variables, this model accounts for differences in income by level of study (bachelor's, master's, PhD, or medical degree), field of study (education, humanities, agriculture, commerce, fine arts, engineering, nursing, health, science, and social sciences), and year in which the income was received (1986, 1991, or 1996).[1] In contrast to Vaillancourt and Bourdeau-Primeau, we do not allow the slope of the age-income profile to vary by field of study, and we assume retirement at age 65. (This difference is one reason our rate-of-return estimates are somewhat lower than theirs.) Using coefficients estimated by the ordinary least squares method for the above log-earnings equation (see Appendix A), we constructed a lifetime earnings stream from age 18 to the assumed retirement age of 65 for each degree-program combination.

We pooled three cross sections of microdata from the censuses (3 percent sample) for 1986, 1991, and 1996 (Statistics Canada 1986; 1991; 1996). All earnings data are deflated into constant (1992) dollars. The data set is restricted to individuals ages 18 to 65 who had completed a university degree, who were paid employees, and who had worked for at least 26 weeks in the census year.[2] We excluded self-employed individuals due to the complexities of interpreting the reported their labor income.[3] Our earnings/income variable is thus based on employment income only, unlike that of Vaillancourt and Bourdeau-Primeau, who use the sum of employment income and self-employment income.[4]

---

1 For a list of variables, see the full regression results in Appendix A.

2 We excluded employed individuals who reported no income despite working more than half the year.

3 With self-employed individuals, reported income may not actually represent earned income due to "income hiding" — whereby some personal expenses are claimed as business expenses in order to reduce reported income for tax purposes. Self-employed individuals may also be able to "split" their incomes with a spouse or other family member who is a co-owner of the business. Finally, self-employment income may also accrue to nonhuman capital.

4 This difference is another factor — probably the main one — causing our rate-of-return estimates to be generally lower than theirs. They acknowledge that the inclusion of self-employment income may introduce an upward bias in the measured rates of return to education, since some portion of self-employment income may be accruing to nonhuman capital. We, in turn, believe that our procedure may result in some downward bias. Our study and theirs together, therefore, define a plausible range within which these rates of return probably actually fall.

Costs

Our calculations include costs for both the individual and society: forgone earnings during the period of educational investment, university operating costs for teaching, and books and supplies; for the student's individual cost, tuition fees are also included. All costs are expressed in constant (1992) dollars.

Forgone Earnings

Forgone earnings are a cost of educational attainment because they represent the opportunity cost of obtaining higher education. Following Dodge and Stager (1972); Vaillancourt (1986; 1995); and Allen (1998), we assume the earnings forgone to obtain a bachelor's degree to be 67 percent of a high school graduate's estimated earnings at age 18 for those ages 18 to 21. The figure of 67 percent follows from the assumption that students work from May through August, and so receive income for one-third of the year. The earnings forgone to obtain a master's degree are assumed to be 50 percent of the bachelor's degree earnings at age 22 for those ages 22 and 23, and the forgone earnings to obtain a PhD are assumed to be 50 percent of the master's degree earnings at age 24 for those ages 24 to 27. We decreased the percentage of forgone earnings included for the graduate degrees to account for fact that graduate students provide a labor supply to universities as teaching and research assistants, so their income is not restricted to the summer months.

Operating Expenses

The cost calculations for the breakdown of university degrees by field of study are calculated using fact books from seven Canadian universities.[5] Rathje (2000) breaks the costs down into two components: a common cost for all faculties in the university and a faculty-

---

5 The seven universities are Victoria, Saskatchewan, Manitoba, Western Ontario, Memorial University of Newfoundland, Calgary, and Alberta. See Rathje (2000) for the detailed university cost calculations.

specific cost. The program-specific cost is the sum of these two components; the program cost used in the IRR calculations is the mean value for a given field of study's costs across the seven institutions. Details of the construction of these costs appear in Appendix B.

Books and Supplies

These costs come from the University of Calgary calendar for the 1992-93 academic year, and are broken down by program. No supply costs were reported for agriculture or health; we assumed that they were equivalent to those for science and nursing, respectively. The same costs were used for both society and the individual.

Total Rates of Return to University Education

Our calculated total rates of return by level and field of university program are presented in Table 1.

Our results show, as do those of other studies, that the total rates of return to university education are higher for females than for males, and that they decline by the level of study. The highest rates of return are in the technical/scientific and professional programs at the bachelor's level.

We found rates of return to be notably lower than those calculated by Allen (1999) and Vaillancourt and Bourdeau-Primeau (in this volume). The difference is not a result of differences in program costs; in fact, the costs we use are lower than those used by Vaillancourt and Bourdeau-Primeau. Rather, their higher calculated total rates of return result from their inclusion of self-employment income in the earnings measure used to construct the age-earnings profile, their prediction of both higher peak earnings for all programs and a larger annual rate of increase in the age-earnings profile.

We found that, at the bachelor's degree level, relative to a benchmark rate of return of 4.25 percent, investment in the education of males within humanities, fine arts, and nursing cannot be

Table 1: *Total Rates of Return to University Education*

	Bachelor's Degree		Master's Degree		PhD	
	Males	Females	Males	Females	Males	Females
			(percent)			
Education	4.24	9.48	7.19	10.45	–0.12	–8.23
Humanities	2.35	7.39	—	2.92	2.45	0.76
Agriculture	4.34	6.37	—	–0.69	2.94	0.13
Commerce	8.53	9.23	10.53	12.07	–2.84	—
Fine arts	–2.51	4.65	3.18	–2.65	1.86	2.97
Engineering	10.68	10.80	–6.50	—	–0.36	–0.43
Nursing	1.02	10.91	4.25	2.48	7.31	–12.47
Health	7.09	10.78	8.22	1.88	–4.73	–4.32
Science	8.61	10.42	—	0.90	–2.04	–2.46
Social sciences	7.08	7.98	2.49	6.12	0.42	–1.68
Medicine	0.33					–3.41

Note: (—) indicates that the resulting rate of return was so negative as to be undefined.
Source: Authors' calculations.

justified on the basis of pecuniary benefits alone.[6] In contrast, for females, all fields surpass a 4.25 percent annual real rate of return. At the master's and PhD levels, rates of return for society are lower, and in many cases negative. Graduate education cannot therefore be justified on the basis of monetary returns alone for either sex. This result reflects the fact that both the opportunity costs and the resource costs are high for a graduate education. Interestingly, for males, three of the four highest returns at the PhD level come from liberal arts programs: education, humanities, and social sciences.

---

6 The choice of benchmark rate for evaluating the investment in university education is somewhat arbitrary. Vaillancourt and Henriques (1986) use 10 percent since it is often the choice of government agencies. Constantos and West (1991) use 6.5 percent since they feel it reflects the real rate of return to physical capital. Allen (1998) uses a 5 percent benchmark. Following Rathje (2000), we use 4.25 percent that reflects the historical range for the real rate of return to capital in Canada between 1964 and 1998.

At this level, science and technical programs have lower rates of return (with the exception of engineering). This is because the forgone earnings costs for these technical programs are higher than those of the liberal arts programs at the same level.

Medical degrees, which one would expect to have high rates of return given the incomes of the medical profession, actually yield low rates of return for both males and females. This surprising result may be, in part, because our study omits self-employed individuals. Many medical professionals, such as dentists, physicians, and veterinarians, own their own practices, and these self-employed individuals may, on average, earn more than their colleagues who are employees. Another factor contributing to the low rates of return in this area is the high operating cost of the programs; Rathje (2000) estimates the cost of a medical education at over $453,000 for four years of study. Finally, given the ability of Canada's public single-payer health insurance systems to control the incomes of physicians and other health care professionals, income-based IRRs probably understate the true total rate of return to a medical education.

Externalities

Some of the programs considered do not, based on monetary benefits alone, warrant the level of investment that society is currently providing. This is particularly true of master's and PhD programs. It is often argued, however, that the rate of return to a university education is underestimated because the calculation omits intangible benefits, or spillover effects.

To address this question sensibly, we need to distinguish between two types of nonpecuniary benefits. There are nonpecuniary benefits of working in some fields that accrue to the workers themselves, such as flexible working conditions or dental plans. These benefits represent an omitted component of the benefits of education that would increase the calculated total rates of return to education were they accounted for, but they are not actual external benefits (that is, benefits accruing to a third party) of advanced education that can be used to justify subsidizing it.

The nonpecuniary benefits we are interested in quantifying are those that are generated by educational investment in an individual, but that accrue to some individual other than the university graduate or indeed to society at large.[7] To that end, and assuming that private, nonpecuniary benefits omitted from the rate-of-return calculations are negligible, we can quantify an upper boundary for the value of the external benefits of a university education as the extra income needed each year to yield a 4.25 percent rate of return. The formula we use is

$$0 = \frac{(B_t + E_t) - C_t}{(1 + r)^t},$$

where r is 4.25 percent. B_t and C_t still represent the benefits (income) and costs for each year (t). E_t represents the additional earnings that would be needed in each year (t) to ensure that $r = 4.25$ percent.

We estimated the amount of external benefits (as a percentage of income) for the degree-program combinations from Table 1 that did not meet a 4.25 percent rate of return. We summarize the percentage of extra income that would be needed each year to ensure a 4.25 percent rate of return in Table 2.

As the table shows, the percentage of income each year that would be needed to obtain a 4.25 percent rate of return varies greatly depending on the degree and program. In most cases, they seem to us reasonable enough, remembering that these amounts, particularly at the graduate level of study, are anything but negligible. Additional external benefits to society may also be accruing in the form of spillover effects such as increased political involvement. However, the taxpaying public may need to be convinced that investing in these programs is worthwhile.

---

[7] If students could choose to pursue studies in whatever program they desired, we would expect that, in equilibrium, the total private rates of return to students would be equalized across all fields. In other words, a lower monetary rate of return for social sciences graduates than for commerce graduates would be compensated for with higher levels of nonwage benefits, such as greater job satisfaction for the social sciences graduate. This theoretical situation does not describe access to all university programs, however. The disciplines with high private monetary rates of return, such as commerce, law, medicine, and engineering, limit their enrollments. The likely outcome in a world where demand for space in these programs exceeds supply is an artificially high rate of return.

Table 2: *Percentage of Annual Income Attributable to External Benefits*

	Bachelor's Degree		Master's Degree		PhD	
	Males	Females	Males	Females	Males	Females
			(percent)			
Education	0.03	—	—	—	12.05	24.56
Humanities	5.54	—	14.64	2.56	7.29	14.04
Agriculture	—	—	14.99	9.05	4.87	16.42
Commerce	—	—	—	—	16.82	32.93
Fine arts	16.01	—	2.25	12.52	10.03	6.17
Engineering	—	—	9.23	17.13	12.88	15.96
Nursing	9.00	—	—	3.25	—	30.75
Health	—	—	—	4.31	20.30	23.92
Science	—	—	11.36	5.72	19.32	22.93
Social sciences	—	—	2.91	—	11.79	9.25
Medicine	25.83					53.04

Note: (—) indicates that the program met the assumed "risk-free" investment benchmark of 4.25 percent.
Source: Authors' calculations.

Private Rates of Return

To calculate private rates of return, we followed the same method used to calculate rates of return for individuals. After-tax income was used to estimate the private monetary benefits of university education, since it is after-tax income that really represents the increased disposable income enjoyed by the individual.[8] (From a

---

[8] Rathje (2000) uses tax rates from 1992, a basic personal credit of $6,456, and a maximum unemployment insurance and Canada Pension Plan contribution of $1,803. There is also a federal surtax of 4.5 percent of the basic federal tax, plus another 5 percent over $12,500. Each province has an individual provincial surtax; this situation poses a problem for trying to estimate taxes for Canada as a whole. Therefore, a population-weighted average of the provincial surtaxes for 1997 was calculated and used for estimating tax payable. The...

social perspective, taxation has the effect of reallocating the benefits of education between the individual with the human capital and the rest of society.)

We also use tuition fees[9] (rather than total operating costs) in the private rate of return calculations. Since the fees that students pay represent only a fraction of total university operating costs, the cost to the individual is lower than for society. We use tuition fees for 1998 which are much higher levels than those of the early 1990s used in many other studies. Our results for the private rates of return are summarized in Table 3.

Vaillancourt and Bourdeau-Primeau's estimates of the private rates of return are generally higher than ours. Presumably, this is due to the higher private costs in our calculations (our estimations of tuition fees and forgone earnings are higher) and the lower levels and rates of increase in after-tax incomes underlying our results. Indeed, quite unlike those of Vaillancourt and Bourdeau-Primeau, our results indicate that, at the bachelor's level, the private rates of return to undergraduate education are lower than the social rates of return. At the master's and PhD levels, the opposite is true: the returns to the individual are higher than to society. This is because, although the total resource costs of education increase dramatically from the bachelor's to the graduate level, the tuition fees paid by graduate students do not reflect this increase. Thus, the gain in income to graduate study is not particularly large relative to the resource cost of the program, but it is large relative to the student's tuition costs.

Note 8 - cont'd.

...number of observations in the data set from each province, as a percentage of the total number of observations, was used to calculate a weighted average tax rate: 54.32 percent. Rathje ignores deductions for items such as charitable donations, child care, and registered retirement savings plans, so the level of after-tax income may be underestimated.

9 The annual tuition costs are for the 1998-99 academic year. The information on tuition and fees came from the websites of the universities used: www.uvic.ca; www.ucalgary.ca; www.ualberta.ca; www.usask.ca; www.umanitoba.ca; www.uwo.ca; and www.mun.ca. In calculating the IRR, the fees were converted to constant 1992 dollars.

Table 3: *Private Rates of Return to University Education*

	Bachelor's Degree		Master's Degree		PhD	
	Males	Females	Males	Females	Males	Females
	(percent)					
Education	3.40	8.95	9.24	12.99	0.75	−7.51
Humanities	1.75	7.31	—	5.22	6.13	3.68
Agriculture	3.90	6.58	—	1.52	5.59	2.37
Commerce	7.40	8.60	11.88	14.83	−2.46	—
Fine arts	−2.91	4.94	6.55	−0.30	5.53	7.80
Engineering	9.62	10.35	−6.19	—	0.32	1.38
Nursing	0.46	10.28	7.05	4.26	10.35	−11.91
Health	6.39	10.51	11.00	3.67	−4.11	−2.95
Science	7.89	10.25	—	2.43	−0.29	−0.65
Social sciences	6.18	7.63	4.07	9.36	1.74	0.51
Medicine	5.39					1.26

Note: (—) indicates that the resulting rate of return was undefined.
Source: Authors' calculations.

As shown in Table 3, females experience higher rates of return than males from all programs at the bachelor's level, and from most programs at the master's level. At the PhD level, males experience a higher rate of return than females. These differences in rates of return may help to explain some features of university enrollment and participation. In particular, the high private rates of return at the undergraduate level of study for females combined with the lower — in some programs, marginal — rates of return for males may explain why university enrollment has grown faster among women than men, to the point that there are now more female university students than male university students in Canada. Similarly, the fact that many PhD programs are dominated by male students may be a result of the fact that a PhD is an unprofitable investment for females.

Implications for Tuition Policy

In the current climate of funding cutbacks to education, a "user-pay" argument has emerged. Universities want to increase tuition fees to try to recover revenue lost through cutbacks to government funding. Davenport addresses such a user-pay approach in recommending ways for Ontario universities to restructure, while still maintaining the goals of quality education, accessibility, and affordability to all. He comments that "the universities have the option of requiring students in faculties with relatively high costs and/or relatively high earnings expectations to pay a larger share of the costs of their programs" (1996, 30). Implementing this type of system would allow high-cost, high-income programs to pay more of their share of the cost of the education.

Table 4 shows the level at which tuition fees for bachelor's degree programs could be set each year (based on a four-year program) while still allowing a 4.25 percent private rate of return.

As the table shows, only fine arts programs would require a subsidy. All the other programs could endure an increase in tuition and still be worthwhile investments — that is, they could offer students, on average, at least a 4.25 percent private rate of return.

These results suggest that Davenport's proposal for differential tuition fees is workable. Tuition fees could be linked to both the cost of the program and expected earnings after graduation. Under differential tuition fees, programs such as engineering, where the cost per student is high and graduates earn high average incomes, would have higher fees than a program such as humanities, in which both the costs and expected average incomes are lower. As Davenport states, the result is that students with higher costs and higher expected average earnings would be paying an average share of the program costs. Lowering fees for programs with lower teaching costs and lower average potential future income would lead to a more uniform return over degree programs.

Conclusions

The results of this study are somewhat different from previous findings: we found generally lower returns to university educa-

Table 4: *Tuition Levels Needed to Render a 4.25 Percent Private Rate of Return (Bachelor's Programs)*

	Average of Male and Female Private Rate of Return	Tuition Currently Charged	Tuition Needed to Result in a 4.25% Private Rate of Return	Percentage Change
	(%)	(1992 $)	($)	(%)
Education	6.18	3,332	11,073	232.31
Humanities	4.53	3,201	5,085	58.86
Agriculture	5.24	3,138	6,625	111.12
Commerce	8.00	3,873	19,050	391.87
Fine arts	1.02	3,282	–3,320	–201.16
Engineering	9.99	3,382	27,900	724.96
Nursing	5.36	3,278	10,340	215.44
Health	8.45	3,293	20,200	513.42
Science	9.07	3,221	22,700	604.75
Social sciences	6.91	3,207	13,100	308.48

Source: Authors' calculations.

tion. We also offer a clearer breakdown of how expenses per student vary from undergraduate to graduate degrees. In most cases, our results suggest that undergraduate education is a worthwhile investment for both society and the individual acquiring the education. They also imply that, if tuition fees continue to rise, they should rise differentially according to program rates of return rather than uniformly across all programs as they have in the past.

Within Canada, proposals for educational reform continue to rely primarily on the tax system for funding (see, for example, Donnelly, Welch, and Young 1999). Thus, it is interesting to note how government policy toward advanced education in Canada reflects the levels of social rates of return that we calculate. Governments have responded to taxpayer demands for the maintenance (if not expansion) of access to undergraduate university education. Our estimates suggest that resources for undergraduate teaching are the easiest to justify, since undergraduate education generates the largest and most concrete social returns of all of the levels of university education. Universities have had to work much harder to convince governments that resources for research and graduate student training is worthwhile. Our estimates suggest that the reason for this may be that, although the benefits to society from such spending may exist, they are not as obvious to the public as monetary returns are. Where the federal government has increased resources for graduate students for research and development activities through the creation of the Canada Foundation for Innovation, it has targeted these resources in the areas of health, the environment, and science and engineering — fields of study where the monetary returns are clear.

Appendix A:
Regression Results for Canadian University Graduates

Table A-1: Regression Results for Canadian Male University Graduates

Variable	Coefficient	T-statistic	Standard Error
constant	7.7571*	348.195	0.0223
age	0.1218*	104.208	0.0012
age2	−0.0012*	−84.994	0.0000
bach	0.2759*	35.163	0.0078
mast	0.3567*	25.179	0.0142
phd	0.4846*	20.167	0.0240
medical	0.6092*	32.606	0.0187
ba*educ	−0.0991*	−8.510	0.0117
ba*humm	−0.1493*	−11.399	0.0131
ba*agri	−0.0857*	−4.909	0.0175
ba*mngt	0.0614*	5.958	0.0103
ba*art	−0.2352*	−7.347	0.0320
ba*engg	0.1568*	14.421	0.0102
ba*nurse	−0.1795*	−2.813	0.0638
ba*health	0.0102	0.378	0.0270
ba*science	0.0710*	5.974	0.0119
D91	−0.0528*	−11.731	0.0045
D96	−0.1305*	−28.467	0.0046
ma*educ	−0.0220	−1.169	0.0188
ma*humm	−0.2557*	−11.899	0.0215
ma*agri	−0.1899*	−5.993	0.0317
ma*mgnt	0.2050*	11.102	0.0185
ma*art	−0.2010*	−3.599	0.0558
ma*egg	0.0831*	4.257	0.0195
ma*nurse	−0.1397	−0.622	0.2245
ma*health	0.1246*	3.075	0.0405
ma*science	−0.0152	−0.642	0.0236
phd*educ	−0.0449	−0.954	0.0471
phd*humm	−0.1501*	−3.940	0.0381
phd*agri	−0.0969*	−2.528	0.0383
phd*mngt	0.1331*	2.176	0.0612
phd*art	−0.1065	−0.911	0.1169
phd*engg	0.0575	1.574	0.0366
phd*nurse	0.1284	0.404	0.3178
phd*health	0.0335	0.713	0.0470
phd*science	−0.0583**	−1.850	0.0315

Note: F–statistic = 1307.76; R^2 = 0.3074; n = 108,525.

* Statistically significant at the 5 percent level.

** Statistically significant at the 10 percent level.

Table A-2: *Regression Results for Canadian Female University Graduates*

Variable	Coefficient	T-statistic	Standard Error
constant	8.0273*	285.222	0.0281
age	0.0940*	61.635	0.0015
age2	−0.0010*	−51.667	0.0000
bach	0.3876*	40.959	0.0095
mast	0.5676*	28.089	0.0202
phd	0.7637*	15.370	0.0497
medical	0.6617*	19.537	0.0339
ba*educ	0.0675*	5.671	0.0119
ba*humm	−0.0168	−1.144	0.0147
ba*agri	−0.0523*	−2.547	0.0205
ba*mngt	0.0620*	4.365	0.0142
ba*art	−0.1173*	−4.211	0.0278
ba*engg	0.1413*	4.870	0.0290
ba*nurse	0.1339*	7.111	0.1339
ba*health	0.1455*	6.515	0.0223
ba*science	0.1270*	6.638	0.0191
D91	−0.0320*	−5.390	0.0059
D96	−0.0707*	−11.730	0.0060
ma*educ	0.1401*	5.338	0.0262
ma*humm	−0.0879*	−2.959	0.0297
ma*agri	−0.1734*	−3.579	0.0485
ma*mngt	0.1836*	5.598	0.0328
ma*art	−0.2568*	−3.652	0.0703
ma*engg	−0.0787	−1.446	0.0544
ma*nurse	0.0509	0.937	0.0544
ma*health	0.0539	1.236	0.0436
ma*science	0.0182	0.389	0.0469
phd*educ	−0.0401	−0.417	0.0963
phd*humm	−0.0909	−1.168	0.0778
phd*agri	−0.2138*	−2.531	0.0845
phd*mgnt	−0.0542	−0.260	0.2082
phd*art	−0.1254	−0.637	0.1970
phd*engg	−0.1406	−0.954	0.1473
phd*nurse	−0.1413	−0.423	0.3339
phd*health	−0.0882	−1.008	0.0875
phd*science	−0.0829	−0.812	0.1022

Note: F–statistic = 613.18; R^2 = 0.2275; n = 76.888.
* Statistically significant at the 5 percent level.

Appendix B: Costs

All costs are in 1992 dollars. For each university, Rathje (2000) obtains the total operating costs, faculty operating costs, and enrollment figures. She subtracts faculty expenses and graduate studies expenses from the total operating cost of the university, then, following Allen's (1998) procedure, multiplies the remaining figure by 67 percent, as this amount is attributable to actual "teaching" costs of the university. The remaining 33 percent of costs are attributed to costs for research and community service; under the user-pay theory (that students should pay for costs of their education), these costs are not attributable to the student, and should be deducted from the total costs of education.[10] The resulting teaching cost is divided by the full-time equivalent enrollment (FTE)[11] of the university to come up with an operating cost per FTE student. Similarly, the graduate studies expense, which is assumed to be mostly the administrative cost of operating the graduate program, is taken in its entirety. This expense is then divided by the FTE enrollment of graduate students to come up with a cost per FTE for graduate programs only. The FTE operating costs for both the total expenses and

---

10 It may be useful to note here that the assumption that all programs have the same average percentage of research and capital costs (33 percent) means that the capital costs may be overstated in some programs and understated in others. For example, the capital costs of an engineering or science program, which requires labs and research facilities, may be higher than 33 percent of the total operating costs, while programs such as humanities or fine arts may have less than 33 percent of total costs attributable to capital. The over- or underestimation of research and capital costs will bias the resulting rates of return and the net present values downward (or upward). Similarly, research capital subsidizes operating costs, so science and technical programs, which have larger amounts of research capital, have higher subsidized operating costs than the less technical programs, resulting in rates of return that may be biased upward.

11 FTE = number of full-time enrolled students + (0.25 × number of part-time undergraduate students) + (0.33 × number of part-time graduate students). For example, a full-time undergraduate student would represent 1 FTE student. A part-time graduate student would represent 0.33 FTE student. This calculation is based on the assumption that part-time students do not use as much of a university's facilities as full-time students.

the graduate expenses for each of the seven universities considered is averaged to estimate an average operating cost for Canada.

The faculty-specific costs are calculated in a similar fashion. We assume 67 percent of the faculty expense to be teaching costs only; this amount is taken and divided by that faculty's weighted full-time equivalent (WFTE) number of students to come up with a cost per WFTE at the bachelor's level.[12] Since the weighting system assumes that master's and PhD degrees are four and six times more expensive, respectively, than a bachelor's degree (Allen 1998), the cost per WFTE is multiplied by four or six to calculate the cost per year of each master's or PhD student. Again, the WFTE operating costs for each program considered for each of the seven universities is averaged to estimate an average program cost for Canada.

As indicated in the main text, the operating expenses payable by the individual are not the same as those payable by society outlined above. The private operating expenses are represented by the tuition fees, which are only a fraction of total university operating costs. The annual tuition costs used here are for the 1998-99 academic year; for the purposes of the IRR calculations, they were converted to 1992 dollars.

The costs used in the rate of return calculations are shown in Tables B-1 through B-6.

---

12 WFTE = (number of full-time bachelor's students) + (0.25 × number of part-time bachelor's students) + (4 × [number of full-time master's students + 0.33 × number of part-time master's students]) + (6 × [number of full-time PhD students + 0.33 × number of part-time PhD students]). For example, an individual who is a full-time undergraduate student would represent 1 WFTE student. A part-time graduate student would represent 1.32 (= 4 × 0.33) WFTE student; a part-time PhD student would represent 2 (= 6 × 0.33) WFTE student. This is based on the assumption that part-time students would not be using as many of the facilities or as much of a professor's time as a full-time student.

Table B-1: Social Costs for a Bachelor's Degree

	Forgone Earnings, Males	Forgone Earnings, Females	Books and Supplies	Operating Costs	Total Cost of Education, Males	Total Cost of Education, Females
	Annual Costs					
	(dollars)					
Education	7,776	7,197	758	7,700	64,936	62,620
Humanities	7,776	7,197	643	8,579	67,992	65,676
Agriculture	7,776	7,197	643	9,427	71,384	69,068
Commerce	7,776	7,197	758	8,094	66,512	64,196
Fine arts	7,776	7,197	1,009	9,986	75,084	72,768
Engineering	7,776	7,197	859	8,326	67,844	65,528
Nursing	7,776	7,197	792	8,915	69,932	67,616
Health	7,776	7,197	792	8,714	69,128	66,812
Science	7,776	7,197	643	8,775	68,776	66,460
Social sciences	7,776	7,197	734	7,756	65,064	62,748

Source: Rathje 2000.

Table B-2: Social Costs for a Master's Degree

	Forgone Earnings, Males	Forgone Earnings, Females	Books and Supplies	Operating Costs	Total Cost of Education, Males	Total Cost of Education, Females
	Annual Costs					
	(dollars)					
Education	9,291	10,534	758	16,334	52,766	55,252
Humanities	8,836	9,682	643	19,853	58,664	60,356
Agriculture	9,416	9,344	643	23,224	66,566	66,422
Commerce	10,909	10,476	758	17,914	59,162	58,296
Fine arts	8,109	8,756	1,009	25,481	69,198	70,492
Engineering	12,000	11,340	859	18,839	63,396	62,076
Nursing	8,573	11,256	792	21,194	61,118	66,484
Health	10,364	11,388	792	22,156	66,624	68,672
Science	11,014	11,180	643	20,634	64,582	64,914
Social sciences	10,259	9,846	734	16,561	55,108	54,282

Source: Rathje 2000.

Table B-3: Social Costs for PhD and Medical Degrees

	Forgone Earnings, Males	Forgone Earnings, Females	Books and Supplies	Operating Costs	Total Cost of Education, Males	Total Cost of Education, Females
	(dollars)					
Education	12,385	14,905	758	21,217	137,440	147,520
Humanities	9,804	11,866	643	26,495	147,768	156,016
Agriculture	10,471	10,893	643	31,582	170,784	172,472
Commerce	15,540	15,567	758	23,587	159,540	159,648
Fine arts	10,355	10,022	1,009	34,937	185,204	183,872
Engineering	13,758	11,975	859	24,975	158,368	151,236
Nursing	11,010	13,633	792	28,507	161,236	171,728
Health	14,341	13,674	792	27,304	169,748	167,080
Science	12,470	13,194	643	27,667	163,120	166,016
Social sciences	12,661	12,956	734	21,558	139,812	140,992
Medicine	11,014	11,180	1,461	100,828	453,212	453,876

Source: Rathje 2000.

Table B-4: Private Costs for a Bachelor's Degree

	Forgone Earnings, Males	Forgone Earnings, Females	Books and Supplies	Tuition Fees, Each Year	Total Cost of Education, Males	Total Cost of Education, Females
	(dollars)					
Education	6,857	6,513	758	3,332	43,788	42,412
Humanities	6,857	6,513	643	3,201	42,804	41,428
Agriculture	6,857	6,513	643	3,138	42,552	41,176
Commerce	6,857	6,513	758	3,873	45,952	44,576
Fine arts	6,857	6,513	1,009	3,282	44,592	43,216
Engineering	6,857	6,513	859	3,382	44,392	43,016
Nursing	6,857	6,513	792	3,278	43,708	42,332
Health	6,857	6,513	792	3,293	43,768	42,392
Science	6,857	6,513	643	3,221	42,884	41,508
Social sciences	6,857	6,513	734	3,207	43,192	41,816

Source: Rathje 2000.

Table B-5: Private Costs for a Master's Degree

	Annual Costs						
	Forgone Earnings, Males	Forgone Earnings, Females	Books and Supplies	Tuition Fees, 1st Year	Tuition Fees, 2nd Year	Total Cost of Education, Males	Total Cost of Education, Females
	(dollars)						
Education	6,782	7,690	758	3,590	1,093	19,763	21,579
Humanities	6,451	7,068	643	3,590	1,093	18,871	20,105
Agriculture	6,874	6,821	643	3,836	923	19,793	19,687
Commerce	7,964	7,674	758	4,531	1,745	23,720	23,140
Fine arts	5,960	6,392	1,009	3,590	1,093	18,621	19,485
Engineering	8,760	8,278	859	3,590	1,093	23,921	22,957
Nursing	6,259	8,217	792	3,590	1,093	18,785	22,701
Health	7,566	8,314	792	3,564	1,067	21,347	22,843
Science	8,040	8,161	643	3,590	1,093	22,049	22,291
Social sciences	7,489	7,188	734	3,590	1,093	21,129	20,527

Source: Rathje 2000.

Table B-6: Private Costs for PhD and Medical Degrees

	Annual Costs							Total Cost of Education, Males	Total Cost of Education, Females
	Forgone Earnings, Males	Forgone Earnings, Females	Books and Supplies	Tuition Fees, 1st Year	Tuition Fees, 2nd Year	Tuition Fees, 3rd Year	Tuition Fees, 4th Year		
					(dollars)				
Education	9,041	10,849	758	3,533	1,021	948	949	45,647	52,879
Humanities	7,157	8,663	643	3,533	1,021	948	948	37,650	43,674
Agriculture	7,644	7,952	643	3,849	1,021	948	948	39,914	41,146
Commerce	11,132	11,143	758	3,532	1,019	947	947	54,005	54,049
Fine arts	7,559	7,316	1,009	3,533	1,021	948	948	40,722	39,750
Engineering	10,044	8,742	859	3,533	1,021	948	948	50,062	44,854
Nursing	8,037	9,952	792	3,533	1,021	948	948	41,766	49,426
Health	10,469	9,982	792	3,533	1,021	948	948	51,494	49,546
Science	9,103	9,632	643	3,533	1,021	948	948	45,434	47,550
Social sciences	9,242	9,458	734	3,533	1,021	948	948	46,354	47,218
Medicine	8,040	8,161	1,461	6,334	5,685	4,347	4,176	58,546	59,030

Source: Rathje 2000.

References

Allen, Robert C. 1998. "The Employability of University Graduates in the Humanities, Social Sciences, and Education: Recent Statistical Evidence." University of British Columbia. Mimeographed.

———. 1999. "Education and Technological Revolutions: The Role of Social Sciences and Humanities in the Knowledge Based Economy." Social Sciences and Humanities Research Council. Mimeographed. Available at Internet website: www.sshrc.ca.

Constantos, Christos, and Edwin G. West. 1991. "Measuring Returns from Education: Some Neglected Factors." *Canadian Public Policy* 17 (2) 127–138.

Davenport, Paul. 1996. "Deregulation and Restructuring in Ontario's University System." *Canadian Business Economics* 4 (July–September): 27–36.

Dodge, David A., and David A.A. Stager. 1972. "Economic Returns to Graduate Study in Science, Engineering and Business." *Canadian Journal of Economics* 5: 182–198.

Donnelly, Maureen, Robert Welch, and Allister Young. 1999. "Registered Education Savings Plan: A Tax Incentive Response to Higher Education Access." *Canadian Tax Journal* 47 (1): 81–109.

Rathje, Kelly Ann. 2000. "Rates of Return to Advanced Education in Alberta and Canada." Calgary: University of Calgary Master's thesis. Unpublished.

Statistics Canada. 1986. *Census Public Use Microdata File on Individuals*. Ottawa.

———. 1991. *Census Public Use Microdata File on Individuals*. Ottawa.

———. 1996. *Census Public Use Microdata File on Individuals*. Ottawa.

University of Calgary. 1996. Office of Institutional Analysis. *The University of Calgary Fact Book 1995-96*. Calgary.

———. 1997. Office of Institutional Analysis. *The University of Calgary Fact Book 1996-97*. Calgary.

University of Manitoba. 1997. Office of Institutional Analysis. 1997. *IS Book: Institutional Statistics*, 23rd ed., *1996-1997*. Winnipeg.

University of Saskatchewan. 1996. University Studies Group. *University of Saskatchewan Statistics*, vol. 22. Regina.

Vaillancourt, François. 1995. "The Private and Total Returns to Education in Canada, 1985." *Canadian Journal of Economics* 28 (3): 532–554.

———, and Irene Henriques. 1986. "The Returns to University Schooling in Canada." *Canadian Public Policy* 12 (3): 449–458.

Comments on
Chant and Gibson, Finnie,
Vaillancourt and Bourdeau-Primeau,
and Rathje and Emery

Jeffrey Smith

I have the happy task of commenting on four fine bits of empirical economics related to higher education in Canada. My discussion is divided into three parts. First, I discuss the three papers on the general theme of returns to higher education, either overall or to particular courses of study at the undergraduate level — namely, those of Finnie, Rathje and Emery, and Vaillancourt and Bourdeau-Primeau. In the next section, I discuss Chant and Gibson's novel study of research productivity at Canadian universities. Finally, I draw some links from these papers back to the themes raised in David Laidler's introduction to this volume, and suggest some profitable avenues for future research on higher education in Canada.

Returns to University Education and to Particular Fields of Study

The three essays on the returns to higher education in general and to various fields of study present evidence that higher education is a "good buy" both for society and for the individuals who undertake it. In this context, a good buy means that the discounted present value of education's labor market payoff exceeds the discounted value of its social or individual cost, respectively. Two of the papers also present evidence that certain fields of study — mainly those that include a strong technical component or prepare students directly for particular well-defined careers — yield better labor market outcomes than others. The findings outlined in these three papers generally comport with those in the existing literature for both Canada and the United States for earlier cohorts. These papers also extend the existing literature in various directions with, for example, Rathje and Emery paying closer attention to the details of the cost and tuition data than has been the norm. Finnie's somewhat startling (for economist readers, in any case) analysis of students' satisfaction with their chosen fields of study also represents a new finding.

Selection Bias

The findings in these essays all spring from relatively straightforward statistical analyses. What is tricky is determining what they mean, both in scientific and policy terms. The first important consideration in regard to all three essays is that students choose their fields of study. Imagine for a moment a counterfactual world in which students arrived at university and, after partying their way through orientation week, got assigned at random to a particular field of study. In this imaginary world, the field-of-study effects estimated in these essays would represent true causal effects — they would indicate the effect of studying in a given field on any randomly selected student.

Now consider instead our actual world. In the world that generated the data used in these essays, students select themselves into particular fields of study based on their goals, interests, and aptitudes, subject in some cases to entrance requirements or capacity constraints. In this world of nonrandom selection, the field effects measured in these essays combine the causal effects of the fields of study with differences across fields in factors that would affect the labor outcomes of students regardless of what they chose to study. These factors include ability, motivation, quality of primary and high school education, parental background, family environment, and so on. Casual empiricism suggests, for example, that some of the high returns reported for technical fields such as computer science and engineering actually represent returns to ability, specifically mathematical ability, that would likely also have a high return in other areas. That is to say, if, for example, you took all the computer science students and switched them with all of the economics students, the returns to economics as measured in these essays would increase, while the returns to computer science would fall.

The simplest way to disentangle the effects of nonrandom self-selection into fields of study is to collect data on as many of these factors as possible and then include them in the regression equation as conditioning variables. In this way, you get the effects of various fields of study on later earnings, "holding constant" the observable characteristics of the students. Unfortunately, no existing Canadian data sets provide information on labor market outcomes, field of study in university, and the various factors likely to affect both of these areas. Constructing such a data set, or adding the necessary questions to an ongoing data set such as the Survey of Labour and Income Dynamics, would greatly improve the evidence available on which to base higher education policy in Canada.

In the absence of better data, we can still reason indirectly. Students care a lot about their labor market outcomes following graduation. They also have at least some knowledge of the type of evidence regarding returns to different fields of study presented here by Vaillancourt and Bourdeau-Primeau, and by Finnie. Given this fact, if the differences among fields of study in later earnings represent causal effects and are not just an artifact of the non-random selection of students, we would expect a migration of students into the fields with higher labor market payoffs. Yet, in stark contrast to this prediction, Finnie reports in his paper an astounding stability in the fraction of students selecting the various fields of study over the three cohorts (spanning eight years) that he considers. I read Finnie's findings on stability in the distribution of fields of study as indicating that all, or almost all, of the differences that he and Vaillancourt and Bourdeau-Primeau estimate do not represent the causal effects of particular fields of study. Rather, they indicate a substantial nonrandom sorting of more able, better-prepared, or more motivated students into particular fields.

Capacity constraints represent one potential alternative explanation for the higher estimated returns to fields such as computer science. At some schools, the number of slots in these fields is limited. Such limits have two effects. First, to the extent that migration into Canada is not costless, so that immigrants do not represent perfect substitutes, and to the extent that students from other fields are not perfect substitutes either, capacity constraints raise the labor market return received by students in the constrained majors by artificially reducing their supply in the labor market.

This effect holds even if the limited slots are allocated by lottery, so that no additional selection is induced. But of course, most programs with capacity constraints do not allocate slots by lottery but rather by some measure of ability and effort, such as performance in various screening courses. This is the second effect of limiting the number of slots, and it creates an obvious bias in the estimated returns to the field of study by deliberately inducing the type of nonrandom sorting already discussed. What we lack in regard to this explanation, however, is evidence. A very useful endeavor for a graduate student would be to collect data on the capacity constraints and slot allocation rules in place in universities across Canada. These data, when compared to the estimated returns by discipline, would allow an evaluation of the relative importance of this factor in explaining the observed differences.

Individual Heterogeneity and the Question of Interest

Heterogeneity is the second important factor to keep in mind in interpreting the findings of the three papers on returns to post-secondary education and to fields of study within university programs. It seems quite likely that the effects of going to a university at all, as well as the effects of particular majors within university, will differ among individuals. One person might flourish in a university environment while another might find the experience stultifying and baffling. One person might discover an important new material while studying chemical engineering, while another might discover only that you should not spill acid on your lap.

To the extent that individuals have some idea about how much they would benefit from making different choices about university attendance and field of study, we would expect them to sort themselves accordingly. Thus, the set of persons we observe attending university should, on average, benefit more from it than would the set of persons not attending university. The same holds true among fields of study: we would expect that the students currently majoring in, say, economics believe they will benefit more from it than they would from another choice of field.

Thinking about heterogeneity in this way has important implications for how we interpret the estimates presented in the three essays under discussion. In particular, we must take care to formulate the question of interest exactly. One potentially interesting question concerns the effects of going to university, or of choosing a particular field of study, on those presently observed to make these choices. For example, we might ask what the return is to studying engineering for those who presently do so. A different question, one that in a world of heterogeneous returns would have a different answer, consists of the effect of studying engineering on those who would be induced to do so in response to particular policy changes. Simple economics suggests that students induced to choose engineering at the margin by a policy change will benefit less from it, on average, than those who chose it prior to the policy change. Similarly, in the absence of credit constraints, we would expect that students on the margin between attending university and not will reap lower rewards, on average, from doing so than students who would attend even if the price were much higher. To make things even more complicated, the same students need not be the marginal ones for all policy reforms. For example, the marginal student who would be induced to attend university by a reduction in tuition may differ from the marginal student induced to attend by the introduction of an income-contingent loan program. Identifying the correct margins for particular policy reforms, and estimating the effects at those margins, remains an important topic for future research. The interested reader should consult Card (1999) and Heckman and Vytlacil (1998) for more technical presentations of these ideas.

Compensating Differences and Mediating Variables

One of the ways in which economics helps our thinking is by providing useful base states against which to compare the actual world.

Simple economics would suggest that, given reasonably good information and in the absence of capacity constraints, the marginal university student should be indifferent to the choices of attending and not, and the marginal student in each field of study should be indifferent to the choice between that field and his or her next best alternative. Yet the estimated rates of return to a university education in general and to particular fields of study presented in these three papers seem to contradict this simple economic model; university has a large positive private return and some fields of study yield much higher labor market earnings than others.

Why does reality fail to match the simple model? The differences between marginal and average returns play a key role, as has already been discussed. Another important factor, however, consists of the nonmonetary returns to both university educations and to fields of study. The simple economic model does not imply that marginal individuals would have the same monetary return to the alternatives they face, but rather that they expect to receive the same utility from them.

This point about what exactly should be equalized at the margin has two aspects. First, casual observation suggests that different fields of study imply different mixes of consumption and investment while in school. If on a Friday night we surveyed both the students in the university library and those at the local dance club, we would find differences in the two distributions of fields of study. In addition to differences in the time and effort required to complete particular degrees, some fields of study involve activities that most people enjoy, such as reading novels, while others involve activities that most people do not enjoy, such as solving differential equations. We would expect these differences among fields during university to be compensated for in the labor market after university.

Second, different fields of study typically lead to different jobs, and those different types of jobs vary in their nonmonetary compensation. Some jobs involve lots of travel, flexible hours, and interesting colleagues. Other jobs involve being outdoors. Still others involve high levels of stress. Indeed, there is a whole literature in labor economics, ably surveyed by Rosen (1986), on the subject of compensating differences — the extent to which persons in jobs with less desirable characteristics receive a wage premium to compensate them. Studies that look only at monetary compensation overstate the differences between fields to the extent that such compensating differences play an important role in labor market outcomes.

A related issue, which has particular relevance to returns to education for women, is differences across education levels and among fields of study in employment and unemployment rates. A standard finding of studies in virtually every developed country is that unemployment rates fall — and employment rates rise — with the level of schooling. Thus, part of the difference in earnings between high school graduates and university graduates arises from the fact that the latter group will spend, on average, more of its time working and less of it being unemployed or out of the labor force. Studies that leave out the "zeros" — that is, studies that omit persons with zero earnings, as do all three studies in this book — miss part of this component of the effect of university completion. They do not miss all of it, because some of those who work less as high school graduates than they would have as university graduates still have positive earnings. Studies that use questions based on annualized earnings, such as Finnie's, miss more of this employment effect than studies that rely on actual earnings as their dependent variable.

Increased employment is not an unambiguous good, of course, particularly for the individual decisionmaker. More work means less leisure. Such tradeoffs complicate individual cost-benefit calculations related to university attendance and field of study. These employment effects are likely to be particularly important for women, who exhibit much more flexibility in their labor supply than do men in the years immediately following university completion. These differential employment effects may help to account for the somewhat surprising differences in returns to different fields of study between men and women. It would be an interesting research exercise to decompose the effects for both men and women into effects on employment and effects on earnings conditional on employment.

General Equilibrium Effects

Large policy changes have large effects — effects that work through the entire economy in different ways. In the current context, the most important of these so-called general equilibrium effects consist of changes in relative skill prices in response to policies that change the mix of skills produced by the educational system. For example, consider a move from the current regime of heavily subsidized tuition to a regime combining higher tuition, more reflective of the costs of providing a university education, with an expanded government student loan program. Such a reform would raise the private cost of attending university and should thereby reduce the number of students who do so. This in turn would diminish the supply of university-educated labor, which would have the countervailing effect of raising its market price.

In this example, a failure to consider this price increase would lead to an overestimate of the negative effect of the tuition increase on university enrollment. In their study of a US program to subsidize university tuition (the policy debate in the United States is moving in the opposite direction from that in Canada in this area), Heckman, Lochner, and Taber (1998) find that taking account of changes in skill prices reduces by 90 percent the estimated impact of a subsidy on enrollment. The lesson here is that general equilibrium effects can be important, and should play a role in analyses of large-scale policies.

Some Smaller Issues

I now consider a number of smaller issues — small not necessarily in their substance but in the sense that I have only a bit to say about each one. The first concerns the inclusion or exclusion of those who go on to a graduate degree from the sample used to estimate the returns to an undergraduate degree. Finnie excludes them in his paper, but I am not sure that I would have. Consider the following imaginary scenario.

Suppose that the only reason anyone studied political science was a desire to go to law school. Once they obtained their bachelor's degree, we might then imagine, all political science graduates would immediately apply to law school. Those that get into law school go on to become lawyers (a discipline with, perhaps, externalities of a different sign from those of many others) and those that did not get in would do something else. In this hypothetical but not completely unrealistic world, excluding persons obtaining a graduate degree would substantially understate the returns to political science, which, in my scenario, consist mainly of the returns to, perhaps, later becoming a lawyer. To return to a more general view, part of the causal effect of certain majors is a heightened probability of going on to graduate school; this effect is something both individuals and society should consider in their calculations.

The second smaller issue consists only of a reminder that none of these three studies has much in the way of longitudinal data. The two studies that use census data rely on a so-called synthetic cohort assumption to estimate the life-cycle returns to both university completion and to specific fields of study. Under this assumption, the outcomes of older persons today proxy for the outcomes that younger people today will experience when they get older. In a world of rapid change, where different cohorts have different skill mixes (and are of different sizes), this assumption may be problematic. Finnie projects earnings profiles beyond the five-year follow-up provided by his data by assuming that the age-earnings profile has a specific functional form. The functional form he adopts is not an unreasonable one, but it would be interesting to know (another topic for future research) the sensitivity of the estimates to the specific functional form he assumes.

Finally, I have a couple of remarks about taxes. First, in the presence of a nonlinear tax schedule such as the one in place in Canada, the expected value of taxes paid does not equal the number that you get by applying the tax schedule to expected income, as is done in all three studies. Second, as is well known but often ignored in cost-benefit exercises of this sort, it costs society more than a dollar to raise a dollar in tax revenue. One source of extra costs is the overhead associated with administering the tax system and with "voluntary" compliance on the part of the long-suffering Canadian taxpayer. A more important source is the set of behavioral distortions induced by the tax system, distortions that reduce the size of the pie for everyone. Estimates of these deadweight costs, or "excess burden" to use the public finance jargon, vary widely, but none of them is zero, and they are large enough in some cases to affect the social cost-benefit calculations in these papers.

Policy Implications

How do the issues raised so far affect the advisability of the various policy proposals raised in the introduction and discussed in some of the chapters?

Consider first a policy, suggested by the findings in Finnie and in Vaillancourt and Bourdeau-Primeau, of increasing the number of students undertaking technical fields of study, such as engineering. In the case of capacity-constrained disciplines this could simply mean loosening the constraints. In other cases it could mean differentially low tuition or perhaps some sort of bonus on degree completion. The arguments above about nonrandom selection into fields of study, individual heterogeneity, and general equilibrium effects all suggest that the returns realized by the new, marginal graduates who would be drawn to these fields would be lower than the estimates in this volume suggest, perhaps substantially lower. There is, as usual, no simple spell to cast in order to make all things wonderful. This does not mean that reducing capacity constraints where they exist is not a good idea; the evidence is consistent with fairly high marginal returns in some disciplines. But the reasoning here does suggest a cautious approach to expensive subsidy programs.

Now consider the policy suggested in the introduction of replacing subsidized tuition with a tuition level more reflective of the costs of providing the education, combined with a more extensive student loan program. The reasoning above about the heterogeneous effects of university suggests that such a reform would reduce the total number of university students, as at the margin some students who previously found it privately worthwhile to attend no longer will. This would (through a compositional effect) increase the average return among those still attending. Whether this is a good or a bad idea in efficiency terms depends on the extent of the externalities associated with university education; keep in mind that those externalities may well be lower for students on the margin between attending and not attending.

Next, consider the very popular recent proposal of a system of higher tuitions combined with income-contingent student loans (loans in which the amount students have to pay back depends in part on how much they make after graduation). Such a reform would have several effects. First, it would increase the relative attractiveness of disciplines that have a high consumption value, leading, one would predict, to more crowded campus pubs and emptier libraries. Second, it would increase the relative attractiveness of majors that lead to jobs with relatively high nonmonetary compensation. This is because the income contingency in the loan payments would increase the tax rate on monetary compensation but not on nonmonetary compensation. For the same reason, it should lead employers who hire university graduates to alter their compensation packages to include a higher relative level of nonmonetary compensation. Thus, we would predict lower paychecks and more corporate "retreats" in Hawaii and Whistler. Third, because the program would provide a sort of *de facto* income insurance for university graduates, it would increase the relative attractiveness of occupations with high variances in earnings. The predicted result of this factor is more athletes and artists relative to other, less variable, occupations. Finally, and perhaps most important, income-contingent loans would raise the already very high marginal income tax rate facing most university-educated workers. This would lead them to work less and enjoy more leisure. Taking all these predictions into account, I confess that I find it tough to see the point to this particular reform.

Finally, consider the related reform proposal of discipline-specific tuitions, as suggested by Rathje and Emery. The effects of this policy would depend crucially on the details of implementation. Basing tuitions on estimated earnings differences that fail to adjust for nonrandom sorting could lead to all sorts of fascinating distortions. To the extent that, for example, the higher earnings of engineers mainly reflect a sorting by ability, higher tuition for this discipline would chase people out of engineering, as the more able could now make more, net of tuition, doing other things. The less able did not find engineering worthwhile before, so they certainly would not with a higher tuition. Such a system would also require periodic updating in response to general equilibrium effects, as the supply changes in response to the initiation of the system would act to change the earnings effects associated with different fields of study, which would then require further changes in the tuition levels, and so on. Technology shocks affecting the relative demands for different skills would also lead to a need for updating tuition levels.

Setting tuition levels based on program costs raises another set of issues. In this regard, it is worth noting (and studying further) the fact that private universities in the United States, which can set their tuitions however they like, in fact set more or less standard tuitions for undergraduate education in any field, and then price discriminate like mad based on family income and assets. This behavior suggests that there may be good reasons for not differentiating tuition too finely by discipline — such as the administrative costs of keeping track of the tuition level for students who wander through four or five majors before settling on the one they will ultimately finish. Students would also have an incentive to exploit such a system by switching at the last possible moment from a low-tuition field to a high-tuition field, so that much policing of who took what courses when would be required.

The Research Output of Canadian Universities

Chant and Gibson take their paper in a different direction from the other three discussed here. Rather than the labor market returns to a university education, they look at the research output of Canadian universities, an exceedingly important topic. This paper lays a fine foundation and provides an interesting (and intuitively plausible) finding: that Canadian universities seem to be holding their own in terms of the volume of publications but not of their impact.

Plenty remains for future work: refining the output measures; expanding the comparisons across disciplines in an attempt to explain differences in performance across time and in the cross section; and delving further inside the black box of particular disciplines that may provide especially useful insight.

In regard to the first of these research areas — refining output measures — the most obvious refinement would be to weight both publications and citations by journal quality. At least in some disciplines, such as economics, relatively standard rankings of journal quality should be available. The arduous part of the task, obviously, would be combining these rankings with the publication and citation data. I suspect that the same basic picture will emerge, but the question is important enough that getting all the details down deserves researcher time and attention.

In regard to the second direction for future research, it is notable that the authors find some fairly wide swings over time in the rankings for particular disciplines. It would be nice to try to link those swings to observable characteristics of the discipline — in particular, to whether or not it operates in an international labor market. If the labor market for a discipline is confined largely to Canadians, then it can better retain its quality in the face of rising salaries in the United States, the United Kingdom, and elsewhere. Other field characteristics worth examining would include the location of the top doctoral programs in the world. Presumably, fields in which one or more of the top doctoral programs is found in Canada will have an easier time retaining quality faculty in the face of labor market competition.

In regard to the final suggested research direction I mentioned, a look at particular disciplines, I offer the somewhat self-serving suggestion that a detailed examination of the case of economics would provide some useful lessons. The economics profession has a truly international labor market. As a result, many economists at Canadian universities are not Canadian by birth, and many of the best-known Canadian economists work at US universities. As is well known within the profession, in recent years the low exchange rate for the Canadian dollar, combined with provincial budget problems, has led to a lot of departures for warmer and more remunerative climes. Studying this field in detail to learn "what went wrong" could provide guidance in reducing the impact of similar changes on fields that may be earlier on in the process.

Concluding Remarks

I now return to some of the main themes raised by David Laidler in his fine introduction to this volume, and then offer up a short list of topics related to higher education in Canada that deserve further research attention. It goes without saying that evidence-based policy-making requires evidence. This volume provides a wealth of evidence on several important questions, but much work remains to be done on these questions to provide the knowledge base required for making coherent and effective higher education policy.

As Laidler notes, the two primary economic justifications for government intervention in higher education markets are externalities and credit constraints. We know very little about externalities, but we could learn more through some clever research on the topic. While it is handy for those of us who make our living in the higher education sector to point to the shimmering hope of externalities to justify our funding, the taxpayer would be better served with some hard empirical estimates.

A lively literature already exists, however, on the subject of credit constraints. Most of it focuses on the United States, but the institutions and participation levels are similar enough that it can probably be generalized to Canada. Two notable recent contributions are Cameron and Heckman (1998) and Stinebrickner and Stinebrickner (2001). Both suggest that, given the current institutional setup and funding levels in the United States, credit constraints are less important than is commonly thought. There does not appear to be a large pool of smart kids being kept away from university by funding issues, nor does it appear that credit constraints alone account for higher rates of dropping out among students from low-income families. This evidence does not necessarily indicate that current student funding programs should be eliminated, but it suggests little need for expansion beyond the levels currently provided in the United States and Canada.

A third broad issue, one that has received relatively little attention in either the United States or Canada, is the rationale for having government operate universities. Consider a system like that outlined in the introduction, in which schools set their own tuition in a competitive higher educational marketplace, and students shop for the school that best matches their needs in the context of a system of government-guaranteed student loans. In such a regime, one could find economic justifications for government to subsidize research, particularly basic research, and to provide student loans and perhaps grants. But no obvious economic justification exists, in either this hypothetical regime or the existing one, for having government actually operate universities. Both theoretical research on why and how we would expect public and private universities to behave differently, and empirical research comparing public and private universities in the United States or using historical data from the period prior to the socialization of Canadian universities, would have great value.

I now offer some additional policy-related topics that would repay further research attention. First, and perhaps most important, one of the main characteristics that differentiate Canadian from US universities is that the faculty at many Canadian universities, even some fairly good ones, is unionized. Several questions arise immediately. Why has this occurred in Canada and not in the United States? Is it because of differences in labor laws? Or some difference in the way in which public universities operate in the two countries? Is it the lack of private sector competition in Canada? What are the likely effects of unionization in Canada over the long term on research output and quality, and on instructional quality? One hears many anecdotes and horror stories, but systematic evidence is largely lacking.

Second, Canadian higher education has a number of other distinctive features not present in the US system. One is the strong separation between honors and general degrees, with, at least in Ontario, an extra year spent obtaining the honors degree. These honors programs are expensive in terms of faculty time but provide a higher quality undergraduate education to the cream of the undergraduate population. In economics, at least, such degrees appear to carry a labor market premium. Is that premium sufficient to justify the extra cost?

Finally, three quick topics for consideration within the context of the current government-operated university system. First, what value, if any, would there be to spending the money it would require to have a true "Harvard of Canada" — that is, a Canadian university of the same research stature as one of the elite private or public universities in the United States. Second, and not unrelated, what is the effect of university quality — as measured by, for example, the variables employed in the annual *Maclean*'s rankings — on labor market outcomes? An as yet unpublished paper by Betts, Ferrall, and Finnie (2001) examines this question, and finds some labor market effects of quality-related university characteristics for male Canadian graduates. Further research, particularly of a kind that was allowed to "name names" by indicating the relative labor market performance of specific universities, would be helpful in thinking about the optimal array of qualities to provide within the public system. Third, and also related, we now know something about the extent of peer effects in university education from the US literature on the effects of peer quality measures on labor market outcomes (see, for example, Datcher Loury and Garman 1995). What do these findings imply for the centralized student allocation mechanism presently used in Ontario? Could changes in the assignment rules increase overall educational attainment?

References

Betts, Julian, Christopher Ferrall, and Ross Finnie. 2001. "The Role of University Quality in Determining Post-Graduation Outcomes: Panel Evidence from Three Recent Canadian Cohorts." University of California at San Diego. Unpublished manuscript.

Cameron, Stephen, and James Heckman. 1998. "Life Cycle Schooling and Dynamic Selection Bias: Models and Evidence for Five Cohorts of American Males." *Journal of Political Economy* 106 (2): 262–333.

Card, David. 1999. "The Causal Effect of Education on Earnings." In Orley Ashenfelter and David Card, eds., *Handbook of Labor Economics*, vol. 3A. Amsterdam: North-Holland.

Datcher Loury, Linda, and David Garman. 1995. "College Selectivity and Earnings." *Journal of Labor Economics* 13 (2): 289–308.

Heckman, James, Lance Lochner, and Christopher Taber. 1998. "Explaining Rising Wage Inequality: Explorations with a Dynamic General Equilibrium Model of Labor Earnings with Heterogeneous Agents." *Review of Economic Dynamics* 1 (1): 1–58.

———, and Edward Vytlacil. 1998. "Instrumental Variables Methods for the Correlated Random Coefficient Model." *Journal of Human Resources* 33 (4): 974–987.

Rosen, Sherwin. 1986. "The Theory of Equalizing Differences." In Orley Ashenfelter and Richard Layard, eds., *Handbook of Labor Economics*, vol. 1. Amsterdam: North-Holland.

Stinebrickner, Todd, and Ralph Stinebrickner. 2001. "The Relationship between Family Income and Schooling Attainment: Evidence from a Liberal Arts College with a Full Tuition Subsidy Program." London, Ont.: University of Western Ontario. Unpublished manuscript.

The Contributors

Sandrine Bourdeau-Primeau holds a BSc (Honours) in Economics and Mathematics and an MSc in Economics from the Université de Montréal. She worked as a research assistant on human resources issues for the university's Centre de recherche et développement en économique and is currently employed as an economist with the Department of Fisheries and Oceans in Ottawa.

Joel Bruneau is an Assistant Professor at the University of Saskatchewan, where he teaches Resource and Environmental Economics, International Trade, and Microeconomics. He was born in Yellowknife, NWT, and after high school moved to Saskatchewan, where he found the prairie winters both warm and short. He has a BA and MA in Economics from the University of Saskatchewan and a PhD from the University of British Columbia.

John Chant has a BA from the University of British Columbia and a PhD from Duke University. He taught at the University of Edinburgh, Duke University, Queen's University, and Carleton University, before going to Simon Fraser University in 1979, where he was Chair of the Department of Economics. He served as the Director of the Financial Markets Study Group at the Economic Council of Canada and as Research Director of the Task Force on the Future of the Canadian Financial Services Sector (the MacKay task force). He has written widely on such topics as the Bank of Canada, the theory of financial intermediation, and the regulation of financial institutions. Professor Chant is now serving as Special Adviser at the Bank of Canada.

Paul Davenport is President of the University of Western Ontario and Professor of Economics there. He taught economics at McGill University (1973–89), and was President of the University of Alberta from 1989 to 1994. He served as Chair of the Association of Canadian Universities and Colleges of Canada (1997–99) and Chair of the Council of Ontario Universities (1999–2001). A graduate of Stanford University (BA, with Great Distinction) and the University of Toronto (MA, PhD), he has honorary degrees from the University of Alberta (1994) and the University of Toronto (2000), and in 2001 was named Chevalier de la Légion d'Honneur by the government of France. His research in economics has centered on economic growth, fiscal federalism, and the knowledge-based economy.

Stephen T. Easton is Professor of Economics at Simon Fraser University, where he has taught since 1975. A graduate of the University of Chicago, he is the author of *Education in Canada* (Fraser Institute, 1988), and was series editor for a set of monographs on education published by the Institute for Research of Public Policy. His work on secondary schooling inspired the popular Fraser Institute Report Cards on secondary education for British Columbia, Alberta, Quebec, and Ontario. He currently serves as Chairman of the Board of the Society for the Advancement of Excellence in Education, and is a Senior Scholar at the Fraser Institute.

J.C. Herbert Emery received his PhD (Economics) from the University of British Columbia in 1993. Since then, he has taught in the Economics Department at the University of Calgary, where he is currently an Associate Professor and Director of the Research Unit for the Study of Civil Society. His research has primarily been in the fields of economic history and labor economics.

Ross Finnie was educated at Queen's University, the London School of Economics, and the University of Wisconsin, where he received his PhD. For the past five years, he has been a Research Fellow and Adjunct Professor in the School of Policy Studies at Queen's, and a Visiting Fellow at Statistics Canada. His research interests include the labor market experiences of postsecondary graduates, student debt and the financing of postsecondary education, and the brain drain. His publications for the C.D. Howe Institute include "Measuring the Load, Easing the Burden: Canada's Student Loan Programs and the Revitalization of Canadian Postsecondary Education" (November 2001); and *Student Loans in Canada: Past, Present, and Future* (with Saul Schwartz, 1996).

William Gibson holds a PhD in economics from Simon Fraser University. He has taught at Simon Fraser and the University of Lethbridge and has been a guest lecturer at the University of Montana and St. Cloud State in Minnesota. In addition to work on the economics of higher education, he has written on public debt, inflationary finance, Canadian economic history, and the economics of gratuities. Current interests include the economics of universities and the importance of research, government spending (and reducing it) and the corpus of public choice economics. In his spare time, he writes satire and humor and takes bird photographs.

David Laidler is Bank of Montreal Professor at the University of Western Ontario, and a Fellow-in-Residence and Canadian Bankers Association Scholar at the C.D. Howe Institute. In 1998 and 1999, he was Visiting Economist and Special Adviser at the Bank of Canada. His fields of interest are monetary economics and the history of economic thought. His most recent large-scale academic publication is *Fabricating the Keynesian Revolution: Studies of the Interwar Literature on Money, the Cycle and Unemployment* (Cambridge University Press, 1999). His book *The Great Canadian Disinflation: The Economics and Politics of Monetary Policy in Canada, 1988–93* (with William Robson, C.D. Howe Institute, 1993), was awarded the Canadian Economics Association's Doug Purvis Memorial Award for excellence in writing on Canadian economic policy.

Melville L. McMillan is a Professor in the Department of Economics and a Fellow of the Institute of Public Economics at the University of Alberta. He served as Chair of the Department from 1987 to 1997 and in various other administrative roles within the university. He has a BA and an MSc from the University of Alberta and a PhD from Cornell University. His research and teaching interests are in public economics — in particular, urban and local economics, fiscal federalism, and the demand for and supply of publicly provided goods and services. His publications include a recent article on measuring university efficiency.

Alice Nakamura holds the Francis Winspear Chair of Business at the University of Alberta. She is the academic co-chair of the Canadian

Employment Research Forum, and she heads up the Canada-wide volunteer university faculty initiative that created www.CareerOwl.ca, an Internet recruiting information system. She has published widely, and has served on numerous federal and provincial task forces and advisory committees. In 1996, Professor Nakamura received an Honorary Doctorate of Law from the University of Western Ontario, and in 1995 she served as President of the Canadian Economics Association.

Kelly A. Rathje graduated from the University of Calgary with a BA (Honours) and an MA, both in Economics. Her master's thesis, "The Rates of Return to Advanced Education in Alberta and Canada," examined the social and individual returns to postsecondary education. Since September 1999, she has been a consultant with Economica, an economic consulting firm specializing in the provision of litigation support in personal injury and fatal accident cases.

Jeffrey Smith is Associate Professor at the University of Maryland. He received his PhD in Economics from the University of Chicago in 1996 and joined the Maryland faculty in 2001. Before that he was Associate Professor and CIBC Chair in Human Capital and Productivity at the University of Western Ontario. In 1997, he received the Polanyi prize, awarded each year to an outstanding young Ontario economist. His research centers on methods for the evaluation of social programs such as job training for the disadvantaged.

François Vaillancourt is Professor of Economics in the Département de sciences économiques, Université de Montréal. He was educated at the Université de Montréal and Queen's University, where he obtained his PhD. His research interests include public economics, human resources and social behavior, and language economics. His publications for the C.D. Howe Institute include "Le statut du français sur le marché du travail au Québec, de 1970 à 1995: les revenus de travail" (with Christine Touchette, 2001); "Taxes, Transfers, and Generations in Canada: Who Gains and Who Loses from the Demographic Transition" (with Philip Oreopoulos, 1998); and *Survival: Official Language Rights in Canada* (with John Richards and William G. Watson, 1992).

Members of the
C.D. Howe Institute[*]

Corporate and Association Members

AGF Management Limited
AON Consulting Inc.
ARC Financial Corporation
AT&T Canada
ATCO Gas Services Ltd.
Acklands Grainger
Air Canada
Alberta Chambers of Commerce
Alberta Energy Company Ltd.
Alberta Treasury Branches
Altamira Investment Services
Arthur Andersen LLP
BCE Inc.
BMO Nesbitt Burns
BP Canada
Bank of Montreal
Bank of Nova Scotia
Barrick Gold Corporation
Bell Canada
Bennett Jones
Birks Family Foundation
Bombardier Inc.
The Boston Consulting Group
Brascan Corporation
Brookfield Properties Corporation
Burgundy Asset Management Ltd.
Business Council of British Columbia
Business Development Bank
 of Canada
CAE Inc.
C.M. Harding Foundation
Cadillac Fairview Corporation
 Limited
Canada Deposit Insurance Corporation
Canada Life Assurance Company
Canada Overseas Investments Limited
Canada Post Corporation
Canadian Association of Insurance
 and Financial Advisors
Canadian Association of Petroleum
 Producers
Canadian Bankers Association
The Canadian Institute of Chartered
 Accountants
Canadian Council of Chief Executives
Canadian Federation of Independent
 Business
Canadian Finance & Leasing
 Association
Canadian Imperial Bank of Commerce
Canadian Life and Health Insurance
 Association Inc.
Canadian National
Canadian Tax Foundation
Canadian Western Bank
Candor Investments Ltd.

---

[*] The views expressed in this publication are those of the authors, and do not necessarily represent the opinions of the Institute's Board of Directors or members.

CanWest Global Communications Corp.
Capital Alliance Ventures Inc.
Cargill Limited
Citibank Canada
Clarica Life Insurance Company
Cogeco inc.
CompCorp
Crown Investment Corporation of Saskatchewan
Crown Life Insurance Company Limited
Deloitte & Touche LLP
Desjardins Ducharme Stein Monast
Deutsche Bank Canada
Dofasco Inc.
The Dominion of Canada General Insurance Company
Donner Canadian Foundation
DuPont Canada Inc.
EDCO financial Holdings Ltd.
ENSIS Growth Fund Inc.
Economap Inc.
Economic Development Edmonton
Empire Financial Group
Enbridge Inc.
Ernst & Young
Export Development Corporation
Fairmont Hotels and Resorts
Falconbridge Limited
Fidelity Investments
Finning International Inc.
Forest Products Association of Canada
Four Seasons Hotels Limited
G.T.C. Transcontinental Group Ltd.
General Electric Canada Inc.
George Weston Ltd.
Gibson Petroleum Company Limited
Gluskin Sheff + Associates Inc.
Goal Group of Companies
Goldman Sachs Canada Inc.
Goodmans

Great-West Life Assurance Company
HSBC Bank Canada
HSD Partners Inc.
Harvard Developments Limited, A Hill Company
Hergott Duval Accounting Services
Hewlett-Packard (Canada) Ltd.
Hollinger Inc.
Honeywell Limited
Hydro One Networks Inc.
IPSCO Inc.
Imperial Oil Limited
Imperial Tobacco Canada Limited
Inco Limited
Inland Group
Insurance Bureau of Canada
Investment Dealers Association of Canada
The Investment Funds Institute of Canada
Investors Group
J.P. Morgan Chase Bank
The Jackman Foundation
Jarislowsky Foundation
The John Dobson Foundation
K.P.A. Advisory Services Ltd.
KPMG LLP
Kolter Property Management Limited
La Jolla Resources International Ltd.
Lazard Canada Corporation
Lombard Canada
Maclab Enterprises
McCarthy Tétrault
McClean Watson Capital Inc.
McDonald's Restaurants of Canada Limited
McMillan Binch
Magellan Aerospace Limited
Manulife Financial
The Maritime Life Assurance Company
Marsh Canada Limited
Max Bell Foundation

Merrill Lynch Canada Inc.
Monitor Company
Moosehead Breweries Limited
Morneau Sobeco
National Bank of Canada
Nexen Inc.
Noranda Inc.
Norske Skog
Nova Chemicals Corporation
Onex Corporation
Ontario Hospital Association
Ontario Medical Association
Ontario Power Generation Inc.
Ontario Securities Commission
Ontario Teachers' Pension Plan Board
Osler, Hoskin & Harcourt
Petro-Canada
Pfizer Canada Inc.
Phillips, Hager & North Investment Management Ltd.
Pirie Foundation
Power Corporation of Canada
Pratt & Whitney Canada
PricewaterhouseCoopers LLP
Princeton Developments Ltd.
Procor Limited
RBC Dominion Securities
RBC Financial Group
Rogers Communications Inc.
Roy-L Capital Corporation
The S. Schulich Foundation
SNC Lavalin Group Inc.
The Samuel Group of Companies
Sceptre Investment Counsel
Shell Canada Limited
Sherritt International Corporation
Southam Inc.
Stikeman Elliott
Sun Life Assurance Company
Suncor Energy Inc.
Syncrude
TD Bank Financial Group
Talisman Energy Inc.
Teck Cominco Limited
Telesystem Ltd.
TELUS
Thomson Corporation
The Toronto Stock Exchange
Torstar Corporation
Torys
TransAlta Corporation
TransCanada Pipelines Limited
Utilicorp Networks Canada
VIA Rail Canada Inc.
The Westaim Corporation
Westcoast Energy Inc.
Weston Forest Corporation
William M. Mercer Limited

Individual Members

Michael J. Adams
James E. Arnett
Harry Baumann
Stanley Beck, Q.C.
Robert Birgeneau
David E. Bond
R.A.N. Bonnycastle
Pierre Brunet
Helen Burstyn

Robert C. Caldwell
Barry Campbell
Russell Campbell
Ken Christoffel
Ian D. Clark
Jack Cockwell
Marshall A. Cohen, O.C., Q.C.
E. Kendall Cork
Marcel Côté

John Crispo
Glen E. Cronkwright
Paul R. Curley
Catherine Delaney
Jean-Claude Delorme
Steven Devries
James Doak
Wendy Dobson
Bill Empey
Morrey M. Ewing
Angela Ferrante
Aaron M. Fish
Dr. James D. Fleck
L. Yves Fortier, C.C., Q.C.
Joseph F. Gill
Ross W. Glenn
Martin Goldberg
Peter Goring
Dr. John A.G. Grant
Dr. Geoffrey E. Hale
Susan J. Han
G.R. Heffernan
Lawrence L. Herman
Robert A. Hill
William Holt
H. Douglas Hunter
Lou Hyndman, Q.C.
Edwin W. Jarmain
Thomas E. Kierans
Joseph Kruger II
R. John Lawrence
Jacques A. Lefebvre
J.W.(Wes) MacAleer
W.A. MacDonald

James P. McIlroy
The Hon. Frank McKenna
Georg Marais
Bruce E. Mintz
Russell J. Morrison
Dr. F.W. Orde Morton
John P. Mulvihill, CFA
Dr. Edward P. Neufeld
James S. Palmer
Andy Perry
Philip G. Ponting
Grant L. Reuber
Nicholas Ross
Davide Rossi
David Santangeli
Guylaine Saucier
Dick Schmeelk
Hugh Segal
Lindsay Shaddy
Gordon Sharwood
Philip Spencer, Q.C.
James Stanford
Wayne Steadman
Harry Swain
Christopher Sweeney
Thomas Symons
Frederick H. Telmer
Bruce Terry
Robert J. Turner
G. Douglas Valentine
Jack H. Warren
David J. S. Winfield
Alfred G. Wirth
Adam H. Zimmerman

Honorary Members

G. Arnold Hart
David Kirk